CW00537832

Private Rights of Way

Private Rights of Way

Stephen Bickford Smith
Barrister, Landmark Chambers

Andrew Francis
Barrister, Serle Court

Christopher Jessel
Solicitor

Dr Keith Shaw
Associate, Pinsent Masons LLP

JORDANS

Published by
Jordan Publishing Limited
21 St Thomas Street
Bristol BS1 6JS

British Library Cataloguing-in-Publication Data

A catalogue record for this book is available from the British Library.

ISBN 978 085308 852 3

Typeset by Letterpart Ltd, Reigate, Surrey

Printed in Great Britain by CPI Antony Rowe, Chippenham and Eastbourne

PREFACE

As the title states, this is a book about *private* rights of way. Such rights of way are not to be confused with *public* rights of way. There are many differences in the law that apply to each of those rights. The law of *public* rights of way and public access to land is covered in excellent terms by Angela Sydenham in her book *Public Rights of Way and Access to Land* published by Jordans; now in its 4th Edition. Therefore, any reader needing assistance about what may be a *public* right of way, or some other *public* right over land should consult that book. This book does not deal with that subject and Chapter 2, para **2.72ff** of this book briefly describes the distinction between public and private rights over land. In addition and for the avoidance of doubt we have not dealt with private rights of 'way' (ie rights of navigation) over, or under water, whether natural, artificial or tidal.

We perceived the need for this book given the complications of the law relating to private rights of way (as easements) and the desire to provide something clear and practical on the subject. To that end we have set out how private rights of way may be acquired and lost, how the rights and obligations under them may be enforced, and how general disputes over them, such as obstructions and lack of repair, may be dealt with under the law.

It is an often overlooked fact that most human beings in this country will need to use a private right of way on a frequent basis, whether he or she is a town dweller, or one who lives in the country. To get to your (or someone else's) house, flat, garage, office, field, or yard, or to walk, or drive over any land off a public footpath, or highway, invariably requires a private right of way to be present for lawful access. Many public spaces and buildings require the use of a private right of way for access; eg the Temples and Inns of Court, most railway stations, shopping centres, cinemas, car parks and sports venues. One example may be given of the importance of such rights when a large number of disputes arose over private rights of way over a decade ago. At that time many house and flat owners were shocked to discover that the private rights which they and their predecessors had enjoyed for generations to access their properties were no longer valid. Large sums of money were being demanded by landowners to allow such access to continue. The Government legislated on the topic to try and solve the problem. On 1 April 2004, the House of Lords put the matter to rest in favour of the users of the private rights of way when it decided *Bakewell Management Ltd v Brandwood* [2004] 2 AC 519. Thus, unlike other easements and property rights, or obligations (eg restrictive covenants, or rights of light which may only trouble a relatively small number of landowners) private rights of way are pretty near universal in importance to many.

The importance of such rights in an overcrowded island and in the context of increasing pressure on land use, especially in built-up areas, means that disputes over private rights of way and the rights and obligations associated with them are always potentially, if not actually, present. Parking spaces, use of roadways with increased numbers of vehicles and obstructions, such as gates, barriers and fences can all cause tempers to flare. The need to determine who has the rights and responsibilities is thus of vital importance before things get out of hand. The tendency for disputes over private rights of way to litigate is shown by the fact that there are over a dozen private rights of way cases noted on Westlaw between March and October 2012. Next to boundary disputes, these claims are capable of producing a great deal of costly tension and aggression between neighbours, but little common sense. Perhaps fewer disputes might arise if there was clear guidance as to the law and as to how to avoid litigation over these rights and the obligations that run with them. This book has that aim.

We hope that this book will assist in providing some answers to those in search of an understanding of the law on this subject. In addition it should be a guide to the resolution of disputes over private rights of way, whether latent, or patent. Finally, it contains precedents which are designed so that rights and obligations within the subject of the book are clearly defined when agreements over private rights of way are being made.

We have tried to assist the reader with not just the law of private rights of way, but also the way in which disputes can be resolved. We stress (in Chapter 12) the need to seek a resolution of conflict in a neighbourly manner, such as by mediation, before launching into what are often expensive and lengthy court proceedings. In addition, in Appendix 2 David Andrews (a former Ordnance Survey surveyor and now a Cartographic Survey and Mapping Expert) provides an insight into the way in which evidence relating to plans, maps and aerial photographs should be interpreted and presented. This is invaluable material when disputes are in court.

This book sets out the law for both England and Wales. In general that is the same but occasionally a statutory provision may be brought into force on different dates in the two jurisdictions. We have attempted to state the law as at 15 October 2012. While this book was in press Land Registry Practice Guide 52 (Easements by Prescription) was revised and the changes, which are minor and administrative, have not been reflected in the text. It is now much clearer about procedures such as automatic entries where both dominant and servient titles are registered. It also updates references to certain railway and canal lands to include the Canal and River Trust.

There are also two changes which are due to come into force in 2013. As the final rules etc are either not yet published, or in final form, we cannot incorporate these changes into the text but we have flagged them in Chapters 11 and 12 in particular.

First, in 2013 the current Land Registration Adjudication procedure will be the subject of new rules. The current office and jurisdiction of the Adjudicator to Her Majesty's Land Registry will be transferred to a new First-tier Tribunal Property Chamber; probably by mid 2013. There will be new procedural rules applicable to that Tribunal. But the jurisdiction under the Land Registration Act 2002 and rules made thereunder to resolve disputes under that Act will not alter. The change will be in the procedure and in the identity of the body resolving those disputes once they are the subject of a reference by the Land Registry. See the flagged up notes to this effect in Chapters 11 and 12.

Secondly, so far as any disputes are in court and are governed by the Civil Procedure Rules (as they invariably are), extensive changes as to costs are planned to come into force on 1 April 2013 as part of the implementation of the Report by Lord Justice Jackson on civil litigation costs published in 2010.

The relevant website in both instances is www.justice.gov.uk so that up to date information can be obtained when these changes take effect.

In addition, as to the future, the Law Commission's Report and Draft Bill on the reform of the law of easements, covenants and profits a prendre, published in June 2011 (Law Com No 327) is mentioned in this book at certain points. Aspects of that Report and the draft Bill will, if enacted, have a drastic effect on the law of easements, including of course private rights of way. At the time of writing there is no indication when any such Bill will be introduced into Parliament.

We thank most sincerely all who have assisted us with the writing of this book. Such thanks go to our colleagues, our instructing solicitors and clients (who often provide the inspiration for legal problems which we do our best to resolve), our partners, families and friends. Their encouragement and forbearance is much appreciated. As is often said 'they know who they are' and we hope they will not mind being in this general Roll of Honour. They can all take individual credit in the role they have played in bringing his book to publication.

We are very much indebted to David Andrews for his contribution in Appendix 2. This will assist readers on the complex questions arising from maps and mapping, especially when expert evidence is required in court.

Naturally we are immensely grateful to all those at Jordan Publishing who have managed to get us safely into harbour with this book. Amongst them we must thank specifically Tony Hawitt and Claire Banyard and of course all their associates. It has been a long voyage and without their expert navigation skills and tactful encouragement, our ship (in the form of this book) would have foundered long ago.

Finally, we are very willing to receive comments on this book via the publishers, whether in terms of praise, or criticism. Such comments will of course be grist to our mill when we come to prepare a second edition!

Note as to the use of potentially gender-specific words.

The use in this book of the words 'he', 'she' or 'it' or any other words which are capable of a gender-specific meaning, is not to be taken as having a gender-specific meaning.

Stephen Bickford Smith

Andrew Francis

Christopher Jessel

Dr Keith Shaw
October 2012

CONTENTS

TABLE OF CASES

References are to paragraph numbers.

TABLE OF STATUTES

References are to paragraph numbers.

TABLE OF STATUTORY INSTRUMENTS

References are to paragraph numbers.

Chapter 1

THE PROPERTY LAW CONTEXT

SCOPE OF THE SUBJECT

1.1   The scope of this book is, as its title suggests, private rights of way. The term 'private' is intended to draw a distinction between those rights of way which exist for the benefit of the owners of particular parcels of land over other land, and rights of way enjoyed by the public at large over public roads, footpaths and bridleways.[1] English law has since time immemorial developed the law relating to highways, of which the law relating to public rights of way is part, separately from the law relating to private rights of way. The law relating to private rights of way forms part of the law of easements.

1.2   Public rights of way are to a large extent regulated by statute. The most important provisions are the Highways Act 1980,[2] and in relation to non-vehicular ways, the National Parks and Access to the Countryside Act 1949,[3] the Countryside Act 1968,[4] the Wildlife and Countryside Act 1981,[5] the Countryside and Rights of Way Act 2000,[6] and the Natural Environment and Rural Communities Act 2006.[7] Public rights of way are, as the name suggests, rights enjoyed by the public at large. They can be acquired in various ways, including by long user for 20 years, or dedication to the public of a right of way by the owner of the land over which the way leads. Liability to repair falls by statute on the relevant highway authority.[8] The stopping up and diversion of highways are subject to statutory procedures. Even in modern times, many public highways, principally footpaths and brideways, have arisen by long user or dedication.[9] However, vehicular public highways normally arise either through compulsory purchase by public authorities of land required for

---

[1]   For the avoidance of doubt, customary ways are also outside the scope of the book. These are rights of a local public or class of persons as the inhabitants of a parish 'to some use or quasieasement of land, as to have a way to a church or market'. See *Brocklebank v Thompson* [1903] 2 Ch 344.

[2]   1980 c 66.

[3]   12 & 13 Geo 6 c 66.

[4]   1968 c 41.

[5]   1981 c 49.

[6]   2000 c 37.

[7]   2006 c16.

[8]   Though certain classes of public paths arising from dedication or long use are not publicly maintainable under the relevant statuory provisions. See generally *Rights of Way A Guide to Law and Practice* 4th edn, published by The Ramblers Association.

[9]   The Natural Environment and Rural Communities Act 2006, Part 6 precludes new public rights of way for mechanically propelled vehicles except pursuant to express creation or the construction under statutory powers of a road intended to be used by such vehicles.

new roads, or as a result of agreements between developers and local authorities incidental to development of land requiring new roads to service it. Under such agreements the developer constructs the new road to a suitable standard, and the local authority then 'adopts' the road as a public highway, accepting at the same time liability for future repair.

1.3   There are some overlaps and similarities between public and private rights of way. For example, public rights like private rights may be acquired by prescription after 20 years of use, and private rights of way can co-exist with public rights of way. The rules as to what constitutes permissible use of the public highway are similar to those which govern private rights of way, though the influence of public law regarding such matters as the right to peaceful assembly has also led to important differences. Nevertheless, an attempt to synthesise the two areas of law would be over-ambitious and detract from the utility of a book primarily aimed at property professionals. The object of the present work is to give an account of the law relating to rights of way as easements. They will be referred to simply as rights of way rather than 'private' rights of way, except where it is necessary to discuss and distinguish between public and private rights. The practical importance of the subject in an increasingly crowded and urbanised world needs little emphasis. Scarcely a month goes past without a significant reported decision on rights of way from the courts in England. Other common law jurisdictions also produce much material of relevance to the subject.

ESSENTIALS OF EASEMENTS

1.4   The purpose of the present Chapter is to set rights of way in context. Private rights of way are an example of those rights known to the law as easements. An easement is defined in *Halsbury's Laws of England*[10] as:

> '... a right annexed to land to utilise other land of different ownership in a particular manner (not involving the taking of any part of the natural produce of that land or any part of its soil) or to prevent the owner of the other land from utilising his land in a particular manner.'

1.5   An easement has been said judicially to be 'a familiar creature of English land law'.[11] Strictly, in English law, servitudes encompass both easements and profits a prendre.[12]

1.6   The essential idea behind the concept of a right of way, as with other easements, is a *right over land belonging to another*, falling short of full ownership or possession. In Roman (and Scots) law the analogous concept is that of the *servitude*, a burden imposed on the land of one owner in favour of land belonging to another. The English law relating to easements is 'perhaps

---

[10]   4th edn, vol 16(2), para 1.
[11]   *Per* Hoffmann LJ in *Willies-Williams v National Trust* (1993) 65 P&CR 359 at 361, CA.
[12]   *Dalton v Angus* (1881) 6 App Cas 740 at 796, *per* Lord Selbourne LC.

the most Roman part of English law'.[13] This results from extensive borrowings from Roman law. This can be traced to Bracton, but grew in importance during the early part of the 19th century, when England was increasing rapidly in population, urbanisation, and wealth, and the need for a developed system of rights over land belonging to others became acute. The same historical process also accounts for the fact that most of the important decisions of the courts in this field date from the late 19th and early 20th centuries. From the Roman law derive the English expressions *dominant land (or tenement)*. This expression is adapted from the Latin *praedium dominans (dominus* = master). The land benefiting from the easement is termed the *servient land (or tenement)*. The Latin original is *praedium serviens (servus* = slave, servant). Hence this refers to the land which is subject to the easement. The Roman law divided easements (*servitudes*) into rural and urban categories. Rights of way were recognised as 'rustic' servitudes and were divided into four categories: *iter, actus, via and aquaeductus*,[14] the last of these relating to the free passage of water. The remaining three are differentiated in developed Roman law according to the extent of the right granted. *Via* is the right to use a prepared roadway across another's land. *Iter* is the right to walk or ride across such land not involving the driving of boats or vehicles, and *actus* the right to drive cattle or vehicles. He who enjoyed a right of *via* was also entitled to *actus* and *via*. And he who enjoyed *actus* also automatically enjoyed *iter*, but the converse was not the case. These rights ran with the land. With regard to *via*, the ancient Roman law of the XII Tables also laid down a fixed width for the roadway of 8 feet, (16 feet at the bends) and provided that if the road were not kept in repair, the dominant owner might deviate from the road.

1.7   From the Roman law also probably derives the rule that an easement can only exist to benefit the dominant land.[15]

1.8   The theoretical legal basis of easements (including that of way) is therefore based on very entrenched legal concepts. The legal incidents of easements are further examined below.

1.9   Despite some recent changes in the law, notably by the Land Registration Act 2002[16] and impetus for general reform, easements remain a category of legal rights over land which enjoys two characteristics which are a recipe both for survival and for ability to cause mischief. They can be acquired by prescription based on long use, and can exist outside the land registration system. Issues relating to the existence, creation, and transmission of rights of way do frequently turn on general concepts of real property law. A brief

---

[13]   Nicholas: *Roman Law* Oxford University Press,1962, p 148. See also Nicholas and Metzger An *Introduction to Roman Law*, Oxford University Press, 1975 and Borkowksi's *Textbook on Roman Law*, 4th edn, Oxford University Press, 2010, para 6.3. For discussion of the influence of the Roman law of servitudes on the English law of easements, including rights of way, see Chapter 11 of the latter work.
[14]   Institutes 2.3.1.
[15]   *Ideo autem hae servitudes praediorum appellantur, quoniam sine praediis constitui non possunt*, Institutes 2.3.3.
[16]   See Chapter 13.

overview of the relevant salient features of the area may therefore be helpful. The Law Commission has examined the area of easements and published some proposals for reform.[17] No immediate legislative action is likely, however.

Easements as interests in land

1.10 Easements are a species of what the law terms 'incorporeal hereditaments'. In *Re Christmas*,[18] Cotton LJ, citing Blackstone's classic *Commentaries on the Law of England*, defined an incorporeal hereditament in the following words:

> 'a right issuing out of a thing corporate, whether real or personal, or concerning or annexed to, or exercisable within, the same. It is not the thing corporate itself, which may consist in lands, houses, jewels, or the like; but something collateral thereto, as a rent issuing out of these lands or houses, or an office relating to those jewels.'

1.11 In another passage, Blackstone then said:

> 'Their existence is merely in idea and abstracted contemplation; though their effects and profits may be frequently objects of our bodily senses.'

1.12 The term 'hereditament' (from late Latin *haereditas* = inheritance) refers to property which devolved to the heirs at law of the owner, ie real property as opposed to personal property which could be disposed of by will. For present purposes, it may be equated to an interest in land.

1.13 Incorporeal hereditaments are, in law, contrasted with 'corporeal' hereditaments; medieval lawyers drew a distinction between interests in land giving rights to full possession which were said to be 'corporeal' and other such interests. Ownership of a 'corporeal' hereditament gave control over the *corpus* (body) of the land. An incorporeal hereditament gave lesser, intangible, rights over land. Modern technology would use the term 'proprietary interest' to describe a corporeal hereditament.[19]

1.14 Incorporeal hereditaments include both easements and profits. Easements are traditionally divided between positive and negative. Positive easements are those which entitle the dominant owner either to do some act on the servient land. A right of way falls within this category. Negative easements require the servient owner to abstain from certain activities or uses on his land. A right of light, for example, is a negative easement, since it obliges the servient owner to restrain from erecting buildings on his land which obstruct the light received by the dominant tenement. However, as a general rule easements do

---

[17] Law Commission Paper 327 'Making Land work: Easements, covenants and profits a prendre', 2011.

[18] (1886) 33 ChD 332.

[19] For a case on the distinction between corporeal and incorporeal rights, see *Brackenbank Lodge Ltd v Peart and Others* (1993) 67 P&CR 249, CA (concerned with whether stint holdings were corporeal or incorporeal hereditaments).

not impose on the servient land any positive obligations. The duty of the servient owner is generally limited to refraining from doing anything which impedes the enjoyment of the easement by the dominant owner. Positive obligations can be imposed by contract or covenant but will not generally bind successors in title.[20] So for example in *William Old International v Arya*[21] it was held that where there was an easement to allow the dominant owner to lay pipes and cables across the servient land, the servient owner was under no obligation to grant an easement to allow the local electricity provider access to lay cables to connect the dominant owner to the electricity supply.

1.15 The category of rights over land which are capable in law of constituting easements is wide, and still growing and adapting to changes in economic and social conditions affecting land use.[22] A recent example is the right to park vehicles.[23] However, as will be seen below, this does not mean that the incidents of established types of easements will be extended by the courts simply because it is reasonable or desirable to do so. Further, the courts have declined to recognise certain proposed species of easement on various grounds, either because they lack precedent or because they are insufficiently clear or too widely restrictive of the servient owners' rights to be accepted:

> 'Incidents of a novel kind cannot be devised, and attached to property, at the fancy or caprice of any owner.'[24]

1.16 A right of way, like other easements, is said to be an 'appurtenant' incorporeal hereditament. This means simply that, however created, it is annexed to land. One cannot enjoy a right of way *in gross*, except as an incident of ownership of an interest in the land to which the right of way belongs.[25]

1.17 No exhaustive definition of the terms 'easement' or 'right of way' exists, and it is therefore necessary to consider the decided cases to establish the nature, extent, and limitation of such rights. Recognition of the fact that easements are interests in land is provided by the Law of Property Act 1925 (LPA 1925) and the Land Registration Act 2002. By section 205(1)(ix) of the LPA 1925, 'land' is defined as including easements. By section 1(2)(a) of the same Act, as an interest in land, an easement is required to be:

---

[20] See generally *Moncrieff v Jamieson* [2007] 1 WLR 2620, HL; *Rhone v Stephens* [1994] 2 AC 310.

[21] [2009] EWHC 599 (Ch).

[22] In *London & Blenheim Estates v Ladbroke Retail Parks Ltd* [1993] 1 All ER 307, a right to park vehicles was recognised as an easement. This is now established following *Moncrieff v Jamieson* [2007] 1 WLR 2620.

[23] See above and Colby, *Easing into a defined space*, Estates Gazette, 2009, No 935, p 100. See further para **1.43**.

[24] See *Ackroyd v Smith* (1850) 10 CB 164 at 188 per Cresswell J citing Lord Bingham CJ in *Keppell v Bailey* (1834) 2 My & K 517 at 535.

[25] *Rangeley v Midland Railway Co* (1868) LR 3 Ch App 306 at 310–311; *King v David Allen & Sons Billposting Ltd* [1916] 2 AC 54; *London & Blenheim Estates Ltd v Ladbroke Retail Parks Ltd* [1993] 4 All ER 157.

'for an interest equivalent to an estate in fee simple absolute in possession or a term of years absolute.'

1.18 Section 132(1) of the Land Registration Act 2002, which contains a definition of 'land', does not repeat the provision of section 3(viii) of the Land Registration Act 1925 which expressly included easements as 'land', but there can be no doubt that under that statute easements are treated as interests in land. By section 187(1) of the LPA 1925:

'Where an easement, right or privilege for a legal estate is created, it shall enure for the benefit of the land to which it is intended to be annexed.'

1.19 The effect of this is that, once a legal easement is created, it attaches to the dominant land even if the actual interest benefiting from the easement at any time is equitable only.[26]

1.20 The characterisation of easements as land for some purposes has effects in certain statutory contexts. Firstly, under section 23 of the Landlord and Tenant Act 1954 (as amended by the Regulatory Reform (Business Tenancies) England and Wales Order 2003) a right of way has been held not to be capable of being occupied by a tenant of business premises for the purposes of that provision.[27] Again, an easement does not fall within section 44(1) of the LPA 1925, which provides for statutory commencements of roots of title.[28] Thirdly, easements are not land for the purposes of certain provisions of the Limitation Act 1980, by virtue of section 38 thereof.[29]

Express creation of rights of way

1.21 The express grant of a legal easement requires and can be effected only by deed.[30] In the case of registered land, when both dominant and servient titles are registered, an easement takes effect in equity only until registered.[31] Where the servient title alone is registered, the existence of the easement requires protection by entry of a notice against the servient title. A legal easement passes on transfer of the land to which it is appurtenant, without any express words, and irrespective of the provisions of section 62 of the LPA 1925.[32] A legal easement cannot be overreached, and does not require

---

[26] See Barnsley 'Equitable Easements – Sixty Years On' (1999) 115 LQR 84.
[27] *Land Reclamation Co v Basildon District Council* [1979] 1 WLR 767 CA.
[28] *Barclays Bank v Lougher* (1996) 51 Con LR 75.
[29] Whether hereditaments referred to in statutes include easements is a question of construction in each case – *Southport Corporation v Ormskirk Union Assessment Committee* [1894] 1 QB 196 CA. *Metropolitan Railway Co v Fowler* [1893] AC 416 HL *Holywell Union and Halkyn Parish v Halkyn Drainage Co* [1895] AC 117 HL.
[30] LPA 1925, s 52(1). In *Sweet v Sommer* [2005] 2 All ER 64 it was conceded that an easement reserved by an assent under hand only took effect only in equity.
[31] Land Registration Act 1925, ss 19(2) and 22(2).
[32] See *Godwin v Schweppes Ltd* [1902] 1 Ch 926 for creation of rights of way under s 62 of the LPA 1925.

registration under the Land Charges Act 1972. The formalities are examined in more detail in Chapter 3. Rights of way may also be created by statute.[33]

Registration of rights of way

1.22 Registration of easements has been affected by the Land Registration Act 2002. Under section 70(1)(a) of the Land Registration Act 1925, legal easements constituted overriding interests and hence did not require registration. Equitable easements required registration. This was subject to an exception where the easement was 'demised, occupied or enjoyed' with land (Land Registration Rules 1925, r 258, *Celsteel v Alton House Holdings*[34]). In practice, many expressly granted easements are not registered. Under the 2002 Act the basic principle is that title is created by registration, and in due course by e-conveyances. The basic rule is that the express grant or reservation of a legal easement is a registrable disposition.[35] An effort has been made to curtail unregistered easements, by limiting 'interests which override'. Where the servient land is unregistered, and the easement is equitable, it must be protected by registration as a land charge.[36]

1.23 The 2002 Act distinguishes between interests overriding first registration (Sch 1) and registered dispositions (Sch 3).[37] The basic idea is that first registration should neither improve nor worsen the registered proprietor's situation. Equitable interests which have not been registered are excluded from both Schedules (Reversing *Celsteel v Alton House Holdings*) the effect of this is that impliedly created *equitable* easements of necessity, common intention or under the rule in *Wheeldon v Burrows* will no longer be overriding. Further:

(a) Easements arising by virtue of proprietary estoppel are no longer beneficial interests, which override. *Quaere* whether the dominant owner could be in actual occupation of an easement.[38]

(b) On registered dispositions a legal easement will in principle be an overriding interest, but only if:

(i) it is registered under the Commons Registration Act 1965 (which has its own system of registration); or

---

[33] For example under Enclosure Acts, Canal Acts, and various other provisions. See e g Highways Act 1980, s 129, and Natural Environment and Rural Communities Act 2006, s 67(5).

[34] [1985] 1 WLR 204. See further para **13.24**.

[35] See Land Registration Act 2002, s 27(2)(d).

[36] Land Charges Act 1972, s 2(5).

[37] See Land Registration Act 2002, ss 11(4)(b), 12(4)(c), 29(2)(a)(ii) and 30(2)(a)(ii).

[38] See *Saeed v Plustrade* [2001] EWCA Civ 2011. In *Chaudhary v Yavuz* [2011] EWCA Civ 1314 a claim for a right of way which had not been incorporated in the contract or registered was held not to be valid against the purchaser of property. The way was one on foot via an external stair leading to upper parts of adjacent properties. The purchaser of one property removed the connection from the stair to the other property. It was held that the 'dominant' owner was not in actual occupation of the stair. There was no basis for imposing a constructive trust on the purchaser because he had not undertaken any new obligation to give effect to the right of way.

(ii)   it is actually known of by the purchaser; or

(iii) it is obvious on a reasonably careful inspection of the land over which the easement is exercisable; or

(iv)   it has been exercised within one year prior to the relevant disposition – see Land Registration Act 2002, Schedule 3, paragraph 3. This is intended to cover such matters as easements of drainage through pipes, which may not be visible or known to either vendor or purchaser.

1.24   For a period of three years beginning on 13 October 2003 these provisions were disapplied, by virtue of Schedule 12, paragraph 10. The effect was that during this period any legal easement remained an overriding interest. The aim was to protect the continued existence of potential easements in the course of being acquired by prescription. These provisions are now long spent.

1.25   These provisions should bring about a curtailment of unregistered easements. How far the provisions of the 2002 Act may be circumvented by proprietary estoppel is not yet established, but section 116 of the 2002 Act recognises that estoppel-based rights are inherently proprietary even before being made binding by the court.[39] The same probably applies under the 2002 Act.

1.26   A legal estate is not capable of existing or being created in an undivided share of land.[40] However, section 187(2) of the LPA 1925 provides that:

'Nothing in the Act affects the right of a person to acquire, hold or exercise an easement ... over or in relation to land for a legal estate in common with any other person, or the power of creating or carrying such an easement.'

1.27   There is therefore no conceptual difficulty in the same rights being enjoyed by diverse dominant tenements, or separate interests in the dominant tenement enjoying rights over the same servient tenement.

Creation of rights of way by implication

1.28   In many situations, the grant of an easement may arise by implication, for example under the rule in *Wheeldon v Burrows*,[41] or by virtue of section 62 of the LPA 1925.[42]

1.29   Where the owner of a single piece of land disposes of part of it and retains the remainder himself, or disposes of the whole to different owners by simultaneous or near-simultaneous conveyances, rights of way may arise by

---

[39]   Rights of persons in actual occupation arising in this way have been held to bind purchasers under the previous regime of the Land Registration Act 1925, s 70. See *Lloyd v Dugdale* [2001] 1 EWCA Civ 1754.

[40]   LPA 1925, s 1(6); Land Registration Act 1925, s 3(viii), (ix).

[41]   (1879) 12 Ch D 31.

[42]   See Chapter 3.

implication of law, or under section 62 of the LPA 1925, in favour of the purchaser of a piece of land having buildings on it, against the vendor. Thus if a vendor owns land with buildings on it, and divides the land into two plots, A and B, and sells plot A, on which there are buildings which gain access across plot B, the purchaser may acquire a right of way across the route of access.

1.30 Acquisition in this way may also occur under the rule in *Wheeldon v Burrows*.[43] Acquisition of rights of way under section 62 of the LPA 1925 and under the rule in *Wheeldon v Burrows* is covered in Chapter 3.

1.31 By section 27(7) of the Land Registration Act 2002, the creation of an easement under section 62 of the Law of Property Act 1925 does not require to be completed by registration. However, it is capable of being registered and there may be circumstances where this is desirable.[44] Technically the creation of an easement in these ways involves an express grant, but in reality the situation closely resembles an implied grant. Often the parties may not appreciate the effect of the statutory provisions until long after the event.

The essentials of easements

1.32 There are four requirements to be satisfied before an easement (including a right of way) can be shown to exist. These are the following:

(1) There must be a dominant and a servient tenement.

(2) The easement must accommodate the dominant tenement.

(3) The dominant and servient tenements must be in separate ownership.

(4) The easement must be capable of forming the subject-matter of a grant.[45]

The need for a dominant and a servient tenement

1.33 The first requirement means that there must be separate parcels of land which benefit and are subject to the easement. It is, however, not uncommon for two neighbouring properties to enjoy cross-easements over each other, as in the fairly common arrangement whereby two houses share a common driveway, legal title to which is divided between them at the mid-point. An incorporeal hereditament can be a dominant tenement. So for example in *Hanbury v Jenkins*[46] it was held that a right of way could validly be appurtenant to a right of fishing.[47]

---

[43] (1879) 12 Ch D 31.
[44] See paras **13.13** and **13.14**.
[45] See generally the judgment of Lord Esher MR in Re *Ellenborough Park* [1956] Ch 131; *Rangeley v Midland Railway Co* (1868) LR 3 Ch App 306; *Hawkins v Rutter* [1892] 1 QB 668.
[46] [1901] 2 Ch 422.
[47] See also *Sussex Investments Ltd v Jackson* [1993] EGCS 152.

The need for the easement to accommodate the dominant tenement

1.34 Turning to the second requirement, easements are rights appurtenant to land and hence cannot exist unless they benefit a particular area of land. It is, therefore, not possible to create an easement recognised by the law in gross, ie as a freestanding right, not appurtenant to land. For example, it would not be possible to create a right of way, which did not benefit any particular land (where there is no servient tenement). It is therefore said that:

> 'It is trite law that there could be no easement in gross'.[48]

1.35 This principle is illustrated by *London and Blenheim Estates v Ladbroke Retail Parks Ltd*,[49] a case concerning the purported grant of a right to park vehicles. In that case a transfer of land to the plaintiff contained the grant of an easement entitling the plaintiff to park on certain land retained by the transferor. The transfer further provided that if the plaintiff purchased other land and gave notice to the transferor within five years of the original transfer, such other land would (provided the plaintiff was the owner of the originally transferred land at the date of the notice) also benefit from the same easement. The plaintiff purchased additional land. The transferor then sold the retained land (the servient tenement), and it subsequently vested in the defendants. Subsequent to the sale of the servient land by the transferor, the plaintiff gave notice under the terms of the original transfer to it that the other land it had purchased subsequent to the original transfer should benefit from the easement of parking on the land retained by the transferor. The plaintiff sought to establish that it had an enforceable easement against the defendants. The claim was rejected on the ground that at the date of the original transfer to the plaintiff there was no identified dominant tenement (apart from the original land transferred to the plaintiff), and, therefore, the terms of the original transfer did not create an enforceable option to create an easement. Since the servient land had been disposed of by the transferor before the dominant tenement had been created, the terms of the original transfer had not created an enforceable option. The court rejected a further argument that an easement was created when the plaintiff gave notice of acquisition of the further land, on the ground that by the time such notice was given the grantor had disposed of the servient land.

1.36 In *Hill v Tupper*[50] a canal company granted the plaintiff a lease of land adjoining a canal and the exclusive right to operate pleasure boats on the canal. The defendant also put pleasure boats on the canal. The plaintiff sought an injunction. It was held, dismissing the plaintiff's claim, that the right claimed was not an easement because it was not connected with the plaintiff's land.

---

[48] See *London and Blenheim Estates Ltd v Ladbroke Retail Parks Ltd* [1993] 4 All ER 157 at 162h per Peter Gibson LJ, citing *Rangeley v Midland Railway Co* (1868) LR 3 Ch App 306 at 310–311; see also para **1.10**. See further *Voice v Bell* [1993] 68 P&CR 441.

[49] [1993] 4 All ER 157, CA.

[50] (1863) 2 H & C 121.

1.37   In the Australian case of *Clos Farming Estates v Easton*[51] a claim for an easement to enter the servient land, carry out viticulture, harvest grapes and sell them failed because inter alia the claimed right did not directly benefit the allegedly dominant land. It merely facilitated the use of the dominant land for farm management.[52]

1.38   The easement must confer practical benefit in fact on the dominant tenement.[53] But it is not necessary that the dominant and servient tenements be contiguous.[54]

1.39   The importance of the requirement is that the easement must directly benefit the dominant tenement. So, for example, if in the case of a right of way the dominant tenement in fact derives no access over the servient tenement, the purported creation of an easement in favour of the dominant tenement will be invalid. There must be some connection between the existence of the easement and normal enjoyment of the dominant tenement.[55] The right must, however, have a necessary connection with the dominant tenement as such, and not merely facilitate the dominant owner's business.[56] However, it is not fatal to the validity of an easement that it in fact benefits a business carried on the dominant land and will be of no use if the business ceases.[57]

In *Kennerley v Beech*[58] it was held that a grant of a right of way over a path was not a valid easement because having regard to the location of the end of the path it did not accommodate the dominant tenement.

The dominant and servient tenements must be in separate ownership

1.40   As to the third requirement, it is well established that an easement cannot exist in circumstances where the same person both owns and occupies the 'dominant' and 'servient' tenements, on the ground that no person can have a right against himself.[59] However, an owner can grant a tenant of part of his land an easement over the remainder, and it seems that where a person owns two parcels of land, one as beneficial owner and the other as trustee, he may

---

[51]   2002 NSWCA 389.

[52]   See also *Hansford v Jago* [1921] 1 Ch 322; *Rangeley v Midland Railway Co* (1868) 3 Ch App 306; *Hawkins v Rutter* [1892] 1 QB 668; *Beckett v Lyons* [1967] Ch 449; *London and Blenheim Estates Ltd v Ladbroke Retail Parks* [1994] 1 WLR 31.

[53]   See e g *Macepark (Whittlebury) Ltd v Sargeant* [2003] 1 WLR 2284.

[54]   *Todrick v Western National Omnibus Co* [1934] Ch 561; *Pugh v Savage* [1970] 2 QB 373; *Hamble Parish Council v Haggard* [1992] 1 WLR 122.

[55]   *Re Ellenborough Park* [1956] Ch 131 at 153.

[56]   *Farming Estates v Easton* [2002 NSWCA 389.

[57]   *Copeland v Greenhalf* [1952] Ch 488 where, however, the claim failed as being in substance a claim of exclusive possession of land, as to which see below. See also *Moody v Steggles* (1879) 12 Ch D 261.

[58]   [2012] EWCA Civ 158.

[59]   *Ladyman v Grave* (1871) 6 Ch App 763; *Roe v Siddons* (1888) 22 QBD 224; *Bolton v Bolton* (1879) 11 Ch D 968; *Metropolitan Railway Co v Fowler* (1892) 1 QB 165; *Attorney General of Southern Nigeria v John Holt & Co (Liverpool) Ltd* [1915] AC 599 at 617–618, PC.

grant an easement in favour of one parcel over the other, on the ground that beneficial ownership of the two parcels is in different ownership even though legal title is not.[60]

The easement must be capable of forming the subject matter of a grant

1.41   The fourth requirement derives from the fact that the basis of the law of easements is a grant by one landowner to another of a recognised right over land capable of subsisting as a legal estate. It is not necessary to examine at length all the cases where the courts have declined to recognise rights of various kinds.

1.42   In the context of rights of way, the following appear to be established points. Firstly the law probably recognises a right to walking in a garden for recreational purposes, based on the much discussed decision in *Re Ellenborough Park*,[61] at least provided that it is appurtenant to an identified dominant tenement.[62]

1.43   Secondly, the easement cannot amount to a grant of exclusive possession. So in *Batchelor v Marlow*[63]a claim that an easement by prescription had arisen to park cars on a strip of land on weekdays during business hours was rejected since its effect would have been to render the rights of the owner illusory. The same conclusion was reached in the earlier case, also concerning car repairs, of *Copeland v Greenhalf*.[64] In *Mulvaney v Gough*[65] a right to use land as a communal garden was held not to give an exclusive right of occupation, nor to prevent the owner from building a driveway across the land. In *Kettel v Bloomfield Ltd*[66] it was held that the express grants in leases of individual flats of sole rights to use designated parking spaces to park a car or motor bike did not amount either to a demise of the spaces or give rise to a situation where the landlord had not left itself with no reasonable use of the land. The rights granted were therefore valid easements. The court had regard to the facts that the leases did not include the spaces in the premises demised and that the rights were limited to parking in the spaces: there was also an express reservation of the right for others to park across the spaces. The issue of easements and parking is considered in further detail in Chapter 4.

1.44   On the other hand, in *P & S Platt v Crouch*[67] an argument that a right to use moorings was not capable of being an easement was rejected. In the context

---

[60]   *Ecclesiastical Commissioners v Kino* (1880) 14 Ch D 213.
[61]   [1956] 1 Ch 131.
[62]   See Baker: *Recreational privileges as easements: Law and Policy*, Conveyancer and Property Lawyer, (20122), p 37.
[63]   [2001] 1 EGLR 119. The citation given is to the first instance decision, which is reversed by the Court of Appeal: [2001] EWCA Civ 1051; [2003] 1 WLR 764.
[64]   [1952] Ch 488.
[65]   [2002] 3 EGLR 72.
[66]   [2012] EWHC 1422 (Ch).
[67]   [2004] 1 P & CR 18.

of rights of way, a right to park vehicles on clearly defined land is now established as capable of constituting an easement. This was held at first instance in *London and Blenheim Estates Ltd v Ladbroke Retail Parks Ltd*.[68] The existence of an easement of parking was likewise recognised in *Batchelor v Marlow*, where the Court of Appeal noted that the possibility of an easement of parking was common ground between the parties. The claim for such an easement failed on the facts. *Moncreiff v Jamieson*[69] appears to put the possibility of such an easement existing beyond doubt, even if its scope is unclear.[70] In *Hair v Gillman*[71] a permission given to a tenant of part of the landlord's property to park on adjacent land was held to have been converted into a right to park by virtue of section 62 of the LPA 1925 when the landlord subsequently sold the premises let to the tenant to the tenant.

1.45 However, in *Saeed v Plustrade*[72] it was said in the Court of Appeal that there was no decision of the Court of Appeal to this effect. The court in this case appears not to have been referred to *Batchelor v Marlow* except at first instance, and it is suggested the preponderance of authority clearly favours the right to park as coming within the category of easements recognised. *Kettel v Bloomfield*,[73] already noted, is consistent with the modern view.

1.46 A grant of rights which are in impermissibly wide and undefined terms is inimical to the concept of an easement. So in *Magrath v Parkside Hotels Ltd*[74] it was argued that a right to use a fire escape was not a valid easement due to it allowing entry to the servient tenement at any convenient point, and permitting the dominant owner to range widely over the servient land at all levels from ground to roof. The court held that read reasonably the grant was not impermissibly wide and undefined.

OTHER CATEGORISATIONS OF EASEMENTS

1.47 Easements are sometimes divided into *continuous* and *non-continuous* easements depending on whether the easement confers a right to do something of a continuous and constant nature. A non-continuous easement is one where enjoyment is of its nature only possible from time to time, by a series of acts. Easements of way come into the category of continuous easements, as do easements of the right to receive water through a water course, and (perhaps anomalously) a right of way if exercised over a formed road.[75]

---

[68] [1993] I All ER 307 affirmed [1994] 1 WLR 31 CA.
[69] [2007] 1 WLR 2620 HL.
[70] See Spark: *Easements of parking and storage: Are easements non-possessory interests in land?*, Conveyancer and Property Lawyer, (2012), p 6.
[71] [2000] 3 EGLR 74.
[72] [2002] 2 EGLR 19 CA.
[73] [2012] EWHC 1422 (Ch).
[74] [2011] EWHC 143 (Ch).
[75] *Watts v Kelson* (1870) LR 6 Ch App 166 at 174 per Mellish LJ. See also *Brown v Alabaster* (1887) 37 Ch D 490.

1.48 The distinction was at one time of importance in conveyancing, since upon severance of tenements easements used as a necessity, or in their nature continuous, would pass by implication of law without any words of grant, but easements which were discontinuous did not pass unless the owner by appropriate language showed an intention that they should pass.[76] However, the importance of the distinction has been lessened by section 62 of the LPA 1925.[77]

Easements and licences

1.49 A right of way is, like all easements, an interest in land. A licence, by contrast, does not create an interest in land. A gratuitous licence may be revoked at any time on reasonable notice without liability.[78] In other cases, whether a licence may be revoked depends on the terms agreed.[79] A licence will not in general bind successors in title to the parties.

1.50 In *Colchester and East Essex Co-Operative Society Ltd v The Kelvedon Labour Club and Institute Ltd*[80] the question arose whether a licence was terminable and if so on what terms. Buxton LJ said:

> '[9] The proper approach to that enquiry is, in my respectful judgement, to be found in the judgment of Lord Justice Goff in this court in *Staffordshire Health Authority v South Staffordshire Waterworks Co* [1978] 1 WLR 1387, 1399 H, where Lord Justice Goff cited from the judgment of Mr Justice Buckley in *re Spenborough Urban District Council's Agreement* [1968] Ch 139, in which reference was made to the speech of Lord MacDermot in Winter Garden Theatre.[81] Lord Justice Goff continued, quoting with approval Mr Justice Buckley:
>
>> "Since ex hypothesi such an agreement contains no provision expressly dealing with determination by the party who asserts that this should be inferred, the question is not one of construction in the narrow sense of putting a meaning on language which the parties have used, but in the wider sense of ascertaining, in the light of all the admissible evidence and in the light of what the parties have said or omitted to say in the agreement, what the common intention of the parties was in the relevant respect when they entered into the agreement. It is of the nature of this problem that he who asserts that the parties intended something which they omitted to state expressly must demonstrate that this was so .... An agreement which is silent about determination will not be determinable unless the facts of the case, such as the subject matter of the agreement, the nature of the contract or the circumstances in which the agreement was made, support a finding that the parties intended that it should be determinable, but there is, in my judgment, no presumption one way or the other."'

---

[76] *Polden v Bastard* (1865) LR 1 QB 156 at 161 per Erle CJ.

[77] Considered in Chapter 3.

[78] *Armstong v Shephard and Short Ltd* [1959] 2QB 384.

[79] *Colchester and East Essex Co-Operative Society Ltd v The Kelvedon Labour Club and Institute Ltd* [2003] EWCA Civ 1671.

[80] [2003] EWCA Civ 1671.

[81] *Winter Garden Theatre (London) Ltd v Milennium Productions Ltd* [1948] AC 173.

1.51 In *IDC Group Ltd v Clark*[82] a deed granted to owners of premises a right to use a fire escape route which led over neighbouring premises. The words used were 'grant licence'. It was held that the words used were not apt for the grant of an easement. Therefore, the rights created were only a personal licence which did not bind successors in title of the grantor. The benefit of a licence may be assignable provided that it is not a purely personal licence or a bare (gratuitous) licence. But the burden of a contractual licence does not pass to the successor of the licensor. However, where a licence expires and the licensee continues to use the facility in question it is possible for an easement to arise by prescription. This was the case in *London Tara Hotel Ltd v Kensington Close Hotel Ltd*.[83] In *Magrath v Parkside Hotels Ltd*,[84] another case concerning rights to use a fire escape route, the court considered but did not decide whether the right might be binding on successors by virtue of estoppels.

GRANT OF FUTURE EASEMENTS

1.52 The grant of future interests in land was formerly restricted by the rule against perpetuities. This is a doctrine evolved by the courts intended to discourage attempts by owners of property from devising schemes of settlements and trusts whose terms have the effect of resulting in interests in land or other property vesting at remote times in the future.[85] The rule was extensively modified by the Perpetuities and Accumulations Act 1964 ('the 1964 Act').[86] The Law Commission recommended further changes.[87] These are incorporated in the Perpetuities and Accumulations Act 2009.[88]

1.53 The rule for dispositions made before the 1964 Act came into force is as follows (this statement is taken from the Law Commission Report, para 1.7):

(a) A future interest in any type of property will be void from the date that the interest which attempts to create it takes effect, if there is any possibility that the interest *may* vest or commence outside the perpetuity period.

(b) For these purposes, the perpetuity period consists of one or more lives in being plus a period of 21 years and, where relevant, a period of gestation. In the case of an interest created after the 1964 Act came into force (15 July 1964) the rule is modified in that:

---

[82] [1992] 2 EGLR 84 CA.
[83] [2010] EWHC 2749 (Ch). See Chapter 6.
[84] [2011] EWHC 143 (Ch).
[85] The ramifications and refinements of the rule were the subject of much study. The most comprehensive and authoritative work on it is still *Gray on Perpetuities*, a monumental work first published in 1886 by the Boston Lawyer John Chipman Gray.
[86] 1964 c 55.
[87] See Law Commission: *The Rules Against Perpetuities and Excessive Accumulations* (HMSO).
[88] 2009 c 18.

(i)   the interest will only be void where it *must* vest or take effect (if at all) outside the perpetuity period;

(ii)   it is therefore necessary to wait and see if need be for the whole perpetuity period, to determine whether the interest is valid; and

(iii) an alternative perpetuity period of up to 80 years may be employed instead of a life in being plus 21 years.

1.54   These provisions were introduced by the 1964 Act, sections 1(1) and 3(1).

1.55   The rule applied to dispositions providing for future grants of easements. So in *Dunn v Blackdown Properties Ltd*,[89] conveyances of 1926 and 1938 granted the plaintiff's predecessors in title the right to use the sewers and drains *now passing or hereafter to pass* under a private road belonging to the defendant's predecessors. At the date of the conveyances, no sewers or drains existed, although one was constructed after the second conveyance. It was held that the plaintiff had no right as against the defendant to make use of the sewer actually constructed. The words of the conveyances purported to create a grant of an easement to arise at an uncertain date in the future, not limited to take effect within the perpetuity period, and the grant was therefore void. Had the case come to court after the 1964 Act, the effect of section 3(1) would have been that the 'wait and see provisions would have applied for the duration of the perpetuity period, so that if a sewer was in fact constructed within the perpetuity period the grant would have been valid to that extent'.

1.56   The main difficulty the rule caused is in relation to the grant of future rights of way and analogous rights, for example to use drains or sewers not yet constructed. It can be avoided to an extent by specifying a perpetuity period (for which purpose 80 years is usually selected, since this eliminates the need to track down dates of deaths of persons specified as lives in being) but this only helps to an extent, as it is certainly possible for future easements to be required commercially to vest beyond this time.

1.57   The 2009 Act removes this difficulty The 1964 Act is limited to existing instruments and no longer applies to easements. Therefore many of the problems of the old law will become of limited importance.

1.58   However, the distinction between immediately granted easements and ones arising in the future remains important in relation to older grants and of course also on the question as to the extent of the rights if any granted. In some cases, a distinction is to be drawn between the grant of a future easement, the grant of an immediate right the use of which is subject to conditions. In *Chaffe v Kingsley*[90] a conveyance of land showed a projected extension of a road from the land of the vendor. The vendor argued that there were to be implied into the conveyances reservations of the right to construct and use of the projected extension of the road. The vendor's claim failed both at first

---

[89]   [1961] Ch 433.
[90]   (1999) 77 P & CR 281.

instance and on appeal[91] on the ground that the conveyances did not contain such implied reservations. However, at first instance the court accepted that the implied reservations contended for by the defendant would not be avoided by the rule against perpetuities. The right to enter the land to construct the road was only exercisable within a reasonable time, which would on any view be far less than 21 years (the default period under the 1964 Act) and the right to use the road would vest immediately notwithstanding that it might not be exercisable until outside the perpetuity period.

1.59   In *Adam v Shrewsbury*[92] the issue arose whether the claimant/respondent had been granted a right of way, when she purchased her house, over retained land of the vendor. The conveyance provided as follows:

> 'The purchaser (ie the claimant) hereby covenants with the vendor (ie Mr Thomas) that within a reasonable time after the vendor has at his own expense excavated the garage space hatched blue on the plan hereto annexed to the level indicated on the site plan she will erect a stock proof fence along the (south-eastern and south western) boundaries (including the three protruding sides of the site hatched blue) separating the property hereby conveyed [ie Tan-y-Ffordd] from the adjoining land of the vendors (ie Bryn Coed) and the purchaser further covenants that she and her successors in title will thereafter be responsible for maintaining and repairing the said fence.'

1.60   The site of the garage space was included in the conveyance. The whole site sloped steeply uphill from the road. Planning permission had been granted for a development including the construction of a garage, and of a road leading to it, but neither had been built. At the time of the conveyance the garage site was virgin rock, and the road petered out at the hairpin bend which would have led to the site of the garage. It was held that the claimant had no right of way over the route of the road to the garage space, because whilst the parties shared an intention that she should have a right, this was only to arise when the road and the space were constructed. Neuberger LJ said:

> 'As I see it, that implied right was either a contractual entitlement to claim a right of way over the whole of the road if and when the relevant work was carried out, or, as seems to me to be the better analysis, an immediate right of way, but one which could only be enjoyed once the north-western section of the road had been constructed. Unfortunately for the claimant, whichever of those two is the proper analysis, her claim must fail.'

1.61   In *Magrath v Parkside Hotels Ltd*[93] a case concerning rights to use a fire escape route under a grant dating from 1947, it was held that an ancillary right to erect alter existing staircases and erect new staircases contravened the rule against perpetuities.

---

[91]   [2000] 1 EGLR 104.
[92]   [2005] EWCA 1006.
[93]   [2011] EWHC 143 (Ch).

1.62 In *Changeinvest Ltd v Rosendale-Steinhausen*,[94] the conveyance contained a reservation of a right of way subject to a proviso that the vendor would make up a road along the strip of land by a certain date. Two points arose. Firstly, whether the successor in title of the vendor could exercise the right of way at all, since the obligation to make up the road, so it was argued, being a positive one, could not bind the successor. Therefore, since the obligation to make up the road was a condition precedent to the right to exercise the right of way, the right of way was now defunct. The second argument was whether the obligation to make up the road within the time limit was a condition precedent to using the right of way at all. The court held that this was not the case, but that the right of way could not be exercised until the road was made up. On the first point, he construed the terms of the conveyance not as imposing a positive obligation but as creating a framework for the exercise of the right of way.

1.63 In the earlier case of *South Eastern Railway Company v Associated Portland Cement Manufacturers*[95] it was held that the grant of a right to construct a tunnel was on the terms of the relevant conveyance an immediate right directly the conveyance was executed.

NO EASEMENT ON AN EASEMENT

1.64 The servient owner has no right to require the dominant owner to continue to exercise the easement.[96] So in *Mason v Shrewsbury and Hereford Railway Co*[97] a stream which had previously been diverted from its natural course into a canal under statutory powers was rediverted on closure of the canal into its natural bed which by that time was silted up. It was held that the plaintiff's claim for flooding of his land failed. Cockburn CJ said:

> '... it appears to me beyond doubt that the servient owner acquires no right to the continuance of the easement and the incidental advantages arising to him from it, if the dominant owner thinks proper to abandon it.'

1.65 Thus there would presumably be no right for a servient owner of a private road to complain if the dominant owner abandoned use of the way, resulting in it becoming overgrown or full of rubbish or a haunt of drug dealers, for example. This is subject to the possibility of specific stipulations in the terms of the grant.[98] But where the servient owner allows a nuisance to occur by reason of third parties fly tipping it may be liable to the dominant owner for failing to take reasonable steps to abate it.[99]

---

[94]   [2004] EWHC 264.
[95]   [1910] 1 Ch 12.
[96]   See e g *Schwann v Cotton* [1916] 2 Ch 459; *Bartlett v Tottenham* [1932] 1 Ch 114; *John S Deed & Sons Ltd v British Electricity Authority* (1950) 66 TLR (pt 2) 567.
[97]   (1871) LR 6 QB 578.
[98]   See generally Chapter 8.
[99]   *Crane Road Properties LLP v Hundalani* [2006] EWHC 2066 (Ch).

Chapter 2

RIGHTS OF WAY DEFINED AND CONTRASTED

2.1   This Chapter is about those rights which are, in some sense, private rights of way but which are not legal easements of the type discussed generally in this book. As explained in Chapter 1, an easement of way is an incorporeal right, granted for a legal estate in fee simple or for a term of years absolute, accommodating a dominant tenement and subsisting over a defined or definable route across a servient tenement in separate ownership. There are other legal concepts which are similar to such easements. They may either be confused with them or interact with them to modify the rights of parties under the law of easements.

2.2   This Chapter therefore considers a number of rights comparable to private rights of way but which differ from legal easements. They can be corporeal rather than incorporeal; subsist as terminable personal relationships rather than as rights of property; last for an indefinite period rather than in fee simple or for a term of years; be enforceable as equitable rights rather than as legal interests; involve taking something from a servient tenement rather than doing or being able to restrain the doing of something on it; allow people to wander over an area rather than pass from one point to another; or benefit an undefined and fluctuating class of persons rather than a dominant tenement.

2.3   Rights of way can also originate by statute rather than grant. Statutory rights of way are considered in Chapter 7. They comprise easements in the normal sense as well as wayleaves and rights of access.

OWNERSHIP OR EASEMENT

2.4   It can sometimes be difficult to ascertain whether a person using a path or track does so because he is the owner of the way (or of a share in it) or because he has a right of way over it. The owner of a legal estate in land (a corporeal hereditament, see para **1.13**) in possession normally has the right to use his property for any lawful purpose. Sometimes he may be out of possession as when he has granted a lease, or a mortgagee has taken possession, or a body having compulsory powers has issued a notice of entry, but those are exceptions to the general rule. As a person cannot have a legal right over his own land, such ownership is incompatible with the existence of an easement; the owner not only cannot acquire a right of way over his land but, if he already has such a right, and then acquires the servient land in the same capacity as he owns the dominant land, the easement will be extinguished by merger (see para **9.18**).

Physical division of way

2.5   The owner of land adjacent to a track or path is presumed to own the soil of the way up to the middle line or *medium filum*. This is most often met with in relation to highways but the same principles apply to a private way where it runs between two properties, and the boundary is, as a general rule, a line drawn along the middle of the way.[1] It is only a presumption and may be rebutted.[2] Where it applies, the owner of property abutting on the road will be entitled to use the half of it adjacent to his land by virtue of his right of ownership although it may be subject to rights of way for the benefit of other properties. He will usually have a right of way, often prescriptive, over the other half.

2.6   The presumption was considered in *Paton v Todd*.[3] In his judgment Morgan J quoted from the judgment of Brightman J in *Giles v County Building Constructors (Hertford) Ltd*[4] which was in these terms:

> 'As I understand the law, there are two presumptions relative to the ownership of the soil of a roadway. One presumption operates in certain circumstances when the conveyancing history of the land and the road is unknown. This presumption supplies a fact of which there is no direct evidence, namely, the ownership of the road. The presumption is that the owner of the land abutting on the road is also the owner of the adjoining section of road up to the middle line, There is no room for this presumption when the conveyancing history of the land and the road is known from the time when they were in common ownership as in the case before me. In such a case, there is, in certain circumstances, a totally different presumption which is more in the nature of a canon of construction that a conveyance of the land includes half the adjacent roadway. The distinction between the two presumptions, if the second one can properly be called a presumption, is clearly drawn by Joyce J in *Mappin Brothers v Liberty & Co Ltd* [1903] 1 Ch 118. I need not refer to that case because Mr Jopling, in his able argument, accepted the distinction and told me that he based his submission only on the second presumption, as indeed I am sure he must. Mr Jopling relied on *Norton on Deeds*, 2nd edn (1928), p 252, for a correct statement of the nature of the second presumption.

> A conveyance of land abutting on a highway, or a non-tidal river, passes the adjoining half of the highway, or of the river bed.

---

[1]   *Holmes v Bellingham* (1859) 29 LJCP 132; 141 ER 843; *Smith v Howden* (1863) 14 CBNS 398; 143 ER 500.
[2]   *Pardoe v Pennington* (1996) 75 P & CR 264, CA; *Commission for the New Towns v JJ Gallagher Ltd* [2003] 2 P & CR 3.
[3]   [2012] EWHC 1248 (Ch) (31 EG 48).
[4]   (1971) 22 P & CR 978 at 981–982.

The presumption may be rebutted, but it is not rebutted: (i) by the land being described as containing an area which can be satisfied without including half the road or river bed; (ii) by the land being described as bounded by the road or river bed; (iii) by the land being referred to as coloured on a plan, whereon the half of the road or river bed is not coloured; (iv) by the grantor being owner of the land on both sides of the road or river; or (v) because subsequent events not contemplated at the time of the grant show it to have been very disadvantageous to the grantor to have parted with the half of the road or river bed, but which if contemplated would probably have induced him to reserve it.

It is a well-settled rule of construction that, where there is a conveyance of land, even although it is described by reference to a plan, and by colour, and by quantity, if it is said to be bounded on one side by a public thoroughfare, then half of the road passes unless there is enough in the expressions of the instrument or in the surrounding circumstances to show that this is not the intention of the parties': per Swinfen Eady J, *Central London Railway v City of London Land Tax Commissioners* [1911] 1 Ch 467, 474.'

2.7   Morgan J in *Paton v Todd* went on to say:[5]

'It is clear that both presumptions apply in the case of a public road. There is no distinction between a highway in the country and a street in a town: see *In re White's Charities* [1898] 1 Ch 659. There is authority for the first presumption applying in the case of "a private or occupation road": *Holmes v Bellingham* (1859) 7 CBNS 329. This case was applied in *Smith v Howden* (1863) 14 CBNS 398, where the land in question was a green lane leading to only one parcel of land, which had the benefit of a private right of way over the lane. In *St Edmundsbury v Clark* (No 2) [1973] 1 WLR 1572, it was considered that the second presumption applied to "an easement of way" as well as to a highway. In *Pardoe v Pennington* (1996) 75 P&CR 264, it was held that the second presumption applied to a bridleway. In that case, the strip of land was described as a bridleway but also as a road or a farm track. There were private rights of way over the track: see at page 266. It was common ground that the second "highway" presumption applied (see at page 269) but on the facts it was held that the presumption was rebutted. I was not referred to any case which discussed the possible application of either presumption to land which was subject to a right of way on foot only (whether a public or a private right of way).

Both presumptions may be rebutted. The first presumption may be rebutted by acts of ownership inconsistent with the result achieved by applying the presumption: *Holmes v Bellingham* (1859) 7 CBNS 329; *Beckett v Leeds Corporation* (1872) 7 Ch App 421.

Many of the cases which discuss the second presumption also discuss what suffices to rebut the presumption. Many of the relevant cases on that point were considered in *The Commission for the New Towns v JJ Gallagher Ltd* [2003] 2 P&CR 24. The decisions in many of those cases turned on matters of detail and involved some fine distinctions. The presumption may be rebutted by internal

---

5   At [35].

evidence within the relevant conveyance itself or by reference to practical and common sense factors which would have been known to the parties at the time of the conveyance: see at [41]'.

2.8   Building estates are often laid out with a shared driveway between each pair of houses. *Williams v Usherwood*[6] illustrates the type of device and some of the problems. It concerned a 1930's housing estate on which two houses, No 31 owned by the defendants and No 33 owned by the plaintiffs, had a common driveway between them. Each owned half the drive way and had a right of way for motor cars over the other half. A fence was erected not down the middle of the drive (which would have prevented use) but on the land of No 33. Part of the foundations of No 33 lay under the drive and its windows opened on to it but the drive was only used by No 31 as No 33 had another means of access. Over the years the owners of No 31 carried out acts of ownership. In 1977 the plaintiffs claimed to assert their rights of ownership of half the drive and their right of way over the rest. The claim was dismissed. The Court of Appeal held that there was evidence on which the judge could find that there had been sufficient acts of adverse possession and abandonment of the right of way. The title by adverse possession to the surface of the driveway was consistent with an implied reservation to the eaves of No 33, the right to use drains under it and the right to open and maintain windows.

2.9   Where the roads on a housing estate are not adopted highways, each house may own half the roadway to which it fronts. *Jaggard v Sawyer*[7] (see para **2.69**) involved a cul-de-sac of ten houses served by a private road. Each house owner also owned the part of the road to which his house fronted up to the middle line and each had a right of way over the parts of the road belonging to the owners of the other houses. The defendant required access over the road (including part where the plaintiff owned half of it) to a building plot which did not enjoy a right of way. The Court of Appeal held this would amount to a trespass but approved the judge's exercise of discretion to refuse an injunction and confirmed his award of damages in lieu (see para **11.141**).

Ways owned in undivided shares

2.10   Prior to 1925, roadways used by several properties were often owned in undivided shares. The effect of the LPA 1925 was to convert undivided shares into beneficial interests under a trust for sale and subsequently the Trusts of Land and Appointment of Trustees Act 1996 changed that into a trust of land. Up to four persons[8] hold the legal estate in trust for the various owners. It is possible that a built and surfaced driveway on the boundary between two properties might be regarded as a boundary structure for the purposes of LPA 1925, s 38 and therefore if before 1926 it was owned in undivided shares it would now be severed vertically subject to rights of user. However, many roads

---

[6]   (1983) 45 P & CR 235 CA.
[7]   [1995] 1 WLR 269.
[8]   Or sometimes the Public Trustee under transitional provisions for such properties so held in 1925. See the LPA 1925, s 39 and Sch 1, Part IV. See also s 34.

set up in this way are not suitable to be so divided, particularly where they serve several properties and will accordingly be held on a trust of land.

2.11 It may be difficult to determine who now have the beneficial interests in a driveway subject to a trust of land. While an incorporeal easement of way automatically passes with the dominant tenement without having to be assigned, the same is not true of a trust interest which needs to be assigned specifically in writing under LPA 1925, s 53. If, therefore, a house was transferred but the seller did not include the beneficial interest under the trust in the driveway, he would retain the equitable title although there could be an argument that by virtue of the sale contract and LPA 1925, s 63 he was a trustee of that beneficial interest for the buyer.

2.12 The legal estate in the shared road would vest in the last surviving trustee and, unless new trustees were appointed, in his executor if one proved his will and title would pass along the chain but if legal title vested in a person who died intestate it would vest under the Law of Property (Miscellaneous Provisions) Act 1994, s 14 in the Public Trustee (formerly in the President of the Family Division). It could therefore be difficult to trace the legal estate in the driveway. It may be possible for either the owners of all the shares to appoint new trustees under the 1996 Act or for some of them to apply to the court for an appointment under the Trustee Act 1925, s 41.

2.13 Defects in title cannot be cured by claiming the benefit of the Limitation Act 1980. A shared driveway in use by several persons will not be in the possession of any one of them sufficiently to ground a claim to adverse possession and, even if they claimed as joint tenants, their possession would not be adverse to the trustees. The beneficial owner of an undivided share has rights of access over the land in the trust. The Trusts of Land and Appointment of Trustees Act 1996, s 12(2) deals with rights to occupy land subject to a trust. A way is not suitable for occupation but the trustees would be bound to permit beneficiaries to make use of it as that is the purpose of the trust.

2.14 Since the legal title to land held in undivided shares is vested in trustees, an adjacent landowner who has a share could, in principle, even though as shareholder he has a proprietary right of access, have a legal easement over the land if it derived from an independent source. For example he might have an undivided share along with his ownership of plot 1 but have purchased plot 2 which already had a separate express right. This will remain the case even if he becomes, perhaps by survivorship, the sole trustee, since his capacities will differ and there will be no merger. However, since he has a right of access by virtue of his share, he could not acquire a prescriptive right of way.

Ownership of roads under inclosure Acts

2.15 In the case of roads laid out under an inclosure award (para **7.10**) the general rule came to be that if the lord of the manor shared in the general allotment under the Act (which was the usual case) then the roadway would be regarded as belonging to the owners of the land to either side up to the *medium filum*. Where the lord of the manor did not receive any allotment under the Act, the soil of any ways laid out remained with him, whether use of them was private to the allottees or whether they were dedicated as public ways.[9] This can be relevant if land initially allotted as agricultural land is subsequently developed so that the private road needs to be made up or services need to be laid in it.

General boundaries rule for registered land

2.16   Registered land is defined both by a description in the property register, which is normally brief (eg 15 Acacia Avenue, Barset) and by reference to an official plan which forms part of the register. The plan usually shows the land in the registered title as bounded by a red line. Whether or not a way is included within the red edging, the official plan is not normally conclusive of the extent of ownership. Most titles are subject to the general boundaries rule in s 60(1) and (2) of the LRA 2002:

> '(1)   The boundary of a registered estate as shown for the purposes of the register is a general boundary, unless shown as determined under this section.
>
> (2)   A general boundary does not determine the exact line of the boundary.'

2.17   This replaces the former rule 278 of the 1925 Rules which provided that the exact line of a general boundary was undetermined and gave examples including 'whether or not the land registered includes the whole or any portion of an adjoining road or stream'. Although those words have not been repeated in the current legislation the principles remain the same. Section 60(3) and (4) provide for fixed boundaries to be determined but in practice those provisions are rarely invoked.

2.18   Frequently the red line of the plan will exclude an adjacent private road or path. Even if so, in the absence of other evidence (such as an express right of way which would be inconsistent with ownership), it may not be possible to tell from the register whether or not the title includes the land comprising the way. Conversely even if a way is shown as within the red line, evidence may be produced to show it belongs (in whole or part) to someone else.

2.19   Occasionally the position is evident, for instance where land to be comprised in a housing estate was registered before plots were laid out and new estate roads dedicated so that when houses were sold the land transferred excluded the roads and footpaths which therefore remained in the developer's title. It may then transfer them to the local highway authority. Such instances largely relate to recent building estates. In other cases it may be necessary to investigate the history of the property. In the absence of any other indication the *medium filum* presumption will be applied.

---

[9]   *Poole v Huskinson* (1843) 11 M and W 827 per Parke B; cf *R v Inhabitants of the Tithing of East Mark* (1848) 11 QBR 877, 116 ER 701, 152 ER 1039.

POSSESSION OR EASEMENT – UNLOADING AND PARKING

2.20 If a person has the right to exclusive possession of some land that cannot be an easement.[10] If complete use of land is conferred exclusively on the owner of one property that may take effect as a grant of a freehold[11] but if use is consistent with other uses by the servient owner it will not. Use as a way will not normally exclude the servient owner from other uses of the land.

2.21 A discontinuous easement, such as a right of way, cannot amount to exclusive occupation of the servient tenement (see para **4.114**). A continuous easement such as a water pipe may do so but provided that the servient owner is not excluded from all benefit from his land it will still be an easement. In the case of a buried pipe he will still have the use of the surface. A right to store goods is also recognised as being capable of being an easement, again provided the right is not so extensive to exclude the servient land owner.[12] In *Wright v Macadam*[13] the right to use a shed for storing coal was recognised as an easement which could pass under the LPA 1925, s 62.[14] The fact that exercising a right involves the temporary exclusion of the servient landowner is not incompatible with the right being an easement.[15] Although such issues are unlikely to be relevant for a right of way on its own, related aspects can arise in connection with loading and unloading and with parking.

Loading and halting

2.22 Issues often arise as to how far the user of a right of way may halt for a short or long time (see para **4.96**). In *Cannon v Villars*[16] Sir George Jessel MR said in the context of a grant of a right of way:

> '... if the road is not to a dwelling-house but to a factory, or a place used for business purposes which would require heavy weights to be brought to it, or to a wool warehouse which would require bags or packages of wool to be brought to it, then a grant of right of way would include a right to use it for reasonable purposes, sufficient for the purposes of the business, which would include the right of bringing up carts and waggons at reasonable times for the purpose of the business.'

---

[10] *Copeland v Greenhalf* [1952] Ch 488.
[11] *Reilly v Booth* (1890) LR 44 Ch D 12.
[12] *Att-Gen of Southern Nigeria v John Holt & Co (Liverpool) Ltd* [1915] AC 599.
[13] [1949] 2KB 744.
[14] But see the discussion of this case in *Grigsby v Melville* [1972] 1 WLR 1355.
[15] *Miller v Emcer Products Ltd* [1956] Ch 304.
[16] (1878) 8 ChD 415.

2.23 That passage was quoted with approval in *Bulstrode v Lambert*[17] in the context of a claimed right to halt to load and unload. In *McIlraith v Grady*[18] a right to stop for a reasonable time to load and unload was held to be ancillary to a right of way.

Parking vehicles

2.24 In addition to a right to halt for a short time, the dominant user may wish to remain longer. This issue tends to arise in the context of rights of way where the dominant owner claims to have the right to keep a motor car more or less permanently in a given place. Parking a vehicle on a specific place for a long period of time, or repeatedly, may amount to an ouster of the servient owner (see para **4.110**).

2.25 In *London and Blenheim Estates v Ladbroke Retail Parks*[19] it was held that the right to park vehicles can be established as an easement provided that it is not so great as to amount to an effective exclusion of the owner of the servient land from its land. In *Saeed v Plustrade Ltd*[20] the Court of Appeal considered *London & Blenheim* and expressly left open the question whether the right to park could exist as an easement. On the facts of the case the claimed right was an overriding interest since the car park area was registered land and the tenant was in occupation of it at the time the landlord acquired the land so that the same facts governed the issue of interference with the right, whether it was an overriding interest or an easement.

2.26 In *Batchelor v Marlow*,[21] the Court of Appeal held that the test was whether the servient owner still retained reasonable use of his land. If the claim to park was so extensive a right that ownership of the servient land was rendered illusory, then it could not be an easement. In *Moncrieff v Jamieson*[22] (a Scottish case on the parallel concept of servitudes), the House of Lords criticised the Court of Appeal's decision in *Batchelor* and obiter suggested an alternative test, namely whether the servient owner retained control and possession of the land but did not overrule *Batchelor*, which is therefore still binding authority in England.

2.27 *Virdi v Chana*[23] again considered if an easement of parking was known to the law. Judge Purle QC held that he was bound by *Batchelor*, but also applied the test in *Moncrieff*, and found that such an easement was capable of existing. The judge said that the servient owner could still plant a tree on the land and:

---

[17] [1953] 2 All ER 728, [1953] 1 WLR 1064.
[18] [1968] 1 QB 468, [1967] 3 All ER 625, CA.
[19] [1994] 1 WLR 31 (1994) 67 P & CR 1.
[20] [2002] 02 EG 102 (CS).
[21] [2003] 1 WLR 764.
[22] [2007] UKHL 42.
[23] [2008] EWHC 2901 (Ch).

'could also come on to the servient land for the purpose of maintaining or repairing the fence which abuts it, or replacing the fence with a wall. She could also go onto the gravelled area (so far as within her ownership) to erect signs, or place decorative flower pots on the land, subject again to not obstructing the ability to park on the gravelled area, which none of this need do.'[24]

2.28 It therefore appears that whether the right to park or the right to storage can exist as an easement will depend on the facts and the extent to which the servient owner is excluded from enjoyment of his land. The issue can in part turn on identifying what the servient tenement is. A right to park vehicles may be a heavy burden on a small area but reasonable in a greater one.

2.29 The period of use may also be relevant to the way in which the person claiming the right to park formulates his claim. In order to establish a possessory right to land it is necessary to demonstrate possession for twelve years for unregistered land[25] and at least ten years followed by an application to the Land Registry (which the registered proprietor has a good chance of defeating) for registered land.[26] For an easement it is usually necessary to show 20 years prescription and, if the land is registered, to satisfy the conditions in LRA 2002, Sch 3, para 3. Thus a person seeking to retain the right to park a car which he has exercised for some time may have to consider whether it is better to claim ownership or an easement.

2.30 Although a contractual right to park can exist on its own, an easement to park cannot be a right in gross but must be appurtenant to a dominant tenement. A right to park will need a means of reaching the parking space. This right of access may be seen as ancillary to the parking or as a separate easement, itself appurtenant to the dominant tenement. Where a separate right to park is created by a licence (for instance in a city centre car park) a right of way to the parking space will be implied as a matter of contractual efficacy. It may also be implied in an express grant of a right to park, at least if the area has previously been used for parking, since 'conveyance' in LPA 1925, s 62 by virtue of s 205(1) includes any assurance of an interest in property. A right to reach the parking space may be a way of necessity.

OTHER EASEMENTS AND NON-DEROGATION FROM GRANT

Continuous or discontinuous

2.31 Easements may be continuous, such as a right to receive light or a right to maintain a water pipe, or discontinuous. Strictly the Rule in *Wheeldon v Burrows* applies only to continuous easements.[27] A right of way is only used

---

[24] See also *Kettel v Bloomfold Ltd* [2012] EWHC 1422 (Ch).
[25] Limitation Act 1950, s 18.
[26] LRA 2002, Sch 6.
[27] *Titchmarsh v Royston Water Co Ltd* (1899) 81 LT 673; *Ward v Kirkland* [1967] Ch 194, [1966] 1 All ER 609 (right to enter servient tenement to maintain a wall not continuous).

from time to time and is not a continuous easement.[28] However, if the way is obvious[29] or is over a made up surface,[30] the right to use it may nevertheless be treated as if it were continuous for the purpose of the Rule (see para **3.33**).

2.32   The discontinuous nature of a right of way is important for the purposes of the LRA 2002. A legal right of way which is not entered on the register of the servient title can be an overriding interest under Sch 3, para 3(2) if (among other conditions) 'the person entitled to the easement or profit proves that it has been exercised in the period of one year ending with the day of the disposition' (see para **13.6**). If a legal right of way does not satisfy that condition (and if it is not obvious or known to the disponee) then, even if it has been exercised in the past, it may cease to take priority after a disposition for valuable consideration if it has not been used during the year preceding the disposition.

Positive or negative

2.33   A right of way is a positive easement, namely a right to do something (pass along) on the land of another as distinct from a negative easement to stop another doing something (such as obstructing the light). The right also has negative aspects since the dominant owner can prevent obstructions or diversions of the way. It appears that at one time there may have been a rule that positive easements could not pass by implication of law, but even if so that appears no longer to be the case.[31]

2.34   *Rance v Elvin*[32] concerned a claimed right to a flow of water. It came through a pipe from a meter and the servient owner paid the water company for the water supplied. The issue was whether the servient owner was bound to continue to provide (and pay for) the meter. The court held there was only a negative duty not to obstruct the supply, and there was no duty to perform positive acts. The dominant owner had a right to such supply as was in the pipes and the servient owner should not interfere but it was not itself bound to pay for the water and if it did not, following which the water company cut off the supply, the dominant owner could not complain. This was followed in *Duffy v Lamb*[33] where a servient owner cut off an electricity supply and the court held he could not do so. He was not bound to take positive action but must not actively interfere. The rule is similar to those on maintenance (see para **8.1**). However in *Konstantinidis v Townsend*[34] there was a right to take water from a borehole through a pump which needed regular maintenance. The parties cooperated over the functioning and cost of the system but the case

---

[28]   *Worthington v Gimson* (1860) 2 E & E 618; 121 ER 232; *Pheysey v Vicary* (1847) 16 M & W 484; 153 ER 1280.

[29]   *Borman v Griffith* [1930] 1 Ch 493.

[30]   *Brown v Alabaster* (1887) 37 Ch D 490; *Millman v Ellis* (1996) 71 P & CR 158 CA.

[31]   See *Ward v Kirkland* [1967] Ch 194 per Ungoed-Thomas J at 224; *Wheaton v Maple & Co* [1893] 3 Ch 48.

[32]   (1985) 50 P & CR 9.

[33]   (1998) 75 P & CR 364; [1997] EG 50 (CS) CA.

[34]   [2003] EWCA Civ 537 CA.

concerned whether there was a proprietary arrangement binding future owners. The Court of Appeal held that such a positive obligation could not so bind. The servient owner's corresponding obligation for a right of way would be to do nothing to obstruct it, but if the way is interfered with in some other fashion, for instance by the local highways authority taking steps to prevent access on to a highway, he has no duty to provide the dominant owner with another means of access. Likewise, if a way was physically destroyed, for instance by erosion of a riverside path, the servient owner would have no duty to provide a replacement.[35]

Derogation from grant

2.35   Where one person grants a right to another, the grantor will not then be permitted so to act that the grantee is deprived of the benefit. This rule applies to many types of legal transaction including leases and it is fundamental to the nature of easements which lie in grant, whether freehold or by demise. The concept of an implied grant in *Wheeldon v Burrows* is an instance of this[36] (see paras **3.30** and **3.72**). Although in *Woodhouse & Co Ltd v Kirkland (Derby) Ltd*[37] Plowman J said:

> 'It may be, I think, that a purely negative right over the servient tenement or quasi servient tenement such as a right of light can be acquired under the doctrine forbidding derogation from grant in a manner which is indistinguishable from an implied grant, but I am not satisfied that this is true of a positive right such as a right of way.'

Nevertheless many rights of way have been recognised under that rule.

2.36   Similarly, where a grant is made, the grantor can not lessen the nature of it, for example by granting a right of way and then erecting a gate across it (see para **10.16**).

USER BEYOND THE DOMINANT TENEMENT

2.37   An easement which is granted for the benefit of a specified dominant tenement is not available to be used for the benefit of other land. This is sometimes called the principle in *Harris v Flower & Sons*[38] (see paras **4.80**,

---

[35]   Compare *R (On the Application of Gloucester Country Council) v Secretary of State for the Environment, Transport and the Regions* (2001) 82 P & CR 15 which concerned an eroded public footpath.

[36]   See *Sovmots Investments Ltd v Secretary of State for the Environment* [1979] AC 144 at 175, [1977] 2 All ER 385 at 396, HL; *Williams v Usherwood* (1983) 45 P & CR 235.

[37]   [1970] 1 WLR 1185 [1970] 2 All ER 587.

[38]   (1904) 74 LJ Ch 127; see also *Skull v Glenister*: (1864) 16 CB NS 81;143 ER 1055; *Lawton v Ward* (1696) 1 Ld Raym. 75; 91 ER 946; *Howell v King* (1674) 1 Mod 190; 86 ER 821; *Allan v Gomme* (1840) 11 Ad & El 759; 113 ER 602; *Senhouse v Christian* (1787) 1 Term Rep 560; 99 ER 1251.

9.110). In that case[39] the defendant owned land (the 'white land') immediately adjacent to the dominant tenement (the 'pink land') served by the way. He erected a single building, partly on the white land and partly on the pink land. The court had to decide whether use of the way to access the building as a whole by passing through the pink land would be for the purpose of obtaining access to the white land; and held that that was the case. Romer LJ said: 'If a right of way be granted for the enjoyment of Close A, the grantee, because he owns or acquires Close B, cannot use the way in substance for passing over Close A to Close B'. This derives from the principle that a grant of easement is limited to its own purposes.[40]

2.38   In *London & Blenheim Estates Ltd v Ladbroke Retail Parks Ltd*[41] a company granted a right to park cars on its land. The contract provided that if it acquired other land the plaintiff, as dominant owner, could require the right to park on that land as well. The company acquired such land and then sold it on to the defendant. The judge at first instance held, and counsel for the defendant on appeal conceded, that there could be an estate contract for the grant of a future easement over land to be acquired in the future, so this point was not decided by the Court of Appeal. They did, however, hold that it was not possible to have an easement where the servient land was disposed of (by the company to the defendant) before the easement was granted. Peter Gibson LJ said:

> 'If one asks why the law should require that there should be a dominant tenement before there can be a grant, or a contract for the grant, of an easement sufficient to create an interest in land binding successors in title to the servient land, the answer would appear to lie in the policy against encumbering land with burdens of uncertain extent. As was said by Fox LJ in *Ashburn Anstalt v Arnold*[42] "In matters relating to the title to land, certainty is of prime importance". A further related answer lies in the reluctance of the law to recognise new forms of burden on property conferring more than contractual rights. Thus in *Ackroyd v Smith*,[43] Cresswell J, giving the judgment of the judges of the Court of Common Pleas, after referring to the impossibility of a grant of a right of way in gross said "nor can the owner of the land render it subject to a new species of burden, so as to bind it in the hands of an assignee. 'Incidents of a novel kind cannot be devised, and attached to property, at the fancy or caprice of any owner:' per Lord Brougham LC, in *Keppell v Bailey*".[44] A right intended as an easement and attached to a servient tenement before the dominant tenement is identified would in my view be an incident of a novel kind.'

---

[39]   As summarised in *Das v Linden Mews Ltd* [2002] EWCA Civ 590 [2003] 2 P & CR 4. See also *Bracewell v Appleby* [1975] Ch 408.

[40]   *Wimbledon and Putney Commons Conservators v Dixon* (1875) 1 Ch D 362; *Bradburn v Morris* (1876) 3 Ch D 812, CA.

[41]   [1994] 1 WLR 31 CA.

[42]   [1989] Ch 1, 26.

[43]   (1850) 10 CB 164, 188.

[44]   (1834) 2 Myl & K 517.

2.39 Where the excessive use is trivial then there may be no objection[45] but the way cannot substantially benefit the non-dominant land[46].

LICENCES AND CONTRACTUAL RIGHTS

2.40 A means of access to property can exist by virtue not of a grant of easement but under a licence, either gratuitous or contractual. A licence is a personal arrangement and does not create an interest in land (see para **1.49**). In *Street v Mountford*[47] the House of Lords held that while a document might be labelled as a licence, if the true nature was that it created some other estate or interest it would be construed and take effect as its substance required. Often the issue is whether a right creates an interest in land which is capable of extending to successors as an easement would.

2.41 A licence which is coupled with a grant[48] or which is granted as part of a contract[49] may be irrevocable as long as the grant or contract continues, but apart from that its nature is to be revocable.

2.42 Landowners, whether private such as farmers, public such as local authorities or charitable such as the National Trust, often create permissive paths over their land which can be used by any member of the public to walk along a route, usually for recreation. Commercial landowners also do so, for instance between a railway station and a parade of shops or a supermarket. It is common for the landowner in such a case to erect a notice under the provisions of Highways Act 1980, s 31 to make it clear that the way is not dedicated to the public, that consent to use it can be withdrawn at any time[50] and usually that persons use it at their own risk. Even though made available for use by the public,[51] such licenced ways remain private and do not create rights.[52]

Shopping centres

2.43 Licences over private land were involved in the Shopping Centre cases in both the UK courts and the European Court of Human Rights (ECHR). *CIN Properties v Rawlins*[53] concerned the nature of the rights of the public to use pedestrian malls within a shopping centre. The defendant had, with others, frequented the centre until CIN barred him for causing a nuisance by writing a

---

[45] *Macepark (Whittlebury) Ltd v Sargeant* [2003] 1 WLR 2284 *Peacock v Custins* [2002] 1 WLR 1815 *Massey v Boulden* [2003] 1 WLR 1792.

[46] *Das v Linden Mews Ltd* [2002] 2 EGLR 76 CA.

[47] [1985] 1 AC 809.

[48] *Wood v Leadbitter* (1845) 13 M & W 838; 153 ER 351.

[49] *Hurst v Picture Theatres* [1915] 1 KB 1.

[50] See *R(Beresford) v Sunderland City Council* [2004] 1 AC 889 at [45] and [72].

[51] Many will be a 'public place' for the purposes of the criminal law such as disorder, drunkenness, drug trafficking and so forth so that the police have powers there.

[52] *Gardner v Hodgson's Kingston Brewery Co Ltd* [1903] AC 229 at 231.

[53] (1995) 69 P&CR D36.

letter revoking any licence that he might have had to come into the malls. He kept coming back and CIN applied for a declaration and injunction. The county court judge found there was no formal agreement[54] giving the public the right to use the pedestrian malls. He did, however, hold that the defendant had an equitable licence to use the malls, exercisable whenever the doors were open and revocable not at will, but only for good reason. The Court of Appeal held CIN could revoke the licence and had done so. In principle, equity can restrict the revocation of a licence where the licensee has acted in reliance on a representation by, or the acquiescence of, the licensor. Here there was no representation by either the local council or CIN that the public would have irrevocable rights to use the malls nor that any member of the public had altered his or her position in reliance on such a representation. The principle had no application to the case. Balcombe LJ expressed:

> '... the gravest doubts whether this principle could ever apply so as to create rights in favour of the public at large, since it is difficult to see how the acts or omissions of those individuals who rely on a representation could create rights in favour of the public.'

2.44 The individuals involved applied to the ECHR in *Anderson v UK*[55] but their application failed:

> 'The Commission notes that the applicants had no history of using the Centre for any form of organised assembly or association. The Commission thus finds no indication in the present case that the exclusion of the applicants from the Centre interfered with their rights under Article 11 of the Convention.'

2.45 In *Appleby v UK*[56] the applicants wanted to collect signatures for a petition, again in a shopping centre. Postel, the private company which owned the centre, refused permission. They applied on the grounds of freedom of expression and the ECtHR found against them on the basis that this was private property and the government was not involved.

2.46 Although these decisions related to shopping centres which were actively managed, the same principles would apply to access by licence across open country or along a private road. It follows that such permission extends only to those persons permitted to be on the private premises or land. The invitation may be extended to the public generally but the landowner retains the right to exclude anyone and it is therefore not a public but a private permission.

Fire escapes

2.47 The issue of how far an apparent licence creates an interest in land capable of binding and benefiting successors in title has been litigated in the context of the right to use a fire escape which is similar to a right of way in that

---

54   Within section 18 of the Highways Act 1971.
55   (1998) 25 EHRR CD 172.
56   (2003) 37 EHRR 38.

it permits people in a building on fire to pass through adjoining premises to escape. In *Norwich Union Pensions Ltd v Friends Provident Assurance Ltd*[57] Neuberger J held that a licence which could be used by successors in title of the original licensee and by its tenants was not a proprietary right. Similarly in *The IDC Group Ltd v Clark*[58] a document granted a licence to use a fire escape, again referring to successors, but was held to be a licence.

2.48 Although in practice most fire escapes appear to be permitted under licence, there seems no reason in principle why they should not be capable of being easements. They would be unusual in that the dominant owner would hope never to have to exercise the right (except perhaps for a fire practice) and the use would be conditional on fire breaking out on the dominant land so that the right might be regarded as equitable. As it would to some extent reflect the structure and layout of the dominant building, so that it was liable to change if that was altered, such a right might be indefinite in nature and therefore be equitable rather than create a legal interest on that basis as well.

Roadway licence

2.49 In *London Tara Hotel Ltd v Kensington Close Hotel Ltd*[59] the owners of one hotel granted a licence to the owners of an adjacent one to use a roadway. Unknown to the licensors, the ownership of the second hotel subsequently changed. More than 20 years after the change the owners of the second hotel claimed a prescriptive right of way. The Court of Appeal upheld the claim on the basis that the licence, being personal, did not extend to users of the roadway other than the company to which it had been given and successive use by later owners of the hotel was a trespass which gave rise to a prescriptive right. It indicated that a prudent licensor in such a case should take steps every few years to check that the terms of the licence were still running and being observed, otherwise the licensor ran the risk of finding that a new right had been created.

Contractual rights

2.50 It is possible to create a right by contract which may endure for some years. In *Senhouse v Christian*[60] in 1722, Mr Senhouse senior granted to Mr Christian senior 'a free and convenient way' over a strip of land as a right in gross. The case in 1787 involved the defendant who was the grandson of the original grantee and the plaintiff who seems to have been a descendant of the grantor. The defendant claimed to have become seised of the right as a way in gross. The nature of the right was not disputed in the case which turned on the extent to which the defendant could make improvements and carry out repairs (which he was held entitled to do) and whether he could construct 'tranverse roads' across the strip to a newly acquired piece of land (which he was held not

---

[57]   (Unreported) 7 June 2001, (2001) WL 1422914.
[58]   (1993) 65 P & CR 179 CA.
[59]   [2010] EWHC 2749 (Ch) at first instance; [2011] EWCA Civ 1356 in CA.
[60]   (1787) 1 Term Rep 560; 99 ER 1251.

entitled to do). The second point seems to be an instance of the rule in *Harris v Flower & Sons* (see para **2.37**) and it is not clear how far this should be seen as a right in gross despite the pleadings. It appears to have been accepted that the benefit and burden descended down the generations on both sides, but as a right in gross it would seem not to be alienable or take effect as an easement. However, there seems no objection in principle to a right to pass along a way being created as a contractual licence for value. It could subsist between the parties and be inherited by their successors. Even if the burden would not bind a purchaser of the 'servient' land, the benefit could now pass under the Contracts (Rights of Third Parties) Act 1999.

NATURAL AND HUMAN RIGHTS

Natural rights

2.51 Natural rights are those which the law imputes to landowners irrespective of any agreement, although they can be excluded by suitable words. These are limited by the law and only recognised in rare cases, specifically a right to the support of land in its natural state and a right to the flow of water. It is possible that a way of necessity may be seen as a similar right on the basis that any person has a natural right to reach his property.

Human rights

2.52 Article 1 of the First Protocol to the European Convention of Human Rights, incorporated in English Law by the Human Rights Act 1998, provides that: 'Every natural or legal person is entitled to the peaceful enjoyment of his possessions.' There is an exception in the public interest subject to conditions (such as payment of compensation on compulsory purchase). There is also a provision that the right does not impair the power of a State to control the use of property. This Article has been held to protect a variety of property rights. In *Parochial Church Council of the Parish of Aston Cantlow v Wallbank*,[61] Lord Hobhouse observed that: 'possessions applies to all forms of property and is the equivalent of assets'. The ECHR has interpreted the Article widely to include many intangible rights.[62] In *Posti and Rahko v Finland*[63] the court held that the applicants' right under a lease granted by the state to engage in fishing on state-owned waters constituted a possession within the scope of the Article, and in *Chassagnou v France*[64] it was applied to the right to hunt on land. Thus an interest in land such as a right of way will be a possession for the purposes of the Convention. Accordingly, it would be a breach of the

---

[61] [2004] 1 AC 546 at para 91.
[62] See *Mellacher v Austria* (1989) 12 EHRR 391, at paras 43–44; and Application 10741/84: *S v United Kingdom* 41 DR 226 (1984), E Com HR (benefit of a restrictive covenant and entitlement to annual rent).
[63] (2003) 37 EHRR 6.
[64] (1999) 29 EHRR 615.

Convention for the State to interfere with a right of way except in the general interest as provided in the Article, for instance on compulsory purchase subject to compensation.

2.53 Article 8, respect for family life and the home, may also be engaged for residential property. There is an argument for saying that if someone's home life is to be respected they must also have a right to get there by physical means.

2.54 The Convention does not itself protect a potential right to acquire property in the future.[65] Therefore, if land does not already have a right of way, it would not provide a means of obtaining one so that the possibility of prescribing for a right of way is not itself a human right. However, prescription is not an infringement of the servient owner's enjoyment of his possessions. By analogy with *JA Pye (Oxford) Ltd v UK*[66] (which concerned limitation), it would appear that once the conditions laid down by domestic law for a right to come into existence by prescription have been satisfied, this would be not a 'deprivation of possessions' but a 'control of use' of the servient land.[67]

2.55 In *Stretch v United Kingdom*[68] a lessee was granted an option to renew by a local authority but, when he wanted to exercise it, it turned out to be ultra vires and void under domestic law because the authority did not have the capacity to grant it. The ECtHR held that it had breached his human rights by interfering with the peaceful enjoyment of his possessions, namely the option, which, although operating in the future, was a present right. The court said[69] 'Possessions' can be existing possessions or assets, including claims in respect of which the applicant can argue that he has at least a legitimate expectation of obtaining effective enjoyment of a property right. By contrast, the hope of recognition of the survival of an old property right which it has long been impossible to exercise effectively cannot be considered as a 'possession'. Nor can a conditional claim which lapses as a result of non-fulfilment of the condition.

2.56 Provided the legitimate expectation is satisfied, the detailed rules are a matter for domestic law. It follows that a person expecting to acquire a right of way by prescription cannot complain if state action breaches that expectation before the right has accrued. However, once the right has crystallised, typically after 20 years, his right of way becomes a possession protected under the Convention and in that case the servient owner cannot complain that the existence of the new right breaches his human rights to enjoyment of his possessions. Correspondingly, if the conditions for abandonment of a right of way are satisfied, then recognition of that by a court would not be a breach of the dominant owner's human rights.

---

65   *Anheuser-Busch Inc v Portugal* [GC] (2005), no 73049/01, ECHR 2007-I; see also *Kopecký v Slovakia* (2004) [GC], no 44912/98, s 35, ECHR 2004-IX.
66   (2008) 46 EHRR 45.
67   At para 66.
68   (2004) 38 EHRR 196.
69   At H3(a).

PROFITS A PRENDRE

2.57 A profit a prendre is a form of servitude or right in the land of another. It comprises the right to take something from the servient land, such as pasture (to take grass through the mouths of cattle, sheep or horses) or fishing rights or mineral rights. Rights of common are profits. Unlike easements which must accommodate a dominant tenement, a profit can either be appurtenant to land, in which case it will pass along with it, or be held in gross, that is as a right which can be sold and bought on its own without any land.

2.58 A profit will normally involve a right of access. Thus pasture requires the right for a herdsman to take animals to graze on the fields or common lands. Similarly, mineral rights involve the operator with its employees and heavy machinery entering and digging the minerals and carrying them away.

2.59 Apart from these unavoidable consequences it may be possible for a right of way to be appurtenant to a profit a prendre.[70] In principle there appears no objection in English law to an incorporeal right being the dominant tenement, although clear authority appears to be lacking. Such as there is relates to fishing. A right of fishery in a river which is in separate ownership from the bank may only involve casting out from the bank without any right to enter the water. However, where the river and its banks are in the same ownership, the fisherman will need the right to walk along and stand on the banks. In *Ecroyd v Coulthard*[71] Chitty LJ said 'I agree that what is claimed is not an ordinary right of way. What is claimed is claimed as incidental to the fishery, but no authority has been cited to shew that there is such an incidental right.' In *Hanbury v Jenkins*[72] Buckley J considered the limited authority and concluded obiter that there could be a right appurtenant to a fishery. It appears there may be such rights in Scotland where fishing law is well developed.

2.60 Apart from fishing, there is limited authority in *Gatewards Case*[73] which concerned the claim of inhabitants of a locality, who had rights of common of grazing, to a customary right of way. Where under the Natural Environment and Rural Communities Act 2006, s 67 rights for mechanically propelled vehicles have been terminated over certain green lanes but a private right of way is created for persons interested in land to use a lane for access with such vehicles (see para **7.38**), the definition of 'interest' in section 71 includes rights of common and sporting rights. The statutory right of way would subsist for the benefit of the servient land, not for the rights as such, but could be used by the owner of the rights. Express grants of mineral rights often include rights of way, together with rights to construct roads, tramways and conveyors but these are better described as wayleaves.

---

[70] *Tilbury v Silva* (1890) LR 45 Ch D 98; see also *Re Salvin's Indenture, Re, Pitt v Durham County Water Board* [1938] 2 All ER 498.

[71] [1898] 2 Ch 358.

[72] [1901] 2 Ch 401. See also *Barton v Church Commissioners for England* [2008] EWHC 3091 (Ch) at [32].

[73] (1606) 6 Co Rep 59b.

WAYLEAVES

2.61   This term is found frequently in Scots law where it can apply to a right to pass over land. It has been taken into English law in two contexts. One is in mining cases where one party may be granted the right to convey minerals underground through the land of another.[74] In this context it is also applied to cases where the conveyance or working has been without consent and the court has to assess the damages, usually related to the value of the minerals taken.[75]

2.62   The second use derives from the Electricity Act, Sch 4 (see para **7.81**) where the term is used for a statutory right to have cables and other plant in land. From that it has been extended to other rights for statutory undertakers to install plant in, over or under land, and these will include the right to pass over adjacent land to install, inspect and maintain the apparatus.

EQUITABLE RIGHTS

Equitable easements

2.63   An easement may be either equitable or legal (see para **3.82**). An equitable easement can correspond to a legal one, save that it may lack some formal element such as registration (see para **13.63**) or creation by deed or certain duration as under LPA 1925, s 1(2)(a) a legal easement must subsist as an interest equivalent either to a fee simple absolute in possession or to a term of years absolute.

2.64   Rights similar to easements can also arise by the application of the principles of equity (see para **3.88**). In *ER Ives Investment Ltd v High*[76] the foundations of a development encroached on an adjoining property. The builder and the adjoining owner agreed that in return for the foundations being allowed to remain, the owner would have a right of way across the development. The Court of Appeal held this created an equity, either on the principle of burden and benefit or acquiescence. An easement of necessity which endures only so long as the necessity subsists will also be equitable.

2.65   An equitable easement may also be created deliberately as for the lifetime of the dominant owner or to subsist until an alternative route, such as access to a highway, is available. Where a private roadway is held by trustees, the rights of the users will subsist in equity under the trust.[77]

---

[74]   Eg *Dand v Kingscote* (1840) 6 M & W 174; 151 ER 370.

[75]   *Martin v Porter* (1839) 5 M & W 351; *Jegon v Vivian* (1871) LR 6 Ch App 742, see *Attorney General v Blake* [2001] 1 AC 268 at 278F.

[76]   [1967] 2 QB 379.

[77]   *Austerberry v Corporation of Oldham* (1885) LR 29 Ch D 750; *Halsall v Brizell* [1957] Ch 169. See also para **2.10**.

Restrictive covenants

2.66 A right of way may be supported by a restrictive covenant which operates in equity. It is common on a grant of an express right of way to impose a covenant not to obstruct the roadway or not to use it except as an access to a defined property or restricting the use, for instance to not more than one dwelling. This may be done with a large house which might be divided or with a large garden which might be built on. Such a covenant will normally be expressed to bind the dominant tenement rather than the incorporeal right of way.

2.67 It is not clear if a restrictive covenant can bind an incorporeal hereditament directly[78] but a grant for a limited purpose will normally achieve the same result. Sometimes the use of the way itself is limited by reference to a covenant binding the dominant land. If such a covenant is varied either under LPA 1925, s 84 or by deed, the purpose governing the right of way will automatically be varied with it and if it is released the way will be for any use.[79]

2.68 It is possible that an exclusion of any grant or reservation of an easement may be construed as a restrictive covenant. In *CGIS City Plaza Shares 1 Ltd v Britel Fund Trustees Ltd*[80] some land was sold for development and the transfer contained provisions that neither the sold land nor the retained land should acquire rights of light over the other. The court held this to be an effective provision excluding the acquisition of an easement of light but considered obiter it might also take effect as a covenant not to claim such an easement. The common practice of including in a transfer a statement that the transferee will not thereby acquire any rights over the retained land of the transferor is therefore capable (depending on the wording) of taking effect in that way. It is possible that a grant for a restricted purpose might also be so interpreted. There is little difference in substance between a way granted for the limited purpose of use by private motor cars only and a way subject to a covenant not to use it for any vehicles other than private motor cars. If so, it might be possible to invoke the jurisdiction of the Upper Tribunal under LPA 1925, s 84 but as there is a difference in form it is likely the Tribunal would not accept jurisdiction.

2.69 The courts will give a limited scope to a covenant invoked to support a right of way. *Jaggard v Sawyer*[81] (see para **2.9**) involved a cul-de-sac of ten houses served by a private road. Each house owner also owned the part of the road up to the middle fronting on the house and each had a right of way over the parts belonging to the owners of the other houses. Each house also had the benefit of a covenant that any unbuilt land in the development should not be used except as a private garden. The defendant required access over the road to

---

[78] The position of the benefit of a covenant is obscure. See *Gaw v Coras Iompair Eireann* [1953] IR 232 but also *Grant v Edmondson* [1931] 1 Ch 1 CA.

[79] *Hotchkin v McDonald* (2004) 18 EG 100 (CS).

[80] [2012] EWHC 1594 (Ch) [2012] All ER (D) 62 (Jun).

[81] [1995] 1 WLR 269.

a new access to be constructed over their garden to an adjacent building plot which did not enjoy a right of way. The Court of Appeal, in addition to refusing an injunction to prevent the trespass, also declined to enforce the covenant. In *Smith v Garrard*[82] land was sold subject to a reservation of a right of way and the seller imposed a covenant to prohibit parking which obstructed the use of the way. The Court of Appeal construed the covenant narrowly so as not to prevent parking which did not cause an obstruction.

RIGHTS OF ENTRY

2.70 A right of entry is almost invariably reserved on a lease and in some cases is conferred or required by statute.[83] It may also subsist on an assurance such as assignment of a lease or a conveyance where it may be used to support the right to collect a service charge (see para **5.58**). Such a right cannot be an easement as it does not benefit a dominant tenement. While sometimes coupled with a right to forfeit a lease or take back property sold, it can subsist simply as a right to view the property, for instance to discover any disrepair.

2.71 There are also innumerable rights of entry granted by statute for public purposes. These include those of planning authorities, on compulsory purchase, for fire prevention, by the police, for health and safety, for inspection of food premises, in case of human or animal disease and many others. They confer on officials a right to pass through premises to inspect them.

HIGHWAYS

2.72 Use of land for passage by the public is, on the face of it, similar to use by private owners and at one time a view developed that they were in effect the same. It was therefore natural for judges to see the right of the public as being somewhat in the nature of an easement. There are many cases in the books which refer to highways in such terms. However, the concept of an easement is not suitable. This was made clear by Lord Cairns LJ in *Rangeley v Midland Railway Company*:[84]

> 'But I must also observe that it appears to me to be an incorrect expression to speak of this as an easement. There can be no easement properly so called unless there be both a servient and a dominant tenement. There is in this case no dominant tenement whatever. It is true that in the well known case of *Dovaston v Payne*,[85] Mr Justice Heath is reported to have said with regard to a public highway that the freehold continued in the owner of the adjoining land subject to an easement in favour of the public, and that expression has occasionally been repeated since that time. That, however, is hardly an accurate expression. There can be no such thing according to our law, or according to the civil law, as what I

---

[82] [2004] EWCA Civ 1655 CA.
[83] See Landlord and Tenant Act 1985, s 11; Settled Land Act 1925, s 42(1)(iii).
[84] (1867-68) LR 3 Ch App 306 at p 310.
[85] (1795) 2 Sm L C 132, 6th Edn; 2 H Bl 527 126 ER 684.

may term an easement in gross. An easement must be connected with a dominant tenement. In truth, a public road or highway is not an easement, it is a dedication to the public of the occupation of the surface of the land for the purpose of passing and repassing, the public generally taking upon themselves (through the parochial authorities or otherwise) the obligation of repairing it. It is quite clear that that is a very different thing from an ordinary easement, where the occupation remains in the owner of the servient tenement subject to the easement.'

2.73   The first three of the four characteristics of an easement are that there must be a dominant and servient tenement, that the easement must accommodate the dominant tenement and that the two tenements must be held by different persons. None of those apply to highways. The fourth is that the easement must be capable of forming the subject matter of a grant. A public right of way is created not by grant but by dedication, although, like a grant, it may be express or implied. In addition an easement is an incorporeal hereditament. A hereditament is a right which before the Land Transfer Act 1897 passed on the death of the holder to his heir. The right to use a highway belonged to all subjects of the Crown whether or not they were anyone's heir. It follows from all these rules that the concept of easement cannot apply. However, despite Lord Cairns' comments, judges continued to use the language of private rights. Perhaps the best known instance is by Lopes LJ in *Harrison v Duke of Rutland*[86] who said:

'if a person uses the soil of the highway for any purpose other than that in respect of which the dedication was made and the easement acquired, he is a trespasser. The easement acquired by the public is a right to pass and repass at their pleasure for the purpose of legitimate travel, and the use of the soil for any other purpose, whether lawful or unlawful, is an infringement of the rights of the owner of the soil...'

2.74   In that case Mr Harrison went on to certain highways across land owned by the Duke in order to disrupt grouse shooting. This was held to be a trespass against the Duke as he owned the soil of the ways and the court considered the public right was only one of passage. The case was followed in *Hickman v Maisey*[87] where the defendant stayed some time on a highway to watch horse trials on the plaintiff's land. *Harrison v Duke of Rutland* and *Hickman v Maisey* were considered in, and their authority weakened by, *DPP v Jones (Margaret)*[88] where Lord Hope of Craighead said:

'It may be convenient to begin an examination of this subject with some general statements. A highway is a way over which there is a public right of way. A public right of way is similar to but not in all respects the same as an easement of way. The right is exercisable by anyone whether he owns land or not, whereas an easement is a right exercisable by the owner of land for the time being by virtue of his estate in the land of which he is the dominant proprietor. There are other differences. But a public right of way closely resembles an easement of way in

---

[86]   [1893] 1 QB 142 at 154.
[87]   [1900] 1 QB 752.
[88]   [1999] 2 AC 240 at p 268.

regard to the nature of the user from which its creation may be inferred and the nature of the use which may be made of it.'

2.75 In *R (Godmanchester) v Secretary of State for the Environment, Food and Rural Affairs*, Lord Scott of Fortescue referred to the comparison of easements and public rights of way:[89]

> 'It is said that the Prescription Act 1832 provided a model for the [Rights of Way Act 1932]. This is no doubt correct but analogies drawn from the rules about prescription of private easements can, if applied to dedication of paths as public rights of way, go astray. For example, private easements, under common law, are private rights in rem and can only be created by grant.... The creation of a public right of way, by contrast, is brought about by dedication of the way as a public way by the landowner.'

2.76 Recent developments in the law of public rights of way that permit use for other purposes such as public demonstrations, exercise and similar functions[90] do not extend to private ways which can be used only for the purpose for which they were granted.

LOCAL AND CUSTOMARY RIGHTS

2.77 In the past, many rights of access subsisted for the benefit of an undefined and fluctuating class of local people. These do not amount to highways as they are not for all the Queen's subjects. Such a right can subsist only by custom or statute. Customs can either be secular or ecclesiastical. Secular customs must in theory have existed since 1189, although in practice the courts will recognise an ancient practice which complies with the conditions for being a custom unless it can be shown that it must have arisen more recently. Ecclesiastical practices could arise until the Reformation.[91]

2.78 *Gatewards Case*[92] concerned a claim to pass over a track in order to exercise a right of pasture. As a general rule a profit, such as a right of common of pasture, cannot be claimed by custom for the inhabitants of a locality since their numbers can fluctuate and if they grew they might exhaust the produce of the soil. However, a right associated with it may be and the court stated that 'the custom that every inhabitant of such a town shall have a way over such land, either to the church or market, &c. that is good, for it is but an easement and no profit'.

2.79 Although described as an easement it does not comply with the requirements that there must be a dominant tenement which it accommodates nor that there must be a competent grantee. *Brocklebank v Thompson*[93]

---

[89]   [2008] 1AC 221 at para 62.
[90]   *DPP v Jones (Margaret)* [1999] 2 AC 240.
[91]   Ecclesiastical Appeals Act 24 Henry 8 c 12 1532/3, see *Harthan v Harthan* [1949] P 115.
[92]   (1606) 6 Co Rep 59b.
[93]   [1903] 2 Ch 344.

concerned a way leading to Irton parish church. The plaintiff was lord of the manor of Irton in Cumberland and the defendant was the owner of land within the adjoining manor of Santon but also within the ecclesiastical parish of Irton. Although there was some indication that a few local people believed the way to be a public highway, the evidence was against that and both parties accepted it was a customary way – the dispute being whether those who could benefit were the tenants of Irton Manor or the parishioners of Irton Parish. The judge found it was a parochial churchway. He held that a customary way was not a highway and was to be regarded as a private way.

2.80 Such rights cannot now be created even by diversion. *Farquhar v Newbury Rural District Council*[94] concerned a claimed new customary way. Before 1743 there had been a way to the church at Shaw at Newbury in Berkshire. The church was near Shaw House and the way passed through a farmyard. In 1841 the church was pulled down and rebuilt and in 1842 the owner of Shaw House made a new road along a different route. Thereafter people used the new road to get to the church. Mrs Farquhar who owned Shaw House at the time of the case admitted that parishioners had the right to go along the road but denied it was a public highway and locked two gates. The Council removed the locks. The court found there was evidence of general public use since 1842 so that the way was deemed to have been dedicated as a public highway. It held that it was not possible to create a new customary churchway at common law even if it was by way of substitution and diversion of an old one. The Court of Appeal relied on *Poole v Huskinson*.[95] In that case there had been a private carriage road at East Bridgeford in Nottinghamshire set out under an Inclosure Act. There was a claim by local parishioners that it had become a churchway but not a public highway. Parke B said 'There may be a dedication to the public for a limited purpose, as for a footway, horse-way, or drift-way; but there cannot be a dedication to a limited part of the public.'

2.81 In the highway case of *Fairey v Southampton County Council*[96] the landowner argued that he had permitted local residents to use a path but had warned off strangers. In the event, that was not relevant to the decision but Denning LJ considered obiter that if it had been then it should have been made clear 'not only to strangers, that they had no right to use the path, but also to local residents, that they only used it by tolerance of the owner' otherwise use could be assumed to have been by the public at large. In *Oxfordshire County Council v Oxford City Council* at first instance[97] Lightman J applied the reasoning in *Fairey* to a town or village green but this aspect was not considered further when the case went to the Court of Appeal or House of

---

[94]   [1909] 1 Ch 12.
[95]   (1843) 11 M & W 827 152 ER 1039.
[96]   [1956] 2 QB 439 at 457.
[97]   [2004] Ch 253 at [100]. The case went on appeal and then to the House of Lords but the point was not considered in the higher courts.

Lords. In *Fortune v Wilts CC*[98] the Court of Appeal assumed Lightman J's view was correct but it does not appear that the point has been subject to full argument.

2.82 Inclosure Acts sometimes granted rights of way for the benefit of local inhabitants. *R v Richards*[99] concerned a claim that such a way was a highway and therefore repairable by the inhabitants at large. The court held it to be a private way and not repairable.

2.83 Although customary and local ways are private rights of way they must now be rare. It is likely that any which were in use after the National Parks and Access to the Countryside Act 1949 introduced the requirement that all footpaths and bridleways must be recorded on the Definitive Map would have been treated as public highways. After use by the public for 20 years they would have become such under the provisions now in the Highways Act 1980, s 31. It is, however, possible that if any of these customary green lanes were vehicular ways which have not become highways then the Natural Environment and Rural Communities Act 2006, s 67 will not apply to them and it will still be lawful to drive mechanically propelled vehicles on them, but such rights will apply only to the residents of the locality.

2.84 Churchways may still subsist but they will not be a matter for the ordinary courts. In *Batten v Gedye*[100] the Rector and churchwardens of Barwick in Somerset removed certain ancient steps leading from the churchyard up to the highway. Some parishioners claimed a mandatory injunction for the steps to be restored. The court found the steps were not a public highway but constituted an ancient churchway and therefore the matter fell within the jurisdiction of the Ecclesiastical Court (which had power to grant a faculty to remove the steps) and was not a matter for the High Court.

RIGHTS OF EXERCISE, RECREATION AND AMUSEMENT

2.85 The right to take recreation on the land of another person, whether in a town square, a private park or a stretch of countryside (often known by the Latin term *jus spatiandi*) can be an easement but does not constitute a right of way. In *A-G v Antrobus*[101] Farwell J said 'The public as such cannot prescribe, nor is *jus spatiandi* known to our law as a possible subject-matter of grant or prescription'. While that remains true at common law for rights of the public it was held in *Re Ellenborough Park*[102] that such private easements can be acquired, at least by express grant. Such rights resemble rights of way save that they confer a right to wander over an area rather than simply pass from one

---

[98] [2012] EWCA Civ 334 at [13].
[99] (1800) 8 Term Reports 634; 101 ER 1588 cited in *Race v Ward* (1887) 7 E&B 384 119 ER 1289.
[100] (1889) LR 41 Ch D 507.
[101] [1905] 2 Ch 188.
[102] [1956] Ch 131.

place to another. The case established that the right to use a private pleasure ground was an easement known to the law. The court relied among other cases on *Duncan v Louch*.[103] That was decided in 1845 on the terms of a right granted in 1675 over an area known as the Terrace Walk. The easement was proved to be a right to pass forwards and backwards over every part of the land, and not merely between two points, and was enjoyed subject to an obligation to pay a proportion of the cost of repairing and amending the Terrace Walk.

2.86 Similar private rights can also exist by statute. The Kensington Improvement Act 1851[104] allows two thirds of the owners of houses around a garden in the locality to choose that the garden will be maintained though a garden committee and the costs collected through the council tax by the local authority which then passes the money to the committee. Residents who contribute are entitled to a key to the garden.

Town and village greens

2.87 It is well established that by custom the inhabitants of a locality could have the right of access for sports and pastimes on town or village greens but it had (in theory) to have subsisted since 1189. Such a right is now statutory.[105] Similar rights could be conferred by local Acts such as inclosure Acts and municipal Acts. They can also be acquired after 20 years' use by inhabitants of a locality or of a neighbourhood within a locality under the Commons Registration Act 1965, s 22 and the Commons Act 2006, s 15. There has been substantial litigation on the subject[106] as well as statutory amendment and the law is still far from settled.

Public rights to roam

2.88 There is a great variety of other rights for the public, notably the of access for open air recreation (the Right to Roam) over registered common land and areas mapped as mountain, moor, heath or down under the Countryside and Rights of Way Act 2000 and a coastal strip under the Marine and Coastal Access Act 2009. There are other rights over common land under the Commons Act 1899 or the LPA 1925, s 193. There is also a right to pass along long distance routes under the National Parks and Access to the Countryside Act 1949. There may be rights over town squares under the Town Gardens Protection Act 1863,[107] over recreation grounds under The Public Health Act 1875, s 164, in open spaces under the Open Spaces Act 1906 and in

---

[103] (1845) 6 QB 904, 115 ER 341.

[104] See *Herrmann v Royal Borough of Kensington and Chelsea and Wainwright as treasurer of Ovington Square Garden Committee* [2010] EWHC 1706 (Ch).

[105] *Oxfordshire County Council v Oxford City Council* [2006] 2 AC 674 at [19].

[106] Including *R v Oxfordshire County Council ex p Sunningwell Parish Council* [2000] 1AC 335; *R (on the application of Beresford) v Sunderland City Council* [2004] 1 AC 889; *Oxfordshire County Council v Oxford City Council* [2006] 2 AC 674; and *R (on the application of Lewis) v Redcar and Cleveland Borough Council* [2010] UKSC 11.

[107] See *Tulk v The Metropolitan Board of Works* (1867–68) LR 3 QB 682.

country parks under the Countryside Act 1968, ss 6–8. The Housing Act 1985, s 12(1)(b), allows a local housing authority, with the consent of the Secretary of State, to provide and maintain recreation grounds in connection with housing accommodation provided by them[108] and if so there will be a right to use the ground. Most of these are by right.[109] There are numerous similar rights under local Acts although some may be at the discretion of the municipality.

2.89 There is also public access by licence such as to the Royal Parks, see Parks Regulation Acts 1872–1974. Providing recreation for the public benefit is a charitable purpose[110] and large areas of the country as well as parks and gardens are opened by the National Trust and other charities.[111]

---

[108] See *R (Barkas) v North Yorkshire County Council* [2011] EWHC 3653 (Admin).

[109] *Hall v Beckenham Corporation* [1949] 1KB 716; *R (Barkas) v North Yorkshire County Council* [2011] EWHC 3653 (Admin).

[110] *Shillington v Portadown UDC* [1911] 1 I R 247; *Bath and North East Somerset Council v HM Attorney General/The Treasury Solicitor (Bona Vacantia)* [2002] EWCA 1623 (Ch) 32. 'It is now well settled that a trust of land for its use for the purposes of public recreation is charitable'.

[111] See Charities Act 2011, s 5, formerly Recreational Charities Act 1958. See also para **2.42**.

Chapter 3

ACQUISITION BY ACTS OF THE PARTIES

INTRODUCTION

3.1   The law of easements has practical implications for a large number of landowners. Recent Land Registry figures suggest that at least 65 per cent of freehold titles are subject to one or more easements. These interests can be fundamental to the enjoyment of property. For example, many landowners depend on easements in order to obtain access to their property, and indeed rights of way and the more modern phenomenon, a right to park, are the types of easement most frequently encountered in practice.

3.2   It is well established in the case of *Re Ellenborough Park*[1] that a right cannot be an easement unless four requirements are satisfied:

(1)   there must be a dominant tenement and a servient tenement;

(2)   the easement must accommodate the dominant tenement;

(3)   the dominant and servient tenements must be owned by different persons; and

(4)   the easement must be capable of forming the subject matter of a grant.

3.3   In practice there is little difficulty with the application of these principles in relation to rights of way. However, there has been a debate as to whether a right to park can fulfil the fourth criterion. It is a debate which has now been resolved in favour of such a right being recognised as an easement.

3.4   These principles have been dealt with in two comparatively recent cases of *Kent v Kavanagh*[2] and *Moncrieff v Jamieson*.[3]

3.5   All easements are deemed to 'lie in grant', that is to say they must be granted expressly, impliedly or by prescription. In the case of implied and prescriptive easements there is no express grant, but the grant is nevertheless assumed or presumed. The various methods of creation are examined in turn in this Chapter, along with formalities associated with agreements for easements

---

[1]   [1956] Ch 131 (at 163).
[2]   [2001] Ch 1.
[3]   [2007] UKHL 42.

and equitable easements, the acquisition of easements by estoppel and the past and present rules against perpetuities and the grant of future rights of way.

EXPRESS CREATION

3.6   An easement is an 'incorporeal hereditament'; that is, it belongs to a defined list of rights recognised by the law of property as being, like land itself, a species of 'real property' to which the rules of land law apply. If created expressly, such rights should be granted by deed if they are to take effect as legal interests.[4] They can also be granted by written instrument, provided that the instrument complies with section 2 of the Law of Property (Miscellaneous Provisions) Act 1989. However, if the written instrument is not also a deed, then they only take effect as equitable interests.[5] An uncompleted agreement to grant a legal easement is a classic example of an equitable easement.

3.7   For an easement to be validly granted, the grantor must have sufficient interest in the servient land to create a valid easement over it. Easements granted over land belonging to third parties may, however, take effect by way of acquiescence, or estoppel in some circumstances.[6] For example, where the third party allows access over his land in return for a right in return such as the maintenance of encroaching foundations. Likewise, if there is an express grant of an easement over land to which the grantor has no title, but he then acquires title, he and his successors will be bound by estoppel.[7] Where the grantor has only a limited interest in the land over which he purports to grant the easement, the extent of the easement will be determined by his interest at the time of the grant, without taking into account subsequent events. So in *Booth v Alcock*,[8] the grantor of an easement of way had at the time of the grant only a lease over the servient tenement. He subsequently acquired the fee simple, but it was held that the grant was restricted in duration to the length of the lease which the grantor had at the date of the grant.

3.8   Where the rights of the grantor to dispose of his land are subject to statutory constraints, he cannot lawfully grant an easement in excess of his powers. This point used to be taken on dispositions by trustees for sale, and may still be taken by tenants for life under the Settled Land Act 1925.[9] The importance of these restrictions, insofar as they apply to former trustees for sale, has been greatly reduced by the Trusts of Land and Appointment of Trustees Act 1996. Trustees of land now have all the powers of an absolute owner unless expressly restricted.[10] It remains the position that when authority is required the grant of an easement which is not authorised will be of no

---

[4]   LPA 1925, s 52.

[5]   LPA 1925, s 53.

[6]   See *ER Ives Investments Ltd v High* [1967] 1 All ER 504, CA.

[7]   *Rowbotham v Wilson* (1857) 8 E&B 123; 8 HLC 348.

[8]   (1873) 8 Ch App 663.

[9]   See eg Settled Land Act 1925, s 49(1), which authorises the grant and reservation of easements, and s 41 of the same Act in regard to the grant of leases.

[10]   Trusts of Land and Appointment of Trustees Act 1996, s 6(1).

effect.[11] *Housden v Conservators of Wimbledon and Putney Commons*[12] concerned a claim to a right of way by prescription by over 40 years' use. The Conservators argued that the statute under which they held the servient land limited their powers of disposal and prevented any grant of such a right. The Court of Appeal construed the statute as authorising the grant. However, in a detailed consideration (albeit obiter) following *Staffordshire and Worcestershire Canal Navigation v Proprietors of Birmingham Canal Navigations*,[13] the court considered that in the absence of a statutory power to make the grant it would not have been possible for the claimant to prescribe. See para **6.111** for more details.

3.9   In the same way as a competent grantor is required, no easement can be granted in excess of the interest of the grantee in the dominant tenement. This is consistent with the general principle that easements are appurtenant to land, so that they can only subsist for as long as the interest in land to which they relate subsists. Where the grant is to someone with a limited interest, who subsequently becomes the owner of the dominant tenement, the easement may endure for the benefit of the freehold only if the terms of the grant contemplated that this should be the case.[14]

3.10   An easement of way may also be reserved by a transferor over land sold.[15] The reservation must normally be in clear terms.[16] Apart from this, an easement may be held to have been reserved by implication but such a reservation will be found to exist only where the facts are not reasonably consistent with any explanation other than such an easement was intended to be reserved.[17]

3.11   An express easement of way may be granted by a lease. The effect of such a grant was considered in the context of a right to light in *Frogmore Developments Ltd v Shirayama Shokusan Co*[18] in the context of its (alleged) inconsistency with intended development of nearby land, which adjoined the former GLC County Hall in London. It was held that the grant of 'the right to free and unobstructed passage of light and air to the premises at all times' entitled the lessee to receive a right of light at a level which did not fall below that required for the ordinary purposes for which the premises could be used. This authority demonstrates how important it is to advise clients where reservations are on the title (whether reserved in transfers of the freehold, or on

---

[11]   See eg *Oakley v Boston* [1976] QB 270 (consent required to grant of an easement under Ecclesiastical Leases Acts 1842 and 1858 but not obtained). See also *Re St Clement, Leigh-on-Sea* [1988] 1 WLR 720.
[12]   [2008] 1 WLR 1172.
[13]   (1866) LR 1 HL 254.
[14]   *Rymer v McIlroy* [1897] 1 Ch 528. See also *Alford v Hannaford* [2011] EWCA Civ 1099.
[15]   See LPA 1925, s 65.
[16]   *Wheeldon v Burrows* (1879) 12 Ch D 31 at 49 per Thesiger LJ.
[17]   *Re Webb's Lease* [1951] Ch 808 at 829 per Jenkins LJ. *Peckham v Ellison* (1998) 77 P&CR D27, CA (right of way).
[18]   (1997) ChD, unreported.

grants of leases) that such reservations (eg of way) may impose a severe constraint on the client's development or building plans.

Interpretation of grants

3.12 One can question whether there are any special rules applicable to the interpretation of documents purporting to create easements.

3.13 Until recently, the view had been that there were special rules applicable to the interpretation of transfers of land. For example in *Scarfe v Adam*[19] Griffith LJ had set a limit on the situations in which extrinsic evidence was available to interpret a transfer of land:

> 'The principle may be stated thus: if the terms of the transfer clearly define the land or interest transferred extrinsic evidence is not admissible to contradict the transfer. In such a case, if the transfer does not truly express the bargain between vendor and purchaser, the only remedy is by way of rectification of the transfer.'

3.14 However, in *Moncrieff v Jamieson* (at paragraph 113 of the judgment) in relation to the implication of rights in a conveyance, Lord Neuberger stated that the conceptual basis of implication is rooted in the general law of contract:

> 'That principle is that the law will imply a term into a contract, where, in the light of the terms of the contract and the facts known to the parties at the time of the contract, such a term would have been regarded as reasonably necessary or obvious to the parties.'

3.15 Lord Neuberger's references to contract are indicative of a growing judicial tendency 'to rest the right to an easement on supposed intention of the parties to the contract or, if there was no contract, on the intention of the testator or grantor'.[20] Further evidence of this tendency can be seen in *Adam v Shrewsbury*[21] where Lord Justice Neuberger (as he then was) said (at paragraph 28):

> 'In my judgment, therefore, the resolution of the issue raised on the present appeal turns on the proper analysis of the common intention of the parties, as gathered from the terms of the conveyance, the position on the ground, and the communications passing between the parties before the execution of the conveyance, which would include the provisions of the contract. Although this court excluded as legally irrelevant any communications between the parties outside the conveyance (unless, of course, there is a claim for rectification) in *Scarfe v Adams* [1981] 1 All ER 843 at 851, it seems to me that such a conclusion is inconsistent with the general principle that when construing a document (whether or not it relates to land) all the surrounding circumstances should be taken into account. That this aspect of Scarfe's case is not the law was decided by this court in *Partridge v Lawrence* [2004] 1 P & CR 176 at 187.'

---

[19]   [1981] 1 All ER 843 (at 851).
[20]   See *Gale on Easements* (17th edn, para 3-120).
[21]   [2006] 1 P&CR 27.

3.16 Thus the current position seems to be that there are few if any special rules applicable to the interpretation of documents said to create easements. When examining a document to see whether, for example, a vehicular (as opposed to a pedestrian) right of way has been granted or to ascertain the width or exact route of a right of way, one applies the general principles set out by Lord Hoffmann in *ICS v West Bromwich BS*.[22] In order to divine the intention of the parties, one starts with the words of the conveyance and any plan annexed to it and one can then look at the situation on the ground at the date of the conveyance and (even) any contemporaneous documents. As Moore-Bick LJ said in the recent case of *ETG Developments v Noah*:[23]

> 'The primary task of the court in a case of this kind is to construe the grant itself. But it is common ground that, in doing so, the court is entitled to take into account not only the language of the grant but also the plan attached to it and evidence by way of background of the condition of the land at the time of the grant and other matters including, in this case, documents submitted for the purposes of obtaining planning permission...'

3.17 The only rule of construction peculiar to easements appears to be as follows: an easement may be created by express grant or by express reservation. In the case of a grant, the rule that a grantor may not derogate from his or her grant is applied, and the grant is interpreted against the grantor (see e g *Williams v James*[24]). In the case of a reservation, although one would expect the words to be interpreted similarly, that is, against the person making the reservation, the currently accepted position, as set out by the Court of Appeal in the case of *St Edmundsbury & Ipswich v Clark*[25] is that a reservation of an easement by a vendor of land is to be interpreted against the purchaser on the basis that the purchaser is treated as the grantor.

3.18 In that case, in a 1945 conveyance of a portion of land an easement was reserved by the Church to Mr Clark. The conveyance was expressed to be 'subject to a right of way over the land coloured red on the plan to and from [the] Church'. The scale plan indicated that the red land equated to an area that was approximately nine feet wide. The conveyance did not expressly state whether a pedestrian right of way or a more extensive vehicular right of way was intended. The Court of Appeal held that, interpreting the conveyance in light of the surrounding circumstances, it was clear that a pedestrian right of way only was being reserved, and the appeal was dismissed. However, the court declared (albeit obiter) that, in view of the reservation still being based on re-grant, the words of the easement should still, in cases of ambiguity, be interpreted against the purchaser and in favour of the vendor. The court did emphasise, however, that this was to be a recourse of last resort to be used in cases when the other principles of contractual interpretation still lead to genuine ambiguity.

---

[22] [1998] 1 WLR 896.
[23] [2008] EWCA Civ 259 (at para 12).
[24] (1867) LR 2 CP 577.
[25] (No 2) [1975] 1 WLR 468.

RIGHTS OF WAY BY IMPLICATION

3.19 Quite often, a conveyance, or other document, will expressly prevent easements of way arising by implication. A document may include a list, expressed to be exhaustive, of all easements and other rights created at the time of the transfer. Alternatively, the document may include an express provision that prevents implied rights from being inferred (see below).

3.20 Where an exclusion is not expressly provided, an easement may be inferred where a conveyance or other document does not grant the easement expressly, but uses terms consistent with the existence of the easement. In *Roberts v Karr,*[26] the description of land in a release as abutting a road was held to preclude the grantor from asserting that the grantee was not entitled to access over a verge which separated part of the land from the road.

3.21 Another example would be how an easement may be held to have been granted by implication, based on the intended use of the property which was the subject of a lease for sale.[27] In *Browne v Flower,*[28] Parker J considered the position of an implicit grant of an easement of light, saying:

> 'Once again, though possibly there may not be known to the law any easement of way for special purposes, still the lease of a building to be used for a special purpose requiring an extraordinary amount of light might well be held to preclude the grantor from diminishing the way passing to the grantee's windows, even in cases where the diminution would not be such as to create a nuisance within the meaning of recent decisions...'

3.22 There seems no reason in principle why these words should be limited to the situation where the lessee or other grantee is claiming an extraordinary quantity of light. It is, however, possible to envisage circumstances where it might be argued that since the contemplated purpose for which premises were being leased or purchased involved at least some obligation on the part of the purchaser to provide adequate access to the work places of those whom he proposed to employ there, there was by implication a grant of an easement of way.[29]

3.23 Implied easements are most likely to arise when land has been divided into two parts and either one or both parts are sold or let.

3.24 When seeking to ascertain whether an easement has been implied it is, however, important to work out whether the claim being made is to an implied grant or an implied reservation.

---

[26] [1809] 1 Taunt 495.
[27] *Lyttleton Times Co Limited v Warners Limited* [1907] AC 476; *Yankwood Limited v Havering London Borough Council* [1998] EGCS 75.
[28] [1911] 1 Ch 219 at 226.
[29] For a case where the grant in a lease of a right of way was held not to be limited by implication from surrounding circumstances, see *Frogmore Developments Ltd v Shirayama Shoku-san Co Ltd* (1997) ChD, unreported.

3.25 An implied grant may occur where A sells or lets land to B retaining some neighbouring land of his own. If B contends that he has an easement over A's land which is neither express nor prescriptive, the claim must be on the basis of an implied grant.

3.26 An implied reservation may occur if A contends that he has an easement over B's land (for the benefit of the land which A has retained), and no such easement has been expressly reserved or prescriptively acquired.

3.27 As a general rule, the law is readier to imply a grant than a reservation. As Lord Justice Thesiger stated in the seminal case of *Wheeldon v Burrows*:[30]

> 'if the grantor intends to reserve any right over the tenement granted, it is his duty to reserve it expressly in the grant.'

3.28 There are four methods by which easements can be created by implication. The first two methods take effect only on grant; the third and fourth can take effect both on grant and on reservation (hence why it is so important to distinguish between a grant and a reservation). They are:

(1) the rule in *Wheeldon v Burrows*;

(2) section 62 of the LPA 1925;

(3) easements of necessity; and

(4) easements of intended use.

3.29 The rule in *Wheeldon v Burrows* and section 62 of the LPA 1925 both give rise to the acquisition of easements as a result of the use of the grantor's land prior to the relevant transaction. They are therefore broadly based on the past exercise of particular rights. Easements of necessity and easements of intended use, on the other hand, are forward looking. In each case, the court is required to examine what the parties to a transaction were contemplating in terms of the future use of the properties in question.

The rule in *Wheeldon v Burrows*

3.30 This case[31] finds its foundations in the principle of implied grant. It is, in effect, an early formulation of section 62 of the LPA 1925 but the rights that

---

[30] (1879) 12 Ch D 31, at 49. See *Walby v Walby* [2012] EWHC 3089 (Ch) at para 25ff per Morgan J. for a full and very useful review of the authorities on the implication of easements by grant and by reservation.

[31] (1879) 12 Ch D 31.

pass are limited by comparison to that section.[32] Again, it is common place for a conveyance to expressly provide that no rights under the principle are capable of being acquired.

3.31   In 1878, Lord Justice Thesiger set out the rule as follows:

> '... that, on the grant by the owner of a tenement or part of that tenement as it is then used and enjoyed, there will pass to the grantee all those continuous and apparent easements (by which, of course, I mean quasi-easements), or in other words all those easements which are necessary to the reasonable enjoyment of the property granted, and which have been and are at the time of the grant used by the owners of the entirety for the benefit of the part granted.'

3.32   The rule sets out the circumstances in which easements may be impliedly granted where the dominant and servient lands were previously owned by the same person. It is said to be based on the doctrine of non-derogation from grant.[33]

3.33   The following three requirements must be satisfied in order for there to be an implied grant under the rule:

(1)   the right must be 'continuous and apparent'. This is taken to mean that it is 'seen on inspection' and 'is neither transitory nor intermittent';[34]

(2)   the right must be necessary for the reasonable enjoyment of the property granted. This requirement is not as narrowly interpreted as it is in the context of easements of necessity. The question is whether the right will contribute to the enjoyment of the property for the purpose for which it was transferred;

(3)   at the time of the grant the quasi-easement was being used by the common owner for the benefit of the part granted.

3.34   The following points should be noted:

(1)   the rule can only grant as easements rights that are capable of fulfilling the requirements of an easement. It cannot transform into easements rights that do not satisfy the necessary characteristics;

(2)   the estate transferred may be legal or equitable. If an easement is implied, it will assume the same status as the estate that was transferred and to which it pertains. For example, if the estate transferred was an equitable lease, the easement will be equitable too;

---

[32]   An exception being the agreement for a lease which does not count as a conveyance for the purposes of section 62. See *Borman v Griffith* [1930] 1 Ch 493.

[33]   See e g *Sovmots v Sec Of State* [1979] AC 144.

[34]   *Titchmarsh v Royston Water Co Ltd* (1899) 81 LT 673; *Ward v Kirkland* [1967] Ch 194, [1966] 1 All ER 609 (right to enter servient tenement to maintain a wall not continuous).

(3) the transfer of the land from the common owner may be a sale, a devise or a gift. It does not therefore have to be for value. However, it must be voluntary (as opposed to being made pursuant to the exercise of compulsory purchase powers);

(4) the land granted and the land retained must have been in <u>both</u> common ownership **and** common occupation before the grant.

3.35 The rule, therefore, usually operates on the sub-division of a parcel of land. For example, if a parcel of land under common ownership is divided into part A, which is retained and part B, which is disposed of, the rule confers by implication on the transferee of part B the benefits of any rights to way over part A that the former owner of both parts exercised over the land prior to its sub-division. The rule also applies where the common owner subdivides and sells the subdivided property simultaneously, retaining no land himself.

3.36 *Wheeldon v Burrows* was itself a case that concerned the right of access to light over the servient tenement. Access to light is regarded as both continuous and apparent and necessary for the reasonable enjoyment of the land and does not therefore suffer from the problems of easements (such as rights of way) which are only in discontinuous use (as and when the dominant owner needs to pass along it) for which proof of use or necessity is required.[35] This is important in the context of a disposition for value of registered land where an easement which is neither known to the disponee nor obvious on inspection takes priority as an overriding interest only if it has been exercised during the year before the disposition (see para **13.8**).

3.37 Thus, in *Swansborough v Coventry*,[36] Trindall CJ said:

> 'It is well established by the decided cases, that where the same person possesses a house, having the actual use and enjoyment of certain rights, and also possesses the adjoining land, and sells the house to another person, although the ways be new, he cannot, nor can anyone who claims under him, build upon the adjoining land so as to obstruct or interrupt the enjoyment of those ways.'

3.38 Two specific scenarios arise under this rule.

Sale of part of land, where vendor retains the remainder

3.39 Where buildings yet to be built on the land being disposed of have but the vendor is aware of, either at the time of the disposition or during any prior agreement for the disposition, that the land is being acquired for building

---

[35] For example, *Borman v Griffith* (above) – the case itself provides a useful review of the rule in *Wheeldon v Burrows* (above) at 499.

[36] [1832] 9 Bing 305 at 309.

purposes, the principle applies equally and the right over the retained land can be used by the buildings when built on the land (ie the implied grant is for the benefit of the land).[37]

3.40   The transfer of rights by implication may be negatived or modified by circumstances, but the onus of establishing this is on the grantor. Therefore, where the grantor makes it clear in express terms that he intends to build on part A (the retained land), the grantee cannot complain if his access to way is restricted by such construction.[38] If, however, the grantee is aware of only a general intention to build, such as by describing the retained land as 'building land', then this is insufficient to negative the implication.[39]

3.41   Where a grantor who sells part of his land does not expressly reserve in that grant an easement of way in favour of the part he has retained, he will normally not be held to have reserved such a right by implication.[40] Such reservation should, therefore, be expressly stated in the grant. The general rule is that grants are construed against the grantor, and this principle applies to exclude, in general, the implication of reservations in favour of the grantor. The correct approach is for the court to interpret the terms of the grant by considering the instrument and the surrounding circumstances in conjunction.[41]

3.42   However, where a vendor disposes of two plots of land simultaneously, which are adjacent to each other, both conveyances are treated as grants under the rule in *Wheeldon v Burrows* and therefore each part acquires by implication the same easements over the other as it would if that other part had been retained by the vendor.[42] This rule applies equally to testamentary dispositions and voluntary conveyances inter vivos.[43]

Lease of part of land, where the landlord retains the remainder

3.43   As with an outright sale of land, the grant of a lease over part of the land of the lessor, will allow the lessee to acquire by implication, for the term of the lease, any right to the access of way over the lessor's retained land, which it can be shown was actually enjoyed by the part let at the date of the lease.

---

[37]   *Frederick Betts Ltd v Pickfords Ltd* [1906] 2 Ch 87.
[38]   *Birmingham, Dudley & District Banking Company v Ross* (1888) 38 Ch D 295.
[39]   *Broomfield v Williams* (1897) 1 ChD at 602. *Frogmore Development Ltd v Shirayama Shokusan Co Ltd* (1997) ChD, unreported.
[40]   *Wheeldon v Burrows* (1879) 12 ChD 31 at 49. See also **5.6**. For the effect of a reservation, see Law of Property Act 1925, s 65.
[41]   *St Edmundsbury and Ipswich Diocesan Board of Finance v Clark (No 2)* [1975] 1 All ER 772, CA; *Frogmore Developments Ltd v Shirayama Shokusan Co Ltd* (1997) ChD, unreported. For the extent of 'surrounding circumstances' see, generally, *Investors Compensation Scheme Ltd v West Bromwich Building Society* [1998] 1 All ER 98, HL.
[42]   *Russell v Watts* (1884) 25 ChD 559 – see especially Fry LJ at 584.
[43]   *Phillips v Low* [1892] 1 Ch 47.

3.44 During the term of that lease, any later lease or grant of the retained land must take effect subject to the right to the access of way to the let land.[44] If, however, there was never any formal grant of the original lease over the let land (eg there was an agreement only to create a lease), the rights of the original informal lessee may still be protected by registration or actual occupation of the part let.

3.45 The application of the principle of implied grant was described by Mellish LJ in *Leech v Schweder*[45] as follows:

'It is perfectly established that if a man owns a house, and owns property of any other kind adjoining that house, and then either conveys the house in fee simple or demises it for a term of years to another person, a right to way unobstructed by anything to be erected on any land which at the time belonged to the grantor passes to the grantee.'

3.46 The implication may be negatived by surrounding circumstances, as where it is well known to the lessee that the lessor intends to develop his retained land in a way which may interfere with the way to the buildings (actual or proposed) on the land let.[46] The onus of negativing the implication of an easement lies on the lessor.[47] Care should therefore be taken when granting leases in particular to ensure that any reservation of the right to build on adjoining land (whether by the lessor or third parties) is wide enough to prevent contrary rights from being implied.

3.47 This principle applies to the implied grant of an easement but not to the reservation, for example, where a lessor, in demising part of his land over which a way exists to his retained land, fails to reserve in favour of the part retained an easement of way over the part demised, the retained land will normally enjoy no right to way during the term of the lease.[48]

Law of Property Act 1925, section 62

3.48 This is now the main way in which the right to easements which are not mentioned in the conveyance are impliedly granted and overlays the rule in *Wheeldon v Burrows*. The section applies to conveyances made after 31 December 1881 which was when section 6 of the Conveyancing Act 1881, which preceded section 62 of the LPA 1925, came into effect.

3.49 It is common practice to expressly exclude section 62 with wording such as:

---

44 *Thomas v Owen* (1888) 20 QBD 225.
45 (1874) 9 Ch App 463 at 472.
46 *Birmingham, Dudley and District Banking Co v Ross* (1888) 38 ChD 295; *Godwin v Schweppes Ltd* [1902] 1 Ch 926.
47 *Broomfield v Williams* [1897] 1 Ch 602; *Pollard v Gare* [1901] 1 Ch 834; *Swansborough v Coventry* (1832) 9 Bing 305; *Myers v Catterson* (1889) 43 ChD 470.
48 *Re Webbs Lease* [1951] Ch 808; *Frogmore Developments Ltd v Shirayama Shokusan Co Ltd* (1997) ChD, unreported. See also *Peckham v Ellison* (1998) 77 P&CR D27, CA.

'Exclusion of Section 62 Law of Property Act 1925

The parties hereby agree and declare that the Transferee is not entitled to any right or easement over the Retained Land other than those specifically granted by this Transfer and accordingly section 62 of the Law of Property Act 1925 [and the rule in *Wheeldon and Burrows*] does not apply to this Transfer.'

3.50 An express exclusion of *Wheeldon and Burrows* may also be included. Section 62 therefore applies only in so far as a contrary intention is not expressed in the conveyance.

3.51 Section 62(1) of the 1925 Act provides that a conveyance of land shall be deemed to include and shall operate to convey, with the land:

'all buildings, erections, fixtures, commons, hedges, ditches, fences, ways, waters, water-courses, liberties, privileges, easements, rights, and advantages whatsoever, appertaining or reputed to appertain to the land, or any part thereof, or, at the time of conveyance, demised, occupied, or enjoyed with, or reputed or known as part or parcel of or appurtenant to the land or any part thereof.'

3.52 Whilst section 62(2) provides:

'A conveyance of land, having houses or other buildings thereon, shall be deemed to include and shall by virtue of this Act operate to convey, with the land, houses, or other buildings, all outhouses, erections, fixtures, cellars, areas, courts, courtyards, cisterns, sewers, gutters, drains, ways, passages, ways, watercourses, liberties, privileges, easements, rights, and advantages whatsoever, appertaining or reputed to appertain to the land, houses, or other buildings conveyed, or any of them, or any part thereof, or, at the time of conveyance, demised, occupied, or enjoyed with, or reputed or known as part or parcel of or appurtenant to, the land, houses, or other buildings conveyed, or any of them, or any part thereof.'

3.53 A conveyance is virtually any instrument which transfers or creates a *legal* estate in freehold or leasehold land.[49] The term does not include, therefore, agreements which create equitable interest only.[50] Where they apply, the general words of section 62[51] can only be excluded by express terms.[52]

3.54 Section 62 has the effect of passing to the transferee of land the benefit of existing easements, profits, privileges and rights which appertain to the land conveyed, or are indeed reputed to appertain to it, or which at the date of the conveyance are enjoyed with that land. This will include rights of way in the course of being acquired, even though precarious.[53]

---

[49] LPA 1925, s 205(1)(iii).
[50] *Borman v Griffith* [1930] 1 Ch 493. Which is of itself sufficient to create an express equitable easement.
[51] Law of Property Act 1925, s 62(4) – *William Hill (Southern) Ltd v Cabras Ltd* (1987) 54 P&CR 42 at 46.
[52] For recent authority on the scope of section 62 see *Kent v Kavanagh* [2006] EWCA Civ 162.
[53] *Midtown v CLRP Co* [2005] EWHC 33 Ch at para 23 per Peter Smith J.

3.55 It is not thought that the *benefit* of a written consent within section 3 of the Prescription Act 1832 will pass under section 62.[54] As appears in Chapter 6, such a consent (if effective) prevents the assertion of a prescriptive claim to way by the dominant owner 'A'. The benefit of such a consent will pass to any successor of A ('B') because B acquires the dominant land with the benefit of the consent and no prescriptive claim can arise while that consent is in force and unrevoked. Section 62 simply has no part to play here. The same observation is made as to the effect of section 63 of the LPA 1925 considered below.

3.56 As an owner of land cannot have an easement over his own land, there is clear authority that section 62 operates only where there has been diversity of tenure, as under a lease of part, or occupation of the dominant or servient tenement prior to the conveyance. This is because where no such divergence exists there can be no easement to pass under section 62.[55]

3.57 In the case of quasi-easements of way, as opposed to other easements, it appears in any event that where there is unity of occupation, section 62 is still capable of applying. This was decided in *Broomfield v Williams*,[56] although that case has been frequently distinguished and an alternative basis for the decision was on derogation from grant. Where there has been diversity of occupation, as where adjacent farm cottages have been occupied by farm workers under licence and the occupants have needed access over one anothers' gardens, if individual cottages are subsequently sold separately section 62 can apply.

3.58 As with the rule in *Wheeldon v Burrows*, the presence of way over land is not difficult to show. Therefore, a right to the access of that way will be transferred under section 62 even where there has been a unity of ownership provided the right has been exercised by and for the benefit of the land conveyed and not just for the common benefit of the two properties. Where the land is not in common ownership no such problem arises.[57]

3.59 The following conditions must therefore be fulfilled for section 62 to operate so as to benefit a buyer:

(1) the right must have been exercised over land retained by the grantor;

---

[54] This point arises where there is a consent provision in a lease (falling within *Haynes v King* (1893) 3 Ch 439) where the successor in title to the landlord acquires the freehold. Section 62 does not operate to pass the benefit of the consent proviso in the lease to the new owner of the freehold.

[55] *Sovmots Investments Ltd v Secretary of State for the Environment* [1979] AC 144 at 176C per Lord Edmund Davies. Lord Wilberforce expressed the same view. But see a contrary view expressed by the Court of Appeal in *P&S Platt v Crouch* [2003] EWCA Civ 1110.

[56] [1897] 1 Ch 602.

[57] It should be noted that the court retains an equitable jurisdiction to rectify any conveyance which mistakenly transfers to a grantee more rights than were intended in a relevant contract for sale.

(2)　the right must have been appurtenant to or 'enjoyed with' the quasi-dominant tenement;

(3)　the right must have already been enjoyed 'at the time of the conveyance';

(4)　the conveyance must be of a legal estate;

(5)　(what are now) the dominant tenement and the servient tenements, must have been in separate occupation prior to the grant.

3.60　However, the operation of the section is subject to the following important limitations:

(1)　the right in question must be capable of being an easement;

(2)　the grant must be within the competence of the grantor;

(3)　the user must not be excessively personal, excessively precarious, merely temporary or a 'mere memory';[58] and

(4)　the section applies only in so far as no contrary intention is expressed in the conveyance or lease.

3.61　The point and indeed danger about section 62 is that it is capable of converting what have hitherto been merely precarious benefits or mere informal licences into permanent property rights. Take the facts of *Hair v Gilman*.[59] In that case, landlord 'L' allowed tenant 'T' to park her car anywhere on the forecourt owned by L in front of the demised property, although there was no express term to this effect in the tenancy agreement. Subsequently, T purchased the freehold of the property she had leased (but not the forecourt) from L. The conveyance of the house was silent on parking rights, but it did not expressly exclude the operation of section 62. T was held to have acquired an easement to park on the forecourt retained by L for the same duration as the freehold estate. It was irrelevant that neither L nor T contemplated that L allowing T to park during the term of the lease would have this result on the conveyance of the freehold.

3.62　In general terms, it is easier to succeed under section 62 than the rule in *Wheeldon v Burrows* as there is no need to prove either that the right was continuous and apparent or that it was necessary for the reasonable enjoyment of the property conveyed. However, as a counsel of prudence, it is often sensible to base a claim on both methods of implication in the alternative. Moreover, in the absence of a 'conveyance' triggering section 62, the rule in *Wheeldon v Burrows* may be the only recourse available to the person claiming an easement.

---

[58]　*Penn v Wilkins* (1974) 236 EG 203.
[59]　(2000) 80 P&CR 108.

Easements of necessity

3.63 An easement of necessity is implied only where the right is essential for the use of the land granted or retained. The question is not whether it is necessary for the reasonable enjoyment of the land but whether the land can be used at all without the implied grant or reservation. A claim will only be successful where the land is 'absolutely inaccessible or useless' without the easement (see e g *Union Wayerage v London Graving Dock* [1902] 2 Ch 577). An easement will not be implied by this route merely because it makes it more convenient to use the land. For example a right of way will not be implied by necessity where there is some other means of access, even if that route is difficult and expensive to use (see e g *Barry v Haseldine* [1952] Ch 835). As an easement of necessity will end if the necessity ends it can not subsist as an absolute fee simple interest and therefore must be equitable.

3.64 The most obvious example of a situation in which an easement of necessity may be implied is where a grantor conveys a piece in the middle, which is completely surrounded by an entire plot of land retained by the grantor. The land in the centre would be completely landlocked, if no implied right of way is granted.

Easements of intended use

3.65 The classic statement here is that of Lord Parker in *Pwllbach Colliery v Woodman* [1915] AC 634 (at 646–7). His Lordship grouped implied easements under two heads: first, those implied because they are ancillary to rights expressly granted; and, second, those implied because they are necessary to give effect to the manner in which the land retained or demised was intended to be used:

> 'The law will readily imply the grant or reservation of such easements as may be necessary to give effect to the common intention of the parties to a grant of real property, with reference to the manner or purposes in and for which the land granted or some land retained by the grantor is to be used. ... But it is essential for this purpose that the parties should intend that the subject of the grant or the land retained by the grantor should be used in some definite and particular manner. It is not enough that the subject of the grant or the land retained should be intended to be used in a manner which may or may not involve this definite and particular use.'

3.66 There are thus two requirements for the implication of an easement of intended use:

(1) the parties must, at the time of grant, have shared an intention, either express or implied, that the land demised or retained should be used for a particular purpose; and

(2) the easement must be necessary to give effect to that intended use.

3.67 In *Moncrieff v Jamieson* Lord Neuberger (at paragraphs 110 and 112) distinguished rights implied under the rule in *Wheeldon v Burrows* from rights which arise under the preceding principle, namely that:

> "'the grant of an easement is prima facie also the grant of such ancillary rights as are reasonably necessary to its exercise or enjoyment" – per Parker J in *Jones v Pritchard* [1908] 1 Ch 630 at 638. Subsequently, in *Pwllbach Colliery Company Ltd v Woodman* [1915] AC 634 at 646 to 647, the same judge, then Lord Parker of Waddington, described the decision in *Jones v Pritchard* as being within a "class of cases in which easements impliedly may be created", not because of "the terms of the grant itself", but because of "the circumstances under which the grant was made"… there are cases where a right is implied because it is "reasonably necessary" for the "exercise or enjoyment" of an expressly granted right (as in *Jones v Pritchard*). In the [this] type of case, it seems to me important to focus on the dual nature of the requirement that the alleged implied right be "reasonably necessary".'

3.68 Lord Hope went as far as to say that, although the extent of any right granted must be construed in the way of the circumstances at the date of the grant:

> 'it is not necessary for it to be shown that all the rights that are later claimed as necessary for the comfortable use and enjoyment of the [easement] were actually in use at that date. It is sufficient that they may be considered to have been in contemplation at the time of the grant, having regard to what the dominant proprietor might reasonably be expected to do in the exercise of his right to convenient and comfortable use of the property.'

3.69 In *Waterman v Boyle*[60] an attempt (successful at first instance) was made to argue for an implied grant into a right of way of a right for private and trade visitors to park cars on an entrance drive for the duration of their visit. The Court of Appeal rejected the claim on the facts. It held the test was whether the right was reasonably necessary at the time of the transfer, as opposed to merely desirable. At the time of the transfer the property in question had some parking spaces, and if the parties had intended any further right of parking there would have been an indication to that effect in the transfer. *Moncreiff* was distinguished on this ground.

LAW OF PROPERTY ACT, SECTION 63

3.70 There have been attempts in two recent authorities to use section 63 to pass the benefit of a break clause in a lease and the benefit of a restrictive covenant over freehold land. In each case the argument failed.

3.71 Section 63 is really designed to deal with a situation where the grantor has a lesser estate than he purports to grant. It is therefore respectfully

---

[60] [2009] EWCA Civ 115.

suggested that in the light of these two authorities section 63 does not operate to pass any right of way which would otherwise pass under section 62.[61]

CREATION UNDER THE OBLIGATION NOT TO DEROGATE FROM GRANT

3.72 This principle is a general rule applying to all conveyances and is not restricted to cases involving easements. It is based upon the presumed intention of the parties to the relevant grant. Therefore, the principle has been described as one 'of common honesty',[62] in that a grantor should not do anything to render a disposal nugatory. The rights acquired pursuant to an application of the principle bind successors in title of the grantor and are available to successors in title of the grantee.

3.73 The principle finds clear judicial expression in the judgment of Parker J in *Browne v Flower*, where His Lordship said:

> 'But the implications usually explained by the maxim that no one can derogate from his own grant do not stop short with easements. Under certain circumstances there will be implied on the part of the grantor or lessor obligations which restrict the user of the land retained by him further than can be explained by the implication of any easement known to the law. Thus, if the grant or demise be made for a particular purpose, the grantor or lessor comes under an obligation not to use the land retained by him in such a way as to render the land granted or demised unfit or materially less fit for the particular purpose for which the grant or demise was made'.[63]

3.74 Therefore, the immunities acquired by virtue of the principle depend upon the common intention, to be gathered either from the express words of the grant or the circumstances in which it was made. No complaint can be made if an act by the grantor does not make the land granted unfit for a particular purpose or only achievable at a greater expense or with less convenience.[64]

3.75 The principle has been applied so as to bind those deriving title from the grantor, irrespective of whether they have notice of the grantor's obligation.[65] In *Johnston and Sons Ltd v Holland*,[66] in which earlier cases were reviewed, the principle was held to apply to acts done by the grantor on land which he did not own at the date of the grant. This may be of considerable importance in rights of way situations, and may effectively preclude a vendor of land on

---

[61] See *Harbour Estates v HSBC Bank PLC* [2005] Ch 194 and *Sugarman v Porter* [2006] EWHC 331 Ch at paras 31–44.

[62] *Harmer v Jumbil (Nigeria) Tin Areas Ltd* [1921] 1 Ch 200 at 235 and see *Johnston and Sons Ltd v Holland* [1988] 1 EGLR 264.

[63] [1911] 1 Ch 219 at 225.

[64] *O'Cedar Ltd v Slough Trading Company Ltd* [1927] 2 KB 123 at 127.

[65] *Cable v Bryant* [1908] 1 Ch 259.

[66] [1988] 1 EGLR 264, CA.

which a building exists, or on which the erection of such a building is contemplated, from using land which he later acquires so as to interfere with the way over it to the purchasers of the building, whether existing at the date of the sale or contemplated at that time. It is immaterial whether the purchaser's building would otherwise enjoy a prescriptive right to way. See also *Paragon Finance v CLRP Co.*[67]

CREATION UNDER STATUTORY PROVISIONS

3.76 Easements may be granted expressly by statute, or may arise by the exercise or performance of powers or obligations contained in those statutes. One example of this is where a public body which compulsorily purchased land under a statutory power may need additional rights over adjoining land in order to carry out the purposes for which the land is being purchased. However, it should be noted that there is no implied right to create new easements which did not exist prior to the compulsory purchase[68] except insofar as they may exist as quasi-easements under either the rule in *Wheeldon v Burrows*, or section 62 of the LPA 1925. This lack of creative power is confirmed by silence in the Acquisition of Land Act 1981, which is the primary Act by which the Government, local authorities and other bodies obtain land by compulsory purchase. Therefore, it is now the norm for specific Acts to contain express provision for the creation of new rights within their powers for compulsory purchase. The Acquisition of Land Act 1981, section 7, defines 'land' as including hereditaments but reference will normally be needed to the extent of powers in the special act which authorises the acquisition in question.

3.77 Where land which has existing easements is compulsorily purchased, these are transferred in the normal way under section 62 and the usual implications for successors in title apply. There are not many circumstances under which it would be envisaged that a right to way would specifically be required in an Act of Parliament, except, for example, insofar as DEFRA requires land for experimental farm purposes. However, a common situation arises where the effect of a compulsory purchase (for example for a new trunk road) is to deprive the owner A of an existing access to the highway or to sever parts of his land from one another. An alternative route may be available over the land of another owner B. In such cases it is common for the compulsory purchase order to include the soil of the access route over B's land but for the acquiring authority to inform B that they will not actually take his land if voluntarily he grants the necessary right of way to A.

3.78 Another form of statutory provision which creates an easement of sorts, is that which permits the laying and repairing of pipes, wires and cables. These are not strictly easements because the statutory undertaker does not acquire the land and as such there is no dominant tenement. This was considered in

---

[67] [2002] 1 EGLR 97.
[68] *Sovmots Investments v Secretary of State for the Environment* [1979] AC 144.

Newcastle-under-Lyme Corporation v Wolstanton Ltd[69] where Morton LJ agreeing with and quoting Evershed J at the first instance stated:

> 'They have by force of the statute the exclusive right to occupy for the purposes of their statutory undertaking the space in the soil taken by the pipes ... but that exclusive right of occupation which continues so long as the Corporation carry on their undertaking, does not depend upon or involve the vesting in the plaintiff corporation of any legal or equitable estate in the land'.

3.79 The conclusion reached by JF Garner[70] is that these 'rights given by statute are *sui generis*, and fit in with no known other jurisprudence concept and amount to an exclusive right to occupy the space or can be occupied by the actual pipes themselves'. Acts which enable these activities include: the Electricity Act 1989,[71] the Telecommunications Act 1984,[72] and the Water Industry Act 1991,[73] but once again in terms of rights to way these types of provisions are of little or no significance. See paras **7.81–7.92**.

CREATION BY WILL

3.80 Easements of way (like any other easement) can also be created by will in cases of a testator leaving dominant and servient land to different people or legal entities The easement will take effect only in equity until the written assent has been made by the personal representatives. In cases where the easement arises by implication it is prudent to refer to that in both the assent of the dominant land and the servient land. An assent of unregistered land need not be a deed[74] and can grant[75] or reserve[76] a right of way.

3.81 It is also possible for a testator to make the land being left by the will subject to an easement in favour of land owned by a third party at the time of the will taking effect (ie to grant an easement in the will).

THE CREATION OF EQUITABLE EASEMENTS

3.82 An easement can be a legal interest in land and will be if the following criteria are satisfied:

(1) it is held for 'an interest equivalent to an estate in fee simple absolute in possession or a term of years absolute';[77] and

---

[69] [1947] Ch 427 at 456.
[70] 20 *Conveyancer* 208 at 213.
[71] Schedule 4.
[72] Schedule 2.
[73] Section 159.
[74] Administration of Estates Act 1925, s 36(4).
[75] *Sweet v Sommer* [2005] 2 All ER 64 CA.
[76] *Thompson v Bee* [2009] EWCA Civ 1212.
[77] LPA 1925, s 1(2)(a).

(2)   it is created by statute, deed or prescription; and

(3)   in the case of the express[78] grant or reservation of an easement over registered land, it is completed by registration.[79]

3.83   In cases where these three criteria are not satisfied, the easement may instead be equitable. Equitable easements can arise in one of three main ways:

(1)   easements which are expressly granted by deed and which must be registered under the Land Registration Act 2002 but where registration is not so effected;

(2)   easements which arise by virtue of proprietary estoppel; and

(3)   equitable easements which arise pursuant to contracts and agreements intended to create legal easements.[80]

These three are considered in detail below.

3.84   Easements not registered remain equitable.

The three main ways in which equitable easements can arise, as stated in para **3.83** above, are considered in detail below.

Non-registration of a legal easement

3.85   With the exception of cases which fall under the Commons Registration Act 1965, an express grant or reservation of an easement will amount to a disposition which must be completed by registration.[81] The grant of an easement pursuant to the operation of section 62 of the LPA 1925 does not amount to a disposition that has to be completed by registration.[82]

3.86   In cases where a disposition of a registered estate has taken place, and must be registered, it does not have legal effect until registration has been

---

[78]   The registration requirement applies only to easements created by express grant or reservation. This does not therefore include easements created by implied grant or reservation, or prescription. For these purposes an easement created by the operation of LPA 1925, s 62, is not an express grant and therefore does not require to be registered: LRA 2002, s 27(7).

[79]   Land Registration Act 2002, s 27(2)(d). A notice of the interest must be entered in the register of the title of the servient tenement and (if the dominant tenement is also registered) the proprietor of the dominant tenement must be entered in the register as proprietor of the easement: Sch 2, para 7. It should be noted that the express grant of a legal easement is a registrable disposition regardless of the duration of the grant; even if granted for the benefit of a lease for seven years or less which is not itself required to be registered, the easement must still be registered.

[80]   See New Brunswick Court of Appeal in *Salisbury (Village) v Collier* (1998) 169 DLR (4d) 560.

[81]   Land Registration Act 2002, s 27(2)(d).

[82]   Land Registration Act 2002, s 27(7).

completed.[83] Schedule 2 to the 2002 Act sets out the relevant requirements,[84] which include how notice of the disposition must be entered in the register. Land Registry Practice Guide 62 explains the procedure in more detail.

3.87 An easement granted or reserved by a lease also amounts to a registered disposition. Land Registry Practice Guide 62 confirms the necessary procedure to effect registration in cases both of registered and unregistered leases.

Proprietary estoppel

3.88 Operation of the principles of equity relating to proprietary estoppel can result in the formation of an equitable easement, including an easement of way.

3.89 Proprietary estoppel affects and creates property rights. Use of the term 'equitable' refers to the equitable jurisdiction of the court to interfere in cases where the assertion of legal rights can be seen to be inequitable or unconscionable. Principles of equity are known to remain flexible and as such, a prescriptive explanation of them is not possible, but there are a number of fundamental principles associated with the doctrine of proprietary estoppel which can be expounded to explain how equitable easements can be created by them.

3.90 Broadly speaking, an equity will arise in cases where a landowner induces another, or by his conduct encourages or so allows the other party to believe, that they will have the benefit of some right over the owner's land or property and that, in reliance on such assurances, the other party acts to his detriment, such acts being known to the owner. The owner then purporting to take an unfair or unconscionable advantage over the other by subsequently denying the said party the right or benefit which he believed he would receive based on the conduct of the other party and their assurances, encouragement and conduct.

3.91 Creation of the equity will give the other person the right to seek relief from the court, such claim being subject to normal principles governing the court's jurisdiction to award equitable remedies. The court has a wide discretion and in deciding whether to grant relief it will have regard to all the circumstances of the case, including the conduct of both parties.

3.92 Where the court determines that the operation of these equitable principles gives rise to an order that the owner should grant the other party a right in the form of an equitable easement, an equitable easement is created by the operation of the principles of proprietary estoppel.[85]

---

[83] Land Registration Act 2002, s 27(1).

[84] Land Registration Act 2002, s 27(4), Sch 2, para 7.

[85] See *Ward v Kirkland* [1967] Ch 194; *ER Ives Investments Ltd v High* [1967] 2 QB 379; *Crabb v Arun DC* [1976] Ch 179, and *Bexley LBC v Maison Maurice Ltd* [2007] 1 EGLR 19. Relief can also be negative, and restrain an owner from asserting a legal right, as well as positive. See also the recent case of *Joyce v Epsom & Ewell BC* [2012] EWCA Civ 1398.

3.93   In *Crabb v Arun District Council,*[86] Scarman LJ said that the law was correctly stated in Lord Kingsdown's dissenting speech in *Ramsden v Dyson.*[87] Whilst referring to the landlord and tenant scenario, the remarks of Lord Kingsdown have been accepted as being of general application, those being:

'The rule of law applicable to the case appears to me to be this: If a man, under a verbal agreement with a landlord for a certain interest in land, or, what amounts to the same thing, under an expectation, created or encouraged by the landlord, that he shall have a certain interest, takes possession of such land, with the consent of the landlord, and upon the faith of such promise or expectation, with the knowledge of the landlord, and without objection by him, lays out money upon the land, a court of equity will compel the landlord to give effect to such promise or expectation.'

3.94   In *Willmott v Barber* the requirements of an estoppel were set out in a speech by Fry J that referred to 'five probanda',[88] however the courts have not always seen such five elements as essential and have taken a broad and pragmatic approach over time in seeking to determine whether the behaviour of the person alleged to be estopped is unreasonable or unconscionable. For example, in *Taylors Fashions Ltd v Liverpool Victoria Trustees Co Lt,*[89] Oliver J. said:

'The more recent cases indicate that the application of the *Ramsden v Dyson* principle – whether you call it proprietary estoppel, estoppel by acquiescence or estoppel by encouragement is really immaterial–requires a very much broader approach which is directed rather at ascertaining whether, in particular individual circumstances, it would be unconscionable for a party to be permitted to deny that which, knowingly, or unknowingly, he has allowed or encouraged another to assume to his detriment than to inquiring whether the circumstances can be fitted within the confines of some preconceived formula serving as a universal yardstick for every form of unconscionable behaviour.'

3.95   The doctrine of proprietary estoppel is subject to limits, like any other doctrine. The doctrine cannot be used by a party to effectively create a right not contemplated by the acquiescing party. In *Bankart v Houghton*[90] Sir John Romilly MR said it was:

'impossible to be reasonably contended that, because a man has acquiesced in the erection of certain works which have produced little or no injury, he is not afterwards to have any remedy, if, by the increase of the works, at a subsequent period, he sustains a serious injury'.

---

[86]   [1976] Ch 179 at 193, 194.
[87]   (1866) LR 1 HL 139 at 170.
[88]   (1880) 15 Ch D 96 at 105–106.
[89]   [1982] Q 13, 133n.
[90]   (1860) 27 Beav 425.

A further example is contained in *Bankart v Tennant*,[91] where a tenant ran a copper factory under an agreement for lease. In the course of his activities he used surplus water from the lessor's canal, and no agreement for the use of this had been documented or agreed. The canal water was not essential to the factory and no right to take it was established under equitable principles.[92]

3.96   Quite often a party will claim that the right to a right of way arises by the principles of proprietary estoppel and most commonly this may be in the course of negotiations of the grant of property rights that are expressly agreed to be '*subject to contract*'. If a party asserts a right in such cases, it would be necessary to satisfy the court that the parties had effectively agreed, in the course of these negotiations, to convert the negotiations into a contract for the grant of the easement of way, or alternatively that some form of estoppel had arisen which now prevented the parties from being able to refuse to proceed with the proposed transaction, involving grant of the right of way. This could possibly take the form of the parties expressly agreeing not to withdraw from the transaction.[93] In cases where negotiation are labelled as being '*subject to contract*', it will be necessary to consider the precise use of the words '*subject to contract*', and whether these amount to an express reservation of either party to withdraw from negotiations at any time (the normally intended purpose of such wording); in such a case, a claim for an estoppel based on expectation will be difficult to make out.[94]

Contracts and agreements for easements

3.97   Parties can enter into an agreement to create a right of way or other legal easements. In such cases, for the agreement to effectively create the easement, the dominant land must be clearly identifiable. The law is clear that before there can be a grant, or the contract for a grant, there must be a dominant tenement of an easement in order to create an interest that can be binding on the servient land (for the current owners and successors in title).

3.98   In *London & Blenheim Estates Limited v Ladbroke Retail Parks Limited* the Court of Appeal held that the grant of a right to nominate some additional land as the dominant tenement for car parking did not create an interest in land which bound successors in title to the servient tenement.[95] In *Voice v Bell*,[96] a clause provided that, if the transferor were to acquire property at the rear of the land transferred, the transferees and their successors should not object to him demolishing a wall so as to provide access for motor vehicles to the

---

91   (1870) LR 10 Eq 141.
92   The contrary is expressed in *Pwllbach Colliery Co v Woodman* [1915] AC 634.
93   *Attorney General of Hong Kong v Humphreys Estate (Queen's Garden) Ltd* [1987] AC 114 at 127H-128B; *Cobbe v Yeoman's Row Management Ltd* [2006] 1 WLR 2964 at [57].
94   *Cobbe v Yeoman's Row Management Ltd* [2005] WTLR 625 at 118–122 (Etherton J) and [2006] 1 WLR 2964 at 53–57 (Court of Appeal). In *Kilcarne Holdings Ltd v Targetfollow (Birmingham) Ltd* [2005] 2 P & CR 105 it was said at [229] that in this respect equity follows the law; the point was not considered on appeal at [2006] 1 & CR D55.
95   [1994] 1 WLR 31, at 38D-E.
96   [1993] EGCS 128.

property in question. The court held that the clause was enforceable only as a matter of contract and that it did not bind successors to the servient tenement.

3.99 Whilst the dominant land must clearly be identified, and whilst there must be a dominant and servient tenement for the grant of an easement, it can be the case that the affected parts of the servient land remain to be identified in the future. This will be subject to any applicable rule against perpetuities being complied with – see below.[97]

3.100 In cases where an agreement is entered into between the parties for the grant of an easement of way, and such an agreement is compliant with any necessary statutory formalities (ie the Law of Property (Miscellaneous Provisions Act) 1989 Act – see below), and is made for valuable consideration, then a valid easement which can be exercised against the servient party and his successors in title (not being a purchaser for value without notice)[98] is created in equity. In similar terms, an agreement not made for valuable consideration but involving cost and work undertaken on the part of the dominant party[99] may, as a result of an estoppel, create an equitable easement.[100] Equitable easements should be perfected by registration (as appropriate) to become legal in nature.

FORMALITIES: THE LAW OF PROPERTY (MISCELLANEOUS PROVISIONS) ACT 1989

3.101 Prior to 27 September 1989, agreements for the grant of an easement were unenforceable unless section 40 of the LPA 1925[101] had been complied with. This provided that it was not possible to bring an action on an agreement for the sale or other disposition of an interest in land, unless the agreement or some memorandum or note thereof was in writing. It also had to be signed by the party or by some other person lawfully authorised by the person concerned. It was possible to avoid having to establish a memorandum or note in writing[102] if the person seeking to enforce the agreement was able to show part performance by him of the said agreement.

3.102 With effect from 27 September 1989, section 2 of the Law of Property (Miscellaneous Provisions) Act 1989 is the relevant provision, superceding section 40 of the LPA 1925. Section 2 of the Law of Property (Miscellaneous Provisions) Act 1989 provides that a contract for the sale or other disposition of an interest in land can only be made in writing and only by incorporating all

---

[97] See *London & Blenheim Estates Limited v Ladbroke Retail Parks Limited*.
[98] See *Thatcher v Douglas* [1996] NLJ 282; *Smith v Curry* (1918) 42 DLR 225; *Leon Asper Amusements Ltd v Northmain Canvash* (1966) 56 DLR (2d) 173.
[99] In *ER Ives Investment v High* [1967] 2 QB 379. The Court of Appeal found that there was a concluded agreement which the parties contemplated would be put into force, but this was not the ratio decided in that case.
[100] See *James Jones & Sons Ltd v Earl of Tankerville* [1909] 2 Ch 440 at 443.
[101] Replacing Statute of Frauds 1677, s 4.
[102] See Megarry & Wade, *The Law of Real Property* (6th edn, 2000), 12.015–12.017.

the terms expressly agreed by the parties in one document or in cases where contracts are exchanged, in each part of the contract.[103] An easement falls within the definition of 'interest in land'[104] and the grant of an easement is a 'disposition'.[105] Quite often the terms will be set out in one document or will be incorporated by reference to an ancillary document.[106] All documents incorporating the relevant terms must be signed by each party to the contract, or someone lawfully on their behalf,[107] that is, the contract must be signed[108] by each party to it and not merely by the party against whom the contract is sought to be enforced.

3.103 Accordingly, section 2 of the Law of Property (Miscellaneous Provisions) Act 1989 completely reforms the previous position under section 40 of the LPA 1925. It is no longer sufficient to have a note or memorandum which evidences the contract. All the agreed terms must be set out in the single document (or in each part of the exchanged documents) in writing. Section 40 of the LPA 1925 allowed a contract to be formed by exchange of informal letters, which is now not possible under section 2 as where there is more than one document, each must contain all the terms. This must be accompanied by the requisite intention of the parties to become bound contractually at the point when contracts are exchanged.[109]

3.104 Subsequent alterations and amendments to an existing contract must also comply with section 2, otherwise such purported alterations become null and void and the contract remains binding in its original form given that no legally binding alteration has superseded it.[110]

3.105 Under the LPA 1925, it was possible to avoid having to establish a memorandum or note in writing[111] if the person seeking to enforce the agreement was able to show part performance by him of the said agreement for the purposes of section 40 of the Act. The doctrine of part performance has since been abolished.[112] However, section 2 of the 1989 Act does not affect the creation or operation of resulting, implied or constructive trusts,[113] as explained in Gale on Easements:

> 'Thus, in a case where the parties made an oral agreement under which one party was to carry out building works on a house and was then to be granted a lease of

---

[103] Law of Property (Miscellaneous Provisions) Act 1989, s 2(1).
[104] Law of Property (Miscellaneous Provisions) Act 1989, s 2(6).
[105] Law of Property (Miscellaneous Provisions) Act 1989, s 2(6) incorporating the definition in s 205(1)(ii) of the LPA 1925.
[106] Law of Property (Miscellaneous Provisions) Act 1989, s 2(2).
[107] Law of Property (Miscellaneous Provisions) Act 1989, s 2(3).
[108] 'Signed' is to be given its ordinary meaning: *Firstpost Homes v Johnson* [1995] 4 All ER 355.
[109] *Commission for the New Towns v Cooper* [1995] Ch. 259.
[110] *McCausland v Duncan Lawrie Ltd* [1997] 1 WLR 38.
[111] See Megarry & Wade, *The Law of Real Property* (6th edn, 2000), 12.015–12.017.
[112] LPA 1925, s 40(2), which preserved the doctrine of part performance, is repealed by the Law of Property (Miscellaneous Provisions) Act 1989, s 2(8); *Yaxley v Gotts* [2000] Ch 162 at 172F, but see *Singh v Beggs* (1995) 71 P & CR 120.
[113] Law of Property (Miscellaneous Provisions) Act 1989, s 2(5).

the house and where that party performed his side of the agreement, the circumstances were such that he was entitled to an interest in the house, applying the principles of proprietary estoppel, and the same facts could be relied upon to establish a constructive trust which had effect notwithstanding section 2 of the 1989 Act.'[114]

PROTECTION OF LEGAL AND EQUITABLE EASEMENTS

3.106   Creation of a legal or equitable easement is not where the matter ends. Once created, an easement must be protected based on the applicable registration rules. There is a difference between the way in which legal easements and equitable easements are protected in order to bind successors of the original parties, and the status of the land as registered or unregistered is also relevant.

Unregistered land

3.107   In the case of unregistered land:

(a)   A legal easement will be valid as a legal interest in land under section 1 of the LPA 1925 and no registration under the Land Charges Act 1972 is required.

(b)   An equitable easement created since 1925 is void against a purchaser for money or money's worth of a legal estate in the land subject to it, unless registered prior to completion of the purchase.[115] The fact that the purchaser has notice of it will not prevent the easement being void against him.[116]

3.108   In cases of unregistered land the first step will therefore be to consider whether the equitable right was created before or after 1926, to determine whether it falls within the scope of the Land Charges Act 1972. Assuming it falls within the scope of the Act, the second step is to consider whether it falls under any class for which registration is required. Normally easements of way will fall into either class D(iii) (equitable easement) or C(iv) (estate contract). An equitable easement is defined as 'an easement, right or privilege over or affecting land created or arising on or after 1 January 1926, and being merely an equitable interest'. An estate contract under the Act is 'a contract by an estate owner or by a person entitled at the date of the contract to have a legal estate conveyed to him to convey or create a legal estate, including a contract conferring either expressly or by statutory implication a valid option to purchase, a right of pre-emption or any other like right'.[117]

---

[114]   Cited from *Gale on Easements*, 2-26, p 103, 18th Edn, 2008. See also *Yaxley v Gotts* [2000] Ch 162.

[115]   Land Charges Act 1972, s 4(6).

[116]   LPA 1925, s 199(1)(i).

[117]   Land Charges Act 1972.

3.109 If not so registered, it is void against a purchaser for money or money's worth of a legal estate in the land subject to it.

Registered land

3.110 On first registration of the title to land or on a disposition the following rules, in summary, apply.[118]

3.111 On first registration a legal easement will be an overriding interest under Schedule 1, para 3 to the Land Registration Act 2002; 'the 2002 Act'. However, in practice, the title deduced *should* refer to such a legal easement and the easement will be noted on the title under the Land Registration Rules 2003 (LRR 2003), rules 35 and 38.

3.112 An equitable easement does not qualify as an interest which overrides under the law in force after 12 October 2003. So any existing equitable easement over unregistered land must have been registered under the Land Charges Act 1972, or it will not be entered on the register. A new equitable easement does not need to be registered under that Act if it is created by an instrument which induces compulsory first registration.[119] Equitable easements created before 13 October 2003 which had the status of overriding interests under section 70(1)(a) of the Land Registration Act 1925 will continue to do so by virtue of the provisions of Schedule 12, para 10 to the Land Registration Act 2002.

3.113 Easements created by estoppel are not seemingly subject to any particular means of protection under the LRA 2002. In practice they may be the subject of a notice on the register if referred to in panel 13 of the FR1 form.

3.114 An express grant or reservation of an easement must be completed by notice on the register under section 27 of the LRA 2002 until which point it takes effect in equity only.[120]

3.115 On dispositions of registered titles, easements (either legal or equitable) entered or noted on the register will bind the disponee. Legal easements may also bind the disponee if not entered or noted where they satisfy the factual conditions in Schedule 3, para 3 to the LRA 2002 and thereby take effect as interests which override. Equitable easements, even if they satisfy the conditions,[121] will not bind a disponee if not so noted – this presents a trap for the unwary.

---

[118] See Chapter 13 for fuller discussion.
[119] Land Charges Act 1972, s 14(3).
[120] This is so only if the title to the servient tenement is registered. Land Registration Act 2002, s 132. See also Ruoff & Roper, *Land Registration*, Chapter 36.
[121] *Chaudhary v Yavuz* [2011] EWCA Civ 1314; [2012] 2 All ER 418; [2012] 1 P & CR 9.

3.116 Indeed, when conveying land it is therefore important to note carefully the definition of title matters to which a transfer is subject. A definition will often refer to:

> '"Title Matters" means the matters, covenants and stipulations contained, mentioned or referred to in the [Property and Charges] registers at the Land Registry of Title Number [ ] so far as they are subsisting or capable of being enforced and affect the Property.'

3.117 If an equitable easement of way is not noted on the title, a purchaser will take free of such equitable easement regardless of actual knowledge.

3.118 Accordingly, it is better for such a definition of title matter to also include:

> 'and the deeds and documents listed in Schedule [x]'

in which equitable easements of way should be referred to. In the event that equitable easements (including easements of way) are not noted on the title, or referred to in a separate schedule, then a purchaser will take free of them.

3.119 Quite often, for these purposes, a document will contain a indemnity covenant in respect of incumbrances on behalf of the transferee:

> 'Transferee's Indemnity Covenant in Respect of Incumbrances
>
> The Transferee covenants with the Transferor [by way of indemnity only and not further or otherwise] that the Transferee will at all times hereafter perform and observe the Title Matters and will keep the Transferor [and the Transferor's Successors] fully indemnified from and against all actions, claims, demands, losses, costs, expenses, damages and liability [in any way relating thereto] [in respect of any future breach or non-observance or non-performance of them].'

3.120 Crucially, this will not refer to any equitable easements of way which were not on the register or otherwise disclosed. In such a case, this will leave the party with the benefit of the equitable easement left with a claim against the transferor to the transfer. This highlights the need to ensure that an accurate list of title matters, including all known equitable easements, are noted on the title when acting for the transferor. Equitable easements are a particular trap for the unwary and are best protected by way of unilateral notice on the register under the new 2002 rules. If the transferor knows of an equitable easement which is not mentioned but which might be binding on him personally, for example if it was created by a contract to which he was a party, then, as well as procuring an indemnity from the transferee, he should consider himself applying for it to be entered on the title.

RULE AGAINST PERPETUITIES IN GRANT OF FUTURE RIGHTS OF WAY

3.121 Perpetuity rules have applied to instruments expressly granting or reserving future easements. Easements may also be granted by implication, prescription or by statute at some point in the future and following the completion of any one of a number of instruments effecting property transactions.

3.122 The enactment of the Perpetuities and Accumulations Act 2009 substantially changed the law of perpetuities. An easement which 'comes into effect' on or after 6 April 2010 will be governed by the 'new regime' introduced by the Perpetuities and Accumulations Act 2009. Easements granted before 16 July 1964 are governed by the 'common law rules'. Easements granted before 6 April 2010 and on or after 16 July 1964 are governed by the 'old regime' under the Perpetuities and Accumulations Act 1964 and the common law rules not disapplied by that Act or qualified by contrary intention. A typical grant of a future easement before 6 April 2010 might have arisen on the sale of a development site such as 'the right within the perpetuity period [defined] to enter on the Seller's adjoining land to construct roads and footpaths and the right at all times after construction for all owners and occupiers of the Property to pass over them'. There can often be mistakes in drafting, for instance accidently limiting the period of use to the perpetuity period, so that any such wording needs to be carefully examined.

The common law rules

3.123 Easements granted before 16 July 1964 are governed by the 'common law rules'.

3.124 Under the common law rules, any *future* easement created by an instrument was void against third parties, if it was inevitable or possible that the easement would 'vest' after an applicable perpetuity period had expired. For those instruments completed before 16 July 1964, the applicable perpetuity period is a 'life in being', that is a person who was alive at the date of instrument, plus 21 years. The person did not necessarily have to be involved in the transaction and before the 1964 Act it was common to use a Royal Lives clause whereby the right had to be exercised within the period of 21 years after the death of the last survivor of the descendants of a named monarch. Initially Queen Victoria was frequently named and in determining whether any particular future easement granted at the beginning of the 20th century is still valid it is sometimes necessary to investigate the date of death of minor members of the German aristocracy who share descent from that Queen. Care had to be taken in defining such a perpetuity period – the point in time in which the interest would 'vest' needed to be ascertainable and not subject to a condition that *may have been* satisfied outside of the perpetuity period.[122] In the absence of any such period being defined in the instrument the applicable perpetuity period was 21 years.

3.125 The easement had to 'vest in interest' within the perpetuity period. This did not mean that the interest had to be immediately exercisable or vest in possession. It was sufficient that the grantee was unconditionally entitled to the interest.

The old regime

3.126 The rules set out in the Perpetuities and Accumulations Act 1964 remain relevant for instruments entered into on, or after, 16 July 1964 but before 6 April 2010.

3.127 The 1964 Act restricted the common law rules which rendered void those easements which would or might vest outside the perpetuity period by introducing the 'wait and see'[123] principle. The 'wait and see' principle allowed an interest to vest at any time within 80 years from the completion of the instrument.

3.128 Section 162(1)(d) of the LPA 1925 excepted from the application of the old regime, any right onto land or easement to: (i) exercise mining rights, (ii) fell and remove timber, (iii) carry out repairs, alterations or additions to adjoining land or buildings, or (iv) construct, alter, repair and maintain service media. This provision was repealed by the 2009 Act.[124] It will remain applicable to easements granted pursuant to instruments entered into before 6 April 2010. The provision has been of restricted application since the decision in *Dunn v Blackdown Properties Ltd*[125] which allowed only *ancillary* easements to be exercised outside of the perpetuity period. Such *ancillary* easements must be conferred to give effect to a substantive right or interest which itself satisfies the perpetuity rules. Perhaps most commonly, an *ancillary* easement, is one which is needed to allow the grantee to *connect* to, and take the benefit of the right(s) granted by the substantive easement.

---

[122] *Gale On Easements*, 1.107–1.115, pp 65–69, 18th Edn, (2008) suggests that such perpetuity periods were of little importance to property easements and that such perpetuity rules were more concerned with gifts and distributions from trust instruments.

[123] Perpetuities and Accumulations Act 1964, s 3(1).

[124] Perpetuities and Accumulations Act 2009, s 4(b).

[125] [1961] Ch 433.

The new regime

3.129 In its most rudimentary sense, the 2009 Act provides that where the instrument creating a future easement 'comes into effect'[126] on or after 6 April 2010 it will *not* be subject to any perpetuity rules.

3.130 It is considered an instrument 'comes into effect' upon its completion by due execution.[127] Where an instrument 'comes into effect' on, or after, 6 April 2010 but pursuant to a contract made before that date, that instrument will still benefit from the new regime.

3.131 The circumstances in which the 2009 Act may apply a perpetuity period of 125 years[128] to the creation of future easements are limited to future distributions of property (and easements in connection therewith) held in trust or allocated under will or a power of appointment.[129]

3.132 Due to the wide disapplication of perpetuity rules applicable to easements, parties to any property transaction in which easements may be created at some point in the future (and where section 62 of the LPA 1925 is not excluded) need to be conscious that an easement may be granted at any time in the indefinite future. Parties should therefore be careful to consider and define an express period in which easements may be granted, effectively creating the contractual equivalent of a statutory perpetuity period should they wish to. Many now see no need to create a perpetuity period, however, and completely disregard the need to create a period for interests to vest.

Miscellaneous exceptions

3.133 A lease (and the easements to be granted therein) completed on or after 1 January 1926, cannot be granted for term commencing more than 21 years after the date of completion.[130]

3.134 A contract to renew a lease (and the easements contained therein), completed on or after 1 January 1926, for a term of more than 60 years from termination of the existing lease will be void.[131]

---

[126] Perpetuities and Accumulations Act 2009, s 15(1). It is considered 'comes into effect' means the completion of the instrument or if later, the satisfaction of any condition subsequent (in connection with the grant of the easement).

[127] See *Dyment v Boyden* [2004] EWCA 1586 where a lease executed by one party and delivered in escrow did not 'come into effect' until its due execution by the other party.

[128] Perpetuities and Accumulations Act 2009, s 5.

[129] Perpetuities and Accumulations Act 2009, s 1(2) and 1(6).

[130] LPA 1925, s 149(3). This provision also includes an agreement or an option for a lease.

[131] LPA 1922, s 145 and para 7(2), Sch 15.

Chapter 4

THE EXTENT AND LIMITS OF RIGHTS OF WAY ACQUIRED THROUGH THE ACTS OF THE PARTIES

INTRODUCTION

4.1   In this Chapter the extent and limitations on rights of way created by acts of the parties are examined. These include express grants, express reservations and rights which may arise by implication in transactions relating to land, particularly under section 62 of the LPA 1925. The principles governing rectification of documents are also examined.

4.2   The potential issues of interpretation of documents granting rights of way which may arise are numerous. A reader of a deed of grant will be anxious to obtain clarity on a number of issues from the express words of the document, where there is an express grant or reservation. These will include depending on the circumstances:

(a)   The identity of the servient land.

(b)   The identity of the dominant land.

(c)   The width and route of the way granted.

(d)   The purposes for which the way can be used.

(e)   The points at which the way can be accessed.

(f)   The permissible types of traffic.

(g)   The permissible volume of traffic.

(h)   How far parking, stopping and other associated activities are allowed.

(i)   The extent to which the way can be regulated by the servient owner without infringing the rights of the dominant owner.

(j)   Whether there are any express provisions relating to maintenance of the way or contributions to the costs of this.

(k)   The extent if any of the rights of the parties to deviate from or divert the
       route of the way.

Where the right of way is not contained in an express grant or reservation, but
arises by implication or by virtue of section 62 of the Law of Property Act, the
same issues may of course arise. The general law of interpretation of
documents is in the process of active development. The courts have moved
away from an approach under which not only was the primary source of
interpretation the document itself, but also the admissibility of extrinsic
evidence of surrounding circumstances was generally limited. The modern
tendency is to treat the document as merely the starting point. The court will
strive to give the document what it considers a 'business-like' interpretation, if
possible, on the basis that this reflects the intention of the parties. It will also
allow extrinsic evidence going to the meaning of the document. An obvious
danger of this approach is that third parties who were not involved in the
transaction but who have relied on the document in some way (for example by
advancing money on the security of the property concerned) may be at risk of
discovering retrospectively that their understanding, however correct as a
matter of language, is displaced by some extrinsic evidence of the sense which
the words would have been understood by the parties at the time the document
was concluded. This consideration lies behind the decision of the Court of
Appeal in *Cherry Tree Investments Ltd v Landmain Ltd*[1] in which it was held
that a registered charge could not be interpreted as containing an immediate
power of sale, though the facility letter pursuant to which the charge was
registered provided for this. The Court of Appeal accepted that the facility
letter was admissible extrinsic evidence but held that a reasonable reader of the
charge would give weight to the fact that the charge would be registered on a
publicly accessible register on which third parties might be expected to rely and
hence not attach weight to private documents such as the facility letter which
had not been given effect to in the registered version of the charge.

GENERAL PRINCIPLES OF INTERPRETATION OF INSTRUMENTS

4.3   It is first necessary to give an account of the general principles relating to
interpretation of documents since where the right of way has been created by
express grant or reservation, the starting point in interpreting the grant is to
consider the express terms of the instrument itself, in the light of the admissible
surrounding circumstances.

4.4   The starting point in interpreting a grant or reservation of a right of way
is the words used. In many cases the words used will be expressions in current
conveyancing use, which may well have been the subject of decided cases.
Where the parties have used unambiguous language the court must normally

---

[1]   [2012] EWCA Civ 736.

simply apply the language used to the facts of the case.[2] Where the language is inconsistent or read literally produces absurd results, the court may relatively readily interpret it to produce a common sense outcome.[3] However, there may be circumstances where the express words cannot be read literally nor easily corrected. There are in general two situations which give rise to particular difficulty. The first is where the literal meaning gives rise to an 'uncommercial' result. The second is where the surrounding circumstances require the apparent meaning of words to be modified.

4.5   Dealing first with the situation where the commercial meaning conflicts with the literal meaning, the court may find itself asked to choose between whether there has been bad drafting and whether there has actually been a bad bargain. In the context of grants of rights of way, the court will in principle be prepared within limits to correct imperfect drafting by a process of interpretation. If the bargain was ill-advised (for one or more parties) to start with, the parties will usually be left to their fate, (absent any claim for rectification of the wording of the instrument, as to which see para **4.145** and following.

4.6   However, deciding whether the problem lies in the choice of inept words, or a party being bested or confused in negotiations is difficult, because the court will not always be able to appreciate the underlying commercial factors which drove the original deal. Indeed, it may find its own rules of evidence positively exclude from the court's gaze exactly what the parties' understanding of their own bargain might have been. Moreover, given that the rights and duties under grants of rights of way, unlike many other contracts, may well pass to parties who have no knowledge of the circumstances in which they were created, the court may be unenthusiastic to embark on over-creative interpretation exercises. The most extreme case of reluctance to interpret a document in a reasonable manner is probably the case of *Cherry Tree Investments Ltd v Landmain Ltd*[4] already noted at para **4.2**. Similar reluctance can be expected where the document is a grant which has been relied on by third parties.

> 'The court must not try to [divine] the purpose of the contract by speculating about the real intention of the parties. It may only be inferred from the language used by the parties, judged against the objective contextual background.'[5]

4.7   The basic parameters of the court's approach are well encapsulated in *Arbuthnott v Fagan*. Sir Thomas Bingham MR said:[6]

---

2   *Rainy Sky SA v Kookmin Bank* [2011] UKSC 50, especially Lord Clarke at [23].
3   See para **4.47** below.
4   [2012] EWCA Civ 736.
5   *Deutsche Genossenschaftsbank v Burnhope* [1995] 1 WLR 1580 at 1587, per Lord Steyn.
6   [1995] CLC 1396 per Sir Thomas Bingham MR (CA). The relevant passages are cited in *International Fina Services AG v Katrina Shipping Ltd, The MV 'Fina Samco'* [1995] 2 Lloyd's Rep 344, 350 per Neill LJ, Roch and Auld LJJ agreeing (CA). The latter case is on your reading list because: (a) it is a full CA approval of the *dicta* of Sir Thomas in the earlier case, and (b) the Lloyd's Reports are more easily available.

'Courts will never construe words in a vacuum. To a greater or lesser extent, depending on the subject matter, they will wish to be informed of what may variously be described as the context, the background, the factual matrix or the mischief. To seek to construe any instrument in ignorance or disregard of the circumstances which gave rise to it or the situation in which it is expected to take effect is in my view pedantic, sterile and productive of error. But that is not to say that an initial judgment of what an instrument was or should reasonably have been intended to achieve should be permitted to override the clear language of the instrument, since what an author says is usually the surest guide to what he meant. To my mind construction is a composite exercise, neither uncompromisingly literal nor unswervingly purposive: the instrument must speak for itself, but *in situ* and not be transported to the laboratory for microscopic analysis.'

4.8   The court will also have regard to the quality of the drafting of the document:

'The poorer the quality of the drafting, the less willing any court should be to be driven by semantic niceties to attribute to the parties an improbable and un-businesslike intention, if the language used, whatever it may lack in precision, is reasonably capable of an interpretation which attributes to the parties an intention to make provision for contingencies inherent in the work contracted for on a sensible and businesslike basis.'[7]

So in *Multi-Link Leisure Developments Ltd v North Lanarkshire Council*[8] the Supreme Court interpreted an option to purchase land as avoiding conferring on the option holder a right to a windfall profit. The option agreement set out the assumptions on which the price was to be determined. These included the words 'of agricultural land or open space suitable for development as a golf course'. The land then became zoned for housing development. The Supreme Court held that the wording of the relevant clause did not require this to be disregarded as the words were inconsistent with other parts of the document giving directions as to valuation assumptions.

It is necessary in each case:

(a)   To consider the potential tensions between the literal and purposive construction of the document and how conflicting interpretations are prioritised in terms of likelihood.

(b)   To assess the tension between the purposive approach to construction and the literal approach to construction.

(c)   To consider the possibility of implied terms which may affect the express terms of the document.

(d)   To consider how far a word or phrase may have different meanings.

---

[7]   *Mitsui Construction Co v Attorney-General of Hong Kong* (1986) 33 BLR1 at 14.
[8]   [2010] UKSC 47.

(e)   To allow for the possibility of a drafting mistake which can be corrected by a process of interpretation.

4.9   It is of course now established that the interpretation of a contract is not simply a question of linguistic analysis of the words used by the parties to make their bargain. In interpreting a contract, the court is seeking to identify the parties' objectively assessed intentions and so must be prepared to look, to some extent, behind the dictionary definitions of the words actually used in the contract. The process is not, however, an absolute one. Where 'ordinary English' words are used, they should *prima facie* be given their ordinary English meaning, unless there is any reason to do otherwise.[9] As Lord Upjohn said in *Tophams Ltd v Earl of Sefton*:[10]

> 'The words which the parties have used in the conveyance, being ordinary words of the English language, must be construed in their ordinary and natural meaning unless the context otherwise requires.'

4.10   Four tools for interpretation are particularly useful in interpreting grants:

(a)   *The need to read the deed as a whole.* If one construes a word or a sentence or even a clause in a deed, one has to read it as a whole and see if there are clues elsewhere in that illuminate the meaning of the word in question. An example is *Ibrahim v Dovecorn Reversions Ltd*,[11] in which the *habendum* in a lease excluded 'the main walls and structure' of the building.[12] Did 'main' qualify just 'walls' or did it relate to 'walls and structure'? Rimer J noted that the landlord's repairing covenant expressly extended to the 'main structure', and concluded that he would be unlikely to have an obligation to repair that which he had demised to the tenant, and so 'main structure' in one clause was used to interpret, 'main walls and structure' elsewhere in the lease.

(b)   *A presumption against redundancy.* Courts normally prefer to avoid concluding that any words in a commercial contract are redundant, so the usual practice is to try to give meaning to each word. This is not a universally approved course, when it comes to leases. As Hoffmann J said in *Tea Trade Properties Ltd v CIN Properties Ltd*:[13]

> 'I see the force of that argument, but I have never found the presumption against superfluous language particularly useful in the construction of leases. The draftsmen traditionally employ linguistic overkill and try to obliterate the conceptual target by using a numer of words or phrases

---

9   'Ordinary English' is the English spoken by 'an ordinary speaker of English': *Young v Sun Alliance & London Assurance* [1976] 1 WLR 104, 110 per Cairns LJ, who added, 'giving oneself for the moment the credit of assuming that one is an ordinary Englishman'.

10   [1967] AC 50, 73 (HL).

11   [2001] 2 EGLR 46.

12   [2001] 2 EGLR 46 (Rimer J).

13   [1990] 1 EGLR 155, 158 (Hoffmann J).

expressing more or less the same idea. I cannot, therefore, rely upon the language alone but must, as it seems to me, construe the words also by reference to the commercial effect which would be produced by one construction or the other.'

(c)   *Ejusdem Generis*. The classic formulation of this principle was stated by Vaughan Williams LJ in *Lambourn v McLellan*:[14]

> '... if you can find that the things described by particular words have some common characteristic which constitutes them a genus, you ought to limit the general words which follow them to things of that genus. In the present case all the articles which are described by the particular words have according to the natural meaning of the words the common characteristic of irremovability; and under these circumstances I think the general words should be applied only to articles which possess that characteristic.'

The *ejusdem generis* principle is not a strict rule. It is a principle which can be rebutted by the language of the clause. In that context, look at this bit of tough reasoning from Devlin J, in *Chandris v Isbrandtsen-Moller Co Inc*:[15]

> 'Legal draftsmen are all familiar with the existence of the *[ejusdem generis]* rule, and familiar too with the proper signals to hoist if they do not want it to apply. Phrases such as "whether or not similar to the foregoing" and "without prejudice to the generality of the foregoing" are often employed in legal draftsmanship; and if the draftsman has read the report of *Larsen v Sylvester & Co*, he will know that the addition of "whatsoever" generally serves the same purpose. Commercial draftsmen are not usually taught these rules.'

So in *Lambourn v McLellan*, in which a covenant to yield up in a lease required the tenant to hand to the landlord:[16]

> '... all doors, locks, keys, bolts, bars, staples, hinges, iron pins, wainscots, hearths, stones, marble and other chimney-pieces, slabs, shutters, fastenings, partitions, pipes, pumps, sinks, gutters of lead, posts, pales, rails, dressers, shelves, and all other erections, buildings, improvements, fixtures and things which then were or which at any time during the said term should be fixed, fastened or belong to the said demised message and premises or any part thereof.'

This impressive list had one genus, landlord's fixtures, so the tenant did not have to hand over his trade fixtures.

---

[14]   [1903] 2 Ch 268, 275–6 (CA). *Ejusdem generis* might be translated as 'of the same kind or nature'.

[15]   [1951] 1 KB 240, 245. The point was unaffected on Appeal at [1951] 1 KB 256 (CA), as the appeal proceeded only on a point concerning an arbitrator's power to award interest.

[16]   [1903] 2 Ch 268 (CA).

(d) *Expressio Unius est Exclusio Alterius:* If something specific is named or granted, more general things of a like nature are excluded.[17] So, in a lease the implied covenant for quiet enjoyment is excluded by the grant of an express covenant, even if it is in more restrictive terms: *Miller v Emcer Products Ltd.*[18] In Oceanic *Village v Shirayma Shokusan Co Ltd,*[19] the landlord of County Hall granted a lease of the London Aquarium gift shop, which prevented it from permitting any other gift shops from operating within the building. This, it was argued, did not prevent it from opening a competing shop on the embankment outside the building The argument failed, as the judge held the purpose of the clause – to protect the business of the gift-shop – outweighed any fine points on the drafting of the lease:

> '[53] In my judgment, the fact that the parties have expressly bargained for a restriction relating to gift-shop use generally in the building does not exclude the implication of a further term relating to the sale of aquarium-related products from a gift shop not within the area of the express restriction. The scope of the express restriction – which relates to all gift shops – is substantially different from the suggested implied restriction – which relates only to aquarium products. The express provision protects future opportunity; the latter is to protect the very business which the landlords, as well as OVL, intended would be carried on with an element of exclusivity. It is a short point; in my judgment, OVL succeeds on it.'

4.11 These 'canons of construction' only carry so far, as interpretation of contractual documents is more than rules about words. As has been authoritatively asserted by the House of Lords in *Investors' Compensation Scheme Ltd v West Bromwich Building Society* (the *ICS* case), context is important.[20] In that case, which has been consistently followed and frequently cited subsequently, Lord Hoffmann emphasised that it would sometimes be appropriate to go behind the ordinary English words used in a contractual document, and to interpret them in light of the factual matrix which existed at the time that the contract was made, albeit mindful that the process of interpretation is one of understanding the words used by the parties to discover their intentions at the date on which the contract was entered into, not to re-manufacture their agreement into a different substantive agreement to meet their perceived intentions. Lord Hoffmann described the parameters of this investigation as follows:[21]

> 'The principles may be summarised as follows.

---

[17] 'The express inclusion of one excludes the others.'
[18] [1956] Ch 304, 319 (CA).
[19] [2001] L&TR 478 (Nicholas Warren QC, sitting as a Deputy High Court Judge).
[20] [1998] 1 WLR 896 (HL).
[21] [1998] 1 WLR 896, 912–913 (HL). The citation for *Antaios Compania Naviera SA v Salen Rederierna AB is* [1985] AC 191, 201 (HL). The reference to Lord Wilberforce and the 'matrix of fact' is a reference to *Prenn v Simmonds* [1971] 1 WLR 1381, 1384 *per* Lord Wilberforce (HL).

(1) Interpretation is the ascertainment of the meaning which the document would convey to a reasonable person, having all the background knowledge which would reasonably have been available to the parties in the situation in which they were at the time of the contract.

(2) The background was famously referred to by Lord Wilberforce as the "matrix of fact", but this phrase is, if anything, an understated description of what the background may include. Subject to the requirement that it should have been reasonably available to the parties and to the exception to be mentioned next, it includes absolutely anything which would have affected the way in which the language of the document would have been understood by a reasonable man.

(3) The law excludes from the admissible background the previous negotiations of the parties and their declarations of subjective intent.

(4) The meaning which a document (or any other utterance) would convey to a reasonable man is not the same thing as the meaning of its words. The meaning of words is a matter of dictionaries and grammars; the meaning of the document is what the parties using those words against the relevant background would reasonably have been understood to mean. The background may not merely enable the reasonable man to choose between the possible meanings of words which are ambiguous but even (as occasionally happens in ordinary life) to conclude that the parties must, for whatever reason, have used the wrong words or syntax.

(5) The "rule" that words should be given their "natural and ordinary meaning" reflects the commonsense proposition that we do not easily accept that people have made linguistic mistakes, particularly in formal documents. On the other hand, if one would nevertheless conclude from the background that something must have gone wrong with the language, the law does not require judges to attribute to the parties an intention which they plainly could not have had. Lord Diplock made this point more vigorously when he said in *Antaios Compania Naviera SA v Salen Rederierna AB*:

> "If detailed semantic and syntactical analysis of words in a commercial contract is going to lead to a conclusion that flouts business commonsense, it must be made to yield to business commonsense.'"

4.12 However, one must have proper regard to Lord Hoffmann's *caveat* in his fifth principle: before departing from the obvious meaning of the words used, one must be satisfied that, 'something must have gone wrong with the language'. The court can undo the consequences of bad drafting if the intended meaning is clear, but it cannot undo bad bargains.

4.13 Lord Hoffmann, consciously or not, expressed the tension between the court's task in ascertaining 'the meaning which the document would convey to a reasonable person, having all the background knowledge which would reasonably have been available to the parties' and the principle that 'law excludes from the admissible background the previous negotiations of the parties and their declarations of subjective intent'. Interpretation is an *objective* *process*, which permits some recourse to material which the parties, *subjectively*, may have known. But, it is never wholly *subjective*.[22]

4.14 It is in this context first necessary to examine the refusal of the courts to admit 'subjective declarations of intent'. Many problems might be resolved if the court enquired of the parties what they intended. The parol evidence rule does not allow this. It prevents a party to a contract from giving evidence to explain what it intended a contract to achieve, or to contradict its proper construction, whatever that may be.

4.15 The most well-known formulation is that adopted by Lord Morris, when giving the advice of the Privy Council, in *Bank of Australasia v Palmer*:[23]

> 'The argument at their Lordships' bar did not disclose any difference of opinion between the opposing counsel on any point of law. The learned counsel for the respondent admitted as fully as their opponents could desire that parol testimony cannot be received to contradict, vary, add to or subtract from the terms of a written contract, or the terms in which the parties have deliberately agreed to record any part of their contract.'

4.16 This formulation still represents modern law: so, for example, see *Shogun Finance Ltd v Hudson*, per Lord Hobhouse:[24]

> 'The rule that other evidence may not be adduced to contradict the provisions of a contract contained in a written document is fundamental to the mercantile law of this country; the bargain is the document; the certainty of the contract depends on it. The relevant principle is summarised in *Phipson on Evidence:*
>
>> "When the parties have deliberately put their agreement into writing, it is conclusively presumed between themselves and their privies that they intend the writing to form a full and final statement of their intentions, and one which should be placed beyond the reach of future controversy, bad faith or treacherous memory."
>
> (See also *Bank of Australasia v Palmer*, per Lord Morris). This rule is one of the great strengths of English commercial law and is one of the main reasons for the international success of English law in preference to laxer systems which do not provide the same certainty.'

4.17 There are many grants of rights of way going back to the 19th century. Unless 'the bargain is the document', who knows *now* what the bargain was?

---

[22] See further *Chartbrook Ltd v Persimmon Homes Ltd* [2009] UKHL 38; [2009] 1 AC 1101 (HL) discussed below.

[23] [1897] AC 540, 545. The Board comprised Lord MacNaghten, Lord Morris, Sir Richard Couch, and Mr Way.

[24] [2003] UKHL 62; [2004] 1 AC 919, 944 Para [49]. The reference given to *Phipson* is to the 15th edn (2000), pp 1165–1166, paras 42-11 and 42-12 and that given for *Bank of Australasia v Palmer* is [1897] AC 540, 545.

Moreover, it is strange how recollections generally fade in the direction most advantageous to the party trying to recall.[25]

4.18   As the quotation from *Phipson* referred to by Lord Hobhouse shows, the parol evidence rule is not limited to excluding evidence to 'to contradict, vary, add to or subtract from the terms of a written contract'. It also excludes evidence from a party to the contract which is intended to explain or amplify what the contract means. This evidence is not admissible: the proper interpretation of a contract requires an objective investigation of the meaning of the language, not an investigation of what one or other party intended.[26]

4.19   Again, this is well-established law, restated at House of Lords level by Lord Steyn in *Sirius International Insurance Co (Publ) v FAI General Insurance Ltd*:[27]

> '[18] The settlement contained in the Tomlin order must be construed as a commercial instrument. The aim of the inquiry is not to probe the real intentions of the parties but to ascertain the contextual meaning of the relevant contractual language. The inquiry is objective: the question is what a reasonable person, circumstanced as the actual parties were, would have understood the parties to have meant by the use of specific language. The answer to that question is to be gathered from the text under consideration and its relevant contextual scene.'

4.20   The principle was re-affirmed (albeit *obiter*) by the House of Lords in *Chartbrook Ltd v Persimmon Homes Ltd*.[28] For present purposes, paragraphs [28]–[47] are important:

> '[41] The conclusion I would reach is that there is no clearly established case for departing from the exclusionary rule. The rule may well mean, as Lord Nicholls has argued, that parties are sometimes held bound by a contract in terms which, upon a full investigation of the course of negotiations, a reasonable observer would not have taken them to have intended. But a system which sometimes allows this to happen may be justified in the more general interest of economy and predictability in obtaining advice and adjudicating disputes. It is, after all, usually possible to avoid surprises by carefully reading the documents before signing them and there are the safety nets of rectification and estoppel by convention.
>
> [42] The rule excludes evidence of what was said or done during the course of negotiating the agreement for the purpose of drawing inferences about what the

---

25   '... it would be inconvenient, that matters in writing made by advice and on consideration, and which finally import the certain truth of the agreement of the parties should be controlled by averment of the parties to be proved by the uncertain testimony of slippery memory' *per* Popham CJ, *The Countess of Rutland's Case* (1604) 5 Co Rep 25b, 26a. See also *Onassis v Vergottis* [1968] 2 Lloyd's Rep 403, 431 per Lord Pierce (HL): 'with every day that passes the memory becomes fainter and the imagination becomes more active.'

26   For an example in the right of way context see *Young v Brooks* [2008 EWCA Civ 816. See also para **4.64**.

27   [2004] UKHL 54; [2004] 1 WLR 3251, 3258. Lord Bingham, Lord Nicholls of Birkenhead, Lord Walker and Lord Brown all agreed: see paras [1], [2], [39] and [40] respectively.

28   [2009] UKHL 38; [2009] 1 AC 1101 (HL).

contract meant. It does not exclude the use of such evidence for other purposes: for example, to establish that a fact which may be relevant as background was known to the parties, or to support a claim for rectification or estoppel. These are not exceptions to the rule. They operate outside it.'

4.21 There is evident difficulty in reconciling the second sentence of paragraph [42] with the preceding one and paragraph [41]. The practical position in the present state of the law is that virtually any material which bears on interpretation is admissible, subject to the qualification that it must have been material which would have informed the parties belief,and the belief of the class of persons who would be likely to read the document, as to the meaning of the document at the time.

4.22 As to the second class of exclusion, 'the previous negotiations of the parties'. The rationale for this is found in the process which the court professes to be carrying out. As Sir Thomas Bingham MR stressed in *Arbuthnott*, the modern approach to interpretation tries to balance the literal words used, urged upon it by one party, with the argument of the other party that the literal meaning gives rise to a commercial nonsense. The court is there to interpret the bargain, not remake it. In the rent review case of *Melanesian Mission Trust Board v Australian Mutual Provident Society* the correct approach was said by the Privy Council to be as follows:[29]

'The intention of the parties is to be discovered from the words used. Where ordinary words have been used they must be taken to have been used according to the ordinary meaning of these words. If their meaning is clear and unambiguous, effect must be given to them because that is what the parties are to be taken to have agreed to by their contract. Various rules may be invoked to assist interpretation in the event that there is an ambiguity. But it is not the function of the court, when construing a document, to search for an ambiguity. Nor should rules which exist to resolve ambiguities be invoked in order to create an ambiguity which, according to the ordinary meaning of the words, is not there. So the starting point is to examine the words used in order to see whether they are clear and unambiguous. It is of course legitimate to look at the document as a whole and to examine the context in which these words have been used, as the context may affect the meaning of the words. But unless the context shows that the ordinary meaning cannot be given to them or that there is an ambiguity, the ordinary meaning of the words which have been used in the document must prevail.'

4.23 The emphasis is important. If the parties have made themselves reasonably clear, the fact that the consequences may be hard for one side or another, or that the result is contrary to some pre-conceived commercial purpose, is nothing to the point. Commercial law grants autonomy to the contracting parties: the parties are perfectly free to agree whatever terms for a rent review they choose. This is a pure question of construction, which is not subject to any preconceptions or presumptions.[30] Bargains which are clearly

---

[29]   [1997] 2 EGLR 128, at 128F per Lord Hope (PC).
[30]   See generally *Rainy Sky SA v Kookmin Bank* [2011] UKSC 50.

and obviously the expressed intention of the parties are to be upheld for the important reason given by Hoffmann J in *MFI Properties Ltd v BICC Group Pension Trust Ltd*:[31]

> 'The court has no option but to assume that [the provision in question] was a *quid pro quo* for some other concession in the course of negotiations. The court cannot reject it as absurd merely because it is counterfactual and has no outward commercial justification.'

4.24 However, where the wording is not clear, one may ask should the court *not* then look at the parties' negotiations, to identify the real bargain? The House of Lords has endeavoured to explain why the 'matrix of facts' is included but evidence of negotiations is still excluded, in *Chartbrook Ltd v Persimmon Homes Ltd*.[32]

4.25 The case concerned an 'overage clause' or 'overage agreement' a form of agreement commonly used in the sale of land for prospective development. The essential features of an overage agreement are the sale by the landowner to a developer at a given price, which does not reflect the value of the land if and when development is either granted planning permission or has actually been carried out. The developer then endeavours to develop the land by obtaining planning permission and carrying out works. At a certain point, which may be typically when planning permission has been obtained or the development has been constructed, the developer then pays the landowner a further sum representing the added value of the land, but adjusted to allow the developer to recover his costs in the development, and a profit. This is termed 'overage'. In *Chartbrook*, the event triggering payment of the overage was the carrying out of the development.[33]

4.26 In *Chartbrook* the landowner, Chartbrook, entered into an agreement with a developer, Persimmon. Under the agreement Persimmon would obtain planning permission and then, pursuant to a licence from Chartbrook, would take possession and build a scheme of commercial premises with flats above and with parking in the basement. Chartbrook would grant the leases directly to the tenants, at Persimmon's direction, and then the proceeds would be divided up. The overage clause was complex: when all the leases were granted, Persimmon would pay to Chartbrook a single sum made up of the 'total land value' and the 'balancing payment'. The 'total land value' was made up of three parts:

(a) the 'total residential land value', of £76.34 per ft^2, multiplied by the area for which planning permission for flats was granted;

---

[31] [1986] 1 All ER 974, 976 (CA).
[32] [2009] UKHL 38; [2009] 1 AC 1101 (HL).
[33] Such clauses were in the past referred to as 'clawback clauses', and the concept as 'deferred consideration conveyancing'.

(b)   the 'total commercial land value', of £38.80 per ft², multiplied by the area for which planning permission for shops and other commercial uses was granted; and

(c)   The 'total residential car parking land value' of £3,024.00, multiplied by the number of spaces for which planning permission was granted.

4.27   The Agreement also makes provision for a 'balancing payment', which was defined in the Agreement as the 'ARP', It was defined as '23.4 per cent of the price achieved for each residential unit in excess of the minimum guaranteed residential unit value, less the costs and incentives'. In other words, the parties had agreed a minimum price for each flat. If Persimmon managed to do better than that price, it would give Chartbrook 23.4 per cent of the uplift, less any additional costs and expenses it incurred in inducing someone to buy the flat, such as fittings better than specification or paying legal expenses.

4.28   The issue was where the deduction of costs and expenses came in the calculation. Chartbrook argued the clause meant '24.3 per cent x (actual sale price – minimum guaranteed residential unit value – the costs and incentives)'. This formula generated a 'balancing payment' to Chartbrook of £4,484,862.00. Persimmon contended on the other hand that the expression meant '24.3 per cent x (actual sale price – the costs and incentives) – minimum guaranteed residential unit value. This formula generated a 'balancing payment' to Chartbrook of £897,051.00.

4.29   Lord Hoffmann held at [12] that an application of the rules of grammar and syntax would not support one construction any more than the other: the construction was so ambiguous that 'something had gone wrong with the language'.[34] Therefore, he went on to construe the contract as a whole, and look at the commercial factors which would have been driving the parties' bargain. He tried to accommodate both the commercial common-sense of the agreement and the draftsman's use of language.

> '[16] I think that to interpret the definition of ARP in accordance with ordinary rules of syntax makes no commercial sense. The term "minimum guaranteed residential unit value", defined by reference to total residential land value, strongly suggests that this was to be a guaranteed minimum payment for the land value in respect of an individual flat. A guaranteed minimum payment connotes the possibility of a larger payment which, depending upon some contingency may or may not fall due. Hence the term "additional residential payment". The element of contingency is reinforced by Para 3.3 of the sixth schedule, which speaks of the "date of payment *if any* of the balancing payment"
>
> [17] The judge declined to regard the terms "total land value" and "minimum guaranteed residential unit value" as indicative of an intention that MGRUV was

---

[34]   See Lord Walker at [84]. However, the majority in the Court of Appeal thought the meaning of the clause was 'clear, certain and unambiguous and its arithmetic is straightforward'. Many draftsmen now use algebra to draft mechanisms for calculating reviewed rents and overage payments in the belief that such formulas are more accurate and less open to challenge.

to be the minimum Chartbrook would receive as the land value of a flat because both terms were defined expressions. They might just as well have been algebraic symbols. Indeed they might, and I strongly suspect that if they had been, they would have made it clear that the parties were intending to give effect to Persimmon's construction. But the contract does not use algebraic symbols. It uses labels. The words used as labels are seldom arbitrary. They are usually chosen as a distillation of the meaning or purpose of a concept intended to be more precisely stated in the definition. In such cases the language of the defined expression may help to elucidate ambiguities in the definition or other parts of the agreement.'

4.30 In relation to rights of way, there are few, if any, special rules applicable to the interpretation of documents creating such instruments. Evidence of surrounding circumstances which would have been known to the parties is readily admitted. So when examining a document to see whether, for example, a vehicular (as opposed to a pedestrian) right of way has been granted or to ascertain the width or exact route of a right of way, one applies the general principles set out by Lord Hoffman in the *ICS* case.[35] In order to divine the intention of the parties, one starts with the words of the conveyance and any plan annexed to it and one can then look at the situation on the ground at the date of the conveyance and (even) any contemporaneous documents. As Moore-Bick LJ said in *TETG Developments V Noah*:[36]

'The primary task of the court in a case of this kind is to construe the grant itself. But it is common ground that, in doing so, the court is entitled to take into account not only the language of the grant but also the plan attached to it and evidence by way of background of the condition of the land at the time of the grant and other matters including, in this case, documents submitted for the purposes of obtaining planning permission ...'

4.31 So in *Todrick v Western Omnibus Co*[37] the court took account of the physical characteristics of the way and the use to which it was being put or might reasonably be put in construing its extent. In *Mills v Blackwell*[38] Morritt LJ said:

'Thus, the process of construction does not just start with a consideration of the words, but one has to consider the words, one has to consider the surrounding circumstances, and then one must reach a conclusion as to what the parties' intention was as expressed in the deed. The surrounding circumstances to which the court is entitled to have regard include, but are not limited to, the physical limitation on the exercise of the right of way. The decided cases indicate that those physical circumstances may or may not be sufficient to enable the court to find that the wide words of the grant are in fact restricted by the surrounding circumstances.'

---

[35] This view is supported by *Young v Brooks* [2008] EWCA Civ 816 and *Davill v Pull* [2009] EWCA Civ 1309.
[36] [2008] EWCA Civ 259 (at para 12).
[37] [1934] Ch 190.
[38] [1999] EWCA 1852.

4.32 The same principle was applied in *Moncreiff v Jamieson*.[39] In *Oliver v Symons*[40] the court had to construe a right of way which included the right 'to go pass and repass with or without motor vehicles and agricultural machinery or on foot...'. This was construed by reference to the physical characteristics of the track in question. In *Carpenter v Calico Quays Ltd*[41] it was held that a deed granting a right of way over 'the Roadway' should be construed in the light of the background circumstances to the grant reasonably known to both of the parties (applying *Investors Compensation Scheme*). Accordingly based on the evidence, the right was found to include both a right to use road and also the grass verges. In *Dutta v Hayes*[42] it was held that a right of way for agricultural purposes extended to recreational equestrian use, having regard to what a reasonable person having all the background knowledge available to the parties would have understood the document to mean.

IMPLICATION OF TERMS

4.33 There are different ways in which a term might be implied into a grant of an easement. For these purposes, the normal contractual principles apply. Lord Wilberforce summarised these in *Liverpool City Council v Irwin*:[43]

'To say that the construction of a complete contract out of these elements involves a process of "implication" may be correct; it would be so if implication means the supplying of what is not expressed. But there are varieties of implications which the courts think fit to make and they do not necessarily involve the same process. Where there is, on the face of it, a complete, bilateral contract, the courts are sometimes willing to add terms to it, as implied terms: this is very common in mercantile contracts where there is an established usage: in that case the courts are spelling out what both parties know and would, if asked, unhesitatingly agree to be part of the bargain. In other cases, where there is an apparently complete bargain, the courts are willing to add a term on the ground that without it the contract will not work – this is the case, if not of *The Moorcock* itself on its facts, at least of the doctrine of *The Moorcock* as usually applied. This is, as was pointed out by the majority in the Court of Appeal, a strict test – though the degree of strictness may vary. There is a third variety of implication, that which I think Lord Denning MR favours, or at least did favour in this case and that is the implication of reasonable terms. But though I agree with many of his instances, which in fact fall under one or other of the preceding heads, I cannot go so far as to endorse his principle; indeed, it seems to me, with respect, to extend a long, and undesirable, way beyond sound authority. The present case, in my opinion, represents a fourth category, or I would rather say a fourth shade on a continuous spectrum. The court here is simply concerned to establish what the contract is; the parties not having themselves fully stated the terms. In this sense the court is searching for what must be implied.'

---

[39] [2007] 1 WLR 2620.
[40] [2011] EWHC 1250 (Ch).
[41] [2011] EWHC 96.
[42] [2012] EWHC 1727 (Ch).
[43] [1977] AC 239, 253–4 (HL).

4.34 It may be that there is no single 'test', as such, for interpretation of contracts, although there are a number of tools. Even Lord Hoffmann would not go that far, with his speech in *ICS*.[44] But there are discernible tests for implying a term. So in *Liverpool City Council v Irwin* Lord Cross said:[45]

> 'Sometimes, what the court is in effect being asked to do is to rectify a particular – often a very detailed – contract by inserting in it a term which the parties have not expressed. Here it is not enough for the court to say that the suggested term is one the presence of which would make the contract a better or fairer one; it must be able to say that the insertion of the term is necessary to give – as it is put – business efficacy to the contract and that if its absence had been pointed out at the time both parties – assuming them to have been reasonable men – would have agreed without hesitation to its insertion.'

4.35 Lord Cross is in this passage combining two elements in a single test:

(a)   the 'Business Efficacy' test, as derived from '*The Moorcock*';[46] and

(b)   the 'Officious Bystander' test, as from *Shirlaw v Southern Foundries (1926) Ltd*.[47]

4.36 Taking the first limb, the courts will imply a term which will give a contract 'business efficacy', because it can be assumed that the parties would have intended the contract to be efficacious: per Bowen LJ in '*The Moorcock*':[48]

> 'In business transactions such as this, what the law desires to effect by the implication is to give such business efficacy to the transaction as must have been intended at all events by both parties who are business men; not to impose on one side all the perils of the transaction, or to emancipate one side from all the chances of failure, but to make each party promise in law as much, at all events, as it must have been in the contemplation of both parties that he should be responsible for in respect of those perils or chances.'

4.37 The other test outlined by Lord Cross derives from the intervention of the famous 'officious bystander', who was born in the speech of MacKinnon LJ, in *Shirlaw v Southern Foundries (1926) Ltd*:[49]

> '*Prima facie* that which in any contract is left to be implied and need not be expressed is something so obvious it goes without saying; so that if, while the parties were making their bargain, an officious bystander were to suggest some express provision for it in their agreement, they would testily suppress him with a common "Of course".'

---

[44]   [1998] 1 WLR 896, 912–913 (HL).
[45]   [1977] AC 239, 256 (HL).
[46]   (1889) 14 PD 64 (CA).
[47]   [1939] 2 KB 206 (CA).
[48]   (1889) 14 PD 64, 68 (CA).
[49]   [1939] 2 KB 206, 227 (CA).

4.38 The court will also require that the term it is being asked to imply is reasonable,[50] and is capable of clear and unambiguous formulation.[51] Also, as Lord Parker put it in *Tamplin Steamship Co v Anglo-Mexican Petroleum Products Co Ltd*:[52]

'It is, of course, impossible to imply in a contract any term or condition inconsistent with its express provisions or with the intention of the parties as gathered from those provisions.'

4.39 But it is still important to keep in mind that no term is to be implied simply because it would be *reasonable* to insert it. See Lord Wilberforce, in the *Liverpool* case:[53]

'In my opinion such obligation should be read into the contract as the nature of the contract itself implicitly requires, no more or less: a test, in other words of necessity.'

4.40 It is also important to ask if these apparent tests are separate or cumulative. In *Philips Electronique Grand Public SA v British Sky Broadcasting Ltd*, Sir Thomas Bingham MR reviewed the authorities and set this test for whether a term should be implied:[54]

'For a term to be implied, the following conditions (which may overlap) must be satisfied: (1) it must be reasonable and equitable; (2) it must be necessary to give business efficacy to the contract so that no term will be implied if the contract is effective without it; (3) it must be so obvious that, "it goes without saying"; (4) it must be capable of clear expression; (5) it must not contradict any express term of the contract.'

4.41 Note that this formulation of the test is cumulative in its effect: all five requirements must be satisfied.

4.42 It ought to follow that implication of terms is relatively inflexible: on Sir Thomas' formulation, there are five cumulative steps in the implication of a term, which may be hard to make out in any given case, especially given that 'business efficacy' is equated with the test of necessity.

4.43 However, if the view of Lord Hoffmann, as expressed in *Attorney General of Belize v Belize Telecom Ltd*[55] is accepted,[56] Sir Thomas' view might

---

[50] *Liverpool City Council v Irwin* [1977] AC 239, 262 per Lord Salmon and also per Lord Edmund-Davies at 265.

[51] *Shell UK Ltd v Lostock Garage Ltd* [1976] 1 WLR 1187 (CA), especially per Ormrod LJ.

[52] [1916] 2 AC 397, 422 (HL).

[53] [1977] AC 239, 254.

[54] [1995] EMLR 472, 481 (CA).

[55] [2009] UKPC 10; [2009] 1 WLR 1988 (PC). The Board comprised Lord Hoffmann, Lord Rodger, Baroness Hale, Lord Carswell and Lord Brown. Are English courts bound by decisions of the Privy Council as they are by decisions of the House of Lords or Supreme Court?

[56] In *Westpac Banking Corporation v The Bell Group Ltd (In Liquidation) (No 3)* [2012] WASCA

become seen to be too rule-driven. Lord Hoffmann suggests that the implication of terms is just a point on the spectrum with interpretation, as did Lord Wilberforce in the *Liverpool* case. Lord Hoffmann said:

'[16] Before discussing in greater detail the reasoning of the Court of Appeal, the Board will make some general observations about the process of implication. The court has no power to improve upon the instrument which it is called upon to construe, whether it be a contract, a statute or articles of association. It cannot introduce terms to make it fairer or more reasonable. It is concerned only to discover what the instrument means. However, that meaning is not necessarily or always what the authors or parties to the document would have intended. It is the meaning which the instrument would convey to a reasonable person having all the background knowledge which would reasonably be available to the audience to whom the instrument is addressed: see *Investors Compensation Scheme Ltd v West Bromwich Building Society*. It is this objective meaning which is conventionally called the intention of the parties, or the intention of Parliament, or the intention of whatever person or body was or is deemed to have been the author of the instrument.

[17] The question of implication arises when the instrument does not expressly provide for what is to happen when some event occurs. The most usual inference in such a case is that nothing is to happen. If the parties had intended something to happen, the instrument would have said so. Otherwise, the express provisions of the instrument are to continue to operate undisturbed. If the event has caused loss to one or other of the parties, the loss lies where it falls.

[18] In some cases, however, the reasonable addressee would understand the instrument to mean something else. He would consider that the only meaning consistent with the other provisions of the instrument, read against the relevant background, is that something is to happen. The event in question is to affect the rights of the parties. The instrument may not have expressly said so, but this is what it must mean. In such a case, it is said that the court implies a term as to what will happen if the event in question occurs. But the implication of the term is not an addition to the instrument. It only spells out what the instrument means.'

Indeed, it could be said that the question has now become what would the contract as a whole be taken to mean by a reasonable person?[57] The process of implying terms has become more creative but also more uncertain. In *Belize*, Lord Hoffmann held [27]:[58]

157, Lee AJA considered [342] criteria such as those set out in *BP Refinery (Westernport) Ptd Ltd v Shire of Hastings* (1977) 180 CLR 266: that a term will be implied in an informal contract only where it can be seen that it is necessary for the effective operation of the contract or is so obvious as to go without saying. Lee AJA noted that 'Although dicta of Lord Hoffman [sic] included in [*Belize*] cautioned against criteria such as those set out in *BP Refinery* being given a "life of their own" (presumably a warning against treating those requirements as restrictive), implication of a term in an informal contract is not a licence to improve a contract without regard to the need to restrict implication of a term to the extent necessary to give business effect to the contract and thus the presumed intent of the parties.'

57 See [2011] CLJ 607 (McCaughran).
58 The New Zealand Court of Appeal agreed with this approach in *Hickman v Turn and Wave Ltd* [2011] NZCA 100. Randerson J held [248] 'We agree that the approach adopted in the *BP*

'The Board considers that this list is best regarded, not as a series of independent tests which must each be surmounted, but rather as a collection of different ways in which judges have tried to express the central idea that the proposed implied term must spell out what the contract actually means or in which they have explained why they did not think that it did so. The Board has already discussed the significance of "necessary to give business efficacy" and goes without saying". As for the other formulations, the fact that the proposed implied term would be inequitable or unreasonable, or contradict what the parties have expressly said, or is incapable of clear expression, are all good reasons for saying that a reasonable man would not have understood that to be what the instrument meant.'

Implication of terms into grants of rights of way

4.44 The circumstances in which terms will be implied in instruments creating rights of way are in practice likely to be limited in most cases to those implied in law, such as not to cause unreasonable obstructions etc, discussed elsewhere,[59] which consider the circumstances in which a grant of a right of way will be subject to implied terms.

4.45 The courts have, however, been prepared to imply terms in grants of rights of way of ancillary rights. So in *McIlraith v Grady*[60] a right was granted 'with or without horses, carts and carriages to pass and repass through over and along' a yard at the rear of a pub to shop premises. Subsequently the shop also became a sub-post office and the pub became a home. It was held that the grant of the right of way for vehicles, construed in the light of the circumstances of the premises at that date included a right for vehicles to stop for a reasonable time to load and unload. Lord Denning MR said:

'There was necessarily imported, in addition to the actual right to pass and repass, also a right to stop for a reasonable time for the purpose of loading and unloading.'

In *Moncrieff v Jamieson*[61] a case relating to implication of rights of parking ancillary to a right of way granted by a conveyance, Lord Neuberger (at [113]) stated that the conceptual basis of implication is rooted in the general law of contract:

'That principle is that the law will imply a term into a contract, where, in the light of the terms of the contract and the facts known to the parties at the time of the contract, such a term would have been regarded as reasonably necessary or obvious to the parties.'

Refinery case should not necessarily be regarded as a cumulative list of elements all of which must be satisfied before a term may be implied. However, each element is a useful indicator relevant to the ultimate question of what a reasonable person would have understood the contract to mean. This is to be construed objectively by a notional reasonable person with knowledge of the relevant background.'

59 See generally Ch 10.
60 [1968] 1 QB 468.
61 [2007] 1 WLR 2620.

4.46 Lord Neuberger's references to contract are indicative of a growing judicial tendency to rest any implied terms on the supposed intention of the parties to the contract or, if there was no contract, on the intention of the testator or grantor. Further evidence of this tendency can be seen in *Adam v Shrewsbury*[62] where Lord Justice Neuberger (as he then was) said (at [28]):

> 'In my judgment, therefore, the resolution of the issue raised on the present appeal turns on **the proper analysis of the common intention of the parties, as gathered from the terms of the conveyance, the position on the ground, and the communications passing between the parties before the execution of the conveyance, which would include the provisions of the contract**. Although this court excluded as legally irrelevant any communications between the parties outside the conveyance (unless, of course, there is a claim for rectification) in *Scarfe v Adams* [1981] 1 All ER 843 at 851, it seems to me that such a conclusion is inconsistent with the general principle that when construing a document (whether or not it relates to land) all the surrounding circumstances should be taken into account. That this aspect of Scarfe's case is not the law was decided by this court in *Partridge v Lawrence* [2004] 1 P & CR 176 at 187.'

Emphasis added.

Correction of mistakes

4.47 Where there is an obvious mistake on the face of the document, a court might be willing to correct the mistake as a matter of contractual interpretation, rather than resorting to the equitable remedy of rectification, is examined below. As Lord Hoffmann commented in *Mannai Ltd v Eagle Star Assurance Co Ltd*:[63]

> 'It is a matter of constant experience that people can convey their meaning unambiguously although they have used the wrong words. We start with an assumption that people will use words and grammar in a conventional way but quite often it becomes obvious that, for one reason or another, they are not doing so and we adjust our interpretation of what they are saying accordingly. We do so in order to make sense of their utterance: so that the different parts of the sentence fit together in a coherent way and also to enable the sentence to fit the background of facts which plays an indispensable part in the way we interpret what anyone is saying. No one, for example, has any difficulty in understanding Mrs Malaprop. When she says "She is as obstinate as an allegory on the banks of the Nile", we reject the conventional or literal meaning of allegory as making nonsense of the sentence and substitute "alligator" by using our background knowledge of the things likely to be found on the banks of the Nile and choosing one which sounds rather like "allegory".'

4.48 Lord Hoffmann may well of course have been aware that the Nile is not home to alligators, but only to crocodiles. Be that as it may, the starting point must be to question whether the terms of the document do, as a matter of

---

[62]   [2006] 1 P&CR 27.
[63]   [1997] AC 749, 774 (HL).

proper construction, mean what at first sight they seem to mean. According to Brightman LJ in *East v. Pantiles (Plant Hire) Ltd*, such an approach will only be justified where:[64]

(a)   there is a 'clear mistake on the face of the instrument'; and

(b)   it is 'clear what correction ought to be made in order to cure the mistake'.

4.49   The *ICS* case shows there is a limit to what evidence may be adduced as to the pre-contractual negotiations. Lord Hoffmann said this:[65]

> 'The law excludes from the admissible background the previous negotiations of the parties and their declarations of subjective intent. They are admissible only in an action for rectification. The law makes this distinction for reasons of practical policy and, in this respect only, legal interpretation differs from the way we would interpret utterances in ordinary life. The boundaries of this exception are in some respects unclear. But this is not the occasion on which to explore them.'

4.50   It may therefore be that the crucial evidence (such as exchanges of correspondence evidencing pre-contractual negotiations) is simply inadmissible in a dispute about the construction of the lease, and therefore a claim for rectification would provide the only successful course of action.

4.51   However, sometimes the mistake is so plain that it matters not that the background material is of limited admissibility. An example is *Littman v Aspen Oil (Broking) Ltd*, where the landlord's solicitor inadvertently put the word 'tenant' in a break clause where he meant to write 'landlord'.[66] The effect was that, on its face, the lease provided that the *landlord* could only exercise *his* right to break if the *tenant* had fully complied with the covenants in the lease. The tenant's solicitor noticed the error but, concluding that the insertion of the provision was in any case a 'try on' on the part of the landlord which had gone wrong, did not bring it to the landlord's attention.[67]

4.52   The Court of Appeal upheld the judge's finding that the word 'landlord' should be construed as if it said 'tenant', because the ordinary meaning was absurd in context. If the lease meant what it literally said, the tenant could defeat the landlord's break option by the simple expedient of breaching one of its own covenants. That would just be uncommercial to the point of obviously wrong. It was further held (albeit *obiter*) that rectification could probably have

---

[64]   [1982] 2 EGLR 111, 112. Approved by Lord Hoffmann in Chartbrook, at [22]–[23], subject to a point made in *KPMG LLP v Network Rail Infrastructure Ltd* [2008] 1 P&CR 11, per Carnwath LJ at [48]–[50] (CA), 'Both in the judgment, and in the arguments before us, there was a tendency to deal separately with correction of mistakes and construing the paragraph "as it stands", as though they were distinct exercises. In my view, they are simply aspects of the single task of interpreting the agreement in its context, in order to get as close as possible to the meaning which the parties intended.'

[65]   [1998] 1 WLR 896, 912–913 (HL).

[66]   [2006] 2 P&CR 2 (CA).

[67]   This sort of thing never goes down well, oddly enough.

been granted if the construction argument had failed: to deliberately take advantage of an obvious drafting error was plainly inequitable.[68] Similarly, in *Holding and Barnes PLC v Hill House Hammond Ltd (No 1)*[69] a repairing covenant was interpreted contrary to its express wording to apply to the whole building and not merely the demised premises which formed part of the building. In *Littman v Aspen Oil Broking Ltd*[70] a provision for determination of a lease prior to the term date provided that in the case of a notice given by the landlord the notice would only be effective if the tenant had paid the rent and duly performed the covenants of the lease. It was held that there was a clear error of drafting, since the clause as drawn allowed the tenant to escape its obligations. There was no commercial purpose in this, and the clause would be read as if the word 'tenant' was substituted for 'landlord'.[71]

4.53 On the other hand, in *Churchill v Temple*[72] the question arose whether a restrictive covenant which prevented the building of a house without the approval of 'the vendors or their surveyor' and prevented any structural alteration or addition to a permitted house without their consent meant the vendors **or their successors in title** or their respective surveyors. The High Court preferred the literal construction and further decided that after the vendors' deaths the restrictions ceased to apply.[73] The judge, Nicholas Strauss QC at [37], correctly emphasised the difficulty in attempting to identify the facts known to the parties when the issue of construction arises long after the contract was entered into:

> '(a) In many cases, including this one, the issue of construction arises long after the contract was entered into, and as between parties who are not the original parties to the contract. It is then usually impossible to know what were all the facts known, or reasonably available, to the parties, to which investors compensation requires the court to have regard, because the parties are not there to provide the evidence. Some of the facts may be clear, but there is a real risk that the court is proceeding on the basis of incomplete evidence as to the relevant background, and that it may therefore misunderstand it.'

4.54 He went on to hold that the parties should be assumed to have thought of all the contingencies which would have been apparent to a reasonable outsider with knowledge of the relevant factual background. They would therefore be assumed to have addressed the issue as to whether the restrictions would be enforceable by successors in title. He concluded that reading the covenants in accordance with their literal terms, which restricted the right to withhold consent to the original vendors, made perfectly good sense and involved no absurdity. This case, while not failing to loyally follow *ICS* in theory, suggests that the court should avoid disregarding the plain words where

---

[68]   This technique of reading out obvious errors is sometimes called 'common law rectification' in practice, but it does not seem the terminology is readily found in the texts.

[69]   [2002] 2 P & CR 145.

[70]   [2005] EWHC 1369 (Ch).

[71]   See also *JIS (1974) Ltd v MCP Investments Ltd* [2002] EWCA Civ 721.

[72]   [2010] EWHC 3369 (Ch).

[73]   Applying *Crest Nicholson Residential (South) Ltd v McAllister* [2003] 1 All ER 46.

the evidence of surrounding circumstances is lacking or equivocal. One is reminded of *Scarfe v Adams*[74] in which Griffiths LJ had set a limit to the situations in which extrinsic evidence was available to interpret a transfer of land:

> 'The principle may be stated thus: if the terms of the transfer clearly define the land or interest transferred extrinsic evidence is not admissible to contradict the transfer. In such a case, if the transfer does not truly express the bargain between vendor and purchaser, the only remedy is by way of rectification of the transfer.'

4.55   That this no longer represents the law is clear from the judgment of Peter Gibson LJ in *Partridge v Lawrence*[75] at paragraph 29, following the *ICS* case. But caution is required when going beyond them where the transaction took place many years ago in circumstances which cannot be reconstructed.

GENERAL RULES OF INTERPRETATION APPLIED IN RELATION TO GRANTS OF RIGHTS OF WAY

4.56   The courts have evolved principles of interpretation which apply to documents creating rights of way. They are generally well established, though would yield to contrary express provision or application of *ICS* principles. The following paragraphs summarise the most important general rules. They are in some cases dealt with in more detail in other Chapters.

The width of the right of way

4.57   Following the ICS case, the court will normally begin by considering the terms of the grant itself. Frequently these will not be clear. If the document refers to a particular road or track, extrinsic evidence of the configuration of the topography at the time of the grant may resolve the matter. Where the document incorporates a plan, sometimes this is inaccurately marked and/or to no definable scale. The court may then see if there is any other indication in the surrounding circumstances of the parties' intention. So in *Partridge v Lawrence*[76] regard was had to the original of a plan drawn to scale, a reduced and unscaled copy of which had been attached to a deed, to ascertain the width of a right of way. A somewhat analogous problem may arise where the question is whether parking by the servient owner is allowed. The question then becomes how much of the width of the way must be left unobstructed. In *Smith v Garrard*[77] the issue arose whether an injunction should be granted to restrain parking of vehicles on a private road. A covenant had been imposed in the following terms:

---

[74]   [1981] 1 All ER 843 (at 851).
[75]   [2004] 1 P & CR 176.
[76]   [2004] 1 P & CR 176.
[77]   [2004] EWCA Civ 1655.

'Not at any time to park vehicles upon or place any articles upon or in any way obstruct the free passage of any part of the Roadway over which other persons have rights of way.'

4.58 The Roadway included verges and the right of way extended to these as well as the metalled portion. The defendant claimed to be entitled to park on the verge since it did not obstruct free passage, and the Court of Appeal agreed.

Chadwick LJ at [32] said:

'The words are there to indicate that the parts of the Roadway on which vehicles are not to be parked are those parts on which the parking of vehicles would obstruct rights of way. They are not there to impose an absolute obligation against parking vehicles which do not interfere with the rights of way but which may be regarded as aesthetically unattractive or an annoyance.'

Where a right of way is granted along a track with verges, some degree of tolerance is allowed for deviation where required for example to allow vehicles to pass.[78]

Traffic permissible

4.59 *Cannon v Villars*[79] lays down the general rule:

'Prima facie, the grant of a right of way is the grant of a right of way having regard to the nature of the road over which it is granted and the purpose for which it is intended to be used; and both circumstances may be legitimately called in aid in determining whether it is a general right, or a right of way restricted to foot passengers ...'

4.60 In *St Edmundsbury and Ipswich Diocesan Board of Finance v Clark (No 2)*[80] a right of way was reserved in a conveyance in general terms over a strip of land. At the time of the grant the strip was wide enough for vehicles, including lorries, and its surface sufficiently firm. However, it was not in fact used in this way, and looked like an abandoned path. The Court of Appeal upheld the judge's decision that regard was to be had in interpreting the grant to the surrounding circumstances at the date of the conveyance. The right was for foot traffic only.

4.61 In *Minor v Groves*[81] the issue arose as to the type of traffic entitled to use a strip of land in front of a house as a right of way. It was held that this was impliedly limited by reference to the width of the right of way.

---

[78] *V T Engineering v R Borland Ltd* (1968) 19 P&CR 890, 895.
[79] (1878) 8 Ch D 415.
[80] [1975] 1 WLR 468.
[81] (2000) 80 P & CR 136.

4.62 In *Oliver v Symons*[82] it was held that an express grant of a right of way over a farm track was impliedly limited by the physical characteristics of the track. There was no right to use it for large tractors and wide load farm machinery. Pulling over on to the verge to use it as swing space was a trespass. In *Dutta v Hayes*[83] the same principle was applied to the interpretation of another right of way for agricultural purposes. In *London Tara Hotel Ltd v Kensington Close Hotel Ltd*[84] it was held that a licence to use a way for vehicles which were of such size as to be unable to leave a parcel of land by any other exit imposed implied limits on the vehicles which were permitted to use it.

4.63 In *Alford v Hannaford*[85] clause 2 of a transfer granted the transferee a right of way along a track 'at all times and for all purposes with or without vehicles and animals'. It was held that this included a right to drive animals along the track and was not limited to pedestrian and vehicular use. In *Todrick v Western Omnibus Co*[86] a vehicular right of way was held to be limited to light vehicles only, having regard to the purposes for which the road was used or might reasonably have been expected to be used in the future. In *Young v Brooks*[87] it was held by the Court of Appeal that a right of way over a footpath serving the rear of the dominant owner's property should not be limited by implication to being exercised only in circumstances where the use of the front door for leaving or entering the property was not reasonably practicable. The judge at first instance had erred in taking account of documents showing how the grantor had interpreted the wording. These were inadmissible, as doing no more than evidencing the intention of the grantor or alternatively how the grantor interpreted the rights granted.

Rights created by grant and reservation may be construed differently

4.64 An easement may be created by express grant or by express reservation.

4.65 In the case of a grant, the rule that a grantor may not derogate from his or her grant is applied, and the grant is interpreted against the grantor.[88]

4.66 In the case of a reservation, whether a reservation is to be implied where it is not expressly included, depends on the application of the rule set out by Jenkins LJ in *Re: Webb's Lease*.[89] The test is whether the circumstances raise a necessary inference of an intention common to both parties that the vendor should have the right of way reserved to it .For such an inference to be drawn

---

[82]   (2011) LTL 18/5/2011.
[83]   [2012] EWHC 1727 (Ch).
[84]   [2010] EWHC 2749 (Ch). The case was appealed [2011] EWCA Civ 1356 but the appeal is not concerned with this point.
[85]   [2011] EWCA Civ 1099.
[86]   [1934] Ch 190.
[87]   [2008] EWCA Civ 816.
[88]   See e g *Williams v James* (1867) LR 2 CP 577.
[89]   [1951] Ch 808 at 829.

the person claiming the right of way must demonstrate that the facts are not reasonably consistent with any other explanation – it is not enough that they are simply consistent with such an explanation.[90] As to the interpretation of reservations, the position as set out by the Court of Appeal in the case of *St Edmundsbury and Ipswich Diocesan Board of Finance v Clark (No 2)* is that a reservation of the easement by a vendor of land is to be interpreted against the purchaser on the basis that the purchaser is treated as the grantor.

4.67   In that case, an easement was reserved on a 1945 conveyance of a portion of land by the Church to Mr Clark. The conveyance was expressed to be 'subject to a right of way over the land coloured red on the plan to and from [the] Church'. The scale plan indicated that the red land equated to an area approximately nine feet wide. The conveyance did not expressly state whether a pedestrian right of way or a more extensive vehicular right of way was intended. The Court of Appeal held that, interpreting the conveyance in light of the surrounding circumstances, it was clear that a pedestrian right of way only was being reserved, and the appeal was dismissed. However, the court declared (albeit obiter) that, in view of reservation still being based on re-grant, the words of the easement should still, in cases of ambiguity, be interpreted against the purchaser and in favour of the vendor. The court did emphasise, however, that this was to be a recourse of last resort in cases when the other principles of contractual interpretation still lead to genuine ambiguity.

Change in purpose of the right of way acquired by grant

4.68   Where the purpose for which the right of way acquired by grant is used changes, it was decided in *White v Grand Hotel (Eastbourne) Ltd*[91] that:

(a)   A right of way granted for general purposes was held not to be restricted to access to the land for such purposes as were reasonably required at the date of the grant; therefore a right of way for general purposes to a private house was not affected by the house becoming a hotel:

> 'Unless there is some limitation to be found in the grant, in the nature of the width of the road or something of that kind, full effect must be given to the grant, and we cannot consider the subsequent user as in any way sufficient to cut down the generality of the grant.'

4.69   It is necessary to establish what was in contemplation at the time of the grant. Despite this width of presumption, there are limits so that in *Milner's Safe Company Ltd v Great Northern & City Railway Co*,[92] a right of way was granted in 1832 in favour of several buildings in London which were at that stage being used as dwelling houses and/or warehouses. About 70 years later, two of those buildings were pulled down and the defendants erected a railway

---

[90]   See also *Peckham v Ellison* (1999) 31 HLR 1030. *Colquhoun v Harris* (High Court of Justice Chancery Division) 19 March 2010 LTL 8/4/2010.

[91]   [1913] 1 Ch 113.

[92]   [1907] 1 Ch 208.

station. The consequence was that at all times of the day and especially in the morning and evening peak hours, a large number of persons were using the right of way to leave the railway station to get to the surrounding streets. The plaintiff sought an injunction to prevent substantial interference with the right of way.

4.70 Counsel for the defendant submitted (at page 217), that 'When once buildings used for trade purposes are on land in a city it is not possible to suppose that the grantor meant to limit his grant to the purposes for which the premises were then used. No clear-sighted man would so tie his property up. In 1812, Moorfields, the site of this property, were waste, and the testator must have foreseen to some extent at any rate the progress of London'.

4.71 Kekewich J did not agree, however he did use that test saying at page 227:

'Not only was the erection of a railway not contemplated by the grantor, but it could not possibly have been within his contemplation, and a railway station is not merely in its construction, but in its mode of occupation, something entirely different from any dwelling-house, warehouse, or even manufactory, which could have been erected on the land.'

4.72 Thus each case depends on the terms of the grant and the surrounding circumstances.

4.73 See also *Robinson v Bailey*[93] in which a right of way granted for all purposes was held not affected by change of use from single dwelling to storage of building materials for business purposes. The general rule is that the way can be used for the new development provided the nature of the use is not radically altered. So in *Giles v County Building Contractors (Hertford) Ltd*[94] a prescriptive right of way led to a convent. It was held it could be used when two buildings were developed into a three-storey block of flats, a bungalow, a house and eight garages. This was described as 'evolution rather than mutation'. On the other hand, in *McAdams Homes v Robinson*[95] an implied easement of drainage through a pipe for a building used as a bakery was not capable of being used for a redevelopment to two four-bedroom houses. This was held to represent a change in character rather than intensification. The Court of Appeal defined the issues as:

(a) Whether the development of the dominant land, ie the site represented a 'radical change in the character' or a 'change in the identity' of the site ... as opposed to a mere change or intensification in the use of the site ...'.

(b) Whether the use of the site as redeveloped would result in a substantial increase or alteration in the burden on the servient land.

---

[93] [1948] 2 All ER 791.
[94] (1990) 22 P & CR 978.
[95] [2004] 3 EGLR 93 CA.

4.74   Neuberger LJ summarised the position as follows:

> 'In my opinion, the effect of the authorities in relation to the present case is that it would only be if the redevelopment of the site represented a radical change in its character and would lead to a substantial increase in the burden, that the dominant owner's right to enjoy the easement of passage of water through the pipe would be suspended or lost.'

4.75   In *Davill v Pull*,[96] rights of way had been granted 'for all reasonable and usual purposes' by conveyances between 1919 and 1921. The dominant tenements were cottages, each of which included a plot of 'garden ground' to which the rights of way gave access. It was held that the phrase 'for all reasonable and proper purposes' interpreted against the factual background in accordance with the *ICS* case did not import the limitation on the grants to use for garden purposes. No draftsman wishing to limit the use of the rights of way to garden purposes would have used those words. The words permitted use of the way for all purposes which were from time to time reasonable and usual. Use of each plot for a house for which planning permission had been granted was reasonable and usual.

Extent of right of way acquired by prescription

4.76   Rights of way may be acquired by prescription in various ways, discussed in Chapter 6. All require that the use be as if as of right and to have continued for a long period, 20 or 40 years depending on the basis on which the right is claimed. Where a right has been acquired in this way, the extent of it is determined by the user which has been continuous during the prescriptive period.[97]

4.77   In *British Waterways Board v Glass*[98] it was held that a prescriptive right of way over a track used for access to a caravan site for six caravans did extend to the use of the dominant land for a substantially increased number of caravans on the ground that this did not involve an increase in the burden of the easement beyond what was permissible. Lord Denning MR said:[99]

> 'It is quite clear that, when you acquire a right of way by prescription, you are not entitled to change the character of your land so as substantially to increase or alter the burden upon the servient tenement. If you have a right of way for your pasture land, you cannot turn it into a manufactory and claim a right of way for the purposes of the factory.'

4.78   On the other hand, in the earlier case of *Wimbledon and Putney Commons Conservators v Dixon*[100] it was held that where the use proposed was

---

[96]   [2009] EWCA Civ 1309.
[97]   *British Waterways Board v Glass* [1965] 1 Ch 538. *Attwood v Bovis Homes* [2001] Ch 379.
[98]   [1965] 1 Ch 538.
[99]   At 1965 1 Ch 555B to C.
[100]   [1875] 1 Ch D 362.

for a different purpose than that for which the way had been used, the right did not extend to this. The head-note summarises the decision:

'The immemorial use of a right of way for all purposes for which a road was wanted and the then condition of the property, does not establish a right of way for all purposes in an altered condition of the property where that would impose a greater burden on the servient tenement. Where a road had been immemorially used to a farm, not only for usual agricultural purposes, but in certain instances for carrying building materials to enlarge the farmhouse and rebuild a cottage on the farm, and for carting away sand and gravel dug out of the farm: – Held, (affirming the decision of Jessel MR,) that that did not establish a right of way for carting the materials required for building a number of new houses on the land.'

4.79 James LJ said:[101]

'I said when this case was first opened, that I was strongly of opinion that it was the settled law of this country that no such change in the character of a dominant tenement could be made as would increase the burden on the servient tenement.'

4.80 The same approach was adopted in *Loder v Gaden*,[102] another case of residential development. In *Attwood v Bovis Homes*,[103] a case concerning rights of drainage, the question was whether a prescriptive right of drainage for agricultural purposes extended to use of the dominant land as a housing estate. It was held that it did. Neuberger J identified two possible rules as to whether a prescriptive right of way survived a radical change in the use of the dominant tenement. On the 'strict' rule, any change in the nature of the use resulted in the right being lost. The 'flexible' rule on the other hand had regard to the question whether the burden on the servient land had intensified.

4.81 Neuberger J suggested the rule which should be applied would be that if there was a radical change in the use of the dominant tenement it would be for the dominant owner to prove that no intensification was involved:

'I would tentatively suggest that the rule may be that if there is a subsequent radical change in the use of the dominant tenement, a right of way acquired by prescription can only continue to be used in connection with the dominant tenement, if the court can be satisfied that the change cannot result in the use of the way being greater in quantum or different in character from that which it was for any continuous period of 20 or 40 years during the period of use of the way in connection with the original use of the dominant tenement.'

4.82 In *McAdams Homes v Robinson,* discussed above,[104] it was said by Nourse LJ that in general, authorities on prescriptive easements also apply to implied easements and *vice versa.* In relation to prescriptive rights of way, the cases fell into two categories:

---

[101] [1875] 1Ch D 368.
[102] (1999) 78 P & CR 223.
[103] [2001] Ch 379.
[104] See para **4.73**.

(a)   Those where there had been a change in the character of the dominant
       tenement, where the use of the right has been restrained.

(b)   Those where there has been no such change, but the burden has
       intensified. In general the intensified use is considered lawful.

A right of way can only be used for the dominant tenement

4.83   The general rule is that a right of way only extends to the land for which
it was granted. So a right of way to land A does not allow access via the way to
A, and then across it, to B. See *Harris v Flower*.[105] This rule does not apply
where the purposes of the use of B are 'merely adjuncts to the honest use' of
A.[106] The Court of Appeal accepted a submission in *Massey v Boulden*[107] that
'the critical question is ... whether the use made of [B] is more than merely
ancillary to that made of [A].' The use will be merely ancillary when there is no
benefit to B, or the benefit to B is insubstantial, so the access is in substance
used for the benefit of A.[108] In *National Trust v White*,[109] it was held that a
right of way could be used to access a car park which was separate to the
attraction which it served. However, in *Jobson v Record*,[110] the Court of Appeal
found that a right of way benefiting A could not be used to transport timber
from B, even where the timber had been stored on A. In *Das v Linden
Mews Ltd*[111] owners of mews houses used a private road over which they had a
right of way to their houses to gain access to park on a piece of land which was
originally a garden. It was held this was not permissible. Buxton LJ held that,
in order to fall outside *Harris v Flower*, the use of the easement to reach B must
be 'extension of the enjoyment of the *access to* the dominant tenement, rather
than ... extension of *enjoyment of* the dominant tenement'. *National Trust* was
distinguished as, on the facts of that case, the use of the car park was part and
parcel of the use of the way for the purpose of the original grant, and it was
not possible to say that the real use of the right of way was to access land that
was not part of the dominant tenement. However, the Court of Appeal
remitted *Das* to the County Court with a strong hint that the case might not be
suitable for an injunction. The High Court of Australia has concluded that the
rule in *Harris v Flower* is, in fact, merely a starting-point for considering the
terms of the grant.[112].

4.84   There is a limited exception to this rule, as was given by Megarry V-C in
Nickerson v Barraclough.[113] Suppose that Lot A is a narrow footpath running
from Lot X (the other side of which is a public road) to Lot B. The owner of
Lot X grants a right of way over Lot X to the owner of Lot A (who also owns

---

[105]   (1904) 74 LJ Ch 127.
[106]   [2002] 28 EG 130 *Peacock v Custins* [2002] 1 WLR 1815, 1824, Schiemann LJ.
[107]   [2003] 1 WLR 1792.
[108]   *Macepark (Whittlebury) Ltd v Sargeant* [2003] 1 WLR 2284.
[109]   [1987] 1 WLR 907.
[110]   (1998) 75 P & CR 375.
[111]   [2003] 2 P & CR 4.
[112]   *Westfield Management v Perpetual Trustee Company* [2007] HCA 45.
[113]   [1980] Ch 325 at 336.

or later acquires Lot B) for the benefit of Lot A. According to Megarry V-C, the grant would be construed as authorising the dominant owner to use the right of way as a means of access to Lot B, since Lot A is a footpath which constitutes a means of access to Lot B. His Lordship said the same result would flow if Lot A were not used as an actual means of access to Lot B but as between the parties to the transaction it was intended to be used in that way. On the other hand, in *Giles v Tarry*[114] it was held that the general rule could not be evaded by a token use of a public highway in the course of accessing land other than the dominant tenement. The correct course was to look at the substance and intention of the user in question.

However, there is no requirement that the use of a right of way has to be by the occupier of the dominant land or his agents. It is sufficient that the use accommodates, or benefits, the dominant land in the sense of being closely connected with the normal enjoyment of the dominant land.[115]

No implied obligation to do repairs

4.85 By a grant of a right of way, neither the dominant nor the servient owner is bound to repair the way, but the dominant owner can carry out reasonable repairs. Grants often provide for contribution by users of a fair proportion of the cost of repair. Such provisions are normally enforceable against the successors of the grantee, on the basis that the exercise of the right of way is conditional on the person using the right making the stipulated contribution.

4.86 So in *Thamesmead Town v Allotey*[116] rights of way over roads and footpaths were granted by a transfer, with the grantees covenanting to pay on demand a fair proportion of all costs in relation to cleansing all roads and footpaths and also to maintenance of communal areas. The grantees had no right to use the communal areas and the Court of Appeal held that positive covenants were enforceable against successors in title if two conditions are satisfied:

(a) The condition of discharging the burden has to be relevant to the exercise of the rights that enabled the benefit to be retained.

(b) The successors in title had to have the opportunity to choose whether to take the benefit of having taken it to renounce it even if only in theory.

4.87 The claim succeeded as regard the roadways and footpaths but failed as regards the communal areas, because in fact the original transfer granted no rights over the communal areas, and Thamesmead Town the grantor had no obligation to maintain them.

---

[114] [2012] EWCA Civ 837.
[115] Compare *Polo Woods Foundation v Shelton-Agar* [2009] EWHC 1361 (Ch). See also *Kennerley v Beech* [2012] EWCA Civ 158 (grant of right of way over path held not to be a valid easement as it did not run to or accommodate the dominant tenement).
[116] (2000) 78 P & CR 557.

Dominant owner's right to repair

4.88   Where the way becomes out of repair, the dominant owner is entitled to carry out repair works. Where the proposed works involve resurfacing or upgrading the road, the rights of the dominant owner to form road surfaces seem established by the decision in *Newcomen v Coulson*,[117] a decision of Jessel MR, with whom James LJ and Baggallay JA concurred. In that case a right of way had been created over a strip of land 11 yards wide when the land having the benefit of the right of way was used only for agriculture. More than a century later the then owner set about building 26 dwellings on the land and forming a street for the purpose, including creating a metalled surface over the right of way. Jessel MR said at pages 143–144:

> 'Then it was said admitting the owner of each house to have a right of way, still the grantees have no right to enter upon the allotments over which the right of way is granted for the purpose of laying down a metalled road. Now it was conceded to be the principle of law that the grantee of a right of way has a right to enter upon the land of the grantor over which the way extends for the purpose of making the grant effective, that is, to enable him to exercise the right granted to him. That includes not only keeping the road in repair but the right of making a road. If you grant to me over a field a right of carriage-way to my house, I may enter upon your field and make over it a carriage-way sufficient to support the ordinary traffic of a carriage-way, otherwise the grant is of no use to me, because my carriage would sink up to the naves of the wheels in a week or two of wet weather. It cannot be contended that the word "repair" in such a case is limited to making good the defects in the original soil by subsidence or washing away, it must include the right of making the road such that it can be used for the purpose for which it is granted. Therefore I think the defendants have a right to make an effective carriage-way going, as they are doing, by the shortest route, and not interfering with the land to a greater extent in width than the width of the street pointed out by the deed itself.'

4.89   The continuing authority of this decision was recognised in the Court of Appeal in *Mills v Silver*[118] where Dillon LJ said:

> 'In the second place, if the first and second defendants or their predecessors had been expressly granted a right of way for all purposes with or without vehicles over the disputed track that would have entitled them not merely to repair the disputed track but to improve it to make it suitable for the accommodation of the dominant tenement even if the dominant tenement was to be used for some purpose not in contemplation at the time of the grant: see *Newcomen*. This is founded on the presumed intention of the grant. In the simplest case, if a general right of way is granted with or without vehicles, which is to be the principal access to a house, it is permissible for the grantee to improve it by making it up as a carriageway: see for instance *Gerrard v Cooke*.'[119]

---

[117]   (1877) 5 ChD 133.
[118]   [1991] Ch 271 at 286–287. See also *Clifford v Dove* [2003] NSWSC 938.
[119]   (1806) 2 Bos. & Pul NR 109.

Does the dominant owner have an implied right to form new access points?

4.90 In *Pettey v Parsons*[120] it was said that it was a question of construction of the grant whether a right of way was limited to access to the dominant owner's land via the openings existing at the date of the grant or whether the dominant owner had a right to form new openings. In the latter case the right is limited to what is reasonable, ie a right of access to a private road is such as would give reasonable opportunity for the exercise of the right of way.

4.91 In *Carder v Davies*[121] it was held that the grant of a right to pass and repass along a road adjoining the boundary of the dominant tenement for all purposes connected with the use of the property as a private residence gave the dominant owner the *prima facie* right to enter the roadway at any point on the boundary, and further that he had the right to change his access point at will, provided this did not result in undue interference with the rights of others. On the other hand in *Mills v Blackwell*[122] it was held that the dominant owner was restricted to use of an existing point of opening. The distinction between the two cases appears to be that in *Mills v Blackwell* the boundary wall was a substantial construction with an existing opening in it at the date of the grant. This led the court to infer that the route of the right of way must be limited to the one existing at the time, which passed by a particular gateway in the wall.

4.92 In *Perlman v Rayden*,[123] a bitter neighbour dispute about access over a shared drive, there was held to be a right to make a new access to the drive to serve a new front door. In the particular case, the court thought that it was significant that the dominant owner was obliged to contribute to the repair of the way.

4.93 In *Well Barn Shoot v Shackleton*[124] an interesting problem arose. The facts were that:

(a) The claimant owned a shooting estate.

(b) The defendant owned a farm on the edge of the estate, and a track 10 feet wide bordered by a grass verge.

(c) The claimant had a right of way over the track which was expressed to be 'over and along the roadway shown coloured brown on the plan attached hereto'. There was a proviso that where the use was for agricultural purposes the claimant would contribute a fair proportion of the cost of repairing and maintaining the roadway, but this did not apply where the use of the roadway was for shooting 'or care of the game or the like'.

---

[120] [1914] 2 Ch 653.
[121] (1998) 76 P & CR D 33.
[122] (1999) 78 P & CR D 43.
[123] [2004] EWHC 2192.
[124] [2003] EWCA Civ 2.

(d)   The brown land clearly only included the track, not the verges.

(e)   The claimant claimed the right to come through a fence and hedge adjacent to the track over the verges and on to the right of way from its land. This was disputed by the defendant. If the defendant was right it would make the right of way useless.

4.94   The High Court (and on appeal the Court of Appeal) held that:

(a)   The grant could not be interpreted as including a right over the verges.

(b)   A claim for rectification failed as there was no evidence to support it.

(c)   The right of way included by implication a right of reasonable access to the field. The proviso in the reservation which imposed an obligation to contribute to the maintenance of the track where it was being used for agricultural purposes, gave rise to the obvious implication that the right of way was also for use by such vehicles.

(d)   A reasonable access across the verge into the field was one 24 feet wide, to allow for manoeuvring of large agricultural vehicles.

(e)   There was no need to imply a right for more than one access point.

4.95   In *Volta Developments v Waltham Forest Friendly Society*[125] it was held that having regard to surrounding circumstances, a deed conferring a right of way over property defined as 'lands' did not have the effect of granting to three separate dominant owners whose land abutted the way. Their entitlement was limited to a single point of access.

Extent to which loading and unloading on the way are permitted by a grant

4.96   In *Bulstrode v Lambert*,[126] a conveyance reserved a right of way 'to pass and repass with or without vehicles over and along the land coloured brown on the plan for the purposes of obtaining access to the building at the rear of the said premises and known as the auction mart'.

4.97   A dispute arose as to whether the owner of the dominant owner could make use of the yard over which the right of way applied, for loading and unloading. Some vehicles halted for appreciable periods of time. The court held that reasonable stopping for loading and unloading vehicles was permitted:

'The whole question is: What is the true construction of the reservation in the conveyance? Mr Campbell says, and with much force, that it is a right "to pass and

---

[125]   [2008] EWHC 1295 (Ch).
[126]   [1953] 1 WLR 1064.

repass ... over and along the right of way. That is something which connotes motion: a right to pass and repass ... He concedes that of course in the case of the ordinary putting down of a passenger there must be a halt for a brief moment, but that is a matter of de minimis ... In my judgment ... the vehicles must be entitled to remain in the yard for such time as is necessary to enable the plaintiff to enjoy his easement of bringing vehicles into the yard; that is, for such time as it takes to load and unload the vehicles. It is only an incident of the right of way expressly granted and may be described as ancillary to that easement, because without that right he cannot substantially enjoy that which has been reserved to him.'

4.98 In *McIlraith v Grady*[127] a right was granted 'with or without horses, carts and carriages to pass and repass through over and along' a yard at the rear of a pub to shop premises. Subsequently the shop also became a sub-post office and the pub became a home. It was held that the grant of the right of way for vehicles, construed in the light of the circumstances of the premises at that date, included a right for vehicles to stop for a reasonable time to load and unload. Lord Denning MR said:

'There was necessarily imported, in addition to the actual right to pass and repass, also a right to stop for a reasonable time for the purpose of loading and unloading.'

4.99 On the other hand, any implied right of this kind does not allow persistent obstruction of the way, for example by vehicles or people queuing to use some facility or attraction provided by or authorised by the dominant owner. So in *Fanigun Pty Ltd v Woolworths Ltd*[128] the supreme court of Queensland held that where a service station was used in a way which resulted in vehicles queuing on the way to enter the service station, such stopping being impliedly authorised by the dominant owner, there had been breaches of an easement which granted *full and free right and privilege at all times hereafter by day or night with or without horses cattle or other animals carts carriages motor cars and other vehicles of any description laden or unladen for all purposes to go pass and repass along through and over [the servient land]*. Both grantor and grantee covenanted not to obstruct the right of way or park or leave any vehicle thereon. Mullins J said:

'[76] Each of the words "go pass and repass" imply motion. That is reinforced by condition 1 of the grant which prohibits both the grantor and the grantee from obstructing the subject land for the purpose of the right of way that is exercisable by the grantee in common with the grantor. It was suggested on behalf of Woolworths that condition 1 should be construed so that the obligation not to obstruct in any way the use of the subject land was limited to obstruction of the subject land involving things other than vehicles on the basis that there was included in condition 1 a specific obligation not to park or leave any motor vehicle, plant or machinery on the subject land which exhausted the restrictions proposed in respect of motor vehicles. I reject that construction of condition 1. The obligation of the parties not to obstruct in any way the use of the subject land

---

[127] [1968] 1 QB 468.
[128] [2006] WSC 28.

supports the intention of the parties to the grant that the subject land be used by the grantee to gain access to Lot 1 in common with the grantor continuing to use the subject land to gain access to the balance of Lots 7 and 8. The inclusion in condition 1 of the specific prohibition on parking or leaving of motor vehicles, plant or machinery on the subject land does not, in the context of the easement, limit the general prohibition contained in condition 1 against obstructing in any way the use of the subject land for the purpose of the right of way in common with the rights of access exercisable over the subject land by the grantor. Conditions 2 and 4 of the easement also serve to emphasise the importance of the right of access to the balance of Lots 7 and 8 retained by the grantor.

[77] Construing the easement according to its terms suggests that queuing of vehicles which results in the vehicles being stopped for a measurable time (even if it is measurable only in seconds or a minute or a few minutes) on a repetitive basis does not fall within the right "to go pass and repass" over the subject land. That makes relevant another principle of construction of an easement which permits reference to be made to the circumstances existing at the time the grant was made for the purpose of construing the easement where an assertion is made that the easement provides for rights beyond those expressly described in the easement'.

4.100 The court rejected various arguments put forward by the dominant owner, including that:

(a)   the dominant land was used and intended to continue to be used as a service station with the subject land as the sole means of entry to it;

(b)   the terms of the easement contemplated that it would still be used by the occupier of other land thereby creating the potential for congestion which might result in vehicles stopping on the subject land;

(c)   the easement was granted to widen and replace the area that had been the subject of a prior lease to facilitate the operation of the service station on the dominant land;

(d)   it was common ground at the time of the grant that the grantee intended to expand the service station substantially; and

(e)   a significant sum was paid for the grant of the easement.

In *Chatham Industries Ltd v Incorporated Owners of Gold King Industrial Building*[129] it was held that a right to use a way for vehicles included the ancillary rights to stop to pick up and set down passengers and to load and unload vehicles. Although the plaintiffs had a right to the use of a car parking space it was non-exclusive. Sometimes they would have to stop temporarily on the road to pick up and set down.

---

[129]   [2011] HKEC 605 CA.

Bulstrode was distinguished by Millett J in *London and Suburban Land and Building Co (Holdings) Ltd v Carey*,[130] on the grounds that in *Bulstrode* there was an express grant of a right of way to bring vehicles carrying furniture along the passageway subject to the easement, and take goods from an auction mart along the passageway. Due to the access routes, this was impossible unless vehicles could stop on the passageway. There was no such factor in *London and Suburban Land and Building Co*, and so loading and unloading was not permitted under the easement. It is also possible to prevent loading and unloading from being permitted under the easement, by stating so in the terms of the grant: *Jalnarne v Ridewood*.[131]

The effect of purported grant of rights over the route of roads to be constructed in the future

4.101   The classic statement here is that of Lord Parker in *Pwllbach Colliery v Woodman*.[132] His Lordship grouped implied easements under two heads: first, those implied because they are ancillary to rights expressly granted; and secondly, those implied because they are necessary to give effect to the manner in which the land retained or demised was intended to be used:

> 'The law will readily imply the grant or reservation of such easements as may be necessary to give effect to the common intention of the parties to a grant of real property, with reference to the manner or purposes in and for which the land granted or some land retained by the grantor is to be used ... But it is essential for this purpose that the parties should intend that the subject of the grant or the land retained by the grantor should be used in some definite and particular manner. It is not enough that the subject of the grant or the land retained should be intended to be used in a manner which may or may not involve this definite and particular use.'

4.102   There are thus two requirements for the implication of an easement of intended use:

(a)   the parties must, at the time of grant, have shared an intention, either express or implied, that the land demised or retained should be used for a particular purpose; and

(b)   the easement must be necessary to give effect to that intended use.

4.103   In *Moncrieff v Jamieson*[133] Lord Neuberger (at paragraphs 110 and 112) distinguished rights implied under the rule in *Wheeldon v Burrows* from rights which arise under the following principle, namely that:

---

[130]   (1991) 62 P & CR 480.
[131]   (1991) 61 P & CR 143.
[132]   [1915] AC 634 (at 646–7).
[133]   [2007] 1 WLR 2620.

'the grant of an easement is prima facie also the grant of such ancillary rights as are reasonably necessary to its exercise or enjoyment – per Parker J in *Jones v Pritchard* [1908] 1 Ch 630 at 638. Subsequently, in *Pwllbach Colliery Company Ltd v Woodman* [1915] AC 634 at 646 to 647, the same judge, then Lord Parker of Waddington, described the decision in *Jones v Pritchard* as being within a "class of cases in which easements impliedly may be created", not because of "the terms of the grant itself", but because of "the circumstances under which the grant was made"... there are cases where a right is implied because it is "reasonably necessary" for the "exercise or enjoyment" of an expressly granted right (as in *Jones v Pritchard*). In the [this] type of case, it seems to me important to focus on the dual nature of the requirement that the alleged implied right be "reasonably necessary"'.

4.104 Lord Hope went as far as to say that, although the extent of any right granted must be construed in the light of the circumstances at the date of the grant:

'It is not necessary for it to be shown that all the rights that are later claimed as necessary for the comfortable use and enjoyment of the [easement] were actually in use at that date. It is sufficient that they may be considered to have been in contemplation at the time of the grant, having regard to what the dominant proprietor might reasonably be expected to do in the exercise of his right to convenient and comfortable use of the property.'

4.105 In *Adam v Shrewsbury*[134] the issue arose whether the claimant/respondent had been granted a right of way, when she purchased her house, over retained land of the vendor. The conveyance provided as follows:

'The purchaser [ie the claimant] hereby covenants with the vendor [Mr Thomas] that within a reasonable time after the vendor has at his own expense excavated the garage space hatched blue on the plan hereto annexed to the level indicated on the site plan she will erect a stock proof fence along the [south-eastern and south western] boundaries [including the three protruding sides of the site hatched blue] separating the property hereby conveyed [ie Tan-y-Ffordd] from the adjoining land of the vendors [ie Bryn Coed] and the purchaser further covenants that she and her successors in title will thereafter be responsible for maintaining and repairing the said fence.'

4.106 The site of the garage space was included in the conveyance. The whole site sloped steeply uphill from the road. Planning permission had been granted for a development including the construction of a garage, and of a road leading to it, but neither had been built. At the time of the conveyance garage site was virgin rock, and the road petered out at the hairpin bend which would have led to the site of the garage. It was held that the claimant had no right of way over the route of the road to the garage space, because whilst the parties shared an intention that she should have a right, this was only to arise when the road and the space were constructed. Neuberger LJ said:

---

[134] [2005] EWCA 1006.

'As I see it, that implied right was either a contractual entitlement to claim a right of way over the whole of the road if and when the relevant work was carried out, or, as seems to me to be the better analysis, an immediate right of way, but one which could only be enjoyed once the north-western section of the road had been constructed. Unfortunately for the claimant, whichever of those two is the proper analysis, her claim must fail.'

4.107 In *Davies v Bramwell*[135] an implied grant of the right to drive vehicles over a garage forecourt was held to have been created where land containing a vehicle ramp used by large vehicles was conveyed. The contemplated use of this land for maintenance of such vehicles which could only gain access across the retained forecourt demonstrated the common intention of the parties to make such a grant. However, in *Chaffe v Kingsley*[136] it was held that there was no reservation of a right of way in the absence of clear evidence of the common intention of the parties.

4.108 On the other hand, In *Changeinvest Ltd v Rosendale-Steinhausen*[137] the conveyance contained a reservation of a right of way subject to a proviso that the vendor would make up a road along the strip of land by a certain date. Two points arose. Firstly, whether the successor in title of the vendor could exercise the right of way at all, since the obligation to make up the road, so it was argued, being a positive one, could not bind the successor. Therefore, since the obligation to make up the road was a condition precedent to the right to exercise the right of way, the right of way was now defunct.

4.109 The second argument was whether the obligation to make up the road within the time limit was a condition precedent to using the right of way at all. The judge held that this was not the case, but that the right of way could not be exercised until the road was made up. On the first point, he construed the terms of the conveyance not as imposing a positive obligation but as creating a framework for the exercise of the right of way.

When will a right to park be included in the grant?

4.110 A right of way does not normally include a right to park, although loading and unloading may be permissible. In *J & O Operations Ltd v Kingston and St Andrew Corporation*,[138] the Privy Council found that, even if they had found an easement of way along a road, it would not have led to an easement of necessity for parking: it was not 'necessary for the comfortable enjoyment of an easement of way: commercial premises are commonly operated without the benefit of adjacent private parking'. The right to park may, subject to the points discussed below, be granted as an easement.[139] The same view was taken

---

[135] [2007] EWCA Civ 821.
[136] [2000] 1 EGLR 104.
[137] [2004] EWHC 264.
[138] [2012] 2 P & CR 4.
[139] *London & Blenheim Estates v Ladbroke Retail Parks* [1992] 1 WLR 1278.

by the Court of Appeal in *Hair v Gillman*.[140] In that case, Mrs Gillman successfully claimed a right to park her car on some land beside her property. She had originally been a tenant of her property and was given permission to park on the land during this period. The right was converted into an easement by virtue of section 62 of the LPA 1925 when she purchased her property.

4.111 A right to park in a designated space may amount to a tenancy or an exclusive licence, but normally the right will be one to park in any free space in an area. The question then arises how far these rights extend. *Saeed v Plustrade*[141] shows that excessive loss of spaces is actionable. In *Montrose Court Holdings Ltd v Shamash*[142] the landlord of an estate of houses and flats with car parking sought to impose a paying permit system of one per household. The defendants (S) who owned the freehold of one of the houses sought declarations that they enjoyed an easement of parking and that the proposed system and tariff were unlawful interferences with it. The Court of Appeal held that S had a right to park in common with the tenants of the flats and other home owners on the estate. They had a right to compete for spaces on the service road. This was not reduced by the regulations. The purpose of the regulations was to enable those with the right to park to compete for spaces in an orderly way. Accordingly the scheme was valid, including a provision limiting parking to 72 hours at any one time, and to one permit per household.

4.112 Parking on a way may in practice not be actionable if it does not prevent use of the way by the dominant owner. In *Smith v Garrard*[143] the issue arose whether an injunction should be granted to restrain parking of vehicles on a private road. A covenant had been imposed in the following terms:

> 'Not at any time to park vehicles upon or place any articles upon or in any way obstruct the free passage of any part of the Roadway over which other persons have rights of way.'

4.113 The roadway included verges and the right of way extended to these as well as the metalled portion. The defendant claimed to be entitled to park on the verge since it did not obstruct free passage, and the Court of Appeal agreed. Chadwick LJ at [32] said:

> 'The words are there to indicate that the parts of the roadway on which vehicles are not to be parked are those parts on which the parking of vehicles would obstruct rights of way. They are not there to impose an absolute obligation against parking vehicles which do not interfere with the rights of way but which may be regarded as aesthetically unattractive or an annoyance.'

In *Moncrieff v Jamieson*, a Scottish case, the House of Lords considered a servitude giving a right of way, which led to a house which was, due to its

---

[140] [2000] 3 EGLR 74.
[141] [2002] 2 EGLR 19 CA.
[142] [2006] EWCA Civ 251.
[143] [2004] EWCA 1655.

location, inaccessible by any vehicle. The right of way was vital in order to allow access to a public road. Moreover, the Sheriff had found that the dominant tenement was not reasonably capable of comfortable enjoyment without the right to park cars on the servient tenement. By the time the matter reached the House of Lords, the only remaining issue was whether the right of way included a right to park. The House of Lords held that there could be an implied right to park along the road over which there was a right of way. Further matters were considered by the House of Lords in obiter discussion, considered further below.

In *Waterman v Boyle*,[144] the dominant tenement had a right of way along a driveway, and two parking spaces in front of the house. The question before the Court of Appeal was whether there was also a right to park along the driveway. The Court of Appeal applied *Moncrieff v Jamieson* and held that there was no such right to park on the driveway. An express right of parking had been included in the grant, and therefore there was none to be implied over the driveway. Arden LJ at [31] held:

> 'In my judgment, if the parties had intended any further right of parking there would have been an indication to that effect in the transfer. Nothing in the surrounding circumstances at the time of the transfer supports the implication of any further right. I would indeed go further and hold that, where there is an express right attaching to the same property of a similar character to the right which is sought to be implied, it is most unlikely that the further right will arise by implication. The circumstances would have to be quite exceptional.'

It was held that *Moncrieff* should be viewed as having been decided on its own special facts, in that, due to the unusual access arrangements to the dominant land, it was reasonably necessary to park on the land subject to the right of way. It was not possible to park on the dominant tenement, and the closest it would have been possible to park (otherwise than on the right of way) would have involved a walk of around 150 yards. Lord Hope held at [34] of *Moncrieff* 'In my opinion it is impossible to reconcile such hardships with the use that might reasonably have been expected to be made of the servitude right of vehicular access for the convenient and comfortable use of the property.' This factor did not arise in *Waterman*, and so the result was different to *Moncrieff*. It should be noted that the facts in *Moncrieff* were undoubtedly unusual: Lord Neuberger referred at [124] to 'the unusual facts of the case'.

Grant of exclusive right to use land for parking etc

4.114 An easement is a right over land falling short of ownership. Rights to exclusive possession of land are not recognised as easements, although they may give rise to claims for possessory title.[145] The rule that an easement which amounts to a claim for ownership will not be valid was affirmed in *Mulvaney v*

---

[144] [2009] EWCA Civ 115; [2009] 2 EGLR 7.

[145] See for example *Hanina v Morland* (2000) 97 (47) LSG 41 (exclusive use of a flat roof not an easement passing under s 62 of the LPA 1925).

Gough,[146] a case where the right to use land as a communal garden was held not to give an exclusive right of occupation, nor to prevent the owner from building a driveway across the land. This case also confirms that a prescriptive easement of access to communal gardens for recreational purposes is capable of being acquired.[147]

4.115 In Batchelor v Marlow:[148]

(a) A owned an unadopted dirt road. The public right of way did not extend to the verges.

(b) R owned a garage nearby and claimed by prescription the right to park six vehicles on the verges of the road, Monday to Friday, 8.30 am to 6.30 pm.

(c) There was only space for six vehicles on the verges.

4.116 The Court of Appeal laid down the following principles:

(a) 'There can be no prescriptive right in the nature of a servitude or easement so large as to preclude the ordinary uses of property by the owner of the land affected ...'

(b) 'The essential question is one of degree. If the right granted in relation to the area over which it is to be exercisable is such that it would leave the servient owner without any reasonable use of his land, whether for parking or other purposes, it could not be an easement though it might be some larger or different grant.'

(c) There was some debate (not resolved) as to whether a right to park could be acquired by prescription.

4.117 The issue was reviewed in *Moncreiff v Jamieson*, considered above. This case is unusual in two respects. The first is that it was an appeal from Scotland. The second is that the narrowness of the actual issue in dispute somewhat belies the potential breadth of the principles enunciated in some of the speeches. As the House of Lords noted (see paragraphs 46 and 107), the express grant of a vehicular right of way does not necessarily or indeed usually carry with it a right to park vehicles on the servient land. Courts have, depending on the circumstances and since the case of *Bulstrode v Lambert*,[149] been prepared to allow temporary parking for the purposes of loading and unloading as an implied incident of an expressly granted right of way.

---

[146] [2002] 3 EGLR 72.
[147] For the validity of an express grant of such an easement see *Re Ellenborough Park* [1956] 1 Ch 131.
[148] (2001) 82 P & CR 36.
[149] [1953] 1 WLR 1064.

4.118   However, there has been a debate as to whether a right to park within a defined area can, by itself, constitute an easement. There has always been a conceptual difficulty because of what has become known as 'the ouster principle'. It is generally accepted that an easement cannot give to the dominant owner 'exclusive and unrestricted use of a piece of land'. In *Copeland v Greenhalf*,[150] a claim was made by a wheelwright to a prescriptive easement to use a strip of land belonging to the defendant, and adjacent to a roadway, to store his customers' vehicles awaiting and undergoing repair and awaiting collection following their repair. Mr Justice Upjohn rejected the claim on the following basis:

> 'I think that the right claimed goes wholly outside any normal idea of an easement, that is, the right of the owner or the occupier of a dominant tenement over a servient tenement. This claim (to which no closely related authority has been referred to me) really amounts to a claim to a joint user of the land by the defendant. Practically, the defendant is claiming the whole beneficial user of the strip of land .... He can leave as many or as few lorries there as he likes for as long as he likes; he may enter on it by himself, his servants and agents to do repair work thereon. In my judgment, that is not a claim which can be established as an easement. It is virtually a claim to possession of the servient tenement, if necessary to the exclusion of the owner; or, at any rate, to a joint user, and no authority has been cited to me which would justify the conclusion that a right of this wide and undefined nature can be the proper subject-matter of an easement. It seems to me that to succeed, this claim must amount to a successful claim of possession by reason of long adverse possession.'

4.119   The clearest modern illustration is *Batchelor v Marlow*,[151] the facts of which have already been noted. The Court of Appeal rejected this claim to an easement and asked itself the question: does an exclusive right to park six cars for nine and a half hours every working day leave the defendant without any reasonable use of his land whether for parking or anything else? They answered that question in the affirmative.

4.120   The facts of the *Moncreiff* case were simple. It involved a house called 'Da Store' situated in the Shetland Isles. The house and garden had previously been part of land owned by the defender. It was sold off in 1973. It was situated at some distance from the nearest public highway and thus the 1973 conveyance granted to the owners: 'a right of access from the branch public road.' The house lies at the foot of a steep escarpment on the foreshore. There is pedestrian access over the defender's land by one route. Vehicles cannot be driven onto any part of the land and there was only one means of vehicular access over another defined route. It was common ground both that the owners of Da Store had an express vehicular right of way over the defender's land and that the express right of way carried with it an implied right to stop vehicles on the servient land in order to turn, load and unload. However the dispute arose because the owners of Da Store claimed for themselves and their licensees a right to park vehicles on that part of the servient land closest to Da Store

---

[150]   [1952] Ch 488.
[151]   (2001) 82 P&CR 36.

generally. They claimed it in two subtly different ways. First, they claimed that the right to park was implied as a necessary ancillary right to their expressly granted vehicular right of way (but not an easement in itself). Secondly, and in the alternative, they claimed that the express grant of the vehicular right of way carried with it an implied easement to park.

4.121 The House of Lords, with varying degrees of enthusiasm, held that there was such a right to park implied into the express right of way because it was 'necessary for the comfortable use and enjoyment of the right expressly granted'. Thus far the case is simply an illustration of the grant of an implied easement.

4.122 One of the arguments raised by the defenders was that, as a matter of law, the right to park could not be an easement at all. All of their Lordships held that it could. Lords Hope and Rodger held that it could be so under the law of Scotland (paragraphs 22, 24 and 75) whilst Lords Scott and Neuberger held that the same applied under English law (paragraphs 47, 102 and 136 to 140).

4.123 Lord Scott dealt at length with the ouster principle. He went so far as to suggest that the traditional test was wrong and should be replaced with a test which asks (paragraph 59): 'whether the servient owner retains possession and, subject to the reasonable exercise of the right in question, control of the servient land.'

4.124 In his view, sole use of a tract of land by a dominant owner to park a vehicle was not inconsistent with a servient owner's retention of possession. Thus presumably, in his view, a right to park a single vehicle in a designated spot was capable of being an easement. Nor is there any difference between the characteristics of an easement acquired by express grant and those of one acquired by prescription.

4.125 Lord Neuberger was more circumspect. He said (at paragraph 137):

> 'In my judgment, the grant of a right to park a single vehicle anywhere on a servient tenement which is large enough to hold, say, twenty vehicles, must be capable of being a servitude or an easement. In such a case, there is no specific place where the vehicle is to be parked, so that there is no specific area from which the servient owner can be said to be excluded ....'

4.126 He continued:

> '... If the right to park a vehicle in an area that can hold twenty vehicles is capable of being a servitude or an easement, then it would logically follow that the same conclusion should apply to an area that can hold two vehicles. On that basis, it can be said to be somewhat contrary to common sense that the arrangement is debarred from being a servitude or an easement simply because the parties have chosen to identify a precise space in the area, over which the right is to be exercised, and the space is just big enough to hold the vehicle ... At least as at

present advised, I am not satisfied that a right is prevented from being a servitude or an easement simply because the right granted would involve the servient owner being effectively excluded from the property.'

4.127 He concluded (at paragraph 143):

'Accordingly, I see considerable force in the views expressed by Lord Scott in paras 57 and 59 of his opinion, to the effect that a right can be an easement notwithstanding that the dominant owner effectively enjoys exclusive occupation, on the basis that the essential requirement that the servient owner retains possession and control. If that were the right test, then it seems likely that *Batchelor v Marlow* was wrongly decided. However, unless it is necessary to decide the point to dispose of this appeal, I consider that it would be dangerous to try and identify degree of ouster is required to disqualify a right from constituting a servitude or easement, given the very limited argument your Lordships have received on the topic.'

4.128 In *Holms v Ashford Estates Ltd*,[152] another Scottish case, the Inner House of the Court of Session considered a situation in which there had been a grant of a parking space (no 42), with right of way across an adjoining parking space (no 43). The finding of fact by the Sheriff was that it was not possible to park in the parking space which had the benefit of the servitude if there was a car parked in the servient tenement. Lord Eassie held:

'Servitude rights of vehicular access have long been recognised not only in Roman law and our law, but also in most legal systems. Naturally, the need to allow such access impedes the use to which the owner of the servient tenement may make of the land over which the access route lies. He may only make transient use of it while it is not required for access by the proprietor of the dominant tenement. The argument for the pursuers on the "ouster" issue is, in our view, essentially predicated on the contention to which we have already referred that by conveying to Ms Mason the area of ground described as car parking space 43 the defenders effectively warranted to her that the area of ground was fit for the purpose of parking a motor vehicle and could not be subject to any servitude right which might interfere with that particular user [that contention having already been rejected].'

The Inner House found that the description of parking space 43 as a parking space was not determinative of its use; in fact, it was too small to be used to park a normal car. The space could therefore be used for a number of other purposes, such as setting out a chair or pot plants. The court held that it was not clear that the owner of parking space 43 would unquestionably win any 'battle of the parking spaces' with the users of parking space 42, and therefore the claim for damages for breach of warrandice would likely fail, although the case was in the end put out By Order.

In *RSN v Safestore*,[153] HHJ Cowell held that the claimants could take advantage of prescriptive rights to park on a road over which they had the

---

[152] [2009] CSIH 28; [2009] SLT 389.
[153] [2009] PLSCS 292.

benefit of an easement of way. This was so even though there was an express prohibition on parking. On the facts, the use of the road for parking by the claimants was not exclusive. It could be shared with the dominant owner of the land, since the land was not occupied constantly, and there would generally not be overlap in use between the claimants and the owners. HHJ Cowell was however keen to stress that this was decided the 'unusual circumstance in this case'.[154]

In *RSN*, HHJ Cowell said at [49]: 'I expect any court would be ... reluctant, to recognise, and so would not find, a right to park one's private car on a neighbour's land (except in the most unusual circumstances or "geography" illustrated by *Moncrieff*) for that would involve a high degree of permanent parking: all day and night except when the car is taken out, that being where the car is "kept" in the usual sense of the word.' However, it appears that a right to park in a defined area is now firmly entrenched amongst the panoply (if that is the appropriate word) of easements recognised by English law[155] and not just as an adjunct to a right of way and it can only be a matter of time before the courts recognise a right to park a vehicle in a single designated space as such an easement.

In *Virdi v Chana*,[156] HHJ Perle QC found that *Batchelor v Marlow* had not been overruled by *Moncrieff*, and therefore remained good law. The test applied was therefore whether the owner of the servient land would be left without any reasonable use of the land, thus rendering ownership illusory. On the facts, the level of ownership was found not to be illusory: the uses to which the land could be put were identified as planting a tree and tending it (or any replacement), placing and tending shrubs or plants, having access to maintain or repair a fence, or replace with a wall, and erect signs, and to alter the surface for aesthetic reasons.

In *Kettel v Bloomfield Ltd*[157] it was held that the grant in a lease of a flat of the sole right to use a designated parking space for parking a car or motorbike neither amounted to a demise of the space nor was invalid because the rights granted were so extensive as to deprive the grantor of any reasonable use of the land. The owner retained rights over the land: the owners could 'pass on foot or

---

[154] At [51].

[155] In *Moncrieff*, Lord Scott said at [47]: 'It is convenient to start with the question whether a servitudal right to park appurtenant to some identifiable dominant land, ie a right in rem and not simply a contractual right, is recognised by law. In my opinion there should be no doubt that it is and, if there is any such doubt, that doubt should be now dispelled.' Furthermore, Lord Neuberger said at [137]: 'In my judgment, the grant of a right to park a single vehicle anywhere on a servient tenement which is large enough to hold, say, twenty vehicles, must be capable of being a servitude or an easement.' However, Lord Hope does comment at [22] of *Moncrieff* that 'I doubt whether it is necessary for the purposes of this case to decide whether a right simply to park vehicles on someone else's land can be said to constitute a servitude in its own right, independently of a servitude right of way over that land by means of vehicles. So I would prefer to reserve my opinion on this point.'

[156] [2008] EWHC 2901 (Ch).

[157] [2012] EWHC 1422 (Ch).

by vehicle across the space freely if there is no vehicle parked on it for the time being or avoiding one that is. He may authorise others to do likewise (and has done so in the other estate leases). He may choose, change and repair the surface, keep it clean and remove obstructions (and is obliged to do so in providing the Services). He may lay pipes or other service media under it, as he may wish to do for the benefit of the estate buildings. He may in principle build above it ... or provide overhead projections such as wires.' The rights granted amounted to a valid easement.[158] Under the present approach, it appears that the courts have been creative in contemplating the possible uses to which the land could be used.

Diversion of the way

4.129 There is no unilateral right to divert the route of a private right of way.[159] But it is possible that a court may refuse an injunction to an aggrieved dominant owner if satisfied that he will not be prejudiced. This was the approach of the court in *Greenwich NHS Trust*. The facts involved a diversion of a right of way in order to form a safe road junction. There was no objection. The court issued a declaration that no person with rights over the way would be entitled to an injunction to prevent the diversion. In *Heslop v Bishton*[160] it was further held that the fact that the dominant owner may have a right to deviate on to the servient owner's land to avoid an obstruction does not mean that the obstruction is not actionable.

Reasonable use only

4.130 The general rule is that the grantee is only entitled to reasonable use of the way, not total freedom from obstructions at all times. Gates and traffic humps may be permissible provided that they are properly maintained. In *Saint v Jenner*[161] the servient owner of a lane metalled it, and this lead to vehicles driving too fast. He then installed speed humps which became a nuisance when potholes appeared, by then causing vehicles to bottom on the humps. The county court judge, upheld by the Court of Appeal, refused the dominant owner a mandatory injunction to remove the humps on the servient owner's undertaking to maintain the surface near them.

4.131 Where the issue relates to complaints of parking, other cars on the road, or other reduction of its effective area, the position is that this may in practice not be actionable if it does not prevent use of the way by the dominant owner. In *Smith v Garrard*[162] the issue arose whether an injunction should be granted to restrain parking of vehicles on a private road. A covenant had been imposed in the following terms: 'Not at any time to park vehicles upon or place

---

[158] See also para **1.43**. An ouster argument also failed in *Polo Woods Foundation v Shelton-Agar* [2009] EWHC 1361 (Ch) in the context of a claimed right to graze animals.
[159] *Greenwich Healthcare NHS Trust v London and Quadrant Housing Trust* [1998] 1 WLR 1749.
[160] (2009) 28 EG 86.
[161] [1972] 3 WLR 888.
[162] [2004] EWCA 1655.

any articles upon or in any way obstruct the free passage of any part of the Roadway over which other persons have rights of way.'

4.132   The roadway included verges and the right of way extended to these as well as the metalled portion. The defendant claimed to be entitled to park on the verge since it did not obstruct free passage, and the Court of Appeal agreed.

4.133   However, in *Celsteel Ltd v Alton House Holdings Ltd*[163] it was held that reducing the width of a driveway from 9 metres to 4.14 metres was a substantial interference with a right of way. A particular point taken into account by the court was that it prevented the dominant owners from driving forward or backwards into their garages. On the other hand in *West v Sharp*[164] it was held that there was no actionable interference with a right of way over a strip of land 40 feet wide by permanently narrowing it to a surfaced width of 13 feet or by placing a tree and concrete blocks to prevent driving outside this width.

4.134   In *B & Q Plc v Liverpool and Lancashire Properties Ltd*[165] the claimant had been granted an express right of way over a large service area. Due to a problem of stock thefts, the claimant would only allow one vehicle into its premises at a time to unload, with other vehicles waiting in the service area. The defendant, who wanted to develop part of the service area, argued that the right of way did not allow the claimant to use the yard for waiting vehicles. The claim succeeded. The court said that if a grantee has contracted for the luxury of an ample right, he was not to be deprived of it merely because the reduced non-ample right would be all that was reasonably required. It found that the reduction proposed meant that the right of way could not be exercised as substantially and practically as previously. In *Saeed v Plustrade Ltd*[166] a lessee was granted under her lease 'a right in common with all other persons entitled to the like right to park his private motor car on such part of the Retained Property as may from time to time be specified by the lessor as reserved for car parking when space is available and subject to such regulations as the lessor may make from time to time'. The complete inability of the lessee to park in the forecourt area for a period of over three years whilst refurbishment works were carried out was a clear derogation from grant. A subsequent reduction from 13 spaces to 4 was also a substantial interference with her rights.

4.135   Restrictions in the form of regulations or barriers may be actionable depending on their practical effect. In *Sisters of the Sacred Heart v Kingston upon Thames RBC*[167] a proposal to install an unmanned code-operated barrier was held to be a substantial interference with an express statutory right of way over a road leading to an estate, on the ground that it would impede large categories of authorised visitors who were unaware of the code or who could

---

[163]   [1985] 1 WLR 204.
[164]   79 P & CR 327 CA.
[165]   (2001) 81 P & CR 20.
[166]   [2002] 2 EGLR 19 CA.
[167]   LTL 28/3/08 CA.

not readily ascertain it. In *Montrose Court Holdings Ltd v Shamash*[168] noted above, the landlord of an estate of houses and flats with car parking sought to impose a paying permit system of one per household. The defendants (S) who owned the freehold of one of the houses sought declarations that they enjoyed an easement of parking and that the proposed system and tariff were unlawful interferences with it. The Court of Appeal held that S had a right to park in common with the tenants of the flats and other home owners on the estate. They had a right to compete for spaces on the service road. This was not reduced by the regulations. The purpose of the regulations was to enable those with the right to park to compete for spaces in an orderly way. Accordingly the scheme was valid, including a provision limiting parking to 72 hours at any one time, and to one permit per household.

4.136 Where the road over which a right of way is granted includes visibility splays, the servient owner may be liable if he obstructs these for derogating from his grant. This was the situation in *Carter v Cole*[169] where the effect of the derogation was to result in a refusal by the local authority to renew a temporary planning permission, leading to a major commercial tenant of the dominant owner vacating its premises. A mandatory injunction was granted.

4.137 Finally, there are situations where the complaint is that the servient owner is not sufficiently careful enough to stop his tenants or other users obstructing the way by parking. The servient owner may be liable for obstructing the way if he fails to take steps to prevent others doing so.[170] In *Hilton v James Smith & Sons (Norwood)*[171] the servient owner, who had granted the dominant owner, who was one of his tenants, a right of way by the lease, was held liable for failing to take proper steps to ensure that his tenants did not obstruct the road. By failing to take steps to enforce covenants in the leases and suing the tenants for trespass he had caused or continued a nuisance. A prohibitory injunction was granted. In the course of his judgment Ormrod LJ said:

> 'However the matter is framed in law, it seems to me to be plain that there comes a stage when an occupier of land, who is well aware that his tenants, or his licensees, are behaving in such a way as to obstruct a private road and thus to interfere with the rights-of-way that he has granted to other tenants, when the occupier of the roadway comes under a duty to act in the matter.'

4.138 In *Ridewood v Jalarne*[172] the owner of an industrial estate had a right of way over a road which was owned by the defendant who also used it for access to his retained land which he used for business. The defendant was held liable to the plaintiff for enclosing part of the road to use as a compound, and for unlawful parking on the road, and the occupants of the industrial estate were

---

[168] [2006] EWCA Civ 251.
[169] [2009] EWCA Civ 410.
[170] See *Hilton v James Smith & Sons (Norwood)* [1979] 2 EGLR 44 and *Ridewood v Jalnarne* (1989) 61 P & CR 143.
[171] [1979] 2 EGLR 44.
[172] (1989) 61 P & CR 143.

held liable to the defendant for authorising, assisting, procuring or encouraging unlawful parking on the road by vehicles making deliveries. The court granted an injunction to prevent the occupiers of the estate from allowing persons to use the road except if they ensured that such persons did not obstruct the road. The practical implications for owners of large estates who grant rights of way over estate roads are inconvenient. In *Crane Road Properties v Hundalani*[173] Charles Aldous QC held[174] that the same applied if the road was left obstructed by fly-tipping which was attracted by the state of the land. The same case reaffirms the general rule that the servient owner is not liable to repair the way. Where he has an express right to claim a contribution to the cost of repairs he cannot recover costs in respect of works going beyond repairs and which involve upgrading the road.

Extent of easements of necessity

4.139 An easement of necessity is implied only where the right is essential for the use of the land granted or retained. The question is not whether it is necessary for the reasonable enjoyment of the land, but whether the land can be used at all without the implied grant or reservation. A claim will only be successful where the land is 'absolutely inaccessible or useless' without the easement (see e g *Union Lighterage v London Graving Dock*[175]). An easement will not be implied by this route merely because it makes it more convenient to use the land. The right will be strictly limited.[176]

4.140 For example, a right of way will not be implied by necessity where there is some other means of access, even if that route is difficult and expensive to use.[177]

4.141 In *Sweet v Sommer*[178] the facts were slightly unusual. An individual, Mr Lovering, owned three plots of land, one of which could only be accessed over the other two. Two of the plots were put by the individual in the name of himself and his wife, but without reserving rights of access to the third, which he retained in his sole name. Both parcels of land later came into the hands of third parties. Hart J held that the transfer of the first two plots of land reserved by implication a way of necessity which was an overriding interest.

4.142 Hart J, unusually, was prepared to hold that a *vehicular* right of way was a way of necessity, as the Loverings clearly contemplated that the piece of land retained by Mr Lovering alone would be developed by the construction of a house. Hart J also upheld a claim based on proprietary estoppel, on the basis that the Loverings would have been estopped from denying that the right of

---

[173] [2006] EWHC 2066 (Ch).

[174] At [70].

[175] [1902] 2 Ch 577.

[176] See also *Colquhoun v Harris* (High Court of Justice Chancery Division 19 March 2010 LTL 8/4/2010.

[177] See e g *Barry V Haseldine* [1952] Ch 835.

[178] [2004] EWHC 1504 (Ch).

way existed, and their successors were bound as the right fell within Rule 258 of the Land Registration Rules 1925, as it was, openly exercised and enjoyed.

4.143 On appeal[179] the decision was upheld on other grounds, essentially that the land enjoyed overriding rights of way which entitled the claimants to seek rectification of the register.

4.144 The most obvious example of a situation in which an easement of necessity may be implied is where a grantor conveys an entire plot of land except for a piece in the middle, which is completely surrounded by the part conveyed. Unless the reservation of a right of way over the land granted is implied, the land in the centre would be completely landlocked.

RECTIFICATION

4.145 Generally, the remedy of equitable rectification is available in the following circumstances:[180]

(a)   there is a written instrument;

(b)   which fails to record with the true agreement between the parties;

(c)   which failure to record arose either:

  (i)   from a common mistake (sometimes, 'mutual' or 'bilateral mistake'); or

  (ii)   from a mistake by one party which the other remained silent about so as to profit therefrom ('unilateral mistake'); and

(d)   where no other remedy is suitable to correct the mistake.

4.146 The courts always approach the remedy of rectification with real caution. As Lord Chelmsford LC said, in *Fowler v Fowler*:[181]

'The power which the court possesses of reforming written agreements where there has been an omission or insertion of stipulations contrary to the intention of the parties and under a mutual mistake is one which has been frequently and most usefully exercised. **But it is also one which should be used with extreme care and caution. To substitute a new agreement for one which the parties have deliberately subscribed ought only to be permitted upon evidence of the clearest and most satisfactory description.** It is clear that a person who seeks to rectify a deed upon the ground of mistake must be required to establish, in the clearest and most satisfactory manner, that **the alleged intention to which he desires it to be made**

---

[179]   [2005] EWCA Civ 227.
[180]   ·McGee, *Snell's Equity* (31st edn, 2000 and 5th supplement, 2009), paras 14-14 to 14-18.
[181]   ·(1859) 4 De G&J 250; 45 ER 97, 264–5; 103.

conformable continued concurrently in the minds of all parties down to the time of execution, and also must be able to shew exactly and precisely the form to which the deed ought to be brought.'

4.147 It follows from this caution that claims in rectification require very convincing evidence and strict proof.

4.148 Useful guidance as to the standard of proof required to found a claim in rectification can be found in *Thomas Bates and Son Ltd v Wyndham's (Lingerie) Ltd*:[182]

> 'The requisite degree of cogency of proof will vary with the nature of the facts to be established and the circumstances of the case. I would say that in civil proceedings a fact must be proved with that degree of certainty which justice requires in the circumstances of the particular case. In every case the balance of probability must be discharged, but in some cases that balance may be more easily tipped than in others.'

4.149 Buckley LJ then cited with approval Denning LJ's rejection, in *Hornal v Neuberger Products Ltd*, of the application of the criminal burden of proof to civil cases.[183]

4.150 Although the burden of proof is, therefore, 'on the balance of probabilities', the courts are still very reluctant to rectify a negotiated and professionally drafted document without strong and convincing proof of there being a defect which causes the document to *not* reflect an aspect of the agreement reached between the parties, especially when it is a professionally drafted document. An expression often used in the older cases is 'strong, irrefragable evidence'.[184] The underlying rationale for the 'balance of probabilities' being actually more onerous in some cases than in other has been recently explained in these terms by Chadwick LJ in *Fuller v Strum*:[185]

> '[70] ... Lord Nicholls of Birkenhead *[said]* in *Re H (minors)* that "Where matters in issue are facts the standard of proof required in non-criminal proceedings is the

---

[182]   [1981] 1 WLR 505, 520, per Buckley LJ, with Brightman LJ agreeing (CA).

[183]   [1957] 1 QB 247, 258. The criminal standard is, of course, 'beyond reasonable doubt'.

[184]   *Countess Dowager of Shelburn v Earl of Inchiquin* (1784) 1 Bro CC 338, 341; 35 ER 137, 356 'the evidence which goes to prove that the words, taken down in writing were contrary to the concurrent intention of all parties must be strong, irrefragable evidence' per Lord Thurlow LC. The term has more recently applied by Neuberger J in *Oceanic Village Ltd v Shirayama Shokusan Co Ltd* [1999] EGCS 83. The learned judge found himself unable to give credence to the evidence of the crucial witnesses for either party, and had no documentary evidence which supported either party. Accordingly, the Judge dismissed the case on the ground that the 'strong, irrefragable evidence' required was simply not made out by the party seeking rectification.

[185]   [2001] EWCA Civ 1879; [2002] 2 All ER 87 (CA). The relevant citations for the cases cited are *Re H (Minors)* [1996] AC 563, 586–7 *per* Lord Nicholls and *Wintle v Nye* [1959] 1 WLR 284, 291 *per* Viscount Simonds. *Fuller v Strum* is a probate case, not concerning rectification, but the point made about the inherent flexibility of the civil burden of proof is a general one. *Re H* was a case under the Children Act 1989, relating to care orders, and *Wintle v Nye* was a probate case.

preponderance of probability, usually referred to as the balance of probability". But, as Lord Nicholls went on to point out there was *"[b]uilt into the preponderance of probability standard … a generous degree of flexibility in respect of the seriousness of the allegation"*. Lord Nicholls said:

> "This approach also provides a means by which the balance of probability standard can accommodate one's instinctive feeling that even in civil proceedings a court should be more sure before finding serious allegations proved than when deciding less serious or trivial matters."

[71] It is, I think, this flexibility of approach within the civil standard of proof which lies behind the observations of Viscount Simonds in *Wintle v Nye*:

> "In all cases the court must be vigilant and jealous. The degree of suspicion will vary with the circumstances of the case. It may be slight and easily dispelled. It may, on the other hand, be so grave that it can hardly be removed. In the present case, the circumstances were such as to impose on the respondent as heavy a burden as can well be imagined.'"

4.151 So, for example in *George Wimpey UK Ltd v VI Construction Ltd*, the case foundered on a lack of minutes of the relevant board meetings which discussed the contract of which rectification was sought.[186] The court thought it 'a matter of speculation' whether the board was, in fact, mistaken as to the terms of the contract.[187]

4.152 The first condition for a claim founded on mutual (or bilateral) mistake is that a party seeking rectification must show that there was a common mistake in the document of which rectification is sought. The alleged mistake here must be the result of an error common to both parties, not the result of one party changing its mind. Rectification is a way of undoing an error in the drafting of a document, so that it accurately reflects the bargain struck between the parties: it is *not* a way of preventing one party to a negotiation from changing its mind prior to the execution of an agreement: see Lord Chelmsford LC, above, in *Fowler v Fowler*.[188]

4.153 The elements which a party seeking rectification by reason of a bilateral mistake must prove have been most conveniently summarised by Peter Gibson LJ, when giving the leading judgment in *Swainland Builders Ltd v Freehold Properties Ltd*:[189]

> '[33] The party seeking rectification must show that:

---

[186] [2005] EWCA Civ 77; [2005] 2 P&CR DG5, per Blackburne J, at [83].
[187] Why should the courts be so concerned about evidence in rectification claims, whereas they ascribe all sorts of intentions to parties in construction cases without any evidence at all?
[188] (1859) 4 De G & J 250; 45 ER 97, 264–5; 103.
[189] [2002] 2 EGLR 71, 74 (CA). Jonathan Parker LJ agreed; there was no third Lord Justice.

(1)   the parties had a common continuing intention, whether or not amounting
      to an agreement, in respect of a particular matter in the instrument to be
      rectified;
(2)   there was an outward expression of accord;
(3)   the intention continued at the time of the execution of the instrument sought
      to be rectified;
(4)   by mistake, the instrument did not reflect that common intention.

[34] I would add the following points derived from the authorities:

(1)   The standard of proof required if the court is to order rectification is the
      ordinary standard of the balance of probabilities: "But as the alleged
      common intention ex hypothesi contradicts the written instrument,
      convincing proof is required in order to counteract the cogent evidence of
      the parties' intention displayed by the instrument itself..." (See *Thomas
      Bates & Sons Ltd v Wyndham's (Lingerie) Ltd* per Brightman LJ).
(2)   While it must be shown what was the common intention, the exact form of
      words in which the common intention is to be expressed is immaterial if, in
      substance and in detail, the common intention can be ascertained:
      Co–operative Insurance Society Ltd v Centremoor Ltd per Dillon LJ, with
      whom Kerr and Eveleigh LJJ agreed.
(3)   The fact that a party intends a particular form of words in the mistaken
      belief that it is achieving its intention does not prevent the court from giving
      effect to the true common intention: see *Centremoor* and *Re Butlin's
      Settlement Trusts (Rectification)* per Brightman J.'

4.154 There is another, additional preliminary point: for the remedy of
rectification to be available, the error has to be in the recording of the prior
agreement or prior accord. Rectification is not available where the bilateral
mistake is as to the substance of the agreement, or the legal effect of the
agreement, even if both parties were equally mistaken.[190] As Mustill J said in
*Etablissements Georges et Paul Levy v Adderley Navigation Co MV Panama SA
(The MV 'Olympic Pride')*:[191]

'The remedy of rectification is available only for the putting right of a mistake in
the terms of a document which purports to record a previous transaction. It is not
an appropriate remedy where the mistake relates to the transaction itself rather
than to the document which purports to record it.'

4.155 Going back to the Peter Gibson LJ formulation, his reference to an
'outward expression of accord' is traditional,[192] but contentious. It has been
held that this requirement for an 'outward expression of accord' is merely an
evidential factor and not a legal hurdle which must be surpassed: *Munt v
Beasley*.[193] However, in *Chartbrook*, albeit *obiter*, Lord Hoffmann declined to
approve *Munt*, instead approving the classic formulation in *Swainland*

---

[190]   Snell, *op cit* 14-14(3).
[191]   [1980] 2 Lloyd's Rep 67, 72.
[192]   *Joscelyne v Nissen* [1970] 2 QB 86, 98 per Russell LJ giving the judgment of the Court of
        Appeal.
[193]   [2006] EWCA Civ 370, per Mummery LJ at [36].

Builders.[194] Perhaps the best rationale for the 'outward expression' requirement is that it is part of identifying whether the parties were objectively *ad idem*. In other words, it is a version of the parol evidence rule. See Lord Hoffmann in *Chartbrook*, approving this passage from Mustill J in *The 'Olympic Pride'*:[195]

'The prior transaction may consist either of a concluded agreement or of a continuing common intention. In the latter event, the intention must have been objectively manifested. It is the words and acts of the parties demonstrating their intention, not the inward thoughts of the parties, which matter'.

4.156 In *Daventry District Council v Daventry District Housing Ltd*[196] Etherton LJ noted that in *Chartbrook* Lord Hoffmann had said that the 'common continuing intention' is not a mere subjective belief but rather what an objective observer would have thought the intention to be.[197] He continued:

'81 Three further points of principle should be noted. First, as Lord Hoffmann said (at [65]), evidence of a party's subjective belief or understanding is not inadmissible. It may have some evidential value as to what was actually said and agreed, although, where the prior consensus is expressed entirely in writing, it is likely to carry very little weight.

82. Secondly, and which is really an aspect of the same point, a party can always give evidence that the wording of the document was the result of a mistake. That is an essential part of the cause of action. Whether or not the mistake is such as to give rise to a right to rectification will, however, depend on the objective assessment of whether there was a common continuing intention to which the document failed to give effect.

83. Thirdly, rectification is a discretionary remedy. In the case of unilateral mistake, the claimant's conduct, such as its own carelessness, may preclude refusal of the remedy: see, for example, *Agip SpA v Navigazione Alta Italia SpA* [1984] 1 Lloyd's Rep 353. That consequence may simply be the result, as it was in that case, of the inability of the claimant to show that it was the defendant's unconscionable conduct rather than the claimant's own deficiencies, which caused the mistake: as Stuart-Smith LJ explained in *Commission for the New Towns v Cooper (Great Britain) Ltd* [1995] Ch 259 at p.279:

"It is important to realise that in that case [viz *Agip*] the defendants did not know of the plaintiffs' mistake, and the mistake was not in any way attributable to the defendants' conduct, but solely to the plaintiffs' carelessness in not reading the charter carefully. In these circumstances, it is plain that it would be quite inequitable to foist upon the defendants a contract they did not intend to make."'

---

[194] [2002] 2 EGLR 71, 74 (CA). *Munt* was cited to the House in *Chartbrook*, so one must assume the choice of *Swainland* was deliberate.
[195] [1980] 2 Lloyd's Rep 67, 72. See Lord Hoffmann at [60]–[61].
[196] [2011] EWCA Civ 1153.
[197] See *Chartbrook* at [60].

4.157 In the *Daventry* case, a majority of the Court of Appeal upheld a rectification claim based on mutual mistake despite the parties never sharing any mistake apart from believing that the executed document accorded with their previous agreement (which, however, each believed contained different terms). The parties had during their pre-contract negotiations produced and discussed various drafts of the agreement. One of these involved one of the parties undertaking a significant liability which had previously been intended to be borne by the other party. The majority approach was to ask whether at this stage a reasonable person would have understood himself to be involved in the negotiation of a different deal from the one originally agreed. Since at this stage the party who was originally intended to assume the burden had not signalled a departure from the prior accord, it would be unconscionable to deny a remedy by way of rectification.

4.158 It is only very exceptionally that a mistake by one party only may lead to rectification: as was recently pointed out by Lightman J in *Rowallan Group Ltd v Edgehill Portfolio No 1 Ltd*, when striking out claims for rectification based on unilateral mistake:[198]

> 'The remedy of rectification for unilateral mistake is a drastic remedy, for it has the result of imposing on the defendant to the claim a contract which he did not, and did not intend to, make. Accordingly the conditions for the grant of such relief must be strictly satisfied'.

4.159 Absent fraud,[199] the conditions for the grant of relief on the ground of unilateral mistake may be summarised thus:

(a) if one party observes that the document as drafted does not accurately record the agreement made between the parties; and

(b) that party does not inform the other party of the inaccuracy; and

(c) the other party acts in a way which is either:

    (i) detrimental to that other party; or
    (ii) is beneficial to the party observing the mistake; then
the mistaken party is entitled to rectification and the party observing the mistake cannot oppose rectification on the grounds that it intended that the agreement should read as it was drafted.

4.160 So, in *Thomas Bates Ltd v Wyndham's Ltd*, Buckley LJ said this:[200]

---

[198] [2007] EWHC 32 (Ch); [2007] 4 EG 187 (CS), at [14].
[199] *George Wimpey UK Ltd v VI Construction Ltd* [2005] EWCA Civ 77; [2005] 2 P & CR DG5, per Sedley LJ at [54], 'if a party's conduct amounts to deception or fraud, there is no need to resort to doctrines of mistake' to grant rectification.
[200] [1981] 1 WLR 505, 515–6 *per* Buckley LJ (Brightman LJ agreeing) and 520–1 *per* Eveleigh LJ (CA).

'For this doctrine ... to apply I think it must be shown: first, that one party A erroneously believed that the document sought to be rectified contained a particular term or provision, or possibly did not contain a particular term or provision which, mistakenly, it did contain; secondly, that the other party B was aware of the omission or the inclusion and that it was due to a mistake on the part of A; thirdly, that B has omitted to draw the mistake to the notice of A. And I think there must be a fourth element involved, namely, that the mistake must be one calculated to benefit B. If these requirements are satisfied, the court may regard it as inequitable to allow B to resist rectification to give effect to A's intention on the ground that the mistake was not, at the time of execution of the document, a mutual mistake.'

4.161 Note the emphasis on the requirement that the party against whom rectification is being sought must have observed the mistake.[201] It is this observation of the mistake (which need not amount to 'sharp practice') which gives the court the jurisdiction to rectify, as it is 'unconscionable' for one party to profit from the mistake of the other.[202]

4.162 These conditions were considered in detail by the Court of Appeal and approved in *George Wimpey UK Ltd v VI Construction Ltd*.[203] In that case, Wimpey had bought land from VI for the development of over 200 residential flats. The agreement contained an overage provision based on a share of the sale price of the flats achieved above a base price.[204] The base price was to be determined by a complex formula. As originally drafted, the formula for base price included a figure for certain 'enhancements' in particular flats, which would increase their value.[205] In the final draft of the documentation (prepared by VI's agent) the figure for enhancements was omitted. The result was that the base price was deflated, leading to a higher overage payment.

4.163 Wimpey sought rectification to insert the value for enhancements, initially on the footing of mutual mistake and then on the footing of unilateral mistake. The claim for rectification was rejected by the Court of Appeal. Wimpey failed to show that they had made a mistake, and failed to show that VI had acted improperly. Some key points of the court's judgment on rectification for unilateral mistake can be summarised as follows:

(a)   The jurisdiction to rectify for unilateral mistake is 'exceptional'.[206]

(b)   Knowledge by one party of the mistake by the other party may consist of:

---

[201]   See also *Agip SpA v Navigazione Alta Italia SpA* [1984] 1 Lloyd's Rep 353 (CA).

[202]   *Thomas Bates and Son Ltd v Wyndham's (Lingerie) Ltd* [1981] 1 WLR 505, 515, per Buckley LJ; approved in *Commission for the New Towns v Cooper (Great Britain) Ltd* [1995] Ch 259, 278 per Stuart-Smith LJ (Evans and Farquharson LJJ agreeing).

[203]   [2005] EWCA Civ 77; [2005] 2 P & CR DG5.

[204]   See para **4.25** above for a definition of 'overage'.

[205]   These 'enhancements' were a premium for a river view of 10 per cent over the basic price, a premium of £2,000 for undercroft parking and an uplift of £1,000 for every floor the flat was above ground level.

[206]   Peter Gibson LJ at [51].

(i)   actual knowledge;

(ii)   wilfully shutting one's eyes to the obvious;

(iii) wilfully and recklessly failing to make such inquiries as an honest
       and reasonable man would make.[207]

(c)   However, the latter two categories *may* be dependent upon a finding of
       dishonesty on the part of the person being wilfully blind or wilfully failing
       to make inquiries.[208]

(d)   There is uncertainty as to the type of conduct which can properly be
       considered unconscionable in this context. The question is whether the
       party not mistaken was 'honest and reasonable', but that phrase is
       paradoxical in the sense that honesty and rationality may not be 'on
       speaking terms' in the commercial context.[209]

(e)   The court's approach is necessarily 'case-sensitive', because 'sharp practice
       has no defined boundary'.[210]

(f)   An arm's-length negotiation between parties of unequal competence and
       resources may well place greater constraints of honest and reasonable
       conduct on the stronger party than on the weaker.[211]

(g)   In the field of rectification for unilateral mistake, 'one is looking for a
       mistake on the claimant's own part which the defendant was
       honour-bound, despite his own legitimate business interests, to point out
       to him'.[212]

4.164 The interaction of these principles can be complex. For example, in
Witney Golf Club v Parker, rectification was sought of a deed of variation to a
lease on the grounds of unilateral mistake by the lessor.[213] A lease of land for a
golf club was varied to allow the lessee to undertake a substantial
redevelopment of the site. The deed of variation included a formula by which
the landlords would share in the profits from the development: a form of
'overage'. The landlords' solicitor introduced a formula to the deed of variation
which was actually less profitable for the landlords than that previously
negotiated with the tenant. The landlords accused the tenant of willfully failing
to highlight the effect of the changed formula, and sought rectification
accordingly.

---

[207] Peter Gibson LJ at [45].

[208] Blackburne J, at [79]. This may not be right, as it sits uneasily with *Commission for the New
       Towns v Cooper (Great Britain) Ltd* [1995] Ch 259, 281 per Stuart-Smith LJ, approving *Baden
       v Société Générale pour Favoriser le Développement du Commerce et de l'Industrie en France SA*
       [1993] 1 WLR 509 (Peter Gibson J).

[209] Sedley LJ at [58].

[210] Sedley LJ at [63]–[65].

[211] Sedley LJ at [65].

[212] Sedley LJ at [61].

[213] [2006] 2 P&CR DG18, (Peter Leaver QC, sitting as a Deputy High Court Judge).

4.165 The judge held that there was 'a degree of conceptual difficulty with the "willful failure" formulation, particularly in the context of an arm's-length commercial negotiation'. The court would have to consider whether there was a *duty* on the tenant to ensure that the landlord was happy with the terms of the revised profit-sharing formula. It held that there was not, because:

(a) the advantages of the new formula were not immediately obvious to the tenant;

(b) the landlords' solicitor had introduced the formula; and

(c) to require the tenant to confirm that the landlords were happy with the deed in the terms proposed would put 'an unrealistic burden on any party to an arm's-length and commercial transaction'.

Chapter 5

PRACTICAL DRAFTING ISSUES

EXPRESS WORDING

5.1 Many of the problems which arise under the general law (see Chapter 4) can be resolved by proper drafting of an express grant of a right of way. Elementary wording such as 'together with a right of way over the track coloured brown on the plan' can lead to disputes as it leaves some matters uncertain. Normally in case of doubt a grant is construed in favour of the grantee; where a reservation is ambiguous it is construed in favour of the seller[1] but drafting should aim to avoid ambiguity.

5.2 A transfer of an existing registered title automatically includes and is subject to existing rights of way which should not be mentioned. On a transfer of part Form TP1, panel 12 contains sections 'Rights granted for the benefit of the property' and 'Rights reserved for the benefit of other land' which should in most cases be used if a new right of way is granted or reserved. If the terms of the grant are complex and link to covenants or other rights it may be preferred to put all the provisions together in one part of panel 12. Other forms such as AS3 (Assent of part) have similar sections. The prescribed terms of leases of land include a clause cross-referring to the provision in a registrable lease of land which grants or reserves an easement but prescribed terms do not apply to leases of purely incorporeal rights (see para **13.60**). There is no prescribed Land Registry form for a grant of rights of way on its own.

5.3 In unregistered conveyances it is good practice to mention existing rights (even though they will be implied) as well as the creation of new ones. Land will be conveyed 'together with' the benefit of either an existing or a new right. It will be 'subject to' an existing right. Where a right of way is being taken for the benefit of retained land of the seller it will be a reservation not an exception, but normal practice (in both registered and unregistered conveyancing) is to use the words 'except and reserving'. Although most conveyances of unregistered land will lead to first registration, and common practice is to use a form of transfer, there are still occasions when a conveyance may be used.

5.4 A right in a new grant might be in the following terms:

---

[1] *St Edmundsbury & Ipswich Diocesan Board of Finance v Clark* (No 2) [1975] 1 WLR 468 applying LPA 1925, s 65(1). The issue was whether a reserved right of way was pedestrian or vehicular.

'A right of way at all times and for all purposes with or without vehicles in common with the grantor and all others now having or hereafter granted the like right over the track coloured brown on the plan for the benefit of the grantee's land edged blue on the plan.'

5.5   For convenience, reference is made to grantor and grantee although the context may require transferor, landlord or some other capacity.

'A right of way'

5.6   The word 'right' should be used to make it clear that a legal right is being created, rather than relying on an inference from the context. Wordy expressions such as 'full right and liberty' are unnecessary. Although such phrases as 'The right to pass and repass' or 'a right of ingress and egress' are sometimes used, this wording is clearest. The words 'over and along' the route are often used but are superfluous.

5.7   Wording such as 'together with a way [or passage] along the land ...' can be ambiguous as to whether title to the land itself is being conveyed or simply a right over it and is best avoided. Sometimes a piece of land is reached by a means of approach such as an accommodation road with unregistered title and it may be unclear whether the seller owns the approach. In such a case it is best to include such right title and interest as the seller may have as that will carry title to the land if he has it and if not it will include the easement (to the extent that is not already implied).

At all times

5.8   A legal right of way in fee simple has to be permanent but may be exercisable at limited times.[2] The words 'at all times' may be superfluous but are often included to make clear the nature of the interest granted. The times of exercise can be limited by a condition,[3] provided it is clear and does not derogate from the grant. They can either be specified or can be subject to designation or approval by the servient owner.

5.9   It is common for leasehold rights to be at defined times such as 'between the hours of 07:00 and 20:00 from Monday to Saturday in each week' in a lease of offices in a block.

Purposes

5.10   It is common to restrict the use to which the right can be put (see para **4.68**ff). The right may be 'for agricultural purposes' or 'for residential purposes' or 'for the benefit of not more than ten dwellings'.

---

[2]   See *Collins v Slade* [1874] 23 WR 199 approved in *Lawrence v Fen Tigers Ltd* [2012] EWCA Civ 26, [2012] All ER (D) 180.
[3]   See *Trustees Ltd v Papakyriacou* [2009] EWCA Civ 1089.

5.11 Sometimes the use is limited by reference to a covenant binding the dominant land. If such a covenant is varied, the purpose governing the right of way will automatically be varied with it and if it is released the way will be for any use.[4] The draftsman may therefore prefer to spell out the use in the clause describing the easement even though this involves duplication.

5.12 A right 'for all purposes' will be widely construed (see para **4.73)** but in order to make the position clear (and this will often be desired where the use of the dominant land may change) it could be 'for all present and future uses and development of the dominant land and with liberty to increase and vary such uses'.

Means of use and nature of users

5.13 The wording sometimes specifies what or who can use the way (see para **4.59**). A footpath will be 'on foot only'. A traditional form was 'with or without animals' or the animals might be specified as horses, cattle or sheep. That is now rare, although access to a field let for a pony paddock might refer to horses. Vehicles may need to be specified, particularly if the route is narrow or includes a bridge with a limited weight bearing capacity. The wording may refer to 'private motor vehicles' or 'agricultural machinery' or impose a weight limit. A route used to extract timber will need to specify the necessary machinery so that there is no dispute about use by heavy lorries capable of carrying tree trunks, especially as use may be infrequent if decades may pass between felling operations. The words 'with or without' vehicles are usual to clarify that there is a right on foot as well.

5.14 Unless a way is specifically personal (in which case it may be for life and equitable or may be for a legal term of years terminable on death) it will extend to future proprietors of the dominant land. On a simple grant, therefore, it is unnecessary to define the parties as including successors in title. Where there are other provisions such as maintenance obligations, such a definition may be necessary.

5.15 Sometimes a right will be granted for the grantee and his visitors or his servants or employees and agents or with or without workmen. Often such words are superfluous but much depends on the context and the draftsman may wish to include them to avoid any doubt. Likewise, there may be a limit on who can use the way. For example, a grant of a right of way to trustees of a sports club might restrict use to the trustees, their employees, members of the club and sporting visitors to prevent general public access. If there is a restriction, care should be taken not to breach the Equality Act 2010.

---

[4]   *Hotchkin v McDonald* (2004) 18 EG 100 (CS).

In common or exclusive

5.16 If the right is not granted in common with the grantor then it may take precedence over the grantor's rights over the same route if the burden becomes too great. This may prevent similar rights being granted in future. The right can therefore be granted in common with the grantor (and future grantees).[5] Although this will not affect those who have rights pre-dating those of the current grantee, the draftsman may wish to make it clear such rights already exist by saying the new right is in common with existing rights.

5.17 Occasionally, the parties may wish to make the right of way exclusive. If complete use of land is exclusive to one property, that may take effect as a grant of a freehold[6] but if use as a way is consistent with other uses by the servient owner it will not. For example, a farmer may grant to a house owner a right of way over part of a field. In order to protect the privacy of the house it may be an exclusive way so that, while the farmer may continue to graze animals there or trim the hedge, no-one else will be entitled to pass over it. The wording should make this clear by indicating the right of way is exclusive as such but also including a provision that use is limited to a way and perhaps also a covenant not to interfere with other uses by the servient owner.

Dominant and servient tenements

5.18 The land benefiting from the right should be defined (see para **4.83**). This can be by title number or plan. If it is in a transfer then it will usually be for the benefit of the whole of the land transferred (if by grant) or the retained parts of a title (if by reservation) but in case of doubt it should be made clear. That is particularly important for a reservation where the seller is proprietor of land registered in several adjacent titles. A reservation such as 'for the benefit of the transferor's retained land' could be void for uncertainty.

5.19 A right of way can be granted for the benefit of only part of the land in a transfer. For instance, the sale of a farm may include a terrace of cottages and a specific right might be granted over a retained footpath leading to the terrace for the benefit of the cottages and no other part of the farm. Correspondingly, a right granted in a transfer of one piece of land may be expressed to benefit other land already owned by the buyer and in that case the other land will need to be defined.

5.20 It used to be customary, where the grant was in a separate deed, to define the dominant land in a recital and then in the body of the deed to state that the right is appurtenant to that defined land, but recitals are now less common and it may be preferred to incorporate a definitions clause.

5.21 A similar practice has sometimes been to define the servient tenement by reference to all the land of the grantor (or perhaps the whole of a field) but

---

5   See LPA 1925, s 187(2).
6   *Reilly v Booth* (1890) LR 44 Ch D 12.

then to say that the right is over a defined track forming part of that land. In the absence of special reasons, such as a right to vary the route, that is confusing and should be avoided. It is sufficient for the servient land to be the same as the route over which rights are granted.

ROUTE

5.22 The route is best shown on a plan. Although the use of the colour brown is customary, any suitable colour or other designation such as hatching may be used. The route may also be defined by points such as 'over the track between points A, B and C on the plan'. A plan is normally essential and can only be dispensed with in unusual cases, for example:

(a) If the dominant land is an isolated farmhouse three miles from the highway it may be sufficient to refer to an existing track in words.

(b) If the grantor does not own the soil of the whole route and a sale includes a right of way over land where he only has an easement, in which case the grantee's rights may need to be stated by reference to the grantor's existing rights (which may themselves be prescriptive and therefore undefined in a document).

(c) If the servient tenement only comprises a roadway with its own registered title and the way is over the whole of it.

(d) Where the right is access over a garden to repair an adjacent house.

5.23 As rights affecting registered land are shown on the register of title by reference to official plans, the land registry will usually wish to see a plan. The plan should be drawn with care and avoid ambiguity. There must be no conflict between a verbal description and the plan and expressions such as 'for identification only' should be avoided.

5.24 The land over which the right is exercisable may be indicated as 'way', 'land' or 'route' or may be described as 'road', 'driveway', 'track', 'passage' or 'footpath'. Where it has not been made up it may be 'intended road'. There are no special words. 'Road' indicates a wider use than 'footpath'. If a landowner is granting a private vehicular right over a route which also has highway status as a public footpath, it would be best to spell this out.

5.25 It is sensible to specify the width of the way as this has given rise to many disputes (see para **4.57**) especially as a plan may be on too small a scale to be clear or it may be uncertain how far the right subsists to swing over a verge.[7] In that case the land registry should be asked to quote the specific wording or file

---

[7] *Oliver v Symons* [2012] EWCA Civ 267.

the copy deed of grant rather than simply state that the land is subject to a right of way. Dimensions may either be marked on the plan or stated in the text.

5.26 If the grantor is likely to wish to make use of the airspace, for instance for an arch or an overhanging tree, the deed may specify a height dimension for the right of way.[8]

Diversion and termination of route

5.27 The servient owner may wish to retain freedom to rearrange the use of his land (for example for future redevelopment) while accepting that the dominant owner is entitled to a secure access. In principle this can done in two ways. It may be a flexible route over a large servient tenement which can be crossed along several lines. Or it may be a defined route which can be diverted such as a driveway which has to be constructed and maintained (see para **4.129**).

5.28 A flexible route may be 'such convenient route between points A and B as shall from time to time be designated by the grantor'. If the effect of this is to grant a permanent right of way but over a route that might vary with circumstances, such as across a car park where vehicles might be in different places, then it may be a legal right. The decided cases on variable rights relate to prescriptive rights[9] but the same principles should apply to express grants. If the true construction is to enable the grantor to vary the right, so long as the end points are fixed (such as an entrance to the dominant land and an access to the highway), then it may be equitable.

5.29 An alternative is the express right to divert a defined route. It may be adapted from the 'lift and shift' clauses often found in easements for pipes and cables. This provides that the grantor may construct a suitably convenient alternative access (either over his own land or that of others) and if he serves notice on the grantee the original right of way (or a specified section of it) will cease and be replaced by the new one. This has not been tested and its legal analysis is uncertain but it appears the courts will in principle accept the concept of such a right provided it is agreed.[10]

5.30 It may operate as:

(a) An option to determine and replace the route, in which case it will be subject to the normal rules for options.

8   *VT Engineering Ltd v Richard Barland & Co Ltd* (1968) 19 P & CR 890.
9   *Propertypoint Limited v Kirri* [2009] EWHC 2958 (Ch); *Payne v Shedden* (1834) 1 Mood & R 382; *Wimbledon and Putney Commons Conservators v Dixon* (1875–1876) LR 1 Ch D 362; *Davis v Whitby* [1974] Ch 186.
10   *Heslop v Bishton* [2009] EWHC 607 (Ch).

(b)   A positive covenant on the part of the grantee to release the right of way over the original route in return for a similar right over a new one, in which case it needs a mechanism to protect it (such as a restriction on the register) or it will not be enforceable against a successor in title.

(c)   An equitable right of way, determinable at the instance of the grantor on terms that a replacement is provided.

5.31   The safest course would be a restriction on the register with a chain of covenants, but this is cumbersome and incurs expense every time the dominant land changes hands.

5.32   If in practice the parties accept the new route then that may be sufficient evidence without further formalities. It is possible that the court might presume an abandonment of the old route coupled with a lost modern grant or an implied grant over the new one. However, until the law is clarified it would be best for it to be formally documented as a release and new grant and these will then need to be registered.[11]

5.33   A different approach is to use a long leasehold right of way with a break clause exercisable only if an alternative route is provided. The lease can include provision for prior consultation and, since both the landlord's obligation to construct any new access to a suitable standard and the tenant's to surrender the old route and take a new grant are positive covenants, enforcement against successors in title to the original parties is simpler.

Bridges and tunnels

5.34   A right of way need not subsist only over the surface of land. Buildings may be connected by bridges or tunnels and suitable rights can be granted. Although a reference in words to the physical structures may be sufficient, it will avoid disputes if, in addition to a plan showing the lateral extension of the right, some definition of the vertical dimension is given. This may be a section drawing, or the height or depth of the upper and lower limits of the right may be defined. It is best for this to be by reference to Ordnance Datum Newlyn but if that is not practicable it maybe by reference to some other level which is unlikely to change such as the existing surface of any road under or over the way granted.

5.35   If the dominant owner has main or exclusive use of the bridge or tunnel then it will be responsible for maintenance. In that case it will need rights of access on adjoining land and above or below the easement in order to construct and then maintain it as an ancillary easement for the benefit of the principal right of way. If the servient owner wishes to take obligations, for instance that the bridge will be kept in repair or that the surface above the tunnel will be supported, then it will run into the normal problems associated with flying

---

[11]   See *Heslop v Bishton* [2009] EWHC 607 (Ch).

freeholds and positive covenants. Such an arrangement may be better documented as a lease of the bridge or tunnel and if the servient owner has the right also to use it that can be covered by a reservation.

Rivers

5.36 Although the public right of navigation exists over certain navigable waters, in general inland waters are private and anyone wishing to pass over or along them will need a legal right. A private right of way can be granted along or across a river.[12] A right across may exist at a ford and will be documented in the same way as any other right. The parties may wish to include special provisions, for instance against polluting the river.

5.37 A right of way may exist by boat. This could be a private ferry across the river, for instance to allow the owner of a house on one bank to reach a field on the opposite bank coupled with a right to moor or anchor. The owner of foreshore or of the bank of a navigable river can grant the right to launch boats in the water, possibly coupled with the right to construct and use a slipway or landing stage.

PARKING AND TURNING

5.38 If the route is wide then issues may arise as to whether the user can park on part of it[13] (see paras **2.24** and **4.106**). The deed of grant can state expressly whether or not that is the case. If so intended then a right to park in a defined place should be specifically granted and that grant may be subject to its own terms and conditions, such as keeping the parking place tidy or paying any local authority rates. If it is not to be included then if there is any possible ambiguity it is best to say '(but not including any right to park or place vehicles on any part of the land)'. Similarly if the dominant owner may wish to use a turning space the deed should make it clear whether that is so. If parking as such is not permitted but there is a right for a temporary halt to load and unload, that should be stated (see paras **2.22** and **4.93–4.94**). If wished there could be a maximum duration by analogy with street parking, such as one hour at a time.

5.39 Where a right of parking is granted appurtenant to a piece of dominant land, then the dominant owner will need a right to get to and from the parking space and this may be expressed to be ancillary to the parking right. Often the right to park will be by a grant of an incorporeal lease or licence and the right of way to the parking space will be included in the grant so that when the right to park expires, so will the right of way. Alternatively there may be a lease of (or more rarely a freehold in) a corporeal defined parking space with a right of way to it across the parking lot.

---

[12] *A-G (ex rel Yorkshire Derwent Trust Ltd) v Brotherton* [1992] 1 AC 425 at 434.
[13] *Moncrieff v Jamieson* [2007] 1 WLR 2620 HL.

RIGHTS OF WAY APPURTENANT TO OTHER RIGHTS

5.40 The dominant tenement need not be land but may be incorporeal (see para **1.33** and **2.57**). Thus on the grant of a profit in gross such as fishing, those exercising the right will need a right to walk along the river bank and a right to stand and fish. There may also be a right to use a boat. A right to take game will include the right for the grantee and his guests and gamekeepers to enter the sporting land to rear live birds and collect shot ones. This may be drafted subject to limits such as a restriction on numbers or a provision that the dominant owner or his agent must accompany any visitors.

5.41 Nineteenth century grants and reservations of incorporeal rights to work minerals often included long and detailed easements to construct and use roads and tramways on the overlying and adjacent surface, but the modern tendency is to grant rights in general terms. If the owner of the minerals and the owner of the surface are the same, then a grant of mineral rights (either freehold or by lease) will include rights of access. If not, the mineral operator will need a separate grant.

5.42 On the grant of an express right for a house owner to repair his building from an adjoining garden, he will need a right of way appurtenant to that right to reach the site of the repairs, together with surveyors, workmen, scaffolding and equipment, conditional on doing as little damage as possible and making good damage caused.

BARRIERS AND SECURITY

5.43 Issues can arise (see para **4.135**) where the terms of a right of way do not deal with gates and barriers and a deed should provide for such matters. The grant may be made subject to the right of the grantor to install gates provided he gives a key to the grantee. Some gates can be operated by electronic code, which must be supplied.[14] If there are only two users it is possible to have a barrier consisting of a chain connecting two posts. Each end of the chain is attached to the post by a padlock and each party provides one padlock so that either party can unlock one side of the chain.

5.44 If the way is also used by the public but is not a highway, the servient owner may wish to close it on certain days in the belief that this prevents the acquisition of prescriptive highway rights by demonstrating lack of intention to dedicate. Although there are other means of doing this,[15] many landowners prefer the custom of annual closure, often on Ascension Day. This will need to be covered by the terms of the grant, otherwise the dominant owner could object to the closure.

---

[14] See *Sisters of the Sacred Heart of Mary Ltd v Kingston upon Thames Royal Borough Council* [2007] EWHC 563 (Ch) John L Powell QC, 14 March 2008.
[15] See Highways Act 1980, s 31.

5.45 On an industrial estate or a gated private housing estate it may be necessary to have the entrance permanently manned by security staff so that any person using the access needs to have express clearance. This arrangement will often be included in a leasehold structure as part of the management scheme.

MAINTENANCE AND REGULATION – GENERAL

5.46 A way over which a right subsists will need maintenance (see para **4.85**). Although a right for a single dominant owner to enter and maintain the route may be implied, it is best to govern this by express terms, particularly if there are multiple users. If users are to share the cost then either the servient owner or one of the dominant owners or a third party such as a management company will need to take primary responsibility and it will be necessary to provide for contributions by other users. This can be done either by making use of the way conditional on payment or by a duty to pay.

5.47 Another possible approach is that different owners are responsible for separate sections of the way adjacent to each property. This will oblige each owner to repair a given section and perhaps also to provide lighting or a direction sign. This could result in different sections of a road being maintained to different standards and is best avoided.

5.48 A direct obligation involving the expenditure of money, either by doing works or by contributing to the cost of works done by others, is a positive covenant and therefore in the case of a freehold grant needs a mechanism to be made binding on successors to the original covenantor. A leasehold grant can contain a positive obligation to do works (although this may be difficult to enforce) or a covenant to pay, or a contribution may be taken as service charge or rent.

5.49 There may also need to be regulations. Negative ones, such as not to obstruct or not to use for certain purposes, can be imposed by restrictive covenants. For freehold land these may be seen either as binding the use of a freehold right of way itself as a legal interest or, since an easement can not subsist in gross, as binding the dominant land but applying to the easement. There may also be positive obligations, such as to shut a gate.

5.50 A number of methods are in use to attach contribution and other positive obligations to a freehold right. The benefit and burden rule is the simplest and most frequently used and works as a conditional grant. The other methods involve securing a positive covenant.

Maintenance under the benefit and burden rule in *Halsall v Brizell*[16]

5.51 A common form is to make the right:

'Subject to and conditional on the grantee paying on demand a fair proportion according to use of the cost incurred by the grantor in maintaining, repairing and renewing the surface of the track'.

5.52 An alternative is:

'Subject to and conditional on performing and observing the covenants set out in the Schedule'

5.53 Such covenants will include provisions for contribution and regulation. The consequence is that if the grantee does not contribute (or perform the other covenants) then the grantor is entitled to suspend the grantee's use of the way until payment is made (or breach remedied) see para **8.20**. If this is to be a condition precedent it should be made clear,[17] for example where a roadway is to be made up and contributions are needed before work starts. This will not generally be suitable for existing roads and a subsequent condition may provide that if the dominant owner does not contribute on demand then the right to use the road will be suspended until payment is made.

5.54 This does not rely on privity of contract. In the first version above there is no express covenant to pay. In the second there may be but (in the absence of a mechanism to secure fresh covenants on change of ownership – see para **5.59** below) it will only bind the first grantee. Therefore, if the dominant owner does not pay, the servient owner will not be able to sue him for the contribution. If he continues to use the way, the servient owner will need to seek an injunction to prevent use until payment or take other action such as locking a gate. The dominant owner will be entitled to relief against suspension on payment.[18]

5.55 A conditional right, such as one dependant on payment, may be regarded as equitable because it is not absolute.[19] An alternative, sometime used on building estates (as was the case in *Halsall v Brizell*[20]), is to establish an express trust whereby the roads are vested in trustees on trust to permit the dominant owners to use them subject to contribution and the dominant owner has the rights of a beneficiary of the trust. The terms of the trust may provide that the beneficiary can require the trustees to carry out a duty of repair, but the terms should not be drafted so as to impose an unconditional liability on them so that their duty will arise only if there are adequate funds in the trust.

---

16 [1957] Ch 169. See also *Thamesmead Town Ltd v Allotey* (1998) 30 HLR 1052 CA.
17 *Yorkbrook Investments Ltd v Batten* (1986) 18 HLR 25, (1986) 52 P&CR 51.
18 *Shiloh Spinners v Harding* [1973] AC 691.
19 LPA 1925, s 1(2)(a) and (3).
20 [1957] Ch 169.

5.56 As the burden relates to the benefit, if the dominant owner does not need to use the way he will be entitled to cease contributing thus throwing a greater burden on those who do use it.[21]

Maintenance and regulation through positive covenants

5.57 Where a positive covenant is imposed on the dominant owner (eg to contribute to costs of repair) a mechanism is required to ensure this can be enforced by subsequent owners after the original covenantor has disposed of the dominant land. This can also be used for other positive covenants (eg to keep a gate closed). Similarly, the dominant owner will need a mechanism to enforce the servient owner's obligation to repair the way although a right to enter and repair in default of the servient owner doing it may be implied or expressed. A number of methods are in use as discussed in the following paragraphs.

Estate rent charge under section 2(4) of the Rentcharges Act 1977

5.58 This can be used on developed housing and industrial estates (see para **8.18**). It frequently also covers a variety of common facilities other than access such as the cost of gardens, cable and other telecom services and staff for porterage or security. Under section 2(5) of the Rentcharges Act 1977 the level of payment must be 'reasonable'.[22] As the principal remedy under section 121 of the LPA 1925 is re-entry on the land charged, this device can be used for a sale of land together with a right of way. It cannot be used for a grant of a right of way on its own as a rentcharge may not at common law be reserved out of an easement.[23]

Restriction on the register with chain of covenants

5.59 This provides that no disposition of the dominant land is to be registered without the consent of the grantor (see para **8.15**). There is a separate maintenance deed under which the grantee covenants to make contributions. The deed will also provide that if the grantee wishes to transfer the dominant land the grantor is obliged to give consent on production of a deed of covenant by the transferee to observe the terms of the maintenance deed. Sometimes the grantor will then expressly release the previous proprietor of the dominant title. The new deed of covenant will contain an application to the Land Registry to enter a similar restriction on the new transferee's title and a provision that the transferee will not further transfer the dominant title without obtaining a covenant from the further transferee and a further restriction and so on.

5.60 The maintenance deed can be as detailed as circumstances require. In addition to an obligation to contribute to costs of maintenance it can set out,

---

[21]   *Thamesmead Town Ltd v Allotey* (2000) 79 P & CR 557.

[22]   *Orchard Trading Estate Management Ltd v Johnson Security Ltd* [2002] EWCA civ 406, [2002] 2 P&CR DG 13 CA; *Smith Brothers Farms Ltd v Canwell Estate Co Ltd* [2012] EWCA Civ 237.

[23]   See *Re Lord Gerard and Beecham's Contract* [1894] 3 Ch 295 at 315.

or incorporate by reference, related user covenants and an obligation to join a management company with service charge provisions comparable to those in a lease of a flat such as the production of audited accounts.

5.61 Although it is likely that the benefit of such positive covenants will automatically pass with the land under section 78 of the LPA 1925 it will be prudent on any transfer of the servient tenement to assign the benefit of covenants by dominant owners to contribute to maintenance or do other positive acts.

Commonhold

5.62 Under the Commonhold and Leasehold Reform Act 2002, freehold units (such as flats in a block or houses on a residential estate or units on an industrial estate), can have the benefit of common services, including a right of way, with a continuing obligation to pay (see para **8.29**). However, it is likely to be unduly expensive to set up a commonhold just to repair a right of way.

Leasehold right of way

5.63 This is discussed below.

Standard of maintenance and amount of contribution

5.64 Maintenance of a private road is normally a simple matter provided it has been properly constructed in the first place, and the sums involved will usually be modest and repair infrequent. The brief provision above refers to 'a fair proportion according to use' and is payable on demand. That form of words is in wide use and will cover most straightforward situations, for instance where a few houses share the use of a short private roadway.

5.65 If major works could be required or where there is potential for a dispute, the draftsman may need to consider more elaborate provisions. On a private residential estate there may be street lighting or weekly street cleaning or mowing of grass verges. Such arrangements involve regular payments and will be organised under a service charge. In a particularly complex situation there could be a management company of which all the users of the way are obliged to be members, with a similar structure to service charges used in blocks of flats. There may need to be provisions for consultation, obtaining competitive estimates and auditing of costs.

5.66 Instead of a general contribution according to use, each property may pay a defined percentage. This could be equal or it might be fair for those whose properties are more remote from the highway (and therefore use a greater length of the drive) or those with bigger houses to pay a larger share. If the properties are part of a development under construction over a long period of time or if there is potential for them to be divided into several units, the draftsman may wish to include provision to adjust the percentages to reflect future changes as otherwise they cannot be varied.[24]

5.67 The various users may want the way to be maintained to differing standards. For instance, on the sale of a remote farmhouse without its fields, the buyer of the house may want a rural retreat to which he and his guests can take private cars designed for the city and the motorway. The farmer will only want to keep a rough track suitable for agricultural machinery. The buyer may be willing to make up the surface at his own expense but if the farmer continues to take tractors and trailers on it, it could soon deteriorate. There is no simple solution. One approach is to permit either party to repair or improve the track, provide for the standard of maintenance to be sufficient for a rough track but provide that if it can be shown that either party has caused material damage then they will make it good.

LEASEHOLD RIGHTS OF WAY

Rights of way included in leases of land

5.68 A demise of premises will often include a right of way to them (see para **8.23**). Many of the same practical maintenance issues will arise as on a freehold grant but as a lease may include positive covenants enforceable by both landlord and tenant the scheme is widely understood and drafting is simpler.

5.69 A lease of part of a building, for instance a flat or an office in a block, will need a pedestrian right of way over the entrance, stairs, lifts and corridors and perhaps vehicular access to parking spaces. A unit on an industrial estate or business park will need a right over the estate roads. The right may be included in the parcels clause or in a separate schedule of easements and if the lease is registrable the right must be mentioned in the prescribed clauses (see para **13.48**). Use will be regulated by covenants either in the body of the lease or in a schedule of regulations relating to common parts. Maintenance of steps, corridors, driveway, parking spaces and so on will be covered by a service charge subject to usual rules.

5.70 This can be used for a normal investment lease, for example for 15 years at a market rent. An alternative is a 'virtual freehold' where a freely assignable lease of an industrial unit is granted for 999 years for a premium and at a peppercorn rent with rights of way over the roadways and parking areas and a service charge (often reserved as a separate rent) to cover maintenance.

Leases of rights of way as incorporeal rights

5.71 A lease of an incorporeal right will be used where the servient tenement is itself leasehold since the leaseholder can not grant a greater right than he has. It may also be used where the dominant tenement is leasehold and the

---

[24]   *Halsall v Brizell* [1957] Ch 169.

leaseholder does not wish to confer a benefit on the landlord or the landlord does not wish to accept any obligations (such as maintenance) which go with the grant. However, that could store up problems for the future as when the lease expires the property may be left without access.

5.72 A leasehold right of way can be used for a maintenance scheme for freehold units on an industrial estate or freehold houses on a residential estate where the roads are not adopted (see para **8.24**). The developer retains the common parts and each buyer takes a lease of a right of way over the estate roads (often as well as other services). Each lease will include management and contribution covenants and the reversion will be passed either to an investor (if there is a profit rent) or to a management company.

5.73 Since a leasehold incorporeal right of way on its own will need to be created by deed in order to comprise a legal interest,[25] it is not possible to grant a legal right of way (separately from land) by a parol tenancy for less than three years at the best rent without a premium. Such a parol grant may take effect in equity[26] but will need to be protected like any equitable right.

5.74 Since the landlord can sue a successor of the original tenant on positive or restrictive covenants in the lease, that may be sufficient to secure performance of any duties without resorting to forfeiture. If a forfeiture clause is desired it cannot be enforceable by re-entry in the normal way as there is no corporeal hereditament on which to enter, but the same effect can be attained by notice to determine. If the leasehold right of way is appurtenant to a freehold title, forfeiture should only be for non-payment of rent or service charge or breach of covenant and the tenant will be entitled to relief on normal terms. If the tenant has a duty to repair the road, section 146 of the LPA 1925 and the Leasehold Property (Repairs) Act 1938 may apply. Forfeiture should not extend to insolvency of the tenant since a mortgagee of the dominant freehold will need to be able to include the right of way on any sale.

5.75 A leasehold easement can no more exist in gross than a freehold one (see para **1.34**). It can only be appurtenant and therefore will in principle automatically pass along with an assurance of the dominant tenement. If the dominant land is freehold then that land will be freely transferable and the benefit of the lease must pass with it; even if the dominant land is leasehold the right must pass with a permitted assignment. Therefore, it is not appropriate to provide for the landlord of the right of way separately to consent to assignment. However, the servient owner/landlord may still wish to impose conditions. There will normally be a covenant to register the passing of the benefit. There may be an obligation to enter into a direct covenant with the servient owner/landlord or with the (freehold or leasehold) owners of the other properties in the scheme to observe restrictions and pay a service charge.

---

[25] *Duke of Somerset v Fogwell* (1826) 5 B&C 875; *Mayfield v Robinson* (1845) 7 QB 486.
[26] *Lowe v Adams* [1901] 2 Ch 598; *Mason v Clarke* [1955] AC 778, [1955] 1 All ER 914, HL.

5.76   It follows that as the dominant land may be sold off in parts there can be no restriction on assignment of part of the benefit of the leasehold interest. In order to avoid an excessive burden on the roads the landlord may wish to restrict the right of way to use in connection with use of the dominant tenement as a single unit or a specified number of units.

5.77   The Landlord and Tenant (Covenants) Act 1995 (LTCA 1995) can apply to any tenancy, including one of incorporeal rights. However, sections 3 and 5 which deal with transmission of benefit and burden of covenants and release of assignors both relate only to 'premises' which are not defined for this purpose. The word probably does not include an incorporeal hereditament although the point remains to be decided. The lease could contain provisions to mirror the statute but if not the parties to an assignment will need to include indemnities.

5.78   Although the transfer of the dominant freehold will carry the appurtenant right with it, as the leasehold right of way cannot have its own registered title, it may be desired that the buyer of property having the benefit of the right takes a formal deed to confirm title, possibly expressed as a confirmation of assignment. An assignment will be required of rights which do not pass automatically such as some types of option or break clause since the benefit of certain covenants may not pass under where section 3 of the LTCA 1995 does not apply. In order to avoid disputes a chain of deeds will be desirable as evidence of title even if not legally necessary. The deed may be kept separate from the contemporaneous land registry transfer so that the buyer can retain the original. The deed can include any appropriate provisions such as an indemnity against future breaches or a direct covenant with the landlord.

5.79   A lease of an incorporeal hereditament on its own is not normally 'premises' for the purposes of Part 2 of the Landlord and Tenant Act 1954.[27] A tenant of business premises may be able to claim a new lease under that Act. If the leasehold is reached by a right of way over the land of the same landlord, the tenant will be entitled to a renewal of that right and if the landlord has a freehold right over other land it will be included as an appurtenant right.[28] However, where the right of way was a leasehold held by the tenant over land of a different landlord (often where the reversion has been split since the original lease was granted) he will not be entitled to a renewal of the easement. He will need to secure any necessary rights from the different servient owner.

5.80   If the separate ownership (or the possibility of a future split reversion) is clear at the outset, the tenant might wish to have a right which would outlast any number of statutory renewals, but it would not be possible to have a right of way for (say) 100 years appurtenant to a lease for 15 years. The tenant may be able to obtain an option binding the servient land that if he (or a person deriving title through him) is entitled to renew a lease of the dominant holding then the servient landlord will renew the right of way, but this needs careful

---

[27]   *Land Reclamation Co Ltd v Basildon District Council* [1979] 2 All ER 993, [1979] 1 WLR 767 but see *Pointon York Group plc v Poulton* [2006] 29 EG 153 (CS), [2006] All ER (D) 175.

[28]   Landlord and Tenant Act 1954, s 32(3).

wording to avoid a break in the chain of succession and on any assignment of the lease the benefit of the option will need to be assigned and notice given to the reversioner.[29] An alternative is a covenant by the original landlord of the whole that, on a disposition of land over which a right of way has been granted with the lease, a freehold right will be reserved for the demised premises.

LICENCES

5.81 A licence can be used if the arrangement is personal or ephemeral and a formal grant of a legal or equitable interest may not be appropriate (see para **2.40**). For instance, there may be a temporary permission for an occupier, whose normal access is obstructed while some building work proceeds, to use an alternative over a neighbour's land. Likewise if there is no dominant tenement; for instance the owner of a piece of land may be willing to give a licence for a procession to pass over it on a particular day.

5.82 A common arrangement is that where a landowner sells off part of his land but retains adjacent land he may want to be able to continue a convenient access, for instance for a favourite walk to a view point and the buyer may be prepared to allow the seller personally to do so but not wish this to pass to a later owner of the seller's retained land. If no right is granted but the seller continues to use the access for 20 years, a right might arise by prescription. An express licence is a sufficient consent for the purpose of excluding that. The licence will make it clear who can use the access, for instance members of the seller's family, or permit the buyer to suspend it, for instance if he has guests. As this is a personal arrangement it will not bind any later owner who purchases from the buyer and if the seller is concerned at that risk the seller will need security. This could be by a lease which only subsists for the benefit of named persons and will be terminable say on the death of the seller or his moving elsewhere. An alternative is an equitable easement for the lifetime of the seller or so long as he resides in a specified dwelling and that can be protected either on the register or by a land charge.

5.83 A bare licence is personal and incapable of assignment.[30] Some licences relating to access are drafted so as to be assignable or to pass with a property until determined. To the extent that such a provision were to be upheld, it would probably be seen either as implying a new licence to a new owner given and accepted on the same terms or be construed not as a licence but as a legal interest comprising an assignable tenancy of the right of way[31] or as creating an assignable licence coupled with a grant (of a temporary right of way).[32] In the absence of authority it will be safer that a new express licence should be given each time there is a change in either the licensor or the licensee as

---

[29] LPA 1925, s 136.
[30] *London Tara Hotel Ltd v Kensington Close Hotel Ltd* [2011] EWCA Civ 1356.
[31] Compare *Street v Mountford* [1985] 1AC 809 at 819.
[32] *Wood v Leadbitter* (1845) 13 M & W 838; *Hurst v Picture Theatres Ltd* [1915] 1 KB 1.

otherwise there could be a risk of prescriptive rights arising[33] although provision for payment of a regular substantial licence fee would prevent that (provided it is collected).

5.84 A licence may be in a formal document but it is often given informally orally or by letter. A formal document will make the position clear and will cover the location of the access, the identity of the licensee, the period of notice to determine any payment, exclusion of liability and any other matters desired. A letter will need to be drafted with as much care as a document between parties. An oral licence can lead to disputes and after 40 years may enlarge into a prescriptive right.[34]

CONTRACTS AND FUTURE RIGHTS

5.85 Since a right of way is an interest in land, a contract for the grant is subject to section 2 of the the Law of Property (Miscellaneous Provisions) Act 1989. Similarly, the grant of an option will need to comply with normal formalities.

5.86 It is common practice on sales of development land for the seller to reserve future rights for the benefit of adjacent retained land which may become developable in the future. This may be along the lines of 'A right of way over all roads and footpaths which now exist on the property or are constructed on it at any time hereafter [*or* within 50 years from the date of this transfer]'. This may be coupled with the right to enter on the property sold in order to construct roads and footpaths to connect to those on the retained land and the right (at all times after construction) to use them. These provisions normally also include rights to lay and use services.

5.87 Care must be taken when providing for future rights (see para **3.95**). In particular, the rights need to be for the benefit of a defined dominant tenement and this can present problems if that is not identified or if the servient land is transferred before the right can be crystallised.[35]

RIGHTS OF WAY AND DEVELOPMENT – GENERAL

5.88 Rights of way are a material factor on development of building estates, particularly of houses. A significant proportion of the area of a housing estate will comprise roads, footpaths and passages. The developer may intend to dedicate the major ways as public highways, but there can be a delay before this happens and it is not always desired.

---

[33] *London Tara Hotel Ltd v Kensington Close Hotel Ltd* [2011] EWCA Civ 1356.
[34] Prescription Act 1832, s 2.
[35] *London and Blenheim Estates Ltd v Ladbroke Retail Parks Ltd* [1993] 4 All ER 157, [1994] 1 WLR 31.

5.89 The land to be developed may, prior to development, be crossed by private rights which interfere with the developer's proposed layout. There are established means of stopping up or diverting public rights of way[36] but these cannot be used to remove a private right. If the local authority is prepared to cooperate they may be prepared to use compulsory powers to extinguish a private right.[37] In rare cases '*Greenwich*' type orders may be available where the owner of the dominant tenement is unknown (see para **9.155**).[38] In most cases the developer will need to come to terms with the dominant owner.

5.90 The developer will need full rights to reach the building land. If it cannot be accessed directly from a highway, then a right of way will be required over intervening land. The owner of the land will be in a position to demand a substantial payment[39] and the new access will need to be constructed to a standard to be approved by that owner. The developer may seek to acquire the freehold of the way so that it can be offered to the highway authority for adoption but this will not be invariable especially in the case of an industrial estate. The owner of the access land may wish to retain ownership of a private way in order to control it and possibly profit if it subsequently gives access to other developments.

5.91 It will be evident that a seller of land may wish deliberately to engineer such a situation to provide a ransom or provision of overage rights where land is sold for one current use (such as agriculture) but there may be prospects of future development. This should be treated with care. A court might regard the use of easements for purposes other than amenity of the dominant tenement with some caution. In order for the arrangement to work the seller needs to be sure of obtaining an injunction to enforce its rights. An injunction is a matter of judicial discretion and may not be granted.[40] Retention of a ransom strip between the development land and the highway (subject to a right of way for a limited use) is in widespread use but the reservation of a right of way across the potential development site to secure overage is not recommended.

Rights within the development

5.92 Owners of units will need rights to cross the development to reach the highway. On an industrial estate this will often be by leasehold rights as indicated above. On a residential estate mortgagees will require dwellings either to have access over a dedicated highway or to have enforceable rights of way. Such rights will normally be freehold although lenders may accept leasehold ones for special reasons.[41] During development the final layout may not be known and there may need to be provision for varying the routes of estate

---

[36] Highways Act 1980, Part VIII.
[37] Town and Country Planning Act 1990, s 237 (as amended by Planning Act 2008, Sch 9, para 4).
[38] *Greenwich NHS Trust v London & Quadrant Housing Association* [1998] 1 WLR 1749.
[39] *Stokes v Cambridge Corporation* (1961) 13 P & CR 77.
[40] *Jaggard v Sawyer* [1995] 1 WLR 269.
[41] See *Council of Mortgage Lenders Handbook* (2010 edn), paras 6.8.4 and 6.9.1.

roads. Once the roads are adopted a private right of way will no longer be needed and can be determined. Although variation and determination could be achieved by an equitable right, such a provision may not be acceptable to a mortgagee and a leasehold right with a break clause is more likely to be approved. A leasehold right can also include covenants to contribute to maintenance pending adoption.

5.93 On some estates the residents may prefer that the roads are not dedicated so that they have the security of a network of private ways which they can control. There may in any case be footpaths and shared driveways which will not be suitable for adoption. Some minor ways can still be dedicated but the highway authority will not adopt or be liable to maintain them. A conveyancer acting for the buyer of a house or flat will need to check whether there will be access over an adopted highway and if not to secure it by an easement and to ensure someone is responsible for maintenance. The methods available to secure this for private ways are considered above.

5.94 Most housing developments involve an agreement under section 38 of the Highways Act 1980 whereby the developer agrees with the local highway authority to construct the roads to adoptable standards, provide a sum for future maintenance and then dedicate them as highways. If the roads have not been constructed to the satisfaction of the highway authority they will not adopt until that is done. In the meantime private rights of way will be required. Most section 38 agreements include provision for a bond by the developer to secure liability against the cost of street works in the event of insolvency.

5.95 Where a property fronts on to or adjoins a private street the conveyancer will need to consider if protection is needed against any potential liability of the house owner. Private streets may become publicly maintainable by use of the Private Street Works Code.[42] This re-enacts nineteenth century legislation and is not now widely invoked but it is still available and used, particularly in the north of England. It involves those who own properties on the private street contributing to the cost of making it up to an adoptable standard and the highway authority then accepting responsibility. Although adoption of private streets is now most often by agreement, the legislation is drafted as conferring a compulsory power on the highway authority to levy a charge on property owners.

5.96 A developer will generally not want to retain an interest in an estate after selling the houses. Occasionally it will, where for instance the road might lead to land to be developed in the future and there might be a ransom element. Otherwise, rights of way along unadopted roads can be dealt with in a variety of ways:

(a) The developer does not pass ownership of the roads to anyone. This often happens. Provided the houses have adequate rights of way, it may not

---

[42] Highways Act 1980, s 34 and Part XI.

matter. It can become a practical issue if repairs are needed or if there are wide verges on which travellers may come to squat or if there is persistent obstructive parking. If the developer was a private building company or a single purpose vehicle of a development group it may be dissolved after the development is completed, in which case title to the roadway will pass to the Crown as bona vacantia. The Treasury Solicitor is usually prepared to sell such roadways to one or more residents.

(b) Each house is the owner of the roadway opposite its frontage subject to rights for other houses and with the benefit of rights over other parts of the road. This can lead to disputes[43] but is a simple solution where there are few houses.

(c) The road can be vested in trustees for the benefit of the house owners as equitable tenants in common subject to legal rights of way for each house. This can be complicated to operate. New trustees may need to be appointed from time to time and on any sale of a house the sale should include an assignment of its undivided share in the road (see para **2.10**).

(d) The road can be vested in trustees or in a residents' association company for the benefit of the residents. This is most often linked to maintenance contributions as indicated above.

(e) A commonhold can be established.

DOCUMENTARY EVIDENCE OF PRESCRIPTIVE RIGHTS

5.97 Supporting evidence of a prescriptive right of way may be given by statutory declaration or statement of truth. An application to have a claimed right noted on the register of title (see para **13.45**) must include a statement of truth and comply with rule 215A of the Land Registration Rules 2003 (LRR 2003).

5.98 The statement or declaration will be given by people who have known the land and its means of access for as long as possible. Ideally this will be over the relevant period such as 20 or 40 years. In practice there may be no single person who has been familiar with property for that time. In that case the person claiming the right will need to assemble a number of declarations covering the relevant period.

5.99 A declaration will have standard opening and closing words[44] and will be used for unregistered land. A statement in relation to registered land may be made in Form ST4 although use of that form is not obligatory.[45] The declarant or maker of the statement should state his connection with the dominant

---

[43] See eg *Jaggard v Sawyer* [1995] 1 WLR 269.
[44] Statutory Declarations Act 1835.
[45] LRR 2003, r 73A(4) as amended. See PG 44 and PG 52, para 6.2.

property (as former owner, neighbour, regular visitor or similar), the date he first became familiar with use of the right of way and if relevant the date of his most recent knowledge. He should give as much detail as possible of the nature and frequency of the use and the extent to which it was open and visible. He should state whether he was aware of any challenge to the use of the way or whether there was any conduct by anyone (either the servient owner or an employee or agent or tenant) who might have given consent. A plan should be attached to or exhibited with the declaration and, if possible, photographs, as old as is practicable.

Chapter 6

ACQUISITION OF RIGHTS BY LONG USE

6.1　Prescription refers to title acquired by use or enjoyment during a time, and in a manner, fixed by the law of the relevant jurisdiction – informally and colloquially, people refer to prescription as 'rights obtained by long use'.

6.2　Acquiring rights by prescription (or long user) is generally accepted to be confusing, complex and not all together consistent. The whole concept of prescription can be seen to derive from the underlying tenet of English law that exercising a right for a long enough period of time, without interference from a third party, should enable the right to be capable of being legitimised and thus recognised in law. Further, in some case, this central tenet is combined with an assumption that the right originally derived in a lawful grant by the servient land owner, as grantor, to the dominant land owner, as grantee.

6.3　This Chapter considers the three ways in which an easement of way can be acquired by long use, and the necessary criteria in each case.

THE POSSIBLE ROUTES

6.4　Broadly, an easement of way may be acquired by prescription in one of three ways:

(1)　By showing continuous enjoyment since time immemorial. This effectively requires one to show enjoyment back until 1189. This mode of acquisition is known as Common Law Prescription.

(2)　By claiming that the easement of way has been enjoyed for a period of at least 20 years and that enjoyment has been pursuant to a fictitious grant of the easement (this by a person capable of making such a grant).

(3)　By proving at least 20 years' continuous enjoyment back from when proceedings are issued to assert the right under the Prescription Act 1832.

6.5　Each of these is considered in more detail below.

Common law prescription

6.6　Common law prescription is by far the oldest means of acquiring prescriptive easements, including rights of way. Whilst it still technically exists in law, in all practical terms it has been superseded by the doctrine of lost modern grant and the Prescription Act 1832 for the making of claims to prescriptive rights. Accordingly, many now regard Common Law Prescription as obsolete in all practical respects.

6.7   The origins of common law prescription are grounded in the history of the law on limitation.

6.8   In *R v Oxfordshire County Council Ex p Sunningwell PC* it was summarised as follows:

> '[The common law] did not treat long enjoyment as being a method of acquiring title. Instead, it approached the question from the other end by treating the lapse of time as either barring the remedy of the former owner or giving rise to a presumption that he had done some act which conferred a lawful title upon the person in de facto possession or enjoyment. Thus the medieval real actions for the recovery of seisen were subject to limitation by reference to various past events. In the time of Bracton the writ of right was limited by reference to the accession of Henry I (1100). The Statute of Merton 1235 ... brought this date up to the accession of Henry II (1154) and the Statute of Westminster 1275 ... extended it to the accession of Richard I in 1189. The judges used this date by analogy to fix the period of prescription for immemorial custom and the enjoyment of incorporeal hereditaments such as rights of way and other easements. In such cases, however, the period was being used for a different purpose. It was not to bar the remedy but to presume that enjoyment was pursuant to a right having a lawful origin. In the case of easements, this meant a presumption that there had been a grant before 1189 by the freehold owner.'[1]

6.9   A 60 year period of limitation for a writ of right and 50 years for a possessory action existed under the Limitation of Prescription Act 1540. Under the Limitation Act 1623, the limitation period for the recovery of land was subsequently reduced to 20 years. As noted above, with regard to easements of way (and other easements), 1189 has remained the extent of legal memory for prescription at common law.

6.10   The origin of common law prescription is therefore based in an assumption that any use which was capable of being traced back to before 1189 could be properly acquired by prescription. Given that this was conventionally impossible to establish in the great majority of cases, the presumption that any right, which was capable of being shown to have been exercised for at least a period of 20 years, had commenced before the period of legal memory (that is, 1189, the time of legal memory), was introduced. In *Angus v Dalton* Lush J said:

---

[1]   [2000] 1 AC 335, per Lord Hoffmann at 349G–350B. Cited from *Gale on Easements* 4-05, p 199, 18th Edn, 2008.

'Theoretically an ancient house at this period was a house which had existed from the time of Richard I. Practically, it was a house which had been erected before the time of living memory, and the origin of which could not be proved.'[2]

6.11 Like all other presumptions, this was capable of rebuttal. The presumption could be rebutted if it was possible to show that the right had not in fact been exercised at all times since prior to 1189;[3] or alternatively that, at some time along the way, there has been unity of ownership – that is the dominant and servient tenements had been owned by the same party. As discussed in Chapter 9, unity of possession without unity of ownership would not prevent the establishment of a claim to prescription at common law. Martin B said in *Winship v Hudspeth*,[4] that a claim by immemorial prescription at the common law would be defeated by proof of unity of ownership at any time, must not be taken as applying to mere unity of possession without unity of ownership.

6.12 Whilst unlikely to be relied upon by a claimant, it is common for common law prescription to be claimed in the alternative along with lost modern grant and a claim under the Prescription Act 1832. These are by far the more likely basis of any claim for the reasons discussed below.

Lost modern grant

6.13 The doctrine of lost modern grant provides that, if an easement has been enjoyed for at least 20 years without any other lawful explanation, it is presumed:

(a)   To have had its origin in a deed of grant made after 1189.

(b)   That the deed of grant has been lost.

6.14 A claim of lost modern grant based on 20 years of use is not rebutted even when the use is interrupted after the required 20 years. Lost modern grant can be seen as more convenient than common law prescription because it no longer is necessary to prove enjoyment back to 1189, and further avoids having to show 20 years of enjoyment back from the date that proceedings are issued (as required by the Prescription Act 1832, please see below).

6.15 The doctrine was most noticeably considered in *Angus v Dalton*,[5] and then on appeal in the Court of Appeal and in the House of Lords. In *Tehidy*

---

2   (1877) 3 QBD 85 at 89.
3   For example, see *Wheaton v Maple and Co* (1893) and *Bowring Services v Scottish Widows' Fund and Life Assurance Society* (1995) 11 EGLR 158.
4   (1854) 23 LJ Ex 268, 10 Exch 5.
5   (1877) 3 QBD 85; (1878) 4 QBD 162; (1881) 6 App Cas 740.

Minerals Ltd v Norman Buckley LJ,[6] delivering the judgment of the Court of Appeal, stated the effect of *Angus v Dalton*[7] as follows:

> "In our judgment *Angus v Dalton* decides that, where there has been upwards of 20 years' uninterrupted enjoyment of an easement, such enjoyment having the necessary qualities to fulfil the requirements of prescription, then unless, for some reason such as incapacity on the part of the person or persons who might at some time before the commencement of the twenty-year period have made a grant, the existence of such a grant is impossible, the law will adopt a legal fiction that such a grant was made, in spite of any direct evidence that no such grant was in fact made.
>
> If this legal fiction is not to be displaced by direct evidence that no grant was made, it would be strange if it could be displaced by circumstantial evidence leading to the same conclusion, and in our judgment it must follow that circumstantial evidence tending to negative the existence of a grant (other than evidence establishing impossibility) should not be permitted to displace the fiction. Precisely the same reasoning must, we think, apply to a presumed lost grant of a profit a prendre as to an easement.'[8]

6.16   It follows from *Angus v Dalton* that the presumption cannot be displaced by merely showing that no grant was in fact made; the long enjoyment stops the servient owner from relying on such evidence or take precedence over it when given.[9] Further the court will make a presumption to give that long enjoyment a legal origin.[10]

6.17   The case also confirms that incapacity to grant the easement will rebut the presumption; that is, it will negative the claim so far as it rests on the fiction of a lost grant.[11] It may also be unreasonable to presume a grant when the evidence of user does not support the right that is claimed.[12] The case further suggests that a claim may be challenged on any basis which would prevent the right from being acquired by prescription from time immemorial.[13]

6.18   Unlike Common Law Prescription, the use of lost modern grant is apparent in modern times. The courts often make recourse to the doctrine and apply it in various respects, including in cases concerning easements of way. As Lord Herschell in *Phillips v Halliday* states:

---

6   [1971] 2 QB 528.
7   (1877) 3 QBD 85; (1878) 4 QBD 162; (1881) 6 App Cas 740.
8   [1971] 2 QB 528 at 552. Cited from *Gale on Easements* 4-11, p 203, 18th Edn, 2008.
9   *Cf.Goodman v Saltash Corp* (1882) 7 App Cas 633; *Bass v Gregory* (1890) 25 QBD 481; *Phillips v Halliday* [1891] AC 228.
10   *Att-Gen v Simpson* [1901] 2 Ch 671 at 698; *East Stonehouse UDC v Willoughby Bros Ltd* [1902] 2 KB 318 at 332; *Dawson v M'Groggan* [1903] 1 IR 92 at 98.
11   See *Angus v Dalton* (1878) 4 QBD 162 at 173–175 and the cases which are referred to therein, namely; *Tyne Improvement Commissioners v Imrie* (1899) 81 LT 174; *Neaverson v Peterborough RDC* [1902] 1 Ch 557; *Hulley v Silversprings Bleaching and Dyeing Co* [1922] 2 Ch 268; *Green v Matthews* (1930) 46 TLR 206; *Bakewell Management Ltd v Brandwood* [2004] 2 AC 519.
12   *Alfred F Beckett v Lyons* [1967] Ch 449.
13   See, e g *Roberts & Lovell v James* (1903) 89 LT 282.

'Where there has been long-continued possession in assertion of a right, it is a well-settled principle of English law that the right should be presumed to have had a legal origin if such a legal origin was possible, and the courts will presume that those acts were done and those circumstances existed which were necessary to the creation of a valid title.'[14]

6.19 Indeed, the doctrine of modern lost grant has been resorted to as an alternative not only to prescription at common law but also to prescription under the Prescription Act 1832, which is discussed in more detail below.

Prescription Act 1832, section 2

6.20 The Prescription Act 1982 does not supersede either common law prescription or the doctrine of lost modern grant. Instead, it introduces an additional two new forms of prescription based on 20 and 40 years of use. It also created a separate regime for rights to light.

6.21 The Prescription Act 1832 refers to itself as[15] 'An Act for shortening the Time of Prescription in certain cases'. The preamble states:

'Whereas the expression "time immemorial, or time whereof the memory of man runneth not to the contrary," is now by the law of England in many cases considered to include and denote the whole period of time from the reign of Richard I, whereby the title to matters that have been long enjoyed is sometimes defeated by showing the commencement of such enjoyment, which is in many cases productive of inconvenience and injustice; for remedy thereof be it enacted...'[16]

6.22 Specifically for the acquisition of an easement of way by prescription, section 2 of the Prescription Act 1832 provides that:

'No claim which may be lawfully made at the common law, by custom, prescription or grant, to any way or other easement, or to any watercourse or the use of any water to be enjoyed or derived upon, over, or from any land or water of our said lord the King, or being parcel of the Duchy of Lancaster or of the Duchy of Cornwall, or being the property of any ecclesiastical or lay person, or body corporate, when such way or other matter as herein last before mentioned shall have been actually enjoyed by any person claiming right thereto without interruption for the full period of twenty years, shall be defeated or destroyed by showing only that such way or other matter was first enjoyed at any time prior to such period of twenty years, but nevertheless such claim may be defeated in any other way by which the same is now liable to be defeated; and where such way or other matter as herein last before mentioned shall have been so enjoyed as aforesaid for the full period of forty years, the right thereto shall be deemed

---

[14] [1891] AC 228 at 231. The doctrine of lost modern grant was also applied, by the House of Lords, in *Bakewell Management Ltd v Brandwood* [2004] 2 AC 519.
[15] Formerly known as Lord Tenterden's Act.
[16] Preamble to the Prescription Act 1832.

absolute and indefeasible, unless it shall appear that the same was enjoyed by some consent or agreement expressly given or made for that purpose by deed or writing.'[17]

6.23   It can be noted that this section also applies to positive easements.[18] The section does not apply to easements of light,[19] which section 3 deals with instead. According to *Dalton v Angus*[20] the section does not apply to easements that are purely negative (although some commentators may disagree with such a position).

6.24   As such, after 20 years of use has been enjoyed, a prescriptive right will arise under the statute. This will be a defence to a claim made that the right did not exist in 1189, a requirement of common law prescription.[21] Crucially, however, the 20 years' use must be *immediately before* the court action that crystallises the easement, that is, the commencement of legal proceedings (save that an interruption (in the sense of some obstruction by the servient owner or a third party, preventing use of the right) of up to one year is disregarded.[22] By contrast, under the doctrine of lost modern grant, the use of the easement must have continued for 20 years, but not necessarily the 20 years immediately before the right is challenged in court. For this reason, the claim to an easement by lost modern grant rather than the Prescription Act 1832 may be preferred. The obvious advantage of the Prescription Act 1832 is that a period of 20 years is overtly specified and that proving it did not exist before 1189 (often pretty simple) will not defeat a claim.

6.25   Accordingly, the Act has not superseded either of the pre-existing methods of claiming by prescription. An easement is still capable of being established by prescription at common law, or under the doctrine of modern lost grant[23] and commonly all three methods will be pleaded in the alternatively.[24] The Act merely provides an (additional and statutory) method of establishing an easement in some cases, based on 20 or 40 years user.

6.26   Indeed, although very rarely encountered in practice, section 2 of the Prescription Act 1832 also allows an easement to be established as 'absolute and indefeasible'. This is in the case of the 40 years' use having been acquired, even if the claim would otherwise be defeated, provided that there has been no *written* consent to the use (because the permission must be in writing, an oral permission would not defeat the claim) and the use was still as of right, that is,

---

[17]   Prescription Act 1832, s 2.

[18]   *Dalton v Angus* (1881) 6 App Cas 740 at 798; *Bass v Gregory* (1890) 25 QBD 481; *Simpson v Godmanchester Corp* [1897] AC 696 at 709.

[19]   *Perry v Eames* [1891] 1 Ch 658; *Wheaton v Maple & Co* [1893] 3 Ch 48.

[20]   (1881) 6 App Cas 740 at 798.

[21]   Prescription Act, 1832, s 4.

[22]   Prescription Act, 1832, s 4.

[23]   See *Warrick v Queen's College, Oxford* (1871) 6 Ch App 716 at 728); see also *Aynsley v Glover* (1874) 10 Ch App 283; *Gardner v Hodgson's Kingston Brewery Co* [1903] AC 229 at 238; *Housden v Conservators of Wimbledon and Putney Commons* [2008] 1 WLR 1172 at [43].

[24]   *Tehidy Minerals Lid v Norman* [1971] 2 QB 528.

without force, without secrecy and without permission (*nec vi, nec clam, nec precario*). Indeed, user for either of the two periods of 20 and 40 years must be 'as of right', that is, *nec vi, nec clam, nee precario*,[25] and the right enjoyed must have been enjoyed as an easement[26] – see below.

PERIOD OF USE REQUIRED

6.27 As referred to above, the period of use required is determined by the basis on which the right is claimed.

Under common law prescription

6.28 Under common law prescription, it is necessary to show continuous enjoyment since time immemorial. This effectively requires one to show enjoyment back until 1189 which was the first year of the reign of Richard I. This date was subsequently fixed by the Statute of Westminster in 1275 and remains fixed to this day.[27]

6.29 As noted above, this burden was partially relieved when there was introduced the presumption that any right, which was capable of being shown to have been exercised for at least a period of 20 years, had commenced before the period of legal memory. Most commonly one would rely on the latter if common law prescription were to be asserted in any claim for a prescriptive easement of way.

Under the doctrine of lost modern grant

6.30 Under this doctrine, if an easement has been enjoyed for at least 20 years without any other lawful explanation, it is presumed to have had its origin in a deed of grant made after 1189 and that the deed of grant has been lost (*Angus v Dalton*).[28] A claim of lost modern grant based on 20 years of use is not rebutted even when the use is interrupted after the required 20 years.

6.31 Lost modern grant can be seen as more convenient than common law prescription because it no longer is necessary to prove enjoyment back to 1189 and further avoids having to show 20 years of enjoyment back from the date that proceedings are issued (as required by the Prescription Act 1832).

---

[25] *Harbidge v Warwick* (1849) 3 Exch. 552; *Gaved v Martyn* (1865) 19 C.13. (ns) 732; *Chamber Colliery Co v Hopwood* (1886) 32 Ch. D 549; *Gardner v Hodgson's Kingston Brewery Co* [1903] AC 229.

[26] *Onley v Gardiner* (1838) 4 M & W 496.

[27] See Nash '1189 and the limits of legal memory' (1989) 139 NLJ 1763.

[28] (1881) 6 App Cas 740.

Under the Prescription Act 1832

6.32 Enjoyment of a right of way over a given period (normally 20 years) will give rise to a prescriptive title to an easement under the Prescription Act 1832. Section 4 of the Act states that:

> 'Each of the respective periods of years hereinbefore mentioned shall be deemed and taken to be the period next before some suit or action wherein the claim or matter to which such period may relate shall have been or shall be brought into question; and no act or other matter shall be deemed to be an interruption, within the meaning of this statute, unless the same shall have been or shall be submitted to or acquiesced in for one year after the party interrupted shall have had or shall have notice thereof, and of the person making or authorising the same to be made.'[29]

6.33 In *Bright v Walker*,[30] in which a right of way under the Prescription Act 1832 was asserted, Parke B spoke of the necessary length of time and qualities of enjoyment necessary for a prescriptive right of way to be made out:

> 'In order to establish a right of way, and to bring the case within this section,[31] it must be proved that the claimant has enjoyed it for the full period of twenty years, and that he has done so "as of right", for that is the form in which by section 5 such a claim must be pleaded; and the like evidence would have been required before the statute to prove a claim by prescription or non-existing grant. Therefore, if the way shall appear to, have been enjoyed by the claimant, not openly and in the manner that a person rightfully entitled would have used it, but by stealth, as a trespasser would have done – if he shall have occasionally asked the permission of the occupier of the land – no title would be acquired, because it was not enjoyed, "as of right" For the same reason it would not, if there had been unity of possession during all or part of the time: for then the claimant would not have enjoyed "as of right" the easement, but the soil itself. So it must have been enjoyed without interruption. Again, such claim may be defeated in any other way by which the same is now liable to be defeated; that is, by the same means by which a similar claim, arising by custom, prescription, or grant, would now be defeasible; and, therefore, it may be answered by proof of a grant, or of a licence, written or parol, for a limited period, comprising the whole or part of the twenty years, or of the absence or ignorance of the parties interested in opposing the claim, and their agents, during the whole time that it was exercised.'[32]

6.34 This section is qualified by the provisions as to disability in section 7.

6.35 Section 2 of the Prescription Act 1832 also allows an easement to be established as 'absolute and indefeasible'. This is in the case of 40 years' use having been acquired, even if the claim would otherwise be defeated. This is subject to two provisos, firstly that there has been no *written* consent to the use

---

[29] Prescription Act 1832, s 4.
[30] (1834) 1 CrM & R 211 at 219.
[31] Prescription Act 1832, s 2.
[32] See also *Monmouthshire Canal Co v Harford* (1834) I Cr.M. & R. 614 and *Tickle v Brown* (1836) 4 A & E 369; and *Winship v Hudspeth* (1854) 10 Ex 5. Cited from *Gale on Easements* 4-77, p 240, 18th Edn, 2008.

(an oral permission is generally seen not to defeat the claim when based on 40 years) and secondly that the use was still as of right, that is, without force, without secrecy and without permission. The 40 year claim is similar to the 20 year claim in that the user period must extend up until the commencement of that action.

6.36 It was initially questioned whether section 2 of the Prescription Act 1832 meant a presumed grant did not have to be by a competent grantor to establish a right based on 40 years' enjoyment. In the House of Lords case of *Staffordshire and Worcestershire Canal Navigation (Proprietors) v Birmingham Canal Navigation (Proprietors)*[33] it was held to be necessary to show that the easement *could* in fact have been granted. In the later Court of Appeal decision in *Housden and another v Conservators of Wimbledon and Putney Commons*[34] this was also confirmed. See para **6.109** for a detailed explanation of these issues.

NATURE OF USER

6.37 The user must be 'as of right' along with being continuous and capable of interruption. These are considered in turn below.

As of right

6.38 In order to establish that a prescriptive right of way has been acquired by user as of right, it is necessary to consider use of the term 'as of right' in section 5 of the Prescription Act.

6.39 In cases other than where an easement of light is claimed under section 3 of the Act,[35] the enjoyment claimed by the user must have been 'as of right'.[36] This is the case both for claims based on periods of 20 or 40 years enjoyment. It is also necessary to how that enjoyment was 'as of right' for the claim of a prescription easement at common law or under the doctrine of lost grant (even where the claim is to light).[37] Any manifestation of permission or consent having been given to the user will defeat the claim.[38] Fitzgibbon LJ said (in the context of lost modern grant) that:

> 'The whole doctrine of presumed grant rests upon the desire of the law to create a legal foundation for the long-continued enjoyment, as of right, of advantages which are prima facie inexplicable in the absence of legal title. In cases such as this, where the grant is admittedly a fiction, it is all the more incumbent on the judge to see, before the question is left to the jury, that the circumstances and character of the user import that it has been "as of right". It appears to me, in the present case,

---

[33] [1866] LR 1HL 254.
[34] [2008] EWCA Civ 200.
[35] *Colls v Home and Colonial Stores* [1904] AC 179 at 205.
[36] *Kilgour v Gaddes* [1904] 1 KB 462.
[37] See *Mills v Colchester Corp* (1867) LR 2 CP 476 at 486, discussed below.
[38] *Odey v Barber* [2008] Ch 175 at [36].

that the evidence is inconsistent with right, and that the user is consistent only with permission to enjoy what the supposed grantor did not want, if and so long as that user might be consistent with the rights of third parties, and also with the grantor's right to use his own property from time to time in a reasonable manner. Such a user could never have been "as of right" in its inception; it could never acquire during its continuance any higher than permissive character, and it therefore never could be, or become, a foundation for the presumption of a grant.'[39]

6.40   The party claiming the prescriptive right is required to prove that his user was 'as of right'. The burden thus clearly rests on the party asserting the right.

6.41   There are three essential qualities of the user; in order to obtain an easement by prescription, the user must be as of right – that being 'nec vi, nec clam, nec precario'. As cited by Coke, from Bracton:[40]

'Both to customers and prescriptions these two things are incidents inseparable, viz. possession or usage, and time. Possession must have three qualities: it must be long, continual and peaceable.'[41]

6.42   Willes J more recently has stated:

'In the case of prescription, long enjoyment in order to establish a right must have been as of right, and therefore, neither by violence, not by stealth nor by leave asked from time to time.'[42]

6.43   The precise meaning of the term 'as of right' is commonly misunderstood.

6.44   It was noted in *R (Beresford) v Sunderland City Council*[43] that 'as of right' did not mean 'of right' but was closer to 'as if of right'. This is because it is possible for the user to be 'as of right' even though it is not adverse to the interests of the servient owner.[44] To understand whether an act has been 'as of right' it is necessary to look at the quality and character of the user and question if the user is of a kind which would be enjoyed by a person who has such a right. It is necessary for the user to demonstrate an appearance of the right being asserted by their actions, and subjective views, beliefs or

---

[39]   *Hanna v Pollock* [1900] 2 IR 664 at 671; see per Buckley LJ in *Att–Gen v Horner* [1913] 2 Ch 140 at 178. Cited from *Gale on Easements* 4-82, p 243, 18th Edn, 2008.

[40]   Bracton, Lib 2, f 51b, 52a, Lib 4, f 222b. Cited from *Gale on Easements* 4-80, p 242m 18th Edn, 2008.

[41]   Bracton, Lib 2, f 51b, 52a, Lib 4, f 222b. Cited from *Gale on Easements* 4-80, p 242, 18th Edn 2008.

[42]   *Mills v Colchester Corp* (1867) LR 2 CP 476 at 486.

[43]   [2004] 1 AC 889, Lord Walker of Gestingthorpe at [72].

[44]   Per Lord Walker of Gestingthorpe at [90].

understandings of the person carrying out the user are not relevant. As discussed below, the user does not have to hold a belief that they have the right that they now claim.[45]

6.45　It is therefore important to consider the three elements of 'as of right' in more detail.

Nec vi

6.46　A number of principles apply to *Nec vi* – broadly speaking, the user must not have been by violence, force or contention. Any acts which constitutes am interruption by, or opposition from, the servient owner will be sufficient to show that the user did not enjoy the easement of way rightfully.

6.47　Section 4 of the Prescription Act makes clear that nothing shall be deemed to be an interruption, unless it shall be submitted to or acquiesced in for the space of a year after the party interrupted shall have had notice thereof, and of the person making or authorising the same. This is a common course of ambiguity. In *Eaton v Swansea Waterworks Co*[46] the question was raised as to what would be the effect in law of a state of 'perpetual warfare' between the dominant and servient owners. The Court of Queen's Bench held that interruptions acquiesced in for *less* than a year could still show that enjoyment was never 'as of right'.

6.48　The case of *Newnham v Willison*[47] applied the principle that contentious user was not user 'as of right' in the context of a plaintiff asserting the right to use a 'swept curve', as opposed to a sharply angled curve, at the junction of two tracks over which he enjoyed a right of way. Evidentially the plaintiff was able to show user for 23 years without objection, before the defendant erected obstacles to prevent the continued use of the swept curve. These were removed by the plaintiff and eventually led to the commencement of proceedings (over a year from erection of the first obstacle). The Court of Appeal held that the claim to prescription must fail because of section 4 of the Prescription Act 1832 (there had been an interruption with the user for more than a year) and because the plaintiff was unable to demonstrate a period of 20 years' user as of right immediately before action was commenced.[48] In the context of *Nec vi*, it was held that the purported removal by the plaintiff of the obstacles erected was sufficient evidence of the user no longer being without force or contention.

---

[45]　*R v Oxfordshire CC, Ex p Sunningwell RC* [2001] 1 AC 335, in respect of 'as of right' in the Commons Registration Act 1965.

[46]　(1851) 17 QB 267.

[47]　(1987) 56 P & CR 8. The claim to easement was based on section 2 of the Prescription Act 1832; it is not clear why the plaintiff did not rely on the doctrine of lost modern grant, which would have caused the claim to succeed on the facts.

[48]　(1987) 56 P & CR 8, at 20, per Eastham J, the mere sending of a letter seems to have been accepted as sufficient to constitute a 'contentious' situation which amounted to an interruption with s 4 and prevented further use being 'as of right'. Others may question such a view.

6.49   *Gale on Easements* questions whether *Newnham v Willison* was correctly decided and suggests that the court appears to have lost sight of the requirement of section 4 of the Prescription Act 1832 with respect to defeating a claim to a prescriptive right, namely that an interruption submitted to or acquiesced in for at least one year. In *Newnham v Willison* the plaintiff removed the initial obstructions and protested by way of a letter sent from his solicitor – *Gale on Easements* questions whether either act constitutes submitting to or acquiescing in the acts relied on as an interruption.[49] This is based on the argument that, if the removal of one obstruction is sufficient to defeat the claim (ie by such an action, the user is contentious and by force, and therefore not 'as of right'), this renders unnecessary section 4 of the Act which includes the one year rule. *Gale on Easements* says that:

> 'The judgments in *Eaton v Swansea Water Works Co* are to the effect that interruptions acquiesced in for less than a year may be of importance "on the question whether there ever was a commencement of an enjoyment as of right"[50] and may show "that the enjoyment never was of right",[51] but do not suggest that such interruptions may be relied upon to defeat the claim on the ground that user as of right became "no longer as of right".'[52]

6.50   In *Smith v Brudenell-Bruce* the servient owner objected to continued user of a way by sending forceful letters of protest asserting that such user thereafter was contentious and not as of right. These were not however sufficient to defeat the claim to the prescriptive right of way because 20 years' user 'as of right' has been enjoyed before the letters and thus the plaintiff was able to rely on the doctrine of lost modern grant notwithstanding that a claim under the Prescription Act 1832 could not be made out.

6.51   Accordingly, in practical terms, single acts of contention or protest should never been relied upon as sufficient to assert that the user has now become no longer *nec vi*, and regard to section 4 of the Prescription Act should be had.

6.52   The principles of *Nec vi* have recently been considered in *Taylor v Betterment Properties (Weymouth) Ltd*[53] in the context of town and village greens.

Nec clam

6.53   The essential ingredient to the right being nec clam, is that enjoyment by the user of the right of way must not have been a secret, ie must not have been exercised by stealth, or only in the night.

---

[49]   See *Dance v Triplow* (1991) 64 P & CR 1 at 5.
[50]   (1851) 17 QB 267, at 273, per Lord Campbell CJ.
[51]   (1851) 17 QB 267, at 275, per Coleridge J.
[52]   The expression used by Kerr LJ at (1987) 56 P & CR 19. Cited from *Gale on Easements* 4-86 P244.
[53]   [2012] EWCA Civ 250.

6.54 The issue of secrecy was pertinent to the decision in *Dalton v Angus*,[54] which demonstrates that there must be some knowledge (or means of knowledge) on the part of the servient owner.[55] For example, in *Liverpool Corporation v Coghill*[56] the claimant intermittently discharged borax solution into the plaintiffs' sewers during night-time. This was without their knowledge. It was held to be a secret enjoyment which thus did not entitle them to an easement notwithstanding that the discharging had been undertaken for a period greater than 20 years immediately prior to the commencement of proceedings.

6.55 Accordingly, for enjoyment to be as of right, it must not be 'clam', that is, a claim to a prescriptive easement must be a user of which the servient owner who has knowledge either actual or constructive.[57] In a right of way context, exercising an easement of way over a neighbour's garden by running across it only at night, would not be sufficient to establish a prescriptive title. Continual use at varying times of the day over a 20 year period would however be sufficient for the prescriptive easement to be made out.

Nec precario

6.56 The third essential element to 'as of right' is that the enjoyment must not be 'precarious', or that which depends not on right, but on the will of another person. 'Si autem', says Bracton,[58] 'seisina precaria fuerit et de gratia, quae tempestive revocari possit et intempestive, ex longo tempore non acquiritur jus.'[59]

6.57 For this reason, a user's enjoyment under a consent, permission or licence from the servient owner will prevent the acquisition of the title to a prescriptive easement. A licence or other consent expressly displaces the presumption that enjoyment was had by the user under a claim of right to the easement.[60] This is because, with consent, the user would not have been undertaken with the intention, by that user, or acquiring or exercising the prescriptive right.[61]

6.58 It is important in this context to make a distinction between acquiescence by the servient land owner and licence or permission. If a servient

---

[54] (1881) 6 App Cas 740.

[55] *Union Lighterage Co v London Graving Dock Co* [1902] 2 Ch 557.

[56] (1918) 1 Ch 307.

[57] *Per* Farwell J, *Burrows v Lang* [1901] 2 Ch 502 at 510.

[58] Translated to: 'If seisin shall have been from mere favour and from grace, which can *be* revoked in season and out of season, no right is acquired from a long period of time.' See *Gale on Easements*.

[59] Cited from *Gale on Easements* 4-94, p 248. See also *Monmouthshire Canal Co v Harford* (1834) 1 CM & R 614; *Chamber Colliery Co v Hopwood* (1886) 32 Ch D 549.

[60] *Ward v Kirkland* [1967] Ch 194 at 233, 234.

[61] Under the doctrine of lost grant or on the basis of section 2 of the Prescription Act, permission granted by a tenant who is in occupation of the servient tenement is sufficient to defeat a claim. See *Ward v Kirkland* [1967] Ch 194, 223.

land owner, aware of the user, acquiesces in knowledge of that user, then the user remains 'as of right'; indeed, acquiescence is the foundation of prescription. Conversely, a user who obtains licence, consent or authority from the servient land owner will not be 'as of right'. This distinction lies in the conduct of the servient owner in each case. Whereas acquiescence amounts merely to tolerance of some description by the servient land owner, consent from the servient land owner (in the form of a licence or the giving of permission) constitutes a positive act or affirmation that the user is permitted.

6.59 Permission can also be inferred from acts of the servient land owner, and does not need to be expressly in writing,[62] and may be inferred from overt and contemporaneous acts of the owner.[63] For example, imposing a charge on the user for passing and re-passing or entering onto the land.[64] However, a lack of some positive act is more likely to be treated as acquiescence in the knowledge of the user.

6.60 Any admission (even verbal), that the enjoyment had been had by permission of the owner of the servient tenement, would be sufficient to prevent the acquisition of the right, prior to commencement of the Prescription Act 1832. This was irrespective of however long such enjoyment might have continued for. Following commencement of the Prescription Act, in cases where the act is relied upon to assert the prescriptive title, a claim to an easement of way (or any easement other than of light) under section 2 of the Act on the ground of an enjoyment for 20 years will be defeated by an oral consent given at the beginning of and extending throughout the user.[65] In cases where a period of 40 years user can be established, a claim will still fail by permission given during the period, or by user which continues on a common understanding of a permissive user being had,[66] but not by prior parol permission.[67] Except in cases where the permission is given orally and the user has continued for 40 years, once permission has been given, the user remains permissive and is not capable of developing into a prescriptive right. The only exception to this rule will be a case where the permission was given only for a limited period or where permission is revoked or a change in circumstances is apparent.[68]

---

[62]   [2004] 1 AC 889 at [75].
[63]   *R (Beresford) v Sunderland City Council* [2002] QB 874 (Court of Appeal) at [11]–[12]. [2004] 1 AC 889.
[64]   [2004] 1 AC 889 at [74]–[75].
[65]   *Healey v Hawkins* [19681 1 WLR 1967.
[66]   See *Jones v Price and Morgan* (1992) 64 P & CR 404 at 407, per Parker LJ.
[67]   *Gardner v Hodgson's Kingston Brewery Co* [1903] AC 229, affirming CA [1901] 2 Ch 198; *Healey v Hawkins* [1968] 1 WLR 1967; and see *Tickle v Brown* (1836) 4 A & E 369; *Beasley v Clarke* (1836) 2 Bing NC 705; *Earl De la Warr v Miles* (1881) 17 Ch D 535 at 596. See also *Tickle v Brown*, above, 369 at 383; see *Gardner* v *Hodgson's Kingston Brewery Co* [19001 1 Ch 594, per Cozens-Hardy J; [1901] 2 Ch 213, per Rigby Li; *Lowry v Crothers* (1872) IR 5 CL 98.
[68]   *Healey v Hawkins* [1968] 1 WLR 1967, applying *Gaved v Martyn* (1865) 19 CB (ns) 732.

6.61 In cases where user was with permission from the outset, it is an evidential question of fact, and any appropriate inferences, as to whether that permission has continued throughout the period of user.[69]

6.62 *Gale on Easements* gives the following example:

'The fact that a gate, through which a right of way was claimed, had always been kept locked, the key having been kept by the proprietor of the servient tenement, but always having been asked for by the proprietor of the dominant tenement as a matter of right, when it was required, and never having been refused, did not prevent the acquisition, by prescription, of the easement.[70] But the fact that a gate across a way is installed and kept locked for substantial periods may well show that user was not as of right: the principle is that the party claiming to have acquired a right by prescription will fail if he can show no more than casual user permitted by a neighbour's tolerance and good nature.'[71]

6.63 A servient owner 'tolerating' use by a dominant land owner will not prevent the acquisition of a prescriptive right. Acquiescence by the servient owner is a necessary element of the concept of a user acquiring rights by prescription.[72]

6.64 In *Rose v Krieser*[73] a dominant land owner made use of an accessway which was not the same as the route granted by an agreement between the parties. The court held that the user had given rise to a right of way by prescription, but went on to hold that the user 'found its origin' in the original agreement. The servient owner asserted that this caused the user to be permissive, and that it was not therefore 'as of right' and could not be relied upon for the purposes of prescription. The argument was rejected on the basis that user pertained to land which was materially different from that referred to in the agreement between the parties.

6.65 One question that often arises in respect of permissions being given by a servient owner to a dominant owner is as to the position when either estate is sold on to a successor in title.

6.66 Permission does not create an interest in the land,[74] and therefore the permission will not bind the successor in title to the servient tenement. As such, the majority of permissions are likely to constitute personal agreements between the contracting parties. Accordingly, such permission falls away on the sale of the dominant land to a third party. In such a case, continued use by the

---

[69] *Gaved v Martyn* (1865) 19 CB (n) 732; *Healey v Hawkins* [1968] 1 WLR 1967.

[70] *Roberts v Fellowes* (1906) 94 LT 279.

[71] *Gale on Easements* 4-98, p 252, 8th Edn. See also *Goldsmith v Burrow Construction Limited, The Times*, July 31 1987 (Court of Appeal (Civil) Transcript No 750 of 1987) explaining and applying *Lay v Wyncoll* (1966) 198 EG 182 and *Green v Ashco Horticultural Limited* [1966] I WLR 889.

[72] *Mills v Silver* [1991] Ch 271 at 2790–280B, per Dillon LJ and at 288A-G, per Parker LI.

[73] [2002] 212 DLR (4th) 123.

[74] *Ashburn Anstalt v Arnold* [1989] Ch 1.

successor (if not prevented) will amount to acquiescence of the servient owner in user as of right (and therefore time will run as against the servient owner in acquiring the prescriptive right). This is subject to an assertion that the continued use supports an inference that the original permission has been extended to the successor to the dominant tenement (in such a case, time would not run). In such a case, it is essential to look into the nature and type of the permission carefully to determine whether it remains valid.

6.67   The user will also fail to be 'as or right' if the servient owner is told that no prescriptive right is being sought by the given conduct of the user. For example, the a party with the benefit of a right of way on foot informs the servient owner that he does not intend to acquire any further rights by walking over additional areas to those comprised in his express grant, then no continuous right of enjoyment is being asserted with respect to an area outside of that contained in an express grant, and no prescriptive right will be obtained.[75]

6.68   In terms of presumptions, the law does however presume that a user undertaking an act that will give rise to a prescriptive easement so acted under a claim of right until the contrary has been established.[76]

Capable of interruption

6.69   The above quotations refer to the servient owner being able to interrupt or stop the user, if knowledge of the enjoyment is known. It is necessary for the enjoyment to be such that the servient owner *could* have prevented or interrupted it.

6.70   The case of *Angus v Dalton*[77] concerned a claim of lateral support for buildings. The Court of Appeal noted that an enjoyment physically incapable of interruption would confer no prescriptive right.[78] Lord Selborne[79] said:

> 'That power of resistance by interruption does and must in all such cases exist, otherwise no question like the present could arise. It is true that in some cases (of which the present is an example) a man acting with a reasonable regard to his own interest would never exercise it for the mere purpose of preventing his neighbour from enlarging or extending such a servitude. But, on the other hand, it would not be reasonably consistent with the policy of the law in favour of possessory titles, that they should depend, in each particular case, upon the greater or less facility or difficulty, convenience or inconvenience, of practically interrupting them. They can always be interrupted (and that without difficulty or inconvenience), when a man wishes, and finds it for his interest, to make such a use of his own land as will have that effect. So long as it does not suit his purpose and his interest to do this, the law which allows a servitude to be established or enlarged by long and open

---

[75]   See *Field Common Ltd v Elmbridge Borough Council* [2005] EWHC 2933 (Ch) at [37].
[76]   *Campbell v Wilson* (1803) 3 East 294.
[77]   (1877) 3 QBD 85; (1878) 4 QBD 162.
[78]   (1878) 4 QBD 162 at 175.
[79]   (1881) 6 App Ca. 740 at 796.

enjoyment, against one whose preponderating interest it has been to be passive during the whole time necessary for its acquisition, seems more reasonable, and more consistent with public convenience and natural equity, than one which would enable him, at any distance of time (whenever his views of his own interest may have undergone a change), to destroy the fruits of his neighbour's diligence, industry, and expenditure.'[80]

6.71 Lord Penzance said that the enjoyment must, in order to confer a right, be capable of interruption 'without extravagant and unreasonable loss or expense'.[81]

Definite, continuous and uninterrupted

6.72 The enjoyment must be definite and sufficiently continuous in its character. Whilst non-use in the context of the extinguishment of easements is unlikely to be sufficient alone to evidence abandonment (ie a firm intention never to use the right again is also required), in this context it may well be enough to prevent the acquisition of that right by prescription if it prevents the user having been definite and continuous.[82]

6.73 Continuity may be interrupted by the act of the servient owner, in which case the requirement of section 4 of the Prescription Act 1832 with respect to an interruption submitted to or acquiesced in for at lest one year becomes relevant (see earlier in para **6.48**). An interruption can also take place by virtue of the person claiming the prescriptive right, in which case it will normally be a question of fact and degree as to whether the claimed enjoyment establishes the easement or not (ie was it sufficiently continuous or were periods of non user by the person claiming the prescriptive right too significant to allow the claim to still be made out).

6.74 The enjoyment of an easement of way does not have to be incessant. In cases of continuous easements such as easements of light to windows it often will be, but in discontinuous easements such as is the case with easements of way, which require the repeated acts of the user, it will be sufficient for the user to take place at such regular intervals that afford an indication to the servient land owner that a right is being claimed against him. Here, regular (but not necessarily incessant use) can be distinguished from mere accidental or occasional exercise, which is not sufficiently frequent to evidence that a right over the servient land is so being claimed. Further, casual use coupled with tolerance by the servient land owner, and perhaps their good nature, may also be insufficient to constitute notice that a right is being claimed over the servient land and thus that a prescriptive easement of way is being acquired.[83] In *Mills*

---

[80] (1881) 6 App Cas 740 at 796. Cited from *Gale on Easements* 4-118, p 264, 18th Edn, 2008.

[81] (1881) 6 App Cas 740 at 805.

[82] *Smith v Baxter* [1900] 2 Ch 138, per Stirling J at 146; and see *Hulley v Silversprings Bleaching and Dyeing Co* [1922] 2 Ch 268 at 281; *Hollins v Verney* (1884) 13 QBD 304.

[83] *Ironside, Crabb and Crabb v Cook, Cook and Barefoot* (1978) 41 P & CR 326, CA. See also *Goldsmith v Burrow Construction Ltd, The Times,* July 31, 1987, CA and *Mills v Silver* [1991] Ch 271.

v Silver,[84] the fact that a track was not passable by vehicles in wet weather (five months of the year) did not break the continuity of enjoyment so as to defeat the presumption of a lost grant.

6.75 In *Hollins v Verney* Lindley LJ said that:

> 'a cessation of user which excludes an inference of actual enjoyment as of right for the full statutory period will be fatal at whatsoever portion of the period the cessation occurs; and, on the other hand, a cessation of user which does not exclude such inference, is not fatal, even although it occurs at the beginning, or the end of, the period.'[85]

6.76 A claim to an easement of parking was not made out in *Central Midlands Estates Ltd v Leicester Dyers Ltd*,[86] where the user was seen only as being 'of an occasional nature'.

6.77 For continuity of use to be broken, a lack of enjoyment in the proper manner or cessation of use will normally be looked for. As Parke B said in *Monmouthshire Canal Co v Harford*:[87]

> 'An enjoyment of an easement for one week and a cessation to enjoy it during the next week, and so on alternately, would confer no right.'[88]

6.78 This does not mean a cessation in actual use, for example because the claimant has no occasion to use the easement, would interrupt enjoyment. It means that cessation in the user as of right will interrupt the continuity of the enjoyment being 'as of right'. In similar terms, enjoyment under permissions that were renewed time and time again by the servient owner would prevent the acquisition of a prescriptive title. Such permissions interfere with the continuity of user being 'as of right' and thus the user is not being undertaken in a proper manner.[89] Repeated interruptions, for less than a year in each case, may be evidence to show that the enjoyment has not been 'as of right' under section 2[90] or they may result in the acquisition of a qualified easement only.[91]

6.79 A person asserting an interruption must establish that some notice other than the mere existence of a physical obstruction was given to the person interrupted.[92] Further, a statement by the servient owner that he would or might interrupt the user in the future is not an interruption; if the servient owner acquiesces in the user continuing in the meantime, then that period of

---

[84]　[1991] Ch 271.
[85]　(1884) 13 QBD 314.
[86]　[2003] 2 P & CR D 01.
[87]　(1834) 1 CM & R 631.
[88]　See *Hollins v Verney* (1884) 13 QBD 304.
[89]　*Monmouthshire Canal Co v Harford* (1834) 1 CM & R. 631, per Lord Lyndhurst. See *Tickle v Brown* (1836) 4 A&E 369 at 383.
[90]　*Eaton v Swansea Waterworks Co* (1851) 17 QB 267, applied in *Newnham v Willison* (1988) 56 P & CR 8, followed in *Smith v Brudenell-Bruce* [2002] 2 P & CR 51.
[91]　*Rolle v Whyte* (1868) LR 3 QB 286.
[92]　*Clover v Coleman* (1874) LR 10 CP 108; *Seddon v Bank of Bolton* (1882) 19 Ch D 462.

acquiescence can be relied upon in support of a claim to prescription.[93] In such cases, the statement actually has the effect of showing that the user is as of right, supporting the claim for a prescriptive title.

6.80 Since an interruption is required by section 4 to be acquiesced in for one year, it is generally accepted that an enjoyment for a period exceeding 19 years which is then obstructed can be protected if proceedings are brought after 20 years have run and before the obstruction has been in effect for a period of one year.[94] In cases where the proceedings are brought before the 20 years have run, the claimant's right is treated as being 'inchoate'; as such, the claimant has no protection (eg by way of injunction or otherwise) until the 20 year period has elapsed.[95]

MISTAKEN BELIEF

6.81 Quite often a user will enjoy a right of way under the mistaken belief that they possessed the right to exercise the easement. The fact that enjoyment may take place under such a mistaken view is not sufficient to prevent the enjoyment being 'as of right', and a claim in prescription can still be made out. As noted previously, the subjective belief of the user is generally seen as irrelevant. The essential determination is as to whether the user being undertaken is of a kind that would be carried on if the user did have the right that is being exercised.[96]

6.82 For example, the acquisition of a prescriptive right over a driveway in *Bridle v Ruby*[97] was not defeated simply because the user of the driveway enjoyed the right under the mistaken belief that he had the right, based on the wording in a conveyance of land relating to his property. Here, the fact that enjoyment by the user of the right of way was of a kind that would be undertaken by the user if he indeed had had the right, was sufficient for the claim to the prescriptive right to be made out.

RELEVANT KNOWLEDGE OF THE SERVIENT OWNER

6.83 The servient owner must have either actual knowledge or the means of knowledge of the enjoyment that has given rise to the claim of a prescriptive right.[98]

---

[93] *Samuel v Fatilt*, unreported, Lune 20, 2000, CA.
[94] *Flight v Thomas* (1841) 1 A & E 688; 8 Cl & Fin 231. See also *Bowring Services Ltd v Scottish Widows' Fund & Life Assurance Society* [1995] 1 EGLR 158.
[95] *Bridewell Hospital (Governors) v Ward, Lock Bowden & Co* (1893) 62 LJ Ch 270; *Battersea v London City Sewers Commissioners* [1895] 2 Ch 708.
[96] *R v Oxfordshire CC Ex p Sunningwell PC* [2000] 1 AC 335.
[97] [1989] 1 QB 169.
[98] *Diment v Foot (NH)* [1974] 1 WLR 1427 at 1433, per Sir Jon Pennycuick V-C; *Williams v Sandy Lane (Chester) Ltd* [2007] 1 EGLR 10 at [33].

In the context of discussing acquiescence by the servient owner in that knowledge, Thesiger LJ, said in the Court of Appeal decision in *Sturges v Bridgman*:[99]

> 'The law governing the acquisition of easements by user stands thus: Consent or acquiescence of the owner of the servient tenement lies at the root of prescription, and of the fiction of a lost grant, and hence the acts or user, which go to the proof of either the one or the other, must be, in the language of the civil law, nec vi nec clam nec precario; for a man cannot, as a general rule, be said to consent to or acquiesce in the acquisition by his neighbour of an easement through an enjoyment of which he has no knowledge, actual or constructive,[100] or which he contests and endeavours to interrupt, or which he temporarily licenses. It is a mere extension of the same notion, or rather it is a principle into which by strict analysis it may be resolved, to hold, that an enjoyment which a man cannot prevent raises no presumption of consent or acquiescence.'[101]

6.84   In *Dalton v Angus*, discussing the essential basis of acquiescence, Fry J, said:

> 'I cannot imagine any case of acquiescence in which there is not shown to be in the servient owner; 1, a knowledge of the acts done; 2, a power in him to stop the acts or to sue in respect of them; and 3, an abstinence on his part from the exercise of such power. That such is the nature of acquiescence and that such is the ground upon which presumptions or interferences of grant or covenant may be made appears to me to be plain, both from reason, from maxim, and from the cases.'[102]

6.85   In *Pugh v Savage*[103] the plaintiff owned the freehold of a farm, including field A, access to which from the highway was gained along a lane, part of which bordered his land. A footpath also ran along the lane from the highway to field A, such footpath also crossing field into field B, and across field B into field C. Prior to 1966 a company owned field B and field C belonged to a separate farm. In 1966 the company bought field C and let fields B and C together with a field fronting the highway to the defendant. The defendant was told at the time of the grant of the tenancy that he would be entitled to a right of way over field A and along the lane to the highway. The plaintiff, however, denied the defendant such a right when he sought to exercise it, and ploughed field A and obstructed the lane. The defendant thus used other parts of the plaintiffs land to get to the highway, which led to the plaintiff seeking an injunction and damages for trespass. The defendant asserted a right of way over field A and along the lane, claiming that the right of way has been exercised without interruption by him and his predecessors, the occupiers of field C, for over 30 years immediately prior to the commencement of the

---

99   (1879) 11 Ch D 852 at 863. See also per Stirling LJ, *Roberts v James* (1903) 89 LT 282 at 287. Cited from *Gale on Easements* 4-104, p 255, 18th Edn, 2008.
100   See *Liverpool Corp v Coghill* [1918] 1 Ch 307 at 314.
101   See *Lloyds Bank v Dalton* [1942] Ch 466. Cited from *Gale on Easements* 4-105, p 256, 18th Edn, 2008.
102   (1881) 6 App Cas 740 at 773. Cited from *Gale on Easements* 4-105, p 256, 18th Edn, 2008.
103   [1970] 2 QB 373; applied by Burgess V-C in *Davis v Whitby* [1973] 1 WLR 629 at 630, 631.

proceedings. It was established at the hearing that shortly after 1940, the field has been let on an oral tenancy which was surrendered when the plaintiff bought the farm in 1950.

6.86　The Court of Appeal applied *Cross v Lewis*[104] and *Palk v Skinner*,[105] and held that where a tenancy of a servient tenement came into existence during the course of the period of user, the grant of the tenancy would not prevent the presumption of a grant under the Prescription Act, unless it could be shown that the servient owner had knowledge of the user while the tenant was in possession. The court did distinguish between cases where the tenancy was in existence at the beginning of the period of user and cases when the tenancy came into existence in the course of the period of user. If the tenant was in place at the commencement of the user then it would not be possible to imply a lost grant by the owner at the beginning of the user, for it would not have been possible for him to have stopped the user even if he had knowledge.

6.87　The law was aptly summarised in *Williams v Sand Lane (Chester) Ltd*:

'... it is possible to derive from the decision of this court in *Pugh v Savage* the following principles applicable to cases where the servient land is, or has been, subject to a tenancy.

First, in a case where the grant of the tenancy of the servient land predates the user by or on behalf of the owner of the dominant land, it is necessary to ask whether, notwithstanding the tenancy, the freehold owner of the servient land could take steps to prevent user during the tenancy. The answer to that question is likely to turn on the terms of the tenancy.

Second, if (notwithstanding the tenancy) the owner of the servient land could take steps to prevent the user, then it is necessary to ask whether (and, if so, when) the freehold owner had knowledge (actual or imputed) of that user by the owner of the dominant land. The fact that the freehold owner of the servient land was out of possession when the user began and throughout the term of the tenancy may well lead to the conclusion that knowledge of that user should not be imputed. But if, on the facts, the owner of the servient land does have knowledge of the user and could (notwithstanding the tenancy) take steps to prevent that user, but does not do so, then (prima facie) acquiescence will be established.

Third, in a case where user of the servient land by the owner of the dominant land began before the grant of the tenancy, it is necessary to ask whether the freehold owner of the servient land had knowledge (actual or imputed) at or before the date of the grant. If so, then it is likely to be immaterial whether the terms of the tenancy are such that the owner of the servient land could (or could not) take steps to prevent that user. That is because if (with knowledge of the user) the owner of the servient land grants a tenancy of that land on terms which put it out of his power to prevent that user, he can properly be said to have acquiesced in it.

---

[104]　(1824) 2 B & C 686.
[105]　(1852) 18 QB 568; 17 Jur 372.

Fourth, if the owner of the servient land did not have knowledge of the user at the date of the grant, then the position is the same as it would be if the grant had pre-dated the user. It is necessary to ask whether (notwithstanding the tenancy) the freehold owner can take steps to prevent the user; and, if so, whether (and if so when) the owner had knowledge of the user.'[106]

6.88 In cases where long user *has* been established, then a presumption arises that the owner of the land knew of it, and the burden of proof then shifts to the servient owner who has to establish that he did *not* have knowledge; the dominant owner does *not* have to prove that the servient owner *did* have knowledge.

AGAINST WHOM ENJOYMENT MUST BE HAD – PRESUMED GRANT BY SERVIENT OWNER

6.89 An essential characteristic of any easement is that one tenement is subject to another. The right to the easement of way will exist with respect to that tenement. Accordingly, where an easement is to be acquired by prescription, the continued user which will give rise to the acquisition of the prescriptive easement must be by a person or entity which is in possession of the dominant tenement. As the user is deemed to be evidence of a previous grant, such a grant can only have been made legally by someone who had capacity to impose a permanent burden on the servient property.[107] Furthermore, the owner of the servient tenement must have been aware of the existence of the easement of way, and have been able to interfere with the easement if he so wished, in order for the user to confer the easement.[108] Accordingly, the two essential elements to consider are the servient owner's interest in the servient tenement and their knowledge of the user of the easement of way.

6.90 The common law provided that all prescription presupposes a grant,[109] and (with the exception of easements of light pursuant to section 3 of the Prescription Act), the court must presume the grant of the easement by the absolute owner of the servient tenement to the absolute owner of the dominant tenement in order to establish a prescriptive title to an easement.[110] In respect of any such presumed grant, it is also essential to be able to identify both a competent grantor and grantee. Here the claim to an easement against an

---

[106] *Williams v Sandy Lane (Cheshire) Ltd* (2007) 1 EGLR 10, cited from *Gale on Easements* 4-115, p 262, 18th Edn, 2008.

[107] *Daniel v North* (1809) 11 East 372.

[108] A lack of interference is construed as acquiescence – see *Gray v Bond* (1821) 2 Brod & Bing 667; *Liverpool Corp v Coghill* [1918] 1 Ch 307.

[109] *Goodman v Saltash Corp* (1882) 7 App Cas 654 at 655; *Gardner v Hodgson's Kingston Brewery Co* [1903] AC 229 at 239.

[110] *Wheaton v Maple & Co* [1893] 3 Ch 63; *Kilgour v Gaddes* [1904] 1 KB 466; *Simmons v Dobson* [1991] 1 WLR 720.

owner of the servient tenement who has an interest lesser than in fee simple is generally viewed as being insufficient.[111]

6.91 It is necessary to consider the issue of presumed grant under the three means by which an easement of this nature may be claimed: namely (1) at common law; (2) by presumption of a lost grant; and (3) under the Prescription Act.

Prescription at common law

6.92 Where an easement is claimed by prescription at common law, it is necessary to show enjoyment against the absolute owner of the servient tenement.[112] This was established in *Wheaton v Maple & Co*[113] where it was held that for a right to be claimed by prescription it must be claimed as appendant or appurtenant to land (that is, it could not be for a limited time or terms of years). In cases where the right claimed is not appendant or appurtenant to land, then prescription at common law is not possible. This principle, that the easement can only be claimed between absolute owners was also held to be the case in other cases, such as *Fear v Morgan.*[114] Specifically with reference to easements of way, Mathew LJ in *Kilgour v Gaddes*[115] (referring to a right of way) remarked that:

'Such an easement [of way] can only be acquired by prescription at common law where the dominant and servient tenements respectively belong to different owners in fee. It follows that where the fee simple in both dominant and servient tenements belongs to the same owner no easement can be acquired by prescription at common law.'[116]

6.93 It has also been said that:

'It is well settled that a lessee cannot acquire a right of way over the land of another lessee under the same lessor either by prescription at common law, or under the doctrine of a lost grant, or by prescription under the Prescription Act 1832.'

6.94 Special rules apply in cases where the right to enlargement of a leasehold estate pursuant to section 153 of the LPA 1925 exists as a unilateral right.[117]

---

[111] See also the provisions in sections 7 and 8 of the Prescription Act 1832.

[112] See Lindley in *Wheaton v Maple & Co* [1893] 3 Ch. 63 at 65 that a right claimed by prescription must be claimed as 'appendant or appurtenant to land and not as annexed to it for a term of years; also that an easement for a limited time only cannot be gained by prescription at common law'.

[113] [1893] 3 Ch 63 at 65.

[114] [1906] 2 Ch 415 at 416.

[115] [1904] 1 KB 467.

[116] Per PO Lawrence J in *Cory v Davies* [1923] 2 Ch 95 at 107, citing *Wheaton v Maple & Co* (above) and *Kilgour v Gaddes*. See also *Simmons v Dobson* [1991] 1 WLR 720.

[117] *Bosomworth v Faber* (1992) 69 P & CR 288. In this case the Court of Appeal were prepared to presume a lost modern grant.

Prescription based on lost grant

6.95 Here, the case of *Wheaton v Maple & Co* is also the authority for the same rule as in cases of prescription at common law; enjoyment as against an owner of the servient tenement who does not have an interest in fee simple will be insufficient.[118] The principle was stated in *Bradbury v Grinsell*:

> 'Though an uninterrupted possession for twenty years or upwards should be sufficient evidence to be left to a jury to presume a grant; yet the rule must ever be taken with this qualification, that the possession was with the acquiescence of him who was seised of an estate of inheritance: for a tenant for life or years has no power to grant such right for a longer period than during the continuance of his particular estate. If such a tenant permits another to enjoy an easement on his estate for twenty years or upwards without interruption, and then the particular estate determines, such user will not affect him who has the inheritance in reversion or remainder; but when it vests in possession the reversioner may dispute the right to the easement, and the length of possession will be no answer to his claim.'[119]

6.96 Specifically with reference to easements of way, in *Roberts v James*,[120] it was held that where a tenant for life in possession of land had a lost grant of an easement of way, it was not possible to imply the grant against the reversioner by virtue only of user of the easement of way during the lifetime of the tenant. One reason for this is that the reversioner, as someone not in possession, would have been unable to interfere with or otherwise prevent the user, and accordingly it would thereby be unjust for his reversion to become bound by the easement of way.[121]

6.97 It is important to establish whether a tenancy was in existence when the user first commenced, or whether the tenancy or came into existence in the course of the period of user. In the case of the former, it is unlikely that a lost grant can be implied. However, the coming into existence of a tenancy during the period of user will not prevent the presumption of lost grant, unless there is evidence that the servient owner had no knowledge of the user whilst the tenant was in possession of the property.[122]

6.98 Special rules apply in cases where the freehold interest in the dominant and servient tenement belongs to the same owner.[123]

---

[118] [1893] 3 Ch 69; applied to lost modern grant in *Simmons v Dobson* [1991] 1 WLR 720.
[119] 2 Wms Saund (1871 Edn) 509–512. Cited from *Gale on Easements* 4-62, p 232, 18th Edn, 2008.
[120] (1903) 89 LT 287.
[121] See *Bright v Walker* (1834) 1 Cr M & R 211 at 221 which suggests an alternative position.
[122] *See Pugh v Savage* [1970] 2 QB 373.
[123] See *Simmons v Dobson* [1991] WLR 720; *Bosomworth v Faber* (1992) 69 P & CR 288 can be seen as an exception.

Claims under the Prescription Act 1832

6.99 Claims under the Prescription Act in relation to light are governed by section 3 of the Act. For these, a presumption of an absolute grant is not required and rights can be acquired against the servient tenement owner even if they cannot dispose of the freehold interest. Other than claims of light, and specifically for claims of easements of way, it is necessary to consider the interest of the servient owner in the servient tenement (eg if the servient land leased, or ultimately owned in fee simply by the same person who owns the dominant land too), and specifically whether the enjoyment has been for a 20 or 40 year period.

Interest of servient owner

6.100 The recent case of *Llewellyn v Lorey*[124] centred around a claim to a right of way for agricultural purposes, and also whether the claimant had acquired a prescriptive easement over the defendant's land. The claimants asserted that from 1931 to 1960 the route had been used for various mining activities, until late 1970 to extract mining waste, and then from 1984 for a motor repair business. Accordingly, a claim both under the doctrine of lost modern grant and the Prescription Act 1832 was made.

6.101 The court rejected the claim on the basis that the land over which the prescriptive right was claimed had been subject to a life tenant, and later subject to two further tenancies. In such periods, given that the land was vested in the life tenant, or subject to the leases, the freeholder was not legally empowered to take action. Possession and control of the land over which the right was claimed was vested in the lessee for the time being. As such, prescriptive use had not been enjoyed, as of right, against the freehold owner of the land, who could not be taken to have acquiesced in knowledge of the user. The interest of the servient owner in the servient tenement was not as freeholder during the relevant periods.

Twenty years' enjoyment.

6.102 A claim under section 2 on the basis of 20 years enjoyment will be successful if title against *all* persons having interests in the servient tenement can be shown. In *Bright v Walker*[125] a lessee enjoyed a right of way over the servient tenement without interruption for more than 20 years. The servient tenement was held by the defendant under a lease for lives from the same bishop under which the plaintiff held its lease. The plaintiff's claim for the right of way under the Prescription Act thus failed because the fee simple in both the dominant and the servient tenement belonged to the same owner. As Parke B said:

---

[124] [2011] EWCA Civ 37.
[125] (1834) 1 Cr M & R, 211.

'The important question is, whether this enjoyment, as it cannot give a title against all persons having estates in the locus in quo, gives a title as against the lessee and the defendants claiming under him, or not at all? We have had considerable difficulty in coming to a conclusion on this point; but, upon the fullest consideration, we think that no title at all is gained by a user which does not give a valid title against all, and permanently affect the Fee ... From hence we are led to conclude, that an enjoyment of twenty years, if it give not a good title against all, gives no good title at all; and as it is clear that this enjoyment, whilst the land was held by a tenant for life, cannot affect the [freehold] reversion in the bishop now, and is therefore not good as against every one, it is not good as against any one, and, therefore, not against the defendant.'[126]

6.103 The land was leased, and in any event, owned by the same person who owned the fee simple in the dominant land.

Forty years' enjoyment.

6.104 In cases where enjoyment has continued for 40 years, the right to an easement is conferred unless the reversioner resists the claim. Such resistance must be within three years after the determination of the particular estate. In *Wright v Williams,*[127] Parke B remarked the Prescription Act's intention was that an enjoyment of 20 years should be of 'no avail against an idiot or other person labouring under incapacity'. Conversely, one of 40 years should confer an absolute title'. Lord Abinger held that the enjoyment of an easement for 40 years gave an 'indefeasible title', *even* where a tenancy for life existed. As such, an absolute grant is presumed in cases where a claim under the Act to an easement is derived from enjoyment over a 40 year period.

6.105 However, an exception to this 40 year rule would be a case where the freehold interest of both tenements belonged to the same landlord.[128] In such a case, a prescriptive easement cannot be acquired by either 20 or 40 years user.

6.106 With regard to whether consents can defeat a claim to a prescriptive right based on 40 years use, the position is that any consent, whether oral or written, which have been given from time to time during the period, will defeat a claim based on either 20 or 40 years' use. A consent in writing, given at the beginning of the use (and extending throughout) defeats a claim based on 20 or 40 years' use as well. However, an oral consent given at the beginning of the use (and extending throughout) has been held only to defeat a claim based on 20 years use, but not 40 years' use.[129] *Jones v Price* provides an alternative position however.[130] In *Jones* the use commenced with oral permission, and even though not renewed (orally or in writing), it was held that there was a tacit understanding between the neighbours that the permission was still in force. Use that continues on a common understanding that the use is, and continues

---

[126] (1834) 1 Cr M & R, 211 at 220, 221. Cited from *Gale on Easements* 4-69, p 235, 18th Edn, 2008.
[127] (1836) Tyr & G.375 (see in particular at 392, 393, 400).
[128] See *Kilgour v Gaddes* [1904] 1 KB 457.
[129] Megarry & Wade, *The Law of Real Property* (Sweet & Maxwell, 8th Edn, 2012), para 28-076.
[130] *Jones v Price* (1992) 64 P & CR 404.

to be, permissive could thus be argued to defeat a claim based on 40 years' use, even if the consent given was originally oral in nature.

6.107 In cases where the legal action is brought on the basis of 40 years, the user period must extend up until the commencement of the action, like in the case of a claim based on 20 years.

6.108 The reason why the rules relating to 40 years use are somewhat obscure is largely because the acquisition of a prescriptive easement based on 40 years use is very rarely encountered. It is significantly more common to rely on 20 years use.

Incompetent grantors

6.109 As noted above, is it insufficient to claim a prescriptive title to an easement of way against an owner of the servient tenement who had an interest less than in fee simple. Normally this is caused by a servient owner being only a tenant. However, an inability to dispose of the fee can be caused by other factors including the doctrine of ultra vires or in cases where the owner of the servient tenement is restrained from alienation.

6.110 The servient tenement may be owned by a company with limited powers of disposition causing the grant of an easement by that company to exceed its power. In such cases, no prescriptive title will arise either where an easement is claimed by prescription at common law or under the doctrine of lost grant. This will also be the case where an easement is claimed under the Prescription Act based on 20 years user (other than an easement of light under section 3). The reason for this is that the necessary grant cannot be presumed.[131] In cases where the claim to an easement is that of light, based on 20 years enjoyment under the prescription Act, it would *not* be necessary to presume a grant, and accordingly a right to the easement might be established.[132]

6.111 The position cases where an easement (other than of light) is claimed under section 2 of the Prescription Act based on 40 years user against a company with limited powers of disposition has traditionally been unclear. When considering the exact wording of the Prescription Act, it can be noted that the wording in section 2 relating to 40 years user other than of light bears close similarity to the wording of section 3, which are applied to 20 years enjoyment of easements of light. For this reason, it has been suggested that, just as for easements of light claimed based on 20 years long use, it is not necessary to presume an absolute grant by the servient owner (who may be unable to have lawfully provided such a grant). This is supported by the decision in *Wright v Williams*[133] which also suggests that it is not necessary to

---

[131] *Rochdale Co v Radcliffe* (1852) 18 QB 287 at 315; *Att-Gen v GN Ry* [1909] 1 Ch 775 at 778. See also *Bakewell Management Ltd v Brandwood* [2004] 2 AC 519.

[132] *Tapling v Jones* (1865) 11 HLCL 304; *Jordeson v Sutton, Southcoates and Drypool Gas Co* [1898] 2 Ch 614 at 618, 626.

[133] (1836) Tyr & G 375.

show an absolute grant. However, *Staffordshire and Worcestershire Canal Navigation (Proprietors) v Birmingham and Navigation (Proprietors)*[134] suggested the converse. Here an easement was claimed on the ground of a 40-years' enjoyment. It was argued that the servient tenement was owned by a company which had no power to make a grant. It was said in the House of Lords that, if the prescription Act 1832 applied to the case, it would be necessary to show that the right claimed *could* have been granted, and because of the limited powers of the company in this case, the grant would have been void for being ultra vires.

6.112 The decision in *Housden v Conservators of Wimbledon and Putney Commons*[135] has since clarified the position. Considering the opening words of section 2 which referred to a claim 'which may be lawfully made at the common law', words which did not appear in section 3, the Court of Appeal upheld an earlier decision of the court that neither the 20-year nor the 40-year period referred to in section 2 gave rise to an easement by prescription in the case of grantor *lacking* the power to grant the easement. In both cases the servient owner would need to have been able to grant the easement. Whilst the Court of Appeal considered that the servient owner was not actually prevented from granting the easement claimed based on its actual power, it considered the issue in any case and held that the House of Lords in *Staffordshire* (a case where the servient owner was unable to grant the easement claimed) had regarded the opening words of section 2 as a ground of distinguishing the operation of section 2 from that of section 3.[136]

6.113 Accordingly, where the dominant owner claims 40 years user under section 2 of the Prescription Act 1832, and the servient owner could *not* lawfully have granted the easement, it will be *ultra vires* just as in the case where 20 years under section 2 is claimed against a servient owner who was unable to have lawfully made a grant in similar terms.[137] As the servient owners had no power to grant the right, any grant would have been ultra vires and therefore void.

ILLEGALITY

6.114 A feature of the acquisition of prescriptive easements in recent times has pertained to whether such an easement can be acquired when the said act undertaken was itself unlawful. In other words, can such an easement over the land have been *lawfully* granted by the servient owner?

---

[134] (1866) LR 1 HL 254.
[135] [2007] 1 WLR 2543 (first instance) and [2008] 1 WLR 1172 (Court of Appeal).
[136] [2008] 1 WLR 1172 at [66] and [77].
[137] Section 3 of the Act can be distinguished from section 2 when the claim is based on 40 years' long user for such purposes. See also *Lemaitre v Davis* (1881) 19 Ch D 281 at 291 in respect of a claim of 40 years' long user under section 2.

6.115 The general rule is that one cannot acquire a right to do something that is prohibited by public statute. For example, unless undertaken with lawful authority, under section 34(1) of the Road Traffic Act 1988 and section 193 of the LPA 1925, it is an offence to drive over land which is not a road (including common land).

6.116 Section 34(1) states that:

'34.— Prohibition of driving mechanically propelled vehicles elsewhere than on roads.

Subject to the provisions of this section, if without lawful authority a person drives a mechanically propelled vehicle:

(a) on to or upon any common land, moorland or land of any other description, not being land forming part of a road, or
(b) on any road being a footpath, bridleway or restricted byway,

he is guilty of an offence.'[138]

6.117 In *Hanning v Top Deck Travel Group Ltd*[139] the Court of Appeal held that an easement could not be acquired by prescription where the use was illegal. This remained the case even if lawful authority had been given. It was held that a prescriptive easement could not be acquired by long use under the Prescription Act 1832, or the doctrine of lost modern grant, where the use relied upon in acquisition of the prescriptive right was unlawful.

6.118 The decision in *Hanning* caused considerable problems for landowners who had assumed they had the benefit of prescriptive rights, particularly of access to their properties, because of long use. The effect of the decision in *Hanning* was to confirm that no such prescriptive rights would have been acquired when the use was unlawful. This particular issue was addressed by parliament and section 68 of the Countryside and Rights of Way Act 2000 provided for a statutory easement in certain circumstances where a prescriptive one failed on grounds of illegality.

6.119 Section 68(1) provided:

'Vehicular access across common land etc.

(1) This section applies to a way which the owner or occupier (from time to time) of any premises has used as a means of access for vehicles to the premises, if that use of the way:
(a) was an offence under an enactment applying to the land crossed by the way, but

---

[138] Road Traffic Act 1988, s 34(1).
[139] (1993) 68 P&CR 14.

(b)   would otherwise have been sufficient to create on or after the prescribed date, and to keep in existence, an easement giving a right of way for vehicles.

(2)   Regulations may provide, as respects a way to which this section applies, for the creation in accordance with the regulations, on the application of the owner of the premises concerned and on compliance by him with prescribed requirements, of an easement subsisting at law for the benefit of the premises and giving a right of way for vehicles over that way.

(3)   An easement created in accordance with the regulations is subject to any enactment or rule of law which would apply to such an easement granted by the owner of the land.

(4)   The regulations may in particular:

(a)   require that, where an application is made after the relevant use of the way has ceased, it is to be made within a specified time,

(b)   specify grounds on which objections may be made and the procedure to apply to the making of objections,

(c)   require any matter to be referred to and determined by the Lands Tribunal, and make provision as to procedure and costs,

(d)   make provision as to the payment of any amount by the owner of the premises concerned to any person or into court and as to the time when any payment is to be made,

(e)   provide for the determination of any such amount,

(f)   make provision as to the date on which any easement is created,

(g)   specify any limitation to which the easement is subject,

(h)   provide for the easement to include any specified right incidental to the right of way,

(i)   make different provision for different circumstances.

(5)   In this section:

"enactment" includes an enactment in a local or private Act and a byelaw, regulation or other provision having effect under an enactment;

"owner", in relation to any premises, means:

(a)   a person, other than a mortgagee not in possession, who is for the time being entitled to dispose of the fee simple of the premises, whether in possession or in reversion, or

(b)   a tenant under a long lease, within the meaning of the Landlord and Tenant Act 1987;

"prescribed" means prescribed by regulations;

"regulations" means regulations made, as respects England, by the Secretary of State and, as respects Wales, by the National Assembly for Wales.

(6)   Regulations under this section shall be made by statutory instrument, and no such regulations shall be made by the Secretary of State unless a draft has been laid before, and approved by a resolution of, each House of Parliament.'[140]

This was enacted specifically to deal with the problem that *Hanning* had created.

6.120 Subsequently the position was clarified in the House of Lords decision in *Bakewell Management Limited v Brandwood*.[141] In *Bakewell* the House of

---

[140]   Countryside and Rights of Way Act 2000, s 68.
[141]   [2004] UKHL 14.

Lords made clear that whilst a prescriptive right could not be acquired to do something expressly prohibited by public statute, where that prohibition is attributable to a lack of lawful authority which *could* have been given, but was not, an easement *could* be acquired by prescription.

6.121 In his judgment, Lord Scott said:

> 'In my opinion, if an easement over land can be lawfully granted by the landowner the easement can be acquired either by prescription under s 2 of the 1832 Act or by the fiction of lost modern grant whether the use relied on is illegal in the criminal sense or merely in the *tortious* sense. I can see no valid reason of public policy to bar that acquisition. We have been referred to no case, pre *Hanning*, that decided the contrary. The decision in *Hanning* took the law, in my opinion, in a wrong direction. It follows that, in my opinion, your Lordships should hold *Hanning* to have been wrongly decided and should overrule the various rulings in reliance on *Hanning* that have been made in the subsequent cases.'[142]

6.122 This decision therefore overturned the *Hanning* decision, and made section 68 of Countryside and Rights of Way Act 2000 redundant (indeed, the decision ultimately led to its repeal on 6 September 2007).

6.123 The effect of this with regard to use of land pursuant to section 34(1) of the Road Traffic Act 1988 is clear. Whilst section 34(1) makes it an offence for someone, without lawful authority, to drive mechanically propelled vehicle on to or upon any common land, moorland or land of any other description, not being land forming part of a road, or on any road being a footpath, bridleway or restricted byway, if the servient owner *could* lawfully have given authority to pass and repass over the land for the user which is not permitted by statute, then a prescriptive easement may lawfully be claimed. Subject to other requirements being satisfied, the prescriptive easement is likely to be claimed under either lost modern grant or under the Prescription Act 1832.

6.124 The case of *R (on the application of David and Susan Joyce Hattersley) v Nun Monkton Parish Council* is an example of the misunderstanding that a landowner can exhibit in respect of the grant of rights of way over land. Here, before the matter came before the court, the Defendant Parish Council consented to judgment on all grounds referred to in the detailed statement of grounds submitted with the application for permission to seek judicial review of the Defendant Parish Council's refusal to grant homeowners in the village, Mr and Mrs Hattersley, a right of way over the village green in Nun Monkton. The Defendant Parish Council had refused to grant Mr and Mrs Hattersley an easement because (*inter alia*) they did not consider they were able to grant a right of way over the village green; they believed they were unable to do so given that the act of driving a vehicle over the village green was prohibited. Crucially, such a prohibition was attributable to a lack of authority which the Defendant Parish Council were able to lawfully provide. Accordingly, as the

---

[142] [2004] UKHL 14 at 47.

Defendant Parish Council *could* grant the easement to Mr and Mrs Hattersley (that is, they could legitimise the user), the Defendant Parish Council had erred in law.[143]

6.125 The pertinent issue is therefore whether the servient owner *could* have given lawful authority. This is apparent in a number of cases and in *Bakewell* the House of Lords gave a number of examples of where a landowner could *not* have lawfully given authority to grant an easement, thus barring a prescriptive claim, These included:

(a) Where the grantor does not have the capacity to make the grant.

(b) Where a statutory provision made it unlawful for the authority to be given. To interfere with the rights that commoners have over common land would constitute a nuisance; as such the landowner would not legally be able to authorise the interference.

(c) Where a statutory prohibition is absolute – in these cases the illegality cannot be corrected by the authority given by the landowner, even if they could provide it.

6.126 This is one particular area of the law on prescriptive easements which continues to cause confusion in practice. The key question to ask in any given case is not whether the act was lawful or not under a given statute, but rather whether the landowner *could* lawfully have provided the authority to grant the easement. This combines the central tenet, that exercising a right for a long enough period of time, without interference from a third party, should enable the right to be capable of legitimisation, with an assumption that the right originally derived from a *lawful* grant by the servient owner, as grantor, to the dominant land owner as grantee.

BY WHOM ENJOYMENT MUST BE HAD – COMPETENT GRANTEE

6.127 As noted above, the general rule applicable to the establishment of a prescriptive title to an easement of way (or any easement claimed under section 2) is that there is the presumption of an absolute grant. Whilst it must be shown that there was a competent grantor in respect of the servient tenement (ie the servient owner must have been able to lawfully make the grant), it must also be demonstrated that there was a competent grantee with regard to the dominant tenement.

6.128 For example, it is not possible for a statutory company or undertaker to acquire, by prescription, rights that are more extensive than are conferred upon

---

[143] Unreported, CO/1743/2007 (High Court of Justice, Queen's Bench Division, Administrative Court).

it by relevant legislation. In *National Guaranteed Manure Co v Donald* (1859) a company which has been reconstituted as a railway company was held to be incapable of acquiring water rights by prescription. *Traill v McAllister* (1890) is a similar case to confirm that acts by a dominant owner which are prohibited by statute cannot result in a prescriptive title to an easement.

6.129 A prescriptive easement must be claimed as appurtenant to the fee simple of the dominant tenement. It is, however, possible to claim a prescriptive easement of way if based on enjoyment as of right by the occupiers of the dominant tenement.[144] For example, the enjoyment of an easement by a tenant for life in possession of the dominant tenement will enure for the benefit of the fee simple. Accordingly, there can be the presumption of an absolute grant in such cases.[145] Indeed, with regard to tenants in occupation of a dominant tenement, the possession of the tenant is treated as the possession of their landlord for these purposes.[146] Thus where the dominant land is let to the tenant, who enjoys a right of way over adjoining land, the tenant's enjoyment is held to be for the benefit of its freehold owner. This would not be the case however if the freehold estate of the dominant and servient tenement were owned by the same person of course; given the unity of ownership in the fee simple, a prescriptive right could not arise.

---

[144] *Wheaton v Maple & Co*[1893] 3 Ch 63; *Kilgour v Gaddes* [1904] 1 KB 466.

[145] See also the pre-Prescription Act cases of *Grimstead v Marlowe* (1792) 4 TR 717; *Att-Gen v Gauntlett* (1829) 3 Y & J 93; *Codling v Johnson* (1829) 9 B & C 933.

[146] *Gayford v Moffatt* (1868) 4 Ch App 133 at 135; *Pugh v Savage* [1970] 2 QB 373 at 383, per Cross LJ *Midtown Ltd v City of London Real Property Co Ltd* [2005] 1 EGLR 65 at [15].

Chapter 7

ACQUISITION OF RIGHTS OF WAY BY STATUTORY POWERS

GENERAL CONSIDERATIONS

7.1   Private rights of way can arise by statute as well as by act of parties. While express and implied rights derive from the actual or imputed intention of the parties, statutory and prescriptive ways take their authority from the general law. Although the law implies a grant for prescriptive ways this is a fiction, well recognised as such in relation to lost modern grant. The two most important forms of statutory private rights of way also involve fictions although as they are considered elsewhere they are outside the scope of this Chapter.

7.2   The first is a statutory imputed intention to make a grant under the LPA 1925, s 62 (see para **3.48**) which may or may not correspond to what the parties would have intended if they had considered the matter. Section 62 (and its predecessor in the Conveyancing Act 1881, s 6) is a form of statutory shorthand, to enact and imply the 'general words' which had commonly been included in conveyances before 1881 and therefore it reflects the practice of conveyancers when drafting deeds.

7.3   The second is a fictitious grant under the Prescription Act 1832 (see para **6.20**) which will often be directly contrary to the intentions of the supposed grantor. Such statutory prescription differs from prescription at common law, principally in relation to the period of enjoyment of the right claimed.

7.4   The rules governing statutory rights of way are therefore primarily those of the common law. The provisions of the LRA 2002 have materially affected the extent to which certain easements can be enforced against a proprietor of registered land but the underlying rules remain the same as for unregistered land.

7.5   The concept of statutory easements and statutory wayleaves has recently been the subject of analysis by the Law Commission in Appendix A to their *Consultation Paper No 205: The Electronic Communications Code*, although their discussion goes beyond the electronic code to consider the nature of such rights for water, gas and electricity. They say[1] 'The term "statutory easement" is used generally as short-hand for a nonownership right created through

---

[1]   Appendix A, para A3.

compulsory purchase legislation.' There is then a footnote referring to 'the Acquisition of Land Act 1981, which applies to a compulsory acquisition under the provisions of the Land Compensation Act 1961; and the Compulsory Purchase Act 1965.' As considered below, the concept can be taken much further and indeed has been by the Law Commission themselves in their *Consultation Paper No 194: Level Crossings*. In particular a distinction can be made between two types of right. One is statutory easements as such, which satisfy the requirements for an easement created by grant as where two parts of a property are severed by a compulsory purchase. The other is statutory wayleaves, most often found to benefit undertakings for water, gas, electricity and telecommunications for pipes and cables but which can include rights of access, where there is no dominant tenement.

Nature of statutory right

7.6 A statutory right of way is, in principle, no different from a way by grant. *Newcomen v Coulson*[2] concerned a way authorised under an inclosure Act. At first instance the Vice-Chancellor said that the right was not an easement but a grant of a road. The Court of Appeal disagreed and held it was an easement and they applied the relevant rules of law.

7.7 Where a private right of way is granted by statute, then the dominant owner can renounce or abandon the right. 'In such cases, when the rights given have been only private rights, unless there has been also in the Act of parliament a clause excluding a power of contract, it has been held that by contract or by voluntary renunciation such rights, as far as they are personal rights, may be parted with and renounced.'[3]

7.8 In *Hulbert v Dale*[4] an inclosure award set out a private way along one route. That way was never constructed and indeed buildings were erected across it but a second way, parallel to it, was made and used. The servient owner disputed the existence of the right of way over the second route. The dominant owner, who would have had the benefit of the way in the award, argued that if it was the case that he had not established a right along the second route then the original awarded route should be revived. The court found that a right over the second route arose under a lost modern grant so that it was not necessary to find if the statutory way had been abandoned, but that would appear to follow. In *Midland Railway Company v Gribble*[5] a statutory way across a railway crossing was held to have been abandoned. However, in *Benn v Hardinge*[6] the Court of Appeal, relying on an earlier decision of that court in *Gotobed v Pridmore*[7] held that where an inclosure award of 1818 had appointed a private carriage road, then even though it had apparently not been used by occupiers

---

2   (1877) LR 5 Ch D 133.
3   *Great Eastern Rly Co v Goldsmid* (1884) 9 AppCas 927, per Earl of Selborne LC at p 937.
4   [1909] 2 Ch 570.
5   [1895] 2 Ch 827.
6   (1992) 66 P & CR 246.
7   (1971) EG 759.

of the dominant tenement for 180 years, it had not been abandoned. In doing so they applied the normal rules of abandonment (see para **9.50**) without reference to the statutory origin of the right.

Direct grant or enabling power

7.9   Although the existence of a statutory way is authorised by an Act of Parliament, the terms will vary from case to case. The statute may provide for the way to come into existence by direct immediate creation as under the Natural Environment and Rural Communities Act 2006, s 67. Alternatively the statute may provide machinery, such as a surveyor under an inclosure Act which provides for an award to be drawn up. More often the Act provides a background against which the parties are encouraged, indeed expected, to reach agreement, with recourse to the statute only where they fail to agree. Thus the Railways Clauses Consolidation Act 1845, s 68 allows a landowner whose land is cut off by a new railway to have a right of way across a level crossing but its terms will be incorporated in a conveyance or deed of grant. Likewise, where a tenant acquires the freehold under the Leasehold Reform Act 1967, the detailed terms of the right of way under section 10 will be incorporated in a transfer and only if the parties cannot agree on the wording will they have recourse to a dispute procedure.

INCLOSURE ACTS

7.10   Many private ways still in use derive from inclosure Acts. In the eighteenth and nineteenth centuries large parts of the country were rearranged under these local Acts. They involved converting the open fields of the village and the waste lands of the manor into cultivated enclosed fields and farms. Once the local Act had passed through Parliament, a surveyor had the responsibility to determine how it would be applied on the ground. He was not usually a lawyer although he would have had access to legal advice. He drew up an award setting out who would receive which allotments of land and what rights were to be enjoyed with them. Some of the inclosed lands were allotted to those who previously had rights over the waste, such as rights of common, or rights to tithes, and some to the former freeholder of the waste, usually the lord of the manor.

7.11   Before inclosure, the land was often crossed by a variety of ways, public, private and customary, and, along with all other rights over the land, these were extinguished by the Acts[8] and new ways were laid out as provided in the award. In *Adeane v Mortlock*[9] an inclosure Act specifically provided that while extinguishing a public footpath along a given route it gave a named landowner a new private right of way over the same route.

---

[8]   *Campbell v Wilson* (1803) 3 East 294, 102 ER 610; *Turner v Crush* (1878-79) LR 4 App Cas 221. See Inclosure Act 1845, s 62.
[9]   (1839) 5 Bing NC 236 132 ER 1095.

Drafting and standard provisions

7.12 Initially, each inclosure Act was individually drafted. Although model clauses developed which were incorporated in numerous Acts, and although surveyors tended to use standard wording in their awards, it is always necessary to consult the Act and award in question to ensure there are no special provisions or differences in drafting. Provisions can be tortuously drawn and difficult to interpret. A common problem is to know if a way, either referred to in general terms in an Act or detailed in an award, was intended to be a public highway or a private way usually for a number of allotments.[10] The scope and extent of use may vary and may be limited to agriculture but where an unrestricted right of way is granted it may be used for any purpose and the owner of a dominant tenement may have the right to enter and make up the way.[11]

7.13 Many of the provisions frequently incorporated in private Acts were included in the general Inclosure Act 1845 and its successors. This Act was passed after the main period of inclosure was over and its provisions apply only to a minority of inclosures but it indicates what the previous common terms were although the opportunity was taken (to a limited extent) to improve the drafting. Section 68 provided for the valuer in making his award to set out private ways.

7.14 There is a variety of ownership rights over such roads. Sometimes the soil continued to belong to the lord of the manor, possibly it might be vested as tenants in common in those person entitled to use the ways[12] and sometimes the *medium filum* presumption applies (see para **2.15**) so the soil of the way is vested in the adjoining landowners. It may be necessary to carry out research to determine which applies. If the person having access over the ways is an owner of all or part of the soil he will not have a distinct right of way over his own property but will be entitled to use the way as an incident of ownership.[13]

7.15 Some private inclosure Acts or awards provided for private roads which were in such words as 'set out and awarded for the use of all the owners and occupiers of lands and tenements in [the area of the inclosure] having occasion to use the same'. These are best analysed as a multiple grant of private ways for the benefit of each portion of land (usually the allottees under the inclosure) which might benefit.

7.16 One source of confusion in interpreting inclosure Acts is that they often refer to 'private highways' or to private roads as being available for general use or repairable by the public or with materials from quarries set apart for general

---

[10] *R v Richards* (1800) 8 Term Reports 634; 101 ER 1588 – right of way for inhabitants held private. See also *Dunlop v Secretary of State for the Environment and Cambridgeshire County Council* (1995) 70 P & CR 307.

[11] *Newcomen v Coulson* (1877) LR 5 Ch D 133.

[12] Subject now to the provisions of the LPA 1925 and the Trusts of Land and Appointment of Trustees Act 1996.

[13] For maintenance provisions see para **8.32**.

road repairs. It appears that the expression 'private highways' or even 'private road' could sometimes refer to a way which was to be a highway but repairable not by the public (that is the parish) but by the residents of a hamlet or even by an identified landowner.[14]

Extent of right

7.17   In *Abson v Fenton*[15] an inclosure Act reserved to the lord of the manor (who had been freeholder of the inclosed land), the power to work minerals and 'to do all such other works, acts, and things as might be necessary or convenient for the full and complete enjoyment thereof, in as full, ample, and beneficial a manner' as if the Act had not been made. It was held that he had the right to construct a waggon way 'whether the direction chosen has been such as a person of reasonable and ordinary skill and experience would have selected beforehand, and whether the mode adopted has been such as a prudent and rational person would have adopted if he had been making the road over his own land, and not over the land of another'.[16]

PRIVATE ESTATE ACTS

7.18   A right of way can be conferred by other private acts. *Sisters of the Sacred Heart of Mary Ltd v Kingston upon Thames Royal Borough Council*[17] concerned the Maldens and Coombe Urban District Council Act 1933 which authorised the local council to acquire and to manage roads on a private development estate and to recover the cost by a service charge on proprietors on the estate. The court held that the Act extinguished any rights of way which existed prior to its enactment and granted new statutory ones in their place and accordingly the rights of the dominant owners and of the council were wholly governed by the terms of the Act. The case involved a proposed automatic barrier and it was held that would be an unreasonable interference with the private rights of the proprietors and so the cost of it was not a proper charge but that the cost of a manned barrier would be lawful.

7.19   Another private estate Act is the Wentworth Estate Act 1964 relating to an estate at Virginia Water in Surrey run by the Wentworth Estate Roads Committee (which has corporate status). The estate had been developed by a private company, Wentworth Estates Ltd, but when the Act was passed development was virtually complete. The Act vested in the Committee, the roads over which residents had rights of way but reserved to Wentworth Estates Ltd rights of way over the estate roads for the benefit of land it still retained. The Act also authorised Wentworth Club Ltd, which operated the Golf Course, to close the estate roads (except to residents) for 14 days in any

---

[14]   See Yolande Hodson 'Footpaths and bridleways in inclosure acts 1801–1845', Rights of Way Law Review 99.3, p 179, September 2011.

[15]   (1823).

[16]   Per Abbott CJ at 1 B & C 203; 107 ER 76.

[17]   [2007] EWHC 563 (Ch).

year while special events took place at the golf club. A similar statute is the St George's Hill Weybridge Estate Act 1990 relating to a private estate at Elmbridge in Surrey. The Act vested the roads and open spaces in the St Georges Hill Residents' Association Ltd. The main purpose of these two Acts was to authorise and govern service charges (see para **8.34**).

7.20   The fact that an estate Act authorises the construction of ways will not by itself confer any rights on residents of the estate. In *White v Leeson*[18] a tenant for life was authorised by a private estate Act to lay out a building estate with ways and streets 'for the general improvement of the estate,' and grant leases. He constructed the roads and granted two leases with express rights of way. Tenants under other leases who did not have express grants of rights of way claimed to exercise similar rights over the streets. The court interpreted the Act as allowing the landlord to restrict access, and even though the ways were for the estate generally, those tenants who did not have an express right were excluded from use.

PARTITION OF LAND HELD IN TRUST

7.21   Where land belongs under a trust to more than one person in undivided shares it is possible for it to be physically divided so that instead of all having rights over the whole, each exclusively owns a specific part.[19] If that happens, the owner of one part may need a right of way over another part. Parties of full age and capacity can make a division and resolve any terms between them but it may also be done by trustees with consent of the beneficiaries of full age under the Trusts of Land and Appointment of Trustees Act 1996, s 7 and the court has a concurrent power to do so under s 14 including dispensing with consent. Partition is also a disposition which may be authorised by the court also under the Trustee Act 1925, s 57.

7.22   Before 1926, such land was owned in undivided shares at common law and there were various statutory powers going back to an earlier statute of 1540 but ultimately in Acts of 1868 and 1876 for applications to court for the land to be partitioned. Between 1926 and 1996 the land was normally held under a trust for sale when it was assumed that the land would be sold and converted into money and therefore the interests of the parties were notionally in the proceeds of sale. There was a power under the LPA 1925, s 28(3) for the trustees to partition the land with the consent of all persons interested. Where the parties could not agree, the expected remedy was to sell the land under the trust for sale.

7.23   The current provisions in the Act of 1996 do not include an express power to grant a right of way for the benefit of one part of the land which might be landlocked over another part, but such a power is assumed to be

---

[18]   (1859) 5 Hurl & N 53; 157 ER 1097.
[19]   Beneficiaries having interests in succession may also partition the land between life tenant and remainderman.

implied in the jurisdiction and the Civil Procedure Rules provide for partition of land which under Part 40, r 15(2) includes any interest in or right over land. Under Part 40, r 16(d) in any proceedings relating to land, the court may order the land, or part of it, to be partitioned.

7.24 In *Johnsen v Wilson*[20] a farm was to be partitioned. Wyn Williams J in his initial judgment[21] ordering the partition said:

'55. Essentially, therefore, the order I propose to make is an order for partition and any consequential order which is necessary to make partition efficacious. For example, I understand that there may be a need to confer rights of way upon the land to be conveyed to the First Claimant.'

7.25 The order did not actually include a right of way and the claimant returned to the court five years later to ask for it to be included under the slip rule. His application was dismissed. There was some argument over the merits of the application and the need for a right of way but apparently none over the jurisdiction. It appears that the judge assumed he had power to award a right of way although, in the event, he did not make such an award.

7.26 That is consistent with the earlier pre-1926 law. In *Lister v Lister*[22] Alderson B said:

'And with regard to the easements, though it is not usual to create an easement over another person's land, yet it is otherwise when a separation of property takes place, and it is necessary that a certain part of it should be assigned to a person who cannot have the use of it without a right of way.'

7.27 In *James v Plant*[23] there was a partition of the Park Hall Estate by agreement between two sisters. An issue subsequently arose as to whether a right of way, extinguished by unity of seisin, but apparently enjoyed as a quasi-easement by tenants of the estate, was revived on the partition. The court found that there was a clear intention of the partition that an existing way should be implied under the general words (the predecessor of s 62) but went on further to say that:

'no reason can be suggested, à priori, for supposing that a way which had been always found useful and convenient for the enjoyment of the Park Hall estate, and which, for that purpose, had been always held and enjoyed by the tenants of Park Hall, and which continued so to be up to the very time of the partition made, should after the partition cease to be held and enjoyed for the same purpose by that sister to whom Park Hall was allotted. Indeed, so strong is that inference, that

---

[20] Cardiff Crown Court, 17 Oct 2011.
[21] 20 June 2006 as reported in the 2011 judgment.
[22] (1839) 3 Y & C 540 at 544; 160 ER 816 at 818. See also In *Re Bracken's Settlement* [1903] 1 Ch 265; *Barkshire v Grubb* 18 Ch D 616, 621, 622; *Newcomen v Coulson* (1877) LR 5 Ch D 133 at 141.
[23] (1836) 4 Ad & El 749; 111 ER 967.

authorities are not wanting to shew that, where a way has been extinguished by the unity of seisin of two estates, by the partition of the two the way is revived.'

7.28   However, in *Worthington v Gimson*[24] there was a private way that had run across the whole estate before partition and continued to be used after the division. The deed of partition did not mention it although it did include general words including 'easements'. It was held, after considering *James v Plant*, that the right of way would not be implied. It did not exist as an easement immediately before the date of partition since there had then been unity of possession and it was not an apparent and continuous easement.

7.29   It therefore appears that there is jurisdiction to include a right of way on partition proceedings but if a way is not either mentioned in an agreement between the parties or by the trustees or by the court then no way will be implied unless LPA 1925, s 62 can be invoked.

STOPPING UP OR DOWNGRADING OF PUBLIC HIGHWAYS

Co-incidence of public and private rights

7.30   A route which is a public highway may also at the same time be a private right of way. This most often occurs where private ways are created, by grant or operation of law, over a route that subsequently becomes a highway. This can happen on a housing estate where the house owners are given rights of way over what in the early stages of development are private estate roads. It may be intended that they will be dedicated as highways and adopted by the local highway authority but it can sometimes be several years before that is completed. It can also occur where an existing private road is used by the public for 20 years leading to implied dedication under the Highways Act 1980, s 31 or its predecessors.

7.31   It is unusual for the opposite to occur and for a landowner to acquire a private right over an existing highway, as if a house owner uses a street or road to gain access to his house or business he will do so by (public) right not as of right and will therefore not obtain a prescriptive easement. However, a private way which is greater than the public one may arise by use. Thus, if a house owner drives his car over land comprising a public bridleway for 20 years he may acquire a prescriptive private vehicular right of way over the bridleway.[25] A landowner in such a situation may also grant an express right of way. Several driveways to private houses also constitute public footpaths and if a large house is divided or cottages on an estate sold off, such enlarged private rights of way can be granted over ways the public can use on foot only.

---

24   (1860) 2 El and El 618; 121 ER 232.
25   See *Bakewell Management Ltd v Brandwood* [2004] UKHL 14; [2004] 2 AC 519; [2004] 2 All ER 305.

Protecting private access over former highway

7.32 A highway can only be stopped up or downgraded, for instance from vehicular to bridleway or footpath, by statute. If this occurs the private user may still need access. The general rule is that stopping up or diversion does not affect any private right of way that may have co-existed with the public right.[26] In *Walsh v Oates*[27] Lord Denning LJ (concurring with the principal judgment of Singleton LJ) said:

> 'It is clear law that there may be a private right of way along a road and a public right of way existing at the same time. When an order is made under the [Highway Act 1835] stopping up a highway, that extinguishes the public right but does not affect the private right.'

7.33 However, if there was no separate private right, the effect of stopping up or downgrading can mean that a person who uses the way to gain access to his property will be deprived of that access. Accordingly, the legislation sometimes provides for continued private rights.

Highways Act 1980

7.34 Part VIII (ss 116–129) of the Highways Act 1980 deals with stopping up and diversion both of highways and of means of access to them from premises, and such means of access can include private rights of way. Under s 124(3) and s 125(3) no order may be made under that Part unless the relevant authority is satisfied either that no access to the premises from the highway in question is reasonably required, or that another reasonably convenient means of access to the premises is available or will be provided. Under s 129(1) a highway authority who have stopped up a means of access to any premises or propose to do so or who consider it necessary or expedient in connection with the construction, improvement or alteration of a highway to provide a new means of access to any premises, may provide a new means of access to those premises from any highway or proposed highway. Part VIIIA (ss 129A to 129G)[28] contains similar provisions for Gating Orders restricting access to control crime but may not do so to restrict necessary access to premises.[29]

7.35 Under Part XI of the Highways Act 1980, there is a procedure for private streets (typically on a housing estate) to be made up to adoptable standards and then adopted. The adoption provision is in section 228. That simply provides that the street 'shall become a highway maintainable at public expense'. It does not extinguish the private rights of way which subsisted over what had been private roads and which therefore presumably continue to subsist, as there

---

[26] *Allen v Ormond* (1806) 8 East 4 103 ER 245; *R v Ifield Inhabitants* (1856) 20 JP 262; *Wells v London, Tilbury and Southend Rly Co* (1877) 5 Ch D 126, CA (where an Act extinguishing right of way across a railway was construed as only extinguishing public rights).

[27] [1953] 1 QB 578, [1953] 1 All ER 963, CA.

[28] Added by the Clean Neighbourhoods and Environment Act 2005.

[29] See also the Highways Act 1980 (Gating Orders) (England) Regulations 2006/537 and (Wales) Regulations 2007/306.

would not appear to be any implied merger of the private right in the public one. If therefore the street were at some later date to cease to be a highway, the private right of way could be asserted.

Road Traffic Regulation Act 1984

7.36 This act allows a 'traffic authority' as defined to make a Traffic Regulation Order in respect of a road for various purposes including avoiding dangers, preventing use by vehicular traffic or preserving the character of the road. It can prohibit, restrict or regulate the use of the road by vehicular traffic. Contravention is an offence. 'Road' is defined in section 142 as 'any length of highway or of any other road to which the public has access, and includes bridges over which a road passes'. The wording of the Act is sufficiently wide to cover use under private easements as well as under the public right of way, but if a traffic authority exercised its powers unreasonably it would be subject to judicial review.

Town and Country Planning Act 1990

7.37 The Town and Country Planning Act 1990, s 249 provides that a local planning authority may make an order prohibiting the use of mechanically propelled vehicles on certain highways. Subsections (3) and (4) provide that where a local planning authority adopt a proposal for improving the amenity of part of their area, and the proposal involves the public ceasing to have any right of way with vehicles over a highway in that area, an order may include such provision as the relevant authority thinks fit for permitting the use on the highway of vehicles (whether mechanically propelled or not) in such cases as may be specified in the order, notwithstanding the extinguishment of the public right. Such provision may be framed by reference to (inter alia) particular persons by whom, or on whose authority, vehicles may be used, or the circumstances in which, or the times at which, vehicles may be used for particular purposes. This would appear to be wide enough to allow the authority to create a private right of way, although access may also be protected by a statutory licence.

Natural Environment and Rural Communities Act 2006

7.38 Under the Natural Environment and Rural Communities Act 2006, s 67 existing public rights of way for mechanically propelled vehicles are extinguished over certain footpaths, bridleways, restricted byways (green lanes) and some other routes. However, under section 67(5) where, immediately before commencement, the exercise of an existing public right of way with mechanically propelled vehicles was reasonably necessary to enable a person 'with an interest in land' to obtain access to the land, or part of the land, then the right becomes a private right of way for mechanically propelled vehicles for the benefit of the land or (as the case may be) the part of the land. 'Interest' is defined in s 71 as including an estate in land and also any right exercisable by virtue of a licence or agreement and in particular includes rights of common and sporting rights. This takes place automatically and the right does not need to be granted, although in practice it will often be prudent for a person claiming such a right to obtain written confirmation from the highway authority. The right is not personal so that if for instance a yearly tenant or licensee had been using the lane for access to a field, the right would subsist as an easement for the freeholder or any future tenant. If the green lane does not give direct access to a property, but only to a private right of way over adjacent land leading to the property, that would be sufficient to confer a legal right since an easement is an interest in land.

COMPULSORY PURCHASE – POSITION OF ACQUIRING BODY

General principles affecting easements

7.39 The compulsory acquisition of land can only be authorised by statute and, because it involves an interference with rights of property, the statutory powers are strictly construed. The power to take land is conferred on specific bodies, such as local authorities and statutory undertakers and for specific purposes such as planning under the Town and Country Planning Act 1990, s 226 or the provision of an electricity substation under the Electricity Act 1989, Sch 3. There are some general acts such as the Acquisition of Land Act 1981 and the Compulsory Purchase Act 1985 which set out procedural and other requirements applying to compulsory powers generally, but in all cases it is necessary to consider the specific power to ascertain in particular how far it relates to the continuation, extinction, grant or reservation of an easement.

7.40 In general, a power to acquire land does not include power to acquire new rights over land which is not itself being taken. Similarly, a power to acquire one piece of land does not include a power to extinguish rights, such as a right of way, over that land where such rights subsist for the benefit of other land not itself being taken. In both instances Parliament has in specific instances conferred power to do so, but reference must always be made to the authorising power.

7.41 Where a body which has compulsory powers wishes to take land in private ownership it is normally done in one of three ways:

(1) The acquiring body may approach the landowner without having taken any steps towards a compulsory purchase order and buy the land by private treaty. No doubt the terms and price will have regard to the potential exercise of compulsory powers, but the sale itself will be no different from any other private sale, with a contract and transfer, and the ordinary rules of law, including those about implied rights will apply.

(2) The body may obtain a compulsory purchase order and serve notice to treat and then enter into discussions with the landowner about price,

accommodation works and other matters, such discussions to be concluded with a transfer. In such a case the acquisition will be compulsory so that for instance implied rights will not apply, but otherwise the negotiated terms will be as set out in the transfer, including any express rights granted to the authority (such as to enter over adjoining land in order to repair the works or clear a drain) and any reservation to the transferor (such as an underpass across a road).

(3)   The body may vest the land in itself by vesting declaration in which case there will be no rights granted or reserved on either side (unless the enabling statutes empower the body to acquire rights over the owner's retained land and they are included in the declaration) although it may be possible later to adjust the situation by negotiation and a deed of grant.

7.42   Once land has become vested in a public body, the way it was originally acquired ceases to be relevant to the existence of easements although the body's powers to deal with the land (and therefore grant easements) may be restricted by its constitution or by the general law.[30] Subject to any such constraints, the public body will be able to grant rights, suffer them to arise by prescription or acquire them like any other landowner.

Acquisition of land with the benefit of an existing right of way

7.43 If an authority acquires land by agreement, then under normal principles it will acquire existing easements which go with that land as well as implied easements.[31] If land is transferred to the authority following a notice to treat it will take existing easements but not new implied easements.[32] Just as land is acquired subject to all subsisting rights which are not automatically extinguished by the acquisition, so it would follow that it should be acquired together with existing benefitting rights. While the owner subject to an acquisition of part of his land will not have his retained land burdened by new rights without express powers, a neighbouring servient owner whose land is already subject to a right of way for the acquired land will not have his position altered by the fact of change of ownership of the dominant land even if that change is brought about under compulsory powers.

7.44   The same may not necessarily be true under a vesting declaration under the Compulsory Purchase (Vesting Declarations) Act 1981 where 'land' has the same meaning as in the enactment which confers the relevant power of acquisition. In that case the acquiring authority is not a successor in title in the same way as it would be on a transfer between parties.

---

[30]   See the discussion of capacity to grant easements at para **6.109**.
[31]   *Jary v Barnsley Corporation* [1907] 2 Ch 600.
[32]   See *Sovmots Investments Ltd v Secretary of State for the Environment* discussed below.

Acquisition or creation of a new right of way

7.45   The general rule is that a new right of way cannot be created by the use of compulsory powers (see para **3.77**) but this has been substantially modified by legislation, specifically in relation to local authorities.[33] In principle, a corporation such as a local council which has power to hold land can also hold rights appurtenant to that land. Even if this was not so in the past, the Localism Act, s 1(1) provides that 'A local authority has power to do anything that individuals generally may do'.

7.46   Express power is needed in the authorising legislation to acquire new easements. *Sovmots Investments Ltd v Secretary of State for the Environment*[34] concerned an acquisition of some maisonettes in a block with the corridors and part of the staircases. The maisonettes were unoccupied and therefore had no separate rights of access through the building over part of the staircase nor did they have other ancillary rights at the time the compulsory purchase order was made. The order referred to the property but not to any necessary easements although these were set out in a separate (non-statutory) document. The House of Lords held that that the power of acquisition did not include easements to be implied either under the Rule in *Wheeldon v Burrows* or under the LPA 1925, s 62. The decision turned on the fact that the suggested easements did not exist even as quasi-easements before the compulsory purchase order was made.[35] Although the Acquisition of Land Act 1981, s 7 governing the compulsory purchase procedure defines 'land' as including hereditaments, this is a general provision. The actual scope of any power to acquire will need to be found in the specific enabling Act. Some enabling Acts include such a power.

7.47   Thus section 13 of the Local Government (Miscellaneous Provisions) Act 1976[36] is headed 'Compulsory acquisition by local authorities of rights over land' and provides:

(1)   A local authority which may be authorised by a Minister of the Crown, by means of a compulsory purchase order, to purchase any land compulsorily for any purpose may be authorised by that Minister, by means of such an order, to purchase compulsorily for that purpose such new rights over the land as are specified in the order; and in this subsection 'new rights' means rights which are not in existence when the order specifying them is made.

---

[33]   See also *Great Western Railway Co v Swindon and Cheltenham Extension Railway Co* (1883–84) LR 9 App Cas 787.

[34]   [1979] AC 144, [1977] 2 All ER 385, HL.

[35]   See also *Pinchin v The London and Blackwall Railway Company* (1854) 5 De GM & G 851; 43 ER 1101 but contra *Hill v Midland Railway Co* (1882) LR 21 Ch D 143 where the statute gave express power. The form of conveyance in Schedule A to the Lands Clauses Consolidation Act 1845 includes general words 'together with all ways, rights, and appurtenances thereto belonging'.

[36]   The Act is said to have been passed to reverse the decision in *Sovmots Investments Ltd v Secretary of State for the Environment* supra, but presumably that refers to the first instance decision as the Act was passed before the case reached the House of Lords.

(2)   The Compulsory Purchase Act 1965 shall have effect with the modifications necessary to make them apply to the compulsory purchase of rights by virtue of the preceding subsection as they apply to the compulsory purchase of land so that, in appropriate contexts, references in those Acts to land are read as referring, or as including references, to the rights or to land over which the rights are or are to be exercisable, according to the requirements of the particular context.

7.48   Likewise under section 250(1) of the Highways Act 1980 'A compulsory purchase order made in the exercise of highway land acquisition powers may provide for the acquisition of rights over land by creating them as well as for the acquisition of rights already in existence'.

7.49   Town and Country Planning Act 1990, Part IX, s 226 authorises the acquisition of land and section 336 says '"land" means any corporeal hereditament, including a building, and, in relation to the acquisition of land under Part IX, includes any interest in or right over land'. The definition is not wholly clear. It starts by saying 'means' rather than 'includes' but then applies 'includes' to an interest or right under Part IX. The result appears to be that such an interest or right must be subsisting not newly created by the compulsory powers themselves.

7.50   That interpretation is reinforced by Part 7 of the Planning Act 2008 which applies (inter alia) to the compulsory acquisition of rights over land. Section 159 (Interpretation: land and rights over land) provides that for the purposes of Part 7 'Land' includes any interest in or right over land and under s (3) 'Acquiring a right over land includes acquiring it by the creation of a new right as well as by the acquisition of an existing one'.

7.51   In practice, where an acquiring authority needs a right of way for the purposes of the scheme, it will include the access land in the compulsory purchase order. It may then agree to accept an easement or it may take the land and then return it to the former owner reserving an easement.

Acquisition of land subject to existing rights of way

7.52   Although the compulsory acquisition of land does not by itself extinguish private rights of way over it,[37] provided (as will normally be the case) that the land is acquired for a purpose involving the construction of works, the enabling statute renders lawful both the works and any interference with private rights as a result of their use[38] (see paras **9.129**, **9.133**). In practice, therefore, the easement will be incapable of being exercised at least so long as the land continues to be used for the purpose for which it was acquired.

---

[37]   See *Bond v Nottingham Corp* [1940] Ch 429 – right of support; *Oppenheimer v Minister of Transport* [1942] 1 KB 242 – option.

[38]   In *Ellis v Rogers* (1885) 29 ChD 661 at 670, 672, CA it was assumed that a compulsory acquisition did not extinguish a restrictive covenant.

7.53   Rights of way over acquired land may be subject to special provisions for their extinguishment or special provision enabling them to be overridden. The Town and Country Planning Act 1990, s 236 is headed 'Extinguishment of rights over land compulsorily acquired' and provides '... upon the completion of a compulsory acquisition of land under section 226, 228 or 230 ... (a) all private rights of way ... over the land shall be extinguished'. Section 237 is headed 'Power to override easements and other rights' and section 237(1) provides that:

> '...the erection, construction or carrying out or maintenance of any building or work on land which has been acquired or appropriated by a local authority for planning purposes (whether done by the local authority or by a person deriving title under them) is authorised by virtue of this section if it is done in accordance with planning permission, notwithstanding that it involves ... interference with an interest or right to which this section applies.'

and section 237(2) provides that 'the interests and rights to which this section applies are any easement, liberty, privilege, right or advantage annexed to land and adversely affecting other land, including any natural right to support'.

7.54   In *Thames Water Utilities Ltd v Oxford City Council*[39] the High Court held that the powers in the Town and Country Planning Act 1990 allowed a council to override a restrictive covenant in order to erect a building but not then to use it. Similar logic would authorise an acquiring authority to erect a building across a right of way, but it would follow that the way itself would nevertheless remain exercisable, assuming it to be physically possible to do so. Following *Thames Water* Parliament intervened in the Planning Act 2008, Sch 9, para 4 by inserting a new subsection (1A) into section 237. This authorised the use by permitting the acquisition and therefore extinction of rights over land where the conditions in that Act are satisfied.

7.55   It is not yet clear how far a legal right of way (as by prescription or implication) which is not entered on a registered title will bind an acquiring authority under the LRA 2002. If an easement is neither obvious, nor known to the disponee, nor has been used within a year before the disposition it will not bind a disponee of a registered estate for valuable consideration under Schedule 3, para 3 (see para **13.6**). An authority acquiring purely by agreement will be such a disponee but it is not clear if an acquisition following a notice to treat or under a vesting declaration is a disposition for valuable consideration within the schedule. The former owner is entitled to compensation but that may not be consideration as such in this context. If the acquiring authority is regarded as taking the land for consideration, the effect would be to extinguish the right without compensation, so it is likely that a court would find that the right continued to subsist.

---

[39]   [1999] 1 EGLR 167.

COMPULSORY PURCHASE – POSITION OF FORMER LANDOWNER

7.56 If a body acquires part of a holding under compulsory powers, the owner will not in general be entitled unilaterally to reserve a right of way over the acquired land for the benefit of severed parts. In principle he must accept the fact that part of his land is lost and claim compensation for diminution in value as a result of severance. However, this can cause hardship to the landowner and can unnecessarily inflate the cost to the acquiring body. Accordingly, provision is made for the reservation of access rights either between severed parts or from retained land to a highway.

Railways and level crossings

7.57 When in the nineteenth century major works such as railways were built it was necessary to allow those whose land was severed or cut off from a highway to have access across the line. Private rights of way across railway level crossings have been considered by the Law Commission in their Consultation Paper No 194 'Level Crossings'. They report that in 2009, quite apart from numerous public highways across railways, there also were 2,642 private crossings. The usual pattern was for the enabling Act to indicate in general terms that owners of lands cut off ought to have a right of way, but for the way itself to be created by reservation out of the conveyance by the landowner to the railway company or sometimes by separate grant. Accordingly, it will be necessary to consider the terms of that deed, a copy or the original of which will normally be held in the archives of Network Rail.

7.58 Railways were initially authorised by individual private Acts. Where the infrastructure was built under the authority of such an Act it is necessary to consider the terms of the Act itself in each case. For railways built after 1845 the terms of the Railways Clauses Consolidation Act 1845 were incorporated. Section 53 requires that if the railway crossed or cut through any private road[40] the company must provide a convenient substitute. Section 68 required the company to provide and maintain accommodation works including convenient passages[41] across the railway of the 1845 Act govern the position.

7.59 *South Eastern Railways v Cooper*[42] considered the effect of a specific right. Immediately after the conveyance of the land for the railway and on the same day, the company made a separate deed of grant of a right of roadway and passage. The company argued on the basis of several earlier decisions that the use of the crossing was limited to the use in existence at the time of the grant. The Court of Appeal held it to be an easement in broad terms allowing the dominant owner to use the crossing for any purpose not inconsistent with the operation of the railway. They drew a distinction between the dominant

---

40   See *TRH Sampson Associates Ltd v British Railways Board* [1983] 1 WLR 170 at [174]–[175].
41   See *Great Northern Railway v M'Alister* [1897] 1 IR 587 at 602.
42   [1924] 1 Ch 211.

owner's rights under the deed and the landowner's rights under section 68, which they referred to as 'mere accommodation works' where the permitted use could be restricted.

7.60 Where a way is construed as an easement, the normal rules of construction apply. In *British Railways Board v Glass*[43] the conveyance conferred a right of way for all purposes. Its wording differed from section 68, giving the landowner a right to pass rather than requiring the company to build and maintain a level crossing. Likewise, the facts may lead to the conclusion that a right can be abandoned.[44]

7.61 In *Glover v North Staffordshire Rly Co*[45] a railway company constructed a line across an existing right of way. The way was not obstructed, it became a level crossing but it was now in such a position that it was dangerous to use and the dominant owner was entitled to damages under the normal rules for injurious affection on compulsory purchase.[46]

Highways

7.62 Although new railways are still being constructed, a more common occurrence in modern times is a new trunk road. For instance, where a farm is divided by a new highway it may well suit both the farmer and the highway authority to construct an underpass so that cattle and tractors can cross the road safely. Such accommodation works must be provided by agreement and work by mitigating the amount of compensation. Accordingly they are normally provided where, following a notice to treat, the landowner transfers his land to the acquiring authority and the terms of the easement will be contained in a reservation in the transfer.

7.63 It will often be possible for a highway authority to agree provisions for stopping up an existing private access instead of using compulsory powers and in such a case they have power to provide a new access.[47] Section 127 of the Highways Act 1980 provides:

> 'The highway authority for a highway may agree with the occupier of any premises and any other person having an interest in them that any private means of access to the premises from the highway shall be stopped up by that authority in any way which seems to them appropriate but not so as to obstruct any highway; and an agreement under this section may make provision for the payment by the highway authority to the other party of compensation in respect of the damage (if any) suffered by him in consequence of the stopping up of the means of access.'

---

[43] [1965] Ch 538.
[44] *Midland Railway Company v Gribble* [1895] 2 Ch 827.
[45] (1851) 16 QB 912; 117 ER 1132.
[46] See also *Ford v Metropolitan and Metropolitan District Rly Companies* (1886) 17 QBD 12, CA; *Barnard v Great Western Rly Co* (1902) 86 LT 798; *Furness Rly Co v Cumberland Co-operative Building Society* (1884) 52 LT 144, HL.
[47] See *The Mayor and Burgesses of the London Borough of Bexley v Maison Maurice Limited* below.

Section 129 provides:

> '(1) Without prejudice to their power to provide a new means of access to any premises when authorised to do so by an order made under any enactment, a highway authority—
>
> (a) who by virtue of an order under section 124 above or an agreement under section 127 above have stopped up a means of access to any premises or propose to do so; or
>
> (b) who consider it necessary or expedient in connection with the construction, improvement or alteration of a highway to provide a new means of access to any premises,
>
> may, subject to subsection (2) below, provide a new means of access to those premises from any highway or proposed highway.
>
> (4) The provision of a new means of access to any premises from a highway under this section or under or by virtue of section 124, 125 or 127 above includes the provision of a road, path or other way on those or any other premises.'

New right of way over third party's land

7.64 The position is more difficult where the affected landowner needs a new right of way over land belonging to another landowner. The acquiring authority would need to acquire the land needed for the new access to adjacent private land, construct the access and then dispose of the land or of an easement over it.

7.65 Highways Act 1980, s 246 authorises a highway authority to acquire land for the purpose of mitigating any adverse effect which the existence or use of a highway constructed or improved by them, or proposed to be constructed or improved by them, has or will have on the surroundings of the highway.

7.66 Land Compensation Act 1973 (accommodation works), s 27(3) provides:

> 'A responsible authority may (a) develop or redevelop any land acquired by them under section 26 above, or any other land belonging to them, for the purpose of improving the surroundings of public works in any manner which they think desirable by reason of the construction, alteration, existence or use of the works and (b) dispose of any land acquired by them under section 26 above'.

7.67 In the absence of a definition in the authorising legislation, the definition of 'land' in the Interpretation Act 1978 applies so that 'land' includes building and other structures, land covered with water, and any estate, interest, easement, servitude or right in or over land.

7.68 Where such a power exists it will frequently be possible to short circuit the procedure of acquiring land and disposing of it. The authority will invite the owner of the land required for the new access voluntarily to grant a right of way direct to the landowner whose access has been cut off and only if he refuses will the land be acquired. Such an easement is a private one by grant even though brought about by statutory means.

PLANNING CONSENTS AND AGREEMENTS

7.69 Planning consent is required (with limited exceptions) for any works of development. Such works often involve the need either to stop up an existing access over adjacent land or to create a new one over land in which the applicant for permission does not have any existing rights, although it may hope to have some in the future. Planning authorities have limited powers to impose conditions in the consent but where wider terms are needed they can be arranged by planning agreements (or unilateral obligations) under the Town and Country Planning Act 1990, s 106. Section 106 agreements or obligations will only bind persons who are parties to them or successors in title to such parties (see para **8.31**). They may need to deal with the acquisition or extinction of an access.

Planning consents

7.70 The general rule is that planning conditions must relate to matters in the control of the applicant. In special cases they can extend beyond that but only to a limited extent. In *Grampian Regional Council v Aberdeen City Council*[48] the House of Lords held that a planning condition that development must not be commenced before a nearby public highway was stopped up was valid. Although the stopping up was not in the applicant's direct control, it was a public matter with a defined and reasonably foreseeable procedure to bring it about.

7.71 It seems that similar principles can apply to a private right of way. In *The Mayor and Burgesses of the London Borough of Bexley v Maison Maurice Limited*[49] a local council constructed a new highway which cut premises off from their access. The council retained, alongside the highway, a ransom strip which was not itself part of the public road. The council granted the landowner a new private right of way over the strip but it turned out to be in a dangerous position and the access had to be moved. The removal was undocumented and the council pointed out there was no legal authority for the moved access. Lewison J held that the council was estopped from denying that the owner had a right of way over the new access. He found there was power under the Highways Act 1980, s 127 to agree a substituted access and that had occurred. He said:

> 'It may be the case that despite the form of the condition attached to the planning permission, the old right of way, as a matter of private right, was not in fact extinguished because the extinguishment of a private right is not a proper matter for a condition attached to a planning permission, even though a negative condition preventing development until a highway has been stopped up is unobjectionable.'

and he referred to the *Grampian* decision.

---

[48] (1983) 47 P & CR 633.
[49] [2006] EWHC 3192 (Ch).

7.72   However, this only applies if there is a reasonable prospect of obtaining the event on which the condition turns. In *Jones v Secretary of State for Wales*[50] there was a need for a new access to the proposed development site. It was suggested to the planning inspector that consent should be given subject to a condition that work should not commence until a private right of way over adjacent common land belonging to the Dunraven Estate had been obtained. It was clear that, in the face of opposition from both the commoners and the conservators of the common, the Estate would not have granted the right of way. The inspector therefore refused planning permission. The Court of Appeal held he was correct in doing so. A *Grampian* condition should only be included in a planning consent if there is some reasonable prospect that the condition would be satisfied and that was not likely on the facts.

Section 106 agreements

7.73   In principle a section 106 Agreement (or undertaking) may provide for the creation of private rights. The circumstances are limited. In *Hall & Co Ltd v Shoreham by Sea Urban DC*[51] a developer applied for permission next to a busy highway. The council sought to impose a condition that it should construct a private ancillary road along the highway frontage and allow the public to use it. The Court of Appeal held the condition was unreasonable and void. It is sometimes suggested that while such a result could not be attained by condition, under the decision in *R v Plymouth City Council Ex p Plymouth and South Devon Cooperative Society*[52] a similar result could be reached by a negotiated section 106 agreement provided the terms had a proper planning purpose related to the permitted development. *R v Gillingham BC Ex p F Parham Ltd*[53] concerned the roads on two adjacent housing developments and the extent to which they could be interconnected or a ransom strip left between them under an agreement under the predecessor of section 106.

7.74   It would appear that there is scope for the creation of private rights of way between sites if the requirements of the section are satisfied. Such rights could be conferred on adjoining landowners under the Contracts (Rights of Third Parties) Act 1999 provided the conditions in that Act are satisfied, possibly by an obligation to grant the rights.

LEASEHOLD RIGHTS EXTENDED OR ENFRANCHISED

Security of tenure

7.75   A number of statutes provide for business operators (eg Landlord and Tenant Act 1954, Part 2, Agricultural Holdings Act 1986) or residential occupiers (eg Rent Act 1977, Housing Act 1988) to have security of tenure of

---

[50]   (1991) 61 P & CR 238.
[51]   [1964] 1 WLR 240; (1964) 15 P & CR 119 CA.
[52]   (1994) 67 P & CR 78; [1993] 2 PLR 75; [1993] 36 EG 135.
[53]   See also (1987) 58 P & CR 73.

their leaseholds or, in the case of the Rent Act, of their statutory status. If the former leasehold had a right of way then it will be replicated in the statutory extension or renewal of the former contractual rights. As terms will have been agreed or implied in the original tenancy, the statutory right of way will be in the same terms.

7.76 A lease of an incorporeal hereditament on its own is not normally 'premises' for the purposes of Part 2 of the Landlord and Tenant Act 1954 so that if the reversion to a leasehold is severed and the landlord of the premises is different from the 'landlord' of the right of way a business tenant may not be in a position to obtain a new right to the easement.[54]

Leasehold enfranchisement and right to buy

7.77 Certain leaseholders of residential property have the right, either individually or in conjunction with other tenants of a block, to acquire either the freehold or a long lease. It would not be sufficient to acquire the house or flat on its own if there were no access and the legislation provides for this. The statute most often provides in general terms that there will be a right of way, or even that the benefited person will have all necessary easements, and leaves it to the parties to negotiate the specific terms against that background, but it may be necessary to invoke the statutory jurisdiction to determine the terms if the parties can not agree.

7.78 The Leasehold Reform Act 1967 enables certain lessees of houses to acquire the freehold. The Act specifically deals in section 10(3) with rights of way:

'(3)   As regards right of way, a conveyance executed to give effect to [the right to acquire the freehold] shall include—

(a)   such provisions (if any) as the tenant may require for the purpose of securing to him rights of way over property not conveyed, so far as the landlord is capable of granting them, being rights of way which are necessary for the reasonable enjoyment of the house and premises as they have been enjoyed during the tenancy and in accordance with its provisions; and

(b)   such provisions (if any) as the landlord may require for the purpose of making the property conveyed subject to rights of way necessary for the reasonable enjoyment of other property, being property in which at the relevant time the landlord has an interest, or to rights of way granted or agreed to be granted before the relevant time by the landlord or by the person then entitled to the reversion on the tenancy.'

7.79 The Leasehold Reform, Housing and Urban Development Act 1993 confers a right of collective enfranchisement on the lessees of certain blocks of flats to buy through a nominee. Rights of way are dealt with in Schedule 7,

---

[54]   *Land Reclamation Co Ltd v Basildon District Council* [1979] 2 All ER 993, [1979] 1 WLR 767 but see *Pointon York Group plc v Poulton* [2006] 29 EG 153 (CS), [2006] All ER (D) 175.

para 4 which is in very similar words to section 10(3) of the 1967 Act although using different terminology. Similarly, in relation to the public sector, the Housing Act 1985 (re-enacting provisions formerly in the Housing Act 1980) confers on certain secure tenants of public sector bodies the right to acquire the freehold of their houses. Rights of way are dealt with in Schedule 6, para 3, again in similar wording to section 10(3) of the 1967 Act.

COUNTRYSIDE AND RIGHTS OF WAY ACT 2000

7.80   In *Hanning v Top Deck Travel Group Limited*[55] some heavy long distance buses used a private roadway across otherwise quiet common land at Horsell Common, Woking in Surrey for over 20 years in circumstances where, if the land had not been common land, their proprietor would have obtained a prescriptive right of way (see para **6.117**). The trustees who owned the common obtained an injunction to prevent this on the basis that the use was illegal because the LPA 1925, s 193 prohibits driving across common land 'without lawful authority' and they argued that only they could lawfully permit it. There is a similar provision in the Road Traffic Act 1988, s 34 (formerly the Road Traffic Act 1930). The actual decision in *Hanning* itself protected the amenities of the common but it opened a way for many owners of such land to claim that householders who had been using a route across the common for vehicular access, perhaps for over 50 years, had no right to do so and if they wanted to continue they had to pay for it. If a house owner wished to sell their house and the buyer insisted on a legal right to drive a car to it the house owner had no choice but to meet whatever demands were made by the owner of the common. This aroused resentment and following pressure by several MPs the Countryside and Rights of Way Act 2000, s 68 provided that where the house owner would, apart from the status of the servient land, be able to establish a prescriptive easement then he could insist on having a legal right of way subject to payment of a price determined according to rules authorised by Parliament. The subsequent regulations[56] laid down a scale of payments equal to a percentage of the value of the house varying with the date the house was built. However, in *Bakewell Management Limited v Brandwood*[57] the House of Lords held that *Hanning* was wrongly decided. If someone had used a way for a sufficient time to obtain prescriptive rights then that itself constituted lawful authority. As a result, the need for such ransom payments disappeared and section 68 was repealed by the Commons Act 2006, s 51. Between 3 July 2002 when the regulations were made and 1 April 2004 when the speeches in *Bakewell* were delivered (or possibly the date of formal repeal on 1 October 2006 for England and 6 September 2007 for Wales if the parties' advisers were not aware of *Bakewell*) a number of payments were made and as a result the statutory easements came into existence. There will usually be little evidence of them although some owners of commons were prepared to execute a

---

[55]   (1993) 68 P & CR 14.
[56]   Vehicular Access Across Common and Other Land (England) Regulations 2002, SI 2002/1711.
[57]   [2004] 2 AC 519.

confirmatory deed of grant. A dominant owner who has made the payment will therefore be entitled to rely either on a prescriptive right or a statutory right.

STATUTORY WAYLEAVES

7.81 The nature of wayleaves is considered at para **2.61** (see also para **3.78**). A statutory wayleave is the right conferred by statute to access land for the purpose of carrying out statutory purposes. The term is specifically applied to electricity plants in the Electricity Act 1989, Sch 4, para 6 but similar issues arise for other services such as telecommunications, water supply, drainage, and gas transmission. In *Newcastle under Lyme Corp v Wolstanton Ltd*[58] it was said:

> 'The corporation's right is analogous to an easement and can be most accurately described as a statutory wayleave, the right to pass gas by means of a pipe through another man's land. That is a right giving the corporation sufficient status to maintain their action for nuisance.'

7.82 It will be necessary for the body or person having the benefit of the statutory powers to have a right of way to reach the plant or working area and it would appear that such rights of access share the nature of the statutory wayleave.

Electricity, gas and water, electronic communications

7.83 Electricity, gas and water undertakers are able to acquire statutory easements; but only electricity and water undertakers possess powers to acquire rights in another way. The reasons for this are unclear.[59] In practice, gas pipelines are usually governed by deeds of grant which have all the appearance of easements which will often define the routes the gas company and its contractors can use for access to construct and later inspect and maintain the pipe. Major electricity lines may also be governed by deeds of grant although smaller installations will be erected under brief wayleave agreements. Many water pipes are simply arranged under a statutory notice to the occupier.

7.84 Where there is an easement, such as for gas, then in order to protect the pipe the company may require a covenant by the landowner not to construct or use (or grant to any other person a right to use) a track or road across the line without its consent.[60]

7.85 Schedule 3, para 1 to the Electricity Act 1989 grants to the Secretary of State the ability to authorise 'licence holders' (that is, electricity companies) to acquire compulsorily land or rights over land. Paragraph 5 provides '...the Acquisition of Land Act 1981 shall apply to a compulsory purchase by a

---

[58]   [1947] Ch. 427.
[59]   Electricity Act 1989, Sch 4, para 6(1). Water Industry Act 1991, s 159(1).
[60]   See *Abingdon Corporation v James* [1940] Ch 287.

licence holder of land or rights in England and Wales; and Schedule 3 to that Act shall apply in the case of a compulsory acquisition by a licence holder of a right by the creation of a new right'.[61]

7.86   The Law Commission point out[62] that:

'A.5 A "statutory wayleave" may be hard to distinguish in practice from a statutory easement. It arises from a specific statutory provision. Again, taking electricity as an example, having addressed compulsory acquisition powers in Schedule 3, Schedule 4 enables licence holders to acquire a "necessary wayleave" in order to install lines on, under or over land, and provides a definition: "the necessary wayleave" means consent for the licence holder to install and keep installed the electric line on, under or over the land and to have access to the land for the purpose of inspecting, maintaining, adjusting, repairing, altering, replacing or removing the electric line.

A.6 Conceptually, therefore, a wayleave is a consent for a particular purpose rather than a property right. Obviously the practical distinction is hard to perceive. But Schedule 4 to the Electricity Act 1989 goes on to make specific provision for compensation for the grant of a wayleave; and in practice a wayleave is identified for this purpose as a right acquired by the Schedule 4 procedure rather than the Schedule 3 procedure.

A.7 The equivalent right for water providers is described in the Water Industry Act 1991 as a power: (a) to lay a relevant pipe (whether above or below the surface) in any land which is not in, under or over a street and to keep that pipe there; (b) to inspect, maintain, adjust, repair or alter any relevant pipe which is in any such land; (c) to carry out any works requisite for, or incidental to, the purposes of any works falling within paragraph (a) or (b) above.

A.8 Sometimes, as is the case in the Electricity Act 1989, the legislation will refer specifically to the granting of a "wayleave"; in other cases, such as the powers of water undertakers outlined above, the legislation does not use that term.'

7.87   Likewise, if a right of way is needed to reach the apparatus in order to lay, inspect, repair or replace it, that access must involve a wayleave. In practice most undertakers prefer to secure their rights by positive agreement with the landowner either by deed of grant or by lease. That deed will include any necessary right of way, for instance to approach an electricity substation and where the substation is constructed under a lease (which is common practice) the right of access to it will be a normal easement. However, in the absence of agreement the company will have recourse to the statutory powers.

7.88   Installation of telecommunications and other plant is governed by the Electronic Communications Code in Schedule 2 to the Telecommunications Act 1984 as amended by Schedule 3 to the Communications Act 2003. It includes power to enter and install equipment and inspect it. In default of

---

[61]   Compare the Water Industry Act 1991, s 155(4); Gas Act 1986, Sch 3, para 4.
[62]   *Consultation Paper No 205: The Electronic Communications Code*, Appendix A.

agreement the court has power to grant the necessary rights. Agreements may be documented in a wayleave but major works such as the erection of telecom masts will most often be authorised by a lease which will include a normal access easement.

Mines (Working Facilities And Support) Act 1966

7.89 As explained in para **2.61** the term wayleave has long been used in the context of mineral rights to describe the right for an operator who had either the freehold in a mine or a lease from the freeholder to convey mineral substances across the land of another owner, sometimes over the surface but often underground. This Act confers compulsory powers to work minerals which may be authorised by court order in the national interest.[63] Under section 2 an applicant for an order can obtain ancillary facilities in addition to the rights to the minerals themselves. The section does not specifically mention a right of way but is in general terms, referring to some specific rights, and a right of way would be covered. Section 2(1)(b) includes '(b) a right of air-way, shaft-way or surface or underground wayleave, or other right for the purpose of access to or conveyance of minerals or the ventilation or drainage of the mines'. Such a wayleave is not specifically an easement as it benefits not a dominant tenement as such but simply the right of working. The rights subsist only so long as the working of the minerals continues. Accordingly it could not constitute an interest in fee simple or for a term of years and therefore cannot be a legal easement.

Access to Neighbouring Land Act 1992

7.90 This Act in section 1(1) gives power to apply for an access order to:

'A person (a) who, for the purpose of carrying out works to any land (the "dominant land"), desires to enter upon any adjoining or adjacent land (the "servient land"), and (b) who needs, but does not have, the consent of some other person to that entry.'

7.91 The order is binding on successors in title of the servient owner and section 4(1) provides:

'In addition to the respondent, an access order shall, subject to the provisions of the Land Charges Act 1972 and the Land Registration Act 2002, be binding on (a) any of his successors in title to the servient land; and (b) any person who has an estate or interest in, or right over, the whole or any part of the servient land which was created after the making of the order and who derives his title to that estate, interest or right under the respondent; and references to the respondent shall be construed accordingly.'

---

[63] See *Bocardo SA v Star Energy UK Onshore Ltd* [2011] 1 AC 380.

7.92   It therefore has many of the features of a statutory easement. However, the court can impose terms and conditions and has power to vary the order so that it may be made for a limited period or even for such time as any specified repairs may be necessary.

Chapter 8

RESPONSIBILITY FOR MAINTENANCE AND REPAIRS

GENERAL RULE

8.1   The general rule is that neither the dominant nor the servient owner is responsible for repair and maintenance of a private right of way (see para **4.85**).[1] Thus the servient owner is not bound to construct the way or keep it in good condition even though it is on his land. The dominant owner likewise is under no duty to repair even though he uses it, although he has a right to do so in order to be able to pass over it. He is not entitled to make up or improve the way against the wishes of the servient owner; equally he must not damage the servient owner's land.

8.2   This general rule may be modified by the relationship between the parties, by contract or by covenant as between landlord and tenant, by the terms of a grant or by statute. It may also be modified by the operation of the torts of nuisance and negligence including occupier's liability and by the provisions of Equality legislation and Health and Safety legislation. A duty to repair can be accepted as a personal commitment between contracting parties but the burden of a positive obligation either to spend money on repairs or to contribute to expenditure by another will not normally bind a successor in title to the person undertaking it although techniques have been developed to overcome this general rule (see below).

Servient owner

8.3   At common law in the absence of an express commitment the owner of the servient tenement is under no liability to repair the route over which a right of way has been granted. As the land is his property he is free to repair or improve it so long as the rights of the dominant owner are respected. If he does so, he has no right (in the absence of express provision) to demand a contribution from the dominant owner.[2]

---

[1]   See *Jones v Pritchard* [1908] 1 Ch 630, 637, a case on support for a house, applied to private right of way in in *Vodden v Gayton* [2001] PIQR P4.

[2]   See also *Gaw v Coras Iompair Eireann* [1953] IR 232 but also *Grant v Edmondson* [1931] 1 Ch 1, CA.

8.4   Interference with private rights of way by positive action is considered in Chapter 10. In general, failure to repair is not actionable although as discussed in *Saint v Jenner*[3] the existence of potholes when taken with other factors may amount to interference.

8.5   Exceptionally it has been held that the dominant owner may prescribe that the servient owner repairs.[4] The underlying principle seems to be based on the same rules as the established authority whereby a party can prescribe for maintenance of a fence, but that has been criticised by the Law Commission as an anomaly.[5] The authorities are old and it is unlikely that a new prescriptive claim that a road be repaired would now be accepted.

Dominant owner

8.6   The dominant owner is likewise under no common law duty to repair the way.[6] He is under a duty not to damage the servient tenement.[7] He has the right to repair[8] (see para **4.88**). It has long been established that the person entitled to the use of the way must do such repairs as he requires and has a right of entry upon the servient tenement for that purpose. The judges resolved in *Liford's Case*[9] that: 'The law gives power to him who ought to repair a bridge to enter into the land, and to him who has a conduit in the land of another, to enter into the land to mend it when occasion requires'.[10] In *Taylor v Whitehead*,[11] it was held to be not a good justification in trespass that the defendant had a right of way over part of the plaintiff's land, and that he had gone upon the adjoining land because the way was impassable from being overflowed by a river; Lord Mansfield, CJ, said, 'by common law, he who has the use of a thing ought to repair it. The grantor may bind himself to do so, but here has not done it.' This may in particular apply to a way of necessity.[12]

8.7   The express grant of an easement can imply the grant of ancillary rights reasonably necessary for its exercise or enjoyment. That can include the right of making the road reasonably fit for the purpose for which it was granted: where

---

3   [1973] Ch 275.
4   *Rider v Smith* (1790) 3 Term Rep 766; 100 ER 848; see also *R v Sir John Bucknell* (1702) 7 Mod 54; 87 ER 1091.
5   'Making Land Work: Easements, Covenants and Profits a Prendre': Law Com 327, para 5.93.
6   *Stokes v Mixconcrete (Holdings) Ltd* (1978) 38 P & CR 488, CA.
7   *Mills v Silver* [1991] Ch 271, [1991] 1 All ER 449, CA.
8   *Ingram v Morecraft* (1863) 33 Beav 49; 55 ER 284; *Mills v Silver* [1991] Ch 271.
9   (1614) 11 Co Rep 46b at 52a.
10   Also *Goodhart v Hyett* (1883) 25 Ch D 182; *Gerrard v Cooke* (1806) 2 Bos & PNR 109; 127 ER 565.
11   *Taylor v Whitehead* (1781) 2 Doug KB 745; 99 ER 475. See also *Ingram v Morecraft* (1863) 33 Beav 49; 55 ER 284; *Pomfret v Ricroft* (1669) 1 Wms Saund 321 85 ER 454 (on appeal); *Stokes v Mixconcrete (Holdings) Ltd* (1978) 38 P & CR 488.
12   See *Osborn v Wise* (1837) 7 Car & P 761; 173 ER 332.

a way was conferred by inclosure act for any purpose the dominant owner was entitled to improve an agricultural cart track by laying a granite road to make it suitable for 26 villa residences.[13]

8.8   It is not clear to what extent the dominant owner may be liable, if at all, for damage caused by normal wear and tear. If regular use of an unmetalled way causes the surface to erode to a level lower than the adjacent land so that, for instance, the servient owner can no longer gain access to a field, is the dominant owner liable? It would seem that provided the use is normal there is no such liability and it is up to the servient owner to protect his land.[14] Heavy wear could, however, be seen as imposing an excessive burden on the servient tenement (see para **4.67**).

Dominant owner and improvements

8.9   The dominant owner is not entitled as a general rule to make improvements[15] unless the terms of the grant authorise this (see para **4.88**).[16] The law on construction of an unmade road was reviewed by the Court of Appeal in *Nationwide Building Society v James Beauchamp (a firm)*.[17] This was a claim in negligence against a solicitor. He had acted for the Building Society on ten mortgages of houses on a new self-build housing estate on land purchased from Amberdown plc. The borrowers formed a company, Willen Homesmiths Ltd. The freehold in the road was retained by Amberdown but the house owners were given rights of way and Willen undertook to make it up to adoptable standard. The borrowers all defaulted on their mortgages and Willen went into insolvent liquidation. The Building Society claimed that the solicitor had not obtained security over the road nor the right to build it. In a detailed judgment of the court Peter Gibson LJ reviewed the authorities and concluded that in the circumstances such a right was to be implied. He said:

> '11. For my part I do not think that it assists to refer to a common law right as though the common law recognised some independent right regardless of the particular circumstances of the grant of a right of way. As I understand the authorities, the grant of a right of way is to be taken to carry with it such ancillary and incidental rights as are necessary to make the grant fully effective. This is so whether the right of way is obtained by prescription or by express grant. The law presumes this to have been the intention of the parties.
>
> 20. The extent of the ancillary right must be determined in the light of the particular circumstances of the right of way.

---

[13]   *Newcomen v Coulson* (1877) 5 Ch D 133 at 143–144, CA. See also *Rudd v Rea* [1921] 1 IR 223; affd [1923] 1 IR 55, CA.

[14]   See *Rouse v Gravelworks Ltd* [1940] 1 KB 489, [1940] 1 All ER 26, CA with reference to a claimed right of support.

[15]   *Mills v Silver* [1991] Ch 271, [1991] 1 All ER 449, CA.

[16]   *Gerrard v Cooke* (1806) 2 Bos & P NR 109; 127 ER 565; *Senhouse v Christian* (1787) 1 Term Rep 560; 99 ER 1251; *Re Bidder and North Staffordshire Rly Co Arbitration* (1878) 4 QBD 412, CA.

[17]   [2001] EWCA Civ 275, [2001] NPC 48, [2001] 45 EG 142.

21. ... There is nothing in the Building Plot Transfer which expressly or implicitly negates the ancillary right which Mr Hodge [*counsel for the solicitor*] claims. The fact that the Borrowers did not own the road land and so could not procure the adoption of the road does not detract from finding that they had the right to construct the road to adoption standard. It seems to me to make good sense that in circumstances where Willen has failed to perform its obligations to construct the road and Amberdown is unwilling or unable to do so, each of the Borrowers should have the right to make the grant to that Borrower of the right of way fully effective by entering on the road land to construct the road to the standard agreed by Amberdown, Willen and the Borrowers.'

IMPLIED PROVISION BETWEEN LANDLORD AND TENANT

8.10 In relation to leasehold rights of way there is no general obligation on a landlord by virtue of its covenant for quiet enjoyment[18] although in particular cases such an obligation may be implied from the circumstances.[19] A tenant who requires such an obligation should obtain an express covenant from his landlord.[20]

8.11 However, under the Landlord and Tenant Act 1985, s 11(1A) and (1B) as inserted by the Housing Act 1988, s 116(1) a landlord under a lease for less than seven years of a building which includes a dwelling is bound to keep in repair the structure of the building including any common parts used by the tenant of the dwelling. This would include passages, corridors and stairways in a block of flats over which the tenants had rights of way.[21] The liability is imposed in respect of the relationship of landlord and tenant rather than that of servient and dominant owners. Under the Defective Premises Act 1972, s 4 a landlord may have a wider duty of care – see para **8.50**.

EXPRESS PROVISIONS FOR REPAIR AND MAINTENANCE

8.12 It is common for the parties to a transaction which involves the grant of a right of way to make express provision for the maintenance and repair of the way. As an obligation to carry out works and an obligation to pay for them are both positive covenants, the normal rules which prevent the burden of such a covenant binding a successor in title of the covenantor will apply. A number of devices have been developed to mitigate this problem.

---

18 *Southwark London Borough Council v Mills* [2001] 1 AC 1.
19 *Liverpool City Council v Irwin* [1977] AC 239; *Miller v Hancock* [1893] 2 QB 177.
20 *Duke of Westminster v Guild* [1985] QB 688, [1984] 3 All ER 144, CA.
21 *Liverpool City Council v Irwin* [1977] AC 239; *King v South Northamptonshire DC* (1992) 24 HLR 284 (1992) 64 P & CR 35 CA.

Chain of positive covenants

8.13 The simplest way of providing for maintenance is for the owner of the servient tenement to covenant to maintain it and for the owners of each benefiting property to covenant to pay a contribution to maintenance costs. So long as the original covenantor remains solvent, a claim can be brought against it (even after it has disposed of the servient land, unless the covenant is framed to exclude this) but what is generally required is a procedure binding owners for the time being.

8.14 *Austerberry v Corporation of Oldham*[22] concerned maintenance of what had been a private road vested in trustees. Land for the road was conveyed to them and they covenanted with the adjoining landowners to build the road and maintain it out of tolls. The plaintiff was a successor in title of such a landowner. In 1880 Oldham Corporation, acting under statutory powers, acquired the road from the trustees and ceased to collect tolls, and the road became a public highway although not at that stage maintainable out of public funds. The Corporation resolved to charge the frontagers with the costs of improving and sewering the road. The plaintiff argued that the Corporation was the successor in title of the trustees who had covenanted to maintain the road out of the tolls. The Corporation argued successfully that the maintenance covenant was not binding on them as successors to the original covenantor. The Court of Appeal declined to extend the principle in *Tulk v Moxhay*[23] relating to restrictive covenants to positive ones involving the expenditure of money on repairs. Two members of the court pointed out that the draftsman could have used the technique of a rentcharge (see below para **8.18**) if he had wished, but had not done so. This decision was approved by the House of Lords in *Rhone v Stevens*[24] which involved an attempt to establish the enforceability of a positive covenant, in that case involving an obligation to repair a common roof. The House held that the rule against enforceability of positive covenants was well established and it would require legislation to change it.

8.15 When therefore a positive covenant is to be used, a common solution is to provide for a new covenant between each successive owner of a property and the person responsible for maintenance. This is done by a chain of covenants and novations. In relation to registered land (the device can not be used for unregistered land) this relies on section 40 of the Land Registration Act 2002[25] which provides that a restriction can be placed on a registered title. The most usual one used in this context is in Form M in Schedule 4 to the Land Registration Rules 2003 that no disposition will be registered without the consent of a named person.

---

[22] (1885) LR 29 Ch D 750.
[23] (1848) 2 Ph 774.
[24] [1994] 2 AC 310.
[25] Replacing section 58 of the Land Registration Act 1925.

8.16 The procedure in common use is that the original transfer on the first sale of a unit on a building estate, whether of houses or commercial premises, contains a covenant on the part of a service company to maintain the estate roads and a covenant on the part of the buyer to contribute a share of the cost. There will also be administrative provisions and there may be other estate covenants. Some of these may relate to the road, for instance not to obstruct it. The original transfer will also include a requirement to apply to the Land Registry to enter a restriction that no disposition be registered without the consent of the service company. The company will covenant that if any future transferees of the unit execute a deed to comply with the provision to pay the service charge (and perform any other positive covenants) and also apply for a similar restriction to be put on their title then it will consent to the future transfer. In that way there will always be a direct covenant by each successive owner of the benefited unit to pay the service charge. Although there is some doubt as to whether imposing a restriction in this form might be an unlawful restraint on freedom to dispose of the freehold of each unit, it is likely the court would consider it merely machinery since the company is bound to consent to the transfer if a deed of covenant is produced.

8.17 The recent Law Commission Consultation Paper on *Easements, Covenants and Profits a Prendre* proposes making positive obligations binding on successors without the need to use this machinery. There is no doubt that the need for separate deeds on each transfer which then have to be produced to the company so it can issue a formal consent adds to the cost and complication of dealing with land and causes delay but it is generally considered an acceptable price to pay in the present state of the law.

Estate rentcharge

8.18 An alternative procedure to make positive covenants binding is by estate rentcharge which was originally a common law device but which is now governed by section 2 of the Rentcharges Act 1977. The owner of freehold land such as a unit on an estate can be made liable to contribute to the cost of performance of a covenant for the provision of services, including maintenance of a road. The rentcharge works in two ways. First, there is a continuing obligation to pay a regular nominal sum, such as £1 per year together with an obligation to pay a substantial service charge as and when demanded. Secondly, the rentcharge itself is secured by a right of re-entry. If the contributor fails to perform the covenant to pay, the rent owner can re-enter on the land and either let it or sell it and recoup itself out of the proceeds. The contributor will be entitled to relief against forfeiture if he makes the payment due.[26] Historically most rentcharges secured a profit payment similar to a ground rent. The Law Commission recommended abolition in a report in 1975 which was implemented by the Act of 1977. In their preliminary investigations the Commission found that estate rentcharges were being used to secure the performance of management covenants, although it was not then a common

---

[26] *Shiloh Spinners v Harding* [1973] AC 691.

device, and therefore the Act allowed this type of rentcharge to be created in future. Since the publicity caused by the Act, they have become a recognised feature of securing service charges on freehold sales.

8.19 *Orchard Trading Estate Management Ltd v Johnson Security Ltd*[27] concerned an industrial estate of 15 freehold units at Toddington in Gloucestershire. Each freehold unit was subject to an estate rentcharge securing the cost of contribution to a service charge for maintenance of the common parts. The court interpreted the concept of estate rentcharge widely, applying a broad test to what would be reasonable for the rent owner to recover. *Smith Brothers Farms Ltd v The Canwell Estate Company Ltd*[28] involved a similar service charge obligation in a transfer and whether it covered the cost of maintaining and repairing all the roads on an estate or only those over which the defendant had a right of way. The court held that the services were supplied for the benefit of the estate as a whole, on which many different landowners owned land and from which they all stood to derive some benefit via the estate and therefore the defendant was bound to contribute a share of that total cost.

Benefit and burden

8.20 The right to use a way may be made conditional on contribution to upkeep. The contribution is not a condition precedent to be fulfilled before the dominant owner can use the way but it may be a condition subsequent, permitting the servient owner to exclude the dominant owner until he pays his contribution.[29]

8.21 This approach is based on the principle of pure benefit and burden associated with the decision in *Halsall v Brizell*.[30] On the sale of plots in a housing development each buyer covenanted to pay a 'due and just proportion' of the costs of maintenance of roads on the development and of a sea wall. There were administrative provisions including an annual general meeting of plot owners. The roads were vested in trustees. The plaintiff was a trustee at the time of the case. The court held that the house owner could not take the benefit of using the roads and having the protection of the sea wall without bearing the corresponding burden of paying for them.

8.22 The principle was confirmed in *Thamesmead Town Ltd v Allotey*[31] which concerned a housing estate with some 45,000 residents. The house in question had been acquired by tenants under the Right to Buy in the Housing Act 1980. The transfer to them included the right to use roads and paths on the estate as well as the right to services such as water and drainage and a covenant to pay a service charge for their upkeep. The draftsman of the transfer was aware that such a positive covenant would not bind successors and included a provision

---

[27] [2002] EWCA civ 406 [2002] 2 P&CR DG 13 CA.
[28] [2012] EWCA Civ 237.
[29] *Duncan v Louch* (1845) 6 QB 904, 115 ER 341.
[30] [1957] Ch 169.
[31] (1998) 30 HLR 1052 CA.

that on any further transfer of the property, the transferee must enter into a deed of covenant with the plaintiff to pay the service charge. The house was resold to the defendant but the transfer did not include the requirement for him to enter into a deed with the plaintiff. The defendant refused to pay the service charge on the basis that the obligation was in a positive covenant. The Court of Appeal held him liable to pay for those facilities he used, namely the unadopted roads and sewers. The court accepted that if there was benefit and burden they did not have to be expressly linked by words which referred to the benefit being conditional on the burden – it is sufficient for that to be implied. However, they indicated that there must be what the court called a correlation and it appears that there must be a covenant which the payer can enforce. If the owner of the property does not wish to use the estate roads then he cannot be compelled to do so or therefore to pay towards them.[32] In *Halsall v Brizell* the roads still belonged to the trustee body (even if new individual trustees had been appointed) and in *Thamesmead* it was still the original company so there was not the problem encountered in *Austerberry* that the covenantor obliged to maintain the roads had changed.

Leasehold estates and rights

8.23 The problems with positive covenants arise because the properties are freehold. No such issues occur with leaseholds because positive covenants can be enforced under privity of estate. Leasehold arrangements can be used for business parks or industrial estates or for blocks of flats taking account of all the traditional features of leasehold service charges. The usual practice is to demise the premises for the term together with necessary easements, commonly set out in a schedule, including a right of way over the common parts which may be within a building, as in an office block or block of flats, or outside as on an industrial estate. The ways will be on corridors, stairways, lifts, driveways and through gates and doors. The covenants will include payment of a service charge, which on larger developments will be supported by auditing. There will be arrangements for collection of instalments on account, provision for bank accounts and other administrative matters. In the case of residential schemes the provisions of the Landlord and Tenant Act 1995 as amended will govern the establishment and collection of the service charge, the need to consult tenants and to obtain competitive quotations and other matters.

8.24 An alternative often used both on commercial and on residential estates which comprise separate buildings such as industrial units or individual houses is to dispose of the units freehold but to grant a leasehold right of way for a term of say 1000 years over the estate roads. There is no legal objection to a right of way for a term of years being appurtenant to a freehold estate.[33] The lease is of an incorporeal hereditament and as such cannot be registered with a separate title. As it must be appurtenant and cannot subsist in gross it will be

---

[32] See also *Gaved v Martyn* (1865) 19 CB (NS) 732 at 758; 144 ER 974 at 985 per Erle J 'A right of way is no evidence that the party entitled thereto is under a duty to walk'.

[33] See *Wall v Collins* [2007] EWCA Civ 444 ,[2007] 3 WLR 459; CA per Carnwath LJ at paras [16] and [19].

entered in the property register of the dominant freehold. It will also be included in the schedule of leases referred to in the charges register of the servient title. The lease will be in normal form, including a landlord's covenant to maintain the road and a tenant's covenant to pay the service charge. If the tenant fails to pay the landlord will be entitled to forfeit the right of way by notice to terminate the use of it but the tenant will be entitled to relief from forfeiture on payment of any arrears. This will be either under section 146 of the LPA 1925 if the service charge is taken as a covenant or at common law if it is reserved as rent.

Equitable rights and equities

8.25   If a right of way is conditional on payment for maintenance it will not be an interest in fee simple absolute and will therefore be equitable rather than legal under the LPA 1925, s 1(2)(a). It is arguable that a *Halsall v Brizel* right which is conditional on payment is therefore equitable in its nature. If so it would only bind a purchaser of the legal estate if it is registered either under the Land Registration Act 2002 or the Land Charges Act 1972. It will be sufficient if the covenant to pay is set out in documents which appear on the register. If the right is registered there will in practice be little difference between a legal and an equitable right and the nature of the right will not matter. The LPA 1925, s 7(1) provides that a fee simple subject to a legal or equitable right of re-entry is for the purposes of that Act a fee simple absolute so that it may be that, if forfeiture of an incorporeal right can be equated with re-entry, the right to determine the easement if the dominant owner does not pay will not affect the legal status of the right. Section 146 of the LPA in the context of leases refers to rights of re-entry and forfeiture as distinct but for most purposes they are assimilated and presumably even if the owner of the road did seek to determine the right for non-payment the beneficiary could claim relief under equitable principles against forfeiture on making payment and remedying any other breach.[34]

8.26   In *ER Ives Investment Ltd v High*[35] Lord Denning MR suggested that 'equitable easements' referred simply to that limited class of rights which before the 1925 property legislation were capable of being conveyed or created at law but thereafter were capable of existing only in equity,[36] but that view does not appear to be generally accepted. In principle an interest which could exist only as an equitable right before 1926 might qualify so that where trustees hold a roadway upon trusts that require them to permit residents of an estate to pass along it (subject to contribution to maintenance) that could be used to support a management scheme.

8.27   Both *Austerberry* and *Halsall v Brizell* involved trust deeds with the roadways vested in a body of trustees. In Victorian times equitable rights could

---

[34]   *Shiloh Spinners v Harding supra.*
[35]   [1967] 2 QB 379.
[36]   See *Celsteel Ltd v Alton House Holdings Ltd* [1985] 1 WLR 205 reversed on other grounds at [1986] 1 WLR 512.

be relied on to the same extent as legal ones if the party to be bound purchased with notice. Since the 1925 legislation introduced a new approach to equitable interests they have been less favoured for purposes such as maintenance but in principle there is no objection to their use. The main practical problem is that they are unfamiliar to mortgage lenders who may prefer a legal easement and therefore the need to explain the nature of the right can add to the cost of purchase of a property.

8.28 In *Halsall v Brizell* the judge had concerns about perpetuity. That will only apply to arrangements created before the Perpetuities and Accumulations Act 2009 and only if the interest is contingent. If the right to determine for non-payment is regarded as a contingency then normally the 80 year perpetuity period (or the alternative of a life in being plus 21 years) should have been sufficient for most practical purposes. If the right is regarded as vested there should not be a problem.

Commonhold

8.29 An estate could be established as a commonhold under the Commonhold and Leasehold Reform Act 2002. Precedents of commonhold community statements for residential and commercial estates have been published.[37] If commonhold becomes generally acceptable this could be the simplest method of securing a service charge and providing for maintenance. This type of arrangement was indeed one of the chief motives for the introduction of commonhold.

8.30 The Commonhold and Leasehold Reform Act 2002, s 25 defines 'common parts' in relation to a commonhold as 'every part of the commonhold which is not for the time being a commonhold unit in accordance with the commonhold community statement'. Section 26 requires a commonhold community statement to make provision '(a) regulating the use of the common parts; (b) requiring the commonhold association to insure the common parts; (c) requiring the commonhold association to repair and maintain the common parts'. Thus the unit-holders will have rights of way over the passages, entrances and grounds and the commonhold association will be responsible for maintenance, paid for out of a service charge.

Town and Country Planning Act 1990, s 106

8.31 This provision (see para **7.73**) is used when planning consent is being granted to impose on a developer terms which cannot be incorporated as conditions in a planning consent. The section authorises not only restrictive covenants but also positive ones binding on successors in title of the initial parties. It has to be made with the local planning authority and may require specified activities to be carried out either indefinitely or for a specified period. Such agreements are often combined with agreements under the Highways

---

[37] See *Encyclopaedia of Forms and Precedents*, Vol 8(1), forms 27 and 28.

Act 1980, s 38 for the construction and dedication of a new highway, such as roads serving a housing estate. Until the road has been built and completed to the satisfaction of the highway authority and adopted, it will not be a maintainable highway but will remain a private right of way for the owners of houses on the estate. A section 106 agreement may therefore provide for the developer to maintain the roadway of way until then.

MAINTENANCE UNDER STATUTE

Inclosure Acts

8.32 Rights granted by inclosure Acts are discussed in para **7.12**. The provisions for setting out private rights of way in the first part of the Inclosure Act 1845, s 68 were repealed by the Statute Law (Repeals) Act 1998[38] but the latter part of the section is still in force. This provides that the ways should be maintained and repaired by the owners in such proportions as the valuer should direct.

8.33 It is common for an award to provide that the users will maintain the way jointly and such an obligation is sometimes enforced.[39] In *Marlton v Turner*[40] a provision in an inclosure act of 1808 which required the owners of land at Field Dalling in Norfolk to keep a hedge against the highways in good repair was interpreted by the judge in the same way as a positive covenant in a conveyance. He held that it could not be enforced against a successor to the original allottee even though it was in a statute which imposed the obligation on his heirs, which the judge interpreted as successors in title. However in *Reynolds v Barnes*[41] a provision in an award of 1855 was upheld to enforce a repairing obligation for a road to the standard to which the road was originally constructed. It is considered that the better view is that as the obligation to maintain arises by statute it remains binding indefinitely. This is reinforced by the fact that when obsolete provisions in the Inclosure Act 1845 were repealed the part of section 68 which provides for maintenance was deliberately left on the statute book.[42]

Private local Acts

8.34 It is possible to provide for maintenance of rights of way in other private or local acts although in view of the expense of promoting such an act they will be rare. *Sisters of the Sacred Heart of Mary Ltd v Kingston upon Thames Royal Borough Council*[43] (see para **7.18**) concerned the Maldens and Coombe Urban

---

[38] Although many earlier provisions in individual acts remain in force.
[39] On similar provision for hedges see *Seymour v Flamborough Parish Council* Farm Law 1 Feb 1997; noted also in *Smith v Muller* [2008] EWCA Civ 1425 at [39].
[40] [1998] 3 EGLR 185 but see *Seymour v Flamborough Parish Council* Farm Law 1 Feb 1997; noted also in *Smith v Muller* [2008] EWCA Civ 1425 at [39].
[41] [1909] 2 Ch 361.
[42] See also Inclosure Act 1848, s 4.
[43] [2007] EWHC 563 (Ch).

District Council Act 1933. It authorised the Council to manage the roads on a private development estate and to recover the cost by a service charge on proprietors on the estate.

8.35 The Wentworth Estate Act 1964 and the St George's Hill Weybridge Estate Act 1990 (see para **7.19**) were passed principally to govern maintenance. The company which ran St Georges Hill Estate and its predecessors had covenanted to maintain the roads and the freehold residents on the estate had covenanted to pay a service charge. There were doubts as to the enforceability of these covenants against successors in title of the covenantors and the Act was passed to overcome the doubts. The Act extinguished any obligations then in force and substituted a duty on the part of the company to maintain the roads and gave it power to levy a charge and recover it from the owners of properties on the Estate. Similarly in the Wentworth Estate Act 1964 the Wentworth Estate Roads Committee were made responsible for maintenance and were empowered to charge a road rate on the residents.

8.36 The standard of maintenance of a road under the Manchester Corporation Waterworks and Improvement Act 1875 was held to be limited to the condition in which it was completed and not to improve it even though the burden of traffic increased, despite the fact that a road only made up to such a standard would not last long and would be uneconomic owing to the increase of traffic.[44]

8.37 The burden of a statutory obligation may not always be binding on a successor in title of the original party. In *Re Woking UDC (Basingstoke Canal) Act 1911*,[45] a company was under an obligation in a private Act to maintain the bridges over a canal. It was held that the burden of that obligation did not run with the land after dissolution of the company and a purchaser from the company's liquidator was not bound by the obligation, but that may have related to the specific nature of a canal undertaking.

Street works

8.38 A common problem is that where statutory undertakers dig up a roadway to lay pipes or sewers the road may be left in an unsatisfactory state. Part III of the New Roads and Street Works Act 1991 deals with street works, that is the laying of 'apparatus' such as pipes and mains. It was passed primarily to deal with highways but is not limited to them and where the undertakers have power to operate in a private road the provisions can be relevant. Section 48 provides:

'(1)   In this Part a "street" means the whole or any part of any of the following, irrespective of whether it is a thoroughfare
    (a)   any highway, road, lane, footway, alley or passage,
    (b)   any square or court, and

---

[44]   *Manchester Corpn v Audenshaw UDC and Denton UDC* [1928] Ch 763, CA.
[45]   [1914] 1 Ch 300, CA.

(c) any land laid out as a way whether it is for the time being formed as a way or not.

Where a street passes over a bridge or through a tunnel, references in this Part to the street include that bridge or tunnel.'

8.39 Accordingly, although all highways are streets, many private ways will be as well. Under subsection (2) the application of Part III to streets which are not highways may be made subject to modifications in regulations but this power has been sparingly exercised.[46]

8.40 Every street is under the authority of a street manager and in the case of streets which are not highways section 49(4) provides:

'(4) In this Part the expression "street managers", used in relation to a street which is not a maintainable highway, means the authority, body or person liable to the public to maintain or repair the street or, if there is none, any authority, body or person having the management or control of the street.'

8.41 In the case of private roads this would mean the servient owner. Many statutory undertakers have powers to take wayleaves to place apparatus in private property (see para **7.81**) and it is often placed along private roads. However, under the 1991 Act in broad terms apparatus is to be laid, inspected, maintained or repaired in a street with consent of the street manager and subject to conditions such as time limits for works. The undertaker has a duty to reinstate the street after the works. Part III comprises some 59 sections and reference should be made to it for details.

Leasehold enfranchisement schemes

8.42 When the Leasehold Reform Act 1967 was introduced, landlords of potentially enfranchisable property were given the right under section 19 to apply for a management scheme to cover maintenance costs of matters such as estate roads, and when later the right to enfranchise was extended there was a further opportunity for landlords who became subject to the Act for the first time under the Housing Act 1974, s 118(2) and the Leasehold Reform, Housing and Urban Development Act 1993, s 68, but that applied only to leases which existed when the various enfranchisement rights were introduced and there was a two year time limit for a landlord to apply for a scheme so no new schemes can be made.[47] Many such schemes are still in force.

OCCUPIERS' LIABILITY

8.43 A duty, if not to maintain a way, then at least to see that it is reasonably safe, may be imposed by the law of tort. If a person (whether the dominant

---

[46] See Street Works (Registers, Notices, Directions and Designations) (England) Regulations 2007, SI 2007/1951, reg 13.

[47] See e g *Re Abbots Park Estate (No 1)* [1972] 1 WLR 598 (1972) 23 P & CR 180; *Malone v Bircham & Co Nominees (No 2) Ltd* [2003] EWHC 3173 (Ch); [2003] NPC 166.

owner or a third party) using a private way is injured as the result of the condition of the way he may seek to claim against the servient owner. If the landowner has been negligent or indeed has deliberately set a trap there may be liability under the general law. Claims are sometimes put forward by an injured person under the Occupiers' Liability Acts 1957 and 1984 although with limited chances of success. Under the 1957 Act an occupier of land owes a common duty of care to his lawful visitors, who are those people who, before its enactment would have been regarded as invitees or licensees. Under the 1984 Act the occupier owes a lesser duty to other people whose presence can reasonably be anticipated.

8.44   In *R v Somers*[48] persons entitled to a right of way were held not to be occupiers of the way for the purposes of the Highway Act 1862.[49] *McGeown v Northern Ireland Housing Executive*[50] concerned a person injured on a public right of way. There was a Northern Ireland Act of 1957 in the same terms as the English one. The House of Lords held that she was using the way by right not as a visitor to the owner of the soil and therefore there was no liability. Lord Keith of Kinkel who gave the leading speech considered a number of earlier cases.

8.45   In *Gautret v Egerton*[51] a licensee was injured when on a bridge crossing some docks. They were visitors and had no right of way. The owner of the docks was not liable to the visitor. In *McGeown* the House of Lords confirmed that remained good law. In *Holden v White*[52] there was a terrace of five houses. The owner of the fourth house had a right of way over a path on land owned by the owner of the first house who conceded she was the occupier of that path. A milkman going to the fourth house trod on a defective manhole cover in the path and was injured. He claimed damages against the owner of the servient tenement under section 2 of the Act of 1957 but lost on the basis that he was not a visitor to the landowner. In *Fairman v Perpetual Investment Building Society*,[53] the plaintiff was a tenant of a flat in a block owned by the defendants who retained possession and control of the common staircase leading to the flats. The plaintiff was a lodger with one of the tenants and was injured by a defective staircase. The House of Lords held that the plaintiff was a licensee of the defendants and that they owed her a duty of care accordingly, but decided by a majority that there had been no breach of the duty. In *Jacobs v London County Council*[54] the plaintiff was approaching a shop from the highway over a private forecourt belonging to the defendants, who were landlords of the shop. The House of Lords held that the facts were indistinguishable from those in *Fairman*, and that the plaintiff was a licensee of

---

48   [1906] 1 KB 326.
49   See also *Pimlico, Peckham and Greenwich Street Tramway Co v Greenwich Union Assessment Committee* (1873-74) LR 9 QB 9 at 13 per Blackburn J.
50   [1995] 1 AC 233; [1994] 3 All ER 53. See also *Greenhalgh v British Railways Board* [1969] 2 QB 286.
51   (1866–67) LR 2 CP 371.
52   [1982] QB 679 CA.
53   [1923] AC 74.
54   [1950] AC 361.

the defendants. However, it was decided that the defendants were not in breach of the duty which they owed to the plaintiff as their licensee.

8.46 Lord Keith in *McGeown*, commenting on *Fairman* and *Jacobs* said:

'It is likely that in both these cases, had they arisen after the passing of the Act of 1957, the defendants would have been held to have been in breach of the common duty of care owed to visitors under it. If the pathway on which the plaintiff fell in *McGeown* had not become subject to a public right of way it seems clear that the defendants would have owed her the common duty of care under the Act of 1957 and would have been liable accordingly.'

8.47 However, he also said of the line of cases:

'These authorities, though there are others, are sufficient to show that the rule in *Gautret v Egerton* is deeply entrenched in the law. Further, the rule is in my opinion undoubtedly a sound and reasonable one. Rights of way pass over many different types of terrain, and it would place an impossible burden upon landowners if they not only had to submit to the passage over them of anyone who might choose to exercise the right but also were under a duty to maintain them in a safe condition. Persons using rights of way do so not with the permission of the owner of the solum but in the exercise of a right. There is no room for the view that such persons might have been licensees or invitees of the landowner under the old law or that they are his visitors under the English and Northern Irish Acts of 1957. There may indeed be a question whether the owner of the solum is occupier of the right of way for the purposes of these Acts. Doubts about that were expressed in *Holden v White* but it is unnecessary for present purposes to decide it.'

8.48 Although the case involved a public right of way the decision is not limited to that. It follows that a person using a private right of way, whether the dominant owner himself or a visitor to his premises, will not be a visitor to the servient owner. Equally, as the dominant owner is not the occupier of the way then he also will not be liable under the 1957 Act.

8.49 The position under the 1984 Act is not so clear. It provides a lesser duty owed by the occupier of premises to persons who are not visitors but those whom he knows or has reasonable grounds to believe may be on land in his occupation. Although it is sometimes suggested that may be sufficient to ground a claim by either the dominant owner or by a visitor to him against the servient owner it remains open whether the freeholder or tenant of land subject to a right of way is to be regarded as the occupier.[55] A piece of land used as a path or road will not normally be suitable for occupation in the ordinary sense and indeed any positive acts of occupation such as cultivating it or building on it could amount to an obstruction of the way.

---

[55] See *Vodden v Gayton* [2001] PIQR P4.

DEFECTIVE PREMISES ACT 1972

8.50 Section 4 of the Defective Premises Act 1972 provides that where premises are let under a tenancy which obliges, or in certain circumstances permits, the landlord to carry out repairs or maintenance, then he owes a duty of care to any person who might reasonably be affected by a defect in the state of the premises to see they are reasonably safe from personal injury or damage to their property caused by a relevant defect. This extends not just to tenants but to any person including visitors and licensees.[56]

DISABILITY AND SAFETY

Equality Act 2010

8.51 The Disability Discrimination Act 1995 as amended by the Disability Discrimination Act 2005 and supported by a Code of Practice, imposed certain obligations relating to means of access to premises. The provisions of those Acts have been consolidated with other provisions against discrimination in the Equality Act 2010. The rules apply to those who provide services to the public, including central and local government, commercial undertakings, charities and some clubs. They can also apply to the letting of accommodation. There is a breach of the duties under the Act if those to whom it applies either treat a disabled person less favourably than others or if they unjustifiably fail to comply with a duty (imposed by the Act) to make reasonable adjustments. This may involve making physical changes to a feature over which a person has a right of way, for instance replacing or supplementing a flight of steps with a wheelchair ramp. The duty is owed by a service provider, which might include a landlord.

8.52 In the case of most private rights of way the servient owner is not providing a service and is in any case not doing so to the public. Thus while a shopping centre which confers rights of way for all shops within it will be a place which members of the public are permitted to enter, a private block of flats will normally not be. Where the duty applies it may fall on both the controller of the building – the landlord – and on the persons supplying facilities – such as shop owners.

8.53 Some provisions of the Act apply to the disposal of premises, including tenancies and sales, but they do not apply to disposals by owner-occupiers. If a developer is selling a housing estate this may affect the design of rights of way. There is a separate duty on landlords and managers to make reasonable adjustments to premises when they are managed or let but this duty does not apply to the sale of premises. It may therefore apply to the grant of a new lease but not to the assignment of an existing lease. This duty (as distinct from the one to make adjustments) does not extend to the removal or alteration of a physical feature but erection of signs or changing a door handle is not an

---

[56] *Clarke v Taff Ely Borough Council* (1980) 10 HLR 44.

alteration for this purpose and there can therefore be a duty to do this. There is also an exemption for certain small dwellings, subject to strict conditions typically relating to premises such as houses converted to multiple occupation. The detailed rules of the equality legislation interact with other provisions of the law and further reference should be made to specialist works.

Health and safety

8.54 The Health and Safety at Work etc Act 1974 contains protections for employees and others in relation to premises including means of entry and exit. Accordingly an employer whose staff reach their office or workshop along a path where he has a right of way will have a responsibility to ensure it is safe. So also will a shopkeeper who invites the public over a forecourt he does not own. Again, reference should be made to specialist guidance as the relevant law is subject to review. In particular there are proposals to reduce a former strict liability to one dependent on negligence.

Chapter 9

EXTINGUISHMENT

9.1 Easements are capable of extinguishment or termination in a number of alternative ways, whether expressly, impliedly, by operation of law or by statute. Differing considerations apply in each case, as this Chapter explains.

EXPRESS RELEASE

9.2 An express release can give rise to the termination of an easement of way at law. In cases where the express release does not prove effective, an equitable release may take effect in the alternative.

Release by Deed in writing

9.3 A right of way can be expressly released by Deed. Since a right of way is an easement, and thus an interest in land, it is necessary for the release to be in writing.[1] Such a written release must take effect as a Deed, rather than simply a written agreement, in order to comply with the Law of Property (Miscellaneous Provisions) Act 1989.[2]

9.4 There is technically no prescribed form or specified type of release document that must be used, but documents which are not executed as a Deed will fail to take effect in law. In order for a document to take effect as a Deed, it will need to say on the face of it that it is a Deed and be correctly executed in such terms. Accordingly, other purported forms of express written release, which do not take the form of a Deed should be avoided, as they will not take effect at law and may only serve to create an estoppel between the parties (see below) or have no effect at all.

9.5 If it is desired that the easement of way is to be completely extinguished, care must be taken to ensure that all parties with the benefit of the right, and all parties subject to the easement, are named in the Deed. For example, if two persons have the benefit of the easement of way in their capacity as legal owners of the dominant tenement, failure to include both parties in the Deed will result in the deed being ineffective at law. This is common in cases where land is held in the name of two joint tenants and where only one of the joint tenants signs the Deed. Further, if benefitting land is sold off in part, all

---

[1] LPA 1925, s 53.
[2] See Law of Property (Miscellaneous Provisions) Act 1989, s 2.

current owners for the time being of each part will need to give effect for the release to be fully effective in releasing the servient land from the easement of way.

9.6   A particular problem can arise due to a failure to correctly identify the servient land in any Deed that purportedly releases a right of way. For example, where only three of four parcels of servient land are named as being released by the dominant owner, the right of way will still attach, and remain in full force and effect, with respect to the missing servient tenement. Relying merely on a description of the land, which can be inherently ambiguous and uncertain, can often be insufficient, and create problems on registration of the Deed and thereafter if a dispute arises as to the extent of the terms of the release by reference to the land that the parties intended it to concern. The problems of identification associated with historic rights of way in ancient documents are particularly likely to cause this situation to occur, and to obviate the difficulties a detailed plan should always be attached to the Deed identifying precisely the servient land to which the release relates. The plan should be initialled or signed by all parties and the release should make clear that the plan, rather than the wording in the Deed, takes precedence in interpreting the document; the plan should not simply be incorporated 'for the purposes of identification only'.

9.7   It is also essential that any purported release is by reference to the land and not a specific purpose for the land (ie a development as defined by the Deed). It can be common practice to purport to release rights of way to facilitate a development (as defined by the agreement), and then find that, following the release, the development materially changes or alters in such a way as to vitiate the release for the specified purpose. This is also apparent with respect to other easements, such as rights of light, which can commonly be released for the 'Proposed Development', only then to find that the development changes in a way which causes the release to be only partially effective, or not effective at all. Again, proper reference to the dominant and servient tenements is essential in each given instance, and any reference to a development or specific purpose should only appear in a recital to the Deed and not the main body of the Deed and the legally operative provisions.

9.8   Formalities associated with an express release will include an application to the Land Registry for removal of the easement which should have been noted on the registered title of the servient land (if the land was registered).[3] In such a case, the Deed of Release will need to be submitted at the Land Registry. A copy will be placed on file for public viewing given that a third party purchaser may wish to view the purported release on a subsequent disposition of the estate to ascertain its extent and validity. The Land Registry may remove the entry referring to the easement or else include a further entry noting that a later deed purports to release the easement or part thereof. This is common in cases other than where the Land Registry can be certain that the only parties with the benefit of the easement of way have given effect to the release. Again,

---

[3]   In unregistered land, legal easements, being legal interests, bind the world regardless of notice.

where benefitting land has been sold off in part, evidentially it can often be difficult to show that all potentially benefitting parties have given effect to the release in order for the right of way to have been definitively extinguished.

9.9 If formalities for the release of a right of way are not complied with correctly, the purported release will fail to take effect at law, and may only bind in equity.

Equitable release

9.10 Commonly, an agreement that purports to expressly release a right of way will fail to take effect in law. It may fail to comply with the requisite formalities, whether because the document is not executed as a Deed or for other reasons such as the document not being sufficiently certain to take legal effect. It may also not have been executed by all of the correct parties, or pertain to less land than the parties understood it to be referring to. In such cases, the parties will need to look to whether it can be argued that an estoppel has arisen pursuant to the understanding or agreement between the parties that, whilst intended, had not in fact been manifest in a binding legal document.

9.11 Equitable principles of estoppel, which can be applied to a variety of contracts and agreements relating to land, can be applied to purported express releases of rights of way in similar terms. In the case where an agreement to release a right of way has been executed, but has failed to take effect in law, the effect of an estoppel arising would be to prevent the other party from reneging on their agreement to release the right of way, or denying its acquiescence.

9.12 The estoppel would be asserted in a case where a party seeks to enforce a right of way and has either:

(1) entered into some form of agreement or understanding (albeit not taking effect at law) by which they undertook not to use or enforce use of the right of way that they were purporting to give up; or

(2) allowed the servient owner to infringe the easement pursuant to a belief (genuinely held) that no attempt to rely on or enforce the right of way would be made by them in relation to such an infringement.

9.13 Equity will not always come to the aid of a third party who seeks to claim that a right of way had been released by agreement when it did not take effect in law, and thus failed to be appropriately noted on the relevant registered titles. In *Allen v Jones*[4] the parties agreed to the release of an easement. The dominant land, subject to the purported agreement between the parties, was however sold before a deed could be entered into. Whilst the seller of the dominant land was bound in equity, by virtue of having agreed to release the

---

4   [2004] EWHC 1119 (QB).

right of way, the court held that the purchaser of the dominant land, who had no knowledge of the agreement, was not bound in equity to release the easement (notwithstanding that the previous owner had agreed with the servient owner to release the right of way). It was also held that the purchaser had done nothing to cause the principles of proprietary estoppel to become applicable in this instance. Accordingly, equity did not assist the party seeking to enforce the purported agreement to release the easement (that had been made prior to the sale), against the third party purchaser, who thus retained the easement of way.[5]

9.14 An estoppel may also not arise if the circumstances of the agreement subsequently change. *Salvage Wharf Ltd v Birmingham Development Company Ltd and G & S Brough Ltd*[6] concerned the construction of a new building and an easement of light. Under the Prescription Act 1832, a right to light can be acquired by prescription after twenty years' enjoyment. This is unless there has been a written consent or agreement. The appellants contended that the terms of an agreement that had been reached between the parties had the effect of an agreement in these terms, thus preventing acquisition of the right of light. Here, the development, as originally envisaged by the developer and documented with the neighbouring landowner, had altered and thus resulted in a greater diminution of light to the affected property. Accordingly, the court held that the prior agreement did not have the effect of extinguishing the right to light and no estoppel could be relied upon.

9.15 With respect to rights of way, this could come about in a situation where the party with the benefit of a right of way agrees to release the right of way in order to allow an extension to an existing house on the servient land, only then to find that the servient owner seeks to rely on that prior agreement to estop the dominant land owner from then protesting to his or her building on the servient land of an entirely new and additional dwelling, rather than the extension to the existing house. The effect of *Salvage Wharf* should be to prevent an estoppel being created in such an instance. Accordingly, in cases where a Deed fails to release a right of way due to referring to the release only for a specified purpose that has been exceeded, changed or modified, it is also likely that equity will fail to assist either. In practical terms, it can also be extremely difficult to evidence an estoppel.

9.16 These cases and examples therefore act as important illustrations of the need to ensure that any purported agreement to expressly release a right of way is documented in writing, including all material terms, and correctly executed by the parties as a Deed. Equity will only assist in certain limited circumstances, and these will normally be cases where the parties to the agreement remain the actual owners of the respective tenements to which the purported release of the right of way pertains. Third parties, without knowledge of an agreement correctly formed or, as appropriate, registered in

---

[5]   See *Robinson Webster (Holdings) Ltd v Agombar* [2002] 1 P & CR 243.
[6]   [2009] EWCA Civ 21.

the normal way, will take free of such a purported agreement or understanding on the sale of the land which is ostensibly subject to such an agreement. Further, where the circumstances of the situation materially change, a prior agreement between the parties will be unlikely to be sufficient to extinguish the rights in the amended context (whether at law or in equity).

EXTINGUISHMENT BY OPERATION OF LAW

9.17 An easement can be extinguished by operation of law in a number of alternative ways.

Unity of ownership

9.18 Fundamentally, an easement must be understood as a charge that is imposed on the servient tenement for the advantage or benefit of the dominant tenement. If the ownership *and* possession of the freehold estate of both the dominant and servient lands vests in the same party, the easement will be extinguished and become merged in the general rights of property. This is on the basis that 'a man cannot have an easement over his own land'.[7]

9.19 This principle should be understood as absolute, and will apply even if the unity of ownership and possession only becomes apparent for just a moment in time. Unity of possession *without* unity of ownership is not sufficient to extinguish an easement, however. In *Canham v Fisk*,[8] Bayley B said that unity of possession merely suspends; 'there must be a unity of ownership to destroy the right'.[9] In *R v Inhabitants of Hermitage*[10] rights (in that case common of pasture) which belonged to the Crown over land belonging to the Duchy of Cornwall were not extinguished when the Duchy was vested in the Crown. The report says that for merger to occur 'tis requisite that the party should have an estate in the lands a qua, and in the lands in qua, equal in duration, quality, and all other circumstances of right'. At common law, merger was automatic. Section 185 of the LPA 1925 provides that 'There is no merger by operation of law only of any estate the beneficial interest in which would not be deemed to be merged or extinguished in equity'. The word 'estate' here does not appear to include interest.[11] The general rule in equity was that merger, at least in relation to estates in land and to charges, was a matter of intention but the decided cases do not appear to have considered the rule in relation to legal easements. On the principle that a person cannot have an easement over their own land it would follow that the common law rule applies that where the

---

[7] *Roe v Siddons* (1888) 22 QBD 236. See also *Metropolitan Ry v Fowler* [1892] 1 QB 165 and *Kilgour v Gaddes* [1904] 1 KB 461 R.

[8] (1831) 2 Cr & J 126.

[9] It is always possible that the easement may continue to exist as a quasi-easement and be recreated under the rule in *Wheeldon v Burrows* (1879) 12 Ch 31 if the property is divided again in the future.

[10] (1692) Carth 239 90 ER 743.

[11] Contrast the definition of 'legal estate' in s 205(1)(x) which does include legal interests.

interests are the same then merger is automatic. In *Clark v Barnes*[12] in June 1925 Major Clark purchased a strip of land subject to the reservation of a right of way to some plots. In September 1925 he purchased those plots. In October 1926 he resold part of the plots to Mr Barnes, retaining the strip. Mr Barnes claimed a right of way over the strip and the court found against him. The decision turned on rectification but it was accepted that the original right of way had been determined by merger. In *Thomson v Waterlow*[13] Lord Romilly MR suggested obiter that if a landowner had a right of way for the benefit of a park through some closes and then purchased the closes and later sold the park on terms incorporating the general words (the predecessor of section 62 of the LPA 1925) the conveyance could be construed so as to grant a right of way, but he was clear that the original right of way would have been 'destroyed by unity of possession'. In relation to registered land, where the dominant and servient titles have come into the same ownership in the same right and subsequently been separated (but without the right having been cancelled on the register) it would therefore follow that the right is nevertheless extinguished (see para **13.98**).

Easements of necessity – exception to the general rule

9.20   Normally where there is unity of ownership and possession the easement of way will extinguish, but certain circumstances may cause that default position to change in the case of an easement of necessity.

9.21   A right of way of necessity is limited by the necessity which thereby created it. In *Holmes v Goring* (1824)[14] the court confirmed that a way of necessity is limited to the necessity that brought about its original creation. The court was clear that the way of necessity would cease if, at any subsequent time, the party entitled to the easement of necessity could approach the place to which it led by passing over their own land (ie an alternative route).[15] In such a case, the right of way would no longer be necessary:

> 'A way of necessity, when the nature of it is considered, will be found to be nothing else than a way by grant; but a grant of no more than the circumstances which raise the implication of necessity require should pass. If it were otherwise, this inconvenience might follow, that a party might retain a way over 1000 yards of another's land, when by a subsequent purchase he might reach his destination by passing over 100 yards of his own. A grant, therefore, arising out of the implication of necessity, cannot be carried farther than the necessity of the case requires, and this principle consists with all the cases which have been decided.'[16]

---

[12]   [1929] 2 Ch 368.
[13]   (1868) LR 6 Eq 36 at p 42.
[14]   2 Bing 76.
[15]   See also *Packer v Welstead* (2 Siderf 39); *Staple v Heydon* (6 Mod 4); *Huckvale v Aegean Hotels* (1989) 58 P & CR; *Proctor v Hodgson* (1855) 10 Exch 824 and *BOJ Properties Ltd v Allen's Mobile Home Park Ltd* (1980) 108 DLR (3d) 305.
[16]   2 Bing 76, at a84.

9.22 It is therefore important to understand the basis upon which the easement came into existence. As discussed above, prima facie union in the same owner of absolute interests in the dominant and servient tenements will lead to the extinguishment of an easement of way. However, an easement of absolute necessity may be an exception to this rule and thereby not be so extinguished in such terms. It was said in *Pheysey v Vicary* that:

> '[the] principle seems to be, that nothing of absolute necessity to the tenement is extinguished by unity of ownership or possession'.[17]

9.23 This exception was apparent in the New South Wales case of *Margil Pty Ltd v Stegul Pastoral Pty Ltd*[18] where unity of ownership or possession did not cause a right of way to 'disappear' where that right of way was necessary to the use of the land which previously had the benefit of the easement.[19] The case concerned a right of way over adjoining lands held under common law title. Here it was said by Needham J that:

> 'I propose to apply the principle that unity of ownership or possession does not cause to disappear a right of way (or other easement) where that way or other easement is necessary to the use of the land which previously had the benefit of the easement. In the case of a right of way the necessity is access ... the question I am considering is ... whether a right of way validly granted is destroyed by the fact that the servient and dominant tenements have come under joint ownership. If the way is a necessary one, there is no merger'.[20]

9.24 It was further held in this case that, even if unity of ownership caused destruction of a right of way (or other easement), a subsequent transfer of the former dominant tenement may revive the right of way (or other easement). As a right of way of necessity ends when the necessity ends and is therefore equitable, the issue of merger will depend more on equitable principles of merger than a purely common law easement.

9.25 Otherwise, where the absolute owner of a property, who has a right of way over a neighbouring property, purchases an absolute interest in that neighbouring property, the right of way will be extinguished[21] by the unity of ownership and possession on the established principles referred to above.[22]

---

[17] (1847) 16 M&W 484, per Alderson B at 490.

[18] [1984] 2 NSWLR 1, per Needham J.

[19] The doctrine also appears to be applicable to rights in the nature of easements, such as the right to have a fence repaired. See *Sury v Pigot* (1625) Palm 444 and *Boyle v Tamlyn* (1827) 6 B & C 329.

[20] [1984] 2 NSWLR 1, per Needham J at 9F–10B.

[21] *Gale on Easements* at 12-03 suggests that this doctrine is applicable to rights in the nature of easements, such as the right to have a fence repaired. However, *Margil Pty Ltd v Stegul Pastoral Pty Ltd* clearly suggests that it is applicable to rights of way.

[22] See also *Heigate v Williams* (1605) Noy 119 and *James v Plant* (1836) 4 A & E 749 M.

Vesting in one owner having different estates

9.26 In the context of the general rule, unity of ownership refers to the freehold ownership[23] of both tenements, and the position where the party has freehold ownership of one tenement and leasehold ownership of the other depends on the specific situation in question.

9.27 The dominant and servient tenements can become vested in the same owner for different estates or interests. In *Simper v Foley*[24] it was said that the effect of such a union of ownership would *not* be to extinguish an easement, but merely to suspend it for as long as the union of ownership continued. Upon the severance of the ownership, the easement would then be revived.

9.28 It was said by Alderson B in *Thomas v Thomas*:

'If I am seised of freehold premises, and possessed of leasehold premises adjoining, and there has formerly been an easement enjoyed by the occupiers of the one as against the occupiers of the other, while the premises are in my hands, the easement is necessarily suspended, but it is not extinguished, because there is no unity of seisin; and if I part with the premises, the right, not being extinguished, will revive.'[25]

9.29 A number of specific scenarios can arise to demonstrate these principles.

Lease of the dominant land to the owner of the servient land

9.30 In a case where the entirety of the dominant land is leased to the servient land owner, an easement of way will be suspended or become dormant.

9.31 For example, imagine that A owns the freehold of Plot 1 and has a right of way over Plot 2, which is owned by B. A grants a lease of Plot 1 to B together with the right of way. B will thereafter, during the term of the lease, use the right of way over its own land, however, this will technically be based on the unity of possession created by virtue of the demise of the lease, rather than the actual grant of the easement.[26]

Plot 1	Plot 2
A – Freehold	B – Freehold
	Right of Way
Lease granted to B over Plot 1	

---

[23] *Canham v Fisk* (1831) 2 Cr & J 126.
[24] (1862) 2 J & H 555, *per* Page Wood V-C at 563, 564.
[25] (1835) 2 CM & R 34 at 41. See also *Whalley v Tompson* (1799) 1 Bos & P 375 and *Buckby v Coles* (1814) 5 Taunt 314.
[26] *Bolton v Bolton* (1879) 11 Ch d 971. See also *Bright v Walker* (1834) 1 CM & R 219.

9.32 Accordingly, the easement of way does not extinguish. If the lease to B comes to an end or is assigned, the easement will then revive and the respective plots of land will revert to their position immediately prior to the grant of the lease from A to B.

Lease of the servient land to the owner of the dominant land

9.33 An easement of way will be suspended or become dormant in the situation where the servient land is leased to the owner of the dominant land.

9.34 This would happen in the following scenario: A owns the freehold of Plot 1 and has a right of way over Plot 2, which is owned by B. B subsequently grants a lease of Plot 2 to A. The easement of way over Plot 2 is thus suspended whilst A is the tenant of Plot 2. The use by A of the right of way is attributed to the leasehold interest which A has in Plot 2 as occupier, as opposed to the existence of the easement of way.[27]

Plot 1	Plot 2
A – Freehold	B – Freehold
	Right of Way
	Lease granted to A of Plot 2

9.35 A difficulty could arise if the lease granted over Plot 2 had a restriction on user – for example, Plot 2 was to be used as a car park only and with no right of access to and from Plot 1. If the original lease was granted to A the issue will turn on the construction of the covenant and whether it was intended to extend to the use of the access to A's freehold. If A then sells the dominant tenement it would formerly have been regarded as a personal covenant but the effect of section 2 of the Landlord and Tenant (Covenants) Act 1995 is that it will continue to prevent other uses of the way. If the lease was granted to X (a third party) and later assigned to A then, as initially it did not touch and concern A's land and would only have reference to the subject matter of X's tenancy at the time X gave the covenant, it would not apply to A's land.

Lease of the dominant land to a third party tenant

9.36 A scenario can occur where the owner of the dominant land grants a lease to a third-party tenant with the benefit of an easement over the servient land. Subsequently, the dominant owner then acquires freehold title to the servient freehold. In such a case, the leasehold easement will continue to exist and not be affected by the dominant land owner's purchase of the servient land over which the tenant enjoys a right of way.

---

[27] *Simper v Foley* (1862) 2 J&H 555.

9.37   For example, imagine that A owns the freehold of Plot 1 and has the benefit of a right of way over Plot 2, owned by B. A then grants a lease of Plot 1 to Tenant (T). The lease also passes the benefit of the right of way over Plot 2 to T. If, thereafter, A disposes of the freehold of Plot 1 to B (the owner of the servient land), the easement will last for the duration of the lease.[28]

Plot 1	Plot 2
A – Freehold	B – Freehold
	Right of Way
Lease granted to T (with benefit of right of way)	
Disposition of Freehold to B	

Merger of leasehold title with freehold

9.38   Where a lease merges with a freehold, special considerations apply. Prior to the decision of the Court of Appeal in *Wall v Collins*,[29] it was generally considered that when a leaseholder acquired the reversion in the same right and merged the term into the headlease or freehold any easements, even over other land, granted by the lease, were extinguished.

9.39   However, in that case, the Court of Appeal ruled that, whilst an easement must appertain to the dominant land, it did not have to be linked to a particular legal interest in the dominant land. As such, when the lease merged with the freehold, the dominant land did not necessarily lose the benefit of the easements contained in the lease. The effect of the merger was therefore to allow the leasehold easements to continue in existence for the term of the lease, but attach, not to the lease, but instead to the dominant land. By virtue of section 62 of the LPA 1925, a perpetual right will be acquired.[30]

9.40   The benefit of such an easement is not automatically entered on the registered title to the reversionary estate (if registered) by the Land Registry, following the decision in *Wall v Collins*.[31] The tenant is, however, at liberty to apply to register the benefit either at the time of merger or at a point thereafter.[32] It is always advisable to apply to the court for the registration in these terms.

---

[28]   *Richardson v Graham* [1908] 1 KB 39, *per* Kennedy LJ at 46.
[29]   [2007] EWCA Civ 444.
[30]   [2007] 3 WLR 459 at 20–27.
[31]   This has been followed through in Land Registry Practice Guide 26. See also para 4.4 of the Guide. This was a recent amendment to the original Practice Guide 26 and at first was issued separately although now it has been incorporated into the Practice Guide.
[32]   The case of leasehold enfranchisement is also an exception to the general rule on merger in these terms. The case of *Kent and another v Kavanagh and another* [2006] EWCA Civ 162 shows that a leasehold easement will survive enfranchisement under the Leasehold Reform Act 1967.

9.41 The merger only takes effect if an election is made – that is, it is not automatic. If the election is made, then the merger has the effect of causing the leasehold easements to fall away but attach instead to the dominant land. Accordingly, this is not a case where the easement ends by effluxion of time (ie of the lease) – this scenario is a premature termination of the leasehold easement pursuant to the election made.

IMPLIED RELEASE

9.42 The release of a right of way can be implied by the conduct of the parties or by virtue of the surrounding circumstances which should suggest that the right of way has been extinguished. There are various ways in which this could occur.

By licence

9.43 A right of way can be terminated with the implied authority of the dominant owner where, for example, the dominant owner gives consent (whether written or oral) for something permanent to be done on the servient land that is inconsistent with the right of way thereafter being exercised (e g the right of way can no longer be enjoyed because of consent given to erect a building on the land).[33]

9.44 This scenario is also common in cases other than with easements of way, by analogy.

9.45 For example, with respect to easements of light, such an easement may be extinguished by implied agreement where the dominant owner authorises the servient owner to erect a building, which must inevitably interfere with the easements of light. Here, the dominant owner will be estopped from reasserting the right thereafter, given that it would be inequitable to do so.[34]

9.46 In *Armstrong v Sheppard & Short Ltd*[35] the plaintiff had orally informed the defendants that he did not object to the construction of a sewer.[36] It was said by Lord Evershed MR in the judgment in general terms that:

The Court of Appeal held in this case that, after the enfranchisement of both properties, the former tenants of each property continued to enjoy the same rights over each others' land as they did when they were tenants.

[33] See *Winter v Brockwell* (1807) 8 East 308; *Liggins v Inge* (1831) 7 Bing 682; *Davies v Marshall* (1861) 10 CB (ns) 697; *Johnson v Wyatt* (1863) 9 Jur (ns) 1333 and *Bosomworth v Faber* (1992) 69 P & CR 288. See also Cullity, 'The Executed Licence' (1965) 29 Cony (ns) 19.

[34] Cf *Taylor Fashions Limited v Liverpool Victoria Trustees Co Limited* [1981] 1 All ER 897 and *Re Basham Deceased* [1987] 1 All ER 405. See also *Gillet v Holt* [1998] 3 All ER 917.

[35] [1959] 2 QB 384 at 399–401, *per* Lord Evershed MR.

[36] It was not clear as to whether the parties were aware of respective ownership of the lands in question and rights thereof.

'... if A gives authority to B for the doing of an act on A's land, and the act is done and completed, then, whatever be the strict description of the authority, whether it be called a permission or a licence, it is, generally speaking at any rate, too late for A, who gave the authority, to complain of it, and that will go to this extent – that a man may by such means extinguish a proprietary right: for example (to quote an instance from the cases), if I, having an easement of light, permit another to come and build a wall up against my window, so as to extinguish the easement, if the wall is built and completed, that may well be the end of it, and I cannot complain of the infringement of my ancient right or require the wall to be taken down.'[37]

9.47 Similarly, in *Liggins v Inge*[38] a man approved a neighbour altering an embankment to a watercourse so that the water, which had formerly flowed to the plaintiff's mill, was diverted to the defendant's property. It was said that, once the work had been done, then it followed that a previously enjoyed right of receiving water had been lost by virtue of the licence provided and that the approval to alter the watercourse could not retrospectively be withdrawn.

9.48 Provided that the authority is exercised, it is immaterial whether it was given in writing.[39] For the estoppel to be created, however, it will be necessary to demonstrate that the dominant owner was aware of the existence of the right, or at least had some suspicion as to the true position.[40]

9.49 It is unusual to experience an implied release in this way, and many argue that the purported termination of any easement in this way, by virtue of the dominant owners implied consent, is merely one constituent part of claiming that the easement has come to an end by virtue of abandonment and the intention for the right never to be exercised again in the future. This is contrary to other views that a right of way can be terminated in its own right by virtue of an implied licence in these terms.[41]

Abandonment

9.50 The law relating to the abandonment of easements generally, and specifically to rights of way, is rather complicated in nature and form. The basic rule is that a legal interest in land, like a legal estate[42], can under section 52 of the LPA 1925 only be assigned by deed and extinction or release is a form of assignment. However, as with leases which can be surrendered by operation of law, there are circumstances in which the law will recognise abandonment. The principles are similar to those of estoppel which under cases such as *Ramsden v Dyson*[43] (see para **3.90**) a right can be established where if someone entitled to

---

[37] [1959] 2 QB 384 at 399–401, *per* Lord Evershed MR.
[38] (1831) 7 Bing 682.
[39] [1959] 2 QB 384 at 399–401, *per* Lord Evershed MR.
[40] This was a material issue in *Armstrong v Sheppard & Short Limited* [1959] 2 All ER 651. See also *Taylor Fashions Limited v Liverpool Victoria Trustees Co Limited* [1981] 1 All ER 897 at 912B.
[41] See *Armstrong v Shepherd & Short Ltd* [1959] 2 QB 384 and *Liggins v Inge* (1831) 7 Bing 682.
[42] See LPA 1925, s 205(1)(x).
[43] (1866) LR 1 HL 139.

a right stands by and watches the servient owner doing something inconsistent with the right, the court will not permit him later to assert it.

General introduction

9.51 Where an easement has not been used or enjoyed for a significant period of time, the easement may be extinguished by abandonment. For an easement to be extinguished in this way, it must be evidenced that the owner of the dominant land had, or showed, a fixed intention never, at any time in the future, to assert the right to the easement or to attempt to transfer it to a successor.[44] Accordingly, as will be explained, mere lack of use of an easement, even for a significant period of time, is alone insufficient to extinguish the easement by abandonment. Easements are perpetual (unless granted for a term a term of years) and potentially valuable rights; because a dominant owner is unlikely to give one up for no consideration, extinguishment will accordingly not be easily or lightly inferred.

9.52 When considering abandonment of easements, it is necessary to differentiate between those easements which are exercised without the need for human agency, but which require an adaption of the dominant land (continuous easements) and those which require human agency (discontinuous easements). Rights of way fall into the category of discontinuous easements as they must be exercised by a person.

9.53 The cessation of continuous easements is more likely to constitute strong evidence of abandonment. The lack of human agency associated with continuous easements means that any act which causes the use of a continuous easement to cease will normally be seen as unequivocal, and thus strong evidence of an intention for the easement to have been abandoned. An example would be the building of a wall which blocks light to windows to which the dominant owner does not object. In turn, the threshold for abandonment is higher in the case of discontinuous easements which require some form of human agency because, such as in the case of rights of way, there may be many plausible explanations for why the easement has not been used for a long time (for example, an alternative right of way was in existence).

9.54 The law as to the abandonment of easement can be contrasted with the rules of the abandonment of the benefit of a contract. For example, it is not possible to have a unilateral abandonment of the benefit of a contract[45] but the unilateral abandonment of the benefit of an easement is possible, if unusual. It is therefore important not to confuse principles associated with the abandonment of easements with those concerning the abandonment of a contract, as they are quite distinct in their own discipline.

---

[44] *Tehidy Minerals Ltd v Norman* [1971] 2 QB 528) 682.
[45] *The Hannah Blumenthal* [1983] 1 AC 854 and *Collin v Duke of Westminster* [1985] QB 581.

9.55 The law as to abandonment of continuous easements has been settled for some time, whereas the law pertaining to the abandonment of discontinuous easements (including rights of way) has been the subject of several recent decisions. These are considered with reference to the criteria for establishing the abandonment of a right of way.

Criteria for abandonment of a right of way

9.56 As discussed above, lack of use of a discontinuous easement alone, even for a significant duration, will not amount to abandonment.[46] This is because a cessation of use of an easement of way does not require any change in the dominant tenement; accordingly a lack of use alone is unlikely to ever be sufficient to amount to abandonment.

9.57 Non-user, in such cases, will constitute evidence from which abandonment may be inferred, but it will not be definite evidence and must be viewed in the overall context.[47] This is because there may be many reasons for the non-use, for example the dominant owner not needing to use the right of way, which would be directly contrary to a claim for abandonment.[48] In *Benn v Hardinge*, the mere non-user of a right of way for a period of 175 years did not, without more, create a presumption that the right had been abandoned. The court held that mere non-user of a right of way was explicable on the ground that there had never been a need for the plaintiff or his predecessors in title to use the way. That did not mean that they had abandoned the right to use the way for all time. Similarly in *Williams v Sandy Lane (Chester) Ltd*[49] the non-use of a route for 30 years was accounted for by reason of the fact that a more convenient route had been available during this period.

9.58 It is also possible that a dominant owner may not object to the conduct of a servient owner that temporarily prevents the exercise of a right of way in the interests of maintaining good neighbourly relations; again such conduct is inconsistent with abandonment and it would be undesirable for such conduct to potentially cause a dominant owner to lose the right of way for all time. In *Snell & Prideaux Limited v Dutton Mirrors Limited* Stuart Smith LJ remarked that:

> 'As a matter of good neighbourliness, an owner of land may well permit his neighbour to make use of the servient tenement for the time being. The dominant owner does not have any present need to exercise his rights and it is a convenience to the servient owner to store materials or vehicles, to erect machinery or

---

46 *Benn v Hardinge* (1992) 66 P & CR 246; *Ward v Ward* (1852) 7 Ex 838 at 839. See also *Guth v Robinson* (1972) 1 BPR 9,209; *Riley v Pentilla* [1974] VR 547; *Treweeke v 36 Wolseley Rd Pty Ltd* (1973) 128 CLR 274; *Kileel & Kingwood Realty Ltd, Re* 108 DLR (3d) 362; *Grill v Hockey* (1994) 5 BPR 97,365 and *Cavacourt Pty Ltd v Durian Holdings Pty Ltd* (1998) 9 BPR 97,761.

47 *Swan v Sinclair* [1924] 1 Ch 254 at 274, *per* Sargant Li citing *Goddard on Easements* (8th edn) at 521.

48 *Benn v Hardinge* (above) at 257.

49 [2006] EWCA Civ 1738 at [52]–[59].

structures for his business. It would, I think, be undesirable, if this generous and good neighbourly conduct could not be indulged in for fear of losing for all-time rights, which at that moment the dominant owner has no need or wish to exercise'.[50]

9.59 It is therefore appropriate to consider, in more detail, what may and may not be deemed sufficient to constitute an intention to abandon and whether any minimum period of non-use is always required.

No minimum period of non-use

9.60 Whilst it is accepted that non-use alone is insufficient to establish abandonment, it can be asked if any minimum period of cessation of use is fixed by law, in the absence of which, there can *never* be the abandonment of an easement of way.

9.61 It has been suggested that, when a title by prescription was acquired, it could only be lost by non-user during a period equal to that required for its acquisition. Indeed Coke in Bracton said:

'It is to be known that the title, being once gained by prescription or custom, cannot be lost by interruption of the possession for ten or twenty years.'[51]

9.62 In the case of *Moore v Rawson*,[52] Littledale J expressed the view that discontinuous easements could only be lost by cessation of enjoyment for 20 years. He said:

'According to the present rule of law a man may acquire a right of way, or a right of common, (except, indeed, common appendant) upon the land of another, by enjoyment. After twenty years' adverse enjoyment the law presumes a grant made before the user commenced, by some person who had power to grant. But if the party who has acquired the right by grant ceases for a long period of time to make use of the privilege so granted to him, it may then be presumed that he has released the right. It is said, however, that as he can only acquire the right by twenty years' enjoyment, it ought not to be lost without disuse for the same period; and that as enjoyment for such a length of time is necessary to found a presumption of a grant, there must be a similar non-user, to raise a presumption of a release. And this reasoning, perhaps, may apply to a right of common or of way.'[53]

9.63 Lord Tindal CJ in *Bower v Hill*,[54] remarked that an obstruction to a right of way of a permanent character, if acquiesced in for 20 years, would be evidence of a 'renunciation and abandonment of the right'.

---

[50] *Snell & Prideaux Limited v Dutton Mirrors Limited* [1995] 1 EGLR 259, *per* Stuart Smith LJ at 262D.

[51] Bracton, Lib 2, f 51b, 52a, Lib 4, f 222b. Cited from *Gale on Easements* 4-80, p 242m 18th Edn, 2008. At this time the analogy to the Limitation Act 1623 had not been introduced into the law.

[52] (1824) 3 B & C 332 at 339.

[53] (1824) 3 B & C 332, *per* Littledale J at 339.

[54] (1835) 1 Bing NC 555. Cf *Drelveu v Sheard* (1836) 7 C & P 465.

9.64 The judgment of Lord Denman CJ in *R v Chorley*[55] indicates however, that there is no minimum period required. The case concerned the obstruction of a footpath. It was said that, in cases where acquiescence in use of the right was asserted, the court should never rely on a period of less than 20 years before being prepared to find for abandonment in any given case.[56] However, a lesser period of non-use, coupled with any act which clearly manifests an intention to abandon the right, would be sufficient evidence without any reference to time at all, and would effectively be equivalent to an express release.[57] It was said:

> 'As an express release of the easement would destroy it at any moment, so the cesser of use coupled with any act clearly indicative of an intention to abandon the right would have the same effect without any reference to time. For example, this being a right of way to the defendant's malthouse, and the mode of user by driving carts and waggons to an entrance from the lane into the malthouse yard, if the defendant had removed his malthouse, turned the premises to some other use, and walled up the entrance, and then for any considerable period of time acquiesced in the unrestrained use by the public, we conceive the easement would have been clearly gone. It is not so much the duration of the cesser as the nature of the act done by the grantee of the easement, or of the adverse act acquiesced in by him, and the intention in him which either the one of the other indicates, which are material for the consideration of the jury.'[58]

9.65 Indeed, Lord Matins VC in *Cook v Bath*,[59] held that 30 years' non-user alone was insufficient to extinguish a right of way. In the same case, the judgment of Sir R Malins VC noted that it is always a question of fact to be ascertained from the surrounding circumstances as to whether the act amounts to an abandonment, or was intended as such. A period of non-use alone, regardless of how long, was not sufficient.

9.66 Accordingly, it can be understood from the authorities that there is no particular period of non-use which is by itself sufficient to constitute abandonment of an easement of way. Rather, attention should be directed to the circumstances giving rise to the non-use (ie can they be explained in some way) or whether the non-use (of whatever duration) is coupled with a manifest intention to permanently renounce the right of way, whether by words or deeds.

Cessation of user: intention

9.67 The cessation of use of the right of way will be insufficient alone to establish abandonment. Further, the fact that an easement has not been used for a very long time will also, in and of itself, be insufficient to evidence abandonment.

---

[55] *R v Chorley* (1848) 12 QB 515 at 519.
[56] See below for non-use being explained in the wider circumstances in order to create the presumption of an intention to abandon.
[57] *R v Chorley* (1848) 12 QB 515 at 519.
[58] Lord Campbell said of *R v Chorley* (1848) 12 QB 515: 'It is an authority that an abandonment is effectual if communicated and acted upon. It goes no further.'
[59] (1868) LR 6 Eq 177.

9.68 In order to create a presumption of abandonment of a right of way, there must be a substantial duration during which the dominant owner has acquiesced in use of the right of way and the circumstances adverse to the user must be sufficient to explain the non-use.[60] The owner of the dominant land must therefore undertake some act which clearly shows a firm intention that neither the owner nor its successors in title will use the easement for any claim of abandonment to be successful.[61] Alternatively, the surrounding circumstances must otherwise indicate an intention of not resuming the user.

9.69 Indeed, Sir Ernest Pollock MR in *Swan v Sinclair*[62] remarked:

> 'Non-user is not by itself conclusive evidence that a private right of easement is abandoned. The non-user must be considered with, and may be explained by, the surrounding circumstances. If those circumstances clearly indicate an intention of not resuming the user then a presumption of a release of the easement will, in general, be implied and the easement will be lost.'

9.70 In *Cook v Mayor and Corporation of Bath*[63] Maines V-C makes clear that the determination of whether an intention to abandon can be made out:

> '...is always a question of fact, to be ascertained by a jury, or by the court, from the surrounding circumstances, whether the act amounts to abandonment, or was intended as such.'[64]

9.71 Preferably, the dominant owner will undertake some act which clearly indicates a firm intention for him, and any successor in title, never to make use of the easement again.[65] This is always preferable, but less likely in practice. In the judgment of Buckley LJ in *Gotobed v Pridmore* it was said:[66]

> 'To establish abandonment of an easement the conduct of the dominant owner must, in our judgment, have been such as to make it clear that he had at the relevant time a firm intention that neither he nor any successor in title of his should thereafter make use of the easement...'

9.72 It was held by the Court of Appeal, in *Tehidy Minerals Ltd v Norman*[67] that abandonment of an easement or a *profit a prendre* can only be treated as

---

[60] *Swan v Sinclair* (above) at 268 and *McIntyre v Porter* [1983] 2 VLR 439.

[61] *Williams v Usherwood* (1983) 45 P&CR 235 and *Gotobed v Pridmoore* (1971) EG 759.

[62] [1924] 1 Ch 254 at 266.

[63] (1868) LR 6 Eq 177.

[64] (1868) LR 6 Eq 177 at 179.

[65] *Williams v Usherwood* (1983) 54 P & CR 235 at 256, citing *Gotobed v Pridmore* (1971) EG 759 and *Tehidy Minerals Limited v Norman* [1971] 2 QB 528.

[66] (1970 115 SJ 78; (1971) EG 750. The case is not reported elsewhere. Cumming-Bruce LJ was quoting from Court of Appeal (Civil Division) Transcript No 498A of 1970, pp 12D–14D (December 16, 1970). Buckley LJ's judgment was the judgment of the court. See also *Costagliola v English* (1969) 210 EG 1425. The *Gotobed* test was recently applied by the Court of Appeal in *CDC2020 Plc v Ferreira* [2005] EWCA Civ 611; [2005] 3 EGLR 15. In that case a right of way granted expressly for purposes connected with the use of three garages. It was

having taken place where a person entitled to it has demonstrated a fixed intention never at any point in the future to exercise the right himself or seek to pass it to someone else. In particular if abandonment takes place as a result of a licence, whether oral or in writing, that will normally only create a relationship between the parties. A licence for value, for instance on a shared driveway where the parties agreed to give up their respective rights so that the extinction was mutual, might create a binding interest but it would in principle be equitable only and, unless registered on the servient title(s) would not bind a later dominant owner in the absence. It could be otherwise if accompanied by actions such as the building of a wall down the middle.

9.73 It is helpful to consider cases where an intention to abandon, or no intention to abandon, was found by the court. This further highlights that any determination will always be in context and with reference to all surrounding circumstances and inherently a question of fact and degree.

No indication of intention to abandon

9.74 The following cases illustrate that, in cases where there is no intention to permanently renounce the right, intermittence of user or alteration in the mode of enjoyment will fail to establish abandonment.

9.75 In *Payne v Shedden*[68] the line and direction of a right of way had been varied as a result of agreement between the parties and at certain periods, the right had been totally suspended. Patteson J was of the opinion[69] that such occasional substitution of another track could be deemed to be substantially the exercise of the old right and 'evidence of the continued enjoyment of it', and that the suspension by agreement was not inconsistent with the right. No intention could therefore be inferred to permanently renounce the right. This view was adopted by the Court of Appeal in *Davis v Whitby*,[70] in which the route of a passageway had been altered by agreement.

9.76 In *Ward v Ward*[71] a right of way was held not to have been extinguished simply by no use for a period much longer than 20 years. Here the way was not used because the owner had a more convenient mode of access through his own land. Alderson B. said:[72]

---

held not to have been abandoned even though the three garages had been demolished and their site occupied by other structures and used unlawfully for over a period of 30 years.

[67] [1971] 2 QB 528 at 553, applied in *Yateley Common, Hampshire, Re* [1977] I WLR 840. See also *Gotobed v Pridmore* (1970) 115 SJ 78; *Williams v Usherwood* (1983) 45 P & CR 235; *Benn v Hardinge* (1992) 66 P & CR 246; *Bosomworth v Faber* (1992) 69 P & CR 288 and *Snell & Prideax v Dutton Ltd* [1995] 1 EGLR 259.

[68] (1834) 1 Mood & R 382. The defendant failed to establish any right of way. See also *Carr v Foster* (1842) 3 QB 581 and *Hale v Oldroyd* (1845) 14 M & W 789.

[69] (1834) I1 Mood & R 382 at 383.

[70] [1974] Ch 186 at 191.

[71] (1852) 7 Exch 838.

[72] (1852) 7 Exch 838 at 839.

'The presumption of abandonment cannot be made from the mere fact of non-user. There must be other circumstances in the case to raise that presumption. The right is acquired by adverse enjoyment. The non-user, therefore, must be the consequence of something which is adverse to the user.'

9.77 There, a lack of use was not coupled with a requisite intention to renounce the right and no abandonment was found.

9.78 In *Lovell v Smith*[73] a new way over the servient owner's land was agreed between the relevant parties approximately 30 years before the action, and as a result of this agreement, use of the old way was discontinued. The court held that lack of use of the old right in these circumstances, and for a period of over 20 years, furnished no evidence of an intention to abandon the old right. Discontinuance of the old way alone was not sufficient to show an intention to abandon.

9.79 In *James v Stevenson*[74] it was held that mere non-user of some of the roads over which a right of way existed, where no occasion for user had arisen, coupled with the use by the servant owner of those parts of the roads for farm purposes, did not constitute abandonment.[75]

9.80 In *Young v Star Omnibus Co*,[76] it was held that the erection of a summer house which projected over a strip of land which was subject to a right of way only amounted, at best, to a partial abandonment. It was therefore no defence to the action brought in trespass against the defendants. In *Charles v Beach*[77] it was held that there was no evidence of abandonment where the dominant owner failed to create an access in relation to a right of way.

9.81 In *Carder v Davies*[78] it was argued that the construction of a wall by the owner of the dominant tenement resulted in the abandonment of the right of access onto a way at any point adjoining his land. However, Peter Gibson LJ said:

'Where the easement owner is in no way limited by the words of an easement to access at any particular point, it matters not that he builds a wall, erects a fence or grows a hedge, which by its nature would not allow convenient access through onto the easement. He is able, if he wishes, to change the access point at any time.'

9.82 In *CDC2020 Plc v Ferreira*[79] a right of way over land was contained in a conveyance 'for all purposes connected with the use and enjoyment of the three garages erected on' the dominant tenement. The way had been unlawfully used for gaining access to other land for over 30 years, following demolition of the

73 (1857) 3 CB (ns) 120. See *Hulbert v Dale* [1909] 2 Ch 570.
74 [1893] AC 162.
75 See also *Cooke v Ingram* (1893) 68 LT 671.
76 (1902) 86 LT 41.
77 [1993] EGCS 124.
78 (1998) 76 P & CR D33, CA, but cf *Mills v Blackwell* (1999) 78 P & CR D43.
79 [2005] EWCA Civ 611; [2005] 3 EGLR 15.

garages and erection of other structures on the site. The dominant owner subsequently redeveloped the land and constructed three garages on it. It was still held that the easement had not been abandoned as no intention to abandon could be made out.

9.83 All these cases demonstrate that the burden is very much on the party asserting abandonment to evidence an intention by the dominant owner, and that the courts will be slow to find such an intention where alternative explanations for the non-use or inconsistent conduct are available. The burden is therefore a rather significant one.

Indication of intention to abandon

9.84 There are cases where the court has been more willing to infer that an easement of way has been abandoned, normally because a cessation to enjoy has been accompanied by indications of an intention to abandon the right or a disclaimer of the right by the dominant owner.

9.85 In *Midland Railway v Gribble*,[80] it was held that the right to use a crossing between land intersected by a railway was abandoned as a result of the alienation by the owner of the part on one side of the railway without reserving any right of way over it. Here an intention never to use again could be found because of the alienation.

9.86 In *Williams v Usherwood*[81] two houses were built with a shared driveway between them, ownership of which was split down the middle. Rights of way were granted to the original owners of the houses over the parts of the driveway that each did not own. The layout was such that one of the parties did not benefit from the driveway and a fence was erected separating the driveways. It was held that the house owner had acquired title by adverse possession of the half width of the driveway originally owned by the other party who was deemed to have abandoned his right of way over this part of the drive.

9.87 A party can also show an intention to abandon the right of way by effectively disclaiming its future use. In *Norbury v Meade*[82] Lord Elson LC said:

> 'In the case of a right of way over the lands of other persons, being an easement belonging to lands, if the owner chooses to say, I have no right of way over those lands, that is disclaiming that right of way; and though the previous title might be shown, a subsequent release of the right might be presumed.'

9.88 That is, a person can effectively disclaim any entitlement to use a right of way. For example, in *Bosomworth v Faber*,[83] a party entitled to a prescriptive right to a supply of water from a particular tank entered into a licence determinable on notice entitling him to construct a water tank (and use water

---

[80]   [1895] 2 Ch 827.
[81]   (1983) 45 P & CR 235.
[82]   (1821) 3 Bligh 211, 241, 242.
[83]   (1992) 69 P & CR 288.

from this) at a different location to the tank subject to the prescriptive right. The licence was terminated and the Court of Appeal held that the previous prescriptive right was impliedly abandoned when the licence was accepted and the new tank system installed and the old tank demolished. In similar terms, in *Robinson Webster (Holdings) Ltd v Agombar*[84] it was held that a pre-existing right of way was abandoned when the dominant owner accepted a licence to use the way, such licence being terminable by one week's notice and at a nominal fee.

9.89 Accordingly, an intention to abandon can be inferred where:

(a) acts of the parties are consistent with manifesting an intention never to use the right of way again (for example, where a party alienates land without reserving any right of way over it). Here the court is looking for a firm intention for the right to have been given up and will look for unequivocal acts to satisfy itself of such a firm intention never to make use of the right again; or

(b) the party effectively disclaims their right to exercise the easement (for example, by accepting a licence to use the way rather than relying on the right they may previously have had).

Mistaken belief

9.90 A mistaken belief that a right has been lost will not constitute abandonment.

9.91 For example, in *Obadia v Morris*[85] Plowman J held that a mistaken impression that the merger of a lease in the freehold reversion had destroyed a right of way was not consistent with an intention to abandon. The courts will look to some positive intention never to use the right of way again, whether by words or the surrounding circumstances.

9.92 Accordingly, it is essential to ensure that any party purporting to give up a right of way, or manifesting an intention never to exercise a right of way again, is aware that they technically have the right to give it up.

Summary of principles for abandonment

9.93 In *Odey v Barber*[86] Silber J referred to the following principles regarding the approach of the courts to a claim that a right of way has been abandoned. These principles can be summarised as follows:

---

[84] [2002] 1 P & CR 243 at 72.
[85] [1974] 232 EG 333.
[86] [2006] EWHC 3109 (Ch); 2 WLR 618 at 103.

(a) whether an act amounts to abandonment, or a person intends an abandonment by their actions, is always a question of fact to be determined from the surrounding circumstances, it is not a subjective question;

(b) the intention of the person alleged to be abandoning the right of way as perceived by the reasonable owner of the servient tenement is the key consideration. The dominant owner's conduct (by words or deeds) must be such to demonstrate a firm intention (with emphasis on 'firm') at the relevant time, that neither he nor his successors in title should ever thereafter make use of the easement again in the future;

(c) non-user alone does not constitute conclusive evidence that a private right of way has been abandoned, all the surrounding circumstances must be considered in conjunction with the non-use;

(d) abandonment will not be inferred lightly given that property owners will not normally wish to divest themselves of a right of way, regardless of whether they have no present use for it.

9.94 In the context of rights of way, case law seems to indicate that facts most likely to establish an intention never to use the right of way again will include walls and other permanent structures being erected across a right of way, along with other obstructions of a permanent nature. In each case, it must be questioned whether the acts of the dominant owner manifest an intention never to use the way *ever* again, or just not to use it in the short term. The more permanent the obstruction, the more likely the court will prefer to find for abandonment. A willingness not to use the right of way for the time being, or a specified period, will never be sufficient to constitute abandonment, no matter how firm the intention; the dominant owner must renounce the right for ever.

Change in dominant tenement: incapable of still benefitting

9.95 Where there is an alteration in the dominant tenement the question arises as to whether an easement may be lost.

9.96 An easement can come to an end where an alteration has occurred in the character of the dominant land, making it incapable of ever benefiting from the easement again. This is often the case where the easement was granted for a limited or specific purpose.

Specific or limited purpose

9.97 It is common for an easement to be created with an express limitation, or specifically granted for a particular purpose or need. It follows, in such cases, that if the defined purpose ceases then logically the easement will be extinguished automatically.[87]

9.98 This principle was demonstrated in *National Guaranteed Manure Company Ltd v Donald*[88] where the dominant owner had the right to take water in order to supply a canal. The dominant land was subsequently changed and the canal was converted into a railway. As a result of this fundamental change in the dominant land, the court considered that the right to take the water had been extinguished. This was presumably on the basis that there was no longer a canal to have water supplied to, and the railway was a permanent feature of the dominant land moving forward.

9.99 In practical terms it can prove difficult for a party to claim that a particular purpose has come to an end, and that the purpose will never be revived, unless they are also able to show that there has been a fundamental change in the nature of the dominant land. Further, where an alteration has occurred in the character of the dominant land, it is not always clear whether the change in character also needs to be supported by an intention never to assert the right to the easement again (making it similar to abandonment), or whether the change is so significant that it is sufficient on its own.

9.100 In a rights of way context, a right may be created specifically for a certain purpose in respect of a particular circumstance. An example includes the grant of a right of way to facilitate access to a development site during the period of construction of the buildings. Once that purpose no longer exists, the right of way will fall away.

Frustration

9.101 Cases where the dominant land is altered so significantly by nature are uncommon in practice and very rarely the subject of litigation. However, in such cases they could amount to frustration.

9.102 Putting aside historic uncertainties as to the application of the doctrine of frustration to issues pertaining to land, it is a matter of authority that an easement is capable of being extinguished by frustration.[89] This may occur where unexpected or supervening circumstances following the grant or the creation of the easement subsequently cause there to be no inherent likelihood or practical possibility in the future of the easement ever benefitting the

---

[87] Also, where an easement is created by grant for a certain period, when that period has elapsed, the easement comes to an end. See *Beddington v Atlee* (1887) 35 Ch D 323.

[88] (1859) 4 H&N 8.

[89] *Huckvale v Aegean Hotels* (1989) 58 P & CR 163 at 173, *per* Slade LJ.

dominant tenement in the manner that was expressly or impliedly contemplated in the original grant or creation of the easement. Indeed, it was argued in *Huckvale v Aegean Hotels* that:

> '...since [at least] October 1987 the use of the right of way over the red land for this purpose has become impossible and that the right of way has accordingly been extinguished because it has lost one of the four essential characteristics of an easement ... in that it is no longer capable of benefiting the dominant tenement and thus has been frustrated...'[90]

9.103 The facts that a party would have to rely on to claim that an easement of way had been extinguished by frustration are similar in nature to those that would be advanced to claim that the easement has been lost by virtue of abandonment. Accordingly, if a party is unable to claim extinguishment of an easement of way by abandonment,[91] it is unlikely that frustration will act as an alternative argument. The onus of proof is on the party alleging frustration and this is likely to remain a significant burden because:

> '...in the absence of evidence or proof of abandonment, the court should be slow to hold that an easement has been extinguished by frustration, unless the evidence shows clearly that because of a change in circumstances since the date of the original grant there is no practical possibility of its ever again benefiting the dominant tenement in the manner contemplated by that grant.'[92]

9.104 More common are cases where there is a change in the dominant tenement causing use of the right of way over the servient land to exceed that by which it was acquired by long use, thus placing a greater burden on the servient land, as the next section explains.

Radical change in dominant tenement leading to imposition of additional burden on servient tenement

9.105 It is an established principle that the use of an easement must not exceed its grant or the purpose that gave rise to its acquisition by long use. Whilst the case law on excessive user can be explained as having been rather inconsistent and contradictory over time, it has, however, recently being clarified in the Court of Appeal decision in *McAdams Homes Ltd v Robinson*.[93] This case demonstrates that an easement can be suspended or lost where the dominant land is developed in a way that amounts to a radical change in its character or identity and which, in turn, results in a substantial increase or placing of an additional burden on the servient land as a consequence of that change.

---

[90] *Huckvale v Aegean Hotels* (1989) 58 P & CR 163 at 173, *per* Slade LJ.
[91] (1989) 58 P & CR 163, at 170, *per* Nourse LJ.
[92] (1989) 58 P & CR 163, at 171, *per* Slade LJ.
[93] [2004] 3 EGLR 93.

9.106 It is important to note that this debate relates only to easements acquired by long use. See below for the contrasting position relating to easements expressly granted.

Historic position on excessive user

9.107 In the case of discontinuous easements, case law has suggested over time that a previously existing legal right (for example a right of way) should not be affected by acts of excessive user or usurpation, if (as is usually the case) the extent of the excess could be ascertained. For example, if someone with a right of way by foot were to use the right of way as a carriageway, the right thus sought to be challenged would, in the mode of its enjoyment, be distinct from the previous easement.

9.108 In *Graham v Philcox* the Court of Appeal said:

'I doubt whether any excessive user, at least of a discontinuous easement, in whatever respect the use may be excessive, will ever of itself bring to an end or indeed suspend such an easement ... The owner of the servient tenement upon which, ex hypothesi, the excessive burden is placed is entitled to have that excessive user restrained. The fact that a court may grant an appropriate injunction or make a declaration to this end does not in my judgment either extinguish or suspend the easement. Provided that the owner of the dominant tenement subsequently reverts to lawful use of the easement, his prior excessive use of it is then irrelevant.'[94]

9.109 In *Hamble Parish Council v Haggard*,[95] a parish council had the right, by way of express grant, to use a way for access to a field intended ultimately to be used for burials, but not to the existing churchyard or church. It was suggested by the court that one option for the dominant owner to seek to prevent excessive user would be for the dominant owner to erect a fence with a locked gate between the two pieces of land.[96] Millett J said that where it is possible, however difficult, to make lawful use of a right of way or other discontinuous easement, the servient owner is entitled to an injunction to restrain excessive user and put the burden of separating the two users and stopping the excessive user upon the dominant owner, but not to obstruct the user completely.

9.110 In *Harris v Flower & Sons*[97] it was claimed that a right of way to obtain access to buildings erected partly on the land to which the right of way was appurtenant and partly on other land had been abandoned. It was so claimed on the basis that it was practically impossible to separate the lawful use from the excessive user. No abandonment was found by the court. The user of the

---

[94] [1984] QB 747 at 756.
[95] [1992] 1 WLR 122 at 134D.
[96] [1992] 1 WLR 122 at 136E.
[97] (1905) 74 LJ Ch 127. Where a way is used to reach land the use of which is ancillary to the use of the dominant tenement, the user is not excessive: *National Trust for Places of Historic Interest or Natural Beauty v White* [1987] 1 WLR 907.

way for access to the buildings, so far as they were situated on land to which the right of way was not appurtenant, was held to be in excess of the rights of the defendants.[98]

Recent developments

9.111 In recent years the position on excessive use with respect to rights of way has received greater interest. In *Attwood v Bovis Homes Limited*,[99] the defendants were proposing to build 1,000 houses on land previously used for farming. The land had the benefit of an easement of drainage through ditches over the plaintiff's land. The easement had been acquired by prescription. Neuberger J held that in cases of easements of drainage (as with easements of support and eavesdrop), the test is whether there has been a change in the dominant tenement of such a kind as to throw a substantially greater burden on the servient tenement. In the present case, it was held that the development would not have such an effect, and accordingly the right was not so affected.

9.112 Neuberger J tentatively suggested that the rule as to rights of way could be that:

> '... if there is a subsequent radical change in the use of the dominant tenement, a
> right of way acquired by prescription can only continue to be used in connection
> with the dominant tenement if the court can be satisfied that the change cannot
> result in the use of the way being greater in quantum or different in character from
> that which it was [for the period establishing the prescriptive right]. The onus
> would be on the owner of the dominant tenement, and would, I suspect, normally
> be difficult to satisfy in relation to a right of way.'[100]

9.113 *Attwood v Bovis Homes Ltd* (along with *Cargill v Gotts*,[101] a case relating to a right to take water) were both considered, with other cases concerning other easements (principally rights of way), by the Court of Appeal in *McAdams Homes Ltd v Robinson*.[102] Both of the earlier cases were approved of in the judgments in this decision. In *McAdams Homes*, the dominant land consisted of a bakery with an implied right of drainage over the servient land, which was adjoining. The bakery was demolished and replaced with two new dwellings; the effect of this was to increase the drainage flow.

9.114 Neuberger LJ gave the first judgment in *McAdams Homes* and held that:

(a)   where at the time an easement is created, the dominant land is used for a
      particular purpose, any increase in the intensity of *that* use, resulting in a

---

[98]   This analysis of *Harris v Flower* was adopted by the High Court of Australia in *Westfield Management Ltd v Perpetual Trustee Company Ltd* [2007] HCA 45 at 27.
[99]   [2001] Ch 379.
[100] [2001] Ch 379, at 388D.
[101] *Cargill v Gotts* [1981] 1 WLR 441.
[102] [2004] 3 EGLR 93.

concomitant increase in the use of the easement, cannot of itself be objected to by the servient owner (even if the increase is substantial in nature);[103]

(b)   excessive use of an easement by the dominant land will leave him liable to an action in nuisance;

(c)   where there is a change in the use of or the erection of new buildings on the dominant land, *without* having any effect on the nature or extent of the use of the easement, the change, however radical, will not affect the right of the dominant owner to use the easement;[104]

(d)   other cases question the effect of a change in the use of the dominant tenement which results, or has the potential to result, in an alteration in the manner or extent of the easement's use;[105]

(e)   the issue as to the extent of an easement acquired by implied grant or by prescription can be determined by two questions:

   (i)   does the development of the dominant land represent a 'radical change in the character' or a 'change in the identity' of the dominant land as opposed to a mere change or intensification in the use of the dominant land;

   (ii) does the use of the dominant land (as redeveloped) result in a substantial increase or alteration in the burden on the servient land;

(f)   if the redevelopment of the dominant land resulted in a radical change in its character *and* would lead to a substantial increase in the burden on the servient land, the dominant owner's right to enjoy the easement will be suspended or lost;

(g)   in cases of these two requirements being satisfied, the dominant owner's right to enjoy the easement will end, or at least be suspended, so long as the radical change of character and substantial increase in burden are maintained – ie for the duration of this period;

(h)   each case would be a fact specific issue with regard to the particular easement in question. It would be important to take into account the

---

[103]   See *British Railways Board v Glass* [1965] Ch 538 and *Cargill v Gotts* [1981] 1 WLR 441.

[104]   See *Luttrel's Case* (1601) 4 Co Rep. 86a; *Watts v Kelson* (1870) 6 Ch App 166; *Atwood v Bovis Homes Limited* [2001] Ch 371, and *Harvey v Walters* (1873) LR 8 CP 162.

[105]   These cases included *Williams v James* (1867) LR 2 CP 577; *Wood v Saunders* (1875) 10 Ch App 582; *Wimbledon and Putney Commons Conservators v Dixon* (1875) 1 Ch D 362; *Milner's Safe Company Limited v Great Northern & City Railway Company* [1907] 1 Ch 208; *RPC Holdings Limited v Rogers* [1953] 1 All ER 1029; *British Railways Board v Glass*; [1965] Ch 538; *Giles v County Building Constructors (Hertford) Limited* (1971) 22 P & CR 978 and *Ray v Fairway Motors (Barnstaple) Limited* (1968) 20 P & CR 261.

position on the ground at the date of the grant, including all surrounding circumstances, and the nature and effect of the redevelopment subsequently undertaken.

9.115 These principles were then applied to the facts of the case, which concerned a right of drainage rather than a right of way. The Court of Appeal found that the redevelopment had radically changed the character of the dominant land and had also led to a substantial increase in the burden on the servient land. The continued use of the easement amounted to an excessive user. Accordingly, the servient owner was entitled to obstruct the dominant owner's use of the drains.

Test for excessive user

9.116 The decision in *McAdams Homes* thus created the following two-part test for excessive use, which, if satisfied, will allow the court to suspend or terminate an easement:

(1)   Does the development of the dominant land amount to a 'radical change in character' or 'change in identity' as opposed to a mere change, or intensification, in the use of the dominant land?

(2)   Does the use of the dominant land, as redeveloped, result in a substantial increase or alteration in the burden on the servient land?

9.117 It is only if there is a radical change in the dominant land *and* a consequent substantial increase in the burden on the servient land that the dominant owner's right to enjoy the easement will be lost, or at least suspended. The loss or suspension will last for the period in which the radical change in character or change in identity, and substantial increase in burden, are maintained.

9.118 In the context of rights of way, this is most likely be apparent where the dominant land is developed to increase usage or capacity in a way which changes its character – for example, a small agricultural holding becomes a residential estate, or an industrial estate is converted into residential use with multiple flats or apartments. Here the dominant land (as redeveloped) is likely result in a substantial increase and alteration in the burden on the servient land as a consequence of the radical change in character and identity; the nature and extent of the use of the existing right of way over the servient land will drastically change because of the change in character and identity of the dominant land.

Contrast with expressly granted easements of way

9.119   As noted above, intensification of user is apparent with respect of rights of way acquired by prescription, where use of the servient land primarily determines the right acquired. In relation to expressly granted rights of way, the position is entirely different.

9.120   In the recent case of *Davill v Pull*,[106] the Court of Appeal was asked to decide the meaning of an easement that was expressly granted. In this case, a right of way over a track had been granted 'for all reasonable and usual purposes'. The dominant land (ie the land with the benefit of this easement) was described as 'garden ground'. The current landowner of the 'garden ground' obtained planning permission for a residential development on it. The neighbours objected and at first instance it was held that the use of the track for the intended purpose was excessive, and therefore unlawful. The High Court decided that the use of the track was limited to all reasonable and usual purposes relating to the dominant land as 'garden ground', as described in the relevant conveyances.

9.121   The developer appealed. The Court of Appeal based its interpretation on principles which are well established in case law. It looked at the particular words used, and the surrounding circumstances existing at the time of the grant. Their Lordships decided that the phrase 'garden ground' had been used to identify the dominant land, not to limit the purposes for which it could be used. Had the draftsman wished to place a restriction on the future use of the 'garden ground' it could have done so.

9.122   The question remained over the construction of 'for all reasonable and usual purposes'. The court accepted that this phrase is to be interpreted more restrictively than 'for all purposes'. However, there was no question that the use of the dominant land for the building and occupation of a dwelling house in accordance with a planning permission was a 'reasonable and usual' use. The easement could therefore be lawfully used for the construction of the houses and for their occupation afterwards.

9.123   The case highlights how, if one intends to impose limitations on the use of an easement expressly granted, such limitations must be absolutely clear. The court will not imply limitations when it was open to the draftsmen to do so if they had wished. The use of a right of way, which has been expressly granted, can often change, quite legitimately, over time, and the draftsman should consider that. This differs entirely from the position where an easement is claimed by prescription. A prescriptive easement is construed restrictively in accordance with the extent of its usage of the servient land at the time the right arises, as the recent case of *Dewan v Lewis* [2010] EWCA Civ 1382 summarises.

9.124   The case related to the use of a private accessway to a farm. The farmer argued that the dominant tenement was used for agricultural purposes and that

---

[106]   [2009] EWCA Civ 1309.

he should be allowed to use the roadway for any purpose that was reasonably incidental to such use. The court ruled that this would mean that the scope of a prescriptive easement would be defined largely by reference to the use to which the dominant land was put – and not by reference to the use that was actually made of the servient land – and that for that reason the argument was rejected.

9.125 The decision therefore confirmed that the extent of easements created by express (or implied) grant differs from easements created by prescription. Use of the dominant land is an important consideration in the case of express (or implied easements) because the courts will assume that the grant includes rights that are necessary for the reasonable enjoyment of the land.[107] However, conversely, the approach to prescriptive easements is entirely opposite, and the specific use of the servient land will be relevant in such a case. For this reason, arguments about intensification of user become relevant to easements acquired by prescription, where a party later seeks to put the servient land to greater use than it had been put to in the course of the acquisition that gave rise to the prescriptive right. This is because, as easements restrict the rights of servient landowners, the law should not allow land to be burdened by a use which is more onerous than the use that has actually been made of it. This does not mean that the prescriptive rights are limited to the precise user made of servient land over the 20 year period of user however; users may acquire analogous rights (for example, vehicular use based on previous use by horses and carriages) or rights to use the land for other purposes that do not impose a greater burden on the servient land. The imposition of the greater burden on the servient land is the key consideration.

Law Commission recommendations

9.126 The tests referred to above were considered by the Law Commission in a consultation paper.[108] Acknowledging that the application and outcome of the test would not be entirely predictable in any given case, the Law Commission noted that the tests needed to be flexible in order to be capable of adapting to the inherently fact-specific nature of disputed easements such as rights of way.

9.127 The Law Commission has recommended that a test, in very similar terms to the test proposed in *McAdams Homes*, should be used in cases where it is necessary to determine whether there has been excessive use of an easement. The Law Commission also suggests that the court should, where excessive user is determined, be given jurisdiction to either extinguish the easement, suspend use of the easement, or (where it may be possible to do so) to sever the use of the easement in order to allow the original use to continue without the additional excessive burden. This reverts to historic treatment of cases involving excessive user which held that a previously existing legal right (such as

---

[107] Only if express limitations are stipulated, and these are breached or exceeded, will a claim arise.
[108] *Law Commission Consultation Paper No 186: Easements, covenants and profits a prendre*, 28 July 2008.

a right of way) should not be affected by acts of excessive user or usurpation, if (as is usually the case) the extent of the excess could be ascertained. The excess would simply be prohibited leaving the original use to continue as before. The Law Commission also noted that damages in lieu was an available option for any of the above.

9.128 Accordingly, excessive user can be understood as a means by which an easement of way can be suspended (for the duration of the radical change in character or identity of the dominant land, and corresponding substantial increase in burden on the servient land) or ultimately extinguished (if the change is one of a permanent nature).

STATUTORY EXTINGUISHMENT

9.129 Statutes operate to extinguish easements in a number of ways, either expressly or by implication or as a result of provisions regarding compulsory acquisition.

Expressly or by implication

9.130 An easement can be extinguished by express words contained in legislation. Examples of statutes which expressly confer powers to extinguish easements of way include:

(a) provisions in the Town and Country Planning Act 1990,[109] the Planning (Listed Buildings and Conservation Areas) Act 1990,[110] the Requisitioned Land and War Works Act 1948,[111] the New Towns Act 1981,[112] and the Civil Aviation Act 1982.[113] These follow the spirit of the Housing Act 1985.

(b) the Housing Act 1985.[114] Upon the purchase of land by a local housing authority under Part IX of the Act, subject to agreement to the contrary and to provisions governing statutory undertakers and telecommunications apparatus, all private rights of way and all rights of laying down, erecting, continuing, or maintaining apparatus on, under or over that land, and all other rights or easements in or relating to that land will be extinguished. This provision is most commonly seen in regeneration cases or so called 'slum-clearance' programmes.[115]

---

[109] Sections 236 and 237.
[110] Section 51(1).
[111] Section 4(2).
[112] Section19 (as amended by the Telecommunications Act 1984, s 109(1), Sch 4, para 79(3)).
[113] Section 46(2)(c); and see *London Regional Transport v Imperial Group Pension Trust Ltd* [1987] 2 EGLR 20, on the London Transport Act 1964, s 14.
[114] Section 295; see also Housing Act 1988, Sch 10, para 4.
[115] It is, however, important to note that there is no statutory procedure for the extinguishment of an easement equivalent to the procedure under s 84 of the LPA 1925 which governs the express discharge of restrictive covenants.

(c) the extinguishment, by a railway company's private Act of 'all rights of way in, over, and affecting' certain 'footways'. The clause did not extinguish a private right of way,[116] however, and was limited only to public rights.

(d) section 8 of the Inclosure (Consolidation) Act 1801[117] and section 68 of the Inclosure Act 1845, which provided that 'ways shall be for ever stopped up and extinguished'.[118]

9.131 An easement may also be extinguished by implication:

> 'When the Legislature clearly and distinctly authorise the doing of a thing which is physically inconsistent with the continuance of an existing right, the right is gone, because the thing cannot be done without abrogating the right.'[119]

9.132 There are limitations regarding this method of extinguishment. Any Act of Parliament will not be construed so as to interfere with a person's property rights without compensation unless the court is obliged to construct it in this way.[120] Further, an easement may revive and not be permanently extinguished if circumstances changed. For example, where a landlord was obliged to erect a wall for fire safety purposes pursuant to a statutory notice under Part XI of the Housing Act 1985, and this wall blocked the tenant's access to a rear bin area, it was held that the tenant's right was not extinguished once and for all.[121]

Compulsory acquisition

9.133 Public and private bodies are empowered by a number of differing statutes to acquire land compulsorily, which will affect pre-existing easements to which a piece of land is subject. The main statutes governing such acquisitions are the Land Compensation Act 1961, the Compulsory Purchase Act 1965, and the Acquisition of Land Act 1981.

---

[116] *Wells v London, Tilbury and Southend Ry* (1877) 5 Ch D 126.
[117] Repealed by the Commons Act 1899, s 23, Sch 2.
[118] At section 68; *Turner v Crush* (1879) 4 App Cas 221.
[119] *Yarmouth Corp v Simmons* (1878) 10 Ch D 518, where it was shown that the construction of a pier authorised by statute would be physically inconsistent with the existence of a public right of way.
[120] *Jones v Cleanthi* [2006] EWCA Civ 1712; [2007] 1 WLR 1604 at [82]. The common law principle is now reflected in Art 1 of the First Protocol to the European Convention on Human Rights incorporated into British law by the Human Rights Act 1998. The High Court decision in *Jones v Cleanthi* confirmed that the principle regarding extinguishment by implication in *Yarmouth Corp v Simmons* applies to private rights created by covenants as well as public rights created by usage. However, the decision did not say that the easement was permanently extinguished; it was held that there was a possibility in the future that certain events could revive the easement. One can therefore question whether it is more correct to say that the easement was suspended (albeit potentially indefinitely).
[121] *Jones v Cleanthi* [2006] EWCA Civ 1712; [2007] 1 WLR 1604, distinguishing *Yarmouth Corp v Simmons* (above). It was held, however, that because the wall was erected to comply with a statutory obligation, this was a defence to an action in nuisance.

9.134   On such acquisitions, any pre-existing easements benefiting the subject land pass to the acquiring authority.[122] Unless the applicable statute provides for the acquisition of a lesser right (such as an easement of way), generally powers of compulsory acquisition require the purchase of the *whole* of the landowner's interest.[123]

9.135   Subject to the exceptions outlined below, as a general rule, the owner of land benefiting from an easement cannot bring an action for disturbance, nor serve a notice to treat where such easement is disturbed as a result of land being compulsorily purchased pursuant to statute. In these cases, the easement is extinguished provided the land remains vested in the acquiring authority. The easement will not be completely extinguished and will bind the land if the land becomes owned by someone other than the acquiring authority (but see below for cases under the Town and Country Planning Act 1990).[124] The remedy for the loss of the easement will be compensation.[125]

Town and Country Planning Act 1990

9.136   Pursuant to section 226 of the Town and Country Planning Act 1990, a local authority can compulsorily acquire land within its area if it considers that the acquisition will facilitate the carrying out of development or redevelopment or improvement of the land. It may also compulsorily acquire land if it considers such acquisition is required[126] for a purpose which it is necessary to achieve in the interests of the proper planning of an area (in which the said land is situated). Unless it considers that such development is likely to contribute to the promotion or improvement of the economic, social or environmental well-being of the area, the authority will be unable to exercise its powers in relation to the facilitation of development or redevelopment or improvement. Where an acquisition, or appropriation, takes place under section 226, the acquisition or appropriation is known as 'an acquisition or appropriation for planning purposes'.[127]

---

[122]   *Sovmots Investments Ltd v Secretary of State for the Environment* [1977]2 All ER 385, HL.

[123]   Ibid at 393g.

[124]   See *Eagle v Charing Cross Ry* (1867) LR 2 CP 638; *Bedford v Dawson* (1875) LR 20 Eq 353; *Wigram v Fryer* (1887) 36 Ch D 87; *Kirby v Harrogate School Board* [1896] 1 Ch 437; *MS & L Ry v Anderson* [1898] 2 Ch 394; *Long Eaton v Midland Ry* [1902] 2 KB 574 (under the Lands Clauses Consolidation Act 1845); and *Wilson's Brewery Ltd v West Yorkshire MBC* (1977) 34 P & CR 224 (under s 10 of the Compulsory Purchase Act 1965). Cases concerning restrictive covenants, by analogy include *Marten v Flight Refuelling* [1962] Ch 115; *Elm Avenue, Re* [1984] 1 WLR 1398 and *Brown v Heathlands NHS Trust* [1996] 1 All ER 133.

[125]   See *Eagle v Charing Cross Ry* (1867) LR 2 CP 638; *Bedford v Dawson* (1875) LR 20 Eq 353; *Wigram v Fryer* (1887) 36 Ch D 87; *Kirby v Harrogate School Board* [1896] 1 Ch 437; *MS & L Ry v Anderson* [1898] 2 Ch 394; *Long Eaton v Midland Ry* [1902] 2 KB 574 (under the Lands Clauses Consolidation Act 1845) and *Wilson's Brewery Ltd v West Yorkshire MBC* (1977) 34 P & CR 224 (under section 10 of the Compulsory Purchase Act 1965).

[126]   *Chesterfield Properties v Secretary of State of the Environment* [1997] EWHC Admin 709 at 19. 'Required' means less than indispensable but, however, more than simply desirable.

[127]   Town and Country Planning Act 1990, s 246(1).

9.137 Where an interference takes place, compensation will be payable to the injured party. The payment of compensation for loss of the easement will be pursuant to the compulsory purchase legislation,[128] and reflects the diminution in the value of the claimant's land. Accordingly, considerations of ransom or loss of bargaining position (so called 'buy out damages') are not relevant to the calculation of compensation for these purposes.[129]

9.138 Accordingly, if the dominant owner of a right of way refuses to negotiate the release of a right of way, it may be possible for a developer to overcome such a refusal if it works with the local authority to facilitate acquisition of the site by the said authority. The local authority could then transfer the land back to the developer for the purposes of the proposed works (the easement would not revive in such a case – see below). The effect of this would be for the developer to circumvent the outright refusal or the demand for damages on a basis other than that which reflects diminution in value.

9.139 One must appreciate that local authorities do not have an unfettered discretion, and all public bodies exercising public decision making powers are subject to scrutiny and challenge by way of judicial review proceedings. To avoid the risk of judicial review of an arrangement of this kind (on the basis that such acquisition could be seemed ultra-vires because the principal purpose of the acquisition was to save the developer money, or simply circumvent an objection), the pre-acquisition owner may need to be able to establish unreasonableness and intransigence on the part of the dominant owner along with the need for the land to be appropriated or acquired for lawful purposes prescribed by the governing legislation.

9.140 If the dominant owner wishes to mount a challenge to the local authority's decision, in accordance with normal public law principles, it is necessary to act promptly and, if by way of judicial review proceedings, within three months of the decision in any event. If a challenge is not made within prescribed limits following the decision by the local authority to acquire the land, it will not be possible for the aggrieved party to make their complaint at a time in the future when the development works actually create an interference with the easement in questions,[130] other than with respect to any outstanding claim for compensation on the basis of diminution in value.

Section 237

9.141 Section 237 of the Town and Country Planning Act, which is commonly referred to in cases where private easements are to be overridden, provides that:

---

[128] For example under sections 63 or 68 of the Lands Clauses Consolidation Act 1845 or under sections 7 or 10 of the Compulsory Purchase Act 1965.

[129] *Wrotham Park Settled Estates v Hertsmere Borough Council* [1993] 2 EGLR 15 (a restrictive covenant case), approving the reasoning and the analysis of the case-law of Judge Marder QC sitting in the Lands Tribunal reported at [1991] 1 EGLR 230.

[130] *Ford-Camber Ltd v Deaminster Ltd* [2007] EWC civ 458.

'(1) Subject to subsection (3), the erection, construction or carrying out, or maintenance of any building or work on land which has been acquired or appropriated by a local authority for planning purposes (whether done by a local authority or by a person deriving title under them) is authorised by virtue of this section if it is done in accordance with planning permission, notwithstanding that it involves:

(a) interference with an interest or right to which this section applies; or

(b) a breach of a restriction as to the user of land arising by virtue of a contract.

(2) Subject to subsection (3), the interests and rights to which this section applies are any easement, liberty, privilege, right or advantage annexed to land and adversely affecting other land, including any natural right to support.

(3) [...]

(4) In respect of any inference or breach in pursuance of subsection (1), compensation:

(a) shall be payable under section 63 or 68 of the Lands Clauses Consolidation Act 1845 or under section 7 or 10 of the Compulsory Purchase Act 1965; and

(b) shall be assessed in the same manner and subject to the same rules as in the case of other compensation under those sections in respect of injurious affection.

Where:

(i) the compensation is to be estimated in connection with a purchase under those Acts; or

(ii) the injury arises from the execution of works on land acquired under those Acts.

(5) Where a person deriving title under the local authority by whom the land in question was acquired or appropriated:

(a) is liable to pay compensation by virtue of subsection (4); and

(b) fails to discharge that liability;

the liability shall be enforceable against the local authority.

(6) Nothing in subsection (5) shall be construed as affecting any agreement between the local authority and any other person for indemnifying the local authority against any liability under that subsection.

(7) Nothing in this section shall be construed as authorising any act or omission on the part of any person which is actionable at the suit of any person on any grounds other than such an interference or breach as is mentioned in subsection (1).'

9.142 The effect of these provisions is to provide that, where land has been acquired or appropriated by a local authority for planning purposes under section 237, provided any buildings constructed or work undertaken is strictly in accordance with planning permission, this will be authorised even if it involves interference with an easement or breach of a restrictive covenant.[131] This is the case whether such works are undertaken by the authority or by a person deriving title under them.[132]

---

[131] Town and Country Planning Act 1990, s 237.
[132] Town and Country Planning Act 1990, s 236(8).

9.143   There are limitations to the use of this power, however. For example, in *Midtown v City of London Real Property Co Ltd*,[133] the Corporation of the City of London (a local authority) acquired a small area of land and a large area of other land for the purpose of redevelopment following bomb damage. The development of the relevant land was carried out by the subsequent purchaser of the land and the local authority retained the other large area of land which it had acquired and used this for a new road. A successor in title (the defendant in this case) proposed to demolish the earlier development and construct a major new development, a small part of which would be on the relevant land. Accordingly, the defendant sought to rely on section 237 of the Town and Country Planning Act 1990 in relation to the relevant land. The Judge referred to part of the judgement of Dyson J in *R v City of London Council, ex parte Master Governors and Commonalty of the Mystery of the Barbers of London*.[134] In this case it was said, albeit obiter, that if the later development was by a successor in title of the local authority which had originally acquired or appropriated the land for planning purposes, the subsequent development must be 'related' in some way to those planning purposes, in order to rely on section 237. This view was upheld and was said to apply regardless of whether the local authority or successor in title owned the land at the time of the proposed development. In cases where the local authority still owned the land, it could re-appropriate this for the proposed development. In cases where the land was owned by a successor in title, the subsequent development had to be related to the original planning purpose. In this case, the development was not held to be related to the original planning purpose. Accordingly, the defendant could not rely on section 237 in this instance.[135] This demonstrates that the use of section 237 is not automatic, and it does not constitute a so-called 'white-wash' procedure of the land in question.

Repeal

9.144   Where a statute which extinguishes a right is subsequently repealed, usually the right will not be revived because of the repeal.[136]

9.145   An example of this in the context of a public right of way can be found in *Gwynne v Drewitt*[137] where an Act was passed in 1819 and was to continue in operation for 20 years. The Act made it clear that a public bridleway across a farm would, if not stopped up, be the means of enabling persons to evade the tolls granted by the Act. It thus enacted that the bridleway should be vested in the owner of the farm in exchange for land of his taken for the purposes of the Act, and that, after the road had been opened for traffic, the bridleway should be stopped up, and it should be unlawful for the public to use it. Subsequent

---

[133]   [2005] EWHC 33 (Ch); [2005] 1 EGLR 65.

[134]   [1996] 2 EGLR 128.

[135]   In these circumstances, the Judge did not need to deal with an argument based on the Human Rights Act 1998, to the effect that section 237 should be 'read down' so as to avoid an infringement of Art 1 of the First Protocol in Part II of Sch 1 to the 1998 Act.

[136]   See, for example, the Interpretation Act 1978, s 16(1)(a).

[137]   [1894] 2 Ch 616.

statutes continued the operation of the Act till 1856, when it was repealed. Upon repeal, the question of whether the public right of way over the bridleway could recommence being used was raised. The court held that the repeal did not revive the public right to use the bridleway.

9.146   Romer J said:

> 'The Act of 1856, which repeals the Act of 1819, had not, in my judgment, the effect at all of reviving the old ways, which had been stopped up and discontinued. The effect of section 51 of the Act of 1819 is this – that the old ways there referred to were stopped up and discontinued – in my judgment, for ever ... The Act of 1819 contained a variety of provisions which had to be continued from time to time; and, accordingly, the Act was continued only for a term, under section 92; but the provision in section 51 was something which was done once for all, and was not intended to be undone at the expiration of the term referred to in section 92. Now, when the Act of 1856 was passed, and the Act of 1819 repealed, it was not, in my judgment, at all the intention of the Legislature, or the effect of the Act of 1856, to undo that which had been already done during the continuance of the prior Act, or to revive these ways, which had been once for all discontinued and put an end to, as public ways, by section 51.'[138]

9.147   A declaration was accordingly made that there was no public way, and the defendants were restrained from trespassing by use of the (former) bridleway.

Statutory title

9.148   Special considerations also apply in the case of statutory title.

9.149   For example, where an easement has already been acquired by prescription, and this becomes vested in the owner of the dominant tenement by statutory authority, the effect of this is for the prescriptive title to merge in the statutory title. In the event that the operation of the statute is limited to a restricted or limited period, the easement will be lost once that period of time has elapsed.[139]

9.150   In *New Windsor Corporation v Taylor*[140] a municipal corporation had a prescriptive right to take certain customary tolls for the passage of carriages and cattle over a bridge belonging to them. In 1734, a local Act which, after reciting their right to take the customary tolls, stated that the said customary tolls should be and remain vested in them, and empowered them to take the said tolls, with a variation as to the exemption of freemen of the borough. In 1819 the corporation obtained another local Act which repealed the former Act and empowered them to take down the old bridge and build a new one and to take tolls which varied from the old tolls in amount and subject-matter. This Act was temporary and had expired. The House of Lords held that that the

---

[138]   [1894] 2 Ch 616.
[139]   *Manchester Corp v Lyons* (1882) 22 Ch D 287 and *New Windsor Corp v Taylor* [1899] AC 41.
[140]   [1899] AC 41 at 49.

prescriptive right to take tolls had been merged in and extinguished by the statutory right given in 1734, and neither had nor could have been revived by the later Act, and that the right to take tolls expired with the later Act. This affirmed the Court of Appeal's decision.[141]

9.151   Lord Davey said:

> 'I hold it to be an indisputable proposition of law that where an Act of Parliament has according to its true construction to use the language of Littledate J, "embraced and confirmed" a right which had previously existed by custom or prescription, that right becomes henceforward a statutory right, and the lower title by custom or prescription is merged in and extinguished by the higher title derived from the Act of Parliament.'[142]

9.152   Accordingly, statutory extinguishment can be understood as completely ending the easement in such cases.

Land Registration Act 2002

9.153   The Land Registration Act 2002 limits the unregistered interests that will automatically override a disposition of registered land (with a view to ensuring that title registers are as complete as possible). This has an important impact on a particular class of easements. Unregistered easements that have been acquired by prescription or implied grant or reservation since 13 October 2003, in certain circumstances, will not bind a purchaser of registered land.[143] Those circumstances are that the right is not known to the purchaser or obvious on a reasonably careful inspection of the servient land, and the easement has not been exercised within one year of the date of the disposition.[144] The requirement for the easement to not be obvious (was aimed at easements such as drainage rights and so) will restrict the frequency of this exception applying to rights of way.

9.154   Nevertheless, whilst these provisions do not technically extinguish the easement, they mean that the easement ceases to be enforceable against a purchaser of the servient land in cases where the easement has not been exercised for a year and is not known to the buyer or obvious. In practical terms, therefore, the easement has been extinguished or lost.

Possible statutory changes

9.155   There has been much recent discussion as to whether changes in the law may be appropriate to extinguish rights of light which would otherwise have an

---

[141]   [1898] 1 QB 186, affirmed.

[142]   [1899] AC 41 at 49.

[143]   See para 13.6ff.

[144]   Section 29(2) and para 3, Sch 3, LRA 2002. It should be noted, that actual knowledge of the purchaser is what is relevant here rather than mere notice. The effect of this is to mean that easements that are not obvious on inspection are vulnerable.

adverse effect on development following the decision in *HKRUK (CHC) II Ltd v Marcus Heaney*,[145] and the application of such arguments to easements of way is also apparent.

9.156   There are various possible solutions for seeking to address the issue of private rights of way affecting development. These include the Upper Tribunal (Lands Chamber) being given the power to modify or abrogate easements (including easements of way) in circumstances where it already exercises jurisdiction in relation to restrictive covenants under section 84 of the LPA 1925 and Part 6 of its current (2010) rules. The majority of Australian jurisdictions have such provisions, and Parliament could adopt section 181 of Queensland's Property Law Act of 1974, which itself follows the English legislation (as amended) but extend also to easements.

9.157   Alternatively, some may argue for a simpler and more sweeping power to cancel, modify or extinguish easements of way which impede development in the form of a statutory procedure for the extinguishment of an easement of way. This could also be linked to a statutory formula for compensation.

EXTINGUISHMENT BY COURT ORDER

9.158   In *Greenwich Healthcare NHS Trust v London and Quadrant Housing Trust*[146] the NHS Trust owned land which included a road over which several neighbouring owners had rights of way. Planning consent had been granted for a new hospital whose construction would involve realigning the road. All the dominant owners were given notice of the proposal and none objected but neither did they positively give consent. The Trust was concerned that in the future the neighbours or perhaps a successor might seek an injunction in the future to restrain the obstruction to their access. It therefore applied to court for a declaration that no such injunction would be granted and that any remedy would be limited to an award in damages for interference. Lightman J held that in the absence of a clear power a servient owner had no right to alter the route of a right of way[147] but since there could be no reasonable objection to the proposal and the defendants had been given notice the court had jurisdiction to and would grant a declaration that the defendants would not be entitled to an injunction or damages when the plaintiff realigned the road. The judge observed that the application for the declaration extended, not to the proprietary right of the defendants to an easement, but to the remedy of an injunction. He observed that the jurisdiction of the court extended to both and said:

> 'The greatest care must be taken to ensure that no injustice is occasioned to the defendants to the application'.[148]

---

[145]   [2010] EWHC 2245.
[146]   [1998] 3 All ER 437, [1998] 1 WLR 1749.
[147]   See *Heslop v Bishton* [2009] EWHC 607 (Ch); [2009] 2 P & CR DG10.
[148]   [1998] 3 All ER 437, [1998] 1 WLR 1749, per Lightman J at 1756(g).

There is therefore a distinction between the exercise of a right and the right itself. It may be that the courts will be readier to restrain remedies than to extinguish substantive rights. Although on the principle that rights depend on remedies it might appear that there is little practical difference, in this case it seems the plaintiff was prepared to accept the possibility of a future claim for damages. The judge was prepared to order that no such claim could be brought but on different facts a court might consider it right to preserve such a claim and therefore the underlying right, even if it could not be exercised to pass over the land. If the easement was entered on the servient title there should be an application to enter a notice of the court order. If it was overriding then as it will not be obvious, once the way been relocated, nor used for a year and provided any disponee has notice of the order, it will not take priority over the disponee's rights. The servient owner should also enter a notice on the dominant titles.

Chapter 10

WRONGFUL INTERFERENCE WITH RIGHTS OF WAY

WHAT IS WRONGFUL INTERFERENCE WITH A PRIVATE RIGHT OF WAY?

10.1 The answer to this question lies in the concept of an interference which prevents the person entitled to use the right of way from exercising his right to do so, in a reasonable manner, either at all, or as conveniently as before.

10.2 As regards the use of words in this Chapter the phrase 'wrongful interference' will be used, although it means the same as the phrase 'actionable interference' used in other books and sometimes in the cases. As will be seen below the interference is not actionable unless it is wrongful; ie it is a substantial interference with the reasonable user of the right of way. That is why we speak of a 'wrongful interference'.[1]

10.3 As was said by Scott J in *Celsteel Ltd v Alton House Ltd*:[2]

> 'The interference will be actionable if it is substantial. And it will not be substantial if it does not interfere with the reasonable use of the right of way.'

Therefore, whether the interference has been wrongful and thus actionable is a matter of fact and degree, and in all cases will require the following matters to be proved first:

(a) A determination of the extent of the right granted, eg as to width, quality and purpose of user etc. See Chapter 4 above. Defining the extent of the right is a crucial first stage. It is not for the defendant (the party allegedly

---

[1] See the use of this term at para 177 of *Halsbury's Laws of England* (4th edn), Vol 16(2). Note that the law of private nuisance may have a part to play here in terms of the unreasonableness of the interference in its effect on the lawful use of the way. On private nuisance see the textbooks on Tort. What is clear from recent authority is that an activity conducted on land which is not carried on under statutory authority, may be a nuisance even though it may be in accord with planning consent or some other scheme which permits use of land. Thus, a wrongful interference with a right of way (eg a wall permitted by planning consent) will not cease to be a wrongful interference if authorised by planning consent, unless there is a specific statutory authority to put that wall there *and* commit a nuisance; see *Barr v Biffa Waste Services Ltd.* [2012] EWCA Civ 312 and cases cited there. See also *Coventry & Anor v Lawrence & Ors* [2012] EWCA Cov 26 referred to in that case.

[2] [1985] 1 WLR 204, at p 217.

interfering with the right) to reduce the extent of that right.[3] So for example, if the way is 15' wide, the question as to whether there has been a wrongful interference with the way will be assessed by reference to the 15' width.

(b) Resolution of the question (if it arises) whether any user is excessive: see Chapter 4 and Chapter 9, para **9.107** above. Clearly if such a user is excessive the claimant cannot complain about interference with that user. He can only complain about interference with the lawful user of the way. This Chapter assumes that the lawful extent of the user is or can be defined if necessary by the court. In this Chapter the issue is whether the conduct complained about by the dominant owner amounts to interference with the right of way over the servient land which denies the dominant owner's ability in practical terms to enjoy that way. So for example, if the use of the way is on foot only, the question as to whether there has been a wrongful interference with the way will be assessed by reference to that user.

Needless to say, many cases may well present issues on both the extent and whether any user is excessive before the question of whether there has been a wrongful interference is reached. For a recent example of such a case see *Zieleniewski v Scheyd & Anor*.[4]

See Chapter 4 and Chapter 9, para **9.107** above and *Reilly v Booth*.[5]

(c) Evidence of the obstruction, or other act or omission which causes the alleged interference.[6]

(d) How far the interference to the lawful user prevents a reasonable user. The leading case on this question is *B&Q Plc v Liverpool and Lancashire Properties*.[7] The principles set out in that case are examined below.

The matters required to be proved under (a) to (c) above require proof by primary evidence, eg of the terms of the grant, or of a long user defining the way and of the obstruction or other material event which is the subject of the claim. Implication of terms may have to be made; see Chapter 4 above at para **4.33**.

As to (d) (and to a certain extent (c)) above there will have to be a 'value judgment' made by the court from those primary facts in order to decide whether (for example) any user is excessive and how far the interference with the lawful user prevents a reasonable user.

---

[3] See *B&Q plc v Liverpool & Lancashire Properties Ltd* (2001) 81 P&CR 20, referred to below.

[4] [2012] EWCA Civ 247, noting the issues listed at para 4 per Briggs J.

[5] (1890) 44 Ch D 12 at p 26 per Lopes LJ.

[6] Note that a servient owner is not bound to maintain a right of way, but its state may deteriorate to a point at which the way may no longer be reasonably useable. See Chapter 8 above as to the obligation to maintain. See *Saint v Jenner* [1973] Ch 275 for authority on this subject.

[7] (2001) 81 P&CR 20.

10.4   This Chapter, therefore, will consider:

(a)   What is wrongful interference?

(b)   Specific examples of what may or may not amount to such a wrongful interference.

Note that the cause of action is usually in nuisance. However, sometimes the cause of action may be for breach of covenant (eg to maintain a way and keep it unobstructed) or for breach of a covenant for quiet enjoyment (eg as between landlord and tenant) or sometimes for breach of the obligation that there should not be a derogation from grant. As to the latter, see Chapter 3 above.

10.5   In this Chapter it will be assumed that the cause of action is in nuisance. If the cause of action lies under the other headings just mentioned, it is usually the case that the interference must still be no less substantial that in would be in nuisance[8]. The only slight difference might be where there is a covenant in specific terms, eg to make up a roadway to a defined specification, where a breach of that obligation would be actionable without needing to prove substantial interference with the use of the way.[9] (The remedy in such a case is in effect specific performance of the covenant by an Order of the Court directing that certain defined work be carried out. A mandatory injunction can have the same effect.) However, in practical terms in the latter example, no-one would think it sensible to enforce the obligation unless there had been a serious breach of it.

10.6   Notwithstanding the different causes of action, it is usually the case that the remedy will be the same whatever the cause of action, ie specific relief (eg injunction) or damages, either at common law or under section 50 of the Senior Courts Act 1981.

The remedies which lie for wrongful interference are considered at Chapter 11 below.

10.7   This Chapter will also consider, in the context of a wrongful interference, whether the servient owner may divert the right of way without the consent of the dominant owner. The topic is fully dealt with at Chapter 4 at para **4.129**.

---

[8]   See *B&Q plc v Liverpool & Lancashire Properties Ltd.* (2001) 81 P&CR 20, at paras 75 ff, per Blackburne J, where he stated: 'The claim is only material if, to be actionable as a breach of covenant, the interference with B&Q's rights ... requires proof of something different from (and less substantial than) what must be shown to constitute an interference actionable as a nuisance. As to this, I am of the opinion that to constitute a breach of a covenant for quiet enjoyment, an interference with an easement must be "substantial" no less than it must where the claim is brought in nuisance. On the face of it, therefore, an action on L&L's covenant adds nothing to B&Q's claim in nuisance.'

[9]   Thus the contrast may be drawn between a roadway which is in 'general' disrepair where a covenant requires it to be made up to a certain standard of repair, and a roadway where there is no such covenant and the remedy in nuisance would only be activated if the state of the road prevented reasonable user; eg because of large pot-holes.

STEPS TO TAKE WHEN CONSIDERING WHETHER OR NOT WRONGFUL INTERFERENCE HAS OCCURRED

10.8

(a) Step 1: Consideration of the extent of the right of way and its purpose. Is there excessive user relied on by the claimant? See Chapter 4 above.

(b) Step 2: What has been done or not done by the person alleged to have created a wrongful interference?

(c) Step 3: What is the effect on the dominant owner's right to exercise the right of way?

10.9 The principles to apply are set out concisely in *B&Q plc v Liverpool & Lancashire Properties Ltd*:[10]

'Actionable infringement of a right of way

39 What constitutes an actionable infringement of a right of way turns on well established principles. They were most recently summarised by Mummery LJ in *West v Sharp* (already referred to) at p 332:

> "Not every interference with an easement, such as a right of way, is actionable. There must be a substantial interference with the enjoyment of it. There is no actionable interference with a right of way if it can be substantially and practically exercised as conveniently after as before the occurrence of the alleged obstruction. Thus, the grant of a right of way in law in respect of every part of a defined area does not involve the proposition that the grantee can in fact object to anything done on any part of the area which would obstruct passage over that part. He can only object to such activities, including obstruction, as substantially interfere with the exercise of the defined right as for the time being is reasonably required by him."

40 He then cited with approval the following passage from the judgment of Scott J in *Celsteel Limited v Alton House Limited*:[11]

> "There emerge from the three cases I have cited [ie *Clifford v Hoare*;[12] *Pettey v Parsons*[13] and *Keefe v Amor*[14]] two criteria relevant to the question whether a particular interference with a right of way is actionable. The interference will be actionable if it is substantial and it will not be substantial if it does not interfere with the reasonable use of the right of way."

---

[10] (2001) 81 P&CR 20. See also the useful recent summary of the law on this issue in *Zieleniewski v Scheyd & Anor* [2012] EWCA Civ 247 set out by Briggs J at paras 11 and 12.
[11] [1985] 1 WLR 204 at 217.
[12] (1874) LR 9 CP 362.
[13] [1914] 2 Ch 653.
[14] [1965] 1 QB 334.

41 But what exactly is meant by "the reasonable use" of a right of way? The decision in *Celsteel* is illuminating in its approach to this question.

42 In that case, the issue was whether the narrowing of a driveway to garages and parking spaces for use by the residential tenants of a block of flats would constitute an actionable interference. The plaintiffs were the lessees of some of the flats and garages. The two defendants, one of whom was the freehold owner of the block and the other of whom was the tenant of a major part of the ground level of the block, proposed to construct a car wash on the driveway which, if built, would have reduced the width of the driveway for about 10 to 12 metres of its length from 9 to 4.14 metres. Before considering whether this would constitute an actionable interference, Scott J considered the particular circumstances of two of the tenants. In the case of the tenant of garage number 52, the evidence established that if the car wash were built it would no longer be practicable for that tenant to reverse into his garage although he could continue without any particular difficulty to enter the garage in forward gear, reversing only to exit from it. The tenant's preference, however, was to reverse in.

43 In answer to a submission that it was preferable to drive in forwards and reverse out (rather than reverse in and drive out forwards) Scott J observed (at p 217d):

> "There are advantages and disadvantages attached to both of the alternatives. Some may prefer one, others may prefer the other. In my view, a lessee whose right of way permits him to adopt either alternative as he may from time to time choose, suffers actionable interference if one alternative is precluded and he is constrained always to adopt the other. To put the point another way, use of the ... driveway in order to reverse into garage 52 is a reasonable use. An obstruction which prevents that use is, accordingly, in my judgment actionable."

44 Scott J then went on to consider a variant of the same contention in the following passage (at 271 e–g):

> "Mr Laurence [counsel for the defendants] submitted that driving in forwards and reversing out was reasonable use of the ... driveway. I agree with him. He submitted further that the proposed car wash would not substantially interfere with this particular use, and thus would not prevent reasonable access by the ... plaintiff to garage 52. He argued from these premises that the car wash would not, on authority, constitute an actionable interference. I do not accept that authority justifies this argued conclusion. In the present case the test is not, in my view, whether the means of access still possible is a reasonable means of access. The correct test is whether insistence by the ... plaintiff on being able to continue to use the other means of access is reasonable In my opinion, it is. I do not think it is open to the defendants to deprive the ... plaintiff of his preferred means of entry to garage 52 and then to justify themselves by arguing that most other people would prefer some other still available means of entry. Such an argument might avail the defendants if the ... plaintiff's preference were unreasonable or perverse But, in my view, it is neither of these things."

45 In my view those passages justify the following propositions advanced by Mr Gaunt: (1) the test of an actionable interference is not whether what the

grantee is left with is reasonable, but whether his insistence on being able to continue the use of the whole of what he contracted for is reasonable; (2) it is not open to the grantor to deprive the grantee of his preferred *modus operandi* and then argue that someone else would prefer to do things differently, unless the grantee's preference is unreasonable or perverse. I call them Mr Gaunt's first and second propositions.

46 After considering the impact on another tenant's ability to gain access to his garage, Scott J considered whether the narrowing of the driveway would constitute an actionable interference with the tenants' reasonable use of it. At p 218 c–g he said this:

> "There are 56 flats at Cavendish House [the block of flats]. The rear driveway may be used by all of them, their visitors and licensees. Vehicles using the rear driveway may range from small cars to large commercial vans. On occasion, lorries may require to use the driveway. The plaintiffs were granted rights of way over a driveway nine metres or thereabouts in width, but with the usable width capable of being reduced by about two metres in the event of cars being parked along the East side of the driveway. I am reluctant to accept that a grantor, having granted a right of way over a nine-metre driveway, can reduce the width of the way by more than a half over an appreciable distance and then require the grantees to accept the reduction on the ground that what is left is all that they reasonably need. It seems to me that the proposed reduction will materially and permanently detract from the quality of the rear driveway and of the plaintiffs' rights over it .... It does not seem to me possible to say that the permanent narrowing of the rear driveway from nine to 4.14 metres over the length of the proposed car wash would leave the rear driveway as convenient for the reasonable use of the plaintiffs as it was before the reduction. The plaintiffs have been granted a right of way over a nine-metre driveway. The enjoyment thereof to which they are entitled under their respective grants cannot, in my judgment, be limited by requiring them to accept a 4.14 metre driveway. If the freeholders wanted the right to construct a car wash on the driveway and thereby to reduce its width to 4.14 metres it was, in my judgment, incumbent on them to reserve that right in the leases. Not having done so, they are not, in my view, entitled to remedy the omission by arguing that 4.14 metres is all the plaintiffs reasonably need. The plaintiffs are, in my judgment, entitled under their grants to the relative luxury, if that is what it is, of a nine-metre right of way. That, after all, is part of what they have paid for."

47 That passage justifies the following further proposition advanced by Mr Gaunt, which I call Mr Gaunt's third proposition, namely, that if the grantee has contracted for the "relative luxury" of an ample right, he is not to be deprived of that right in the absence of an explicit reservation of a right to build on it merely because it is a relative luxury and the reduced, non-ample right would be all that was reasonably required.

48 In short, the test, as Mr Gaunt submitted, is one of convenience and not necessity or reasonable necessity. Provided that what the grantee is insisting on is not unreasonable, the question is: can the right of way be substantially and practically exercised as conveniently as before?'

10.10 It will be seen from the extract and the principles set out above that what has been done or not done will be crucial when answering the question – 'Provided that what the grantee is insisting on is not unreasonable, the question is: can the right of way be substantially and practically exercised as conveniently as before?'

Note that the question is NOT whether what the grantee is left with is reasonable.

10.11 What is the effect of what has been done or not done? Can the right of way be substantially and practically exercised as conveniently as before? How do you deal with this question in practical terms?

(a) This is a question of evidence. As the principles set out above state, the interference will be actionable if it is substantial. And it will not be substantial if it does not interfere with the reasonable use of the right of way.

(b) Thus in practical terms the facts must support that conclusion, if you are advising the dominant owner. If you are advising the servient owner you will need facts to disprove the allegation made that reasonable user will no longer be possible.

(c) So start with re-examining the first three steps at para **10.8** above. When you have got to the end of that stage you should have in front of you all the evidence you need and if you do not you will need to find it as best you can; see Chapter 12 below on evidence.

(iv) Such evidence will include:

(i) The practical effect on the user, such as any difficulty in walking along the way, or driving, or manoeuvring a car over it. Oral (non-expert) evidence may be perfectly suited to the task. It is not always necessary to have photographic, video or even expert evidence to prove the substantial interference.

(ii) Whether the difficulty will always be there; e g will there be a queue of traffic only at certain times of the day? Will that be significant? (See para **10.16** below under queuing). Even occasional (but regular) interference can be actionable.

(iii) Expert evidence when essential – eg on manoeuvring HGVs and other large vehicles; *B&Q v Liverpool & Lancashire Properties*[15] is a classic instance where such user of the right of way by vehicles had

---

[15] (2001) 81 P&CR 20. See *Zieleniewski v Scheyd & Anor* [2012] EWCA Civ 247 for a recent example of a case where the Court of Appeal emphasised the successful pursuit of claim for wrongful interference by the deployment of purely oral non-expert evidence, especially where it is credible, detailed, based on experience and provides a satisfactory explanation for the difficulties which are encountered by the interference complained of; see paras 34–36 per Briggs J.

to be considered. Note that modern changes to machinery may mean that this has to be taken into account, and it is also important to bear in mind that such changes do not mean that former methods of using the way may be unreasonable or perverse.[16]

(iv) is the way adequate for user by public service vehicles (PSV) such as fire engines, ambulance and refuse collection vehicles? PSV can be larger than domestic vehicles but access by them is vital in emergencies and for the normal enjoyment of property served by the way, eg refuse collection.

Finally, all of this requires a site visit which is crucial if the problems are to be understood fully.

10.12 For practical and 'worked' examples of the detailed evidence required see the *Celsteel* and *B&Q* authorities above. These show the approach which the court will apply to the evidence on both sides.[17]

See Chapter 12 below for a more detailed discussion of matters concerning evidence.

THE EFFECT OF DELAY IN ASSERTING A CLAIM FOR WRONGFUL INTERFERENCE

10.13 Quite apart from the effect of delay in obtaining any remedy, especially an injunction (see Chapter 11 below), delay may have a more serious effect on whether a wrongful interference can be proved at all. This is because of the application of the law of estoppels.

10.14 It is clear that conduct may estop the dominant owner from claiming that the alleged interference is wrongful, eg where that owner has acquiesced in a change of the route of a right of way, or has accepted the presence of a car on a space which has led the servient owner to change the layout of his own land: see para **10.16(e)** below on the right to deviate and Chapter 4 at para **4.129** above for the law on that subject.

---

[16] See, for example, the observations of Briggs J in *Zieleniewski v Scheyd & Anor* [2012] EWCA Civ 247, at para 12 on the extent of a right of way acquired by prescription.

[17] For other modern 'worked' examples on whether the threshold of an actionable interference has been crossed, see *Worth v Turner* [2004] EWHC 1096 (Ch) (the effect of posts on large PSV), *Siggery v Bell* [2007] EWHC 2167 (Ch) (gates), *Hitchman v Wilbraham* (2007) WL 1498548 (rocks and parked cars), *Milebush Properties Ltd v Tameside MBC* [2011] EWCA Civ 270 (security gate), *Maiorello v Ashdale Land & Property Co Ltd* [2011] EWCA Civ 1618 (obstruction to prevent unlawful user), *Barrie House Freehold Ltd v Merie Binmahfouz Company (UK) Ltd* [2012] EWHC 353 (Ch) (proposed light well over garden over which easement existed held not to interfere with limited rights of enjoyment), *Zieleniewski v Scheyd & Anor* [2012] EWCA Civ 247 (wall and fence as an interference to agricultural machinery) and *Oliver v Symons & Anor* [2012] EWCA Civ 267 (gates).

10.15 In such cases the defence goes beyond *laches* (see Chapter 11 below) and may rest on estoppel by acquiescence or convention, or promissory, estoppel. For an example of these principles at work see *Lester v Woodgate*.[18] There, the claimant's (and his predecessor in title's) conduct by acquiescing in the works carried out by the defendant's predecessor which effectively made the right of way (on foot and with a wheelbarrow) unusable was held to be such as to disentitle the claimant as a matter of estoppel from enforcing his legal rights. This was not just a matter of delay (*laches*). The question is, would it be unconscionable to enforce the right?[19]

10.16 Commonly encountered interference with rights of way which may be wrongful will be as follows:

(a) Buildings, walls and other structures. The effect of these should speak for themselves. Illustrative cases include *Celsteeel Ltd v Alton House Holdings Ltd*[20] (car wash installation buildings), *Young & Co's Brewery plc v Gordon*[21] (fire escape which obstructed the right of way) and *Wesleyvale v Harding Homes (East Anglia) Ltd*.[22] For acts narrowing the way by other means see (f) below. See also 'verge space' referred to at (f) below.

(b) Posts and bollards. Illustrative cases include *Woodhouse & Co Ltd v Kirkland (Derby) Ltd*[23] (note the same issues may arise here as they do under gates etc below, where the posts etc are of the lockable or demountable type), and *Worth v Turner*.[24]

(c) Gates, with or without locks or codes, and other barriers which may impede user. In practice. this type of obstruction is the most commonly encountered and the 'knee jerk' reaction of the dominant owner is to say that the gate is a substantial interference in all cases. But that reaction may not be correct in law. It has already been seen above that the test of what is actionable depends upon satisfying the court that the interference interferes with the reasonable use of the right of way; see the words of Scott J in *Celsteel Ltd v Alston House Holdings Ltd*[25] at p 217 B–C:

> 'The interference will be actionable if it is substantial. And it will not be substantial if it does not interfere with the reasonable use of the right of way.'

---

[18] [2010] EWCA Civ 199 at para 20 ff per Patten LJ.
[19] See also *Perlman v Rayden* [2004] EWHC 2192 (Ch) (Patten J) where one of the issues in that dispute was whether the claimant was estopped from alleging trespass by the defendants to the private roadway, and in the context of restrictive covenants, *Harris v Williams-Wynne* [2006] EWCA Civ 104, where the unconscionability question was held to be the vital one to ask.
[20] [1985] 1 WLR 205.
[21] [2001] All ER (D) 56.
[22] [2003] EWHC 2291 (Ch).
[23] [1970] 1 WLR 1185.
[24] [2004] EWHC 1096 (Ch).
[25] [1985] 1 WLR 204.

Gates and other similar obstructions are no different from other instances where an actionable obstruction is alleged.

It was established in *Pettey v Parsons*[26] that whether or not a gate will be actionable will depend on whether it is a substantial interference with the way granted. This is the general principle to be applied in all cases. The application of the principle will be one of fact.

Thus the answer to whether there has been an actionable interference with the right of way by the gate or barrier will depend on the facts of each case.

The broad categories which are usually encountered within this type of obstruction are:

(i)   Unlocked gates or barriers.[27]
(ii)   Locked gates or barriers, locked with keys or codes or swipe cards.
(iii)   Manned   gates   or   barriers: *Milebush   Properties   Ltd   v Tameside MBC*.[28]

And no doubt there may be other varieties.

The key evidential questions in each case will usually be:

(i)   What is the nature of the right of way granted and of the dominant and servient land? Much will obviously depend on the nature and volume of user, and for example security considerations.
(ii)   Are the gates consistent with that right in terms of size etc?
(iii)   Has some form of 'security' regime been in place before the present issue over the alleged obstruction has arisen? (For example does a lease, or licence, or some other agreement, even if not part of the freehold title, contain terms allowing gates, or was there a security regime in place at the date of that earlier lease etc?) See *Milebush Properties Ltd v Tameside MBC*.[29]
(iv)   Are gates etc necessary, or are they merely there out of 'spite' or a desire to be awkward? Such a motive is too often present in neighbour disputes. The motive with which the gate etc was erected (whether a good or bad motive) will be one of the circumstances of the case to which the court must have regard following *Pettey v Parsons* (see above). For an example of the relevance of conduct on two fronts see *Owers v Bailey*,[30] where the unpleasant conduct of the defendant was relevant to the issue of the actionable interference and also led to an award of aggravated damages, the court applying *Perlman v Rayden*[31] on the latter issue.[32] See also *Lister v Rickard*[33] for an example of a case where the closing of gates was no longer

---

[26]   [1914]2 Ch 653.
[27]   The phrase 'gates or barriers' includes doors or other like features, such as moveable poles or rails.
[28]   [2011] EWCA Civ 270.
[29]   [2011] EWCA Civ 270.
[30]   [2007] 1 P&CR DG17.
[31]   [2004] EWHC 2192 (Ch).
[32]   See Chapter 11 at para **11.120** for aggravated damages.
[33]   (1969) 21 P&CR 49.

necessary owing to a change in the use of the servient owners' land from grazing of cattle to arable. But note that considerations such as the security of the servient owner's land will not determine the scope of the right of way as a matter of construction.[34] Such considerations only affect the answer to the question whether there has been an actionable interference with the right of way, once the scope of that right has been determined.

(v)   How many gates etc will there be and where in terms of size and location? See *Siggery v Bell*[35] for an example of a case where two gates were a substantial interference to the trackway.

(vi)   Will they be unlocked, or kept open at certain times as they were ordered to be in *Pettey v Parsons* (see above)?

(vii)   If gates etc are locked are keys or codes or swipe cards provided and to whom? Who is to regulate this? Are there third parties (eg postmen or women) who cannot gain entry?[36]

(viii) Is an appointment necessary (eg with the servient owner, or a commissionaire, or security guard) to gain access? Does personal information have to be given, or identity shown? Are the 'permitted hours' being changed without proper notice or consultation? Is there a reason for any change and if so what is it? (See (xi) and (xii) below.)

(ix)   What are the criteria for issuing keys etc or for granting or refusing entry?[37]

(x)   Is there an 'answerphone' system in place?

(xi)   Is there some other way of protecting the servient owner's legitimate interests (eg in the security of his property) whilst providing reasonable user of the right of way for the dominant owner? (See *Siggery v Bell* for an example of this.)

(xii)   Above all, how will it work in practice?

Illustrative cases include *CP Holdings v Dugdale*[38] (railway level crossing barriers), *Siggery v Bell*,[39] *The Sisters of the Sacred Heart of Mary Ltd v Kingston upon Thames Borough Council*[40] (code operated unmanned barriers, but note that the claimants had the benefit of a wide right to use the estate roads conferred under a private Act of Parliament) and *Milebush Properties Ltd v Tameside MBC*[41] (gates with security guards).

Note the fact that the interference is infrequent does not mean that the interference with user is not actionable. For authority for that proposition

---

[34]   See *B&Q Plc v Liverpool & Lancashire Properties Ltd* (2001) 81 P&CR 20, at para 35, per Blackburne J.

[35]   [2007] EWHC 2167 (Ch).

[36]   Much will depend on who can gain entry without inconvenience to that person or the dominant owner for whose benefit the entry has to be made.

[37]   If the policy is to grant access or issue keys etc on a pretty much unrestricted basis the servient owner should be in a stronger position than where this is not the case; for an example of the former see *Forestry Commissioners for England and Wales v Omega Pacific Ltd* [2000] All ER (D) 17.

[38]   (1998) NPC 97 (Park J, 22 May 1998).

[39]   [2007] EWHC 2167 (Ch) (Gates).

[40]   [2008] (ChD John Powell QC 14 March 2008; LTL 28/3/2008).

[41]   [2011] EWCA Civ 270.

see *B&Q Plc v Liverpool & Lancashire Properties Ltd*[42] at para 73, per Blackburne J, applying *CP Holdings Ltd v Dugdale*[43] (above). The uninterrupted nature of the right granted may be critical, especially in the context of industrial, commercial or retail sites; as in *B&Q*. The effect of interruptions can lead to queuing which of itself may be an actionable interference with the rights of other users. But the fact that some waiting is required (eg at a railway crossing gate, or for pemission to enter) is not in itself objectionable; see *B&Q* at para 74.

Also consider carefully rights of way granted in terms which limit user to the business hours only of the servient owner, outside which gates etc will be locked, or access may be limited; see Chapter 4 where questions of construction are considered.

(d)   Ramps, speed humps and potholes.[44] Ramps and speed humps may be reasonable in all the circumstances where speed control is needed, especially if accompanied by conspicuous warning notices.

As was said in *Saint v Jenner*:

> 'In this connection it is to be observed that in deciding what is a substantial interference with the dominant owner's reasonable use of a right of way, all the circumstances must he considered, including the rights of other persons entitled to use the way: here the rights of the defendants in connection with their property and riding activities; and there was, in our judgment, evidence on which the judge could properly hold, as he did, that the ramps as originally planned and constructed did not constitute a substantial interference.' (Stamp LJ at p 279 C–D).

But if accompanied by potholes (caused by neglect as opposed to deliberately placed there in which case the interference would speak for itself if big enough) or other features on the right of way, so as to impede reasonable navigation of the way, even at very slow speeds, they will be an actionable interference.[45]

As was also said in the same case:

> 'By the time the proceedings were launched, the situation had, however, changed. The condition of the road had changed and pot-holes had developed at the ends of some of the ramps, with the result that the height of the ramps in relation to the bottom of the pot-holes had, as the county court judge in effect found, become so great as to make these ramps a substantial interference with the enjoyment of the right of way by the plaintiffs.' (Ibid at p 279 E–F).

---

[42]   [2001] 81 P&CR 20.

[43]   (1998).

[44]   See *Saint v Jenner* [1973] Ch 275.

[45]   See *Saint v Jenner* [1973] Ch 275 at pp 279–280 per Stamp LJ. There are no compulsory standards for the design and construction of road humps on private roads. But the regulations which apply to highways (Highways (Road Humps) Regulations 1999, SI 1999/1025) are a useful template, especially as to the size and location of such humps as specified under reg 4. But even if compliant, they may well amount to an actionable interference with the exercise of the way.

It is suggested that the same conclusion might be reached if the nature and number of the humps (and the use to which the way can lawfully be put) is such that lawful user cannot be reasonably be enjoyed.

It is to be noted that whilst the servient owner is under no obligation to maintain the surface of the right of way (in the absence of enforceable terms to the contrary, see Chapter 4 at para **4.88** above), there can come a stage where the state of the way becomes such that reasonable user is not possible, and that may amount to an actionable interference with the right of way.[46]

Other illustrative cases include *Lester v Woodgate*[47] at para 11 per Patten LJ.

(e) Redesign of access. Here the effect of the redesign may be to cause an actionable interference. Note that it is not possible unilaterally for the servient owner to realign the right of way.[48]

Illustrative cases include *Celsteel Ltd v Alton House Holdings Ltd*[49] (see above) and *Heslop v Bishton*[50] (wall and pillar erected held a substantial interference and it was no answer that the right of way could be exercised over a different route not within the grant). For the absence of any implied 'right to align' or 'deviate' see Chapter 4 at para **4.129**. This means that in the absence of that right, or legally binding agreement there may be no legal enforceable right to force the dominant owner to use a convenient alternative route. As is made clear at para 23 of the judgment of HHJ Cooke (sitting in the Chancery Division in Birmingham) in *Heslop v Bishton* there is no reason why the servient owner cannot unilaterally execute a deed of grant in favour of the dominant owner conferring on the latter the alternative route. Whilst the dominant owner is not obliged to use this alternative route and can insist on using the old one, but on the assumption that this route is as convenient as the original route, it is likely that the remedy sought by the dominant owner will be affected by the presence of a convenient alternative legally granted; see para 21. So in such a case an injunction may be unlikely. However, it is equally clear that the old route is not extinguished, so in principle obstruction of the old route is in principle actionable, see *Heslop v Bishton* at para 24 and *Deacon v SE Railway*,[51] cited in *Greenwich NHS Trust v London & Quadrant Housing Association* referred to above. (See Chapter 3 for grants of rights of way and Chapter 9 for their extinguishment.)[52]

---

[46] In the context of badly pot-holed private roads and paths, it is worth noting that servient owners of public rights of way need to ensure that their public liability policy covers damage, injury, or death where the state of the way is attributable to their neglect to maintain. Duties may be owed to certain classes of users under the Occupiers' Liability Acts 1957 and 1984; see Chapter 8 above at para **8.43**.

[47] [2010] EWCA Civ 199.

[48] See *Greenwich NHS Trust v London & Quadrant Housing Association* [1998] 1 WLR 1749.

[49] [1985] 1 WLR 204.

[50] [2009] EWHC 607 (Ch). And see *Kettel v Bloomfield Ltd* [2012] EWHC 1422 (Ch).

[51] (1889) 41 LT (NS) 377.

[52] But note that there can be no cause of action if the terms of the grant do allow alternative rights of way, or provision for the exercise of associated rights over alternative land. This type

(f)   Narrowing the right of way, leading to limited height, or width restrictions, or tunnels. As in the instances given above, the question whether the interference is actionable will depend on the application of the principles set out in the *Pettey v Parsons* and *B&Q* authorities.

Thus, whilst the servient owner may build right up to the edge of the right of way, provided that does not interfere with its reasonable enjoyment, if the contrary can be proved, the building will be actionable. For example, certain types of vehicles may need room to manoeuvre laterally, or may need a minimum height for access. HGVs are common examples of where such latitude will be needed.

Illustrative cases include *VT Engineering Ltd v Richard Barland & Co*[53] (tunnel restricting height of vehicles using the right of way) and *B&Q Plc v Liverpool & Lancashire Properties Ltd*[54] (see above).

As to the former case (*VT Engineering*) in *Oliver v Symons*[55] the Court of Appeal held that the notion that there could be sterilised corridors of land either side of the way to allow for the 'swing space' was unsound. The court applied *Minor v Groves*[56] so that *VT Engineering* is no longer good law to support the 'tolerance' asserted by Megarry J there; see *Oliver v Symons* at paras 34–42, per Elias LJ.

It is clear, however, as recognised at para 41 per Elias LJ in *Oliver v Symons*, that the terms of an express grant (or reservation) will be construed as having regard to the purpose for which it was granted, so that there may well be cases where the width of the track required for use must exceed its physical dimensions. But as is stated at that paragraph, there would need to be 'cogent evidence' before a court would be persuaded that a narrow construction could not achieve the objective which the parties to the grant intended. Thus if the grant was made in circumstances when purely domestic vehicles were envisaged as the users, a greater width required to allow lorries would not be allowed. See also the issue over 'verge space' in *Oliver v Symons* discussed at paras 43–48 per Elias LJ.

See Chapter 4 above for the law on the construction of the terms of grants, or reservations of rights of way.

(g)   One way systems.

Illustrative cases include *Globeshaw Ltd v Save Service Stations Ltd*[57] (traffic management system at petrol station an actionable interference with the dominant owner's right of way over the servient land which included the petrol station).

---

of agreement will often be found in leases, or estate schemes, for an example (affecting parking in Princes Gate, London SW7) see *Montrose Court Holdings v Shamash & Ors* [2006] EWCA Civ 251.

[53]   (1968) 19 P&CR 890.
[54]   (2001) 81 P&CR 20.
[55]   [2012] EWCA Civ 267.
[56]   (2000) 80 P&CR 135.
[57]   (1997) Unreported (JV Martin QC, LTL 21/5/1997).

(h)   Disrepair of right of way.
　　　See (d) above.

(i)   Other types of interference:

　　(i)　Parked cars: see *Hitchman v Wilbraham*,[58] held an actionable interference.
　　(ii)　Rocks and boulders: see *Hitchman v Wilbraham* (as above).
　　(iii) Skips: see *B&Q Plc v Liverpool & Lancashire Properties Ltd*.[59]
　　(iv)　Washing away or erosion of the right of way. This is not so much a case of interference (by positive action by the servient owner) but rather some event which causes the right of way no longer to be usable – or easily so. The event may not be the fault of the servient owner. As will be seen from Chapter 4 at para **4.129** above there is no right to deviate, and from Chapter 9 at para **9.105** above, this type of event may lead to the extinguishment of the right of way.

---

[58]   (2007) Unreported (HHJ Hickinbottom, LTL, 1 June 2007).
[59]   (2001) 81 P&CR 20, at para 69, per Blackburne J.

Chapter 11

DEALING WITH DISPUTES AND REMEDIES TO ASCERTAIN RIGHTS AND PREVENT WRONGFUL INTERFERENCE RELATING TO RIGHTS OF WAY

INTRODUCTION

11.1 This Chapter deals with disputes over private rights of way ('rights of way') and how they can either be settled between the parties to this dispute or resolved by the courts, or other bodies such as the adjudicator to HM Land Registry. This Chapter, therefore, deals with the remedies that may be available to the parties. The main headings to this Chapter will be as follows:

- Preliminaries – including self-help.

- Negotiation, meditation, arbitration and other forms of out of court resolution.

- Discharge and modification of rights of way.

- Claims in court – Part 1 – declarations.

- Claims in court – Part 2 – injunctions.

- Claims in court – Part 3 – damages.

- Adjudication by the adjudicator to HM Land Registry.

- Other legal remedies.

Note that this is not a textbook on civil procedure. Procedure is dealt with in Chapter 12 where there is also consideration of the evidence needed in claims concerning rights of way. For detailed treatment see the monographs on this subject and the annual volumes on the Civil Procedure Rules (CPR), such as the White Book.

PRELIMINARIES

11.2   Disputes over rights of way present certain features which, on the one hand may be particular to those rights and on the other hand, may be common to disputes encountered generally in the area of property law. In any dispute it is important to remember the following features so far as they may arise.

11.3   Any agreements relating to the compromise over disputes of rights of way, for example, to record a new grant or reservation must be in writing and in a document which records all the terms of that agreement and is signed by all parties in order to conform with section 2 of the Law of Property Miscellaneous Provisions Act 1989. Otherwise, the agreement will be void. This is because an easement such as a right of way is an interest in land within section 2(6) of that Act. Recent authority such as *Cobbe v Yeomans Row*[1] and *Thorner v Major*,[2] makes it difficult (if not impossible) to avoid the consequences of lack of formal compliance with section 2, even where there may be supporting evidence to prove promissory, or proprietary estoppel.[3]

11.4   The express grant, or reservation of a right of way as a legal interest in land, must be effected by deed. Therefore, when compromising dispute over a right of way, a deed will need to be executed to allow the Land Registry to alter the formal terms of such a legal easement having been granted. Otherwise, the grant or reservation will make effect only as an equitable easement; see Chapter 3.[4] An Order of the Court, for example if in declaratory form, can (according to its terms) take effect without more, and must be produced to the Land Registry for the purpose of entering the terms of the order on the titles to both the dominant and servient land.

11.5   As will have been seen from Chapter 3 at para **3.88**, whilst the court may recognise equitable easements created, for example, by estoppel (see *E R Ives Investments Ltd v High*[5] and see section 116 of the Land Registration Act 2002) care should be exercised in order to avoid creating such easements by conduct, for that would be against the interest of that person. Thus, in the context of a dispute over rights of way it may be important to consider past conduct and promises in order to see whether evidence of that sort will support an independent claim to a right of way. Past conduct may also be material where

---

[1]   [2008] UKHL 55; [2008] 1 WLR 1752.

[2]   [2009] 1 WLR 776.

[3]   See also *Helden v Strathmore Ltd* [2011] EWCA Civ 542, *Whittaker v Kinnear* [2011] EWHC 1479 (QB) and *Francis v F Berndes Ltd* [2011] EWHC 3377 (Ch) for recent authority on the scope of section 2 of the 1989 Act.

[4]   An easement is a legal interest in land within section 1(2)(a) and, therefore, the grant of such legal interest must be by deed; see sections 51–53 of the LPA 1925. An exception to this lies in the rather unusual case of an easement being disposed of by a will, see section 55(a) of the LPA 1925. For the registration of legal in easements under Law Registration Act 2002 see Chapters 3 and 5 above. See also section 1 of the Law of Property (Miscellaneous Provisions) Act 1989 for the formalities of the execution of deeds.

[5]   [1967] 2 QB 379.

there are allegations of extinguishment or actionable interference: see Chapters 9 and 10 and *Lester v Woodgate*.[6]

11.6 But what about self help? Clients often ask (with justification) when confronted with obstructions, invariably erected without any notice or warning, can I simply remove the wretched thing? The answer is invariably 'no' for the reasons set out below. The starting point is always that self help is a 'bad idea'. The short answer to the question is 'don't'.

11.7 Self help is not favoured as a remedy; see *Lagan Navigation Co v Lambeg Bleaching Dyeing and Finishing Co Ltd*.[7] Whilst the old cases state that a nuisance (ie an actionable obstruction to a right of way) may be 'abated' (ie removed, or in some other way stopped), it is generally unwise to take steps which could be criticised in later proceedings, or even lead to criminal charges such as under section 5 of the Criminal Damage Act 1971, or at common law as a conduct likely to lead to a breach of the peace. Removing the obstruction often involves a trespass at civil law. Recent authority limits the rights to remove an obstruction to a right of way, or such other nuisance, or interference with the exercise of the right of way to those where the case for such removal is clear and simple, in cases of particular emergency, and where the cost and expense of litigation could not be justified: see *Burton v Winters*,[8] applied in *Chamberlain v Lindon*.[9] In most cases a speedy application to the local County Court is the best remedy: see *Co-operative Wholesale Society Ltd v BRB*.[10]

11.8 Therefore, while it is tempting to take steps to remove obstructions to rights of way, the person who does that may find it difficult to justify such steps whether taken either in the context of the dispute of the right of way (eg as to its existence or extent) or, whether steps taken can be seen as excessive, eg where solid concrete blocks have been erected in front of a right of way to a residential garage.

11.9 If the case warrants self help, you must not do unnecessary damage when removing any obstruction. That in itself may, of course, lead to a dispute. But, there may be cases where self help can be the only proper course eg in an emergency (safety to the dominant owner, or third parties) or where the case for removal is a simple one in the case of a spiteful and pointless obstruction and where, as stated above, the cost and expense of litigation would be out of all proportion to the steps taken to remove the obstruction. (But even here a judgment call on what is a 'simple' case for removal may be difficult to make and the danger of inflaming neighbourly relations will be obvious if an objective views is taken of the matter, as indeed it should be). In addition, self help may be required as part of a course of action to remove an obstruction where there is a need to avoid losing a right of way such as one enjoyed by

---

6   [2010] EWCA Civ 199.
7   [1927] AC 226 at p 244 per Lord Atkinson.
8   [1993] 1 WLR 1077.
9   [1998] 1 WLR 1252.
10   [1995] *The Times* LR 695 (CA).

prescription under section 2 of the Prescription Act 1832 and when interruption of section 4 could occur in circumstances where a year provided for under section 4 is about to expire, see Chapter 4 above. (Although it should pointed out that written notice by way of objection would suffice under section 4 of the 1832 Act.)

11.10   Other points to note in the context of self help are:

(a)   If you are thinking about self help you will usually be the last person to think objectively and accurately about the true extent of your rights.

(b)   If carried out, it usually leads to a breach of the peace being committed by one side or the other, if not both sides. That leads to a night in the cells, a Police caution with the risk of criminal charges and either fines, community services orders, an ASBO or prison. So it is not worth the risk. (See the guidance given by Lawton LJ in *R v Chief Constable of Devon and Cornwall ex parte CEGB*[11] and see also Denning MR at p 471).

(c)   Self help is not appropriate where the court has refused to grant a mandatory injunction to remove the obstruction. In such a case the sole justification for removal by self help has gone, as the court has decided the point in issue. This applies whether the cause of action is in nuisance or trespass, see *Burton v Winters* (above) at p 1082 C–D, per Lloyd LJ. However, a question mark does arise as to what happens where the court has refused to grant a mandatory injunction and the obstruction remains. What is to happen then? There is (inevitably) no easy answer to this question and it is suggested that the only practical resolution is by amicable agreement between some servient and dominant owners. That may be a pious hope in many cases where relations between neighbours are at rock bottom. This means that the only legal alternative is a claim in damages, either at common law, or in lieu of the injunction under section 50 of the Senior Courts Act 1981 for the loss (if any) caused by the infringing obstruction. It is usually in the interest of both parties to agree some form of resolution, if only to avoid the 'blot' of having to disclose the dispute in pre-contract disclosure on any sale or remortgage of the affected properties.

(d)   If you persist in defying a Court Order you will be usually be committed to prison for contempt, see *Burton v Winters* where the claimant was sentenced to two years in prison for contempt of court.[12]

---

[11]   [1982] QB 458 at p 473.
[12]   The details of the rules which govern committal for contempt for non observance of an Order of either the High Court or the County Court are set out in CPR Part 81, in force since 1 October 2012. The topic is beyond the scope of this book.

(e) Notice of an intention to remove the obstruction is of course always a sensible prior step to take, save in an obvious emergency, see *Delaware Mansions v Westminster City Council.*[13]

(f) You cannot exercise self help if the nuisance has not yet happened. Therefore, merely suspecting that your neighbour may be about to block your driveway does not allow you to put up bollards of your own to block your neighbour especially, for example, if he has a joint right of way over the same land. The preferable course to take (if nothing else will work) is to seek a *quia timet* injunction. This is an injunction sought where it is 'feared' that the interference will occur, hence the word *timet* in Latin: see para **11.68**ff below.

(g) If you are going to exercise self help you will need to do so without delay: see *Burton v Winters*[14] and *Co-operative Wholesale Society Ltd v BRB*,[15] referred to above.

(h) Involving the Police in bringing criminal proceedings (eg under the Criminal Damage Act 1971) is invariably a 'manifestly inappropriate' procedure to adopt in the case of what is usually a civil claim between neighbours. The Police and CPS are not the right people to decide these types of cases. The delay inherent in such proceedings and the fact that the punishment (if there is a conviction) will not assist in the practical resolution of the dispute. Psychologically, seeking to bring criminal charges is not a good move by a neighbour against his other neighbour: see *Chamberlain v Lindon.*[16]

(i) It is clear that where those causing the obstruction are either numerous or where their identities are unknown and cannot be easily traced, self help may not be a practical remedy, eg intermittent parked cars. But a claim in trespass may be possible (eg with the assistance of the records held by DVLA) and protection by the use of lockable or demountable bollards may be a practical cure: see *Hilton v James Smith & Sons.*[17]

(j) In conclusion, modern concepts of neighbourliness suggest that self help is very rarely going to be the proper approach.

NEGOTIATION, MEDIATION AND ARBITRATION AND OTHER METHODS OF RESOLUTION

11.11 The modern trend is to see if disputes can be settled at pre-claim or post-claim pre-hearing. The cost rules under the CPR Part 44, rule 3 encourage

---

[13] [2001] 1 AC 321.
[14] [1993] 1 WLR 1077.
[15] [1995] *The Times* LR 695.
[16] [1998] 1 WLR 1252, at p 1257 A and p 1262 B–C, per Sullivan J.
[17] [1979] 2 EGLR 44, at p 45J–K, per Ormrod LJ.

this and modern authority makes it clear that mediation is a required part of the equipment needed for use by the parties for any piece of litigation. See *Halsey v The Milton Keynes General NHS Trust*.[18]

11.12 There is no reason why disputes over right of way should not be dealt with in this manner. Indeed, it is unusually the case that they should be so dealt with in this way, for otherwise litigation over rights of way, especially between residential neighbours, invariably gets out of hand. As was said by the Court of Appeal in *West v Sharp*[19] and subsequently in many other decisions in the higher courts, these disputes invariably throw up huge amounts of costs, often for very little benefit, and some form of alternative dispute resolution should be deployed at an early stage.

11.13 There are, of course, a number of alternative ways in which negotiations can take place. Some examples are as follows:

(a) Without prejudice negotiations party to party or with a third party facilitating them.

(b) Informal negotiations between solicitors, agents, and counsel etc.

(c) Informal negotiations involving someone in a semi formal role, for example, a local councillor.

(d) Formal mediation.

(e) Joint neutral evaluation – e g before experienced counsel or a surveyor.

(f) A joint reference to counsel for an Opinion.

11.14 All can be on a 'without prejudice' basis. The psychology of mediation and compromise generally is a complex subject and is well covered in the text books on mediation and dispute resolution. No special rules apply to rights of way mediation, or any other form of resolution. But if agreement is reached it is worth noting the formal requirements for the grant of valid and enforceable easements, including rights of way, set out in Chapter 3 above. If there is to be a compromise where damages are payable, or payment of a release, or some other sum, the tax consequences of this must be examined with an expert in that field.

11.15 Formal arbitration under the Arbitration Act 1996 is rare in rights of way cases except where this has been specified in the terms of the grant or reservation. There is no reason why this form of resolution should not be specified, especially where a dispute may conceivably arise over the nomination

---

[18] [2004] 1 WLR 3002.
[19] (2000) 79 P&CR 327, at p 334 per Mummery LJ.

of an alternative right of way as part of the grant and there should be some machinery to deal with this; see Chapter 5 above.

11.16 Expert determination may well be used in these disputes, especially where the deed imposing or granting the right of way specifically provides for such determination. As stated in para **11.15** above, there is no reason why this form of resolution should not be specified, especially where a dispute may conceivably arise over the nomination of an alternative right of way as part of the grant and there should be some machinery to deal with this: see Chapter 5 above. Where expert determination is specified, consideration should be given to the following matters:

(a)   Is the determination to be binding, or non-binding on the parties?

(b)   What are the terms of reference to the expert?[20]

(c)   Who is to be the expert and what timescales are to be involved, if not already set out in the documents requiring the determination?

(d)   What limited rights to challenge or appeal will there be? (Compare the limited right of appeal under the Arbitration Act 1996.)

11.17 Note that under the Party Wall Etc. Act 1996 a Party Wall Surveyor cannot determine a right of way dispute, see section 9 thereof. There is a limited right of access under section 8, which the building owner can exercise, but this must be linked to the purposes of the party wall dispute.[21]

DISCHARGE AND MODIFICATION OF RIGHTS OF WAY

11.18 At present, rights of way can only be discharged by agreement. See the conveyancing formalities set out at Chapters 3 and 5 above. In June 2011, the Law Commission recommended an extension of section 84(1) of the LPA 1925 to encompass easements within the jurisdiction presently conferred on the Lands Tribunal to discharge or modify covenants. See Law Commission Report No 327, para 7.35 and draft Bill Cl 30.

11.19 Note also related to rights of way the following powers which may affect the exercise of existence of the right of way:

(a)   The overriding power of Local Planning Authorities in section 237 of the Town & Country Planning Act and similar legislation.[22]

---

[20]   See *Aviva Life and Permanent UK Ltd v Kestrel Properties Ltd* [2011] (ChD Cawson QC) (LTL 11/11/2011) for recent authority on the nature and scope of the expert's authority.

[21]   See Bickford-Smith & Sydenham, *Party Walls, Law and Practice*, 3rd Edn, (Jordans), for detail on this topic.

[22]   See Chapter 9 at para **9.141** and also Francis, *Restrictive Covenants and Freehold Land, A Practitioner's Guide*, (current edition) Chapter 12.

(b)   The effect of compulsory purchase of land on private rights of way. For details see specialist works on Compulsory Purchase. Chapter 9, at para **9.141** deals with overriding private rights of way under section 237 of the Town & Country Planning Act 1990.

CLAIMS IN COURT – PART 1

Preliminaries

11.20   Before any claim is to be brought in court (whether the High Court or the County Court – and for the purposes of this Chapter 'court' means either of them) the questions must be asked, 'what issue am I seeking to resolve by the claim I am intending to bring?'

11.21   Claims over private rights of way can range widely. There are those which seek a declaration about the meaning of the grant or reservation of the way, or whether a way has been acquired by prescription, or the extent of the way, or the question whether it has been abandoned. There are those claims which seek injunctions to prevent or remove obstructions. There are those claims which seek damages for the breach of the terms of the right of way (e g excessive user) or where damages are sought in place of an injunction where there has been an obstruction.

11.22   It is therefore important to think about the precise way in which the claim arises, because until this is worked out, the claimant may be unsure about what he needs to present to the court in terms of his case, and what remedy he seeks.

11.23   It is possible to summarise the three ways in which private rights of way disputes can give rise to claims. In lawyer's language the issue here is what is the 'cause of action' which is created by the facts of the dispute?

11.24   These causes of action may be as follows:

(a)   A cause of action based on the terms of the grant or reservation, or the nature of the long user on which a prescriptive claim may be based. This type of claim is usually based on a breach of the terms of the grant or reservation or a denial by the servient owner that the right has ripened into a prescriptive one. Such claims may not always require proof that the terms of the grant etc have been broken. There may be a dispute, for example over what the terms of the grant mean – a question of pure construction of words – see Chapter xx above.

(b)   A cause of action based on the tort of nuisance. This arises where there has been an actionable interference with the easement; see Chapter 10 above.

(c) A cause of action based on other facts, such as malicious falsehood; see para **11.190** below.

11.25 The significance of this distinction is because not only what has to be proved to establish the cause of action is likely to be different in each of the three categories at para **11.24** above, but also the limitation periods for bringing any claim may differ; see para **11.146** below.

11.26 The different types of remedy are considered below. It may be that a single cause of action (eg for actionable interference) may engage more than one remedy, eg a declaration as to the extent of the right of way, an injunction to restrain the breach, and damages. There may even be a case where the facts are such that the neighbours' war of words brings in a claim of malicious falsehood; see para **11.190** below.

11.27 Unlike the law of restrictive covenants, because a legal easement is a legal interest in land, it should not matter whether the original parties to the grant or reservation are seeking to enforce the easement, or be liable upon it. As to equitable easements, because they occupy a somewhat uncertain position, if created after 13 October 2003, and are not capable of being overriding interests if created after that date, it may be necessary to ascertain what standing a party may have to enforce the right of way claimed, and likewise what liability a person may have under it if the easement is not noted on the servient title by an agreed or unilateral notice; see Chapter 13 below. If the original parties are enforcing the equitable easement, or making an original party liable under it, the cause of action can be one based on the agreement founding the easement, or in nuisance. If there are successors in title seeking to enforce, or being made defendants to enforcement, in the absence of notice on the register of the servient land, the latter may be able to argue that they are not liable to the easement claimed and no claim on either the agreement or in nuisance can be made against them.

11.28 Finally it should be explained that references below to 'claimant' and 'defendant' are to those claiming the remedy (or disputing it) and it may be that a defendant is seeking a remedy by counterclaim against the claimant: see Chapter 12 at para **12.49** below for counterclaims. For the sake of brevity if not clarity the terms 'claimant' and 'defendant' are therefore used to include those who are also concerned as parties to claims where they may be counterclaiming parties, or defending any such counterclaims, or even third party claims.

Declarations

11.29 The jurisdiction to make declarations as to private rights of way generally is contained in section 19 of the Senior Courts Act 1981. In addition, CPR Part 40, rule 20 confirms the court's power to make declaratory orders, even when no other remedy is claimed. Therefore, declaratory relief may be sought, even where an injunction or damages is not required as part of the litigation. The grant of a declaration is discretionary. There is no *right* to a declaration. This means that even if the jurisdiction is engaged, the court must consider whether it should make the declaration sought.

11.30 The basic preliminary requirements for a declaration being sought or granted are as follows:

(a) Is there an actual, as opposed to a hypothetical, question which needs to be placed before the court? For example, is there a real issue over the right of way, e g as to its user or construction etc? (See *Globeshaw Ltd v Save Service Stations Ltd*[23] for an example of a case where the only dispute before the court (after agreement was reached about a deed of variation of a right of way), was about the costs of the claim.) If there is no dispute, or if the declaration sought would serve no useful purpose, the court will decline to make that order: see *Thomas Brown Estates Ltd v Hunters Partners Ltd*[24] for a recent example of the court refusing to make the declaration sought on these grounds. The following parts of the judgment of the Chancellor on the jurisdiction to grant declarations in the real property context in *CIP Property (AIPT) Ltd v Transport for London & Ors*, are instructive:

> '23 It is convenient to start with reference to the authorities to which I have been referred. They fall into two categories; the principles regarding the grant of a declaration and the principles relating to the grant of quia timet injunctions. They are, as might be expected, broadly similar. In the case of declarations, Civil Procedure Rule 40.20 provides that the court may make binding declarations whether or not any other remedy is claimed. Thus the remedy of a declaration is discretionary.

> 24 I was referred to the decision of Farwell J in *Draper v British Optical Association* [1938] 1 All ER 115. Though decided before the introduction of the CPR, it is not suggested that they introduced any material change. In that case the British Optical Association had adopted a code of ethics in relation to advertising by its members. The claimant was a member and the manager of a shop which had issued advertisements not in accordance with that code. The Association wrote to him seeking an undertaking that he would comply with the code and then convened a meeting of the governing body of the Association to consider whether to remove the name of the claimant from the list of members. The claimant brought an action for a declaration to the effect that the Association was not entitled to enforce its code of ethics on him. The action failed on the ground that it was premature. At page 119 Farwell J said this:

> "In order to entitle himself to any such declaration or injunction as he seeks with regard to that matter, he has got to satisfy the court that the defendant association has done, or is threatening to do, that which he says is ultra vires. If the meeting had been held, if the plaintiff had attended or had not attended, as the case may be, and if the association, as a result of the

---

[23] (1997) Ch D JV Martin QC, 21 May 1997, LTL 21/5/97.
[24] [2012] EWHC 21 (QB). See also *CIP Property (AIPT) Ltd v Transport for London & Ors* [2012] EWHC 259 (Ch).

meeting, had purported to expel him because he had been guilty of an infraction of the code of ethics, then I can well appreciate that he would have a cause of action – though whether he would succeed or not is another matter – which the court would have to try and determine. But that is not the position. The only ground on which it can be suggested, so far as I understand this case, that the defendant association is threatening to enforce on the plaintiff this code of ethics [and then the reference is given to where it can be found] that 'infractions of the above code will be regarded as breaches of professional conduct and dealt with as such,' and in the letter of June 24 in which the secretary calls the plaintiff's attention to the code of ethics and asks for an undertaking that he will not advertise prices or any special method of testing. Those two, taken together, are not, in my judgment, any sufficient evidence that the defendant association is threatening or intending to enforce on the plaintiff this code of ethics. It may be that, if and when the defendants hold their meeting, they may think it right to seek to enforce against the plaintiff the provisions of the code of ethics, and, if they do, it may be that they will be acting ultra vires . But, until they have sought to enforce that code upon the plaintiff, I myself do not consider that it is for me to determine this question in the abstract. It is quite true that, in a proper case, the court will determine matters of this kind in a quia timet action, but there must be before the court, before it will entertain a quia timet action, satisfactory evidence that the defendant is threatening or intending to do that which it is said he is not entitled to do, or that which, it is said, will lead to serious damage to the plaintiff."

Thus in relation to prematurity the rules in relation to declarations are much the same as for quia timet injunctions.

25 In addition I was referred to the statements in relation to the jurisdiction to grant declarations considered recently by Kitchin J (as he then was) in *Arrow Generics Limited v Merck* [2007] FSR 920. At paragraph 49 he quoted with approval from the judgment of Pumfrey J in *Nokia Corporation v Interdigital Technology Corporation* [2006] EWHC 802, summarising the principles to be deduced from the judgment of Lord Woolf (Master of the Rolls) in *Messier-Dowty v Sabena* and Neuberger J in *Financial Services v Rourke*. Pumfrey J there, having referred to those authorities, said they establish three relevant principles:

"The correct approach to the question of whether to grant negative declarations was one of discretion rather than jurisdiction. The use of negative declarations was to be scrutinised and their use rejected where it served no useful purpose, but where such a declaration helped ensure that the aims of justice were achieved, the court should not be reluctant to grant a negative declaration. Before a court could properly make a negative declaration, the underlying issue had to be sufficiently clearly defined to render it properly justiciable."

26 Thus in relation to that part of the claim, that is to say the claim for a declaration, the appropriate questions are: (1) is the claim premature, (2) would the declaration sought serve a useful purpose, and (3) are the issues sufficiently clearly defined to be properly justiciable? As will be seen, though properly formulated as separate considerations, they overlap. Indeed I incline

to the view, but it is unnecessary to decide, that the propositions summarised in paragraphs 2 and 3 are in fact just tests for prematurity under 1.'[25]

(b) Declarations cannot be granted by consent and the court must be persuaded that the order sought is a proper one to make: see *Rolls-Royce Plc v Unite the Union*[26] (applied recently in *Milebush Properties Ltd v Tameside MBC*[27]) for a modern summary and review of the jurisdiction.[28]

(c) The declaration made and any order supplementing it (eg in terms of an injunction) must not go further than is necessary to secure the legal rights of the parties and to prevent unlawful (as opposed to lawful) user: see for example *Maiorello v Ashdale Land & Property Co Ltd*,[29] considering and applying *Hamble Parish Council v Haggard*.[30]

(d) Who should be the parties? Normally the dominant and servient owners will be the parties. The question may arise if anybody else should be a party; eg those with a right (eg under a covenant) to use the right of way. Those who have an obligation to maintain the way, or joint users, tenants and licensees with similar rights that may be affected by the claim, should be joined. In some cases where the potential class of those affected may be numerous, the claim may have to be brought against certain defendants on a representative basis, or with notice under CPR Part 19, rules 6 and 7.

(e) As opposed to a positive order (eg that the right of way over X is enforceable) a negative declaration may be needed in the form granted in *Greenwich Healthcare NHS Trust v London & Quadrant Housing Trust*[31] and in *Well Barn Shoot v Shackleton*[32] (for example, a declaration that that a right of way is not enforceable). This latter type of declaration may be needed if the servient land owner needs, for example, to know whether or not his land is subject to an enforceable right of way. Ideally, if he is planning to develop that land in a way that will interfere with a claimed right of way, he will want the answer to be certain. So the order sought should only be sought if there is a strong case for it.

(f) It is possible to obtain a declaration by summary procedure under CPR Part 24 in clear cases where there is no arguable defence.

---

[25] [2012] EWHC 259 (Ch). The claim arose out of the Crossrail redevelopment of Tottenham Court Road Underground Station in central London and the likely effects of the the 'oversite' developments due to be completed after the Crossrail project is completed in 2017.

[26] [2010] 1 WLR 318, at paras 38–50 (Wall LJ) and 118–120 (Aikens LJ).

[27] [2011] EWCA Civ 270.

[28] See also Snell's *Equity*, 32nd Edn (2010) 14-008 and Zamir and Woolf, *The Declaratory Judgment*, Sweet & Maxwell, 4th Edn (2011), for further details on this jurisdiction.

[29] [2011] EWCA Civ 1618.

[30] [1972] 1 WLR 122.

[31] [1998] 1 WLR 1749. See also *CIP Property (AIPT) Ltd v Transport for London & Ors* [2012] EWHC 259 (Ch) (above) where the claim for a declaration that the defendants were not entitled to obstruct the claimant's rights of light was rejected as premature; see para **11.30(a)** above.

[32] [2003] EWCA Civ 2.

11.31 Costs should follow the event under Part 44, rule 3: see Chapter 12 at para **12.188** below. See Chapter 12 on evidence and procedure, at para **12.107**.

11.32 There is no limitation period for a declaratory relief. But delay in seeking that relief may make the question over the right of way hypothetical; see above at para **11.30**(a) and (b) and see below at para **11.50**.

11.33 A declaration is appropriate where issues over the right of way arise such as:

(a)   Where questions of construction of the terms of the express grant or reservation or, as to the effect of an implied grant arise under either *Wheeldon v Burrows*,[33] or section 62 of the LPA 1925 (see Chapters 3–5 above). The need to issue a claim for a declaration may arise as to the extent of the right of way, eg as to whether or not it serves particular land, or whether or not the principle expressed in *Harris v Flower & Sons*[34] is engaged as regards the identity of the potentially dominant land: see Chapter 4 at para **4.83** above for details.

(b)   Where an issue arises as to whether rights have been acquired by user under the Prescription Act 1832 or lost modern grant: see Chapter 6 above.

(c)   Where an issue arises as to whether a right of way has been abandoned; see for example *Benn v Hardinge*:[35] see Chapter 9 above.

(d)   Where certainty as to the rights of third parties is needed, see, for example, the *Greenwich* and *Well Barn Shoot* decisions cited at para **11.30(d)** above. But note the need to avoid raising the issue prematurely; see para **11.30(a)** above.

(e)   Where there are questions as to the legality of the user and its effect, see for example *Bakewell Asset Management Ltd v Brandwood & Ors*[36] and *Maiorello v Ashdale Land & Property Co Ltd*,[37] considering and applying *Hamble Parish Council v Haggard*.[38] On the question of lawful user see Chapter 6, para **6.114** above.

(f)   Where a declaration is required to provide certainty prior to seeking injunctive or other relief from the court in the same claim. But note the need to avoid raising the issue prematurely; see para **11.30(a)** above.

---

[33]   (1879) 12 ChD 31.
[34]   (1905) 74 LJ Ch 127.
[35]   (1993) 66 P&CR 246.
[36]   [2004] 2AC 519.
[37]   [2011] EWCA Civ 1618.
[38]   [1972] 1 WLR 122.

11.34 Other miscellaneous points on declaration as to rights of way are as follows:

(a)   See Chapter 12 below for the evidence needed to be placed before the court in this type of claim.

(b)   The construction of a grant of an easement may well require consideration, not only of the words used, but also the context in which those words have been used. As will be seen from Chapter 4 at para **4.11** above, the modern approach to the construction of documents as set out in recent cases such as *Mannai Investments Co Ltd v Eagle Star Life Assurance Co Ltd*,[39] *ICS v West Bromwich Building Society*,[40] *Chartbrook v Persimmon Homes Ltd*,[41] and *Rainy Sky SA v Kookmin Bank*,[42] stresses the 'commercially sensible' construction, which, if at all possible, should be reached. (Note that if it is not possible to do this, the result of the literal meaning of the words in context will have to be applied.) This invariably requires the evidence of context to be before the court, so that in rights of way disputes for example, the background to express grants will often be of crucial importance, and the rules as to the admissibility of such evidence will be equally important in claims for declarations as to the meaning and effect of grants. (See *St Edmundsbury and Ipswich Diocesan Board of Finance v Clark (No 2)*[43] and *West v Sharp*[44] for examples of the application of these principles to rights of way disputes.) See further Chapter 4 above.

(c)   Is other relief needed in the same claim, such as an injunction, or a claim for damages?

(d)   Are there any other disputes (eg over boundaries, or covenants) which need to be raised and resolved in the same claim?

CLAIMS IN COURT – PART 2

Injunctions

General considerations

11.35 As was stated at the outset of this Chapter, this is not a litigation handbook, and, therefore, some knowledge will be assumed as to civil litigation and the remedies of an injunction. The up-to-date edition of *Civil Procedure* and other guides can be used to fill the gaps where extra assistance is required. What is emphasised here in Part 2 (and in Part 3 below where damages are

---

[39]   [1997] AC 749.
[40]   [1998] 1 WLR 896.
[41]   [2009] 1 AC 1101.
[42]   [2011] UKSC 50.
[43]   [1973] 1 WLR 1572; [1975] 1 WLR 468.
[44]   (2000) 79 P&CR 327 at p 332 per Mummery LJ.

discussed) is the way in which these remedies, particularly at the interim stage, can be sought or resisted. Such law and practice has a particular significance in the context of restrictive covenants and how they may be enforced.

11.36 Before contemplating bringing a claim for an injunction, the following points can arise and questions based on them should be asked.

11.37 These questions are relevant because the injunction is an equitable, and thus discretionary, remedy. Its grant will depend on all the circumstances of the case which are material. It is all too easy to forget this in the hurly-burly of threatened litigation, and these preliminary questions are better asked at an early stage, rather than later on when the costs penalties of changing course, or abandonment, may be severe.

11.38 Some preliminary questions are:

(a) If you are acting for the potential claimant, is he entitled to use the right of way in the manner claimed?

(b) Whether you act for the potential claimant or defendant (and this question may be more important if you act for the latter), is the defendant's land *bound* by the easement claimed?

(c) Has there been a an actionable interference, or is what is threatened going to be such an interference, and if so to what extent? (See Chapter 10 above). Is there any sense in seeking a declaration?

(d) In addition, consider:

   (i) *How far has the potential defendant gone?* Suppose the obstruction has been in place for months or years and your client has stood idly by. In such a case the court may not grant an injunction quite as readily as if you had sought the injunction at an earlier stage; see para **11.50** below for the effect of delay etc.

   (ii) *Has the claimant indicated (openly) that all he wants is money?* If so, that will usually be fatal to a claim by him for an injunction.[45]

   (iii) *Can you afford to claim or defend?* This is not just a question of costs, but the question touches upon the undertaking in damages a claimant will have to give if he is to get an interim injunction (see paras **11.66** and **11.87** below) and the likely damages a defendant may have to pay if he is found liable in a case where damages are the remedy ordered by the court.

   (iv) *Is this a special case where no injunction can be claimed?* Statutory and other provisions may rule out the remedy of an injunction, as well as damages in lieu, e g where section 237 of the Town & Country Planning Act 1990 applies: see Chapter 9 above.

---

[45] *Gafford v Graham* (1998) 77 P&CR 73.

(v)   *Can your client avoid litigation by other means?* Self help may be out of the question, but what about arbitration, mediation, ADR and all the other modern alternatives to litigation; see paras **11.11–11.17** above.[46]

(vi) Have you complied with the General Pre-Action Protocol?[47]

(vii) Is any claim premature? Note the need to avoid raising the issue prematurely; see para **11.30(a)** above and the *CIP Property (AIPT) Ltd* case referred to there.

11.39   *Prima facie* this is the remedy to seek and which should be granted if the circumstances warrant it where there has been an actionable interference with the right of way: see Chapter 10 above.

When will an injunction be granted?

11.40   In W*est v Sharp*,[48] Mummery LJ made it clear that an injunction will only be granted 'if there is a substantial interference so as to justify the intervention of equity'. Thus an injunction will not be granted in the case of 'trivial or temporary infringements' or where 'there is no continuing interference or threat of interference or in cases where damages would be an adequate remedy'.[49] But once you can show the actionable interference, the injunction will be the starting point as a remedy, the 'default setting' in computer language. You do not need to show specific loss or damage, merely that your rights have been actionably infringed.

General principles as to the grant of injunctions in private rights of way disputes

11.41   An injunction will be granted (almost) as a matter of course to restrain interference with a private right of way. But, as stated above, the court has a discretion in the award of the remedy. The old authorities on covenants, such as *Doherty v Allman*[50] and *Osborne v Bradley*[51] make it clear that a breach of covenant will lead to the grant of an injunction to restrain a breach. Since then

---

[46]   See the guidance given by the Court of Appeal in *Halsey v Milton Keynes General NHS Trust* [2004] EWCA Civ 576, and in *Reed Executive Plc v Reed Business Information Ltd* [2004] EWCA Civ 887 and para **11.11** above.

[47]   No advice should be given in any claim without having considered the alternatives to litigation. The costs risks in not doing so may be significant. See *Halsey v Milton Keynes General NHS Trust*, above.

[48]   (2000) 79 P&CR 327, at p 333, para (3).

[49]   *Ibid op cit*. For a recent example of where an injunction was refused on the ground that the interference was trivial, or temporary, see *Barrie House Freehold Ltd & Ors v Merie Binmahfouz Company (UK) Ltd* [2012] EWHC 353 (Ch); a trench dug over a period of six months in winter months during building works in an ornamental garden serving a block of flats in central London. Not a case of access over the area where the trench was dug.

[50]   (1878) 3 App Cas 709. See also section 37(1) of the Senior Courts Act 1981 which gives the court power to grant an injunction where 'it appears to the court to be just and convenient to do so'.

[51]   [1903] 2 Ch 446.

the modern approach to the exercise of the discretion (prior to the review of the authorities in *Regan v Paul Properties* (below)) may be seen on *Gafford v AH Graham*[52] and *Mortimer v Bailey*.[53] Whilst these were both covenant cases it is suggested that the same principles apply to claims in nuisance against an actionable interference with a private right of way. It is thought that since the review of the authorities in *Regan v Paul Properties* (below) the decision of Peter Smith J In *Midtown v City of London Real Property Co*[54] (a right of light case in which a prohibitory injunction was refused as it would be oppressive to defendants to be prevented from pursuing a large scale and 'worthwhile and beneficial' development east of New Fetter Lane, London, EC4) is not of universal application and turns on its special facts. See para **11.123** below for the principles applicable to damages in lieu of an injunction.

The discretion extends to the terms on which an injunction will be granted

11.42   For a case where the order was suspended in order to allow the claimant to deal with the immediate breach see *Thorn v Madden*[55] (time given to allow paying guests to relocate themselves) and *Achilli v Tovel*[56] (time allowed for removal of structure interfering with light).

The discretion extends to the terms on which an injunction will be granted

11.43   If granted, the court may suspend the order; for example to allow the parties time to agree an alternative route or time for the removal of an offending obstruction.

11.44   The best summary of the principles as to whether to grant an injunction, or damages in lieu in recent years is to be found in the Court of Appeal's decision in *Regan v Paul Properties DPF No 1 Ltd. & Ors.*[57] That was a right of light case, based on the tort of nuisance, so the review of the authorities and the principles set out by the Court of Appeal there apply with equal force to claims where private rights of way are being enforced.

11.45   Mummery LJ stated at para 34:

'Damages in lieu of injunction: the authorities and the general principles

34   A review of the authorities is required to see whether the deputy judge was correct in stating their effect in para 85 of his judgment ...

35   Shelfer[58] is the best known case. It is a decision of the Court of Appeal. It has never been overruled and it is binding on this court. The cause of action was nuisance, as in this case, though in the form of noise and vibration rather than interference with a right of light.

---

[52]   (1998) 77 P&CR 73.
[53]   [2004] EWCA Civ 1514.
[54]   [2005] EWHC 33 (Ch).
[55]   [1925] Ch 847 at p 852.
[56]   [1927] 2 Ch 243.
[57]   [2007] Ch 135; '*Regan*'.
[58]   *Shelfer v City of London Electric Lighting Co* [1895] 1 Ch 287; '*Shelfer*'.

36   Shelfer has, for over a century, been the leading case on the power of the court to award damages instead of an injunction. It is authority for the following propositions which I derive from the judgments of Lord Halsbury and Lindley and A L Smith LJJ. (1) A claimant is prima facie entitled to an injunction against a person committing a wrongful act, such as continuing nuisance, which invades the claimant's legal right. (2) The wrongdoer is not entitled to ask the court to sanction his wrongdoing by purchasing the claimant's rights on payment of damages assessed by the court. (3) The court has jurisdiction to award damages instead of an injunction, even in cases of a continuing nuisance; but the jurisdiction does not mean that the court is "a tribunal for legalising wrongful acts" by a defendant, who is able and willing to pay damages: per Lindley LJ, at pp 315 and 316. (4) The judicial discretion to award damages in lieu should pay attention to well settled principles and should not be exercised to deprive a claimant of his prima facie right "except under very exceptional circumstances": per Lindley LJ, at pp 315 and 316. (5) Although it is not possible to specify all the circumstances relevant to the exercise of the discretion or to lay down rules for its exercise, the judgments indicated that it was relevant to consider the following factors: whether the injury to the claimant's legal rights was small; whether the injury could be estimated in money; whether it could be adequately compensated by a small money payment; whether it would be oppressive to the defendant to grant an injunction; whether the claimant had shown that he only wanted money; whether the conduct of the claimant rendered it unjust to give him more than pecuniary relief; and whether there were any other circumstances which justified the refusal of an injunction: see A L Smith LJ, at pp 322 and 323, and Lindley LJ, at p 317.

37   In my judgment, none of the above propositions has been overruled by later decisions of any higher court or of this court.'

11.46   The principles set out in *Shelfer* as explained in *Regan* have been applied in the following recent cases:

(a)   *Jacklin v Chief Constable of West Yorkshire.*[59]

(b)   *Turner v Pryce.*[60]

(c)   *Site Developments (Ferndown) Ltd v Barratt Homes Ltd & Ors.*[61]

(d)   *Watson & Ors v Croft Promo-Sport*; *'Watson'.*[62]

(e)   *HXRUK II (CHC) Ltd v Heaney*; *'Heaney'.*[63]

---

[59]   [2007] EWCA Civ 181.
[60]   [2008] (Stephen Smith QC sitting as a deputy High Court Judge in Birmingham). Judgment delivered 8 January 2008; LTL ref 17/1/2008.
[61]   [2007] EWHC 415.
[62]   [2008] EWHC 759 (QB).
[63]   [2010] EWHC 2245 (Ch). In addition, other recent cases where the courts have considered whether an injunction should be granted, are: *CIP Property (AIPT) Ltd v Transport for London & Ors* [2012] EWHC 259 (Ch), *Barrie House Freehold Ltd & Ors v Merie Binmahfouz Company (UK) Ltd* [2012] EWHC 353 (Ch), and *Derrick Barr & Ors v Biffa Waste Services Ltd* [2012] EWCA Civ 312.

(f)   *Derrick Barr & Ors v Biffa Waste Services Ltd* [2012] EWCA Civ 312.

Note that in the last case, at para 124, Carnwath LJ stressed the fact *Watson* was not 'the last word' on the scope of the discretion to grant or refuse an injunction bearing in mind the application of the principles in *Shelfer*, especially where important public interest issues are at stake. Thus in private rights of way disputes (whether or not important public issues are at stake) the discretion which lies behind the remedy of the injunction is a paramount factor and *Shelfer* should not be seen as a straight jacket. What is certain is that this area of law is capable of further development and clarification. Such development and clarification of principles is also needed if there is to be any certainty even in a discretionary jurisdiction.

11.47   For an injunction to be granted it is not *necessary* for the claimant to prove pecuniary loss as a result of the actual, or threatened breach, but it may be desirable to do so. *Prima facie* the claimant is entitled to the remedy of the injunction on proof of the actionable interference, see para **11.40** above. However, in respect of the question whether damages in lieu of an injunction will be awarded, the question of loss will be relevant. The modern approach to the exercise of the discretion will inevitably involve a consideration of the loss caused by breach.[64] After all, the jurisdiction is a discretionary one requiring an examination of all the relevant facts. But it must be stressed that in the light of the principles set out in *Regan* and the authorities cited in that case, the court may be unmoved by pleas from the defendant that the loss is really very small. And the court will not be moved by a plea from the same party that the cost of removing the cause of the actionable interference is out of proportion to the loss to the claimant.[65]

11.48   Where there is doubt whether the existence of a private right of way might be the subject of an actionable interference if activity is carried out on the servient land, it is strongly suggested (as with other potentially adverse rights) the prudent party will get the matter sorted out before starting activity which might cause such an interference. If he takes a chance, then it will require very strong circumstances where, if the chance has been taken and lost, an injunction will be withheld.[66]

Specific factors which will hinder or prevent the grant of an injunction

11.49   Whilst each case must be assessed on its own facts, it is suggested that the following principles apply to both interim *and* final applications for injunctions.

---

[64]   See para **11.49** below.
[65]   See *Regan* (above) at paras 64–73, per Mummery LJ.
[66]   This statement is based on the warning given by Jacob LJ in *Mortimer v Bailey* [2004] EWCA Civ 1514, at para 41. Whilst that warning was given in the context of a restrictive covenant dispute, the same warning is, it is suggested, equally applicable to potential disputes over an interference with private rights of way.

Delay or acquiescence

11.50　Time is 'of the essence' if not in legal, then in factual terms when seeking injunctive relief. The remedy is a discretionary one and the court will have regard to how promptly the application for relief was made and in what circumstances. The maxim of equity, that it will assist the vigilant, applies here. See *Shelfer* (above).

11.51　Varying degrees of delay and acquiescence may be found to exist. At one end of the scale is permission openly granted to use a different route of the way, or to consent to an interference with the way in full knowledge of the right, or years of delay in seeking to enforce the right of way. At the other end of the scale, there is conduct which is equivocal, or trivial in terms of time. Failing to object to a planning application for development which might potentially affect the right of way, even if notified, is not usually 'fatal' to a claim to enforce the right. But whilst the response to the local planning authority will need to address matters that are material in planning terms, the opportunity to assert the right to the servient owner should not be lost, and a failure to do that may be significant at a later date when delay has to be explained in an application for an injunction.

11.52　Generalisations can hardly be drawn too far, even from this example. Modern authorities show that the court will look at *all* aspects of the parties' conduct before deciding whether such conduct disentitles the claimant from obtaining injunctive relief. The test of whether the claimant should, or should not, be barred by his conduct from obtaining an injunction has been described as one which requires the question to be asked:

> 'Would it be unconscionable in all the circumstances for this party seeking the injunction to enforce his rights which he undoubtedly had at the date of the breach of covenant by means of an injunction?'[67]

11.53　It is ultimately a question of fact and degree. Detriment is often a strong factor which makes it unconscionable for the enforcing party to obtain the injunction, eg where he has stood by over a long period of time doing nothing about the interference while the defendant spends money on his land in buildings. In the absence of detriment the court needs to find some other factor which makes it unconscionable for the party having the benefit of the covenant to change his mind and enforce.

---

[67]　*Harris v Williams-Wynne* [2006] EWCA Civ 104, at para 36, per Chadwick LJ. See *Shaw v Applegate* [1977] 1 WLR 970 and *Gafford v AH Graham* (1998) 77 P&CR 73, as the earlier leading authorities on this question. See also *HXRUK II (CHC) Ltd v Heaney* [2010] EWHC 2245 (Ch) for the effect of sporadic complaints over a long period of time without any attempt to bring any form of claim in court. For a recent example where delay over many years in seeking to restrain the unlawful use of a right of way led to the injunction being refused at trial and in the Court of Appeal, see *Greenmanor Ltd v Pilford & Anor* [2012] EWCA Civ 756, at paras 36ff per Etherton LJ.

11.54 Under this head of unconscionability may also be placed the various categories of estoppel which might prevent enforcement of the right. Thus, conduct which would allow the servient owner to believe that there will be no objection to the proposed work may amount to an estoppel, eg oral representations – 'that's OK Old Boy – don't worry about the right of way'. One example in specific terms can be the entry into an agreement to consent to works to which the Party Wall Etc. Act 1996 applies, or the acceptance of an Award under that Act. Although that Act specifically excludes private law rights under the law of easements, nuisance etc from its ambit, what the parties have done in the context of party wall matters may be highly significant when the court has to consider conduct in respect of a claim for injunctive relief.

11.55 Merely negotiating should not deprive the potential claimant of the right to seek an injunction, if the negotiations fail. In that context it is important to ensure that open negotiations are kept distinct from any negotiations conducted on a without prejudice basis.

11.56 Each case will always be fact specific. Thus in *Gafford v AH Graham*[68] (which was a covenants case where the principles of unconscionability as expressed in *Taylors Fashion v Liverpool Victoria Trustees*[69] were applied) injunctive relief was refused. It was also refused on the basis of delay and acquiescence in *Harris v Williams-Wynne*;[70] another covenants case. But in *Jacklin v Chief Constable of West Yorkshire*[71] (a right of way case) the defence to an injunction based on delay and acquiescence failed and the injunction was granted. In *HXRUK II (CHC) Ltd v Heaney*[72] sporadic open complaints over a long period of time without any attempt to bring any form of claim in court did not prevent the injured party (the defendant) obtaining a mandatory injunction to remove those parts of the claimant's building which caused the actionable interference to the defendant's light.

Past history

11.57 Past failures to enforce which have led to the disappearance of the right of way or even its abandonment will lessen or remove the prospect of injunctive relief being granted. The court will not restrain a breach where little purpose would be served by specific enforcement. But there may be good ground to preserve the right of way even though it may not have been used for some time and unless abandonment can be shown an injunction may well lie to protect it.

---

[68] (1998) 77 P&CR 73.
[69] [1982] QB 133 (at p 155 per Oliver J).
[70] [2006] EWCA Civ 104.
[71] [2007] EWCA Civ 181.
[72] [2010] EWHC 2245 (Ch). See also *Greenmanor Ltd v Pilford & Anor* [2012] EWCA Civ 756.

The claimant openly indicating that he will take money

11.58 That is usually fatal to a claimant who persists in seeking an injunction, see *Shelfer* (above). Unless there is good reason why a claimant should not be held to an openly declared position, he will get damages in lieu of an injunction.[73]

Parties to claims

11.59 See para **11.20** above for the same issue where a declaration is being sought. The necessary parties will usually be amongst the following classes:

(a) Dominant and servient owners. These will usually be the freehold owners. If there are joint rights of user, all those seeking to enforce (or necessary as defendants) must be joined. The question can arise as to whether the freeholder is in possession or reversion.

(b) If in reversion, the reversioner can be a claimant (if interested in the dominant land) and may need to be a defendant (if interested in the servient land). In the former case, injury to the reversion needs to be proved, eg by virtue of the permanent blocking of the right of way from the dominant land. See *Jones v Llanrwst UDC*,[74] per Parker J. But the injury needs to be permanent in the sense that it will remain unless there is something done to remove it. There are generally taken to be three types of injury to the reversion, these are:

   (i)   Where there is present loss or injury, eg the effect of the obstruction on the passing rent, or at a rent review; although the latter may fall within head (ii) below depending on the date of the next review.
   (ii) Future loss or injury, such as when the lease falls in.
   (iii) Where the damage is clearly of real permanent effect; such as the barring of a claim to a right of way under section 2 of the Prescription Act 1832, because of the effect of the interruption under section 4 thereof (see Chapter 6, paras **6.32** and **6.72** above).[75]

(c) Tenants in occupation should either be claimants or defendants. Whether under a long lease or a periodic tenancy, they should be defendants. A question can arise as to whether tenants at will or licensee should be parties. If it is the tenant at will, or licensee which is causing the obstruction then of course they should be joined as defendants.

---

[73] *Gafford v AH Graham* (1998) 77 P&CR 73, at p 84, per Nourse LJ.
[74] [1911] 1 Ch 393, at p 404.
[75] Note the authorities on the question of whether or not a reversioner should be a party, or can sue, are old. The leading ones are generally taken to be *Rust v Victoria Grading Dock Company* (1887) 36 Ch 113, and *Jones v Llanrwst Urban District Council* [1911] 1 Ch 393. There may be a need for a modern approach to the question of whether reversioners can enforce in this type of claim. It is suggested that there is no good reason why not.

(d)   Third parties who might be affected by the interference should be joined, such as users under a covenant.

(e)   Any other adjoining owners with an interest in the private right of way or its resolution might have to be joined. For example, highway authorities may have adjoining land where persons pass from the highway on to a private right of way. A dispute has arisen as between the location or position of the private right of way and the highway land. In such a case the local highway authority may have to be joined, or at the least, notified of the claim. The same approach may apply to statutory undertakers and other public or quasi public bodies (eg Network Rail) where they have interests in land (eg railways under or over private rights of way) which may be affected by the dispute.

(f)   Unless it seems that the dispute over the right of way is likely to affect the security held by a mortgagee (the identity of the mortgagee(s) being evident from the Official Copies of the Register of the material land or title) it is not usual to join any such mortgagee. However, informing the mortgagee of the dispute is sensible. Where the dispute affects land in the course of development, informing the developer's funder/mortgagee is often a wise step to take as that information may cause the funder to put pressure on its borrower to sort the matter out.

(g)   Defendants without any title to land but causing a nuisance should be joined, as suggested above, such as licensees or trespassers. Others may also have to be joined such as strangers parking cars on the right of way. See *Hilton v James Smith & Sons (Norwood) Limited*.[76] There may be a duty on the landlord freeholder owed to his tenants to take steps to prevent or remove the nuisance to the right of way enjoyed by his tenants.

11.60   Note that claims for an injunction affecting a right of way may also arise in other contexts, but are not dealt with here in any detail. For example:

(a)   Breach of restrictive covenants affecting freehold land.

(b)   Landlord and tenant disputes:

    (i)   breach of covenant for quiet enjoyment;
    (ii)   breach of grant of the terms of a right of way in a lease;
    (iii) breach of covenant in the lease to prevent nuisances. For example see *Hilton v James Smith* (above).

(c)   Contractors, builders etc placing skips on rights of way, or otherwise obstructing the right of way, may also have to be joined as defendants. It will usually be necessary for the freeholder, or long leaseholder who has control over his contractors etc to take steps to remove or lessen the effect

---

[76]   [1979] 2 EGLR 44.

of these types of interference at an early stage before litigation becomes inevitable. For otherwise the contractors etc will have to become defendants (possibly later on in the proceedings at the case management stage) if they are still maintaining the obstruction. See *Jacklin v Chief Constable of West Yorkshire*[77] for an example of this type of claim.

Types of injunction

11.61   There are two types of injunction which can be granted:

(a)   *Prohibitory:* an injunction which restrains a breach which is either anticipated, or threatened[78] (such as an obstruction which is about to be erected) or continuing and which an order is required to stop, eg the proposed revised layout of a forecourt to a block of flats which if implemented will interfere with the right of way actionably.

(b)   *Mandatory:* an injunction which requires a positive act to be done by the defendant to conform with the order, such as the removal of the offending obstruction.

11.62   It should be clear that anyone who delays beyond a point where prohibitory relief will serve no purpose (as in cases of an obstruction which is already in place across the way) will have to consider the prospect of seeking *mandatory* relief. That is not an attractive prospect in many cases, as because of the severity of such an order, the court may be reluctant to grant such relief.[79] This point reinforces that made at para **11.41** above and at para **11.66** below regarding the importance of a quick response to interference with the right of way.

11.63   It is relevant to note that in rights of light cases the court will be prepared to order demolition, or partial demolition, of buildings causing an interference with light, where there has been an actionable interference with the right of light.[80] The same practice should apply with greater force where the effect of an obstruction to a right of way is, or will be extreme.

---

[77]   [2007] EWCA Civ 181.

[78]   Sometimes referred to a '*quia timet*' injunction (the words in Latin meaning 'that which is feared').

[79]   See *Morris v Redland Bricks* [1970] AC 652 for the general principles on which the court will act when applications are made for mandatory relief. In *Gafford v AH Graham* (1998) 77 P&CR 73, the Court of Appeal refused to grant mandatory relief seeking the removal of a riding school where the claimant had stood by and failed to prevent its erection by seeking interlocutory relief at an early stage. By the trial date the building had been up for over seven years. For authority on interim applications for mandatory relief (which is a bold course) see *Nottingham BS Eurodynamics Systems* [1993] FSR 468 and CPR Part 25, rule 1.

[80]   See *Deakins v Hookings* [1994] 1 EGLR 190, *Regan* and *Heaney* (above) for three recent examples where mandatory relief was granted to deal with a nuisance to rights of light. It is suggested that rights of way are to be treated no differently.

11.64 Should an application for interim relief be made? Recent authority, *Mortimer v Bailey*,[81] indicates that a failure to seek interim prohibitory relief is not fatal to obtaining a final mandatory at trial. Furthermore, the Court of Appeal in *Regan* has confirmed that the 'default setting' is that an injunction, whether prohibitory or mandatory, will be the *prima facie* remedy. It is for the defendant to prove that such an order should not be made when the court is being asked to exercise its discretion as to the remedy. See para **11.40**ff above for further discussion of this question.

11.65 What is the effect of the grant of planning consent? As a warning to developers and others who might feel that the existence of planning consent should be the end of the matter, the rule is that adverse interests such as rights of way, will take precedence and remain enforceable (and planning consent documents makes this clear) and the court may grant the injunction whatever the status of any planning consent.[82] It is also important for developers and others who feel inclined to suggest that they can 'buy off' those with the benefit of the covenant, to be aware that the court does not accept the concept that rights are there to be bought off as opposed to being enforced. This point is dealt with below in Part 3 where damages in lieu of an injunction are considered.

The stage at which an injunction should be sought

11.66 The answer which should always be given is 'as early as possible'. But what does this mean?

11.67 To answer this question, consider the following example.

11.68 The defendant (alleged to be about to interfere actionably with the right of way) is engaged in speculative development with borrowed money and he is probably on a tight contract with builders. The mere issue of a claim form may force him to stop building so as to interfere with the right of way and sue for peace. If the claim form seeking an injunction is registered as a pending land action,[83] that will have to be explained to purchasers and the defendant's lender. Anything which threatens the speed at which the development can be completed will be bad news for the defendant and his lender.

11.69 In this example the claimant runs a risk if he does not seek interim relief. It is tempting to think that the claimant can simply wait until trial, but at that stage, when the building is complete and the obstruction is in place, the prospect of obtaining injunctive relief may be more remote.

---

[81] [2004] EWCA Civ 1514.
[82] See *Derrick Barr & Ors v Biffa Waste Services Ltd* [2012] EWCA Civ 312.
[83] In registered titles use the Unilateral Notice under the Land Registration Act 2002, ss 34(2)(b), 35 and 87(1); use form UN1. In unregistered titles, register a pending land action under the Land Charges Act 1972, s 5; see *Ruoff & Roper Registered Conveyancing* (Sweet & Maxwell), Chapter 42.

There is jurisdiction to grant an injunction on a *'quia timet'* basis ('that which is feared') where there is an immediate threat to so something which requires the intervention of the court to prevent it. Note the words 'immediate threat'. For recent authority on that see *CIP Property (AIPT) Ltd v Transport for London & Ors* [2012] EWHC 259.

11.70 For conflicting authority on whether the claimant should be forced to seek interim relief see *Blue Town Investments Ltd v Higgs & Hill plc*[84] (where the claimant was so forced in a right of light case) and *Oxy-Electric Ltd v Zainuddin*[85] (where the court refused, where a breach of covenant was alleged, to require the claimant to make such an election). In *Vardy v Banner New Homes*[86] the court refused to strike out the claim, relying on *Oxy-Electric* and referring to the intimidatory conduct of the defendant prior to the action being commenced without any interim application to pull down the houses already built. It is suggested that since *Mortimer v Bailey*,[87] the failure to apply for interim relief should not prevent the court from granting permanent relief at trial in the absence of compelling factors present, a failure to apply for interim relief should not put the claim at risk of being struck out under CPR Part 3. This is particularly so since the case management powers of the court under the CPR will allow claims to be managed in such a way as, for example, merits their urgency. A Part 23 application can be made at any time seeking directions for an early hearing. In addition, it is suggested that Art 6 of the Convention for the Protection of Human Rights and Fundamental Freedoms 1950 ('the Convention'), now part of Sch 1 to the Human Rights Act 1998 and in force since 2 October 2000, allows a claimant to decide how he wants to pursue his claim (within the rules) and states that he/she should not be forced to make an interim application as a condition of pursuing that claim. *Site Developments (Ferndown) Ltd v Barratt Homes Ltd*[88] is a recent example of an unsuccessful application to strike out on a summary application the injunctive and damages relief sought by the claimant which had a real prospect of success under CPR Part 24, rule 2(a)(i).

11.71 In any claim for interim relief the claimant must consider the problem of the undertaking in damages. This is considered at para **11.87** below.

11.72 In most respects, applications for interim injunctions to protect interest under private rights of way are no different from other types of application for injunctions. You have to satisfy the court that:[89]

(a) there is a serious question to be tried;

---

[84] [1990] 1 WLR 696.
[85] [1991] 1 WLR 115.
[86] (1998) (HHJ Rich QC, Chancery Division, 1 May 1998) (unreported).
[87] [2004] EWCA Civ 1514.
[88] [2007] EWHC 415 (Ch).
[89] See CPR Parts 23 and 25 and the test based on *American Cyanamid v Ethicon* [1975] AC 396. On 'real prospect of success' see *Celador Products Ltd v Melville* [2004] EWHC 2362 (Ch), at paras 6–7, per Sir Andrew Morritt V-C.

(b)   the balance of convenience dictates the grant of the injunction; and

(c)   the claimant can give the undertaking in damages where it is appropriate to require him to do so.

11.73   In view of the way in which the courts now encourage the parties to identify and resolve issues in a claim at an early stage, and the speed with which claims proceed to a full hearing, the significance of the threefold test in *Cyanamid* may be somewhat lessened. However, at the interim stage, the court will be concerned to preserve the status quo, if that is the just course to take, and will often issue directions for the further conduct of the claim; eg as to an expedited hearing date where building work is in issue. See *Mortimer v Bailey*[90] for a claim where interim relief was refused, but the case was ordered to go straight to trial. *Site Developments (Ferndown) Ltd v Barratt Homes Ltd*[91] is a recent example of the way in which the court will assess the merits of an interim application by the defendant to (in effect) strike out claims to injunctive relief where the question is whether there is a real prospect of success in the claimant obtaining the injunctive relief sought. As the court declined in that case to find that there were no real prospects of success in the injunction claims, it did not have to rule on the effect of any infringement of Art 1 of the First Protocol to the European Convention on Human Rights. That issue would have arisen had the court considered it proper to strike out the injunction claims, and the question would then have been how far that would have been a breach of the Article and whether the damages in lieu would be fair compensation for the taking away of any rights and whether a fair balance was struck between the parties' rights under the Article. It is important for any claimant to assess the strength of his claim against any summary application by the defendant to strike out or limit the relief to be sought.

11.74   In private rights of way cases, unless it is plain that the claimant does not have the benefit of the easement, or that the defendant is not subject to it as the servient owner, there will usually be no dispute that there is a serious question to be tried. This will be true not only where the right was the subject of an express grant, or reservation, or an implied grant, but also where the issue may be over whether the right of way has been acquired by longer user; or conversely whether it has been abandoned; see Chapters 6 and 9 above. The court will usually assume that the evidence in support of the claim to the easement will be adequate to do that at trial. On an application for interim relief, the court will not conduct a 'mini trial' on the evidence put forward in the witness statements in support of the application. But the serious question to be tried (eg as to the easement and its interference) must be present on the face of the evidence lodged with the application for the interim injunction.

11.75   As to the balance of convenience, in private right of way disputes it can generally be said that this lies in favour of removing (or preventing) the

---

[90]   [2004] EWCA Civ 1514, [2005] 2 P&CR 9.
[91]   [2007] EWHC 415 (Ch).

obstruction or other interference. However, in some cases the cost or effect of compliance on an interim basis may be too great. In *Gregory v Courtroyal Ltd*[92] (a covenant case), the court refused to grant an interim injunction to restrain building work in breach of covenant. The work was substantially advanced, £2 million had already been spent on the development by the defendant, damages might be an adequate remedy to the claimants, and the claimants did not have the means to satisfy the defendants' losses if they had to stop work which if ordered would seriously jeopardise the defendants' financial position. So there was less risk of injunction if the application for an interim injunction was refused than if it was granted.

11.76 The courts do not like defendants trying to 'steal a march' on the claimant and will take such conduct into account when deciding whether to grant the interim injunction.[93]

11.77 It is much harder to persuade a court to grant a mandatory injunction on an *interim* basis, for in order that the court can do so it must be as certain as it can be that at the trial it will appear that the mandatory interim injunction was rightly granted.

11.78 The view has been expressed recently to the effect that the court should consider whether the *injustice* suffered by the defendant (in a case where the injunction turned out to be wrongly granted) is greater than the injustice suffered by the claimant, if at trial it turned out that he was entitled to a mandatory injunction, having been refused it at the interlocutory stage.[94]

11.79 For the 'injustice' argument see *Films Rover Ltd v Cannon film Sales Ltd*.[95] The principle of who will suffer the greater injustice has been applied in *Nottingham BS v Eurodynamics Systems*[96] where the principles applicable were set out. *In Zockoll Group Ltd v Mercury Communications*,[97] the Court of Appeal held that the summary of principles in the *Nottingham BS* case was 'all the citation that should in future be necessary'. The summary given by the court in the *Nottingham BS* case is as follows:

(a)   As this is an interlocutory (interim) matter, the overriding consideration is which course is likely to involve the least risk of injustice if it turns out to be 'wrong' in the sense described by Hoffmann J in *Films Rover* (see above).

---

[92]   (Unreported) 30 April 2002, Rimer J, Chancery Division. For authority addressing the issue of the balance of convenience in an interim application made in the context of demolition work and nuisance caused by it in the City of London, see *Hiscox Syndicates Ltd & Anor v Pinnacle Ltd* [2008] EWHC 145 (Ch).

[93]   *Shepherd Homes v Sandham* [1971] Ch 340, at p 349.

[94]   See *Shepherd Homes v Sandham*, above.

[95]   [1987] 1 WLR 670.

[96]   [1993] FSR 468.

[97]   [1998] FSR 354.

(b) An order which requires a party to take a positive step at the interim stage may well carry with it a greater risk of injustice, if it turns out to have been wrongly made, than an order which merely prohibits action, preserving the status quo.

(c) It is legitimate for the court to consider at the interim stage whether it feels a high degree of assurance that the claimant will be entitled to establish the right to that order at trial. The greater the degree of assurance, the less the risk of an injustice if an interim mandatory injunction is granted.

(d) However, there may still be circumstances in which it is appropriate to grant an interim mandatory injunction, even where the court is unable to feel any high level of assurance that the claimant will establish this right. These circumstances will exist where the risk of injustice, if the injunction is refused, outweigh the risk of injustice if it is granted. This summary is routinely applied by judges hearing applications for interim mandatory relief.

11.80 In cases concerning *covenants* it may be difficult to assess where the greater injustice lies; for example, where a residential building is to be knocked down, the contrast between the two situations is extreme. In other cases (such as a breach of covenant relating to a small garden wall) the contrast will be far less acute. In many cases money can satisfy the claimant, thereby making it less likely that a mandatory injunction will be granted. The same considerations may *not*, however, apply to *private rights of way* cases where the right of way secures access to the dominant land and injustice will plainly result if the obstruction is not removed without delay.

11.81 The court will have regard to whether an award of damages will be an adequate remedy, if an injunction were refused; see para **11.123** below for such damages.

How to obtain an interim injunction

11.82 Reference should be made as to the procedure to the current edition of the *Civil Court Service* or the *White Book* for the full practice and the forms required; see the caveat as to the scope of this Chapter at the beginning of it. If in the Chancery Division, follow the practice set out in the current Chancery Guide and on the HMCTS website, especially with regard to lodging documents in electronic form.

11.83 In very broad terms, you will need to do the following:

(a) Issue a claim in the High Court (or County Court) using a Part 7 claim form (usually with Particulars of Claim/Statement of Case) alleging the facts on which the claim to the private right of way and the actionable interference is asserted.

(b)   Issue an application under CPR Parts 23 and 25. This will require a witness statement from the applicant (or solicitor) setting out the evidence and stating why the application is for an interim injunction. This will also require a draft order to be drawn with the evidence.

(c)   File and serve all the documents, usually allowing at least two clear days before the hearing date.

(d)   Attend the hearing and seek the order. If it is to be made, the party applying will usually need to give the undertaking in damages, see above.

11.84   Note that in some very urgent cases you can seek the interim order before issuing the claim form at (a) above (on an undertaking to issue forthwith after the first hearing). Additionally, in very urgent cases you can make the application (after issue of the claim form and application under (a) and (b) above) without notice to the other side, or without the full two clear days notice. The civil procedure textbooks must be consulted in these urgent cases.

11.85   Specific to each case will be the need to consider what proper orders to make as regards costs and the future conduct of the claim once any interim order is granted, or not granted as the case may be. In suitable cases the court may expedite the claim for final hearing, eg where there is great urgency because building work is under way.

11.86   The usual practice is:

(a)   If the claimant succeeds in obtaining interim relief he will get his costs as 'claimant's costs in the case', ie if he wins at trial he gets the costs of the interim application (and presumably the other costs of the action), but if he loses at trial he does not have to pay the defendant's costs of that application, although the claimant may have to pay the defendant's other costs of the action.

(b)   If the claimant loses his application for interim relief the order will be 'defendant's costs in the case'. Thus if the defendant wins at trial he will get the costs of the interim application (and presumably the other costs of the action) from the claimant. If, however, the claimant wins at trial and gets an injunction he will get the costs of the action, but not his costs of the interim application.[98]

The undertaking in damages

11.87   The usual practice when seeking interim relief is that the court may require the claimant to undertake to pay the defendant the loss which it has

---

[98]   See CPR Part 44, Practice Direction, Costs.

suffered should it turn out at the trial that the injunction obtained on an interim basis is not to be made final.[99] The undertaking is an absolute one (if given) and is to be liable for that loss.

11.88 For the nature of the undertaking and its enforcement, see the full analysis in *Cheltenham & Gloucester BS v Ricketts*,[100] applied in *Eliades v Lewis*[101] and *Lunn Poly Ltd v Liverpool & Lancashire Properties Ltd*,[102] at paras 42 and 47–50. The conduct of the parties will be relevant and such conduct may disentitle the party seeking to enforce the undertaking from doing so. In *Regan v Paul Properties*[103] the court declined to order enforcement of the undertaking in damages because the defendants had acted unlawfully and the claimant had acted in good faith. For the practice and the problems thrown up by impecunious claimants, see CPR Part 25 and *Allen v Jambo Holdings*.[104] For a general statement on how far the claimant should seek interim relief with the burden of the undertaking in damages in mind, see *Mortimer v Bailey*,[105] see para **11.66** above. For the need to provide credible evidence of loss caused by the existence of the injunction, see *Yukong Line Ltd of Korea v Rendsburg Investments Corp of Liberia (The Rialto) (Injunctive Relief)*,[106] applied in *North Principal Investments Fund Ltd v Greenoak Renewable Energy Ltd*.[107]

11.89 This may be a heavy burden for a claimant to bear and although there are exceptions, any claimant contemplating enforcement of covenants by injunction must be prepared to give such an undertaking. The counterpart to this predicament lies in the fact that a defendant who is faced with a claim for an injunction without any interim application being made, will not be able to recoup any losses pending trial owing to the uncertainty of his position. But that uncertainty 'is no more than a necessary consequence of the existence of a claim which has not yet been adjudicated'.[108]

11.90 What the claimant may have to contemplate is the 'David and Goliath' situation of having to give an undertaking for many thousands of pounds in a case where the defendant is a builder or developer and there are penalties on the contract and other costs following a delay in the execution of the projected development.

---

[99] As with claims for security for costs under CPR Part 25, rule 13 (which might raise issues under Art 6 of the Convention) it could be argued that to require a claimant, or any other party, to give an undertaking which he is financially unable to give is a breach of Art 6. Hence the discretion of the court set out at the opening of the Practice Direction, CPR Part 25, para 5.

[100] [1993] 1 WLR 1545.

[101] [2005] EWHC 2966 (QB).

[102] [2006] EWCA Civ 430.

[103] [2006] EWHC 2052 (Ch).

[104] [1980] 1 WLR 1252.

[105] [2004] EWCA Civ 1514, [2005] 2 P&CR 9 at para 30, per Peter Gibson LJ.

[106] [2001] 2 Lloyd's Rep 113.

[107] [2009] EWHC 985 (Ch).

[108] Per Hoffmann J in *Oxy-Electric v Zainuddin* [1991] 1 WLR 115, at p 120.

11.91 It is clear that in any case of anticipated enforcement of covenants the claimant must be forewarned of the generally accepted need to give an undertaking in damages as the price of obtaining an injunction. Moreover, it is not always prudent to avoid this issue by not seeking interim relief in view of the risk that either the defendant will simply carry on regardless.[109] The defendant should be warned that unless he can obtain an undertaking in damages from the claimant (which is of some value) he will be out of pocket if at the hearing it turns out that the interim injunction should not have been granted.

11.92 It is worth pointing out by way of a final note on this point that even the option of not seeking interim relief, but going straight to a final hearing on a expedited hearing basis, may require the claimant to give the undertaking as to damages as the condition of the defendant undertaking to stop work until the judgment in the trial, or further order.

Final injunctions

How to obtain a final injunction

11.93 Reference should be made as to the procedure to the current edition of the *Civil Court Service* or the *White Book* for the practice and the forms required, see the caveat as to the scope of this Chapter at the beginning of it. See also Chapter 12 at para **12.39** below for procedure.

11.94 It should be noted that (as indicated above) it is not always necessary to seek an interim injunction, and it is possible to issue proceedings and proceed straight to a final hearing and a final injunction.

11.95 In broad terms you will need to do the following:

(a) Issue a claim in the High Court (or County Court) using a Part 7 claim form (usually with Particulars of Claim/Statement of Case) alleging the facts on which the breach of covenant is asserted.

(b) Await the acknowledgement of service and defence (and counterclaim) – within the time limits set by CPR Parts 10 and 16.

(c) Proceed to complete and file the allocation questionnaire (CPR Part 26) (injunction and damages claims for breach of covenant will usually be allocated to the multi-track) and to the case management stages

---

[109] It should not be forgotten that it is a rule of practice (at least in the Chancery Division) that even where the defendant accepts that he should be bound by an interim order until trial and gives an undertaking not, for example, to do the acts alleged to be in breach of covenant, the claimant must still give the undertaking in damages; at least in case where the claimant would otherwise be required to give it, or unless the contrary is agreed. See the current edition of *The Chancery Guide*. (www.justice.gov.uk/guidance/courts-and-tribunals/courts/chancery-division).

(CPR Part 29) with disclosure of documents (CPR Part 31), witness statements (CPR Part 32) and experts (CPR Part 35).

(d)   Attend all pre claim hearings and, assuming mediation or other forms of compromise are not successful, proceed to trial and final order.

Note that there can be many variations of this order of events.

11.96   Two issues which can arise in these claims are:

(a)   Where an interim application is made for an injunction and the court determines that this application is to be treated as the trial of the claim (or of the issue about which the injunction is sought – eg the construction of the grant of the right of way).

(b)   Where there is default of acknowledgment of service, or of defence, or where summary judgment is sought under CPR Part 24 – eg that the injunction should be made final, or conversely that the claim is so hopeless that it should be struck out.

11.97   In each case the court will only make a final order if it is satisfied that it is just to do so on the evidence before it. As these types of hearing invariably last more than two hours they will be listed as interim applications by the order and a timetable for evidence etc and date for a hearing will be fixed by the court.

11.98   Note that at the heart of many disputes over rights of way will be the issue whether the interference with the right of way presents a clear case of substantial (and thus actionable) interference, see Chapter 10 above.

Only if the interference is in that category will a final perpetual injunction be ordered. If a mandatory injunction is ordered, the court will specify in precise terms what it is that the parties have to do in order to avoid an unwitting breach of the order and contempt of court.

Limitation of claims in injunction cases

11.99   There is no period set by the Limitation Act 1980 for claims seeking injunctive relief, and the same would appear to be the case so far as damages in lieu are sought under section 50 of the Supreme Court Act 1981.

11.100   However, as the remedy is an equitable one, the principle of *laches* (or unconscionable delay) will apply and as stated at para **11.50** above, such delay will deprive the party claiming the injunction of that remedy where the principle of *laches* applies.[110] But mere delay in seeking the remedy is not enough. The court must consider whether it would not be reasonable to the

---

[110] For a detailed treatment of this area of the law see *Snell's Equity*, 32nd Edn, Chapter 5,

other party if the injunction was to be awarded, or where the claimant's conduct amounts in effect to a waiver of his rights.

11.101 It is important to separate *laches* from estoppel. The latter is often linked with the former. As was said by Lord Neuberger in *Fisher v Brooker*:[111]

> '... *laches* and estoppel are well established equitable doctrines. However, at least in a case such as this, I am not convinced that acquiescence adds anything to estoppel and *laches*. The classic example of proprietary estoppel, standing by whilst one's neighbour builds on one's land believing it to be his property, can be characterised as acquiescence: see per Oliver J in *Taylor Fashions Ltd v Liverpool Victoria Trustees Co Ltd (Note)*.[112] Similarly, *laches*, failing to raise or enforce an equitable right for a long period, can be characterised as acquiescence.'

11.102 The 'founding principle' of what amounts to *laches* was stated by The Lord Chancellor, Lord Selborne in 1874 in this way:

> 'Now the doctrine of *laches* in Courts of Equity is not an arbitrary or a technical doctrine. Where it would be practically unjust to give a remedy, either because a party has, by his conduct, done that which might fairly be regarded as equivalent to a waiver of it, or where by his conduct and neglect he has, though perhaps not waiving that remedy, yet put the other party in a situation in which it would not be reasonable to place him if the remedy were afterwards to be asserted, in either of these cases lapse of time and delay are most material. But in every case, if an argument against relief, which otherwise would be just, is founded upon mere delay, that delay of course not amounting to a bar by any statute of limitations, the validity of that defence must be tried upon principles substantially equitable. Two circumstances, always important in such cases, are the length of the delay and the nature of the acts done during the interval, which might affect either party and cause a balance of justice or injustice in taking the one course or the other, so far as relates to the remedy.'[113]

11.103 More recently, in *Fisher v Brooker*[114] Lord Neuberger stated:

> 'Fifthly, *laches* is an equitable doctrine, under which delay can bar a claim to equitable relief. In the Court of Appeal, Mummery LJ said that there was 'no requirement of detrimental reliance for the application of acquiescence or *laches*', para 85. Although I would not suggest that it is an immutable requirement, some sort of detrimental reliance is usually an essential ingredient of *laches*, in my opinion. In *Lindsay Petroleum Co v Hurd*,[115] Lord Selborne LC, giving the opinion of the Board, said that *laches* applied where "it would be practically unjust to give a remedy", and that, in every case where a defence "is founded upon mere delay ... the validity of that defence must be tried upon principles substantially equitable".

---

paras 5-016–5-019, and McGee, *Limitation Periods*, Chapter 3, paras 3.014–3.012. See also *Halsbury's Laws of England*, 4th Edn (Reissue), Vol 28, paras 881–884.

[111] [2009] 1 WLR 1764, at p 1780.

[112] [1982] QB 133, 151.

[113] *Lindsay Petroleum v Hurd* (1873–1874) LR 5 PC 221, at pp 239–240 (Judicial Committee of the Privy Council).

[114] [2009] 1 WLR 1764 at pp 1780–1781.

[115] (1874) LR 5 PC 221, 239–240.

He went on to state that what had to be considered were "the length of the delay and the nature of the acts done during the interval, which might affect either party, and cause a balance of justice or injustice in taking the one course or the other, so far as relates to the remedy'.

11.104 A point may arise on the relevance of any defined limitation period which might be applicable by analogy under section 36(1) of the Limitation Act 1980.[116] The issues are as follows:

(a) If the claim is to enforce the terms of the grant directly, where there is a plain breach of the terms of the grant, or reservation (eg user outside permitted hours), the claim may be seen as one based on the enforcement of the terms of the grant or reservation. It may not necessarily be a claim in tort. Thus the analogous period of limitation will be determined according to it being either under seal (to which the 12 year period under section 8 of the Limitation Act 1980 applies) or, if the grant or reservation is under hand, the six year period applies under section 5 of that Act.[117]

(b) If the claim is based in the tort of nuisance (eg actionable interference), the six year period under section 2 of the Limitation Act 1980 may be applied by analogy under section 36(1).

11.105 However, in practice the court will take into account any delay (*laches*) or acquiescence within that period in deciding whether to grant the remedy, which is of course discretionary. Section 36(2) of the Limitation Act 180 specifically recognises this.

11.106 If the right of way claimed is based on long user under lost modern grant, or section 2 of the Prescription Act 1832 ('section 2'), the position would seem to be as follows:

(a) Whether the claim to enforce is based on lost modern grant or under section 2, the principles stated above in respect of delay and estoppel will apply.

(b) If the claim is based on lost modern grant, it may be possible to regard the 6 or 12 year period as applicable by analogy as under para **11.101** above

---

[116] Section 36 states, so far as material: '36 Equitable jurisdiction and remedies. (1) The following time limits under this Act, that is to say: (a) the time limit under section 2 for actions founded on tort; ... (b) the time limit under section 5 for actions founded on simple contract; ... (d) the time limit under section 8 for actions on a specialty; ... shall not apply to any claim for specific performance of a contract or for an injunction or for other equitable relief, except in so far as any such time limit may be applied by the court by analogy in like manner as the corresponding time limit under any enactment repealed by the Limitation Act 1939 was applied before 1 July 1940. (2) Nothing in this Act shall affect any equitable jurisdiction to refuse relief on the ground of acquiescence or otherwise.'

[117] In the discussion of specific periods under the Limitation Act 1980 it is assumed that none of the extension or exclusion provisions in Part II (section 28 and section 32) apply. For details of those see Snell and McGee referred to at footnote 110 above.

and section 36(1) of the 1980 Act as the 'lost' grant will have been presumed to have been under hand (ie not sealed or executed as A Deed – merely signed) or by Deed (ie executed as a Deed in conformity with the rules before and after 1990).

(c)   If the claim is made purely under section 2, the position as to analogous periods under section 36(1) of the 1980 Act is unclear. Because section 2 does not require the proof of any presumption of grant,[118] it seems that no analogous period where a claim may be based on a document under seal or under hand applies. It follows that the only question will be whether there has been delay amounting to *laches,* as discussed above.

(d)   If the claim is based in the tort of nuisance, para **11.104(b)** will apply.

11.107   It is important to note in this context the concept of the interruption under section 4 of the Prescription Act 1832 (see Chapter 6 above) and the need for the claim to be commenced in the year of the interruption, whether or not that claim seeks an injunction, or damages, as the case may be.

11.108   As stated at Chapter 10 at para **10.13** above, and at para **11.101** above, delay may lead to a claim that an estoppel lies against the enforcement of the right of way claimed. See *Lester v Woodgate*[119] for a recent example of this. At paras 39–40 Patten LJ stated:

> 'These authorities, I think, indicate the need to take a flexible and very fact-specific approach to each case in which an estoppel by acquiescence is relied upon. *Shaw v Applegate* confirms that there may be cases where the principle can apply even though the initial interference with the property or legal rights was clearly and perhaps knowingly tortious. In such cases the absence of a mistaken belief of right on the part of the defendant will be one of the factors to be considered in determining whether the claimant's enforcement of his legal rights would now be unconscionable. As explained in *Jones v Stones*, a deliberate act of trespass or nuisance is unlikely to have been influenced by the position taken up by the claimant to the invasion of his legal rights or therefore to have given rise to any detriment on the part of the defendant in terms of the work or expenditure which he carried out. This, I think, is the point made by Lord Cranworth in *Ramsden v Dyson*, although his views are, I believe, closely linked to the relatively conservative approach of the common law as to the circumstances in which a party in the position of the landowner was under a duty to speak. So far as relevant, it is now clear that an obligation to make one's position known is not limited to cases where silence would amount to some form of deception. The commonly accepted test is that set out by Lord Wilberforce in *Moorgate Mercantile Co Ltd v Twitchings*[120] which is whether:

---

[118]   *Tapling v Jones* (1865) HLC 290 (a right of light case on section 3 of the 1832 Act but the principle on which section 2 rests is also that there need be no presumption of any grant).
[119]   [2010] 2 P&CR 21.
[120]   [1977] AC 890 at p 903.

"Having regard to the situation in which the relevant transaction occurred, as known to both parties, a reasonable man, in the position of the 'acquirer' of the property, would expect the 'owner', acting honestly and responsibly, if he claimed any title to the property, to take steps to make that claim known …"

40. If the claimant's conduct at the time takes the form of encouraging the defendant to believe that his otherwise tortious interference with the claimant's property will be waived and not objected to and, in reliance on that, the defendant subsequently acts in a way which can be characterised as detrimental then the position is, I think, different from the facts considered in *Ramsden v Dyson* and the court does then have to decide whether the causative effect of that conduct is sufficient to bar the enforcement of the legal right. In this connection it is important to bear in mind what Robert Walker LJ said about detriment in *Gillett v Holt*:[121]

"The overwhelming weight of authority shows that detriment is required. But the authorities also show that it is not a narrow or technical concept. The detriment need not consist of the expenditure of money or other quantifiable financial detriment, so long as it is something substantial. The requirement must be approached as part of a broad inquiry as to whether repudiation of an assurance is or is not unconscionable in all the circumstances.

There are some helpful observations about the requirement for detriment in the judgment of Slade LJ in *Jones v Watkins*.[122] There must be sufficient causal link between the assurance relied on and the detriment asserted. The issue of detriment must be judged at the moment when the person who has given the assurance seeks to go back on it. Whether the detriment is sufficiently substantial is to be tested by whether it would be unjust or inequitable to allow the assurance to be disregarded – that is, again, the essential test of unconscionability. The detriment alleged must be pleaded and proved.'"

Other points on injunction claims on rights of way disputes

11.109 The order must be endorsed with Penal Notice. See Chapter 12 post.

11.110 Enforcement of any order is under RSC by committal; see para **11.10(d)** above and CPR Part 81 and Chapter 12 below. In so far as any order has a money judgment attached to it the enforcement is by RSC Order 45 as modified by CPR Part 81 since 1 October 2012.

11.111 Insofar as it is necessary to go against assets, particularly assets of directors of companies who are in breach of an order, enforcement of an injunction by way of the issues of a writ of sequestration may be possible under RSC Order 46, rule 5 as modified by CPR Part 81 since 1 October 2012. The fact that assets of company directors may be seized under such an order (in

---

[121] [2001] Ch 210 at p 232.
[122] 26 November 1987.

effect a form of contempt of proceedings) sometimes comes as a surprise to recalcitrant directors and others who seem only concerned to shelter behind the corporate veil of the company in contempt.

11.112 Execution of documents by the court (eg a deed of grant of a deed of relief) of an easement may be applied for under RSC Order 45, rule 8. See also Chapter 12.

11.113 Application can be made in the rare instance where an assessor or assessors should be appointed to sit with the judge; such assessors are appointed under section 70 of the Senior Courts Act 1981 and see CPR Part 35, rule 15 and Part 35, PD, paragraph 10. Application can also be made for court appointed experts to advise on the case under CPR Part 35, rule 7(2); eg where the parties cannot agree on who is to be the single joint expert.

Appeals from judgments

11.114 See Chapter 12.

Costs in claims about private rights of way

11.115 See Chapter 12. See also Part 44, rule 3, applicable to injunction claims.

Timescales for hearings

11.116 Clearly in injunction cases there will be a need for prompt action and a speedy hearing. Interim applications need to be made unless without notice on two clear days notice. See CPR Part 24. The final hearing may well need to be expedited in order that it can come on for hearing quickly in very urgent claims, particularly for injunctions. For lead times on hearing dates consult the list at the appropriate court, or in the Chancery Division on the HMCTS website.

CLAIMS IN COURT – PART 3 – DAMAGES

Introduction

11.117 The cause of action (ie the basis of the claim) for breach of the terms on which a private right of way may be used, whether it be excessive user (see Chapter 4 above) or actionable interference (see Chapter 10 above) is either one based directly on the terms of the grant or reservation, or based on the tort of nuisance. See para **11.130** below.

11.118 Damages for breach of the terms of the grant of the right of way, or its reservation, or a right of way established by prescription (see Chapter 6 above) may be granted either at common law, or in lieu of, or in addition to an injunction under section 50 of the Senior Courts Act 1981. The damages recoverable under either basis should be assessed on the same basis, so that the distinction between damages at common law or in equity should no longer apply with any practical consequence.[123] The distinction between damages at 'common law' and under section 50 (or as sometime referred to 'in equity') is a historic one and a description of that history is beyond the purpose of this book. Suffice it to say that if the claim is brought seeking damages only (without without a declaration) and without seeking an injunction or damages in lieu under section 50, the claim to damages (based no doubt on the tort of nuisance) will be regarded as being a 'common law claim'. If the claim includes a claim for an injunction, and/or damages in lieu, the claim to damages will be based on the jurisdiction under section 50 and may be said to be 'in equity'. Most claims about private rights of way where there has been actionable interference, or excessive user, will seek an injunction and/or damages in lieu under section 50. There are few claims that seek damages only. But irrespective of the way in which the claim is put, it is suggested that there should be no difference in the permissible heads of loss, if they can be proved of course; see the *WWF* case cited at footnote 123.

11.119 The heads of damage for actionable interference with a private right of way, or for breach of its terms (eg excessive user), will include the following, bearing in mind that as stated at para **11.118** above the cause of action is in nuisance:[124]

(a) The diminution in value of the claimant's land by reason of the interference or breach of the terms of the easement.

(b) Financial loss caused by the interference or breach of the terms of the easement.

(c) Loss of quiet enjoyment or amenity caused by the interference, or breach of the terms of the easement.

(d) The value to the defendant of the past breaches such as the unlawful use of the servient land from which a profit has been made.

(e) The value of the ability to claim an injunction to restrain the interference or breach of the terms of the easement. This usually translates into the price of a release. Hence the references in the case to 'release fee' or 'ransom' or 'Wrotham Park' damages.

(f) Aggravated damages.

---

[123] See *WWF World Wide Fund for Nature v World Wrestling Federation Entertainment Inc* [2007] EWCA Civ 286 [2008] 1 WLR 445, at para 41, per Chadwick LJ, for the view that damages may be assessed on the same basis whether at common law or in equity.

[124] See *Hunter v Canary Wharf Ltd* [1997] 2 AC 655.

11.120   For losses to be recovered under any of the above heads, or generally, they must be shown to have been *caused* by the breach of the terms of the easement, or the actionable interference. However, if the claim (or cause of action) is in one in nuisance, damage is not the 'gist' of the action (ie it is not *necessary* to prove damage to be able to sue – unlike in the tort of negligence) and the claim can be brought without proving actual loss. To this extent the cause of action is akin to that in trespass to land where damage need not be proved.[125] In private rights of way claims this is often the case where a future action by the defendant might cause loss in the future, and in some cases the court may presume that such loss may occur. In such cases it may also be appropriate for the claimant to seek a *quia timet* injunction to prevent a future act which would interfere actionably with the right of way or be in breach of its terms; see para **11.69** above. If the breach alleged is one which relates directly to the terms of the grant or reservation (eg a limitation on permitted hours of user), the cause of action may be regarded as either one based on the breach of the terms of the grant, or in nuisance.

Damages at common law

11.121   These will be as stated above, namely:

(a)   The diminution in value of the claimant's land by reason of the interference or breach of the terms of the easement.

(b)   Financial loss caused by the interference or breach of the terms of the easement.

(c)   Loss of quiet enjoyment or amenity caused by the interference, or breach of the terms of the easement.

(d)   The value to the defendant of the past breaches such as the unlawful use of the servient land from which a profit has been made.

(e)   The value of the ability to claim an injunction to restrain the interference or breach of the terms of the easement. This usually translates into the price of a release. Hence the references in the case to 'release fee' or 'ransom' or 'Wrotham Park' damages.

11.122   It will be seen from para **11.118** above and para **11.136(5)** below that the final element at para **11.121(e)** is supported by modern authority as a potential head of recovery in a common law claim.

---

[125]   See *Patel v WH Smith (Eziot) Ltd* [1987] 1 WLR 853. Contrast the position in the case of public nuisance where damage must be proved.

Damages in equity

11.123 When the court has jurisdiction at the date of the issue of the claim form (or service of the counterclaim seeking an injunction, or damages in lieu) to grant an injunction, pursuant to section 50 of the Senior Courts Act 1981, it can award damages in lieu of an injunction.[126] Note that there must be jurisdiction to grant an injunction. So if the conduct of the claimant is such as to disentitle him from an injunction, no damages in lieu can be awarded.

11.124 The discretion to grant such damages is governed by the following 'good working rule' stated in *Shelfer v City of London Electric Lighting Co Ltd*,[127] and setting out the circumstances in which damages in lieu may be given:

(1) where the injury to the claimant's legal rights is small;

(2) one which is capable of being estimated in money;

(3) one which is capable of being compensated by a small money payment;

(4) one in which it would be oppressive to grant an injunction.

11.125 It is clear that the four factors in *Shelfer* do not amount to a 'forensic straight-jacket' for what is ultimately a matter of judgment and discretion in the particular circumstances of the case.[128] But as a 'good working rule' *Shelfer* is the starting point and that was made clear by the Court of Appeal in *Regan* and subsequently in *Heaney*.

---

[126] See *Jaggard v Sawyer* [1995] 1 WLR 269. The date at which the assessment of damages in lieu should be based can be the date before the works in breach of covenant are started; see *Amec Developments Ltd v Jury's Hotel Management (UK) Ltd* (2000) 82 P & CR 286 and *Lane v O'Brien Homes Ltd* [2004] EWHC 303 (QB); see further para **11.124** below on assessment of such damages and the date at which the value is to be assessed. The jurisdiction to grant damages in lieu of an injunction (or specific performance) which was formerly in Lord Cairns' Act 1858, is now contained in the Supreme Court Act 1981, s 50. See *Regan v Paul Properties* [2007] Ch 135 ('Regan') and *HXRUK II (CHC) Ltd v Heaney* [2010] EWHC 2245 (Ch) ('Heaney') for the principles and authorities on which an injunction will be granted.

[127] [1895] 1 Ch 287, at pp 322–3, per AL Smith J. That was a nuisance claim and was brought by both the freehold owner and the tenant of land as a result of the effect on the claimant's land caused by the defendant's generators of electricity which were causing noise and vibration to 'The Waterman's Arms' at Bankside, on the south bank of the River Thames. An injunction was granted by Kekewich J and upheld by the Court of Appeal. Anyone now standing at the southern abutments of the Millennium Bridge and facing what is now the Tate Modern (the former Bankside Power Station) will be very near the location of the parties' properties. The book *The House by the Thames* (Gillian Tindall, Chatto & Windus, 2006) contains not only an evocative portrait of that part of London and its history, but also has a line drawing of the location generally and a photograph of the Waterman's Arms.

[128] *Watson & Ors v Croft Promo-Sport* [2008] EWHC 759 (QB) per Simon J at para 86 (a noise nuisance case). But see *Jacklin v Chief Constable of West Yorkshire* [2007] EWCA Civ 181, referred to below where the Court of Appeal required all four conditions in *Shelfer* to be met. It is suggested that *Jacklin* (as the higher authority) is to be preferred. It seems that Jacklin was not cited in *Watson* as *Jacklin* is not referred to in the judgment of Simon J in *Watson*. It is referred to in *Heaney*.

11.126 It seems from recent authority that all the four factors must be satisfied if the defendant is to escape an injunction and be ordered to pay damages instead. They are cumulative. So satisfaction of the first three factors is necessary, but not sufficient.[129] That is why satisfaction of the fourth factor is so important. To avoid the *prima facie* remedy of the injunction being granted, there must be some additional factor amounting to exceptional circumstances to justify an award of damages, such as oppression to the defendant, if the injunction is granted. Hence the fourth factor.

11.127 The burden is firmly on the defendant to prove that the claimant should not be awarded an injunction; see *Regan*, above and at para **11.41** above.

11.128 It is suggested that the heads of damages in equity will be as in common law (see para **11.121(e)** above) with the emphasis on the final element set out there, namely, the value of the ability to claim an injunction to restrain the interference or breach of the terms of the easement. This usually translates into the price of a release. Hence the references in the case to 'release fee' or 'ransom' or; Wrotham Park; damages.

11.129 Thus in conclusion, care must, therefore, be taken to advise a defendant that the idea that he has the right to 'buy off' the claimant with an offer of damages is wrong. It will fall to the defendant to show why the claimant's *prima facie* right to an injunction should not be granted. In effect, the defendant must show that it is an exceptional case and, for example, it would be oppressive to award an injunction against him.[130] Developers and others ignore this at their peril.

General principles relating to awards of damages in private rights of way cases

11.130 As stated at Chapter 10 above, a claim for actionable interference is based on the tort (civil wrong) of nuisance. That requires proof of substantial interference with the easement; in this case the right of way. Therefore, save as below, the measure of damages awarded will be assessed by reference to placing the victim in the position he would have been had the nuisance not been committed. No actual damage needs to be proved, but in fact damages are not awarded unless there has been substantial interference with enjoyment, see *West v Sharp*[131] where he stated:

---

[129] *Jacklin v Chief Constable of West Yorkshire* [2007] EWCA Civ 181, at para 48, per Buxton LJ.

[130] The fact of oppression was the guiding factor in the decision by the Court of Appeal in *Gafford v Graham* (1998) 77 P&CR 73, in awarding damages in lieu. It is clear from that authority and from *Regan* and *Heaney* (above) that some special case needs to be shown by the defendant to avoid an injunction where there is jurisdiction to grant it. See para **11.40** above for the principles on which injunctions will be granted.

[131] (2000) 79 P&CR 327, at p 33, para (4) per Mummery LJ.

'Wrongful interference with an easement is a nuisance. Although actual damage does not have to be proved, in fact damages are not awarded unless there has been a substantial interference with enjoyment.'

11.131   The aim of such damages is to compensate the wronged party for his loss. No loss means no damages in practical terms.

11.132   As stated above, such damages may be assessed by reference either to the loss suffered by the wronged party (eg the diminution in the value of his property caused by the blocking up of the right of way) or by reference to the sum which the wronged party could reasonably have demanded from the tortfeasor (usually the defendant) for the release of the wronged party's rights. The latter is often called, variously, the 'release fee' or 'ransom' or 'Wrotham Park' measure. But in either case the measure is designed to be compensatory.

11.133   There are two possible exceptions to this rule:

(a)   Where the damages to be sought are assessed on a *punitive* or *exemplary*, or *aggravated* basis as a result of the defendant's *conduct*. For example of the latter see *Perlman v Rayden*.[132] This is a controversial area of the law and the reader is referred to specialist works on damages such as *McGregor on Damages ('McGregor')* for a full treatment of this subject.[133]

Such damages are not compensatory. They are designed to punish and deter. To that extent they have a questionable existence in the civil, as opposed to the criminal, law.

In any event it is suggested that unless the facts warrant it (as they did in *Perlman v Rayden*, above) in view of the jurisdiction to award profit-related, or 'Wrotham Park' based damages, which of course are based on the profit which the unlawful party has made, or will make from the breach. (See the analysis earlier in this Chapter.) So it is suggested that to award exemplary damages in a claim based on breach of covenant would be rare where the remedy in compensatory damages is quite adequate and meets the point that a party in breach should not be allowed to retain all of his unlawful net profits, or gains.[134]

It is suggested that apart from bad conduct cases, the only other ground on which exemplary damages could be awarded for a breach of the terms of a private right of way (assuming jurisdiction to make such an order was present) would be where the wrongful conduct (the breach) was calculated by the defendant to make a profit for himself which may exceed the

---

[132]   [2004] EWHC 2192 Ch.

[133]   18th Edn (2009) and supplements. See also Tettenborn & Wilby, *The Law of Damages*, Butterworths, 2nd Edn (2010) at Ch 2.

[134]   See McGregor, (Chapter 11 at para 11-016) where the discussion makes it clear that one day the court will have to decide whether such damages can be recovered in a breach of contract claim, as opposed to one in tort; the latter usually being the case in claims for damages over private rights of way. The speech given by Lord Scott of Foscote to the Chancery Bar Association on 20 January 2006 ('Damages') contains some useful observations on exemplary damages for those who may want to consider it further.

compensation to be paid to the claimant.[135] But as stated above, why should that be necessary where compensatory damages can be awarded to reflect that element of profit?

(b)   Where the damages are based on the tort of malicious falsehood. For further details of this see para **11.190** below.

11.134 Unless, therefore, damages are being assessed within the execptions under para **11.133(a)** or (b) above, the damages must be compensatory.

11.135 As to how damages are assessed in practice on either of the bases set out at para **11.132** above the law at present may be summarised as follows.

11.136 On the basis of recent authority, the principles of assessment of damages for breach of the terms of a private right of way (including actionable interference) can be stated thus:

(1)   It is axiomatic that any award of damages for breach of covenant should be *compensatory* in its aim and based on the theory that the claimant should be put into the position he would be in had the tort or breach of the terms not occurred.[136] This will be referred to below as 'the breach'.

(2)   *Prima facie* the measure will be based on the diminution in value of the land served by the easement of way by reason of the breach, whether past, or continuing. The date of the breach will usually be taken as the date for assessing the value of that loss. But in some cases where justice requires it and in claims for damages in lieu of an injunction a later date may be taken, especially where the date of a hypothetical negotiation to value the benefit of the right lost may be taken.[137] In this context, the concept of 'parasitic' damages should not be ignored. Damage to part of the benefited land may in fact cause the whole to be diminished in value. This is a concept which is well known in claims to interference with rights of light and there is no reason why a similar approach should not be adopted where a breach of covenant is the subject of the claim.[138]

---

[135] This is the second category set out by Lord Devlin in *Rookes v Barnard* [1964] AC 1129, at p 1226. For the other main cases see *Broome v Cassell & Co* [1972] AC 1027, *Kuddus v Chief Constable of the Leicestershire Constabulary* [2002] 2 AC 122, *The Gleaner Co Ltd v Abrahams* [2004] 1 AC 628. See also *Borders (UK) Ltd & Ors v Commissioner of Police for the Metropolis* [2005] EWCA Civ 197, at paras 20–27, per Sedley LJ. See also the recent Privy Council decision in *Takitota v A-G* [2009] UKPC 11, where the function of exemplary damages is discussed. (Bahamas.)

[136] *Livingstone v Rawyards Coal Co* (1880) 5 App Cas 25.

[137] *Lunn Poly Ltd v Liverpool & Lancashire Properties Ltd* [2006] EWCA Civ 430 at paras 17–29 per Neuberger LJ and in *Heaney* (above) where the date of the start of the potentially infringing works was taken as a likely date at which the developer would have wanted to reach a settlement of any claims. See also *Pell Frischmann Engineering Ltd v Bow Valley Iran Ltd* [2011] 1 WLR, at paras 50–53, per Lord Walker.

[138] See Hudson, 'Parasitic Damages for Loss of Light', 39 Conv [NS] 116; McGregor, Chapter 6 at para 6-110.

(3) There may, however, be cases where the measure at point (2) is not truly compensatory, either because it does not take full account of what the claimant has lost, or because it does not take into account the value of what he would have had retained, or maintained if the rights of way had not been the subject of interference, or some other breach. The latter alternatives may be translated into the right to enforce the covenant at any time by means of an injunction. But as is clear from recent authority the lack of an ability to maintain an injunction claim may not prevent the alternative basis of assessment referred to at point (4) below from being applied.

(4) In cases falling within point (3) the court may award the claimant a sum which represents the amount the defendant would reasonably be willing to pay to secure the release from the private right of way over his land. That sum may be calculated by reference to a fair percentage of the defendant's profit, or by reference to some other benefit which accrues to the defendant from a release, e g a percentage of the uplift in value of his land freed from the adverse right. What the defendant ought to be willing to pay (and the claimant ought to be prepared to accept) depends on the outcome of a hypothetical negotiation. The features of such a negotiation will vary from case to case. This is often referred to as the 'Wrotham Park' basis of assessing damages.[139] This basis of assessment will enable the defendant to recover damages in respect of past breaches even though the defendant could not establish actual financial loss. In *Amec Developments Ltd v Jury's Hotel Management (UK) Ltd*, the court set out the sorts of factors which ought to be considered. The judge stated at para 35:

> 'I am now in a position to consider the effect of the hypothetical negotiation. It would, in my view, include the following features, though in setting them out I should not be taken as leaving other matters out of consideration:
>
> (a) On the one side Amec is a willing seller, but only at a proper price.
> (b) On the other side, Jury is a willing buyer wanting to acquire the right to cross the A-B line and prepared to pay a proper price but not a large ransom.
> (c) In such a negotiation the parties would proceed on common ground, put forward their best points and take into account the other side's best points.
> (d) The negotiations are deemed to take place before any transgression occurs.
> (e) The basis of the negotiation would be a split of the perceived gain to Jury. That gain would not be obvious, and would be the subject of debate within the sort of variables that I have described above.

---

[139] Following the basis of assessment adopted by Brightman J in *Wrotham Park Estate Co Ltd v Parkside Homes* [1974] 1 WLR 798. In fact the origin of such assessment (being related to the defendant's unlawful profit) is much older and is set out in the wrongful user of land and 'wayleave' cases such as *Whitwham v Westminster Brymbo Coal and Coke Co* [1896] 2 Ch 538, as referred to in *Attorney General v Blake* [2001] 1 AC 268.

(f)   The parties are to be taken to know the hotel's actual figures for the purposes of assessing gain.

(g)   In this case, the extent to which Jury would have been able to build more than 240 rooms if they had to confine their hotel to the proper footprint is not clear. I have already held that they might be able to get a small number more, but beyond that the picture is much more murky, and I treat the negotiation as taking place with no clearer a picture than was presented to me. The parties would have, at those negotiations, the case that I had which demonstrates that while Jury could design a hotel of more than 260 or 265 rooms on the proper footprint, but which did not clearly demonstrate that such a hotel would or could be built. One should not assume that it would; it has not even been proved clearly enough that Jury would have found Mr Stevens' design (or any particular alternative design) acceptable. Jury would be able to make a case for extracting some extra rooms from the proper footprint, that case declining in strength as the number arises. This factor is one of the irresolvable points that would be canvassed in the negotiation with no final conclusion being reached on it in terms of deciding an actual number; but it can be said that Jury would not advance a completely convincing case for 265 rooms.

(h)   The numbers arising from these calculations are also debatable because of a genuine difference of view as to discount factors and yields.

(i)   Amec cannot pray in aid any damage to its own property. It is simply trying to extract a benefit from its right to prevent Jury from earning some more money from a larger hotel.

(j)   The additional land which Jury were seeking was not just a few inches – it was almost 4 metres wide, and the area was 11 per cent of the area of the hotel. That is a significant amount of extra building.

(k)   While militating against any sort of *de minimis* figure (at least), the preceding factor also imposes a restraint on very high figures. For example, it shows why Jury would never pay (and Amec could never expect) Mr Uglow's £2.3 million figure. Mr Uglow may be able to get there as a matter of logic, but as a matter of common sense Jury would never pay a sum approaching £2.3 million for the right to build on a £4m strip of land when they had only paid £2.65 million for the whole plot in the first place.

(l)   Jury's costs figures, while perhaps generally in the right area, have not been proved as cleanly and as clearly as one would expect.

(m)   Jury would be fairly keen, though not overwhelmingly anxious, to have the right to build over the A–B line.

(n)   As important as any of the above factors is this. In any negotiation science and rationality gets one only so far. As the end of the day the deal has to feel right. Some of the numbers that have been suggested by Amec in the course of this litigation, while perhaps intellectually justifiable, seem to me to be way over the top of what Jury would be prepared to pay, when set in the context of the rest of the cost of this hotel.'[140]

---

[140] (2001) 82 P & CR 286, at para 35, per Anthony Mann QC.

As the judge said under factor (n) 'at the end of the day the deal has to feel right'. So there can be no fixed formulae, or percentages or 'tariffs'. This is an important point made also at para **11.140** below.

The main recent authorities on the question of 'release fee' damages are:

- *Attorney-General v Blake.*[141]
- *Amec Developments v Jury's Hotel Management (UK) Ltd.*[142]
- *Experience Hendrix v PPX Enterprises Inc.*[143]
- *Severn Trent Water v Barnes.*[144]
- *Lane v O'Brien Homes Ltd.*[145]
- *Tamares v Fairpoint.*[146]
- *Sinclair v Gavaghan.*[147]
- *Lunn Poly Ltd v Liverpool & Lancashire Properties Ltd.*[148]
- *WWF World Wide Fund for Nature v World Wrestling Federation Entertainment Inc.*[149]
- *Forsyth-Grant v Allen*[150] (noting in that case that an account of profits held not available in a nuisance claim).
- *Field Common Ltd v Elmbridge Borough Council.*[151]
- *Pell Frischmann Engineering Ltd v Bow Valley Iran Ltd.*[152]
- *Vercoe v Rutland Fund Management Ltd.*[153]
- *Stadium Capital Holdings (No 2) Ltd v St Marylebone Property Co plc.*[154]
- *Enfield London Borough Council v Outdoor Plus Ltd & Anor.*[155]
- *Kettel v Bloomfield Ltd.*[156]

(5) An award under point (4) is capable of being made both at common law and in equity.[157]

(6) It is probable that a claimant will be able to recover damages based on the price of a release if at the date of the issue of the claim form the court

---

[141] [2001] 1 AC 268.
[142] (2000) 82 P & CR 286.
[143] [2003] EWCA Civ 323.
[144] [2004] EWCA Civ 570.
[145] [2004] EWHC 303 (QB).
[146] [2007] EWHC 212 (Ch).
[147] [2007] EWHC 2256 (Ch).
[148] [2006] EWCA Civ 430, at paras 17ff.
[149] [2007] EWCA Civ 286.
[150] [2008] EWCA Civ 505.
[151] [2008] EWHC 2079 (Ch) at paras 55–92, per Warren J.
[152] [2011] 1 WLR ('*Pell Frischmann*').
[153] [2010] EWHC 424 (Ch).
[154] [2011] EWHC 2856 (Ch).
[155] [2012] EWCA Civ 608.
[156] [2012] EWHC 1422 (Ch).
[157] This was made clear, at least so far as the Court of Appeal was concerned, in *WWF World Wide Fund for Nature v World Wrestling Federation Entertainment Inc* [2007] EWCA Civ 286, at para 41, per Chadwick LJ. See para **11.118** above.

could not have awarded an injunction as matter of jurisdiction, e g because it was not sought, or because the persons to whom any injunction would have been directed were not parties. Both the Court of Appeal and the Privy Council have indicated (without deciding the point) that where the a party has acted breach of his agreement, the court may award damages based on a percentage of net uplift, or profit ('Wrotham Park' type damages) even though there is no claim for an injunction. This is because such 'Wrotham Park' type damages exist at common law (being based on the principle of compensatory damages) and do not depend on the jurisdiction under Lord Cairns' Act, now section 50 of the Senior Courts Act 1981, see para **11.118** above.[158]

If the court *could* have granted an injunction, but chose not to do so because, for example, such an order would have been oppressive to the defendant, or because of the claimant's conduct, the 'Wrotham Park' basis of assessment under point (4) is available.[159]

(7) As a matter of defining the issues in the Particulars of Claim, or other pleadings, it is *not* necessary either to claim either damages in lieu of an injunction (if the claimant is really seeking an injunction) or to claim an injunction if the claimant is really seeking damages in lieu in a case where the chances of obtaining an injunction are non-existent, or very remote. Thus in the claim form and Particulars of Claim, or other pleadings (e g a counterclaim) within CPR Parts 7, 16 and 20, you simply claim the remedy that you are seeking. What is required is a clear indication of whether the claimant is seeking damages for past injury, or damages in substitution for an injunction; if the latter is claimed, it is sensible to put forward how the 'Wrotham Park' figure, or the price of the release is calculated.[160]

---

[158] See *WWF World Wide Fund for Nature v World Wrestling Federation Entertainment Inc* [2007] EWCA Civ 286, at para 54, per Chadwick LJ and *Pell Frischmann v Bow Valley Iran* [2011] 1 WLR 2370 at para 48(5) per Lord Walker. In *Surrey County Council v Bredero Homes* [1993] 1 WLR 1361, the houses built in breach had been sold off by the defendant developer prior to the action, and the house owners were not parties. A claim for damages at common law was brought. Damages based on a Wrotham Park basis were refused as it was held that since the claimants did not seek, nor could it seek an injunction, they had suffered no loss. Thus only nominal damages of £2 were awarded to each of the two claimants. The Court of Appeal's decision in that case refusing substantial (as opposed to nominal) damages, if seen as being based on a wider principle of the basis of assessment, may no longer be regarded as good law in view of the cases at para **11.141** below.

[159] See *Wrotham Park Estate Co v Parkside Homes* above, *Jaggard v Sawyer* [1995] 1 WLR 269, and *Gafford v AH Graham* (1998) 77 P&CR 73. The rationale of refusing damages based on the price of a release expressed in *Surrey County Council v Bredero Homes* [1993] 1 WLR 1361 was rejected by the Court of Appeal in the last two cases referred to above. Therefore the wider basis of the decision to refuse substantial (or Wrotham Park) damages in claims form common law damages, or where no injunction is pursued (see *Surrey County Council v Bredero Homes*) would now appear not to have survived, especially since the *WWF* decision referred to above; see *ibid* at para 41 per Chadwick LJ. There is an interesting discussion of these cases in McGregor in Chapter 12 at para 12-844.

[160] *Jaggard v Sawyer* above, at 285, per Millett LJ. The clearer the case is put as regards damages in the particulars of claim, the better. See CPR Part 16, rule 4 and the Practice Direction, Part 16, for what must be included in the Particulars of Claim. The same applies to a counterclaim

(8) Multiple claimants, or potential claimants.

It seems clear that if there are actually, or potentially a number of persons between whom the right to enforce the terms of the right of way, and, therefore, the right to receive damages may be divided, the product of the Wrotham Park calculation should be so divided. The hypothetical negotiations (in the context of the actual claim) should take into account the numbers of those who may have a claim to the damages. This was the approach taken in *Jaggard v Sawyer*.[161]

This factor may have to be considered when a developer is negotiating to buy out rights. On the one hand he may not want an open settlement to be used as a comparable (see para **11.142** below). On the other hand he may want it to be so used. He may be in dilemma here. Normally the course to take is to keep any settlements confidential as between the parties to them, but as ever is the case, there may be exceptions.

If a 'release fee' measure is taken in rights of way disputes, how will that be assessed?

11.137 The starting point is to look at the anticipated net profit to be made from the activity which causes the breach, eg the actionable interference with the right of way. Alternatively, the net development value of the land can be taken, that being the amount by which the value of the land is increased by virtue of the freedom from the adverse right.

11.138 The percentage to be applied to that net amount is often conventionally expressed as the 'Stokes' percentage, that being one third of the net profit, or uplift.[162]

---

under CPR Part 20. *Amec Developments Ltd v Jury's Hotel Management (UK) Ltd* (2001) 82 P&CR 286, was a claim where the issue was over damages only; the matter being heard as an inquiry into damages under Lord Cairns' Act, the claimant not having pursued the claim in the writ as issued for an injunction.

[161] [1995] 1 WLR 269. See *Small v Oliver & Saunders (Developments) Ltd* [2006] EWHC 1293 (Ch) at paras 90–99; *WWF World Wide Fund for Nature v World Wrestling Federation Entertainment Inc* [2007] EWCA Civ 286, at para 78.

[162] See *Stokes v Cambridge Corporation* (1961) 13 P&CR 77. *See Amec Developments v Jury's Hotel Management (UK) Ltd* (2000) 82 P&CR 286, and *Heaney* (above) referred to at para **11.123** above, for the factors which ought to be considered by the hypothetical negotiators and the 'reality check' which should be applied to any resulting figures. *Stokes* was in fact not a case about damages for breach of covenant, but rather a compulsory purchase case, where unless access to the land being acquired could be achieved, that land could not be developed. So it was necessary to work out the notional price payable to the owner of the access land (which happened to be the acquiring authority) in order to assess that cost and take that into account when assessing the compensation payable for the land being acquired. The 33.3 per cent figure (as a percentage of the eventual profit which the landowner might achieve – with the access) was taken against the background that: (i) the exact proportion of the eventual profit which the landowner would pay for the access was 'a matter for conjecture', (ii) half was too much, and (iii) the owner of the access way would not contribute to the cost of making the access road.

11.139 The percentage is not, however, immutable. It must be a fair one; see para **11.136** above. It is wrong to take one-third as the percentage in all cases.

11.140 The following fluctuations are recorded in the reported authorities:

(a) 'High Water Mark' 50 per cent (*Re SJC Construction Co Ltd's Application*)[163]

(b) 'Low Water Mark' 5 per cent (*Wrotham Park Estate Co v Parkside Homes*).[164]

11.141 In other cases it may be difficult (if not wrong) to apply a *Stokes* percentage and other percentages are taken. For example:

(a) In *Gafford v Graham*[165] the Court of Appeal made an award of £25,000 based on the income generated by the business being carried on breach and the marriage value between the land and the business, that being a realistic guide to what the claimant would have demanded for a relaxation of the covenants.

(b) In *Jaggard v Sawyer*[166] the sum awarded as a fair ransom price was £6,250, where the injury to the claimant was small and where there was no element of speculative development.

(c) In *Tamares (Vincent Square) Ltd v Fairpoint Properties (Vincent Square) Ltd*[167] the stress was on the percentage being a 'fair' one; which in the result was about one-third of the net value of the area of the development which caused the actionable interference with light.[168]

11.142 In practice, the claimant should be warned against over-estimating his expectation of recovery of a *Stokes* payment. The stress is on what is the value of the wrongful use (e g in breach of covenant) to this defendant and not some

---

[163] (1975) 29 P&CR 322. An application to modify a covenant under the LPA 1925, s 84(1) where the issue was the compensation payable for such modification. See further *Winter v Traditional and Contemporary Contracts* [2007] EWCA Civ 1088. The use of the reference to 'high and low water marks' was referred to by Carnwath LJ (at para 27) in that case to show that the percentage of net uplift in value is not fixed, and will certainly not always be determined at the 'Stokes' 33.3 per cent.

[164] [1974] 1 WLR 798.

[165] (1998) 77 P&CR 73.

[166] [1995] 1 WLR 262.

[167] [2007] EWHC 212 (Ch). See also *Field Common Ltd v Elmbridge Borough Council* [2008] EWHC 2079 (Ch) at paras 93–170, per Warren J, for recent example of the evidence set out in a hypothetical negotiation. *Lunn Poly Ltd v Liverpool & Lancashire Properties Ltd* [2006] EWCA Civ 430, is also important in this context as it makes clear the time at which the hypothetical negotiation is to take place and the assumed facts in that negotiation.

[168] See also *Heaney* (above) at paras 86ff of the judgment when assessing damages in lieu of the injunction in a case of interference with rights of light.

hypothetical parties.[169] From the defendant's point of view he may be concerned, particularly in the context of speculative development, where time and money is at a premium, to reach a quick settlement, and he can at least point to the low percentage in *Wrotham Park*. It may be that if there have been payments in settlement of claims by other parties entitled to enforce these can be used as a precedent to show what the 'market value' of the release will be.[170] In practice, both sides need to get their respective surveyors together to see if a sum can be agreed. It is in this context that the importance of testing the outcome of the hypothetical (if not actual) negotiation against the words of the judge in *Amec v Jury's Hotel*[171] that 'at the end of the day the deal has to feel right' is stressed. It is in this context that pre-claim (protocol) letters can be helpful as they can be used to set out the figures which a potential claimant will be seeking and their basis; without prejudice of course to any claim for an injunction.[172]

11.143 The sum must not be so large that it would deter or prevent the development from being carried out.[173]

Interest on damages in private rights of way claims

11.144

(a) Interest on damages may be awarded at the court's discretion under either section 35A of the Senior Courts Act 1981 (if the claim is determined in the High Court) or under section 69 of the County Courts Act 1984. The rate and the period for which interest is ordered is discretionary. It is not limited to the rate used in personal injury claims.

(b) The Special Account rate (tracking Bank of England Base Rates by a margin of between 0%–2.7%) should be chosen as the rate. This is because

---

[169] See *Field Common Ltd v Elmbridge Borough Council* [2008] EWHC 2079 (Ch), at paras 77–78, per Warren J.

[170] This was the approach adopted in *Marine & General Mutual Life Assurance Society v St James' Real Estate Co Ltd* [1991] 2 EGLR 178 (a right of light claim) where the court used a figure reached in settlement with another person affected by the interference (not a party to the claim) as good evidence to support the 'release fee' figure.

[171] See para **11.136(4)** above.

[172] Tactically, defendants can also use pre-claim letters to tempt claimants or their advisers into making *open* statements that they will accept money in lieu of an injunction; for the effect of this, see *Gafford v Graham* (1998) 77 P&CR 73, at para **11.38** above. Of course, communications marked without prejudice will be within the cloak of privilege and cannot be used in court. It is vital to ensure that the protection of such privilege is maintained once used so chains of emails must be marked 'without prejudice'. For authority on what is needed to make any change of status from open to without prejudice and *vice versa*, see *Cheddar Valley Engineering Ltd v Chaddlewood Homes Ltd* [1992] 1 WLR 820, and see CPR Part 31 on disclosure of documents referred to at Chapter 12, paras **12.66** and **12.67** below.

[173] *Tamares (Vincent Square) Ltd v Fairpoint Properties (Vincent Square) Ltd* [2007] EWHC 212 (Ch), [2007] 1 WLR 2148.

the aim of such an award is to compensate the successful party for the fact that that particular party had been kept out of his money which ought to have been paid to him.

(c)   The recent decision of Ramsey J in *Hanifa Dobson & Ors v Thames Water Utilities Ltd*[174] refers to the authorities and on the principles to be applied when awarding interest on damages for nuisance.

(d)   As the gist of a claim for wrongful interference with a private right of way, or excessive user, is based on a claim in nuisance, those principles should apply to this type of claim. The same principles as to interest should also, it is suggested, apply whether damages are awarded at common law or in equity.

Practice and procedure

11.145   See Chapter 12 below.

Limitation in damages claims where there is a breach concerning a private right of way

11.146   The position, in summary, is as follows:

(a)   The claim will be in the tort of nuisance (see para **11.130** above) so the six year period from the date of the accrual of the cause of action will apply under section 2 of the Limitation Act 1980. It is thought unlikely that the extended periods provided for by section 14A of the 1980 Act apply to the tort of nuisance, as opposed to negligence.[175]

(b)   The likelihood will be that the actionable interference to the private right of way will be regarded as a continuing tort (eg while the obstruction is still there) so that the cause of action under section 2 accrues from day to day, and thus until a claim is brought the six year period will continue to move forward on a daily basis. But care must be taken in the case of a 'one off' breach, possibly not a nuisance, but, for example an excessive user. There, the six year period may accrue on the date in question and remain fixed. It has to be said that in most private rights of way disputes the obvious consequences of interference etc leads to claims being issued well within any six year period of limitation.

(c)   As pointed out at para **11.50** above, claims for injunctions and damages in lieu are governed by the equitable rules of *laches* and acquiescence. These principles do not apply to damages claims directly and if damages are

---

[174]   [2012] EWHC 986 (TCC). See also McGregor, Damages, 18th Edn, Ch 15. For the Special Account rate see Court Funds Rules 2011, SI 2011/1734, and for the rules as to the pleading of interest see CPR Part 16, r 4.

[175]   See McGee, *Limitation Periods*, 6th Edn, Chapter 6, para 6.006.

sought simply at common law. However, if damages are sought in lieu of an injunction under section 50 of the Senior Courts Act 1981, the principles of *laches* and acquiescence will apply to any damages claim so brought.[176]

(d)   The periods set out in the 1980 Act may be postponed in cases of fraud, concealment, or mistake; see section 32.

Other points on damages claims in rights of way disputes

11.147   Evidence. See Chapter 12 below for points on evidence, particularly from experts and on valuation of losses.

11.148   Repair of the way. Where there is no obligation to repair the right of way (see Chapters 3 and 4 above and Chapter 10) consider the appropriate measure for the assessment of damages in the claim in nuisance for the effect of the non-repair as an actionable interference. This may not necessarily be linked to the cost of repairing the right of way, but may be linked to possible loss in value of the dominant property by reason of the difficulty of access. If there is an obligation to repair imposed the right of way the measure will effectively be for breach of the covenant to maintain etc. the right of way, which will be the cost of the repair etc.

11.149   In cases of complexity as to the assessment of damages consider the need for assessors, or court appointed experts, see CPR Part 35, rules 7 and 8 and 15.

Appeals in damages claims

11.150   See Chapter 12 below.

Costs in damages claims

11.151   See Chapter 12 below. Note the use of Part 36, or costs offers in 'Calderbank' form will be of special importance in damages claims.

Timescales for hearings in damages claims

11.152   See para **11.116** above. Damages claims are usually of no special urgency and, therefore, a case for expedition of the hearing will not normally be made out. Interim awards of damages may be made under CPR Part 25, rule 1(K) and rule 6.

---

[176]   See *Pell Frischmann Engineering Ltd v Bow Valley Iran Ltd* [2011] 1 WLR, at para 54, per Lord Walker, where the effect of delay on the amount of damages to be awarded under section 50 is considered. It is clear that the effect of 'extraordinary' delay is a reason to moderate damages which are 'quasi equitable' in nature.

ADJUDICATION OF PRIVATE RIGHTS OF WAY DISPUTES BY THE ADJUDICATOR TO HER MAJESTY'S LAND REGISTRY

11.153   This is not a detailed text on this jurisdiction. For the full analysis of the adjudication procedure see Chapter 48 of Ruoff and Roper, *Registered Conveyancing,* Looseleaf, (Sweet and Maxwell) and the *Practical Guide to Land Registry Adjudication*, Brilliant and Michell (2012).

Note the reference to the procedural changes due to take place in 2013 referred to in the Preface.

11.154   This is a fast developing area of law. Those considering seeking the resolution of disputes over rights of way by this means should have regard, not only to the most up to date version of Ruoff & Roper but also to the Land Registry's and the adjudicator's websites, including in particular the decisions found on the latter, www.ahmlr.gov.uk and also at www.bailii.org.[177]

11.155   A Note on the decisions of the adjudicators under this jurisdiction:

The decisions of the adjudicators are not binding as between themselves. But just as in the Upper Tribunal (Lands Chamber) when the President's or Members' decisions under section 84(1) of the LPA 1925 are being referred to in other applications under that jurisdiction, the significance of each decision by an adjudicator is that it is a worked example of the application of the 2002 Act and the Rules made under it and an example of how the jurisdiction has been exercised in that case. The aim is to create a body of principles for future use. It is also the case that, as with the decisions of the Lands Chamber, each case will usually turn on its own facts. Any decisions by the High Court, or Court of Appeal following appeals from the adjudicator will be binding on the latter as a matter of precedent. (See *Knights Construction (March) Ltd v Roberto Mac Ltd*[178]).

11.156   For those who may want to see the way in which the jurisdiction has been exercised in just four recent cases concerning private right of way you could refer to:

* *Fordham v Edscer.*[179]

---

[177]   The major difficulty with finding decisions on the AHMLR website is that there is no easy way to search specifically for rights of way cases other than under category 8 'easements' or the far wider category 2 'alteration and rectification of the register'. There may be other categories which might produce decisions in rights of way disputes, so the process of searching is rather slow and cumbersome and may not be as exhaustive as one may wish. The Bailii list is not a complete record, but it is possible to see the subject matter more easily. Since 2011 the adjudicators' decisions are cited under the citation reference 'EWLandRA' with the year of the decision preceding that citation and the internal adjudication reference at the end. Before that date the cases are cited only by the year of decision and the internal adjudication reference.
[178]   [2009] under adjudicator's ref 2009/1459.
[179]   [2009] ref 2008/0083.

- *Courtney v Cobb.*[180]

- *Laughton v Naylor.*[181]

- *Brown v Collins.*[182]

Background and jurisdiction

Background

11.157 It is important to note the separation between the Land Registry (acting by the registrar usually located at the relevant District Land Registry) and office of the adjudicator to HM Land Registry. The latter office is quite independent from the former.

11.158 In the context of disputes over rights of way, the jurisdiction of the adjudicator is important and is a valuable alternative to cases which might otherwise come have to before the County Court, or High Court.

11.159 In many cases where rights of way are being disputed, particularly as to whether they can be asserted, or where there is an issue over abandonment, the right course to adopt is to consider this jurisdiction first. The advantages are set out below at para **11.181**.

Jurisdiction

11.160 *Note: Changes in procedure under the rules that govern Adjudications are due to come into force in 2013.*

See the Preface for the details of those changes so far as they are known at the time of writing; October 2012.

11.161 Jurisdiction is conferred by section 73 of the Land Registration Act 2002, 'the 2002 Act'. Section 73(7) is particularly in point as it is this provision which obliges the registrar to refer the matter in dispute (usually being an objection to an application to alter the register – eg by the noting of or removal of an entry relating to a right of way – using form AP1) to the adjudicator. Until the objection has been disposed of, the registrar may not determine the application which is the subject of the objection. The application is an important event where, for example, a question arises as to the date when the applicant made the application. This issue can arise under sections 2 and 4 of the Prescription Act 1832; 'the 1832 Act' (see Chapter 6 above at para **6.32**ff). It has been held (in *Wilkin & Sons Ltd v Agricultural Facilities Ltd* [2012] EWLandRA 0420, 10 April 2012) that the date of the application is the relevant date under section 4 of the 1832 Act in order to define when the 'suit

---

[180]   [2010] ref 2009/1434.
[181]   [2010] ref 2009/0239.
[182]   [2011] EWLandRA 2009_1013.

of action' arose and from which the 20 year period will be calculated back and also for the purposes of any interruption; see also para **11.169** below. The date is the entry of the disputed application in the Day List at the Registry.

11.162   The reference then proceeds as follows:

(a)   Once the matter is referred to the adjudicator this is effectively the commencement of separate proceedings and the matter is thereafter outside the Land Registry itself. Note that 'the matter' will include not just the determination of whether the applicant has the relevant right or claim which is the subject of the reference and the adjudication, but also whether, and if so how, an entry should be made on the register of title to protect that right or claim. (See *Jayasinghe v Liyanage*,[183] where Briggs J stated at para 16:

> '16. It follows in my judgment that what has to be referred to the adjudicator under section 73(7) , where an objection which is not obviously groundless cannot be disposed of by agreement, is not merely the question whether the applicant has a relevant right or claim, but the additional question whether the entry of a restriction is necessary or desirable for the purpose of protecting that right or claim. Both of those questions fall within what is described in section 73(7) as "the matter" to be referred to the adjudicator.
>
> 17. It is also apparent from section 73(5) to (7) that determination of the application for the restriction, where there has been an objection, requires the objection to be "disposed of". The disposal of the objection is therefore an integral part of the matter referred to the adjudicator under section 73(7).
>
> 18. It follows from that analysis that the precise nature of the adjudicator's function on any particular reference under section 73(7) will be significantly affected by an examination of the precise restriction sought, the nature of the claim or right thereby sought to be protected, and the basis of the objection which has led to the reference. It is plain from section 110(1) that the adjudicator is given a broad discretion, on a reference under section 73(7) , whether to decide "a matter" himself, or to require it to be decided in a competent court, and it is equally plain from the panoply of procedural powers given to the adjudicator under the Practice and Procedure Rules that a decision to decide a matter himself may properly involve a trial, rather than merely a summary review directed merely to the question whether an asserted claim is reasonably arguable.'

(b)   Rectification of the register under section 65 and schedule 8 to the Land Registration Act 2002 and the payment of indemnity under section 103 of and schedule 8 to the Land Registration Act 2002 is also dealt with by the adjudication route, which must be taken in the first instance.

---

[183]   [2010] 1 WLR 2106, at p 2111.

(c) Therefore, errors on the register in respect (for example) of the noting of rights of way whether on the dominant and servient tenement will of course, at least in the first instance, be referred to the adjudicator for his decision.

(d) Finally, as to who may be party to the adjudication, whilst section 73(1) of the 2002 Act provides that 'subject to subsections (2) and (3), anyone may object to an application to the registrar', it seem clear from recent authority, namely *Wells v Pilling Parish Council*[184] that only those with a private law right (e g as to the right of way) should be parties. The fact that private rights (or possible the absence of them) are recorded (or not recorded) in a public register affects the fundamental nature of the rights and the standing of those who should be party to an adjudication; see *Wells v Pilling Parish Council* (above) at paras 14 and 18 per Lewison J. However, some adjudicators have decided that *Wells v Pilling Parish Council* is not binding on them and that questions of standing may still be decided in favour of those who may not have an estate, right, or interest in the title concerned; see Ruoff & Roper at 48.014 for the discussion of this present controversy. The provisions of section 77(1) of the 2002 Act which impose a duty to act reasonably on (*inter alia*) those who have a right to object to an application to the registrar, with a liability in damages to those who suffer damage by a breach of that duty by virtue of section 77(2) thereof, should also be borne in mind when considering who may have a valid interest in objecting to an application or adjudication. In any event, where there is a question over parties or their standing, the adjudicator has a discretion as to how to proceed taking into account the overriding objective in rule 3 of the Procedure Rules and to add or substitute the appropriate respondent under rule 24 of those Rules. For example if an application (made under Land Registry Form AP1) to enter notice of a private right of way over the land owned in fee simple by A was opposed not by A, but by B, who was simply a residuary legatee under A's will, B should not have standing as an objector. (See *Kent County Council v Fremlin*[185] (Mr Adjudicator Mark) for an example of the way in which the discretion under rules 3 and 24 of the Procedure Rules).

Procedure

11.163 If the parties cannot agree term to allow the application (or have it withdrawn) the initial reference from the registrar to the adjudicator is governed by the Land Registration (Referral to the adjudicator to Her Majesty's Land Registry) Rules 2003, SI 2003/2114, 'the Referral Rules'.

*See the Note at para **11.160** above as to future rule changes.*

---

[184] [2008] EWHC 556 (Ch).
[185] [2011] EWLandRA 2010_0756.

11.164 Rule 3 of the Referral Rules sets out the procedure for referral to the adjudicator.

11.165 The adjudicator then issues the notification to the parties under the Procedure Rules referred to below. Once the matter is referred to the adjudicator neither party can terminate the reference as a unilateral act. However, the parties may come to a consensual agreement which resolves the parties' differences. In addition the beneficiary of the claimed right (eg the benefit of the right of way) can withdraw its objection to the case being advanced by the other party, eg the objection to the cancellation of a unilateral notice under which a right of way is claimed is withdrawn. But even in such a case the adjudicator is still obliged to make a decision on the reference. These principles were clearly stated by the Court of Appeal in *Silkstone v Tatnall*.[186] At para 48ff Rimer LJ gave the following guidance for use in these types of case:

> '48 I would summarise the position in my own words as follows. A reference to an adjudicator of a "matter" under section 73(7) confers jurisdiction upon the adjudicator to decide whether or not the application should succeed, a jurisdiction that includes the determination of the underlying merits of the claim that have provoked the making of the application. If the adjudicator does not choose to require the issue to be referred to the court for decision, he must determine it himself. In the case of an application under section 36 to which an objection has been raised, the relevant issue will be the underlying merits of the claim to register the unilateral notice. Neither party can by his unilateral act (including by his expressed withdrawal of his application, objection or case) bring the reference to an end. Equally, neither party can be compelled to advance a case to the adjudicator that he no longer wishes to advance. A party who conveys such a wish to the adjudicator can be regarded as conveying his wish to "withdraw" his application, objection or case but it is then for the adjudicator to rule in his discretion as to how to deal with any such withdrawal. That will require a consideration of all the circumstances.
>
> 49 It may perhaps, particularly at the early stage of a reference, be regarded by the adjudicator as just simply to permit the withdrawal and to make an order terminating the reference, making any appropriate direction to the registrar and dealing with costs. If the order says no more, it would no doubt leave an objector free to revive the same claim. That may not necessarily be unjust.
>
> 50 In other cases, particularly when the reference is significantly advanced, to deal with a withdrawal on terms like that may be unjust. It may still be appropriate in such cases for the adjudicator to terminate the reference but he may consider it just to do so not only on terms as to costs, but also on the basis of a direction to the registrar requiring him to reject any future applications of a specified kind from the withdrawing party (see rule 41(2) of the AR). The imposition of such a direction is not a matter that requires the consent of the withdrawing party. It may in other cases, particularly those in which the reference is far advanced, such as

---

[186] [2011] EWCA Civ 801; [2011] 41 EG 116.

was the position in the present case, be appropriate for the adjudicator to proceed to the substantive hearing, rule upon the merits of the issue and then make such order as is appropriate.

51 Subject to the qualifications that appear from what I have said, I therefore broadly, and respectfully, agree with the way in which the adjudicator approached his jurisdiction. I would respectfully disagree with the narrower approach to the adjudicator's jurisdiction that the judge favoured.

52 I add this. During the argument, there was some discussion as to whether it is open to an objector, during a reference to an adjudicator, to reflect a change of mind about the maintenance of his objection by applying for a voluntary removal of his unilateral notice under s 35(3). Mr Morshead submitted that the objector could do so. Miss Tipples was more ambivalent about the position but appeared to prefer the view that he could not. The judge's view was that, during the currency of a reference, the s 35(3) door is closed. That was: (i) because as the validity of the objection was before the adjudicator, the registrar's power to permit a removal under s 35(3) was suspended; and (ii) the objector has no right under s 35(3) to withdraw a notice, he has at most a right to apply to withdraw it, whereas the s 36 applicant would be entitled to object on the grounds that as the matter of the notice's cancellation was before the adjudicator it would be unjust to allow such a unilateral withdrawal.

53 I do not, with respect, agree with the judge about that. I do not understand why the fact of a pending reference to the adjudicator excludes the objector's right (improbable though it may be in most cases that he will exercise it) of applying for a removal of the notice under s 35(3) . There is nothing in the Act or the LRR that expressly constrains the exercise of that right during the currency of a reference; nor can I detect anything in the legislation that impliedly constrains it. The removal of the notice under s 35(3) is not, I consider, dependent upon the exercise of any discretion or judgment by the registration. Subject to being the beneficiary of the notice, paying the fee, filling in Form UN2 properly, removal is a matter of right. The discussion in argument about a possible recourse to s 35(3) arose in the context of the consideration of Mr Morshead's example of the objector who, during a reference, has a change of heart and wishes to remove the blight from the applicant's title as promptly as possible. I hope it is clear from what I have said that I would not regard any removal of the notice by an exercise of the s 35(3) right as automatically bringing the reference to an end, any more than does the expressed wish of the objector to withdraw his objection and case. The proceedings before the adjudicator will still remain alive until he has made a decision disposing of them.'

11.166 Once the notification of the reference is made to the adjudicator, the detailed procedure is contained in the adjudicator to Her Majesty's Land Registry (Practice and Procedure) Rules 2003, SI 2003/2171 ('the Procedure Rules'). The key document at this stage will be the preparation of the statement of case by each of the parties under the Procedure Rules, rules 12–14. Of particular note is the need at this stage to list the witnesses which each party will call at any hearing under rule 14(1)(e) of the Procedure Rules.

11.167   Therefore, the summary sent by the registrar to the adjudicator will be the first key document and the statement of case will be the second key document. The adjudicator may direct a claim in court to be issued under section 110(1) of the Land Registration Act 2002 if that is the appropriate course.

Directions for and conduct of hearings

11.168   The manner in which these are conducted is set out at Parts 4 and 5 of the Procedure Rules. Note that the initial burden will be on the party seeking alteration of the register (whether by the addition of or removal or an entry, or its modification) but the burden may shift and the overall result may well be determined by the adjudicator's evaluation of the evidence before him, both written and oral. This is a significant point to bear in mind where adjudications concern private rights of way claims based on prescriptive enjoyment. (See *Baxter v Mannion*.)[187]

The effect of the disputed application leading to the reference to the adjudicator on time running under sections 2 and 4 of the Prescription Act 1832

11.169   Following *Wilkin & Sons Ltd v Agricultural Facilities Ltd* [2012] EWLandRA 0420, 10 April 2012, the right in issue (eg a prescriptive right of way which is being asserted, or challenged under section 2 of the 1832 Act) will be called into question at the date on which the disputed application for the registration of the relevant interest, or other application which is disputed is made and which leads to the reference to the adjudicator. That date is the day on which that disputed application is entered in the Day List at the Registry. See ibid para 113, per the adjudicator to HMLR. That will be the date of the relevant 'suit or action'; see also para **11.161** above. This is also particularly important when considering the concept of the interruption under section 4. See further Chapter 6 above.

Orders that can be made as to rights of way disputes

11.170   These are governed by Procedure Rules, rules 40 and 41.

11.171   In private rights of way disputes the practical outcome will be usually be as follows. The adjudicator may:

(a)   Cancel the entry of the right of way.

(b)   Modify the entry of it.

(c)   Enter a new right of way.

---

[187]   [2011] 1 WLR 1594 at paras 37–40 per Jacob LJ.

No doubt other orders can be made within the rules as the reference admits.

Costs

11.172 This is a VERY important part of the process. These are provided for by Procedure Rules, rules 42 and 43. They are 'compulsory reading' for anyone thinking of engaging in the adjudication process. Consideration of the way costs orders can be made should inform the conduct of an adjudication by any parties both pre-adjudication and during it. Ignorance of them is, as ever, no defence.

11.173 The starting point is that under rule 42(2) the adjudicator may, on the application of a party or of his own motion, make an order for costs.

11.174 The next stage is to consider what factors may be taken into account when making any such order. Under rule 42(3) he must have regard to all the circumstances. By rule 42(1) this will include both pre- and post-proceedings conduct (conduct being defined by rule 42(1)(b)), the extent of success achieved by a party and the representations made to the adjudicator.

The order that can be made as to costs is set out in rule 42(4)

11.175 The order for costs may be directed to be assessed on either the standard or indemnity basis, rule 42(7).

11.176 In short these rules 'mirror' the principles on which costs are ordered in civil claims governed by the CPR; see CPR Part 44, rule 3.

11.177 It is important that parties to adjudications appreciate this and that this is not a 'costs free' or 'costs neutral' jurisdiction.

Appeals

11.178 These are governed by Part 6 of the Procedure Rules.

11.179 With permission of the adjudicator, an appeal lies to the High Court; section 111 of the Land Registration Act 2002 and Procedure Rules, rule 45. Note that there is no appeal to the County Court. The adjudicator may stay implementation of his decision pending the outcome of the appeal, rule 45(1). In practice the Chancery Division of the High Court will hear these appeals.

11.180 Thereafter, any appeal will lie with permission to the Court of Appeal, see CPR Part 52 and onwards, with permission if granted, to the Supreme Court.

Advantages and disadvantages of using the adjudication procedure

11.181

(a) A simple procedure.

(b) A specialist 'tribunal'. The adjudicators (by which is meant both the chief and full time as well as the part time adjudicators) are well versed in land registration and real property matters.

(c) Cost effective.

(d) Deals with a limited issue, eg over the validity of the registration of a right of way.

(e) The adjudicator cannot award damages, or an injunction. However, if that relief is needed there is the right to refer the matter to the court under section 110(1) of the Land Registration Act 2002. The adjudicator can so direct, see rules 6–11 of the Procedure Rules for what happens in such cases. (A party can also bring his own court claim and rules 10 and 11 set out what is to happen in such a case. The aim is to avoid multiplicity and conflict of proceedings.)

(f) This procedure is invariably quicker than proceeding in the County Court, or the High Court.

(g) There is sometimes a disadvantage in the fact that all witnesses, including experts, need to be identified early at the Statement of Case stage, but that should be no real disadvantage given the CPR requirements to put litigation into order at the earliest possible stage.

Limitation in adjudication claims

11.182 There is no specific Limitation Act 1980 period applicable to these claims. So there is no time limit by which a person must cause the registrar to refer the dispute to the adjudicator which might be comparable to a period of limitation, contrast paras **11.99** and **11.146** above.

11.183 There are of course time limits within the Referral and Practice Rules themselves, eg the 28 days allowed for serving the statement of case in answer to an application under Practice Rule 13. But these are not periods of limitation.

11.184 However, there are some time limits and other facts which may apply or be relevant. These are:

(a) Rectification of the register, e g by removing an entry. There is no set period. But of course the longer the matter is left the less likely the right may be able to be asserted if in doubt and be allowed under Schedule 4 of the Land Registration Act 2002.

(b) Indemnity claims. A time limit of six years applies from the date on which the claimant knows or but for his own default would have known the right to claim an indemnity under Schedule 8 of the Land Registration Act 2002 arose, see para 8, ibid, applying the 'simple contract debt' period set out in the 1980 Act. This in turn applies section 5 of that Act.

Other remedies?

Judicial review under CPR Part 54

11.185 This may be relevant in the context of appropriation of private rights of way under section 237 of the Town & Country Planning Act 1990, or under Compulsory Purchase procedure. See Chapter 9 above.

11.186 By virtue of CPR Part 54, rule 5, any application for juridical review must be made 'promptly and in any event not later than three months after the grounds to make the claim first arose'. That time may not be extended by agreement between the parties. This limit does not apply where the relevant statutory enactments specify a shorter time for making the claim for judicial review. This time limit is short and must be observed, especially where, as is discussed at para **11.186** below, an issue may arise over whether a private law declaration is the proper remedy.

11.187 In a case where it may be necessary to seek to challenge the exercise of overriding, or compulsory purchase powers which may affect the continued existence of the right of way there is no specific statutory period beyond that as provided by Part 54, Rule 5.

11.188 Care needs to be taken to check whether either the private law remedy of a declaration or the public law remedy of judicial review is the appropriate remedy. For the full law on this complex issue see the notes to CPR Part 54 in the civil procedure text books, and the textbooks on Judicial review. Recent authority such as *Milebush v Tameside MBC*[188] shows the importance of the need to bear in mind the distinction between private and public law remedies, especially where, for example, the property rights of the parties may be contained in public documents such as section 106 Agreements.

Rectification of documents

11.189 This remedy is one brought in the Chancery Division and either a Part 7 or Part 8 claim (see Chapter 12 below) where it is necessary to rectify a

---

[188] [2011] EWCA Civ 270.

deed of easement or an agreement formally recording an easement in order to accord with the agreement of the parties. Rectification claims may be brought on the footing that the document recording the agreement fails to accurately reflect the parities actual agreement and this is because of a mistake. The mistake may be one which is common between the parties (ie which effectively on the evidence would be regarded as shared) or, alternatively, a mistake which is recognised by one party but, where in effect that party has kept quiet about the error which has crept in to the document. This latter form of mistake is often known as a unilateral mistake and is based on a species of equitable fraud, or estoppel. For full details of the jurisdiction and conditions which are necessary to be satisfied where seeking the rectification of a document see Snell's *Principles of Equity*, 32nd Edn, Chapter 16.

Slander of title

11.190   This is a common law remedy where there has been a statement made about a property right, eg about a right of way.

11.191   The allegation is that the statement is unfounded and is made with malice. There also needs to be proof of special damage caused by the unfounded and effectively malicious statement. Therefore, for example, if in the process of selling his property A discovers that B has made a statement with malice concerning a right of way enjoyed by A over B's land (eg denying the existence of the right without any factual basis whatsoever), A may sue B for slander of title.

11.192   For further reference see *Gatley on Libel and Slander*, (current) 11th Edn.

Applications to restore companies to the register under sections 1024–1029 of the Companies Act 2006

11.193   These types of application may have to be made in the context of private rights of way where it is necessary (eg in the context of defunct management companies) to restore those companies where they have been struck off the register and where (for example) the benefit of an uncompleted contract to grant the right of way has vested in the Crown, either as *bona vacantia*, or is vested in the Crown Estate following a disclaimer by the Treasury Solicitor holding the *bona vacantia* asset.

11.194   Specialist company law works must be consulted under this heading for the details of these types of application. There is a very useful guide to applications under sections 1024-8 on the Companies House website, www.companieshouse.gov.uk, and for those applications as well as court applications under section 1029, the Treasury Solicitor's website (www. bonavacantia.gov.uk) contains court Forms and precedents.

Chapter 12

EVIDENCE AND PROCEDURE

INTRODUCTION

12.1   This Chapter covers two closely linked matters:

(1)   First, the *evidence* needed to deal with disputes over rights of way, in particular the evidence which would be relevant in court or in an adjudication, arbitration, or a mediation to prove, or disprove claims affecting rights of way.

(2)   Secondly, the *procedure* to be adopted when disputes over rights of way have to be dealt with in court, or before the adjudicator.[1] In addition, there will be reference to the way in which material should be presented at a mediation, arbitration, or other formal meetings held to resolve rights of way disputes out of court. In such cases the formal rules of procedure used in court or in an adjudication do not apply, but other rules may.

12.2   Please note this is not a textbook on civil procedure or on the law of evidence. Reference should therefore be made to the current editions of main practitioners' works on such topics. These will include:

(a)   *Civil Court Service* (Jordans, annual edition).

(b)   *White Book* (Sweet & Maxwell, annual edition.)

(c)   *Phipson on Evidence*, 17th edition (and supplements).

(d)   *Hollander on Documentary Evidence*, 11th edition.

(e)   Hodgkinson and James, *Expert Evidence*, 3rd edition.

It is assumed that the reader has access to material on these topics which is up to date.

---

[1]   See Chapter 11 above at para **11.44**. References in this Chapter to 'the adjudicator' mean those who exercise the jurisdiction under Part 11 of the Land Registration Act 2002.

EVIDENCE – THE 'BASICS'

12.3   As a general proposition, the rule is that there is a distinction between *facts* and *evidence*. Thus, it may be a *fact* that A walks over a path from B to C every day for over 20 years, but to prove this fact requires *evidence*. Without evidence, facts cannot be proved. If the fact asserted by one party about A's use of the path is disputed, and other facts are presented that cast doubt upon A's use, that contest must be determined by the presentation of evidence to a court.

12.4   In addition, courts require evidence produced before them to be *admissible*. This means that the evidence must comply with certain rules before the court will look at, or hear, the evidence. Without evidence which is admissible a court, the adjudicator, or an arbitrator cannot find the relevant facts proved. (For example the court will require documentary proof of an express grant, or reservation of a right of way; or in another case it will require evidence to show user from witnesses whose statements are in court and who will attend to be cross-examined on them, unless their evidence is agreed by all parties.) Special rules apply to evidence from expert witnesses. In this Chapter reference to 'the court' or 'courts' will include other bodies such as the adjudicator to HM Land Registry, unless an express distinction is made.

12.5   It may be truism that facts require proof by evidence, but this is often overlooked, particularly in rights of way matters where it is tempting to assume that a certain state of affairs speaks for itself. That is why evidence and the need to prove things by means of *admissible* evidence is so important.

12.6   The standard of proof in civil cases is on *the balance of probability*. This means that if there is a dispute over whether a state of affairs exists (e g whether A used a pathway for over 20 years) the court will assess the evidence for and against that proposition to decide whether, on the balance of probabilities and given all the admissible evidence presented, A did or did not use the pathway for over 20 years.

12.7   Unless the facts are proved, the cause of action or claim will fail. For example, in cases of actionable interference, unless it can be proved that there is an unreasonable interference with a right of way, there can be no cause of action. See Chapter 10 above. This requirement of proof also bears upon the fact that the procedure of presenting cases in the court is an adversarial one. This means that it is for each party to prove his case. The court has no 'inquisitorial' function, unlike Coroners' Courts where the Coroner is required to find certain facts and it is his responsibility to call for evidence that allows him to reach conclusions on those facts. In rights of way disputes and in pretty much all civil claims the court does not investigate the case and call for evidence. It is for the parties to present the best evidence they can and then place that before the court and to test the other party's evidence by way, for examination, of cross-examination of that other party's witnesses. The adversarial system means that parties without legal representation or guidance are often taken by surprise when they discover that it is for them to place their evidence (in admissible form) before the court. The judge does not do that for them.

12.8 It is also worth remembering that the evidence presented to the court must be *relevant* to the dispute. So if the case is all about whether A used the path for 20 years without anyone's consent, the evidence must be relevant to that and not whether A was a good or bad person. In addition, the relevance of the evidence must be set against the *legal issues* which arise in the case. As will have been seen from earlier Chapters, the question whether a right of way can be shown to exist, or whether it does not, and what is its nature, will depend on certain questions of law being answered in a particular way. So for example, if A needs to prove that his use of the path gives him a prescriptive right of way he must satisfy the legal conditions set out in section 2 of the Prescription Act 1832, or under lost modern grant, and his evidence must be relevant to that. So must the evidence of the defendant, who for example may be able to produce a written consent to use the way, which must be in admissible form.

12.9 Thus, without evidence to prove that X or Y as the case is a matter of fact, the contentions of a party to a claim for or against X or Y will fail.

12.10 Some examples are given below as to the evidential issues raised in fairly commonplace rights of disputes.

12.11 Note that evidence and its presentation is not the same as the law and its presentation. For non-lawyers this can be a hard distinction to grasp. For example, a person may say that A has got his right of way because the law says (in broad terms) that 20 years' user gives him the right. But even if that is an accurate statement of the law (which let us assume it is) it doe not get A home unless A produces the relevant admissible evidence which can lead to that contention of law being proved in his favour, on the balance of probabilities.

12.12 There is one final point to note about evidence. As private rights of way cases are heard by a judge alone (it is assumed that no element of malicious falsehood or defamation is involved where a Jury may be required) it will be for the judge to weigh up the evidence and assess it. He will do so observing the following principles:

(a) Is it admissible? (See above.)

(b) If the evidence is disputed, has it been tested? For example by cross-examination of a witness of fact whose testimony deals with that disputed evidence.

(c) Is the evidence credible? For example, a witness can hardly speak of A's use of the path if that witness was abroad for the whole of a period of five years during the 20 years claimed without any communication with A.

Here, the judge will have to assess the credibility of the witness, eg is that witness exaggerating, or is the evidence given by an honest witness doing his best with recollections?

(d)   What weight does the evidence have? Here the judge will have to assess what weight to place on evidence that may or not go to prove the case of any party. For example, if A's claim as to 20 years user is supported by evidence of a host of reliable witnesses, that may be evidence of some weight in support of the claim. Likewise if there is photographic evidence of the state of the path that does so. There may be evidence of little weight where, for example, the recollection of a witness is faint or muddled. In terms of documents the same principles will apply. It is also important to bear in mind that credibility and weight will be assessed against challenges to that evidence and counteracting evidence, eg that a witness has grounds for giving self-serving evidence, or that a document is a forgery, or is incomplete.

(e)   So the key to assessing your client's evidence is to ask whether (assuming it is admissible and relevant) it is going to survive the 'stress test' of credibility and weight and will therefore be of probative value in supporting your client's claim.

      For recent examples of the way in which the court deals with these matters see:

      (i)   *Zieleniewski v Scheyd & Anor* [2012] EWCA Civ 247; noting the importance of the efficient deployment of oral non-expert evidence; see para 34 per Briggs J.
      (ii) *Durden v Aston* [2012] EWCA Civ 636; noting the importance of plans which can often be crucial evidence in rights of way disputes as well as boundary disputes. The two types of claim are often interlinked.
      (iii) *Cameron v Boggiano* [2012] EWCA Civ 157; noting the importance of title documents and not relying solely on topographical features.

EXAMPLES

12.13   A disputes the claim by B that the right of way used by B over A's land:

(a)   goes through a particular field;

(b)   may be used by motor cars;

(c)   may be used for non-agricultural traffic;

(d)   may be accessed to point X.

12.14 A disputes B's claim that there is a right of way by long user over A's land.

12.15 A claims that B cannot use the right of way over A's land because A claims that it has been abandoned by non-user by 50 years and, in addition, a gate across the way has been locked for that period of time.

12.16 Evidence needed in these examples to prove the facts alleged will be as follows:

(a) Documentary evidence, e g evidence of title and any express grant or reservation and of any evidence of an implied grant under section 62 of the LPA 1925, or under non-derogation from grant.

(b) Oral evidence, e g as to long user, or non-user.

(c) Historical or photographic evidence to show the state of the track, or path at periods of time in the past.

(d) Photographic evidence of the current state of the claimed right of way, or of any features on it or across it such as gates etc.

(e) Video or DVD evidence of manoeuvres required to get round obstructions, for example.

SOURCES OF EVIDENCE

Oral evidence

12.17 This will include not just direct oral evidence, but also statements admitted under CPR Part 33 as hearsay and also statutory declarations made under the Statutory Declarations Act 1835 before a solicitor or barrister. Note that the latter are NOT the same as witness statements, or affidavits referred to below. They are simply declarations of fact made by the maker believing the same to be true, in accordance with the form required by the Schedule to that Act, and no more (or less) than that. The mere fact that something is said in a Statutory Declaration does not prove that what is said there is true. Thus in court if the terms of the Declaration are disputed the maker of it can be cross-examined on it and the court can make findings about whether what is said in the Declaration is true or not.

12.18 It is clearly important that any oral evidence shall be given, subject to any direction of the court, or unless the hearsay exception applies, by witnesses who will attend court to give that evidence, on oath or affirmation; CPR Part 32, rules 2 and 5.

12.19 If they are unwilling to make a witness statement, they may have to be served with a witness summons issued by the court under Part 34, rule 3. A summary is usually prepared of the anticipated evidence to be given by the witness summonsed which will be shown to the other parties and to the judge at the hearing. It is of course a factor to be taken into account whether a reluctant, or positively unwilling witness will do more harm than good to your client's case if summonsed. In some cases it may be necessary to call that person, if only to avoid any accusation by one's own client that one was negligent in not doing so; although one must weight up such a possibility and explain to the client the danger that calling such a witness might do to his case. Where a witness is summonsed it is necessary to examine that witness in chief for his evidence in chief to be given orally, as he will usually not have produced a witness statement. (Sometimes the service of a witness summons – which under Part 34, r 5 must be served at least seven days before the date on which attendance at court is required – may lead to a statement being produced given careful handling of that witness by the solicitor responsible for the issue and service of the summons.) A witness who gives evidence following services of witness summons is liable to be cross-examined in the usual way.

12.20 Unless the witness has to be summonsed, the evidence of a witness of fact must be given by means of a witness statement that complies with CPR Part 35 as to content, prior service on the parties and filing in court. Special rules apply to expert witnesses under CPR Part 35.

12.21 Usually the witness statement will stand as that witness's evidence in chief and there is only a limited right to amplify or add new matters to that evidence, CPR Part 32, rule 5(3). The witness may be cross-examined on the whole of his evidence, both in his statement and in any evidence given orally in chief, see Part 32, rule 11.

12.22 Not considered here, but occasionally encountered in rights of way claims, is the way in which evidence can be given by affidavit (Part 32, rule 15) or by examination leading to that person's evidence obtained upon the examination being contained in a deposition and used at the trail; see Part 34, rule 8 ff. The latter is sometimes used when witnesses are too ill or frail to attend court. Likewise, there is power to allow evidence to be given by video link or other means such as by satellite link – Part 32, rule 3.

12.23 Proceedings may be taken for contempt of court against persons giving false evidence in witness statements – Part 32, r 14 and see also CPR Ord 81.

Documentary evidence

12.24 This speaks for itself. However, the usual rule is that the 'best evidence' of a document should be produced. Thus, if the original exists, that should be available for inspection by the parties and in court if required to be looked at by the judge (for example where the plan to a conveyance is such that the right of way is only clearly visible by the drawn lines on the original and where copying or scanning is not clear enough).

12.25 The rules about disclosure and inspection of documents referred to at para **12.67** below should be consulted here.

Specific documentary evidence

Titles, whether registered, or unregistered

12.26 Even in the case of registered titles, pre-registration documents of title if available, may well be of crucial evidential importance, eg to show the line of the route of a way on a conveyance plan which may not be entirely clear on the filed plan.

Land Registry documents

12.27 This will include historic, or closed titles and internal surveyors' reports under Land Registry reference MB16. Any evidence of what was lodged on First Registration of title that will have been retained by the Registry may also be of some significance.

Agents' Particulars

12.28 These are often of background relevance, and often need to be treated with care as they can display inaccuracies and 'puffery'.

Photographic evidence, whether current or historical

12.29 This can be *very* important. Archives such as Aerofilms maintain websites and other records so that this evidence can be produced with their consent and upon payment of their fee. Ordnance Survey evidence is also of potentially high value. The Ordnance Survey will retain not only maps, both current and historic, but also aerial photographs, mapping records and survey records – see Appendix 1 for further information on these sources.

Enclosure awards and tithe maps

12.30 These are often of great value and were of significance in *Benn v Hardinge* (1993) 66 P&CR 246; see Chapter 9 at paras **9.50**ff and **9.56** on abandonment where this case is referred to. (For a useful book on researching this source of information, see *Enclosure Records for Historians*, Steven Hollowell, Phillimore & Co Ltd, 2000 and see Appendix 1 below.)

English Heritage

12.31 Its historic photographic records, especially in major cities is unsurpassed.

Local historical societies

12.32 The evidence that they can produce is often invaluable.

Expert Evidence

12.33 See below at para **12.70**.

Holders of specialist property records

12.34 These will include Network Rail, The National Railway Museum archives, Transport for London, British Waterways Board, Port of London Authority (and other River and Harbour Authorities) The National Trust, Central and Local Government bodies and Public Utility companies.

QUESTIONS TO ASK WHEN CONSIDERING WHAT EVIDENCE TO OBTAIN IN ORDER TO PROVE OR DEFEND THE CLAIM

12.35

(a) What facts need to be proved?

(b) What evidence can be used to prove those facts?

(c) How can that evidence be found?

(d) How can that evidence formally be presented to the court under the rules of the CPR that govern evidence at court?

(e) What evidence will have weight and what will not?

(f) How can the evidence be *tested* pre-claim or pre-hearing? The questions to ask are:

    (i) What propositions of law must be proved by either party to win the claim or its defence?

    (ii) How can those propositions be proved by admissible evidence and in what form?

    (iii) Does that evidence prove the case I need to prove on the balance of probabilities?

    (iv) Where are the strong parts of my case and where are the weak parts and what can be done (if anything) about the latter?

(g) How will proportionality and the cost of obtaining evidence and its relevance be borne in mind and met in terms of ensuring that the cost etc is not disproportionate to the claim, whilst accepting that the claim has to be dealt with justly? Note the overriding objective at CPR Part 1.

EXPERT EVIDENCE

12.36 The rules that apply to the admission of expert evidence are set out in CPR Part 35. There is no attempt here to paraphrase those rules as they are technical and must be complied with if your expert evidence will be admitted at the hearing. If you do not comply with the rules and directions the court may make under Part 35, you will probably not get your expert evidence in; see the prima facie rule that no expert evidence can be called at the hearing without the court's permission – r 35.4(1). It is also the case that any attempt to get in expert evidence late (ie not within the timetable allowed at the CMC (see para **12.70** below) and near to the trial date will be met with resistance because the other party will usually need time to answer that evidence with its own expert, experts are often committed elsewhere so may be hard to engage and the trial may have to be adjourned with the party whose application it is to let in the late expert evidence paying the costs of the adjournment. See also para **12.70** below.

12.37 The question that can arise in private rights of way cases is whether an expert witness is required and if so what sort of expert is needed?

12.38 There is no standard answer to that question and the parties and the court will be mindful of Part 35, rule 1 which restricts expert evidence to that which is 'reasonably required to resolve the proceedings'. Much may and usually will depend upon the nature of the dispute, the value of what is at stake and the costs of experts. In some private rights of way disputes there may well be no need for any experts, eg where the sole issue is the construction of a grant or reservation in a deed. In others, particularly where long user is required to be proved, or abandonment arises and features on the ground over many years may be in issue, the following may have to be called as experts:

(a) Land Surveyors. This is invariably the case in rights of way disputes, particularly when the right of way dispute may also be linked as is often the case to bad boundary disputes.

(b) Ordnance Survey or Mapping Experts. See Appendix 1 which refers to this type of evidence.

(c) Legal Experts (for example conveyancing experts). But note that questions of law and of construction of documents will be for the court. So the role of legal experts is usually very limited.

(d) Photographic Interpretation Experts. See Appendix 1. These can be of critical significance in a case where aerial photographs have to be interpreted, eg to show features on the ground at a certain date such as gates or trackways.

Note: In all cases where expert evidence might be required, consider the question of its necessity at an early stage (often pre-claim) and what is required and whether X or Y is the right expert for the job.

PRACTICE AND PROCEDURE IN PRIVATE RIGHTS OF WAY DISPUTES

Generally

12.39 The reader is reminded that this is *not* a civil procedure book and, as stated at para **12.2** above, the reader is requested to consult civil practice books and other books relating specifically to evidence referred to in that paragraph. The emphasis below is on providing a 'skeleton' of the stages in a claim and also to refer to specific issues that can arise in private rights of way disputes.

STARTING THE CLAIM (NOT IN ADJUDICATION CASES, FOR THOSE SEE PARA 12.175 BELOW)

12.40 Funding the claim whether by private funding, Public (Legal Aid) funding (if available) or under a Conditional Fee Agreement, needs to be considered at the outset. It will be assumed that the advisers to any party can deal with this. Assistance may be had for those eligible under the Bar Pro Bono Scheme see www.barprobono.org.

12.41 It will be assumed that all pre-claim means of settlement have not succeeded.

Stage 1

12.42 If for the claimant, send *the pre-claim protocol letter*, see the Practice Direction on Pre-Action Conduct, especially paras 6 and 7 and Annex A, para 2. This is invariably an essential step to take. Failure to do so may have an adverse effect in costs, see CPR Part 44, rule 3 referred to at para **12.117** below.

12.43 Other points to consider at this stage are:

(a) Consider at this stage if there has been any previous litigation which might present an issue estoppel problem.[2] This means that if, for example, a court or the adjudicator, or an arbitrator has already decided something about the right of way, or if the parties settled any old claim, that may well prevent further litigation about it.

(b) Consider if pre-claim disclosure is required under CPR Part 31, rule 16, eg the potential defendant's title documents relating to the private right of

---

[2] For the modern law of issue estoppel see *Johnson v Gore-Wood* [2002] 2 AC 1 and section 49(2) and (3) of the Senior Courts Act 1981.

way in issue, which he is refusing to disclose, and it is an unregistered title. The jurisdiction is limited to what is permitted by r 16.[3]

Stage 2

12.44 Should the claim be made using Part 7 or Part 8 claim forms under the CPR? As a general rule the choice is based on the following factors:

(a) If there is likely to be a substantial dispute of fact over the right of way, the use of a Part 7 claim form is required. The issues should be defined precisely in the Particulars of Claim, defence and any reply, see below at para **12.45ff.**

(b) If it is unlikely that the dispute will involve a substantial dispute of fact, a Part 8 claim form may be appropriate; CPR Part 8, rule 2(a) (for example a case where the dispute is purely one of construction of the document granting the right of way). The evidence of the parties (such as it may be given the absence of any substantial dispute of fact) will be capable of being set out in witness statements that must be filed and served with such a claim and in response to it. The evidence in witness statements is followed up by the legal advisers with their submissions of law at the hearing. There are no 'pleadings' in Part 8 claims. It is open to the court to direct that a Part 8 claim is to proceed as if it was a Part 7 claim and direct that Particular of Claim and other pleadings be served and filed; Part 8, rule 1(3). This is sometimes done when it turns out that the claimant has used the wrong claim form, or where, under Part 8, rule 8, the defendant objects to the use of the Part 8 procedure; e g where he says that there is in fact a substantial dispute of fact.

There is no special rule of court which requires disputes over private rights of way to be issued using a specific claim form.

(c) Is an *interim application* needed under CPR Part 25 for an injunction? (For example to stop an access way being blocked up and the remedy is required urgently because of the frequent user, or means of escape in case of fire.) An interim injunction will require special consideration before it is to be sought. See Chapter 11 at para **11.35ff** on the remedy of the injunction.

(d) Who are to be parties? Who is to be the claimant and who will be the defendant? Are other joint users, tenants, licensees, contractors and others to be defendants? See CPR Part 19 for the rules as to who will be necessary parties and how to deal with large classes of parties, e g residents on a private estate all using the right of way.

---

3   For recent authority on this jurisdiction (and the inherent jurisdiction of the court to order disclosure), see *Maltby Investments Ltd v Maltby Holdings Ltd* [2012] EWHC 4 (Ch).

Stage 3

Particulars of Claim

12.45 What must be pleaded to assert the private right of way?

(It will be assumed that the claim is issued under Part 7.)[4]

For matters to consider see the Appendix to this Chapter at para **12.176** below.

12.46 In outline, the possible points which may have to be claimed are as follows. Note this is not an exhaustive list and each case must be treated on its own facts. Other problems may be pleaded, such as claims to other easements, or boundary claims.

For the relevant CPR rules see Part 16:

(a) The express grant or reservation. This will be in the documents of title and/or on the register of title. See Chapter 3 above.

(b) If applicable, a grant under section 62 of the LPA 1925. See Chapter 3 at paras **3.48** and **3.76** above.

(c) If applicable, a grant by virtue of the application of the principle of non-derogation from grant under *Wheeldon v Burrows* (1879) 12 ChD 31; see Chapter 3 at para **3.30** above.

(d) If applicable, a way of necessity.

(e) If applicable, an easement arising by estoppel.

(f) If applicable, prescriptive user leading to a right of way either at common law, or under the fiction of lost modern grant, or under section 2 of the Prescription Act 1832; see Chapter 6 at para **6.20** above.

12.47 This is an important note. The pleaded case which asserts (or denies) the existence of the private right of way must contain the *facts* on which the party will rely *and NOT the evidence*. The evidence will go in the witness statements under Part 32 referred to above. For example, if the claimant asserts the claim that A has the right of way over the path, he need merely plead the fact that a deed of grant dated X granted that right of way. The evidence of that grant will be proven by means of the document or the office copies of the title. The same principle applies to a claim based on long user, e g where it can

---

[4]   Note: although under the CPR the words 'plead' or 'pleading' are out of favour and the words 'statement of case' are now used to mean the claim form, Particulars of Claim, defence, counterclaim (Part 20 Claims) and reply to a defence (see CPR Part 2, rule 3(1)) the use of the words 'plead' or 'pleadings' is used in this Chapter as a shorthand way of expressing all those categories of document where, in effect, each party sets out its 'stall' in single documents.

be pleaded that A has used the path for upwards of 20 years without consent or interruption etc within section 2 of the Prescription Act 1832. Those facts can be pleaded. But you should not plead the evidence which supports those facts, eg that Farmer Giles saw A using the path every morning.

12.48 However, it is worth noting that pleadings must contain a statement of truth under CPR Part 22 and making a false statement can lead to proceedings for contempt of court being brought against the party making the false statement, CPR Part 32, rule 14. So the facts pleaded must be true. Also there is power under CPR Part 18 to request that the other party supplies further information of his pleaded case if it is inadequately pleaded.

Stage 4

The defence and (if necessary) the counterclaim[5] which disputes the private right of way claimed. What must be pleaded to create an effective defence or counterclaim?

12.49 For the relevant CPR rules see Parts 15, 16 and 20. For the rule that facts and not evidence should be pleaded see para **12.47** above.

For materials to consider see the Appendix to this Chapter at para **12.177** below.

12.50 As stated at Stage 3, this is an outline of the possible points which may have to be claimed by way of defence to the private right of way asserted. Note this is not an exhaustive list and each case must be treated on its own facts. As stated above, other problems may be pleaded, such as defences to claims to other easements, or boundary claims:

(a) Denial of the grant or reservation or of its effect, eg as a matter of construction, or, for example, section 62 was excluded expressly or because of common occupation of servient and dominant land.

(b) A failure to meet the requirements of prescriptive user, eg a consent under section 2 or an interruption under section 4 of the Prescription Act 1832.

(c) Facts that would negative a way of necessity, or facts that show that the ingredients for an estoppel easement to arise are not present; see Chapter 3 at para **3.88**ff above.

(d) Abandonment, or extinguishment by other means; see Chapter 9 above.

---

[5] Sometimes referred to as a Part 20 Claim because CPR Part 20 governs counterclaims.

12.51 A counterclaim will be needed to assert a private right of way right if the case requires that or if (for example) a declaration is needed to put the route of the private right of way beyond doubt for the future. See Chapter 11 above for remedies.

Stage 5

The defence to counterclaim and (if necessary) the reply to the defence and requests for further information on the pleaded cases and any further pleadings

12.52 For the relevant CPR rules see Part 15, rule 15, in particular, rule 15.3, 15.4 and 15.8, and Part 16, in particular rule 16.5 and 16.7, Part 18 and Part 20, rule 20.3.

12.53 For the rule that facts and not evidence should be pleaded, see para **12.47** above.

A defence to counterclaim

12.54 This will be required under CPR Part 16.5 and Part 20.3, if there is a counterclaim. Otherwise the claimant will be treated as having admitted that the defendant's defence is correct and the court may make an order on that footing, if necessary in default of defence under CPR Part 12.

12.55 A reply to the defence, or to the defence to counterclaim is not strictly required; see CPR Parts 15.8 and 16.7. This is because failure to serve a reply to a defence (or to a defence to counterclaim) does not mean that the claimant admits the matters raised in the defence. If a reply is served by the claimant, even if the reply fails to deal with a matter raised in the defence, the claimant shall be taken to require that the matter be proved by the defendant, ibid rule 16.7(2). It is wise to serve a reply where the defendant raises a point in his defence which cannot be met with a simple 'joinder of issue' as it used to be called. For example, if the defendant simply disputes the claimant's case that A has been using the path for upwards of 20 years, because there is evidence which the defendant has to suggest that A has not been doing so (eg because he was in prison for ten years), no reply is needed. There is simply then a dispute between the parties on the evidence of user. But if the defendant raised, for example, a consent under section 4 of the Prescription Act 1832, it might be necessary to plead in the reply that such a consent was not, for example, in writing. Such a 'new point' raised in the defence may not simply be capable of being met by the old 'joinder of issue' principle. It is also in keeping with the CPR that the parties should put their 'cards on the table' at the earliest time, and in terms of the pleaded case of each party, the sooner each party knows what the other side is going to argue, the better. The same is true at trial when the judge needs to know what is in issue. For reasons that concern costs orders under CPR Part 44, it is also prudent to set out one's case in the pleadings openly.

Further information requests under Part 18

12.56   These will be needed if the pleaded case is inadequate in its particulars of the facts relied upon.

12.57   For example, if no adequate facts are pleaded on which a claim based on long user can be assessed, or if there is no date given at which, or dates between which a Lost Grant can be assumed to have been made,[6] a Part 18 letter and if required in the absence of an adequate reply to the letter, a Part 18 request should be made.

Subsequent pleadings

12.58   It is open to the parties to amend their pleaded cases under the rules set out in CPR Part 17, which should be consulted if that needs to be done.

12.59   No further pleading (statement of case) may be filed, or served after the reply without the permission of the court; CPR Part 15, rule 9. It is unusual these days to see any pleading after the reply. However, in a private right of way case it may be necessary for a defendant to serve a further pleading in answer to the claimant's reply if the reply takes a point which is one which raises a new point and which needs a specific answer. This further pleading is usually known as 'rejoinder'. For example, if in the reply the claimant pleads that the consent under section 4 was in some way invalid, if there is a new point to answer the invalidity point (eg based on the authority of a person to give it), that may be a proper case for a rejoinder. Such a further pleading can often be avoided by amending the original defence. These issues are properly dealt with at the first Case Management Conference; see para **12.63** below.

CONTINUING AND MANAGING THE CLAIM

12.60   At this stage of a private right of way dispute, all parties should know not only what is on the 'label' of the jar containing the case, but what is in that jar in terms of real contents. Under the CPR the parties are encouraged and expected to further the overriding objective under CPR Part 1 by bringing out the substance of the case, not only in the pre-claim protocol letters (see para **12.42** above) but also in the pleadings, or if the case is brought under CPR Part 8, in the witness statements that support the claimants' claim or the defendant's defence to it.

12.61   As stated above, this is not a civil practice book, but set out in brief outline below are some of the main points that the parties need to consider once the initial stages set out at para **12.40** above have been concluded.

---

6   See *English Clays Lovering Pochin & Co Ltd v Plymouth Corpn* [1973] 2 All ER 730.

Mediation

12.62 Private rights of way disputes should be capable of being resolved by this means. See Chapter 11 above.

Case Management Conference ('CMC') and directions at the CMC

12.63 The relevant rules on the conduct of the CMC are at CPR Part 29.

It is likely that most, if not all, private rights of way claims will be assigned to the multi-track, and if brought by a Part 8 claim form will automatically be so assigned.

12.64 The CMC should *never* be regarded as the 'cinderella stage' of the litigation. Orders should be sought at the CMC which should enable the claim to be determined with the right evidence and the correct issues before the court at the trial hearing. This means that the focus should be on getting your client's case in order so that at the trial hearing you will have all the means at your disposal to win the case, or defend it successfully. This also means focussing on the terms of the directions you want from the court so that you are not wrong footed at the trial, e g by not having the right experts, see above at para **12.36** and the rules at CPR Part 35; see also para **12.70** below.

12.65 The questions that should be considered in a private right of way dispute will often encompass the following – although this is by no means an exhaustive list.

12.66 All of these points should be dealt with in a case summary with a brief chronology and draft directions set out; see Part 29 PD, paras 5.6 and 5.7. The orders sought should be agreed if possible between the parties and thus subject only to the court's determination that what is agreed is achievable:

(a) Are there any Preliminary Issues? (Eg is the evidence of a grant by deed at all?)

(b) Documents – what will be the timetable for disclosure and inspection under CPR Part 31?

(c) What witnesses of fact will I need?

(d) Will I need any experts? Who should they be in terms of expertise?

(e) Should any experts be joint experts? (See Part 35, rule 7.) When should the experts meet to discuss and identify the issues in the case and as far as possible to agree any points; see Part 35, rule 12. The court may direct such discussions under rule 12(2) and (3). Note that unless the parties agree the contents of the discussions shall not be referred to at the trial and any agreement by experts must have the express agreement of the parties to be bound by any such agreement; rule 12(4) and (5).

(f) Will assessors be needed under Part 35, rule 10? This is not usual in a private right of way case, although it is sometimes encountered if a Party Wall appeal is in some way mixed up in the private right of way dispute.

(g) What timetable should be proposed for the steps to be taken so far? (Think realistically, especially around public festivals and holidays.)

(h) Stay for meditation. This is often a 'standard' direction and should be effective at a time when all the parties' evidence is in the hands of each party so that any mediation can be on a fully informed basis.

(i) Location and duration of trial hearing. (Bear in mind that the judge may well need a view so the court may have to sit near the site of the dispute. If in the County Court the trial can be transferred to a suitable venue – although the County Court in which the claim is issued should be the defendant's 'home' court – so the trial court location should be convenient. In the High Court it may be necessary (if the claim is issued in out of the Chancery Division in the High Court in London) to transfer it to either a local County Court, or a suitably convenient Chancery District Registry. Finally for disputes in the London area the Central London County Court (Central London Civil Justice Centre) (Chancery List) at 26 Park Crescent London W1N 4HT, is often a sensible choice of venue with experienced chancery circuit judges dealing with that List.

(j) Directions for trial and dates; see www.justice.gov.uk to view and download the current Chancery Guide (2009 and subsequently updated) for a template in Appendix 3.

(k) Costs estimates for each party down to the end of the claim need to be exchanged and filed. (See CPR Part 43 Costs, PD para 6). These are *very* important and are designed to ensure that the costs of the parties are proportionate to the issues in the claim, in accordance with the overriding objective under CPR Part 1, rule 1. As part of its duty to manage the claim the court may make a costs capping order under CPR Part 3, rule 1, and Part 44, rules 18–20 and CPR Part 44 Costs, PD Part 24, para 23A. See also *Leigh v Michelin Tyre Plc* [2004] 1 WLR 846, for judicial guidance on the importance of costs estimates, both in terms of the management of the claim but also on the question whether such estimates should bind the party entitled to receive any costs under an order to the court to the amount in the estimate, or a sum taking that estimate into account. The obligation to supply a costs estimate at the CMC is also regarded as one which continues until trial with revised estimates being supplied if and when necessary to the other party and to the court. The obligation to supply an estimate of future costs is also part of the solicitor's ordinary professional duty to his client; *ibid* para 22, per Dyson LJ.

Note that from 1 April 2013 there will be a new costs management procedure under CPR Part 3 and section 6 of the Costs PD and a new Costs PD 3E requiring (amongst other things) the filing and exchange of costs budgets by each party.

Note: there are *severe sanctions for non-compliance* with orders made at the CMC; see generally Part 29 PD, para 7. These may include striking out a claim or defence (CPR Part 3, rule 4) or for the payment of a sum of money into court as a condition of being allowed to carry on with the claim or defence (CPR Part 3, rule 1(5)) or allowing an extension of time for compliance on terms; Part 29 PD, section 7.4.

Disclosure and inspection of documents

12.67 See CPR Part 31.

Witness statements

12.68 These must comply with CPR Part 32. See paras **12.17**, **12.35**ff and **12.44(b)** above.

12.69 In addition here are some guidance points:

(a) Importance of clarity and relevance.

(b) Use the witnesses' own words.

(c) Exhibits should be relevant and clear if copied, especially if in colour. Black and white copies of colour images, or smudged or badly scanned images will NOT do and are an 'own goal' if you prepare them in that state. The cost of modern high quality colour copying is no longer an issue so as to prevent proper images being reproduced. Accurate and clear plans will obviously be essential in private rights of way disputes.

Experts' evidence

12.70 See CPR Part 35 and para **12.36** above.

Reference must be made to Part 35 and the PD for full details of the rules governing the admission of expert evidence.

The rules about additional experts' evidence and substitution of experts were recently set out by the Court of Appeal in *Guntrip v Cheney Coaches* [2012]

EWCA Civ 392. It is very important that parties realise that it is not possible to 'chop and change' one's experts, even if one does not like what they have concluded.

That case contains a useful summary of the duties of experts in the judgment of Lewison LJ which states:

> '15 Whether to grant a party permission to adduce expert evidence, particularly where the application involves a change of expert, is a case management decision. It is a discretionary decision entrusted by the rules to the first instance judge. The discretion must, of course, be exercised judicially having regard to the overriding objective. But the fact that the discretion was a discretion entrusted to District Judge Payne means, in my judgment, that the issue on this appeal is not whether Judge Corrie exercised his discretion correctly, but whether he was entitled to interfere with District Judge Payne's exercise of his discretion.
>
> 16 CPR Part 35.4(1) makes it clear no party may call an expert or put in evidence an expert's report without the court's permission. An expert's overriding duty is to help the court on matters within his expertise. This duty overrides any obligation to the person who instructs or pays him: see CPR Part 35.5.
>
> 17 Under CPR Part 35.12, the court may and usually will direct a discussion between experts. The purpose of the discussion is to identify and discuss the expert issues and where possible reach agreed opinions on those issues. In *Stallwood v David* [2006] EWHC 2600 (QB); [2007] 1 All ER 206, Teare J correctly pointed out in paragraph 17 of his judgment:
>
> > "Thus, the express purpose of a discussion between experts is to reach if possible an agreed opinion on the expert issues: see CPR 35.12(1)(b). It necessarily follows that the rule contemplates that as a result of the discussion an expert may modify or change the opinion he had previously expressed in his report. In the context of trial management that is a most desirable purpose because it will tend to reduce the duration and expense of the trial and encourage a settlement of the case. Thus, the mere fact that an expert has changed or modified his opinion following an experts' meeting cannot by itself be a reason for permitting a party who is disappointed with the change or modification of opinion to adduce evidence from another expert. It would not be possible in such circumstances to suggest that further expert evidence is reasonably required to resolve the proceedings: see CPR P."

The expert's overriding duty applies not only to the preparation of an initial report, but also to the preparation and agreement of a joint statement with an expert advising an opposing party as well as, of course, to evidence given orally in court. If at any time the expert can no longer support the case of the person who instructed him, it is his duty to say so. Indeed, if the expert forms that view it is far better that he says so sooner rather than later before the litigation costs escalate. It is partly because an expert's overriding duty is to the court that the court discourages expert shopping, particularly where a party has had a free choice of expert and has put forward an expert report as part of his case. He must adduce good reason for changing expert. The mere fact that his chosen expert has modified or even changed his views is not enough. The expert may have had good reason for changing his views. He may have been confronted with additional evidence as in *Singh v CJ O'Shea & Co Limited* [2009] EWHC 1251 (QB). His opposite number may have pointed out flaws in his initial report, especially in cases where reports have been exchanged rather than served sequentially. It is not possible to lay down hard and fast rules. Even if permission to change expert is refused, it is always open to a party to put to the other side's expert in cross-examination, if he is called, points raised by his new expert.

18 What can be said, however, is that a judge hearing an application to change experts must exercise his discretion in accordance with the overriding objective. This means that a court must deal with cases justly. Justice involves justice to the defendant as well as justice to the claimant. It also involves saving expense, dealing with the case proportionately and ensuring that it is dealt with expeditiously. Necessarily, this means that decisions are fact sensitive and case specific.'

This guidance is particularly important in private rights of way disputes where experts are, for example, required to give evidence on mapping, or on photographic evidence and on measurements.

Interim applications

12.71   See CPR Parts 23 and 24.

12.72   Questions which may arise in this type of dispute will be:

(a)   Should I apply to strike out the claim under CPR Part 3, rule 4? (eg as disclosing no case).

(b)   Should I seek an interim Injunction under CPR Part 25? See Chapter 11 at para **11.66** above.

(c)   Is there any other application that I should make under Part 23, eg for summary judgment under Part 24, or in default of defence under Part 12?

(d)   Is this a case where security for costs should be the subject of an application under Part 25, rule 12?

Other pre hearing points

Compromise

12.73   It is never too late to try to settle. Seeking to do so is not (in itself) a sign of weakness.

There are any number of ways to settle a claim. See Chapter 11 above at para **11.11** for the negotiated or mediated way out.

In the context of claims that are running it is possible to consider the following options:

(a) Open offers to settle; these can be referred to the Judge at any stage.

(b) Without prejudice offers; these cannot be referred to the Judge at any stage as they are privileged. For details of the law of privilege see the practice and evidence books referred to at the beginning of this Chapter.

(c) Without prejudice save as to costs offers; these can only be referred to the Judge at the stage when costs are in issue and if such offers have a bearing on the order for costs that the court can make. (These are sometime referred to as 'Calderbank offers' after a case in 1975; viz *Calderbank v Calderbank* [1976] Fam 93.

(d) Part 36 offers; see below.

See para **12.123** for further details on the above in relation to costs.

Note: the reference to 'the Judge' includes any judge who is dealing with the case at the pre-trial as well as at the trial stage.

The use of Part 36 offers and 'Calderbank'[7] letters

12.74 See CPR Part 36.

12.75 This is a complex area of law and practice and the rules under Part 36 and the civil procedure books must be consulted for a full treatment.

DO NOT use the Part 36 procedure unless you are fully conversant with it. It is a self-contained 'code' and it is easy for the inexperienced, unwary, or even lazy litigant or adviser to go wrong when using it.[8]

ALWAYS have the up to date text of Part 36 and the Part 36 by your side when considering its use.

The aim of making Part 36 offers is to protect yourself (or your client) against certain orders as to costs, see para **12.107** below.

Thus in a private right of way dispute a Part 36 offer could be put in terms that anticipated what a court might do in its judgment and if such an offer is effectively 'better' under Part 36, rule 14, the offering party may well obtain his costs, or at least avoid having to pay the other side's costs; see para **12.123** below on costs risks in these dispute.

---

[7] Offers to settle made in terms that are without prejudice save on the question of costs. They do not attract the formal rules under Part 36, nor the advantages of Part 36 when used properly.

[8] See *Gibbon v Manchester City Council* [2010] 1 WLR 2081, where the Court of Appeal described Part 36 as a 'carefully structured and highly prescriptive set of rules'. See also the more recent authorities on the formalities of such offers as analysed by the Court of Appeal, namely, *C v D* [2011] EWCA Civ 646; [2012] 1 All ER 302, and *PHI Group Ltd v Robert West Consulting Ltd* [2012] EWCA Civ 588.

Discontinuance

12.76 See CPR Part 38.

12.77 There may come time before the hearing where for any number of reasons (eg that a party no longer has any stomach for the fight or has been advised on clear terms that he will lose) the said party wants to get out of the claim and discontinue. Under Part 38 the usual rule is that the party who discontinues has to pay the other party's costs down to that date, but the court may order otherwise; Part 38, rule 6. It may be that, for example, evidence emerges from the defendant which was previously unknown to both parties. Whilst that evidence means that the claim cannot be pursued, the proper order might be no order as to costs. Alternatively it might be that if the defendant's disclosure of vital documents at a late stage could have been made far earlier, so as to allow the claimant to take a sanguine view of the case at an earlier stage, the defendant should be ordered to pay all, or part of the claimant's costs down to the discontinuance.

Further directions from the court

12.78 CPR Part 29 makes provision so as to allow the parties to seek further directions and to vary those made upon application being made under CPR Part 23.

12.79 Unless the court dispenses with the requirement to do so, the order made on the CMC will contain a requirement on the parties to file a pre–trial checklist by a defined date to ensure that all directions made on the CMC have been complied with. (See Part 29, rules 2 and 6 and Part 29 PD, paras 8 and 9).

12.80 Some courts (eg the Central London Civil Justice Centre – Chancery Business List) will set a date and time for a *Pre-Trial Review* under Part 29, rule 7 about four–five weeks before the start of the trial hearing in order to ensure that all directions have been complied with and that the case is ready for trial. As with the CMC, the parties' advocates should prepare a case summary, brief chronology and a list of any further directions (which, as before at the CMC, should be agreed if possible) and (importantly) an outline timetable for the trial hearing; noting in particular the stages for each part of the trial (eg if there are multi-issues) and the best use of witnesses' time, particularly experts. Once this is done the trial dates and timetable are fixed by the court in consultation with the parties and their advisers; see Part 29, rule 8 and Part 39, rule 4.

12.81 Finally, what about seeking to adjourn hearings of trials that have been fixed? Parties should be aware that moving the date of a trial that has been fixed is not an easy task. Any such application must be made by a Part 23 application under Part 3, rule 1(2)(b). The grounds must be good and strong ones, eg sudden and serious ill health of a party. The mere fact that the parties have decided at the 11th hour to start negotiating to settle the dispute is not a good enough reason for an adjournment. (Although if the parties are really engaged in settlement talks at the start of the trial the judge will usually allow reasonable time for those to run their course, eg to the end of the first day. If there is no settlement at that point the trial will have to start the next day.) The court must be satisfied that any delay to the trial hearing and the outcome of the case will not cause prejudice to the party who wishes to proceed. Prejudice caused by wasted costs of preparation is covered by the order that the costs thrown away by the adjournment are to be paid by the party applying for the adjournment in any event. A first request for an adjournment is usually treated more favourably than a second, or subsequent one. The latter often take on an air of the party seeking the adjournment wishing to put off what might be called an evil day. But any order for an adjournment will often be made on conditions, in order to secure the rights of the other party and to prevent prejudice to that party. The commonest example of such a condition is that the applicant for the adjournment pays the costs thrown away by the adjournment and in any event and usually within a short time; eg 21 days. These costs will usually be assessed summarily on the application for the adjournment, see para **12.130** below for summary assessment of costs.

Advice on evidence and merits

12.82 It is important that at some stage before the hearing, and preferably in good time, there is a full assessment of the claim. This should be entrusted to counsel, if instructed, or should be carried out by the solicitor or other adviser dealing with the claim. The essence of this task is to check that the evidence is all present to support the client's case, and that a proper assessment is made of the other party's case (and its evidence) in order that a proper assessment of merits can be made. If there are deficiencies or weaknesses these may be able to be remedied in good time before the hearing. An ideal time for such advice is once all the evidence is in following the working out of the directions made on the CMC. Even if a party is in person there is no reason why such a party should not ask a sensible friend to have a look at the matter, or ask the Bar Pro Bono Unit to see if a barrister can review the case.

THE HEARING OF THE CLAIM

Preparation for the hearing

12.83 (See CPR Part 39 for the general rules that apply to hearings.)

12.84 In outline (and yet again bearing in mind the scope of this book) the focus of attention should be upon the preparation of:

(a) Bundles and skeletons; observe the Chancery Guide; see www.justice.gov. uk to view and download the current Chancery Guide (2009 and subsequently updated).

(b) Photographs, plans and models not in an expert's report allowed by directions given under CPR Part 35; see permission required under CPR Part 33, rule 6. (This often catches parties out and permission should be sought at the CMC.)

(c) Plans – are they clear? Is there a common or agreed plan – even if for illustrative purposes only?

(d) Proper clear copies of all documents especially photographs; see para **12.29** above.

(e) Bundles that comply with Part 39 of the PDA and the Chancery Guide. Do not overstuff the lever arch or ring files and do not use dangerous sharp brass clips and tags or treasury tags. Keep bundles organised into separate files to contain for example:

   (i) Pleadings, orders and formal court documents.
   (ii) Witness statements.
   (iii) Exhibits to (ii).
   (iv) Experts' reports.
   (v) Other documents (eg of title, etc) which are not at (i) to (iv) but which may be relevant.
   (vi) Open correspondence.

12.85 If there is to be evidence given with the use of video, film or DVD, this should be the subject of specific directions under Part 32, rule 1, at the CMC. The trial court will need to be told, so that proper equipment can be installed.

12.86 In addition to the bundles referred to above there will be the bundles containing the advocates' (or parties') skeleton arguments and the bundle(s) of authorities.

12.87 It is very important to always keep out of the trial bundles any privileged material and any offers which are not open. Costs offers, whether open, or made under Part 36, or in *Calderbank*[9] terms, should go in a separate bundle which should only be shown to the judge after judgment when costs are in issue.

12.88 In complex cases a core bundle should be produced with the core documents, an agreed plan and agreed list of issues. There may also have to be a 'bible' containing all documents in, for example, date order; eg if the dispute over the private right of way involves a claim for rectification and there are documents in files during the conveyancing transaction, that should be kept in date order.

---

[9] See fn 7 above.

12.89 Skeleton arguments should be delivered to the court and exchanged between advocates or with parties (if any are in person) under the terms of the directions given at the CMC. It is usual and sensible for advisers and/or parties (if in person) to agree:

(a)　A timetable for the trial hearing.

(b)　Issues for the court to decide.

(c)　A chronology of material events.

(d)　Authorities (decided cases) and statutes and extracts from text books relevant to the legal argument to be in a common bundle.

12.90 Materials must take into account judges' likes and dislikes, e g the latter will be present where there are poor plans, bad copies and unwieldy bundles in broken files.

12.91 Client care – where is the court? How do I get there and how long will it take? What will the courtroom look like? Is access etc in place for anyone with special needs? The Court Manager or his staff can help with this. Think ahead!

12.92 There will be no Jury.

12.93 Client preparation before and during the case should involve ensuring that the client and your witnesses are ready on the day and that they have read their statements fully before the start of the hearing. Ensure telephone or email communication is open to those who have to stand by. There are sanctions under CPR Part 39, rule 3 for those who fail to attend the trial.

The hearing

Client care immediately prior to the hearing

12.94 Explain to the client what will happen and in what order. The hearing will be held in public, unless special exceptions apply under CPR Part 39, rule 2(3). It is hard to think of any of the exceptions applying in a claim over a private right of way.

12.95 The usual order of events is:

(a)　The claimant's advocate opens the case. (The judge will have had the skeleton arguments so he will usually be aware of what is in issue.)

(b)　There may also be a request from the judge that the defendant's advocate makes a short opening statement of his case, or clears up any points about which the judge is not clear. At this stage the judge may hold the view of the site, see note below at para **12.96**.

(c) The claimant's advocate calls his witnesses and they are asked to confirm (on oath, or affirmation) their evidence in their witness statements as their evidence in chief. With the judge's permission, that witness may given further evidence orally in chief under Part 35, rule 5(3). They may then be cross-examined by the advocate for the defendants(s). Counsel for the claimant may re-examine, for example to clarify something his witness said in cross-examination.

(d) The same applies as under (b) to the experts whose reports have been put in.

(e) It is open to the parties to agree that certain witness statements or reports may be put in as agreed evidence and that the witness either does not need to be called, or if called to prove his evidence, will not be cross-examined. It is of course up to any advocate whether he needs to cross-examine or re-examine.

(f) Once the claimant has called all his witnesses and experts, the defendant will do the same and the process at (c) and (d) is reversed with the defendant calling his witnesses and experts to give evidence in chief and the claimant's advocate cross-examining if necessary with, again if needed, the re-examination by the defendants' advocate of his witnesses and experts.

(g) At this stage, if it has not occurred earlier, the judge may hold the view of the site, see note below at para **12.96**.

(h) Once all parties' evidence is completed, the order of final submissions will usually start with the claimant's advocate and be followed by the defendant's advocate with the claimant's advocate having the right of reply on any points raised by the defendant's advocate not dealt with by the claimant's advocate. Note that once evidence has closed it is very difficult indeed to get further evidence in and parties should be advised that legal submissions are purely on the evidence that has been place before the court, and such submissions are not an opportunity to bring in further evidence by the 'side door'.

(i) As explained below at para **12.96**ff, at the close of legal submissions the judge will either give a judgment (rare in a case of any length) or will reserve his judgment to another date. If any orders or undertakings have to be carried over the judgment (eg interim injunctions), the judge will make the necessary order to allow them to carry over.

The judge's 'view' of the site of the dispute

12.96 This is often a feature of private rights of way trials and some practical points on the judge's view may be worth a few lines.

12.97 The gathering of the judge with the parties on the site is sometime a fraught event for the parties given the emotional background that may be present to the dispute. But with care and planning and the observance of certain ground rules set out below, it should go smoothly and be a useful part of the hearing.

12.98 If there is to be a view by the judge of the disputed area of the private right of way, it is taken either after opening submissions and before the parties' evidence starts, or at the close of evidence and before final submissions. There is no fixed rule about this and much may depend on the case, the judge and the time of year (daylight etc) as to when it will be best to have a view, if one is needed. It is important for the parties to remember that the view is carried out in order that the judge may have the advantage of seeing the site and appreciating aspects of the case that papers and photographs cannot really demonstrate. During the view (and this is often agreed beforehand) the judge will be shown the chosen 'list' of things that the parties would like him to see, as being relevant, and of course the judge may express a desire as to what he may want to see. The view is carried out in the presence of the parties and their immediate advisers and sometimes the experts. It is not usual to have all the witnesses present and the view should not be conducted with so many people present that its management becomes difficult. The parties to the claim should also be aware and be advised that if they are present they should not use the view as a chance to give evidence, or bring in irrelevant material. The judge will not treat anything he hears, or sees in such a manner as evidence in the case. If the parties are represented they should indicate through their advisers if there are any matters which the judge should see. There should, of course, be a degree of courtesy between the parties, however fraught the case may be. If any party feels he cannot be in the presence of the other party on the site, he should retire and leave it to his advisers to point out features on his behalf.

12.99 If there are to be 'test' manoeuvres carried out in the presence of the judge, these should be agreed in advance and arrangements put in hand to ensure that the manoeuvres take place on time. Health and safety may have to be observed with an on site safety briefing and with hard hats and high visibility jackets issued to all present, e g on an industrial estate, or building site, or where a HGV or large farm vehicle manoeuvre is part of the 'test'. On farms, steps should be taken to ensure no breach of any bio-security rules.

12.100 This may seem like common sense, but in the author's experience a lack of planning can cause problems with views.

12.101 It is improper for the judge to view the site on his own. The judge will usually travel to the site on his own (with his clerk).

Timetable of evidence and submissions

12.102 Check that your experts are able to attend and that you ensure that time is not wasted. They will usually not be required on the first day of any case of length. Usually experts will give their evidence 'back to back' so that each can assist the client's advisers (when not giving evidence) by hearing the other expert give evidence. Ensure that all persons on standby can be contacted immediately by phone, text, or email.

JUDGMENT AND AFTERWARDS

The trial is over. How is the judgment given?

12.103   The judge will either give his judgment:

(a)   immediately after the close of the hearing. This is usually referred to as an 'unreserved' judgment; or

(b)   at a date and time to be fixed, often referred to as the 'handing down' of the judgment.

12.104   In complex cases, or those which last more than one day, the second course is more usually adopted. When that is done there are special rules in CPR Part 40, PD 40E, about the procedure to be followed before the formal handing down, and in particular to whom a draft judgment may be disclosed before that date. Parties who have legal advisers must be told about these rules, as must others concerned with the case who may have an interest in the outcome. There are also technical rules in CPR Part 40, rule 2 about what a judgment must contain.

After judgment in the trial. Part 1 – the order of the court – its substantive terms

12.105   Given the variety of cases that lead to judgment, a short checklist is the best that can be provided at this stage.

12.106   Other than terms as to costs you will need to deal with the following matters:

(a)   What will be the terms of the order? In private rights of way disputes, unless the award is for damages, the substantive part of the order will invariably be for some form of declaration as to rights, or an injunction. So either the terms need to be worked out in advance (eg as in the pleadings) or to follow the judgment. The judge will usually encourage, or require the parties or their advisers to deal with these terms and present a draft to the judge for his approval so that he can make the order in those terms.

(b)   Are the terms clear and will they work in practice? (eg as to the width, or definition of the right of way in question as declared, or as to the terms of any injunction).

(c) Can they be agreed? Do undertakings have to be given? If so, are these clear and workable? Note that undertakings given to the court are equivalent to an injunction, and breach of such an undertaking may be punishable in the same way, eg by contempt – see RSC O. 45 and O 52. Care must be taken in the giving of and in the wording of undertakings for this reason. Thus, legal advice must be taken if any undertakings are being proposed.

(d) Is there to be permission to apply back to the court in case of difficulty? (This is invariably sensible and should be in any order where terms need to be implemented.)

(e) How will the judgment to do or not do something be enforced? See RSC 45, rules 5–8 and section 36 of the Senior Courts Act 1981. For committal applications see CPR Part 81.

(f) Execution of documents. If a party will not execute a document, the court can appoint someone do it on that person's behalf, see section 39 of the Senior Courts Act 1981.

(g) What happens if there is a breach of the order, or any undertaking given to the court? Consider the power to the court to commit the party in breach to prison, this is a complex subject dealt with under RSC Order 52.

(h) Note the very *limited* power to correct errors in orders under CPR Part 40, rule 12; see *Johnsen v Johnsen*[10] for a recent example of the limits of that power in connection with an order about a right of way.

(i) If there is to be an inquiry as to damages (eg for damages in lieu of an injunction), terms in the order will have to deal with further directions as to the conduct of that enquiry. Usually the case is directed back to the Master or District Judge for a case management conference to work out what directions are required; eg as to valuation experts.

(j) If an undertaking as to 'damages' (ie compensation for loss suffered by the respondent to an injunction application if it turns out that the injunction was wrongly granted) was given by the applicant seeking and obtaining an interim injunction (see Chapter 11, at para **11.87** above) the court will need to decide before any final order is made what is to happen about the applicant's liability on that undertaking. There are usually two issues, first whether there is a any liability on the applicant on his undertaking, and secondly, if there is such liability, how that is to be determined. The terms of any order and as to a further hearing on these discrete issues will need to be in the order following trial if not dealt with

---

[10] [2011] EWHC 2623 (Ch).

on that event. (See *Cheltenham & Gloucester BS v Ricketts*,[11] *Eliades v Lewis*[12] and *Regan v Paul Properties*[13] for the principles).

(k)   Is the order to be noted on any Land Registry titles? If so, the Order must provide for that and the parties must be ordered to allow the relevant entry to be made as an agreed (or unilateral) notice under sections 32–39 of the Land Registration Act 2002; see Ruoff & Roper, *Registered Conveyancing*, 42-023 ff. The order should provide that the parties are to proceed by way of an agreed form of application to enter the form of notice on the titles affected in order to record the material terms thereon; e g the terms of a declaration as to the width and user of a private right of way.

(l)   Is any party going to try to *set aside the order* under Part 39, rule 3? Note that this is not the same as seeking to *appeal* under Part 52 which is dealt with below at para **12.138**. (Such an application is often made by a party who for one reason or another did not attend the trial.) For the relationship between seeking to set aside an order under Part 39, rule 3 and an appeal where useful guidelines are set out by Lord Neuberger MR at paras 36–48 and by Lloyd LJ at paras 77–83, see *Bank of Scotland v Pereira*,[14] and applied in *Williams v Hinton*.[15]

After judgment in the trial. Part 2 – the order of the court – costs

12.107   As with other topics covered in this Chapter, a full treatment of the principles applicable to costs in civil claims is not to be found here. To cover every angle of the law of costs would require a separate book to be written. The reader must consult the civil procedure texts referred to at the start of this Chapter for such treatment. In addition, monographs, such as *Cook on Costs* (Butterworths – Annual Edition) and *Civil Costs, Law and Practice*, Friston (2nd Edn, Jordans, 2012) should be consulted. What follows is, therefore, only a very bare outline of the points that should be considered in the context of costs at the conclusion of a claim over a disputed private right of way. However, the points made, even if shortly, are important, as the costs of any litigation are invariably the most important part of it and focus needs to be on the principles applicable even before any claim is begun.

Note that from 1 April 2013 there will be substantial changes as to the way in which costs are to be managed (at the CMC stage – see para **12.66(k)** above) and as to what costs are proportionate under CPR Part 44 and as to what costs will be recoverable from the losing party under Conditional Fee Agreements. See para **12.2** above as to the need to consult at all time up to date practice books.

---

[11]   [1993] 1 WLR 1545.
[12]   [2005] EWHC 2966 (QB).
[13]   [2006] EWHC 2052 (Ch).
[14]   [2011] EWCA Civ 241.
[15]   [2011] EWCA Civ 1123.

12.108 There are four principles which lie at the heart of any costs order. These are:

What is meant by 'costs' in this context?

12.109 In general terms, costs in the context of an order made by the court will be the costs actually incurred by a party to the claim and which arise from it.

12.110 These costs will not only be the solicitor's costs, but also the costs of counsel and any experts and the costs (conduct money) of any witnesses who have to be required to attend court on a witness summons. These costs are often referred to as 'party and party' costs.

12.111 Other expenses of litigation will not be treated as 'costs'. These will include those incurred as between the solicitor and his client and which may go beyond the costs required for the conduct of the litigation. These are often referred to as 'solicitor and own client' costs; see *Smith v Buller*.[16] Other examples of charges which are not costs are out of pocket expenses such as travel expenses, or the cost of time by the litigant, or his loss of profit because he has had to attend to the claim.

12.112 Where a party is acting in person, his costs will include those items allowed under Part 48, rule 6. (See also Part 44, rule 2(1)(a).)

12.113 Finally, any damages ordered to be paid in the claim (with any interest on them) are not costs. In respect of costs incurred *before* a claim is started these may be recoverable if they are of use and service in the claim, or where it is of relevance to the issues in the claim or where the work was required because of the acts or omissions of the party liable to pay those costs, see *Re Gibson's Settlement Trusts*.[17]

12.114 The overriding principle is that costs are *not* imposed by one party upon the other under the court's order as a punishment. The further principle is that unless an indemnity order for costs is made (see below at para **12.127**) the party receiving his costs is only entitled to a reasonable and proportionate sum of costs. Finally, in any event (and ignoring any interest on unpaid costs ordered to be paid) the person receiving his costs is not entitled to more costs than he has to pay his solicitor; this being based on the principle that an order for costs to be paid is an indemnity to the party who has to pay his own solicitors and no more than that.

12.115 Note that no-one can be obliged to pay a sum of 'costs' unless there is a court order to prove that liability to pay. Therefore, the nasty little notices sent by official looking entities claiming 'costs' for the alleged infraction of the

---

[16] (1875) LR 19 Eq 473.
[17] [1981] Ch 179.

rights claimed by them, seeking 'costs' or 'costs at law' or similar, have no legal force; eg where there has been a dispute over the exercise of a private right of way and the servient owner engages the services of an agency to recover a 'fine' with 'costs'.

The issue over whether there has been nuisance to the easement is one matter, but no right to 'costs' can be asserted by such means without an order of the court.

12.116 Finally, no attempt is made here to deal with complex issues which arise in respect of costs where there are Conditional Fee Agreements (CFA) or where costs are recoverable under contracts or where an advocate has been engaged under the Pro Bono Scheme, or where the claim is for costs only under Part 44, rule 12A. See para **12.107** above for the changes on 1 April 2013 affecting the recovery of costs under a CFA.

What order should the court make – if any?

12.117 The guiding principles are set out in CPR Part 44, rule 3. Costs are ultimately at the discretion of the court, see section 51 of the Senior Courts Act 1981. Part 44, rule 3 supplies the principles upon which that discretion should be exercised. It will be assumed that the claim is being dealt with under the multi-track.

12.118 The principles are so important that they are also set out in full below (so far as material in civil claims about private rights of way) in order to assist the reader of this Chapter.

'44.3

(1)   The court has discretion as to –
       (a)   whether costs are payable by one party to another;
       (b)   the amount of those costs; and
       (c)   when they are to be paid.
(2)   If the court decides to make an order about costs –
       (a)   the general rule is that the unsuccessful party will be ordered to pay the costs of the successful party; but
       (b)   the court may make a different order.
(3)   The general rule does not apply to the following proceedings –
       ...
(4)   In deciding what order (if any) to make about costs, the court must have regard to all the circumstances, including –
       (a)   the conduct of all the parties;
       (b)   whether a party has succeeded on part of his case, even if he has not been wholly successful; and
       (c)   any payment into court or admissible offer to settle made by a party which is drawn to the court's attention, and which is not an offer to which costs consequences under Part 36 apply.
(5)   The conduct of the parties includes –

(a)   conduct before, as well as during, the proceedings and in particular the extent to which the parties followed the Practice Direction (Pre-Action Conduct) or any relevant pre-action protocol;

(b)   whether it was reasonable for a party to raise, pursue or contest a particular allegation or issue;

(c)   the manner in which a party has pursued or defended his case or a particular allegation or issue; and

(d)   whether a claimant who has succeeded in his claim, in whole or in part, exaggerated his claim.

(6)   The orders which the court may make under this rule include an order that a party must pay –

(a)   a proportion of another party's costs;

(b)   a stated amount in respect of another party's costs;

(c)   costs from or until a certain date only;

(d)   costs incurred before proceedings have begun;

(e)   costs relating to particular steps taken in the proceedings;

(f)   costs relating only to a distinct part of the proceedings; and

(g)   interest on costs from or until a certain date, including a date before judgment.

(7)   Where the court would otherwise consider making an order under paragraph (6)(f), it must instead, if practicable, make an order under paragraph (6)(a) or (c).

(8)   Where the court has ordered a party to pay costs, it may order an amount to be paid on account before the costs are assessed.

(9)   Where a party entitled to costs is also liable to pay costs the court may assess the costs which that party is liable to pay and either –

(a)   set off the amount assessed against the amount the party is entitled to be paid and direct him to pay any balance; or

(b)   delay the issue of a certificate for the costs to which the party is entitled until he has paid the amount which he is liable to pay.'

12.119 So the starting point, and in effect the end point too, is that orders for costs will be made following the principles set out above.

12.120 This means that in disputes over private rights of way it follows that in the vast majority of cases, and subject to what is said at para **12.122** below about offers, costs will follow the event.

12.121 However, it is worth bearing in mind that the facts set out below *may* require a different approach:

(a)   Where the claim is in reality not contentious, but where the parties are concerned to have their rights and obligations determined by the court. This may happen where a Part 8 Claim (see para **12.44** above) is issued seeking declarations as to the construction of a grant of a right of way.

(b)   Where the issues in the claim are separate and an 'issue led' approach to costs, reflecting the degree of success or failure of the parties on the issues, may be the correct approach. Only if it is practicable to separate the costs relating to the issues in terms of percentages of total costs, or time spent, will the court usually follow this approach. The guidance of Jackson J in

Multiplex Constructions (UK) Ltd v Cleveland Bridge UK Ltd[18] is worth stating in full as it is usually applicable to private rights of way disputes and not just to the commercial litigation referred to at the start.

'(i)   In commercial litigation where each party has claims and asserts that a balance is owing in its own favour, the party which ends up receiving payment should generally be characterised as the overall winner of the entire action.

(ii)   In considering how to exercise its discretion the court should take as its starting point the general rule that the successful party is entitled to an order for costs.

(iii) The judge must then consider what departures are required from that starting point, having regard to all the circumstances of the case.

(iv)   Where the circumstances of the case require an issue-based costs order, that is what the judge should make. However, the judge should hesitate before doing so, because of the practical difficulties which this causes and because of the steer given by rule 44.3(7).

(v)   In many cases the judge can and should reflect the relative success of the parties on different issues by making a proportionate costs order.

(vi)   In considering the circumstances of the case the judge will have regard not only to any Part 36 offers made but also to each party's approach to negotiations (insofar as admissible) and general conduct of the litigation.

(vii) If (a) one party makes an order offer under Part 36 or an admissible offer within rule 44.3(4)(c) which is nearly but not quite sufficient, and (b) the other party rejects that offer outright without any attempt to negotiate, then it might be appropriate to penalise the second party in costs.

(viii) In assessing a proportionate costs order the judge should consider what costs are referable to each issue and what costs are common to several issues. It will often be reasonable for the overall winner to recover not only the costs specific to the issues which he has won but also the common costs.'

The effect of any offers made which may relate to the order to be made as to costs – whether open offers, made under CPR Part 36, or in Calderbank form[19]

12.122   (These are referred to below in generic terms as 'costs offers'.) See also para **12.74ff** above.

12.123   For the details of how Part 36 and other costs offers should be made, refer to the standard civil procedure and costs text books – see the beginning of this Chapter. In outline the main points to bear in mind are:

---

[18]   [2008] EWHC 2280 (TCC).
[19]   As to *Calderbank* offers see para **12.74ff** above.

(a) Open offers to settle on terms are ones which can and will be seen by the judge at the hearing. They may have the tactical advantage of putting the offeree on the 'back foot' if what is being offered is sensible and likely to be in terms of any court order.

(b) 'Calderbank'[20] offers are those which are expressed to be without prejudice (ie privileged) *save as to costs*. This means that (subject to any waiver of privilege) they can only be looked at by the judge when the question of any costs order arises. These must NOT go into the trial bundle.

(c) Without prejudice offers are fully privileged and (subject to any waiver of privilege) they cannot be looked at by the judge at any stage of the claim, including the stage at which costs are in issue. These must NOT go into the trial bundle.

(d) Part 36 offers must comply with the terms of Part 36 to be fully effective. If they are effective, the receiving party may be entitled not only to indemnity costs but also to interest at a rate not exceeding 10 per cent above base rate on any damages and costs awarded in the claim. As stated at para **12.75** above, the need to ensure that there is compliance with the terms of Part 36 is complex and that is why reference must be made to the practice books dealing with Part 36. Part 36 offers must not be referred to the trial judge prior to the stage at which the costs order is being considered, see Part 36, rule 13. So as under (b) and (c) above these offers must not go into the trial bundle.

(e) Care must be taken at any interim hearing of a claim (or a CMC – see para **12.63** above) to ensure that if any Part 36 offers are referred to, that they are not referred to the judge who may hear the claim at trial and that no note is kept on the court file of any such offers.

(f) Any offer made should be assessed on the basis that before making it (in whatever form chosen) it should represent a fair judgment of the possible outcome of the claim, that it presents a practicable solution (important in private rights of way disputes), that it represents an attempt to save costs and is likely to be sufficiently tempting to the other party to be capable of acceptance, or at the very least, may establish the basis on which settlement can be reached. Derisory offers (on any footing) are a waste of time and the costs of preparing them.

(g) Note: some cautionary words for claimants and defendants:

   (i) Making sensible offers in claims is not a sign of weakness.

---

[20] So named after the practice was clarified in *Calderbank v Calderbank* [1976] Fam 93.

(ii)   Costs are too great a financial burden in many of the disputes over private rights of way for any litigant to be able to throw away the chance to save the costs of such litigation.

(iii) This is so however much the point in issue may be seen as one of 'principle' or 'moral right'.

(iv)   The concepts of 'points of principle' or 'it is my moral right' are far too expensive for all but the most wealthy parties to be able to afford.

(h) Finally, it is worth bearing in mind that litigation generally and in particular claims over private rights of way, carry high risks. The risks of losing are often very high. The chance of success is not and never can be guaranteed. The complexity of the law of easements does not assist those who seek to litigate in this area of law. So no adviser should conduct a claim over private rights of way without a large sign placed in front of the client at all times which states: 'Can you afford to lose? If you think you can, you are probably fooling yourself.'

The basis of assessment of any costs ordered to be paid by the court by any party (or other person) to another party – (standard or indemnity costs?) – summary and detailed assessments

12.124 Note that references to the 'receiving party' are references to the party who has an order for costs in his favour, and references to 'the paying party' are references to those who are ordered to pay costs.

12.125 For the details of these matters refer to the standard civil procedure and costs texts – see the beginning of this Chapter. In outline the main points to bear in mind are detailed in the following paragraphs.

12.126 Costs ordered to be paid will *usually* be assessed (ie the amount payable being decided by the court) on the *standard* basis; Part 44, rule 4(1). This gives the receiving party the right to the costs which are proportionate to the matters in issue (a factor which is sometimes forgotten in hard-fought private rights of way claims) and which resolves any doubt about whether costs were reasonably incurred by the receiving party in favour of the paying party. See also Part 44, rule 5. See para **12.107** above for the changes taking place on 1 April 2013, which will include a new definition of what is proportionate under CPR Part 44.

12.127 However, the court may order the costs to be paid on the indemnity basis under Part 44, rule 4. If it does so, the receiving party is entitled to all his costs and any doubt about whether they were reasonably incurred will be resolved in favour of the receiving party. The circumstances in which the court will order assessment on the indemnity basis are many and varied.

The principes were recently set out by Gloster J in *Euroption Strategic Fund Ltd v Skandinaviska Enskilda Banken AB* [2012] EWHC 749 (Comm).

She stated:

'9. The starting point is section 51 of the Senior Courts Act 1981, which provides that costs are in the discretion of the court, subject to the rules of the court.

10. The relevant provisions of the CPR are those contained in rules 44.3, 44.4 and 44.5. As rules 44.4 and 44.5 make clear, there are two differences between the two bases of assessment. The first difference is as to the party who bears the relevant burden of persuasion in a case of doubt as to whether costs were reasonably incurred or reasonable in amount. On the standard basis of assessment, the burden of proof is on the receiving party: see rule 44.4(2)(b). On the indemnity basis, the burden of proof is on the paying party: see rule 44.4(3). The second difference is that, on the standard basis of assessment, the paying party has the benefit of the limitation contained in rule 44.4(2)(a), namely, that only costs which are proportionate to the matters in issue are recoverable.

The relevant principles.

11. There was virtually common ground between the parties as to the principles to be applied by the court in making its choice between the two bases of assessment. The principles are well-known and have been exhaustively rehearsed in the relevant authorities. The following is no more than a headline summary.

12. First, on either basis, the receiving party is only entitled to recover costs which it has actually incurred, and, further, is only entitled to receive costs which were reasonably incurred and were reasonable in amount. Second, the standard basis is the normal basis of assessment: see *Reed Minty v Taylor* [2002] 1 WLR 2800 at [28]; *Excelsior Commercial & Industrial Holdings Ltd v Salisbury Hammer Aspden & Johnson* [2002] EWCA (Civ) 879 at [19]. This means that there has to be something in the conduct of the action, or about the circumstances of the case in question, which takes it out of the norm in a way which justifies an order for indemnity costs: see Excelsior (supra) and *Noorani v Calver* [2009] EWHC 592 (QB) at [9], per Coulson J. Third, cases vary very considerably, and the Court of Appeal has declined to lay down guidelines on the subject: see Excelsior (supra) at [32]. It is obvious from a reading of the authorities that each case is highly fact-dependent.

13. Fourth, to demonstrate that a case has gone outside the norm of behaviour, it is not necessary to show that the paying party's conduct lacked moral probity or deserved moral condemnation in order to attract recovery of costs on an indemnity basis: see *Balmoral Group Ltd v Borealis (UK) Ltd* [2006] EWHC 2531 (Comm) at [1], where Christopher Clarke J said:

"The basic rule is that a successful party is entitled to his costs on the standard basis. The factors to be taken into account in deciding whether to order costs on the latter basis have been helpfully summarised by Tomlinson, J, in *Three Rivers District Council v The Governor and Company of the Bank of England* [2006] EWHC 816 (Comm). The discretion is a wide one to be determined in the light of all the circumstances of the case. To award costs against an unsuccessful party on an indemnity scale is a departure from the norm. There must, therefore, be something – whether it be the conduct of the claimant or the circumstances of the case – which takes the case outside the norm. It is not necessary that the claimant should be guilty of dishonesty or moral blame. Unreasonableness in the conduct of the proceedings and the raising of particular allegations, or in the manner of raising them may suffice. So may the pursuit of a speculative claim involving a high risk of failure or the making of allegations of dishonesty that turn out to be misconceived, or the conduct of an extensive publicity campaign designed to drive the other party to settlement. The making of a grossly exaggerated claim may also be a ground for indemnity costs."

14. However, as Mr Shivji [counsel for the claimant] emphasised, by reference to paragraph 8 of the decision in Noorani (supra), conduct must be unreasonable "to a high degree" to attract indemnity costs. "Unreasonable" in this context does not mean merely wrong or misguided in hindsight: see per Simon Brown LJ (as he then was) in *Kiam v MGN Limited (No 2)* [2002] 1 WLR 2810. In each case, it is a fact dependent question as to whether or not the paying party's conduct has been unreasonable to a high degree.

15. One example of a case of unreasonable conduct in the conduct of proceedings was *Digicel (St Lucia) Ltd v Cable & Wireless plc* [2010] EWHC 888 (Ch) at [68]–[69]. The claimant had shown no interest in proportionality by casting its claim disproportionately wide, and requiring the defendant to meet such a claim. In such circumstances, Morgan J held there was no injustice in denying the claimant the benefit or an assessment on a proportionate basis, given that, in such circumstances, the claimant had forfeited its right to the benefit of the doubt on reasonableness: at [68]–[69]. Another relevant example of conduct of the paying party which took the case outside the norm was *Re Continental Assurance Co of London plc (in liquidation) (unreported)* 13 June 2001, where Park J approached the question of indemnity costs on the grounds that the liquidators had pursued all issues at full length and right to the end of trial, with the result that the amount of costs incurred was enormous. It was appropriate that the costs of the successful respondents should be assessed on the indemnity basis so that they, and not the liquidators, received the benefit of any doubt as to whether incurring the cost was reasonable.'

12.128 Thus in terms of these principles there are two main areas which are usually the subject of investigation.

First – where the conduct of the paying party in the claim has departed from the norm; see *Excelsior Commercial and Industrial Holdings Ltd v Salisbury Hamer Aspden & Johnson*[21] (eg pursuing a claim to a private right of way (or defending a genuine claim) which either as to the claim or the defence was hopeless from the start). Added to this there can be the over-enthusiastic pursuit of claim with often a harassing manner in correspondence etc, allegations of dishonesty or fraud (unproven at trial) issues over proportionality and failing to comply with court directions or orders. The list is

---

[21] [2002] EWCA Civ 879. See also the useful judgment of Sales J on costs in *F&C Alternative Investments (Holdings) Ltd v Barthelemy & Ors* [2011] EWHC 2807 (Ch) which deals with both the way in which costs were to be paid and the issue of whether the standard or indemnity basis of assessment applied having regard to the Part 36 offers which had been made and withdrawn, and finally the issue of interest on costs.

endless, but it is also important to remember that the mere fact of complete success in the claim, or defence does not in itself entitle the victorious part to costs on the indemnity basis.

12.129 Secondly, where the defendant as the paying party is subject to a judgment in favour of the claimant which is at least as advantageous to the claimant as the receiving party as the proposals contained in the claimant's Part 36 Offer; see para **12.74** above.[22]

12.130 In any claim over a private right of way (dealt with on the multi-track as is assumed at para **12.63** above) which has lasted less than one day, once any order for costs to be paid by one party to the other is made, the judge will usually assess the costs to be paid on a *summary* basis. It is for this reason that costs schedules must be served by each party on the other no later than 24 hours before the time at which the hearing is due to start; Part 44, rule 7 and Part 44 PD, section 13. That is the general rule and for the judge to be persuaded that a detailed assessment is required, with its delay and expense, requires the party so contending to persuade the judge that there is good reason not to do so, eg lack of time, substantial costs, or complex objections better dealt with by the Costs Judge. The importance of having the costs schedule ready under Part 44 Costs PD, para 13.5 cannot be overestimated.[23] On a summary assessment the judge will be concerned with deciding three things. First, the basis of assessment (see para **12.126** above). Secondly, what rates for the solicitors and counsel involved should be allowed (during which the current Guide to the Summary Assessment of Costs under Part 48 must be consulted) and finally what time should be allowed by way of reasonable allowances for the work done. As set out above at paras **12.126–12.127** the difference between standard and indemnity costs will be important during this task.

Detailed assessment

12.131 This is a complex subject and as stated above reference must be made for the detail to the civil procedure books and the text books of Cook and Friston on costs.

12.132 If the costs are ordered to be subject to a detailed assessment, they will have to be assessed by a Costs Judge under Part 47 and its Practice Direction. The significant point about this procedure is that there are costs attached to it and it will take time. It is always sensible for the parties to agree any sum of costs ordered to be payable in advance of a detailed assessement.

---

[22] For the detail see *Civil Costs: Law & Practice*, Friston (Jordans), Chapter 13, para 13.12ff.

[23] See *MacDonald v Taree Holdings Ltd.* [2001] 1 Costs LR 147 for the guidance set out by Neubeger J as to what the judge should do when there has been a failure to serve a costs schedule under section 13.5. Note it is not possible for a costs judge to carry out the summary assessment. The judge who conducted the hearing must do it; see Part 44 Costs PD, section 13.8.

Interest on costs

12.133 Any costs ordered to be paid by the court will carry interest at what is currently 8 per cent unless a different or higher rate is ordered, e g under Part 36 – see above.[24]

Unless the court orders otherwise (or unless a rule of Practice Direction provides otherwise) such interest will run from the date when the judgment is given by the judge and not (if later) when the order is drawn up by the court; Part 40, rule 8 and Part 44, rule 3(6)(g). This is an important point which must not be overlooked by parties ordered to pay costs.

12.134 There is power to disallow interest due to a receiving party under Part 47, rule 8(3) where the receiving party delays in the course of a detailed assessment of costs.

12.135 To avoid any interest it is often prudent for the paying party to make a payment of costs on account if there is going to be a delay in agreeing the total, or in the detailed assessment.

Other points

12.136 For the details under each of these heads refer to the standard civil procedure and costs texts; see the beginning of this Chapter.

12.137 In addition the parties will need to consider:

(a) *Wasted costs orders.*
     This may be appropriate where the conduct of a legal representative warrants an order that any part of his costs are disallowed or that he pays any part of the other party's costs personally (see section 51(6) of the Senior Courts Act 1981 and CPR Part 44, rule 14 and Part 48, rule 7 and (Friston – above) at 7.204 ff).

(b) *Costs orders against third parties.*

---

[24] See Section 17 of the Judgments Act 1838 (High Court) and section 74 of the County Courts Act 1984. It is assumed that the costs are less than £5,000 if ordered by the County Court; see Art 2(1) of the County Courts (Interest on Judgments) Order 1991, SI 1991/1184. See also *Simcoe v Jacuzzi UK Group plc* [2012] EWCA Civ 137; [2012] 2 Costs LR 401 on the application of the rules as to when interest runs on orders for the payment of costs. See also *F&C Alternative Investments (Holdings) Ltd v Barthelemy & Ors* [2011] EWHC 2807 (Ch) at para 71ff per Sales J. It is clear from that judgment that the fact that the receiving party has had to borrow and pay interest on such borrowing in order to fund the litigation will be a relevant factor in determining what rate of interest such a party should receive on the costs due to him. It will, however, be necessary for that party to show that there was need to borrow for that purpose and that the interest rate was the best that could be obtained for that borrowing in the market. See Part 44.3. r 6(g) at para **12.118** above. The interest on these costs will run up to the time when the costs order is made, from which time the Judgment Act interest rate will apply.

For example, those who have funded the claim, or who have been responsible for it, but have not been a party to it.

See CPR Part 48, rule 2. The guidelines are set out in *Symphony Group v Hodgson*,[25] at pp 192–194, per Balcombe LJ. These are:

> '(1) Where a person has some *management* of the action, e g a director of an insolvent company who causes the company improperly to prosecute or defend proceedings: see *In re Land and Property Trust Co Plc*;[26] *In re Land and Property Trust Co Plc (No 3)*;[27] *In re Land and Property Trust Co Plc (No 2)*;[28] Court of Appeal (Civil Division) Transcript No 160 of 1993; *Taylor v Pace Developments Ltd*;[29] *In re A Company (No 004055 of 1991)*[30] and *Framework Exhibitions Ltd v Matchroom Boxing Ltd.*[31] It is of interest to note that, while it was not suggested in any of these cases that it would never be a proper exercise of the jurisdiction to order the director to pay the costs, in none of them was it the ultimate result that the director was so ordered.
>
> (2) Where a person has maintained or financed the action. This was undoubtedly considered to be a proper case for the exercise of the discretion by Macpherson of Cluny J in *Singh v Observer Ltd*,[32] where it was alleged that a non-party was maintaining the plaintiff's libel action. However, on appeal the evidence showed that the non-party had not been maintaining the action and the appeal was allowed without going into the legal issues raised by the judge's decision: see *Singh v Observer Ltd.*[33]
>
> (3) In *Gupta v Comer*[34] this court approached the power of the court to order a solicitor to pay costs under Ord 62, r 11 as an example of the exercise of the jurisdiction under section 51 of the Act of 1981.
>
> (4) Where the person has *caused* the action. In *Pritchard v JH Cobden Ltd*[35] the plaintiff had suffered brain damage through the defendant's negligence. That resulted in a personality change which precipitated a divorce. This court held that the defendant's agreement to pay the costs of the divorce proceedings could be justified as an application of the *Aiden Shipping Co Ltd v Interbulk Ltd*[36] principle: see [1988] Fam 22, 51.
>
> (5) Where the person is a party to a closely related action which has been heard at the same time but not consolidated – as was the case in *Aiden Shipping* itself.

---

[25] [1994] QB 179.
[26] [1991] 1 BCLC 845.
[27] [1991] BCLC 856.
[28] *The Times*, 16 February 1993.
[29] [1991] BCC 406.
[30] [1991] 1 WLR 1003.
[31] (Unreported), 23 September 1992; Court of Appeal (Civil Division) Transcript No 873 of 1992.
[32] [1989] 2 All ER 751.
[33] [1989] 3 All ER 777n.
[34] [1991] 1 QB 629.
[35] [1988] Fam 22.
[36] [1986] AC 965.

(6)   Group litigation where one or two actions are selected as test actions: see *Joseph Owen Davies v Eli Lilly & Co.*[37]

I accept that these categories are neither rigid nor closed. They indicate the sorts of connection which have so far led the courts to entertain a claim for costs against a non-party.

However, it seems to me that the particular circumstances of this case require this court to accept the invitation of Lord Goff in *Aiden Shipping Co Ltd v Interbulk Ltd*[38] and to lay down some principles for the guidance of judges of first instance when they are asked to make an order for costs against a non-party, and in doing so I am well aware of what Lloyd LJ said in *Taylor v Pace Developments Ltd*:[39] "There is only one immutable rule in relation to costs, and that is that there are no immutable rules." I am also aware of the observations warning against laying down rules for the exercise of a discretion in relation to costs generally by Bowen LJ in *Jones v Curling*[40] and by Brett MR in *The Friedeberg*.[41] Nevertheless, I am fortified by the fact that Lord Goff considered that such guidance might well become necessary and I believe that the circumstances of this case indicate the present necessity for guidance. In my judgment the following are material considerations to be taken into account, although I do not suggest that there may not be others which are relevant.

(1)   An order for the payment of costs by a non-party will always be exceptional: see *per* Lord Goff in *Aiden Shipping Co Ltd v Interbulk Ltd*.[42] The judge should treat any application for such an order with considerable caution.

(2)   It will be even more exceptional for an order for the payment of costs to be made against a non-party, where the applicant has a cause of action against the non-party and could have joined him as a party to the original proceedings. Joinder as a party to the proceedings gives the person concerned all the protection conferred by the rules, as to e.g. the framing of the issues by pleadings; discovery of documents and the opportunity to pay into court or to make a *Calderbank* offer (*Calderbank v Calderbank*[43]); and the knowledge of what the issues are before giving evidence.

(3)   Even if the applicant can provide a good reason for not joining the non-party against whom he has a valid cause of action, he should warn the non-party at the earliest opportunity of the possibility that he may seek to apply for costs against him. At the very least this will give the non-party an opportunity to apply to be joined as a party to the action under Ord 15, rule 6(2)(b)(i) or (ii).
       Principles (2) and (3) require no further justification on my part; they are an obvious application of the basic principles of natural justice.

---

37   [1987] 1 WLR 1136.
38   [1986] AC 965.
39   [1991] BCC 406, 408.
40   (1884) 13 QBD 262, 271.
41   (1885) 10 PD 112, 113.
42   [1986] AC 965, 980F.
43   [1976] Fam 93.

(4) An application for payment of costs by a non-party should normally be determined by the trial judge: see *Bahai v Rashidian*.[44]

(5) The fact that the trial judge may in the course of his judgment in the action have expressed views on the conduct of the non-party constitutes neither bias nor the appearance of bias. Bias is the antithesis of the proper exercise of a judicial function: see *Bahai v Rashidian*.[45]

(6) The procedure for the determination of costs is a summary procedure, not necessarily subject to all the rules that would apply in an action. Thus, subject to any relevant statutory exceptions, judicial findings are inadmissible as evidence of the facts upon which they were based in proceedings between one of the parties to the original proceedings and a stranger: see *Hollington v F Hewthorn & Co Ltd*;[46] *Cross on Evidence*, 7th edn (1990), pp 100–101. Yet in the summary procedure for the determination of the liability of a solicitor to pay the costs of an action to which he was not a party, the judge's findings of fact may be admissible: see *Brendon v Spiro*,[47] cited with approval by this court in *Bahai v Rashidian*.[48] This departure from basic principles can only be justified if the connection of the non-party with the original proceedings was so close that he will not suffer any injustice by allowing this exception to the general rule.

(7) Again, the normal rule is that witnesses in either civil or criminal proceedings enjoy immunity from any form of civil action in respect of evidence given during those proceedings. One reason for this immunity is so that witnesses may give their evidence fearlessly: see *Palmer v Durnford Ford*.[49] In so far as the evidence of a witness in proceedings may lead to an application for the costs of those proceedings against him or his company, it introduces yet another exception to a valuable general principle.

(8) The fact that an employee, or even a director or the managing director, of a company gives evidence in an action does not normally mean that the company is taking part in that action, in so far as that is an allegation relied upon by the party who applies for an order for costs against a non-party company: see *Gleeson v J Wippell & Co Ltd*.[50]

(9) The judge should be alert to the possibility that an application against a non-party is motivated by resentment of an inability to obtain an effective order for costs against a legally aided litigant. The courts are well aware of the financial difficulties faced by parties who are facing legally aided litigants at first instance, where the opportunity of a claim against the Legal Aid Board under section 18 of the Legal Aid Act 1988 is very limited. Nevertheless the Civil Legal Aid (General) Regulations 1989,[51] and in particular regulations 67, 69, and 70, lay down conditions designed to ensure that there is no abuse of legal aid by a legally assisted person and these are designed to protect the other

---

[44] [1985] 1 WLR 1337.
[45] [1985] 1 WLR 1337, 1342H, 1346F.
[46] [1943] KB 587.
[47] [1938] 1 KB 176, 192.
[48] [1985] 1 WLR 1337 1343D, 1345H.
[49] [1992] QB 483, 487.
[50] [1977] 1 WLR 510, 513.
[51] SI 1989/339.

party to the litigation as well as the Legal Aid Fund. The court will be very reluctant to infer that solicitors to a legally aided party have failed to discharge their duties under the regulations – see *Orchard v South Eastern Electricity Board*[52] – and in my judgment this principle extends to a reluctance to infer that any maintenance by a non-party has occurred.'

These principles are set out in full because this type of application may well have relevance and must be considered, even as a possible course to adopt, in private rights of way disputes. For example where the dispute has arisen because of the conduct of someone who is not a party to the claims such as a negligent solicitor who drew the grant. Or more frequently cases where 'funders' such as residents' groups, or companies or associations are either controlling, or funding the litigation. The list is potentially a wide one. (See also *Civil Costs, Law and Practice*, Friston, 2nd Edn (2012) (Jordans) at 7.136ff.)

(c)   *Where money (eg damages) is ordered to be paid to a child or protected party.*
      Here the costs payable out of any money the child or protected is to receive must be subject to a detailed assessment; see Part 48, rule 5.

(d)   *Interim costs orders.*
      See Part 44, rule 3(6)(e) and (f). See *Civil Costs, Law and Practice*, Friston, 2nd Edn (2012) (Jordans) at 7.399.

After judgment in the trial. Part3 – appeals

12.138   Appeals are a complex subject and for the details the civil practice books must be consulted. The key (and only) text to be followed is CPR Part 52 and its accompanying Practice Direction ('PD').

12.139   What follows is a summary of the main points to consider if a party wishes to appeal against a judgment against him.

12.140   In this part the reference to 'the lower court' means the court which has made the order against which the appeal is sought. 'The appeal court' refers to the court to which an appeal is made; see Part 52, rule 1(3).

Routes

12.141   The route to be taken by an appeal is set out in Part 52 PD, section 2A.1 and Table 1.

12.142   In private rights of way claims the likely routes will be as follows. It will be assumed that the claim is or has been allocated to the multi-track; see CPR Part 26.

---

[52]   [1987] QB 565.

12.143 The distinctions between routes of appeal lie according to: (a) the claim form used and if issued under Part 7 its allocation, eg to multi-track; (b) the court, and (c) whether the decision against which the appeal is sought is interim or final.

12.144 Where the decision of the court is NOT a final one but an interim one (eg an order on an *interim* application or for directions, see Part 52 PD, section 2A.2) the route will be as follows:

Judge who made the decision	Appeal Court
District Judge in the County Court	Circuit Judge
Circuit Judge in the County Court	Single judge of the High Court
Master of the High Court or District Judge sitting in High Court	
Registry	Single judge of the High Court
High Court Judge	Court of Appeal

12.145 Where the decision of the court is a *final* one (see Part 52 PD, section 2A.2) the route will be as follows:

Judge who made the decision	Appeal Court
If the proceedings were issued by a Part 7 claim form and allocated to the multi track (see above):	
District Judge in the County Court	Court of Appeal
Circuit Judge in the County Court	Court of Appeal
Master of the High Court or District Judge sitting in High Court	
Registry	Court of Appeal
High Court Judge	Court of Appeal
If the proceedings were issued by a Part 8 claim form:	
District Judge in the County Court	Circuit Judge
Circuit Judge in the County Court	Single judge of the High Court

Master of the High Court or District Judge sitting in High Court	
Registry	Single judge of the High Court
High Court Judge	Court of Appeal

12.146 Note:

(a) In all cases of appeals from the Court of Appeal, these will lie to the Supreme Court.

(b) In the rare case where there is some special reason why the appeal should 'leapfrog' the Court of Appeal, the High Court Judge can direct that the appellant applies to the Supreme Court for permission to appeal directly to that court; see sections 12 and 13 of the Administration of Justice Act 1969. (See also Supreme Court Rules 2009, Practice Direction 3, paras 3.1 and 3.6.) In private rights of way cases it is most unusual for a claim to 'leapfrog' this way.

Permission

12.147 Save in certain cases which would never arise on a private rights of way case (save possibly where a committal order had been made) permission to appeal *will always* be required from the lower court and if that court does not grant it, permission will have to be sought from the appeal court; Part 52, rule 3.

12.148 Unless the lower court allows a longer period, the application for permission must be made within 21 days of the decision of the lower court against which it is sought to appeal. Note that this date will usually be the date when the judgment or order is made and not when the court issues the sealed order.

12.149 The criteria for granting permission are set out at Part 52, rule 3(6):

'(6) Permission to appeal may be given only where –
(a) the court considers that the appeal would have a real prospect of success; or
(b) there is some other compelling reason why the appeal should be heard.'

12.150 The court granting permission may limit the issues on which the appeal is to be heard or impose other conditions, eg security for costs.

12.151 The application for permission is usually made at the time the judgment or order is made. If that is refused then the application may be made to the appeal court. It is tactically wise, if instructed to do so, to make the application for permission to appeal at the time the judgment or order is made as otherwise you will have to come back at a later time (and within the 21 day period) before the same judge to make that application, with an increased liability to costs.

12.152 If permission to appeal is refused by the lower court, the application to appeal will have to be made to the appeal court on paper using Court Form **N161**. See Part 52, rule 4.

12.153 If the appeal court refuses to grant permission on the paper application, an oral hearing may be requested under Part 52 PD, section 4.1–4.14A. A respondent may oppose the application for permission on the basis that the grounds of appeal do not meet the threshold in Part 52, rule 3(6) but the opposing party may not be awarded his costs of that application; see *Jolly v Jay*.[53]

12.154 If the appellant is granted permission the respondent may file his own notice of appeal, 'a respondent's notice', see Part 52, rule 5, Court Form **N 162**. He will do this where, for example, he supports the decision of the lower court, but not the reasoning, or where that reasoning may be 'suspect'. He will also need to file a respondent's notice where he wishes to appeal against some part of the order which is against him, e g the award of damages.

12.155 In some appeals the appeal court will decide whether permission should be given and the merits of the appeal at the same hearing. This is often done in urgent cases.

Grounds

12.156 These must be stated in the notice of appeal, which may also have to include the reason(s) for granting permission to appeal; see Part 52, rules 4 and 11 and Part 52 PD, section 3.

12.157 It is important to note that the grounds must state on what basis the decision of the lower court was wrong, or unjust because of a serious procedural, or other irregularity in the lower court. It is not enough to say simply that 'the judge was wrong' or 'I do not agree with the decision of judge X' and leave it at that. This is because under Part 52 PD, section 3.2(2) you must state against each ground whether that ground raises a point of law, or is an appeal against a finding of fact. The distinction can be explained as follows.

12.158 In a case where the lower court has decided that: (a) a right of way exists for the benefit of A over B's land by longer user (section 2 of the Prescription Act 1832), (b) that certain facts led to that conclusion, and (c) an

---

53   [2002] EWCA Civ 277.

injunction should lie against B to prevent his obstruction of the way, the following points by B (appellant) would have to be made in the notice of appeal where the grounds must be set out:

(a)   that the judge was wrong in law in his interpretation of section 2, eg by overlooking a written consent by B to A's user;

(b)   that the judge should not have found on the fact that A's user was continuous for the 20 year period relied upon by A; and

(c)   that it was in any event wrong for the judge to exercise his discretion to grant an injunction.

12.159 What is important in presenting appeals, both when seeking permission and even more importantly when arguing the appeal itself (if permission is given), is to identify clearly the real points in issue. This means that you need to identify either a point of *law*, or a point of *evidence* (fact) or a point of *discretion* where the lower court has gone wrong.

12.160 It is important to separate out the three elements of law, fact and discretion.

12.161 Errors of *law* should be fairly self-explanatory. Did the lower court misapply the law?

12.162 One important question that can sometimes arise where the appeal raises an issue of law is what authority is binding on the appeal court?

12.163 Having regard to the doctrine of precedent (see *Young v Bristol Aeroplane Co*[54] and *Howard de Walden Estate Ltd v Aggio*,[55] was the lower court bound to follow a higher court's decision? Is this appeal court so bound? In a Note to his judgment in the *Howard de Walden* case (above) Mummery LJ set out some useful principles on precedent, or as it is called in Latin, *stare decisis*.

'*Judgment of the court on precedent*

On these appeals the court received submissions on a question of stare decisis that needs to be settled by a ruling from this court.

The question is whether a judge sitting at first instance in the county court is bound by a decision of a judge sitting in the High Court, when that decision has been given not on an appeal to the High Court, but by a High Court Judge

---

[54]   [1944] KB 718.
[55]   [2008] Ch 26. The main decision was reversed by the House of Lords ([2009] 1 AC 39) but not on the point referred to below). On precedent and the importance of defining what is the point of decision in a case (usually described in Latin as the '*ratio decidendi*') see the recent and most instructive judgment of Lloyd LJ in *Frozen Value Ltd v Heron Foods Ltd* [2012] EWCA Civ 473, in particular at para 116ff.

exercising a first instance jurisdiction that has been conferred by statute on both the High Court and the county court (in this case by the Leasehold Reform Acts).

In this case the decision of Mr David Donaldson QC sitting as a deputy judge in the High Court in *Maurice v Hollow-Ware Products Ltd*[56] was treated by Judge Crawford Lindsay QC, sitting in the Central London Civil Justice Centre, hearing the *Earl Cadogan* case, and by Judge Collins sitting in the same Civil Justice Centre hearing the *Howard de Walden* case, as the decision of a court of co-ordinate jurisdiction which was not binding on the county court, although it would, as a matter of judicial comity, usually be followed by a judge in the county court unless convinced that the decision was wrong.

In this context we do not think that there is any relevant difference between the decision of a High Court Judge and the decision of a deputy High Court Judge.

Although both Judge Crawford Lindsay QC and Judge Collins correctly stated the principle of *stare decisis* applicable to decisions of co-ordinate courts of first instance (see *Huddersfield Police Authority v Watson*;[57] *Colchester Estates (Cardiff) v Carlton Industries plc*[58]), this principle does not, in our judgment, apply as between decisions of the High Court and the county court, even when each court is exercising the same first instance jurisdiction. The relationship between the High Court and the county court is that of superior court and inferior court and the decisions of the former, whether made on appeal or at first instance, are binding on the latter.

With the benefit of the research conducted by counsel and by the judicial assistants in the Court of Appeal, we state the position as follows.

In accordance with the well established principles of *stare decisis* the decisions of a higher court are binding on judges sitting in a lower court. This principle serves the interests of legal certainty: see *Broome v Cassell & Co Ltd*.[59] The needs of litigants and their advisers to know where they stand arenot served if a lower court is free to create a conflict of authority by declining to follow the relevant decision of a higher court.

The county court is a lower court than the High Court in the hierarchy of the legal system of England and Wales and is bound by the decisions of the High Court, as well as those of courts above; see *Cross & Harris, Precedent in English Law* , 4th edn (1991), p 123 which refers to an almost invariable assumption to this effect.

The Chancery Division of the High Court does not cease to be a higher court than the county court when it exercises the same first instance jurisdiction as has been conferred on the county court by the Leasehold Reform Acts. The fact that both the High Court and the county court are courts of first instance exercising the same statutory jurisdiction does not justify the creation of an exception to the general rule of *stare decisis* stated in para 92 above.

---

[56] [2005] 2 EGLR 71.
[57] [1947] KB 842, 847.
[58] [1986] Ch 80.
[59] [1972] AC 1027, 1054.

We do not accept the tentative suggestion that it is arguable that a county court judge is not bound by the decision of a judge of the High Court because appeals from the county court can go to the Court of Appeal: see *Salmond's Jurisprudence*, 12th edn (1966), p 163 footnote (w). The fact that both the High Court and the county courts are lower than the Court of Appeal, to which appeals lie, does not mean that the High Court and the county court are courts of co-ordinate jurisdiction for the purposes of the doctrine of *stare decisis*.'

12.164 As to errors of *fact* the Court of Appeal said this in *Assicurazioni Generali SpA v Arab Insurance Group*.[60]

12.165 Per Clarke LJ:

'The approach of the court to any particular case will depend upon the nature of the issues kind of case determined by the judge. This has been recognised recently in, for example, *Todd v Adams & Chope (trading as Trelawney Fishing Co)*[61] and *Bessant v South Cone Inc*.[62] In some cases the trial judge will have reached conclusions of primary fact based almost entirely upon the view which he formed of the oral evidence of the witnesses. In most cases, however, the position is more complex. In many such cases the judge will have reached his conclusions of primary fact as a result partly of the view he formed of the oral evidence and partly from an analysis of the documents. In other such cases, the judge will have made findings of primary fact based entirely or almost entirely on the documents. Some findings of primary fact will be the result of direct evidence, whereas others will depend upon inference from direct evidence of such facts.

In appeals against conclusions of primary fact the approach of an appellate court will depend upon the weight to be attached to the findings of the judge and that weight will depend upon the extent to which, as the trial judge, the judge has an advantage over the appellate court; the greater that advantage the more reluctant the appellate court should be to interfere. As I see it, that was the approach of the Court of Appeal on a "rehearing" under the Rules of the Supreme Court and should be its approach on a "review" under the Civil Procedure Rules 1998.

Some conclusions of fact are, however, not conclusions of primary fact of the kind to which I have just referred. They involve an assessment of a number of different factors which have to be weighed against each other. This is sometimes called an evaluation of the facts and is often a matter of degree upon which different judges can legitimately differ. Such cases may be closely analogous to the exercise of a discretion and, in my opinion, appellate courts should approach them in a similar way.'

12.166 Per Ward LJ:

'... we consider the judgment testing it against the evidence available to the judge and we ask, as we used to ask, whether it was wrong. The Court of Appeal can only interfere if the decision of the lower court was wrong and in deciding whether

---

[60] (Practice Note) [2003] 1 WLR 577, at pp 579 and 584.
[61] [2002] 2 Lloyd's Rep 293.
[62] [2002] EWCA Civ 763.

or not findings of fact were wrong, we take a retrospective look at the case and do not decide it afresh untrammelled by the judge's conclusion.

The trial judge's view inevitably imposes a restraint upon the appellate court, the weight of which varies from case to case. Two factors lead us to be cautious about interfering. First, the appellate court recognises that judging the witness is a more complex task than merely judging the transcript. Each may have its intellectual component but the former can also crucially rely on intuition. That gives the trial judge the advantage over us in assessing a witness's demeanour, so often a vital factor in deciding where the truth lies. Secondly, judging is an art not a science. So the more complex the question, the more likely it is that different judges will come to different conclusions and the harder it is to determine right from wrong. Borrowing language from other jurisprudence, the trial judge is entitled to "a margin of appreciation".

Bearing these matters in mind, the appeal court conducting a review of the trial judge's decision will not conclude that the decision was wrong simply because it is not the decision the appeal judge would have made had he or she been called upon to make it in the court below. Something more is required than personal unease and something less than perversity has to be established. The best formulation for the ground in between where a range of adverbs may be used;"clearly", "plainly", "blatantly", "palpably" wrong, is an adaptation of what Lord Fraser of Tullybelton said in *G v G (Minors: Custody Appeal)*,[63] admittedly dealing with the different task of exercising a discretion. Adopting his approach, I would pose the test for deciding whether a finding of fact was against the evidence to be whether that finding by the trial judge exceeded the generous ambit within which reasonable disagreement about the conclusion to be drawn from the evidence is possible. The difficulty or ease with which that test can be satisfied will depend on the nature of the finding under attack. If the challenge is to the finding of a primary fact, particularly if founded upon an assessment of the credibility of witnesses, then it will be a hard task to overthrow. Where the primary facts are not challenged and the judgment is made from the inferences drawn by the judge from the evidence before him, then the Court of Appeal, which has the power to draw any inference of fact it considers to be justified, may more readily interfere with an evaluation of those facts.'

Note that the appeal court can draw any inference of fact which it considers justified on the evidence; Part 52, rule 11(4).

12.167 The third factor, the wrong exercise of *discretion* by the lower court, as a possible ground of appeal, is harder to use as the basis of a successful appeal. This is because the appeal court is notoriously reluctant to find that the exercise by the lower court of its discretion (eg as to the remedy of an injunction or damages in lieu) is wrong. The statement of Lord Fraser of Tullybelton in *G v G (Minors: Custody Appeal)*[64] is usually relied upon here for guidance where the exercise of a discretion is being subjected to an appeal:

---

[63] [1985] 1 WLR 647 at p 652.
[64] [1985] 1 WLR 647 at p 652.

'... the appellate court should only interfere when they consider that the judge of first instance has not merely preferred an imperfect solution which is different from an alternative imperfect solution which the Court of Appeal might or would have adopted, but has exceeded the generous ambit within which a reasonable disagreement is possible.'

12.168　The skeleton argument which must accompany any notice of appeal (see Part 52 PD, sections 5.9–5.10) is an essential weapon is any appeal. It is the quality of the advocacy in this paper which will often win, or lose appeals; and certainly at the permission stage, the way in which the case for permission is in it put will be crucial.

Appeal from interim or case management decisions

12.169　The appeal courts do not favour these and the rules provide that certain strict conditions must be met for such appeals to have any prospect of success; see Part 52 PD, section 4.4–4.5.

Costs only appeals

12.170　The appeal court rarely disturbs appeals against costs orders. This is because of the nature of the discretion in the lower court under Part 44, rule 3 (see above at para **12.118**).

12.171　As was said in *Adamson v Halifax Plc*:[65]

'Costs are in the discretion of the trial judge and this court will only interfere with the exercise of that discretion on well-defined principles. As I said in *Roache v News Group Newspapers Ltd*:[66]

"Before the court can interfere it must be shown that the judge has either erred in principle in his approach, or has left out of account, or taken into account, some feature that he should, or should not, have considered, or that his decision is wholly wrong because the court is forced to the conclusion that he has not balanced the various factors fairly in the scale."

That statement was approved in *AEI Rediffusion Music Ltd v Phonographic Performance Ltd*.[67] Although that decision was before the CPR came into force, it is clear that the court applied the same principle in relation to interfering with the trial judge's discretion.'

12.172　Note:

(a)　Assessments of costs and appeals against them. (This is in contrast to the substantive order for costs referred to at (i) and (ii) above.) If the appeal is against an order of an authorised court officer who has assessed costs on

---

[65]　[2003] 1 WLR 60 at p 65 per Sir Murray Stuart-Smith.
[66]　[1998] EMLR, 161 at p 172.
[67]　[1999] 1 WLR 1507 at p 1523, per Lord Woolf MR.

a detailed assessment, CPR Part 47, rules 20–23 and PD sections 47–48 will apply to an appeal from that decision. No permission is required, it is complete rehearing, and Part 52 does not apply. If the appeal is from a costs judge following a detailed assessment, the appeal will follow the route under Part 52 PD, Table 1; see para **12.144**ff above. Such an appeal is one to which Part 52 will apply and is a review and not a complete rehearing. Reference should be made to the current editions of the costs text books (*Cook on Costs* (annual) and Friston, *Civil Costs: Law and Practice*, 2nd Edn, 2012) for the details of such appeals against assessments of costs.

(b) If the substantive appeal is allowed (ie the order made below NOT relating to costs is overturned or in some other way varied) the appeal court will have power to review and overturn the costs order made by the lower court; see Part 54, rule 10.

The hearing of appeals and assessing their merits

12.173 In private rights of way claims, and unless a re-hearing of the case is in the interests of justice, an appeal is limited to a review of the decision of the lower court; Part 52, rule 11(1).

12.174 The oral hearing of an appeal will usually adopt the following order:

(1) The appellant opens and present his case. As all parties to the appeal will have been required to file skeleton arguments Part 52 PD the appeal court will usually have read them and will be familiar with the issues in the appeal. So the task of the appellant, or his advocate, is to present his case against that background and deal with the points raised by the court.

(2) The respondent or his advocate will follow with the same task as the appellant.

(3) The appellant or his advocate may reply to any points raised by the respondent which require a reply.

(4) The court may call upon the respondent or his advocate to make submissions on certain points of concern at the stage when the appellant would normally open. This is often done if there are aspects of the respondent's case which require clarification, or where the court is concerned to hear what the respondent's case is on certain points.

(5) The court may decide that it does not want to hear submissions from the respondent if it is satisfied that the appeal is hopeless and without merit.

(6)   Unless certain very strict rules are satisfied, you cannot introduce new evidence in an appeal; see Part 52, rule 11(2) and *Ladd v Marshall*[68] and the numerous cases subsequent to that decision which can the found in the practice books commenting on Part 52, rule 11(2).

LAND REGISTRATION ADJUDICATION PROCEDURE

12.175 *Note: see the Preface as to the changes to the rules due to take place in 2013.*

See also Chapter 11 at para **11.153** above.

The rest of this Chapter must be read with such changes borne in mind.

Stage 1	Dispute over right of way
Stage 2	Correspondence with Land Registry
Stage 3	Resolution?
Stage 4	If resolved end of matter
Stage 5	If not resolved to next stage
Stage 6	Registrar prepared case summary under reference rules 3, not less than 15 business days for comments Registrar then refers to an adjudicator under section 73(7) 2002 Act and Reference Rules 5
Stage 7	Parties may prefer to settle at this stage but note procedural points as to whether or not reference can be withdrawn
Stage 8	Reference handled at initial stages by the adjudicator's office. Note: no longer a Land Registry matter
Stage 9	Notification of parties under Procedure Rules 5(b)
Stage 10	Directions under section 110/1 of the 2002 Act to start claim in court; Procedure Rules 6–11

---

[68]   [1954] 1 WLR 1489.

Stage 11	If no reference to court under section 110/1 of the Statement of Case by Applicant and Respondent under Rules 2–14 of the Procedure Rules
Stage 12	Preparation for hearing and directions; Procedure Rules Part 4
Stage 13	Hearing by adjudicator or deputy adjudicator. Procedure Rules Part 5
Stage 14	Decision. Instructions to registrar at Land Registry
Stage 15	Decision as to costs
Stage 16	Appeal and route of appeal. To High Court Judge. To Court of Appeal. To Supreme Court

APPENDIX TO CHAPTER 12

Forms of pleading

12.176 For details of practice etc, see Chapter 12 above. This is not a book on civil procedure, but certain points on rights of way disputes need to be observed when pleading cases in such disputes. The ground rules are set out in CPR Parts 7, 8 and 16. The essential ingredients of any claim or counterclaim raising title to a right of way are as follows:

(a) plead the title to sue and the grant or reservation which will be any one at least of the following:

   (i)   express terms; see Chapters 3, 4 and 5 above.
   (ii) *Wheeldon v Burrows*; see Chapter 3 above.
   (iii) Section 62 of the LPA 1925; see Chapter 3 above.
   (iv) Section 2 of the Prescription Act 1832. Note the need here to particularise 20 years user and compliance with that section; see Chapter 6 above.
   (v)   Lost modern grant; see Chapter 6 above.
   (vi) Particularise the date, so far as possible, of the alleged Lost Grant; alternative dates can be given; see *Tremayne v English China Clays Lovering & Pochin Ltd.*[69]
   (vii) Abandonment of any grant, or any release, giving particulars; see Chapter 9 above.

---

[69]   [1972] 1 WLR 657.

(b) Plead actionable interference. See Chapter 10 above.

(c) Plead the relief sought. This will include either a declaration, an injunction, or damages and statutory interest; see Chapter 11 above. The claim for damages should include a claim to interest under section 34A of the Senior Courts Act 1981 (if the claim is in the High Court) or section 68 of the County Courts Act 1984 if the claim is in the County Court.

(d) Plead loss and damage. Whilst damage does not establish the cause of action which is usually in nuisance (see Chapter 11 at para **11.117** above) it is usually needed as a matter of principle. A decision has to be taken in terms of tactics at the pleadings stage as to whether to exhibit reports from experts. If obtained at this early stage and they are in final form and if they are going to be relied on at trial, there is no reason not to refer to them in the Particulars of Claim and serve them at the same time (eg reports of the effect of traffic of an obstruction). Particulars will be needed of any loss and damage sought.

(e) If specified work needs to be done under the injunction (effectively in mandatory terms) for example to restore land, or to remove obstructions, this needs to be stated. Any order for work to be done must be in precise terms so that the party ordered to carry it out knows precisely what he has to do.

(f) Consider whether there are any other claims which need to be brought within the pleading, or any other form of relief, for example a declaration as to boundaries to resolve a boundary dispute, or rectification of the transfer, or a dispute over drainage or water supply. Sadly these claims are often found clustered together, especially in residential neighbour disputes.

Defendants

12.177 Defendants will need to file and serve a defence and if necessary a counterclaim, see CPR Part 16, rule 4; para **12.52ff** above.

The defence should plead matters such as consent or illegality of user in a claim based on prescription. A counterclaim is only needed if the defendant is making a counter assertion; eg. for a declaration as to the route of the right of way.

If and so far as there is a counterclaim, the same particulars that need to be set out in a Particulars of Claim need to be set out in a counterclaim; eg setting out the express, implied or prescriptive grant to a right of way.

Reference should also be made here to the provisions in the CPR Part 15, rule 8 as regards the reply to any defence. A reply to a defence is optional. The claimant need not file a reply unless there are matters stated in the defence which go beyond the mere joinder of issue; eg in a right of way case where the defence pleads a release of a right of way which in fact becomes overtaken by a later re-grant. So far as there is any counterclaim, a defence to a counterclaim must be filed and served; see para **12.54** above.

Claim forms

12.178   As stated above at paras **12.44–12.45**, the best course is to adopt the Part 7 claim form with Particulars of Claim annexed.

In cases where the facts are unlikely to be in dispute (eg where matters of pure questions of construction arise) a Part 8 claim form with a witness statement in support is the appropriate course to take.

In the vast majority of cases where there is any evidence of dispute of fact, a Part 7 claim form with fully pleaded particulars will make it easy for the parties and the court to see what is in issue from those particulars and any defence and counterclaim. This is often in stark contrast to the lengthy and often woolly statements found in witness statements which are filed and served in conjunction with Part 8 claims.

Chapter 13

LAND REGISTRATION AND TITLE

GENERAL PRINCIPLES AND OUTLINE

13.1 Where title to land is registered, the rules set out in other Chapters are modified by the law contained in the Land Registration Act 2002 (LRA 2002) and the Land Registration Rules 2003[1] (LRR 2003) which both came into force on 13 October 2003 replacing earlier legislation. The general rule is that a right of way over registered land is not enforceable unless either it is an overriding interest (paras **13.3–13.18**) or it is entered or noted on the register of title. Express rights granted over registered land after 12 October 2003 must be registered (paras **13.19–13.26**). Implied and prescriptive rights may be either registered or overriding (paras **13.27–13.46**). The rules for leasehold easements are similar to freehold but modified (paras **13.47–13.62**). Most rules apply to legal interests, that is those held for an interest equivalent to a fee simple or a term of years. Equitable easements have separate rules (paras **13.63–13.76**). Where a right is neither registered nor overriding it may still have some effect in limited circumstances (paras **13.77–13.84**). The Chapter concludes with some procedural issues (paras **13.85–13.94**), extinction (paras **13.95–13.98**) and commonhold rights (paras **13.99–13.100**).

SOURCES OF LAW

13.2 The law affecting rights of way over registered land is found in LRA 2002 and LRR 2003 as amended:

(a) If the rights existed on 12 October 2003 it may be necessary to refer to the Land Registration Acts 1925 (LRA 1925) to 1997 and the Land Registration Rules 1925[2] (LRR 1925) as amended.

(b) There are a few decisions of the courts specifically affecting registered titles subject to rights of way or easements generally but rulings before 2003 may not still apply.

(c) These sources are supplemented by Land Registry Practice Guides (PG), in particular PG 62 (Easements), PG 52 (Easements claimed by prescription), PG 15 (Overriding interests and their disclosure), PG 19 (Notices, restrictions and the protection of third party interests in the

---

[1] SI 2003/1417 amended by SIs 2005/766, 2005/1982, 2008/1750, 2008/1919 and 2009/1996.
[2] SR&O 1925, No 1093.

register) and PG 64 (Prescribed clause leases) which present an authoritative land registry view although they are not themselves law and are in principle subject to challenge. These are accessible on the land registry website and as they are subject to frequent revision it is important to check the latest version.

(d)   The rules of the general law are to be read subject to the LRA 2002 but will otherwise apply.

RIGHTS OF WAY AS OVERRIDING INTERESTS

General

13.3   The register is intended to be conclusive and contain a reference to all rights affecting the registered estate. In general, a right of way will bind the servient proprietor only if it appears on the title. However, an unregistered right can sometimes subsist as an overriding interest which overrides the lack of mention on the register. In relation to private[3] rights of way there are distinct rules as to those which bind the estate on first registration and those which bind on a disposition.[4]

Overriding interests arising in registered land before 13 October 2003

13.4   Schedule 12, paragraph 9 of LRA 2002 provides that an easement which was an overriding interest before 13 October 2003 in land registered before that date will continue as such (see para **13.15**). This includes all unregistered legal rights of way and certain equitable ones (see para **13.68**).

Position of overriding interests on first registration after 12 October 2003

13.5   Sections 11 and 12 of LRA 2002 incorporate Schedule 1 which sets out those interests which override on first registration. Schedule 1, paragraph 3 reads 'A legal easement or profit a prendre'. This comprises rights existing prior to the disposition (if any) giving rise to registration whether express, implied or prescriptive as well as servient rights implied by reservation out of that disposition. Such rights will bind the first proprietor of the servient tenement. The reason is that under normal rules the right will have bound the owner before first registration. That position is not changed by the fact that at some date (usually a few days but it may be many years in the case of a voluntary registration) after acquiring the land the owner applies to be registered.

---

[3]   Public rights of way are overriding under Sch 1, para 5 and Sch 3, para 5.
[4]   Customary ways (see para **13.14**) will always be overriding: see LRA 2002, Sch 1, para 4; Sch 3, para 4. This appears to be so even if they are also manorial under para 11 and therefore subject to the time limits in s 117.

Position of overriding interests on a disposition

13.6 Sections 29 and 30 of LRA 2002 incorporate Schedule 3, paragraph 3 which sets out those unregistered easements which bind on a disposition and provides (omitting references to profits) as follows:

'3 Easements ....

(1) A legal easement ... except for an easement ... which at the time of the disposition—
   (a) is not within the actual knowledge of the person to whom the disposition is made, and
   (b) would not have been obvious on a reasonably careful inspection of the land over which the easement or profit is exercisable.
(2) The exception in sub-paragraph (1) does not apply if the person entitled to the easement ... proves that it has been exercised in the period of one year ending with the day of the disposition.'

13.7 The effect is (first) that an equitable right of way is not overriding[5] on a disposition and (secondly) that an unregistered legal right of way binds the person taking under the disposition unless it satisfies both of two conditions. One is that it is not obvious on inspection of the servient land. The other is that the disponee does not actually know about the right. This applies as much to express rights as to implied, prescriptive or statutory ones: see para **13.16**.

13.8 However, if the dominant owner can prove he has exercised the right during the year before the disposition then the right of way will still bind even if neither obvious nor known. The day of the disposition here means the day the transfer, lease, grant or charge was completed, not the day of submission for registration. Even though, if the disposition is not registered within the statutory time limits, it does not operate at law[6] it does operate in equity. The right will bind the disponee so long as he retains his estate or interest but (unless it becomes known or obvious) it will not bind another person (such as a lessee) taking under a disposition more than a year after the last exercise.

13.9 It remains to be determined what will be 'obvious'. Presumably the draftsman of the LRA 2002 intended a different meaning from the words 'continuous and apparent' in the rule in *Wheeldon v Burrows*(see para **3.30**). The issue did not arise under LRA 1925 since all legal rights of way (and some equitable ones) were overriding interests without any need to be evident. In most cases the right will be exercisable over a track or path which will lead somewhere and which will be an 'obvious' feature but the identity of the property (or properties) it serves may not be. Suppose the buyer of a mansion house with a metalled drive discovers six months after his purchase that the owner of a holiday cottage in the former grounds has a right of way arising from implied grant after 12 October 2003. The cottage owner has not been there for two years. What would be obvious on inspection? The driveway itself

---

5   Unless preserved by LRA 2002, Sch 12, para 9.
6   LRA 2002, s 27(1).

would be but it also leads to the mansion and other houses. Would knowledge of the existence of the cottage be sufficient? What if it is hidden behind some trees? Or there might be a right of access to a garden to repair an adjacent house where the need to repair only occurs at infrequent intervals. There appears scope for dispute. It is likely this will involve an objective test as to what would be obvious to a reasonable disponee to balance the subjective test of actual knowledge. The right will bind if the disponee either knew under (a) or ought to have known under (b).

13.10   If an interest within Schedule 3 is the subject of a notice on the register at any time after 12 October 2003 then, if it is subsequently removed from the register, it will not revert to being an overriding interest.[7]

13.11   It can happen that the benefit of a right of way is entered on the dominant title but the burden is not registered on the servient title in which case it will only bind the servient owner if it is overriding. A conveyancer for the dominant owner may therefore wish to check the servient title.

Duty to disclose overriding interests

13.12   An applicant for registration must either state that he does not know about any overriding interests or, if he knows his land is servient, he must disclose them. This will normally be in form D1. On first registration (when all legal easements are overriding) rule 23(1) of LRR 2003 requires the use of form FR1 in which panel 11 requires D1 as does rule 28(1). (Strictly a right can not be overriding until the first edition of the register has been issued but the registry uses the expression for convenience.) In addition, panel 12 is a certificate that the applicant has disclosed all known rights. If they are shown up in the documents of title land registry staff should pick them up (rule 28(2)(b)). An equitable right registered as a land charge (see para **13.68**) should also be picked up if it was created or referred to within the period of the title deduced. On a disposition, rule 57(1) requires disclosure in form AP1, panel 11 of which requires form D1. There is no equivalent in form AP1 to panel 12 of FR1 so the duty extends only to overriding interests.

13.13   The wording of Schedule 3, paragraph 3(1)(a) is if the legal easement is 'not within the actual knowledge' of the disponee. If an applicant knows that another person claims an unregistered disclosable right of way but does not admit the right exists, care must be taken in giving a statement that there are no interests as failure to disclose will be a breach of duty[8] and may constitute an offence.[9] It is suggested that the best approach is a balance of probabilities; in case of doubt the claimed interest should be disclosed but on the basis that it is not admitted.

---

[7]   LRA 2002, s 29(3).
[8]   LRA 2002, s 71.
[9]   LRA 2002, s 123.

Legal rights of way existing on 13 October 2003

13.14 Before 13 October 2003 it was not essential to have the right on the register although it was good practice. The benefit could be entered on the dominant property register[10] and the burden on the servient title.[11] A legal easement, however, created or arising, which was not entered on the charges register of the servient title, took effect as an overriding interest binding the servient land either on first registration or if created subsequently.[12] This included express grants and implied and prescriptive rights.[13]

13.15 To preserve the position, a right which was an overriding interest in land registered before 13 October 2003 retains that status under LRA 2002, Sch 12, para 9 unless and until the right is registered. This includes all legal rights of way and certain equitable rights (see paras **13.4**, **13.68**).

13.16 If title to the servient land was not registered before 13 October 2003, paragraph 9 does not apply. On first registration after that date any unregistered legal easement subsisting before that date remains overriding.[14] On a subsequent disposition it will only retain that status if it is known, obvious or recently exercised (see para **13.6**).[15] It is possible on first registration to overlook the effect of a deed especially where the documents of title have become separated or if the grantor did not take a duplicate or counterpart or to overlook an implied or prescriptive right. This may present problems although it is not a nullity (see para **13.77**). A conveyancer acting for an owner with the benefit of an old right should check the servient title.

13.17 Even if the land has become registered without reference to a right of way, the applicant has a duty on any disposition on or after 13 October 2003 (see para **13.12**) to disclose known overriding interests. These include a right of way granted or having arisen before that date over a title registered before that date. On the first disposition following after first registration it also includes a right granted before first registration but after that date. On a later disposition it may not, but this may depend on the estate granted. Thus registration of a lease or charge would not exclude the duty of disclosure on a later transfer of the freehold. If in doubt a conveyancer should consider disclosing any known unregistered rights of way but as this might lead to what would otherwise have been an unenforceable right becoming noted on the register, care should be taken.

---

[10] LRR 1925, r 3(2)(c).
[11] LRA 1925, s 70(2) and (3); LRR 1925, rr 40 and 41.
[12] LRA 1925, s 70(1)(a).
[13] LRA 1925, ss 9 and 20. It also includes customary ways (LRA 1925, s 70(1)(a)) which are regarded as private rights of way. *Brocklebank v Thompson* [1903] 2 Ch 344, see para **2.77**.
[14] LRA 2002, Sch 1, para 3, see para **13.5**.
[15] There was a transitional provision to protect the situation in LRA 2002, Sch 12, para 10. This expired on 12 October 2006, see para **1.24**.

13.18 LRR 2003, r 73A[16] provides that a proprietor of a (dominant) registered estate may apply to be registered as the proprietor of a legal easement which has been acquired over unregistered land however arising.[17] Although possibly aimed at current grants over unregistered land, the wording is not limited to them and extends to rights over land unregistered at the time of grant even if registered later.

EXPRESS LEGAL RIGHTS OF WAY

Created after 12 October 2003 over servient registered titles

13.19 A deed is required for a grant out of registered land as for unregistered land (see para **3.6**). This may be satisfied either by a separate deed of grant or by incorporation by grant or reservation in a transfer, lease or other disposition. A transfer of all or part of a registered title must be in, and a registrable lease must include, one of the prescribed forms which allow for rights of way.[18] There is no prescribed form for a separate grant but it should include the title number of the servient land[19] and of the dominant land (if registered) and normally a plan which must be drawn to land registry standards (PG 40 Land Registry Plans) with a scale and a north point. If the registry considers the document or the plan defective it will reject the application for registration under LRR 2003, r 16(3).[20]

13.20 LRA 2002, s 27(1) and (2)(d) provide that the express grant or reservation of an easement in relation to a registered estate for an interest equivalent to a fee simple or a term of years absolute requires to be completed by registration and does not operate at law until the relevant registration requirements are met. The main requirement is that the burden of the grant is entered in the charges register of the servient title.[21] Other requirements relate to the use of correct application forms.[22] If the grant or reservation is not so completed it is not void but it takes effect in equity (see para **13.63ff**).

13.21 If the grant or reservation is in a transfer or other registrable disposition then it will automatically be registered on registration of the

---

[16] Inserted by Sch 1, para 24 of the Land Registration (Amendment) Rules 2008, with effect from 10 November 2008.

[17] LRR 2003, r 73A(1)(a).

[18] An assent of unregistered land need not be a deed (Administration of Estates Act 1925, s 36(4)) and if under hand can validly grant a right of way (*Sweet v Sommer* [2005] 2 All ER 64 CA). An assent can also impliedly reserve a right of way, see *Thompson v Bee* [2009] EWCA Civ 1212. An assent of part of a registered title granting a right of way must be in form AS 3 which must be executed as a deed. As to short leases see paras **13.51–13.53**.

[19] LRR 2003, r 212(3).

[20] The former practice on plans was strict but as from September 2012 it was it was relaxed to a limited extent. The registry may now accept a plan provided it is possible to identify the land the subject of the application. See PG 49 Return and rejection of applications for registration, para 6.2.

[21] LRA 2002, Sch 2, para 7; LRR 2003, r 9(a).

[22] LRA 2002, s 25; LRR 2003, r 13.

disposition against the servient title.[23] If the grant is in a separate deed the grantee will need to apply for registration using form AP1. If that is not done then, even if the grantee registers an agreed or unilateral notice, that will not be sufficient. A notice by itself is no guarantee of validity. It merely preserves priority of the equitable interest. The registry will put the notice on the servient title but add a note in the following terms:[24]

> 'NOTE: The grant or reservation of the rights ... has not been completed by registration in accordance with section 27 of the Land Registration Act 2002 and so does not operate at law.'

13.22 The duty to disclose overriding interests on registering a disposition does not extend to such an equitable right (see para **13.12** but see also para **3.114**).

Created after 12 October 2003 over servient unregistered land

13.23 If a legal right of way is expressly granted or reserved over unregistered land then until registration the right will take effect under normal rules as a legal interest. On first registration of the servient land the applicant has a duty to disclose known rights (see para **13.12**). The right may be overlooked and not entered on the register but it still takes effect as an overriding interest.[25] If it does not qualify on a subsequent disposition (because not known, obvious or recently exercised) it may be postponed to the rights of the registered proprietor (see para **13.79**).

Created after 12 October 2003 for the benefit of a dominant registered title

13.24 Although LRR 2003, r 5(b)(ii) provides that the Property Register 'must' where appropriate contain details of easements benefiting the registered estate, this provision in delegated legislation should be read subject to the statutory provision in LRA 2002, s 11(3) that registration vests title to the registered estate in the registered proprietor together with all interests subsisting for the benefit of the estate. Accordingly, failure to register the benefit on the title to the dominant land does not invalidate the right of way as a legal interest.

13.25 If the right arises in a registrable transaction then when the transaction is registered against the servient title the benefit will be registered in the dominant title provided the registry is given the dominant title number.[26]

13.26 If the servient land is not registered, the dominant owner may still apply in form AP1 for the benefit of an express grant or reservation to be noted.

---

[23] LRA 2002, s 38.
[24] PG 62, para 3.1.
[25] LRA 2002, Sch 1, para 3.
[26] LRR 2003, r 72C; PG 62, para 4.1.

LRR 2003, r 73A(1)(a)[27] provides that a proprietor of a (dominant) registered estate may apply to be registered as the proprietor of a legal easement which has been acquired over unregistered land however arising.[28] The registrar will require production of the servient title[29] which the applicant will need to prove in the normal way for unregistered land. Although for land this usually begins with a good root of title (sale or mortgage) at least 15 years old that has been held at first instance not to apply to an easement such as a right of way. On appeal the Court of Appeal did not discuss the point.[30] If the registrar is not satisfied as to title he may enter details of the right 'with such qualification as he considers appropriate'.[31] If not disclosed on first registration the right will remain overriding but on a disposition it will only do so if known, obvious or recently exercised. It is therefore sensible to register a caution (see paras **13.85–13.89**).

IMPLIED, PRESCRIPTIVE AND STATUTORY RIGHTS OF WAY

In general

13.27 An unregistered legal right of way subsisting over registered land on 12 October 2003 remains an overriding interest (see para **13.15**) and this includes implied, prescriptive and statutory rights.

13.28 Where an implied or prescriptive or statutory right has arisen (before or after that date) over unregistered land, it will qualify on first registration under LRA 2002, Sch 1, para 3 as an overriding interest.

13.29 Where the land was first registered after that date (irrespective of when the right arose) or where the right arose after that date (irrespective of when the land was first registered), if it has not been entered or noted on the register it will take priority over a disposition for valuable consideration only if it is known to the disponee or obvious or recently exercised (see para **13.6**).

13.30 If not, it may be postponed to the rights of the registered proprietor. An unregistered implied or prescriptive or statutory right remains a legal interest since section 27(2)(d) of LRA 2002 (which converts otherwise unregistered legal interests to equitable ones) applies only to express grants and section 27(7) provides this does not include the operation of LPA 1925, s 62. Such a right therefore retains some significance and may in some cases recover priority (see para **13.84**).

---

[27] Inserted by Sch 1, para 2, Land Registration (Amendment) Rules 2008, with effect from 10 November 2008.
[28] LRR 2003, r 73A(1)(a).
[29] LRR 2003, r 73A(2).
[30] *Barclays Bank v Lougher* (1996) 51 Con LR 75 applying LPA 1925, s 44 as modified by the Law of Property Act 1969, s 23. See para **1.20**.
[31] LRR 2003, r 33(2).

Registering the benefit of implied, prescriptive and statutory rights of way

13.31 A registered title has the benefit of any rights enforceable against other land, whether or not they are noted on the dominant register (see para **13.24**). It is normally good practice to enter the benefit of an implied or prescriptive right on the dominant title, but that is not necessary for its validity. It is unusual for statutory private rights of way to be entered but there seems no reason why this should not be done.

13.32 On first registration, the registrar may enter appurtenant rights if he is satisfied that the right subsists as a legal estate[32] and if he is not satisfied he may enter details of the right with such qualifications as he considers appropriate.[33]

13.33 At any time after first registration (and not necessarily on a disposition), LRR 2003, r 73A[34] provides that a proprietor of a registered estate may apply to be registered as the proprietor of a legal easement which has been acquired over a registered title otherwise than by express grant or reservation[35] or over unregistered land however arising.[36] An express grant does not include the operation of LPA 1925, s 62: r 73A(3).

13.34 A right arising by virtue of statute without a deed is not an express grant (see generally Chapter 7). Several arose under inclosure acts and railway acts. More recent sources of such rights arise from stopping up or downgrading of highways. If a public highway is stopped up or diverted, a new private right may be given to a person affected, for example under section 129 of the Highways Act 1980. Under section 67(5) of the Natural Environment and Rural Communities Act 2006 if an unrecorded vehicular right of way is extinguished a private right may come into existence. These statutory rights arise by operation of law and are similar to implied rights. Where they relate to ancient 'green lanes' the servient title will often be unregistered. Where the adjacent land, such as a field or garden, is registered then the green lane (or half of it up to the middle line or *medium filum*) may be regarded under the general boundaries rule under section 60 of the LRA 2002 as being within the title even though the red line showing the boundary on the official plan may run along the field or garden side of the lane. However, *medium filum* is only a presumption and the soil of the lane may not be in the adjacent title but be vested in some other owner such as a lord of a manor (see para **2.16**).

---

[32] LRR 2003, r 33(1).
[33] LRR 2003, r 33(3). Inserted by Sch 1, para 9, Land Registration (Amendment) Rules 2008, with effect from 10 November 2008.
[34] Inserted by Sch 1, para 24, Land Registration (Amendment) Rules 2008, with effect from 10 November 2008.
[35] LRR 2003, r 73A(1)(b).
[36] LRR 2003, r 73A(1)(a).

13.35 The applicant must supply supporting evidence (see para **13.45**) to satisfy the registrar that the easement is a legal estate which subsists for the benefit of the applicant's registered estate.[37] If the registrar is not satisfied as to the evidence he may enter details in the property register with such modifications as he considers appropriate.[38]

13.36 The mentions in rr 33(1) and 73A of the easement subsisting as 'a legal estate' refer[39] to section 205(1)(x) of LPA 1925, where the expression is defined to include legal interests. The reference in r 73A(1) to being a 'proprietor' of an easement appears odd as it cannot subsist in gross as property on its own. This was added in 2008 and did not appear in the previous version in the rules (rr 73 and 74 repealed) as originally issued in 2003 which referred to a person who 'claims the benefit' of a legal easement. The wording comes from LRA 2002, Sch 2, para 7(2)(b) which also covers a rentcharge which can subsist in gross. The inference is that the proprietor of the appurtenant land is also proprietor of all rights that go with it.

13.37 The registry will consider the evidence and may then enter a note but it will often be phrased to make it clear that the right is claimed but not conclusively proved. A standard form of note[40] is:

> '[Date] The registered proprietor claims that the land has the benefit of a right [terms of right as claimed by claimant]. The right claimed is not included in this registration. The claim is supported by [dates and details of statement(s) of truth or statutory declaration(s) and who has made them].
>
> NOTE: Copy/copies filed.'

13.38 The effect of the right not being included is that it stands alone. As the effect of substantive registration of the benefit of a right is a registry guarantee that the right exists, so that it could be liable to pay compensation if it is wrong, the registrar will not make an unqualified entry unless satisfied of the position.

Registering the burden of implied, prescriptive and statutory rights of way

13.39 Registration of the benefit is not sufficient protection on its own. The right must either be overriding or the burden be entered on the servient title. If the dominant claimant has sufficient evidence to satisfy the registrar that the right exists, he can apply for substantive registration against the servient title in form AP1. In the case of a right (whether statutory as considered in para **13.34** or implied or prescriptive) over a green lane which is not within the red line on an official plan, then if the applicant is unsure whether the lane is treated under the general boundaries rule as being in the registered title or not it would be

---

[37] LRR 2003, r 73A(2).
[38] LRR 2003, r 73A(5), as amended.
[39] LRA 2002, s 132(1).
[40] PG 52, para 7.2.

prudent to lodge a caution (para **13.85**) against the lane itself as well as registering a notice on the title to the adjacent land, and if the land on each side is in separate titles, then on both.

13.40 If the claimant cannot produce satisfactory evidence, he can register a notice under LRR 2003, Part 7 on the charges register of the servient title to protect an implied or prescriptive or statutory right of way in form AN1 or UN1. This does not give full protection since the entry of a notice is not registration for that purpose (see para **13.21**) but if the right exists it preserves priority.[41] If the right satisfies the conditions to be overriding then the conveyancer for a potential applicant should consider whether it is sensible to register a notice. That is because if a notice is lodged, the right ceases to be overriding and if the notice is subsequently cancelled it will not thereupon become overriding again.[42] On balance it will in most cases be preferable to have a notice on the register but that may not always be so.

13.41 If there is sufficient evidence of validity, or if the servient proprietor consents, there can be an agreed notice. If the servient owner accepts that the right exists as claimed, then instead of a notice a substantive entry of the right may be made in the form agreed although in such a case it would be better practice for the parties to enter into an express deed of grant to make the terms clear.

13.42 If an agreed notice cannot be used, the dominant owner will need to protect the right by a unilateral notice. On receipt the registrar will notify the servient proprietor[43] who may object or may recognise only a right in different terms, for instance a right for one dwelling rather than an unrestricted right. In the absence of express objection the unilateral notice will be entered but the servient proprietor can apply at any time for it to be cancelled.[44]

Disputes about notices affecting implied and prescriptive rights of way

13.43 If the servient owner either objects to the original application or later applies for cancellation and the applicant does not agree, the matter will be referred to adjudication. (see para **11.152**).

13.44 Where the benefit and burden have been noted independently as a result of separate disclosures by the two proprietors or by a notice lodged at a time different from first registration of the dominant title, the state of the dominant and servient registers may be different. The registry will not automatically coordinate the entries on the two titles. To the extent that a right is overriding it may exist but in a form different from that for which either party argues. It is therefore unsafe to rely on entries for implied or prescriptive rights of way and

---

[41]   LRA 2002, s 32.
[42]   LRA 2002, s 29(3).
[43]   LRA 2002, s 35(1)(a).
[44]   LRA 2002, s 36; LRR 2003, r 86.

a conveyancer should check the wording on both titles. Even where there is no entry or notice on the servient title it may be prudent to inspect any title which might be thought to claim a right of way.

Evidence supporting a claim to a prescriptive right of way

13.45 The claimant will need to satisfy the registrar of his claim. Unless the right is admitted, the claimant will still have to make a case on the facts. The application must include a statement of truth, which may be made in Form ST4[45] although use of that form is not obligatory[46] but any application must comply with LRR 2003, r 215A.[47] Statutory declarations are often also provided in support (see para **12.17**).

13.46 If title to the servient land is unregistered, the applicant will need to prove it. The dominant claimant may have limited information as to the title and there could be some defect or intervening interest which might prevent prescription. Where an implied grant arises on a disposition leading to first registration, it will usually be sufficient to show that the servient land had been in the same title as the dominant land.

RIGHTS AFFECTING LEASEHOLDS

In general

13.47 The law concerning registered leasehold titles is as far as possible the same as for freeholds but the nature of a leasehold estate involves some adaptations.

13.48 If after 8 January 2006 the right is granted in or reserved out of a registrable lease, then the lease itself must (with limited exceptions) include prescribed clauses.[48] These include a form on the front of the lease, part of which is as follows:

---

[45] LRR 2003, r 73A(4) as amended; see also PG 73 – Statements of Truth.
[46] PG 52, para 6.2.
[47] Inserted by SI 2008/1919, r 4(1), Sch 1, para 72 with effect from 10 November 2008: SI 2008/1919, r 2.
[48] LRR 2003, r 58 and Sch 1A, clause LR 11 as amended by Land Registration (Amendment) (No 2) Rules 2005, with effect from 9 January 2006.

LR11: Easements *Refer here only to the clause, Schedule or paragraph of a Schedule in this lease which sets out the easements*	LR11.1: Easements granted by this lease for the benefit of the property
	LR11.2: Easements granted or reserved by this lease over the property for the benefit of other property

13.49 Leases of less than seven years are not normally registered with their own titles.[49] Occasionally some short leases such as discontinuous tenancies[50] may be registrable. But in general there is no register for short leases on which to note the benefit or burden.

Rights affecting the reversion to a leasehold

13.50 The burden of express rights granted after 12 October 2003 will need to be noted on the title to the registered servient tenement, whether freehold or leasehold. An express right of way affecting the title and not completed by registration is equitable.[51] That includes leasehold rights and it applies even if the dominant lease itself is not registrable (for example because it is a monthly or yearly tenancy).

13.51 If a right of way under a subtenancy (say annual) is granted out of an unregistrable headlease (say for five years) but is not binding on the reversion to the headlease, it cannot be registered. PG 62, para 10 says with some hesitation that if a headlease has the benefit of an easement and grants a sublease of part, there is still a single easement and the subtenant can protect it by unilateral or agreed notice.

13.52 Where the tenancy is created orally or in writing otherwise than by deed, the view expressed by the registry[52] is that any beneficial easement is equitable. However, provided the tenancy of the land takes effect in possession, is for not more than three years and is at the best rent without a fine[53] it will create a legal estate in the demised land and, although an express right of way will be equitable until registered, an implied one will be a legal interest.[54]

13.53 For example, if a landlord of a large house grants a written monthly tenancy of the second floor flat with an express right of way across the front

---

[49]   LRA 2002, s 3(3).
[50]   LRA 2002, s 3(4).
[51]   LRA 2002, s 27(1) and (2)(d) – see para **13.20**.
[52]   PG 62, para 5.3.
[53]   LPA 1925, s 54(2).
[54]   *Wright v Macadam* [1949] 2KB 744.

garden and up the stairs, the tenant ought to register the right. An express right which is not registered is equitable and will not be saved as an overriding interest. If the reversion is sold, the tenant's unregistered right will not bind the new proprietor who can therefore obstruct the access. (Such obstruction may be harassment[55] or may infringe the tenant's human right for respect for his home[56] but that is a separate issue.) However, if the tenancy agreement (if there is one) does not expressly grant a right but it is implied, then there is no obligation to register the implied right and it will subsist as a legal interest and may therefore be overriding. Such a distinction is illogical.

13.54 Where a lease is itself registered or noted on the landlord's title, the register will include a reference to the easements granted by the lease in the following terms:[57]

> 'The parts of the land affected thereby are subject to the leases set out in the schedule of leases hereto. The leases grant and reserve easements as therein mentioned.'

13.55 If the lease contains a provision affecting a disposal by the landlord, for instance by a business tenant to secure a right of way on any disposition of the reversion to the servient land,[58] this should be referred to in clause LR 10 of the Prescribed Terms (because the servient land is not part of the property) but the tenant may also wish to protect the right by notice.

Rights affecting the leasehold

13.56 Leasehold land may be subject to rights of way affecting the superior title before the lease was granted. If the superior estate was registered at the date of grant the registry will automatically copy over any relevant entries. If not, the registry will either require proof of title in order to grant absolute title or will grant a good leasehold or qualified title which is automatically subject to any relevant rights.

13.57 There will also be rights of way benefiting or reserved out of the registered lease under the terms of the grant and the register contains a standard entry:[59]

> 'Unless otherwise mentioned the title includes any legal easements granted by the registered lease(s) but is subject to any rights that it reserves, so far as those easements and rights exist and benefit or affect the registered land.'

---

55   Protection from Eviction Act 1977, s 1.
56   Human Rights Act 1998, Sch 1, Pt I, art 8. This may apply only where the landlord is a public authority. See para **2.52**.
57   PG 62, para 5.1.1.1.
58   To avoid the problem in *Land Reclamation Co Ltd v Basildon District Council* [1979] 2 All ER 993, [1979] 1 WLR 767.
59   PG 62, para 5.1.1.

13.58 Similarly, the lessee may be in a position to grant rights for the residue of the term or rights may be acquired by prescription to endure so long as the term continues or be implied in an assignment of part or in a sublease. These will be treated in a similar way to rights out of freehold land save that they will only be temporary rights.

Leases of rights of way as incorporeal interests

13.59 Section 3 of LRA 2002 provides that title to an easement alone can not be registered. A lease of an incorporeal right of way still needs to be completed by registration under LRA 2002, s 27(1) and (2)(d). The benefit can only be registered as appurtenant to the dominant corporeal title. The burden will need to be noted on the title to the land out of which it was granted in the normal way.

13.60 Unlike a lease of an estate in land, a lease of a right of way on its own as an incorporeal hereditament does not have to include the prescribed clauses. These are required by LRR 2003, r 58A(4)(a)[60] which defines a 'prescribed clauses lease' as one within LRA 2002, s 27(2)(b) which refers to the grant of a term of years absolute. Section 132(1) of LRA 2002 incorporates the definition in LPA 1925, s 205(1)(xxvii) which requires the term to take effect in possession or in reversion and a lease of a right of way does neither. Although under LPA 1925, s 1(2)(a) an easement can subsist for an interest equivalent to a term of years absolute, that does not make it a term for this purpose. This is consistent with LRR 2003, Sch 1A, panel LR4 which refers to the 'land' being leased.

Determination of leases

13.61 When a lease is determined (however this occurs), any beneficial rights of way will usually also determine. The burden of any subject rights over the leasehold belonging to parties other than the landlord may also determine although this may depend on how the lease determined. Where the lease and its easements are all derived out of the same superior title, closure of the leasehold title will normally involve the removal of any reference to the rights of way. Where the right has been noted against another title it will usually be necessary for the proprietor of that title to make an application for removal of any notice of the lease and its rights. However, it appears from *Wall v Collins*[61] (see para **9.37**) that in certain circumstances a leasehold right of way can survive termination of the lease. In such cases, therefore, the applicant may need to satisfy the registry that the right of way has indeed been extinguished. PG 26 (Leases – determination) in para 4.4 refers to beneficial easements affecting a registered estate and gives guidance for noting them.

13.62 If a right benefiting a subtenant has been protected by notice and is to be cancelled (for example on expiry of the subtenancy) then, if it was a

---

[60]   As amended by the Land Registration (Amendment) (No 2) Rules 2005, SI 2005/1982, rule 5.
[61]   [2007] Ch 390.

unilateral notice, the subtenant can do so on his own, but if an agreed notice the registrar will require evidence that the right has ceased to exist.[62]

EQUITABLE RIGHTS OF WAY

In general

13.63 A right may either be equitable in its nature (for instance as being conditional, terminable or arising by proprietary estoppel,[63] see para **13.71**) or may take effect in equity but not as a legal interest because it fails to comply with formalities (in this context particularly registration requirements). In general, the register is concerned with legal rights but the burden of an equitable right may be registrable against the servient title.

13.64 The original requirement of equity that an equitable right was not enforceable against a bona fide purchaser of the legal estate without notice has not adapted easily to the structure of registered conveyancing. For example, on the basis that a way of necessity subsists only so long as the necessity does, it must be equitable and if not registered it will not bind a servient proprietor.

13.65 If the servient land was not registered before 13 October 2003, an equitable right cannot be an overriding interest (because such an interest must now be legal, see paras **13.5** and**13.7**; in contrast to the position before that date see para **13.68**) and therefore there is no duty directly under LRR on an applicant for registration of a disposition to disclose it.[64] However, on first registration form FR1 (required by LRR, r 23(1)) requires disclosure of all rights (see para **13.75**) and under LRA 2002, s 123 if a person suppresses information with the intention of concealing a person's right he is guilty of an offence. An equitable easement is a right for this purpose. It is also possible for the beneficiary to protect it by notice under LRA 2002, s 32 as notices are not limited to legal interests.

Pre-1926 equitable rights of way

13.66 An equitable right in unregistered land arising before 1926 will only be enforceable against a purchaser of the legal estate for value with notice. If the notice was in writing[65] it may still be among the documents of title. Any pre-1926 equitable rights of way which survive will be rare and if they have been in regular use the dominant owner may be able to establish some other form of legal right. Where a right was initially equitable, for instance if it was terminable, and is still exercised, it will remain in force in accordance with pre-1926 law.

---

[62] PG 62, para 10.
[63] *ER Ives Investments Ltd v High* [1967] 2 QB 379.
[64] LRR 2003, r 57.
[65] See *Greaves v Tofield* (1880) LR 14 Ch D 563.

13.67 Under LRA 1862, s 27(2) an easement of any description was treated in a similar way to an overriding interest (although the term was not used) so equitable easements of which notice had been given would have been enforceable.[66] If the easement of which there was notice arose before 1 January 1926, and the land was registered before 13 October 2003, such a right will therefore be overriding.[67] In addition, since a pre-1926 equitable easement could not be protected by registering a land charge[68] the provision of LPA 1925, s 198 (which provides that registration as a land charge is deemed to constitute actual notice) does not apply to it.

Post-1925 equitable rights of way

13.68 The general rule is that equitable easements in registered land arising after 1925 will be postponed to rights registered as a result of a disposition for value unless they have been noted on the register of title.[69] However, an unregistered equitable right which arose between 1926 and 2003 and was openly enjoyed can subsist as an overriding interest[70] and the effect of the judicial interpretation of the relevant provisions is that this was capable of applying to a large class of equitable easements. This rule was reversed by the LRA 2002[71] but the reversal does not affect rights accrued before 13 October 2003.

13.69 An equitable right of way created after 1925 over land not registered under the LRA 1925 or 2002 will be void as against a subsequent purchaser of the legal estate for money or money's worth (and therefore also against persons deriving title through him) unless it has been registered under the LCA 1925 or 1972 at the land charges registry as an equitable easement class D(iii)[72] (or is protected by priority notice against a search and a land charge is subsequently registered). However, where the equitable right arises under an instrument executed after 26 July 1971 which will lead to first registration of the servient tenement under (now) LRA 2002, it does not need to be so registered under the LCA[73] but it will need to be entered on the new register under the LRA 2002.

13.70 It sometimes happens that land charges registered a long time ago are overlooked on first registration under the LRA 2002 as searches may not be made or abstracted against all former estate owners but only against recent

---

[66] Section 33.
[67] LRA 2002, Sch 12, para 9.
[68] LCA 1972, s 2(5)(iii).
[69] LRA 1925, s 59(2) and (5) and 70(1)(a); LRA 2002, s 29.
[70] *Celsteel Ltd and Others v Alton House Holdings (No 1)* [1985] 1 WLR 204. See para **1.22**. The decision was (in part) reversed on appeal on different grounds not affecting this point which turned on the words in LRA 1925, s 70(1)(a) 'not being equitable easements required to be protected by notice on the register'.
[71] By the drafting in Schs 1 and 3 of para 3 which refer to legal easements and para 2 which refers to 'relating to land of which he is in actual occupation'. The claimant will not be in occupation of land over which he claims an easement. See Law Com 271, para 8.55.
[72] LCA 1972, s 4(6).
[73] LCA 1972, s 14(3).

ones. The land charge subsists on the LCA register even though not entered on the LRA register. However, only legal rights can be overriding interests (see paras **13.5** and **13.7**) and therefore an equitable right which is not shown on the LRA register[74] can not qualify as such. Section 11(4) of LRA 2002 does not include interests of this sort. In such a case there may be a right to rectification.[75] Under section 25 of LPA 1969, a purchaser may be entitled to claim compensation from the registrar for the fact that his estate turns out to be subject to a right of which he was not actually aware. In those circumstances it would normally be just for the LRA register to be rectified to reflect the registered land charge.[76] In addition to compensation under LPA 1969, the proprietor may also claim under LRA 2002, Sch 8, para 1(1)(a) and (b).[77]

13.71   Rights of way arising by equitable estoppel (see para **1.25**) which before 1926 would not have been recognised as proprietary interests capable of being created at common law, do not require to be registered under the LCA 1972.[78] However, they are not legal easements and therefore cannot be overriding interests. It can therefore happen that a right arising by estoppel which bound unregistered land will cease to bind on first registration. Where the dominant owner is aware of the position, the interest may be protected by caution if title is not registered, or notice if it is. Under section 116 of LRA 2002 an equity by estoppel and a mere equity are regarded in relation to registered land as having effect from the time the equity arises as a proprietary interest capable of binding successors in title to the servient proprietor and therefore capable of being protected by notice.

13.72   Where there is a contract to grant a right of way, the right itself does not yet exist but the contract creates an equitable right to specific performance. The contract may be protected by notice on the register. In relation to unregistered land it may be protected by land charge, since although section 2(4)(iv) of LCA 1972 refers to a contract to convey a legal estate and legal interest is not mentioned, the effect of section 205(1)(x) of LPA 1925 (incorporated by LCA 1972, s 17(1)) is that 'estate' includes 'interest'.

13.73   It follows that an unregistered equitable right of way, even if obvious on inspection and regularly used, and even if binding on a proprietor for the time being, is not enforceable on a person subsequently taking under a disposition.[79]

---

[74]   Unless created before 13 October 2003 and saved, as mentioned above.
[75]   LRA 2002, Sch 4, para 2(1)(c), 5(c).
[76]   LRA 2002, Sch 4, paras 3(2)(b) and 6(2)(b).
[77]   This may also apply to pre 1926 equitable easements of which notice was given.
[78]   *ER Ives Investments Ltd v High* [1967] 2 QB 379.
[79]   *Chaudhary v Yavuz* [2011] EWCA Civ 1314.

Registering an equitable right of way

13.74 The benefit of an equitable right of way can not be registered[80] but passes automatically.[81]

13.75 The burden should be protected by notice using form AN1 or UN1 except where the right is created in a transfer when it will be entered automatically. On first registration the applicant has a duty (shown in form FR1, panel 12) to disclose all known rights. This includes equitable rights of way. On a disposition only overriding rights (which must be legal) need be disclosed.

13.76 If the equitable right arises under a trust of land (for example if the roadways on an estate are vested in trustees for the benefit of the residents[82]) it cannot be registered[83] because section 33(a)(i) of LRA 2002 says no notice may be registered in respect of a trust of land. Accordingly the disclosure duty in form FR1, para 12 does not extend to such rights. A beneficiary under a trust may be able to register a restriction against the trustees' title.[84]

LEGAL RIGHTS OF WAY NEITHER REGISTERED NOR OVERRIDING ON DISPOSITION

13.77 If a right of way subsists as a legal interest it may still have some force even though it is neither registered nor within Schedule 3, paragraph 3.

13.78 On first registration, any legal right of way remains an overriding interest.[85] Although, on a disposition for valuable consideration of a registered title, unregistered legal rights of way are not overriding if they are not known to the disponee, obvious or recently exercised (see paras **13.7–13.8**)[86] they do not cease to be legal interests. These include express legal rights of way over land not registered at the time of grant and overlooked on first registration and implied and prescriptive rights.

13.79 Section 29 of LRA 2002 provides that on a disposition (of or out of an existing registered estate) for valuable consideration, an unregistered right which does not then qualify as overriding is postponed to the interest under the disposition. The effect of postponing the right of way to the rights of the disponee is that a second or later registered proprietor or a lessee or a chargee in possession would be entitled to prevent exercise (by injunction or by direct action such as obstruction) but it is not to extinguish it.[87]

---

[80] LRA 2002, s 2 and Sch 2, para 7; LRR 2003, r 73A.
[81] LRA 2002, s 11(3).
[82] As in *Halsall v Brizell* [1957] Ch 169 where the trust deed was made in 1851.
[83] LRA 2002, s 78.
[84] LRR 2003, r 93(a) and (c).
[85] LRA 2002, Sch 1, para 3.
[86] Unless affecting a title registered before 13 October 2003.
[87] Contrast LCA 1972, s 4(6) where an unregistered equitable easement is rendered void.

13.80 It may still have some effect. An express right such as that described above retains its status as a legal interest and does not become equitable because LRA 2002, ss 27(1) and 27(2)(d) (which make an unregistered express grant[88] or reservation after 12 October 2003 equitable) applies only to a disposition out of a registered estate. An implied or prescriptive right will be legal in any event. Thus, if the dominant owner actually exercises it during a period when it is postponed, that is not a trespass so that the servient proprietor could not claim the usual nominal damages.

13.81 If the land is disposed of within a year of such exercise, the right may thereupon become an overriding interest. It may also become enforceable if the disponee comes to have actual knowledge before acquiring the title. This is because in registered land each proprietor acquires title by virtue of registration not by virtue of a chain of transactions and, although generally referred to as a successor in title, is strictly not one in the same sense as a person who acquires unregistered land by a conveyance which forms part of his title. The lack of knowledge of a previous owner is therefore not relevant. Although section 28 of LRA provides that priority is not affected by a disposition, that is subject to section 29 which itself refers to Schedule 3.

13.82 The right may also be enforceable against any subsequent proprietor who acquires without giving value, as by gift or inheritance or by adverse possession.[89] Under section 29(1) of LRA 2002, a right that is unregistered and not overriding is postponed only to a disposition made for valuable consideration. This is limited to an interest affecting the estate immediately before the disposition, but such a right may be regarded as affecting even though postponed, although the point is arguable.

13.83 It follows that it may be possible to register such a right following a disposition even though it has been postponed at some earlier time. That will be because it has become overriding (because of the disponee's knowledge or because it has been exercised less than a year before the disposition) or it has ceased to be postponed (because the disponee does not take for value). It may also be registrable if it becomes obvious on the ground.[90]

13.84 For example, a legal right of way was granted by deed in 2006 over Blackacre which was then unregistered. No duplicate was put with the deeds and no memorandum endorsed. The grantor died, his executors sold Blackacre in 2008 and the buyer obtained first registration. The grant was not discovered and not noted on the register. The way is not obvious on inspection, the buyer did not know about it and the right has not been exercised. It still bound the buyer. He granted a ten year lease and it did not bind the registered lessee who could refuse access to the grantee. The lease expires while Blackacre still

---

[88] For this purpose, the operation of LPA 1925, s 62 is not express (see LRA 2002, s 27(7)).

[89] LRA 2002, Sch 6, para 9(2) says priorities are not affected on adverse possession but as the new proprietor did not acquire for value s 29 should prevail.

[90] If, as LRR 2003, r 73A(1) suggests, an easement is property, then rights under HRA 1998, 1st protocol, art 1 may be engaged.

belongs to the original buyer who then goes into occupation. As he was first proprietor he could not claim the right was postponed and it would be exercisable against him. The buyer dies and his executors assent Blackacre to his widow and the assent is registered. That is not for valuable consideration and so the right remains exercisable. She sells Blackacre and the right becomes postponed to the interest of the new registered owner who can refuse access. If, before a later proprietor acquires an interest, he comes to know about the right or the way is actually exercised, the right may become exercisable again. It may also do so if at some later stage the land passes without valuable consideration as by gift or on inheritance.

CAUTIONS

13.85 If the servient land is unregistered, the dominant owner may wish to consider registering a caution against first registration.[91] This applies with particular force where the right is not obvious on inspection and is not regularly used. It applies even if the right was granted by deed (see para **13.26**). Even if the benefit is entered on the register of the dominant title, the registry will not automatically pick it up on registering the servient title. Although it is not in general possible to lodge such a caution to give notice of a registrable legal estate in land, the holder of an interest can do so (LRA 2002, s 15(1)(b) and (3) as the definition in LPA 1925, s 205(1)(x) is excluded by the way section 15 is worded). It is not essential to the validity of the right but is good practice.

13.86 A caution may be essential (in addition to a class D (iii) land charge) where the right of way is or could be equitable. If a right is conditional, for instance on paying contributions to maintenance, then it may be equitable and therefore cannot be overriding even on first registration. A caution will prevent it being overlooked on first registration.

13.87 A caution by itself does not give any legal protection but on the application for first registration the registrar must notify the cautioner[92] who can then ask for the right to be noted on the new registered title. The registrar will consult with the applicant for registration and where the situation is clear the right will be entered.

13.88 Care should be taken before registering a caution. In most cases of express rights, this will not be contentious. A caution may, however, throw up a dispute about implied or prescriptive rights. In such a case there are two issues to consider. First, if a caution is lodged without reasonable cause, any person who suffers damage can claim against the person registering the caution.[93] Secondly, when an application is made for first registration of the cautioned

---

[91] This was recommended by the Law Commission report leading to the LRA 2002. Law Com 271, para 8.72.
[92] LRA 2002, s 16.
[93] LRA 2002, s 77.

land, if the cautioner and the applicant for registration cannot agree the matter will be referred by the land registry to the adjudicator (see para **11.152**). As adjudication involves expense and as non-registration does not affect the validity of a legal right of way granted or existing at the time of first registration (although it may on a subsequent disposition), the cautioner may be prepared to withdraw the contested caution without prejudice to his rights, although if there is a later dispute that might be construed as a sign of weakness.[94] In such a case, once registration is completed he may then consider applying for an entry or a unilateral notice on the title although as the proprietor has to be notified that may itself lead to adjudication.

13.89 If the dominant land changes hands before the servient land is registered, details of the person entitled to be notified should be changed on the cautions register using form AP1.[95]

RESTRICTIONS

13.90 If a restriction on the register is used to secure performance of positive covenants such as contribution to maintenance (see para **5.59**) a specific application will be needed either in form RX1 or one of the other means in LRR 2003, r 92(7). Often the conveyancer acting for the transferee will be prepared to lodge this on behalf of the grantor but the point may need to be confirmed in correspondence.

OPTIONS

13.91 If the dominant owner has an option to acquire a right of way, it must be protected by registration. If the servient land is not registered this will be by a C(iv) land charge and if registered by a notice on the register.

13.92 If a lease contains a right to acquire an interest in other land, such as to call for a grant of a right of way over adjacent land once a road is laid out, it must be mentioned in paragraph LR9 of the Prescribed Clauses. A right to renew an incorporeal leasehold right of way must be noted against the landlord's title and as the Prescribed Clauses do not apply this will need to be the subject of a specific application.

13.93 An incorporeal leasehold right of way may be subject to a landlord's right to 'lift and shift' the way by terminating it in return for a grant over a new route. As the incorporeal lease cannot be registered with its own title, the break clause will need to be protected by a C(iv) land charge.[96]

---

[94] See, however, *Silkstone v Tatnall* [2010] EWHC 1627 (Ch).
[95] LRA 2002, s 21(1)(b); LRR 2003, r 51 – as amended by Sch 1, para 12 of the LR (Amendment) Rules 2008, with effect from 10 November 2008 – see also PG 3, Cautions.
[96] *Greene v Church Commissioners for England* [1974] Ch 467.

ESTATE RENTCHARGE

13.94 If an estate rentcharge, normally with a right of re-entry, is taken to secure performance of a positive covenant such as contributing to repair of a roadway(see para **8.18**), then the beneficiary of the rentcharge should apply on form AP1 for registration at the same time as the application for registration of the first registration or disposition of the land subject to the rentcharge. Substantive registration of the rentcharge as a legal interest with its own title is voluntary,[97] but if the rentcharge is not so registered then, while the burden may be noted on the title to the subject land, it will take effect in equity as will the right of re-entry.[98] Under LRA 2002, Sch 2, para 7(2) the creation, grant or reservation of a rentcharge must be noted on the register.

EXTINCTION OF REGISTERED FREEHOLD RIGHTS OF WAY

13.95 If the registrar is satisfied that a registered right of way has been wholly released and the entry does not relate to any other rights, he will cancel the entry. If the right is part of a bundle of rights or if there is doubt as to the efficacy of the cancellation, then the entry may remain but a note will be entered on the title to that effect.[99]

13.96 If a right is otherwise protected by substantive entry on the register and the entry is cancelled, it must follow that the right is extinguished since it is neither overriding nor registered. The registry will therefore require clear evidence before cancelling such an entry.

13.97 If a notice of what had formerly been an overriding right of way is entered on the charges register of the servient title, it ceases to be overriding. If the notice is subsequently cancelled the right of way will not revert to being overriding.[100]

13.98 An easement will be extinguished by merger which is automatic (see para **9.17**) and the rule applies in principle as much to registered land as unregistered. If title 1 has a right of way over title 2 and the proprietor of title 1 later acquires title 2 in the same right, the registry will not necessarily pick up the merger. The entries will remain on the two titles unless an application is made to cancel them. If title 1 is subsequently sold, it appears that the right will not revive (although a new grant of an identical right might be implied on the sale). The register is normally conclusive as to the identity of the proprietor[101] but not necessarily as to rights. While the effect of section 11(3) of LRA is that

---

[97] LRA 2002, ss 3(1)(b), 4(2).
[98] LRA 2002, s 27(2)(e); LPA 1925, s 1(2)(b) and (e).
[99] PG 62, para 12.
[100] LRA 2002, s 29(3).
[101] LRA 2002, s 58.

the proprietor has 'all interests subsisting for the benefit of the estate', a right which has determined by merger is not subsisting even though it appears to be from the state of the register.

COMMONHOLD

13.99   PG 60 (Commonhold) sets out the registry requirements for registration of commonhold land under the Commonhold and Leasehold Reform Act 2002, Part 1, the Commonhold Regulations 2004[102] and the Commonhold (Land Registration) Rules 2004.[103] The common parts will be registered in a separate title from the units. This will have an entry in the following form:

> 'This title comprises the common parts of the commonhold defined by the commonhold community statement. The land in this title has the benefit of and is subject to the rights and duties conferred and imposed by the commonhold community statement.
>
> NOTE 1: Version ... of the commonhold community statement is dated ...
>
> NOTE 2: Version ... of the memorandum and articles of association of the commonhold association is dated ...
>
> NOTE 3: Copies filed.'

13.100   The rights will be governed by the commonhold community statement and will normally include rights of way over the common parts.

---

[102]   SI 2004/1829 as amended by SI 2009/2363.
[103]   SI 2004/1830 as amended by SI 2008/1920 and SI 2009/2024.

Appendix 1

PRECEDENTS

A1.1

General note

As with all precedents the suggestions below should be treated with care. There are many published precedents for rights of way and most practitioners will have their own preferred house style, layout, system of definition and so forth. The following are therefore intended as illustrations of possible approaches and any specific draft will need to take into account the particular circumstances of the transaction. The forms include some suggestions to resolve a number of problems encountered in practice. These suggested solutions have not been tested in court and may be subject to challenge. The precedents should be considered in the light of the drafting comments in Chapter **5**.

A1.2

Right of way by reference to former grant

Together with the benefit of a right of way granted by a Deed dated *etc* and made *etc* [so far as it benefits the Property] [in common with the Transferor].

A1.3

Land Registry Form TP1 Panel 12

Rights granted for the benefit of the property

Together with a right of way with or without vehicles in common with the Transferor and all others who now have or are granted in the future a similar right over the track coloured brown on the plan for the purpose of a single private dwelling house.

Rights reserved for the benefit of other land

Except and reserving to the Transferor for the benefit of [the remainder of the land comprised in title number XXX] [the land shown edged green on the plan] a right of way with or without vehicles and construction machinery over the track coloured brown on the plan for all present and future purposes and development of the land benefited with liberty to vary or increase the use.

A1.4

Grant of right of way over one registered title for benefit of another

Land Registry

Grant of Right of Way

1.   Title number(s) of the servient property:

2.   Servient Property:

3.   Title Number(s) of the dominant property

4.   Dominant Property

5.   Date:

6.   Grantor:

[7.]   [Chargee:]

8.   Grantee:

9.   The grantor [with the consent of the chargee] grants to the grantee subject to and conditional on performance of the covenants in clause 12 (which shall be a condition of exercise of the right) a right of way for the grantee and all persons authorised by the grantee with or without vehicles over the driveway coloured brown on the attached plan ('the driveway') in common with the grantor and all other persons who now have or are granted in the future the like rights for the benefit of the [use of] the dominant property [as a single private residence]

10.   Consideration
[The grantor has received from the grantee for the right granted the following sum (in words and figures):] [The grant is not for money or anything that has a monetary value] [Insert other receipt as appropriate:]

11.   The grantor grants with [full title guarantee] [limited title guarantee]

12.   Additional provisions:
In this panel 12 references to the parties include their successors in title.
The conditions are observance of the following covenants:

12.1   The grantee covenants with the grantor to pay on demand from the grantor a fair proportion according to use in connection with the dominant property of the cost incurred by the grantor in repairing renewing and maintaining the driveway

12.2   The grantee covenants with the grantor and with the owner of each property [now] having the benefit of the like right of way with intent to bind the [dominant property and each part of it] [exercise of the rights granted] and with intent to benefit each part of the servient property and also each property [now] having the benefit of the like rights of way that those persons using the right of way under the authority of this deed will not obstruct the use of the driveway by other persons

Execution

A1.5

Grant over unregistered land

THIS DEED OF GRANT is made the day of 20 BETWEEN

(1)   of ('the Grantor')
(2)   whose registered office is at ('the Mortgagee') (3) of ('the Grantee')

WHEREAS

(1)   The Grantor is seised for a legal estate in fee simple in possession of the property described in Part 1 of Schedule 1 ('the Roadway') subject to a Mortgage ('the Mortgage') dated the day of 20 between the Grantor (1) and the Mortgagee (2) and subject also to the several deeds of grant of rights of way described in Schedule 2 ('the Existing Rights') but otherwise free from incumbrances and is also seised for a legal estate in fee simple of the property described in Part 2 of Schedule 1 ('the Grantors Land')

(2)   The Grantee is seised for a legal estate in fee simple of the property described in Schedule 3 ('the House')

(3)   The parties have agreed for the grant of the rights described in Schedule 4 ('the Grantees Rights') for the sum of pounds (£)

NOW THIS DEED WITNESSES as follows:

1   The Grantor in consideration of the sum of pounds (£) (the receipt whereof is hereby acknowledged) with full title guarantee hereby grants and the Mortgagee consents to the grant and confirms unto the Grantee the Grantees Rights in common with the Grantor the persons entitled under the Existing Rights and all persons now having or hereafter granted the like rights TO HOLD unto the Grantee in fee simple appurtenant to the House subject to the covenants hereinafter contained

2   The Grantee for himself and his successors in title to the House covenants with the Grantor with intent to bind the House and each part of it capable of benefiting from the Grantees Rights [but so that no person shall be bound after parting with all interest in the House] and with intent to benefit each part of the Roadway and also to benefit each part of the Grantors Land capable of benefiting into whosesoever hands it or such parts may come.

        2.1   Not to obstruct the use of the Roadway by any person lawfully entitled

        2.2   Not to use the Roadway except for access to not more than two residential units on the House

        2.3   Not to park or station vehicles on the Roadway [save in the course of temporary loading and unloading]

3   The Grantee for himself and his successors in title to the House covenants with the several persons now entitled to the Existing Rights and their successors in title to their respective properties with intent to bind the House and each part of it capable of benefiting from the Grantees Rights [but so that no successor in title shall be bound after parting with all interest in the House] and with intent to benefit each part severally of those respective properties into whosesoever hands any of them may come

        3.1   Not to obstruct the use of the Roadway by any person lawfully entitled

3.2 Not to park or station vehicles on the Roadway [save in the course of temporary loading and unloading]

4 The Grantee further covenants with the Grantor (to the intent that the exercise of the Grantees Rights shall be subject to and conditional on performance) to perform the obligations set out in Schedule 5 ('the Positive Obligations') and so that if at any time hereafter the Grantee or any successor in title of the Grantee is in breach of any of the Positive Obligations the rights of the Grantee or such successors under this deed shall be suspended until the breach is remedied

5 For the purposes of the Contracts (Rights of Third Parties) Act 1999 it is agreed that (with the exception of clause 3 and the application to successors in title of the parties) nothing in this deed shall confer on any third party any right to enforce or any benefit of this deed

6 The Mortgagor acknowledges the right of the Grantee to production of the documents of title set out in Schedule 6 and the Grantor covenants with the Grantee that when the Mortgage and those documents come into the Grantors possession he will if required and on payment of his reasonable costs give a statutory undertaking for their safe custody and that in the meantime the Mortgagor and its successors in title will keep the Mortgage and those documents held by it safe, whole and undefaced, fire or other inevitable accident excepted

IN WITNESS etc

SCHEDULE 1 – *Land belonging to the Grantor*

Part 1 – The Roadway

All that roadway at in the Parish of in the County of shown (with the measurements) on the attached plan no 1 and thereon coloured brown

Part 2 – The Grantors Land

Those parts of the Grantors Estate in the County of which are shown on the attached plan no 2 and thereon edged blue

SCHEDULE 2 – *The Existing Rights*

The rights created by the following deeds of grant:

Date	Grantor	Grantee	Benefiting property

The following admitted prescriptive rights:

Approximate date of acquisition	Benefiting property

SCHEDULE 3 – *The House*

The property known as House in the said parish of shown edged red on the attached plan

SCHEDULE 4 – *The Grantees Rights*

A right of way at all times with or without vehicles over the Roadway for the purpose of not more than two private residences on the House

SCHEDULE 5 – *The Positive Obligations*

To pay on demand a proportionate part according to use (to be determined by the surveyor to the owner of the Roadway) of the cost of inspecting maintaining repairing and renewing the Roadway in a condition suitable for use by private motor cars and other vehicles reasonably expected to visit private residences

If any person exercising the Grantees Rights or any other person using the Roadway in connection with the House shall cause damage to the Roadway then at the cost of the owner of the House forthwith to make good such damage to the reasonable satisfaction of the owner of the Roadway

SCHEDULE 6 – *Documents of Title*

Date   Document   Parties

A1.6

Right for benefit of part of property

Together with a right of way on foot only for the benefit of that part of the Property comprising numbers 1 to 3 Farm Cottages shown edged blue on the Plan over the footpath coloured brown on the Plan for residential purposes

A1.7

Where there is a disputed claim to a prescriptive right of way

Together with such right of way as the Transferor is able to grant and without any covenant for title [over the track coloured brown on the plan] [as the Transferor and his predecessors in title have enjoyed for upwards of 20 years over the track between the Property and the Highway known as ...]

A1.8

Variable route

A right of way [continue as normal] between points A and B on the Plan [over the route coloured brown on the plan or such other route as the Grantor may from time to time designate] [over such route as may from time to time be available over the land edged green on the plan]

A1.9

Proviso for diverting route

A right of way [continue as normal – define 'Roadway'] PROVIDED THAT if the Grantor shall wish to divert the route of the Roadway (or any part of it) and shall free of cost to the Grantee provide a new roadway of substantially similar convenience and constructed to no less standard than the Roadway and shall give the Grantee not less than three months notice in writing expiring at any time then on expiry of that notice the Grantor shall be bound to grant (or procure a grant of) and the Grantee shall be bound to take a new grant on the same terms as this Deed (things being changed which ought to be changed) over the substituted route and the Grantee will release the rights over the Roadway (or part of it as the case may be) and the parties will complete all necessary legal formalities to perfect the new grant and on completion of the new grant the rights granted by this Deed (or so much of them as shall relate to the part to be determined) shall determine (but without prejudice to any subsisting claim by either party) [Provided further that if the Grantee shall not have completed the release and new grant within two months after the expiry of the notice then the right to be determined shall determine automatically at the end of those two months and the new right shall thereupon become exercisable by the Grantee]

If the positive obligation to release the existing way is to be enforceable against a successor to the Grantee it will need to be supported by a method such as a restriction on the register with a chain of deeds of covenant.

A1.10

Aerial footway

A right of way on foot over the footbridge whose lateral position is shown coloured brown on the attached plan and whose vertical dimensions [are shown on the elevation drawing number XYZ 123 attached] [lie between A metres and B metres above Ordnance Datum Newlyn] [lie between P metres and Q metres above the surface of the private roadway known as Dale Drive] together with the right on giving reasonable notice (except in emergency) to enter with or without workmen and contractors on the land beneath and the airspace beside the footbridge for the purpose of inspecting maintaining repairing and renewing the footbridge causing no obstruction to users of [the private roadway known as] Dale Drive doing as little damage as practicable making good all remediable damage and paying compensation for all irremediable damage

A1.11

Right of way to parking space

Together with the right to park one private motor car [in the space coloured blue on the plan] [in such space as the Grantor may from time to time designate within the area edged green on the plan] [in such space within the area edged green on the plan as may from time to time be available but without any guarantee on the part of the Grantor that any space may be available at any given time] together also with a right of way with or a private motor car or on foot between the entrance marked A on the plan and such parking space over such routes within the land coloured green as are from time to time available for access

A1.12

Conditional grant

... grants a right of way... [continue as normal] subject to and conditional on the grantee paying on demand a fair proportion according to use of the costs incurred from time to time by the person in possession of the roadway in inspecting maintaining repairing and renewing the roadway PROVIDED (and this grant is subject to this condition) that if the Grantee fails to pay the full sum due on demand then the Grantees right to use the roadway shall be suspended until such time as payment is made

A1.13

Provision for deed of covenant for maintenance with restriction on the register

THIS DEED is made etc

BETWEEN etc (define parties as including successors in title)

1	The Grantor grants to the Grantee *etc. Define* 'dominant land'
2	The Grantee covenants with the Grantor [*maintenance covenants, provision for payment, restrictive and positive covenants relating to the right of way. These may be in schedules. There may also be covenants by the Grantor to maintain and repair*]
3.1	The Grantee covenants with the Grantor on any disposition of the dominant land or any part of it [other than a mortgage or charge or a lease for not more than 7 years] to procure that the person in whose favour the disposition is made enters into a new deed of covenant with the Grantor to pay the sums due and perform the other obligations under this deed (including this clause) at the same time and in the same manner as the Grantee is bound by this deed to pay and perform them
3.2	The parties apply to the chief land registrar to enter in the title to the dominant land a restriction in Form N to the Land Registration Rules 2003 that no disposition of the freehold estate in the dominant land by the Grantee is to be registered without the consent of the Grantor
3.3	The Grantor will consent to the registration of a disposition of the dominant land or any part of it if the person to whom the disposition is made has entered into a deed with the Grantor in the same terms as this deed including this clause (things being changed which ought to be changed) and the Grantor has received the new deed from such person
3.4	If the Grantee has parted with all interest in the dominant land and has paid all sums due under this deed and a new deed in accordance with clause 3.3 has been delivered to the Grantor then the Grantor will release the Grantee from further liability under this deed

A1.14

Estate rentcharge on sale of land

Rights granted for the benefit of the property

A right of way with or without vehicles in common with the Transferor and all others who now have or are granted in the future a similar right over the estate roads shown coloured brown on the plan for the purpose of [specify] and in relation thereto reserving to the Transferor out of the Property by way of perpetual estate rentcharge (first) the sum of ten pence per year payable (if demanded) on 21 June in each year for the purpose of making the Transferees covenants in clause X.3 of this panel in this transfer enforceable and (secondly) the sum due under the Transferees covenant in clause X.3(1) as payment for meeting or contributing to the cost of the performance by the Transferor of the Transferors covenant in clause X.2 of this panel in this transfer to repair the roadway such rentcharge to be charged for ever upon and issuing out of the Property

Other

X.1   The parties declare that (in addition to the statutory powers of the Transferor under the Law of Property Act 1925 to enable the Transferor to enforce payment of the estate rentcharge) if the estate rentcharge or any part of it is at any time in arrears and unpaid for more than 21 days after it has become due and lawfully demanded or if there is at any time a breach of any of the Transferees covenants in clause X.3 then the person entitled to the estate rentcharge may re-enter the Property or any part of it in the name of the whole and repossess and enjoy the Property as if this grant had never been made without prejudice to any right of action or remedy in respect of any previous breach of covenant

X.2   The Transferor covenants with the Transferee for the benefit of the Property and with intent to bind his successors in title to the roadway that subject to contribution by the Transferee in accordance with his covenant in clause X.3(1) he and they will keep the roadway in a reasonable state of repair

X.3   The Transferee covenants with the Transferor for the benefit of the roadway and with intent to bind his successors in title to the Property

        (1)   to pay on demand a fair and reasonable proportion according to the use made of the roadway by the owners and occupiers of the Property of the reasonable cost incurred by the Transferor in performing the Transferors covenant in clause X.2

        (2)   to shut the gate at point G on the plan after passing through it

A1.15

Right of way in lease of offices

This will usually be one of several easements in a schedule.

'Access Areas' means the entrance steps, entrance hall, stairs, lifts and corridors of the Building

A right of way on foot over the Access Areas between the hours of 0700 and 2000 from Monday to Saturday in each week

A1.16

Leasehold right of way appurtenant to freehold unit sold at the same time

The Prescribed Clauses are not required – see 13.20. The draftsman may wish to include them as a matter of course although they do not fit easily with an incorporeal grant. LR4 refers to land but the 'property' here will be the right defined in clause 1; in LR9.3 the lift and shift clause 6 should be mentioned; LR 11.1 is not relevant since an easement is itself the right granted and does not exist for the benefit of the right. LR11.2 will be a duplication of the 'property'. Under LR8 although by operation of law an easement can not be assigned separately from the dominant tenement that restriction is not contained in the lease. If the clauses are not used it will be prudent for the conveyancer lodging the application to lodge a certificate similar to those under LRR 2003 r58A(2) that the lease relates to an incorporeal right of way to avoid possible requisitions.

Title Number of servient land

Servient land

Title number of dominant land [leave blank if not yet registered]

Dominant land

THIS LEASE is made the [date]

BETWEEN

(1)   ('the Landlord')
(2)   ('the Tenant')

NOW THIS DEED WITNESSES as follows:

1   Definitions

    1.1   Reference to the parties include their successors in title [*or other definition as desired for instance to cover immediate reversion where landlord might grant overriding lease*]

    1.2   'The routes' means the ways shown coloured brown on the attached plan

    1.3   'The dominant land' means the [freehold] land [comprised in title number XXX] [comprised in a transfer of even date between the Landlord and the Tenant] [shown edged red on the attached plan] and where the context admits references to the dominant land include part of it

    1.4   'The right of way' means a right of way with or without vehicles over the routes

    1.5   'The maintenance cost' means the cost incurred by the Landlord in maintaining the routes in accordance with Schedule 1

    1.6   'The Tenant's proportion' of the maintenance cost is [Y per cent] [determined in accordance with Schedule 2]

    1.7   'the Estate' means the Dale Industrial Estate edged blue on the plan

2   Grant

In consideration of the [sum of xxx pounds (£xxx) the receipt of which is acknowledged and of the] rents hereby reserved and the covenants and conditions on the part of the Tenant herein contained the Landlord [with full title guarantee] grants to the Tenant a right of way with or without vehicles over the routes TO HOLD unto the Tenant in common with the Landlord and all others now having or hereafter granted the like right [for the benefit of] [appurtenant to] the dominant land for a term of 999 years from the [*date*] YIELDING AND PAYING (first) the rent of [a peppercorn if demanded] [*other rent either fixed or with provision for review*] and (second) the Tenant's proportion of the maintenance cost

3   Tenants Covenants

The Tenant covenants with the Landlord as follows

3.1   To pay the Tenants proportion of the maintenance cost within 10 days of receipt of a demand and if the tenant does not do so then to pay interest at a rate equal to [specify rate of interest or basis of calculation] from time to time on any sum unpaid from the date of demand until payment

3.2   Not to obstruct the routes and not to park or place a stationary vehicle on any part of the routes

3.3   Not to use the right of way except for the use of the dominant land for [*use e.g. not more than two light industrial units*]

3.4   On any transfer of the dominant land to procure that the transferee enters into a direct covenant with the Landlord to observe and perform the obligations of the Tenant contained in this Lease

3.5   Within one month of any disposition of the dominant land to supply to the Landlord a certified copy (or if it is not in writing other evidence) of the disposition and an address for service of demands for payment within the territories of the European Union

3.6   *Other covenants as desired including to pay profit rent if applicable, rates and taxes including VAT, costs of section 146 notices, insurance against public liability, indemnity against claims in respect of use by Tenant or visitors etc. If change of use of dominant land might impact on the routes consider including planning clauses.*

4   Landlords Covenants

The Landlord covenants with the Tenant as follows

4.1   That the Tenant observing the covenants and conditions on the Tenants part contained in this lease may quietly and peaceably enjoy the rights free of disturbance by the Landlord or any person claiming through under or in trust for the Landlord

4.2   Subject to contribution by the Tenant to keep the routes in good repair

4.3   On any disposition of any unit on the Estate to impose upon any disponee who has rights of way over the routes similar covenants to contribute to maintenance to those contained in this Lease

5   Determination on forfeiture

If the Tenant fails to pay [the rents hereby reserved when due] [the Tenants proportion of the maintenance cost within 10 days of demand] or if the Tenant commits or suffers a breach of any covenant or condition on the Tenants part contained in this Lease then the Landlord may by notice determine the right of way but without prejudice to any subsisting right of either party against the other

6   Lift and shift

If the Landlord shall wish to divert the routes or any part of them and shall free of cost to the Tenant provide a new route of substantially equal convenience and constructed to a similar standard as the way over which rights are granted by this Lease and shall give the Tenant not less than three months notice in writing expiring at any time then on expiry of that notice the Landlord shall be bound to grant (or procure a grant of) and the Tenant bound to take a new lease of a right of way over the substituted route on the same terms as this lease (including this clause) (other things being changed which ought to be changed) for a term equal to the residue of the term granted by this Lease and the parties will complete all necessary legal formalities to perfect the new grant and on completion of the new lease this Lease shall determine (but without prejudice to any subsisting claim by either party)

7   Release of parties following assignment

7.1   The Tenant will not be liable to the Landlord for any breach of the terms of this Lease occurring after the Tenant has ceased to be proprietor of any part of the dominant land

7.2   The Landlord shall not be liable to the Tenant for any breach occurring after [the Landlord has ceased to be proprietor of any part of the routes] [the reversion immediately expectant on the determination of the term in all parts of the routes has ceased to be vested in the Landlord]

8   Service of Notices

Notice to be served under this lease may be delivered to the Landlord at the address shown on the register of the Landlords title to the routes and to the Tenant at the address shown on the register of the Tenants title to the dominant land

Include other provisions for service of notices as desired.

IN WITNESS

Schedule 1

Here provision may be set out for maintenance including any procedure for consultation on major works, auditing of costs and so forth

Schedule 2

Here provision may be made for a variable maintenance contribution depending on amount of use, number of units on the estate, burden of heavy vehicles and any other relevant factors

Execution

A1.17

Deed on change of proprietor of dominant land having a leasehold right

THIS DEED is made etc

BETWEEN

(1)   Seller
(2)   Buyer
(3)   Landlord

WHEREAS

(1)   By a Lease ('the Lease') dated *etc* and made between [*original landlord*] (1) and [*original tenant*] ('the Tenant') (2) a right of way was granted [for the benefit of] [appurtenant to] the land comprised in Land Registry Title No ABC 123 ('the dominant land') for the term of 999 years from [*date*]
(2)   The Seller is now the registered proprietor of the dominant land
(3)   The Seller and the Buyer have agreed for the sale of the dominant land
(4)   The Lease contains a covenant that on any transfer of the dominant land the transferee should enter into a direct covenant with the Landlord to observe and perform the obligations on the part of the Tenant contained in the Lease
(5)   By a transfer ('the Transfer') of even date the Seller has transferred the dominant land to the Buyer and that transfer includes [benefiting] [appurtenant] rights

NOW THIS DEED WITNESSES as follows

1   In consideration of the premises the Seller confirms and (so far as an assignment is not contained or implied in the Transfer or by law) assigns to the Buyer ALL the rights granted by the Lease TO HOLD unto the Buyer appurtenant to the dominant land for all the residue of the term granted by the Lease
2   With the object and intention of affording to the Seller a full and sufficient indemnity but not further or otherwise the Buyer covenants with the Seller that he and his successors in title will during the Term perform all the obligations on the part of the Tenant contained in the Lease and keep the Seller indemnified against all actions, claims, demands, losses, costs, damages or liabilities whatsoever by reason of any future breach of such obligations
3   The Buyer covenants with the Landlord to observe and perform the obligations on the part of the Tenant contained in the Lease

To be executed by Seller and Buyer

A1.18

Licence by letter

Dear Darby and Joan

This letter confirms the terms of the licence under which you and your visitors may walk across the land shown edged red on the attached plan over the route shown.

1   This permission is personal to you and your children Jack and Jill and to not more than four other private visitors at any one time to your house The Limes so long as such visitors are accompanied by either of you.

2   The access is to be used for leisure and amenity purposes only and on foot and between the hours of 10.00 am and 6.00 pm. Persons using the access may be accompanied by not more than two dogs.

3   You will do no damage, drop no litter and generally behave in a responsible way. Persons using the access will keep strictly to the route shown on the plan and will not trespass on any other part of my property. Dogs must be kept on a lead. You must shut the gates.

4   Access is at the risk of the persons exercising it and neither I nor any member of my family nor any employees or agents of mine will be liable for any loss damage or injury to persons or property. If exercise of this licence results in any damage or injury to any person or property you will fully indemnify me against any costs and claims.

5   I reserve the right to suspend the permission at any time for not more than a day.

6   The licence will determine automatically if The Limes ceases to be your permanent home or if I dispose of the land edged red. If there is a breach of the terms of this licence I may determine the licence forthwith. Either of us may determine this licence at any time on two months notice in writing to the other.

Yours sincerely

A1.19

Lifetime right of way

Except and reserving to the Transferor during his life until he shall cease to reside at The Limes shown edged blue on the Plan a right of way on foot over the garden of the Property between the gates marked A and B on the Plan during the hours of daylight [but not at such times as the occupier for the time being of the Property shall be entertaining guests in the garden]

A1.20

Licence between companies for right of access

THIS LICENCE is made the [date]

BETWEEN

(1)   ABC Limited whose registered office is at ... (the Owner) and

(2)   DEF Limited whose registered office is at ...(The Licensee)

NOW THIS DEED WITNESSES as follows

1   In consideration of [the licence fee mentioned below and] the obligations on the part of the Licensee the Owner grants licence to the Licensee and persons authorised by the Licensee to have access over the roadway coloured brown on the attached plan ('the Roadway') for the purpose of the occupation by the Licensee of the Licensee's premises ('the Premises') known as [*name*] [shown edged red on the plan].

2   The license fee will be [*state substantive fee if there is one with provisions for review if appropriate*] per quarter payable on the usual quarter days in arrear.

3   The Licensee covenants with the Owner as follows:

         Insert obligations as desired but do not include yield up or assignment provisions.

4

4.1   This licence may be determined

         (a)   by the Owner forthwith if there is any breach of the obligations on the part of the licensee or

         (b)   by either party on giving not less than two months notice in writing to the other expiring at any time

4.2   On determination (whether by act of parties or by operation of law) the Licensee shall cease to make any use of the Roadway)

[4.3   On determination the Licensee will pay an apportioned part of the fee in respect of the time from the last payment up to the date of determination]

5   This Licence is personal to the Licensee and is not capable of assignment

6   This licence does not create any interest in land nor the relation of landlord and tenant

Executed as a deed

A1.21

Reservation of future access rights on sale of building land

Except and reserving for the benefit of [the land edged green on the Plan] [the rest of the land in title no XXX]

(1)   a right of way at all times after construction over all roads and footpaths constructed on the Property [at any time after] [within 50 years from] the date of this transfer and

(2)   the right [at any time after] [within 50 years from] the date of this transfer to enter on to the Property to make connecting roads and footpaths and a right of way over the connections at all times after they have been made.

A1.22

Shared driveway on Form TP1 Panel 12

Rights granted for the benefit of the property

Together with a right of way on foot or with vehicles over the land coloured brown on the plan comprising half of the shared driveway with the adjoining Plot No XX

Rights reserved for the benefit of other land

Except and reserving to the Transferor for the benefit of Plot No XX shown edged green on the plan a right of way on foot or with vehicles over the land coloured blue on the plan comprising half of the shared driveway with the Property

A1.23

Land Registry Statement of truth

Land Registry
Statement of truth in support of an
application for registration and/or
noting of a prescriptive easement

ST4

If you need more room than is provided for in a panel, and your software allows, you can expand any panel in the form. Alternatively use continuation sheet CS and attach it to this form.

If a joint statement is made by two or more persons, consequential amendments can be made to the text in the panels (for example, 'I' can be changed to 'we').

Land Registry is unable to give legal advice but our website www1.landregistry.gov.uk provides guidance on Land Registry applications. This includes public guides and practice guides (aimed at conveyancers) that can also be obtained from any Land Registry office.

Insert full name.	1　I:
Insert full address.	of:
	make this statement in support of an application to Land Registry for registration and/or noting of an easement based upon prescription.
	2　Status of person making this statement
Place 'X' in one box only.	I am
	☐ the legal owner of the benefiting land (other than as personal representative)
This is for cases where the legal owner is a company or firm, someone who has died, or is otherwise incapable of making the statement personally. Insert the name and address of the legal owner.	☐ making this statement on behalf of:
Please specify and enclose any relevant documentation.	who is currently or was previously the legal owner of the benefiting land but who cannot make this statement for the following reasons:
See note above.	☐ other:
Place 'X' in one box only.	3　Type of application
	☐ Registration of benefit of an easement – benefiting land is registered and burdened land is unregistered
	☐ Registration of benefit of easement and entry of notice of burden – benefiting land is registered and burdened land is registered
If applying for entry of a unilateral notice, do not use this form - please use form UN1 instead.	☐ Entry of notice of burden of easement – burdened land is registered and benefiting land is unregistered
	4　Title number(s) of the benefiting land (if registered):

Insert address including postcode (if any) or other description of the property, for example 'land adjoining 2 Acacia Avenue'. If the benefit of the easement is claimed in relation to unregistered land or part only of the land in the claimant's registered title(s), you must identify the benefiting land by attaching a plan showing the relevant land or (if appropriate) by referring to an existing reference on the title plan. Place 'X' in the appropriate box(es) and complete the first statement if appropriate. Enter reference, for example 'edged red'. If the benefiting land is unregistered, enclose any copy title deeds, if available.	**5** Description of the benefiting land: ☐ The land is clearly identified on the attached plan and shown: ☐ The land is unregistered and is comprised in the copy title deeds enclosed
	6 Title number(s) of the burdened land (if registered):
Insert address including postcode (if any) or other description of the property, for example 'land adjoining 2 Acacia Avenue'. If the easement affects unregistered land or part only of the land in one or more registered titles, you must identify the burdened land by attaching a plan showing the relevant land or (if appropriate) by referring to an existing reference on the title plan. Place 'X' in the appropriate box(es) and complete the first statement if appropriate. Enter reference, for example 'edged red'. If the burdened land is unregistered, enclose any copy title deeds, if available.	**7** Description of the burdened land: ☐ The land is clearly identified on the attached plan and shown: ☐ The land is unregistered and is comprised in the copy title deeds enclosed
Insert name and address of any known freehold owner of the land or person thought to be the freehold owner, such as the person having the unregistered documentary title to the land or being the registered proprietor of registered land, and/or any tenants and/or mortgagees. If not known, please state this by inserting 'not known'.	**8** Identity of the freehold owner of the burdened land or person thought to be the owner and related persons:

Describe the easement claimed to have been acquired by prescription as it might be described in the register. For example, 'a right of way with or without vehicles for the benefit of [describe benefiting land] over [describe burdened land]'.	**9 Easement claimed:**
Insert details of the facts relied on to support the claim that an easement has been acquired by prescription.	**10 Details of user:**
Insert details of date and circumstances in which the user in panel 10 started and finished. Any 'gaps' must be specified if the period is not continuous.	**11 Period of user:**
Place 'X' in one box only and complete the relevant statement if appropriate.	**12 User without force, secrecy or permission** I confirm that ☐ to the best of my knowledge and belief, the user has always been exercised without force, secrecy or permission
Insert details, including dates, and attach any available correspondence or other relevant documentation. If you place 'X' in the second box you are unlikely to establish a claim to the easement by prescription.	☐ the user has not always been exercised without force, secrecy or permission because:
Insert details of any past or present contact with the owner of the burdened land or person thought to be the owner and/or any tenants and/or mortgagees of that land, including dates. If none, please state this by inserting 'none'. If there has been any dispute concerning the claimed right, please provide details, including dates. Attach copies of all available correspondence or documents relating to the contact or dispute.	**13 Contact with freehold owner of the burdened land and related persons:**
Insert other relevant details, (if any).	**14 Other relevant details**

If the person making the statement is unable to sign it, this wording will need to be amended to comply with rule 215A(5) and (6) of the Land Registration Rules 2003. In addition, and in cases where the person making the statement is unable to read, there will need to be an appropriate certificate: see rule 215A(4) and (5).

15 I believe that the facts and matters contained in this statement are true

Signature (of person
making this statement): _____

Print full name:

Date:

A1.24

Checklist

- Define parties as including successors if continuing obligations
- Define dominant tenement
- Define servient tenement – is it same as route of way
- Check route against Land Registry plan or plan on deeds
- Permitted use
- Power to vary/increase use in future
- Width of way
- Is turning permitted
- Is parking permitted
- Condition not to obstruct
- Repair – unilateral or by agreement
- Maintenance obligations

    – Contribution according to use

    – Defined proportion of cost

    – Variation of proportions

    – Procedure for approving estimates

    – Date of collection of contributions

    – Bank account

    – Auditing of accounts

- Maintenance to cover resurfacing, mowing verge, street cleaning, lighting
- Power to upgrade surface
- Security – gates, electronic controls, padlocks
- Notices excluding public use
- Termination or diversion

    – Fixed term

    – Deviation across defined area

    – Power to serve notice to substitute new route

- Hours/days of exercise (leasehold or equitable only)
- Check Grantor's freehold title
- If land in tenancy confirm either

    – reservation sufficient (check dominant land) or

    – obtain lessee's confirmation

- Obtain consent of any mortgagees
- Register burden against servient title or lodge caution or enter notice
- Register land charge if equitable and unregistered
- Register benefit

Appendix 2

A2

SURVEY METHODS AND OTHER CONSIDERATIONS TO BE TAKEN INTO ACCOUNT IN THE INTERPRETATION AND COMPARISON OF HISTORIC ORDNANCE SURVEY MAPPING AND AERIAL PHOTOGRAPHY/SATELLITE IMAGERY

INTRODUCTION

A2.1   The object of this Appendix is to present an explanation of the factors that need to be taken into account when interpreting and comparing Ordnance Survey maps of different ages in order to make valid conclusions, whether for the determination of the position and alignment of Property Boundaries and Rights of Way, or for any other reason.

A2.2   Although this text concentrates on Ordnance Survey mapping, the principles covered apply equally to other mapping.

A2.3   This Appendix also covers factors to be considered in the interpretation of aerial photography and satellite imagery.

A2.4   It will be seen that a simple comparison or overlay of maps or aerial images of different ages is fraught with complications, even when the maps and aerial images being compared are at the same nominal scale.

SURVEY METHODS FROM THE EARLIEST YEARS

A2.5   The gestation of the Ordnance Survey is generally accepted to be in the military maps of Scotland designed to help in the suppression of the Jacobite uprisings. These maps were surveyed and printed by the Board of Ordnance, an autonomous department responsible for munitions and armaments. The maps were printed at a scale of one inch to 1,000 yards, (the later true Ordnance Survey maps were at a scale of one inch to one mile).

A2.6   An early print shows a survey party in the Scottish Highlands comprising an Officer, Non-Commissioned Officer and six soldiers as Assistants, (one carried the instrument, two measured with the chain, two for the fore and back stations, and one as batman). The maps showed only those features that were of military significance, roads, hills, rivers, settlements etc.

A2.7   What is considered to be the founding act of the Ordnance Survey was the delivery of a 'Great Circular Instrument' to the Board of Ordnance in 1791. The maker of this theodolite, (for that is what it was), Jesse Ramsden was the greatest instrument maker of the time. He made out his invoice to 'Ordnance Survey', the first time that the name had been used, and it has been used ever since. The first of these instruments had been supplied to the Royal Society and its original task was the observation of a triangulation scheme to connect the two astronomical observatories of Greenwich and Paris in order to try to resolve disagreements between astronomers about their relative positions. Each of these theodolites weighed over 200lbs and had a horizontal circle 36 inches in diameter, needing a four wheeled carriage and up to four horses to transport it around the country. These two theodolites, and several smaller theodolites, were used to complete the first Triangulation of the whole of Great Britain.

A2.8   Triangulation relied upon the accurate measurement of all the angles of the triangles and the accurate measurement of the length of at least one side of one triangle. In those early days the accurate measurement of angles was very much easier and less time consuming than the measurement of distances, so triangulation remained the primary method of providing high order survey control until the development of electronic distance measurement in the 1950s made trilateration a more accurate method of control fixation.

A2.9   The network of Primary triangles was broken down into smaller triangles, (Secondary, Tertiary, 4th order, etc), until the detail of the map could be surveyed by compass traverses, plane table, lines of sight, and chained lines with offsets from the chain lines. The resulting measurements were plotted onto field sheets with pencils, straightedges and scales. (This is the 'Graphic Survey' technique that is the basic method that Ordnance Survey surveyors still use to complete the fine detail on the maps, albeit supplemented by Global Positioning Systems, (GPS), electronic theodolites and pen computers in the place of paper or plastic field sheets).

A2.10   In those early days the maintenance of straight chain lines was challenging, and offsets were often significantly longer than would be accepted in later Ordnance Survey practice. An accurate offset requires not only accurate distance measurements, but also accurate right angles to be raised from the chain line. These were the methods of survey that resulted in the first editions of the 1:2500 scale, (25.344 inches to one mile), and 1:10,560 scale, (6 inches to one mile), 'County Series' maps. These maps proved fit for purpose until the use of GPS by map users became common in the last few years. While the County Series maps were accurate enough **Relative**[1] to local detail they were found to have **Absolute**[2] positioning errors of up to 10 metres or more when tested with modern technology.

A2.11 When the County Series mapping was updated it was revised on a cyclic system based upon the age of the mapping, regardless of the amount of change on the maps. New detail was added and destroyed detail was erased. Methods used were theodolite traversing, plane tabling, chain surveys and graphic survey completion. The revision always included a ground perambulation by the surveyor in which he identified changes and surveyed them using an appropriate method from those listed above, plotting his work directly onto the field sheets.

THE TRANSITION TO NATIONAL GRID MAPPING

A2.12 The County Series maps had been surveyed on several Cassini projections with a different central meridian for each county or group of counties.

A2.13 This had the effect of producing significant discrepancies when adjoining maps across county boundaries were butted together, especially where larger counties such as Yorkshire and Durham met. In order to solve these problems the Davidson Committee in 1938 recommended the following measures, (amongst others):

(a) the adoption of a single projection for the national mapping with a single central meridian, (Transverse Mercator with a Central Meridian along Longitude 2° West);

(b) the adoption of a National Grid referencing system;

(c) the 'Overhaul' of the mapping to eliminate the errors that had crept into the original survey in the course of the various revisions;

(d) the adoption of the scale of 1:1250, (*50.688 inches to one mile*), for the mapping of major towns; and

(e) the adoption of a system of 'Continuous Revision' for the large scale maps.

A2.14 In order to implement the first recommendation it became necessary to survey onto the existing 1:2500 County Series maps the exact positions of the triangulation stations relative to their nearest topographic detail. The maps were then cut up into a 'loose jigsaw' in order that the plotted triangulation stations could be shifted onto their correct National Grid co-ordinates, carrying with them the detail in their immediate vicinity. This often resulted in gaps and misalignment of linework etc which the detail surveyor would have to resolve as part of the 'Overhaul' process. With the advent of the

---

[1] For an explanation of Absolute and Relative Accuracies see the section on Positional Accuracy Improvement later in this Appendix.

[2] As above.

use of aerial photography in the late 1960s this process became more efficient as an overview of an area was now possible, identifying errors which were not apparent from ground inspection alone.

A2.15 The adoption of the scale of 1:1250 for major towns meant that some areas which had previously been surveyed and revised by 19th century methods at 1:2500 scale now had to be Resurveyed at 1:1250 scale using National Grid control and the most accurate survey instruments available. As the major towns developed and grew, more and more of the 1:2500 scale mapping was superseded by Resurvey at 1:1250 scale. Traverses were run between triangulation points to mark and coordinate Revision Points, (RPs), to control Chain Survey. Later these traverses would fix Permanent Traverse Stations, (PTSs), which controlled Tacheometric traverse surveys. Chain and 'Tachy' surveys would provide a skeleton framework of detail for the surveyor to complete the maps by Graphic Survey methods.

A2.16 Aerial photography was also increasingly used to control the 1:1250 scale Resurveys, the detail on the photograph being plotted precisely on stereoscopic Air Photo Plotters with the detail not visible on the aerial photography surveyed graphically by the detail surveyor. Aerial photography was also used for 1:2500 scale Revisions, using overlapping photographs to give the surveyor a stereoscopic virtual model of the terrain.

A2.17 The 1:10,560 scale County Series mapping was replaced in the 1970s by 1:10,000 scale Resurvey mapping of mountain and moorland areas based upon National Grid controlled aerial photography.

A2.18 During Continuous Revision of the 1:1250, 1:2500 and 1:10,000 scale surveys the surveyors used aerial photography and modern instrumentation to maintain accuracy standards where the size of the development required it, with the fine detail completed by graphic survey methods.

A2.19 All of the 1:2500 scale County Series maps, and the first and 'New Editions' of the 1:1250 and 1:2500 scale National Grid maps' (identified by the edition letters A, B, C, D, etc) can be regarded as 'snapshots of the landscape', that is, they were full revisions that captured all the topographic detail on the ground at the time of the survey. The same cannot be said of revisions which resulted in the publication of SUSI®, SIM®, SIP®, Superplan®, Sitemap®, Location Map, OS Mastermap® etc. These will not contain all change, as under Continuous Revision policy only those pockets of change that were economic to survey were included. Ordnance Survey's current policy, however, is that all major change will be surveyed and available to customers within six months of those changes occurring on the ground. In this context 'major change' will include a new house, but not extensions to houses or field boundaries in rural areas.

LATER DEVELOPMENTS

A2.20 In the 1950s new instrumentation began to be available. The Tellurometer was able to precisely calculate distances up to 100Km by measuring the phase differences in a transmitted and reflected radio wave. It also had the advantage that the operators 100Km apart could talk to each other using the radio signal, instead of relying on signal lights or heliograph flashes.

A2.21 Close on the heels of the Tellurometer came:

(a) the Wild DI10 Distomat, a distance measurer using Infra Red (IR) Waves which was small enough to be mounted upon a compact theodolite and with a range of about 2Km;

(b) the AGA 12 Geodimeter, again using IR to measure up to 1.5Km; and

(c) the Kern DM500 family of IR instruments measuring up to 1KM.

A2.22 Each of these instruments was used to provide control for the detail surveyors, mainly in the areas of 1:1250 scale mapping. Later models of the Kern DM500s could download observations of angles and distances into an electronic datalogger, thereby eliminating clerical errors in recording.

A2.23 As these instruments were being introduced there were also developments in the 'drawing' of the maps. From the mid 1960s the maps were being digitised; the surveyor's field sheets were converted into computer files, the data of which could be manipulated to be presented at various scales and specifications, and which could be transmitted electronically. The digital data also stored attributes about the nature of the feature such as whether it was a building, water, kerb line, features over 0.3 m high, feature under 0.3 m high etc as well as the dates of original digitising and any subsequent updates.

A2.24 In the 1980s the digitising of the surveyors' updates began to be undertaken in the surveyors' field offices on Digital Field Update Stations, (DFUS). The surveyors' graphic survey was digitised, stored and transmitted overnight to update the database in Ordnance Survey headquarters. The data was also used to plot out a new field document for the surveyors to use when the next update was undertaken. The up to date digital data was also available for supply to customers.

A2.25 In the 1990s, Global Positioning Systems were developed from Satellite Doppler equipment. The early GPS equipment was very heavy and bulky, and so it was used mainly to fix high order control and for special projects such as the proving surveys for the Channel Tunnel alignment. As the equipment became lighter and more portable it developed into equipment that a surveyor could carry in a small rucksack and was capable of fixing detail positions on National Grid coordinates to better than five centimetres. It also fixed positions in real time by using radio and mobile telephone contact to the Ordnance Survey national database to constantly correct the raw GPS coordinates to the National Grid coordinates of the network of GPS control stations.

A2.26 At the same time there were developments in the digitising of the map detail. DFUS was discontinued in favour of PIES, (Portable Interactive Edit Station), a hand held pen computer that a surveyor could carry in the field and digitise the survey as it occurred on the ground. This was later developed into PRISM, (Portable Revision and Integrated Survey Module), the equipment which all today's Ordnance Survey detail surveyors still use to update the OS Mastermap®.

A2.27 It was then but a small step to link GPS to PRISM, so that as the surveyor positions his GPS antenna over a point he taps the PRISM screen and the antenna position is plotted onto the PRISM screen to an accuracy of better than +/- 5cm.

A2.28 Ordnance Survey developed and distributed a mathematical transformation to convert GPS coordinates (WGS84) to National Grid coordinates (OSGB36). This, and the widespread availability of GPS to map users, had the effect of highlighting the positional accuracy limitations of the 1:2500 scale National Grid mapping when users compared the GPS derived coordinates with the map coordinates.

A2.29 Ordnance Survey's solution to this problem was the Positional Accuracy Improvement programme, completed in 2005. All the 'Overhauled' 1:2500 scale National Grid maps were adjusted to fit GPS controlled National Grid coordinates. This was not a Resurvey process, more of a Revision in which the data was moved to a more accurate National Grid position while retaining the digital attributes of every feature and point in the data so that a history of the point was retained. It may seem a simple task, but there were many problems to overcome to maintain the integrity of the data. The overall effect of the programme was to improve the overall Absolute Accuracy of the 1:2500 scale 'Overhaul' mapping from +/-2.7 metres Root Mean Square Error, (RMSE), to +/-1.1 metres RMSE.

IMPLICATIONS OF THE ABOVE FOR MAP USERS

A2.30 It can be seen from the above that the factors to be taken into account in the interpretation and comparison of Ordnance Survey maps from different epochs can be summarised as follows:

(1) The accuracy and precision standards of the original survey of the 1:2500 and 1:10,560 scale County Series mapping.

(2) The errors and inconsistencies introduced during the various Revisions of the original survey.

(3) Positional shifts introduced during the transformation of the County Series mapping on multiple Cassini projections onto a single Transverse Mercator projection.

(4)   Positional shifts introduced during every Revision when errors were identified and corrected by the Ordnance Survey surveyors.

(5)   Differences between the 1:2500 scale surveys and the later 1:1250 scale National Grid mapping where this covered the same area.

(6)   Positional shifts introduced by the Positional Accuracy Improvement programme of the 'Overhauled' 1:2500 National Grid mapping.

To the above also have to be added:

(7)   Inconsistencies introduced by the instability of the various drafting and storage media of the early surveys.

(8)   *Apparent* inconsistencies introduced by specification changes of the mapping over time.

(9)   Actual changes to the topographic detail on the ground.

(10) Omission of minor detail not surveyed under the specification for Continuous Revision.

A2.31   Taking these topics in order:

(1)   Although the original 1:2500 surveys dating back to the mid 19th century were undertaken with the best instrumentation and knowledge at the time, there can be no denying the accuracy and precision achieved cannot compare favourably with the accuracies and precision achievable today. Nevertheless, the mapped detail is usually locally consistent. If the first edition County Series mapping is examined in isolation for small areas (say less than 3-4 Hectares), then there should be few problems.

(2)   At each Revision of any mapping, new errors would inevitably be introduced. These will be few and relatively minor; major errors would be noticed at the time and rectified.

(3)   The 'Overhaul' process of recasting the County Series mapping from multiple Cassini projections onto a single Transverse Mercator projection involved the 'cutting up' of the mapping and repositioning the segments onto true National Grid coordinates. This was a highly skilled job and great care was taken to avoid cutting through buildings and small enclosures. Whenever possible, cuts through railways, canals etc were made at right angles to the features. This was not always possible, however, and the resolution of the resulting problems could be a major problem for the 'Overhaul' surveyor.

(4)   As each Revision cycle of the 1:2500 County Series mapping took place, the surveyors would be more experienced and trained to more stringent survey specifications. They would also be using the latest technologies available. For these reasons they would identify minor errors in the original survey and correct them as part of the Revision process. Typical examples are likely to be:

(a)   minor changes of shape in fences, hedges etc;

(b)   minor changes to dimensions of enclosures or buildings;

(c)   changes to the spelling of names, (especially frequent in Welsh mapping as attempts to anglicise Welsh names were made at times, followed by attempts to change back to correct Welsh in the 20th century).

(5)   The only Resurvey of the 1:2500 mapping was the First Edition County Series mapping of the mid 19th century. All subsequent updates of the 1:2500 mapping were different forms of Revision, including the 'Overhaul' of the mid 1900s and the Positional Accuracy Improvement programme of the early 21st century. The 1:1250 scale mapping of the 1940s onwards were Resurveys based upon rigid National Grid control. When comparisons are made between the 1:1250 scale mapping and the earlier 1:2500 scale mapping of the same area this has to be borne in mind. One common mistake made in comparing maps at different scales is to enlarge the smaller scale map to the scale of the larger scale map. This creates a false basis for comparison as the enlargement of a map, (including digital data), does not improve the accuracy of the map or the data. A more meaningful comparison can be made by reducing the larger scale map to the scale of the smaller scale map. This in no way degrades the quality of the larger scale map and retains the integrity of the smaller scale map.

(6)   A further positional shift of mapping data occurred during the Positional Accuracy Improvement programme. GPS controlled aerial photography was used to move every feature and data point visible on the photography onto a more accurate National Grid position, retaining all the digital data attributes for each data point and line. Map data not visible on the photography was then moved, with its attributes, to fit in its correct relative position to the surrounding corrected detail. Shapes were retained wherever possible. This has resulted in the possibility of rigidly controlled map detail being in close proximity to detail still containing minor errors because those errors are original and the detail was not visible on the aerial photography.

(7)   For many years the mapping archive was stored on paper media, prone to irregular and unpredictable distortions over time due to temperature and humidity. From about 1950 onwards the archive was stored on more stable glass or plastic media. Only when digital storage was introduced in the 1960s could the archive be regarded as free from any possibilities of further distortion.

(8)   Ordnance Survey mapping specifications have been subject to many changes over the period since the survey of the first County Series maps. These specification changes can result in apparent anomalies when comparing different epochs of mapping. For example, when the First Edition of the 1:2500 County Series mapping was surveyed almost every isolated tree, including those in hedgerows, was surveyed in its actual position. By the time of the first Revision of the mapping, trees in hedgerows were no longer shown. As time progressed fewer and fewer trees have been shown in position and now only avenues of trees are shown, (at a standardised spacing), and trees which are significant landmarks or to which an administrative boundary is mered.

(9)   It must never be forgotten that differences in the detail on the mapping being compared could always be possible to changes to the features on the ground between the dates of survey or revision of the maps.

(10) It must never be accepted that the lack of depiction of minor features from later publications of a map is conclusive evidence that the features did not exist on the ground at the date of the revision of the map.

CONCLUSIONS ABOUT MAP COMPARISONS

A2.32 From everything stated above it would appear that the comparison of different epochs of Ordnance Survey mapping can be a minefield.

A2.33 Indeed it can be; all of the above factors can be present during any comparison, but will not always be apparent at first glance. Indeed, in many cases the individual effects will be negligible to the extent that they may not even be detectable. However, in the worst possible case they will all be present, and their effects could be significant.

A2.34 The golden rules will always be:

(a) If apparent anomalies in comparison are noticed, investigate whether one or more of the listed factors is likely to be the cause of the anomaly. If it is a possibility, then try to quantify the effect of each factor and make a judgement whether it is significant in the particular circumstances.

(b) It is always best practice to make comparisons of mapping at the scale of the smallest scale map.

(c) It is good practice to compare over small areas whenever possible, using fitting points which are with reasonable certainty common to all the maps being compared.

Statement published by Ordnance Survey on the use of Ordnance Survey maps in defining property boundaries

A2.35 The purpose of an Ordnance Survey map is to depict, within the limitations imposed by the particular scale and in accordance with the rules and conventions adopted by Ordnance Survey and which were in being at the time, the topographical features in existence at the time of survey or revision.

A2.36 Whilst parliamentary and local authority boundaries are shown where appropriate, as made clear in the Ordnance Survey Act 1841,[3] Ordnance Survey is not concerned with private property boundaries as such: for example, a fence, if shown, will be located on the map in the position it occupied at the date of survey without prejudice as to whether or not it was erected along a proper boundary of legal ownership.

---

[3] The unrepealed portions of this Act were made permanent by the Expiring Laws Act 1922.

Statement published by Ordnance Survey on the use of Ordnance Survey maps in defining rights of way

A2.37 Some Ordnance Survey small-scale maps depict rights of way which have been derived from Definitive Maps as amended by later enactments or instruments held by Ordnance Survey, and are shown subject to the limitations imposed by the scale of the mapping.

A2.38 Later information may be obtained from the appropriate County Council, Unitary Authority or London Borough Council.

A2.39 The representation of any other road, track or path on an Ordnance Survey map is no evidence of the existence of a right of way.

CONSIDERATIONS TO BE TAKEN INTO ACCOUNT IN THE INTERPRETATION OF AERIAL PHOTOGRAPHY AND SATELLITE IMAGERY

A2.40 The major advantage of aerial imagery over mapping is that it provides compelling evidence of what was actually on the ground at the date of the capture of the imagery. However, there are still factors that must be considered:

(a)   The detail that one wishes to see may be obscured by cloud, haze or vegetation.

(b)   Aerial imagery freely available on various websites, ie:

     (i)   Google Earth.
     (ii)   Google Maps.
     (iii)   Yahoo! Maps.
     (iv)   Flash Earth.
     (v)   Microsoft Virtual Earth.
     (vi)   NASA.
     (vii) Open Layers.
     (viii) Bing Maps 3D.
        The major problem with internet imagery is that the date of the imagery is often not known. A Copyright date is often prominently displayed, but this can be some years after the capture date of the imagery.

(c)   Survey quality aerial photography taken by:

     (i)   Ordnance Survey.
     (ii)   Royal Air Force.
     (iii)   Royal Commissions on Historical Monuments.
     (iv)   County and District Councils.
     (v)   Private aerial photography firms.
        It will be possible to determine the exact date, and often the time of day, that these photographs were taken. They will also be classified as either

'Vertical' or 'Oblique' photography, and details such as the camera lens focal length and the flying height of the aircraft will also be available.

Aerial photography taken for survey purposes will usually be 'Vertical' photography, that is, the aircraft will have been , (within very tight parameters), level (for pitch and yaw) at the time of exposure and consequently the camera lens will have been pointing vertically downwards. This will have had the effect of minimising distortions in the photograph, and such distortions as remain will be predictable and correctable. These photographs are also usually available as overlapping strips, and ground points will be visible on at least two, (and up to six), photographs. With suitable viewing equipment this enables a three dimensional virtual model of the terrain to be seen, greatly improving the interpretation of features such as buildings, walls, hedges and even kerb lines which will appear to have a 'height' over the surrounding ground.

(d)   Oblique aerial photographs are not taken vertically and may have been taken on hand held cameras. They are prone to unknown distortions mainly due to the fact that the technical data available for vertical photographs is either not available, or is not to the same accuracy. They do, however, provide evidence of the existence of a feature at the time if the date of the photograph can be established. Measurements taken from oblique photographs should be treated with extreme caution due to the distortions.

(e)   All aerial photographs, both vertical and oblique, suffer from a phenomenon known as 'overthrow'. Features such as houses and walls that are not directly below the camera at the time of exposure will display the top of the feature displaced from its true ground position away from the Nadir point, (the point vertically below the camera). This is easily recognised on the photograph as the walls of houses can be seen with the eaves and foot of the wall both visible on the photograph on one or two sides of the house and only the eaves line visible on the other two or three sides of the house. The same effect displaces ground features on hills, though the true '(under)ground' position cannot, of course, be seen in this case.

(f)   Modern photography is available in colour which can make for better interpretation of ie crops, nature of a hard surface, vegetation etc.

CONCLUSIONS ABOUT THE INTERPRETATION OF AERIAL IMAGERY

A2.41

(a)   If the date of a photograph is important to prove the age of a feature, then be careful that the age can be confirmed; copyright date is not the same as photography date.

(b)   If measurements are to be taken from aerial imagery then it is better to use true vertical images, capable of being viewed stereoscopically, and interpreted by someone with appropriate training and skills, than to attempt to do it yourself.

(c)   Always remember that all aerial images will have some distortion. In particular the 'overthrow' phenomenon that can cause roofs of buildings to *seemingly* trespass over a neighbour's boundary.

A FULL EXPLANATION OF POSITIONAL ACCURACY IMPROVEMENT (PAI)

A2.42   Description from the Ordnance Survey website: http://www.ordnancesurvey.co.uk/oswebsite/pai/pdfs/PAI_Companion.pdf.

A2.43   The Positional Accuracy Improvement (PAI) programme dealt with improving the Absolute Accuracy from 1:2500 scale 'Overhaul' accuracies to either 1:1250 scale Resurvey standards (for the built-up areas of defined rural towns) or 1:2500 scale Resurvey standards (the remaining rural areas). However, any surveyed changes must also conform to the Geometric Fidelity and Relative Accuracy of those standards of survey. The conformity statements below define these accuracy levels.

A2.44   Note that certain types of feature, such as road centrelines, vegetation and landform limits and underground features, are surveyed to a lesser degree of accuracy. Centrelines and vegetation and landform limits are subjective, while underground features may have been supplied by third parties.

A2.45   The Absolute and Relative Accuracies are measurable and definitive, and statements of the expected errors of these by survey scale are given. Geometric Fidelity cannot be closely defined and is a matter for subjective judgement. The guideline is that the detail must be acceptable in terms of Geometric Fidelity when plotted or displayed at a scale no larger than the storage scale.

A2.46   The reason for undertaking the PAI programme was that the majority of 1:2500 scale mapping was based on 'Overhaul' mapping from the 1950s. The 'Overhaul' process took the existing County Series mapping, based on many separate Cassini projections, and converted it to the National Grid on a single Transverse Mercator projection. There were limitations in that conversion process that resulted in ± 2.8 metres root mean square error (RMSE) Absolute Accuracy. However, the Relative Accuracy of features (distances between features close to each other) was very good at ± 1.2 metres RMSE, and is retained following Positional Accuracy Improvement.

Geometric Fidelity

A2.47   The principle of Geometric Fidelity is that any real-world alignment or shape must be accurately reflected in the data to the required specification, for example:

(a)   detail that is square on the ground must be represented as square in the data, and shapes must be accurate;

(b)   alignments that are straight in real life must be represented as straight lines within the data;

(c)   lines of sight that pass through points on the ground should pass through the map positions of the corresponding points; and

(d)   adjacent features should be in sympathy with each other as regards alignment, distance apart and orientation.

Relative Accuracy

A2.48   Relative Accuracy is a measure of the positional consistency of a data point in relation to other near points of detail. Relative accuracy compares the scaled distance between features measured from the map data with distances measured between the same features on the ground.

Absolute Accuracy

A2.49   Absolute Accuracy is a measure that indicates how closely the coordinates of a point in the map dataset agree with the real coordinates of the same point on the ground in the British National Grid reference system.

BUILT-UP AREAS WITHIN DEFINED RURAL TOWNS

Absolute Accuracy

A2.50   An Absolute Accuracy of ±0.4 metres root mean square error (RMSE) and a normal distribution of errors must exist. This standard is applied to any contiguous area of data as per the following:

(a)   95% of points should be in error by no more than ± 0.7 metres;

(b)   99% of points should be in error by no more than ± 0.9 metres; and

(c)   no point should be in error by more than 1.2 metres.

Relative Accuracy

A2.51   A Relative Accuracy of ± 0.40 metres root mean square error (RMSE), a normal distribution of errors and a maximum error of 0.80 metres must exist. This standard is applied to any contiguous area of data.

Example of Relative Accuracy

A2.52   If the distances between two well defined points of detail 60.0 metres apart were measured in the real world, there would be an expectation that this distance would be represented in the map data by a scaled distance of between 59.2 metres and 60.8 metres.

OUTSIDE OF BUILT-UP AREAS WITHIN DEFINED RURAL TOWNS AND ALL OTHER RURAL AREAS

Absolute Accuracy

A2.53 An Absolute Accuracy of ±1.10 metres root mean square error (RMSE) and a normal distribution of errors must exist. This standard is applied to any contiguous area of data as per the following:

(a) 95% of points should be in error by no more than ± 1.90 metres;

(b) 99% of points should be in error by no more than ± 2.40 metres; and

(c) no point should be in error by more than 3.0 metres.

Relative Accuracy

A2.54 A Relative Accuracy of ±1.00 metres root mean square error (RMSE), a normal distribution of errors and a maximum error of 1.90 metres must exist. This standard is applied to any contiguous area of data.

Example of Relative Accuracy

A2.55 If the distances between two well defined points of detail 100.0 metres apart were measured in the real world, there would be an expectation that this distance would be represented in the map data by a scaled distance of between 98.1 metres and 101.9 metres.

OTHER DIFFERENCES BETWEEN THE PAI OF RURAL TOWNS AND THE PAI OF OTHER RURAL AREAS

Survey tolerances

A2.56 Ordnance Survey map data aims to portray an accurate survey of the features which comprise the detailed topography, so that each feature is correctly depicted in terms of shape, size, orientation and position relative to all the surrounding features. However, the accuracy levels chosen at the basic scales of survey restrict the absolute achievement of this objective.

A2.57 For that reason information is selected for inclusion so that display and graphic plotting of the data gives optimum results at the accuracy of survey. This requires there to be differing tolerances for data capture of similar features at the different accuracy survey levels.

Constraints imposed by survey tolerances

A2.58 Juts and porches which are an integral part of a building, bay windows and recesses are shown when their smallest dimension is not less than:

(a)   1.0 metres – Resurvey of rural towns for PAI.

(b)   2.0 metres – PAI of other rural areas.

A2.59   Nevertheless, smaller juts and projections are shown when they abut onto a public thoroughfare or they carry height information.

A2.60   Rivers, streams and drains are shown at their true scale width or by a single line where their width is less than:

(a)   1.0 metres – Resurvey of rural towns for PAI.

(b)   2.0 metres – PAI of other rural areas.

A2.61   Where the central alignment of an unmade path is less than 1 metre (Resurvey of a rural town for PAI), 2 metres (PAI of other rural areas) from an adjacent building, fence, hedge or wall, the central alignment is shown at that minimum distance away from the feature.

A2.62   The symbol used for square pylons and similar features is shown oriented and true to scale, except where the feature is below the minimum size, in which case the minimum sized symbol is used. The minimum sizes are:

(a)   3 metres square – Resurvey of rural town for PAI.

(b)   6 metres square – PAI of other rural areas.

A2.63   Where the limits of cliffs and slopes are coextensive with features such as fences, the limits of cliff or slope are offset by approximately 0.5 metres at source scale for clarity.

A2.64   Where areas of slope or cliff taper at their extremities, they cease to be shown when the minimum horizontal width is less than:

(a)   1.0 metres – Resurvey of rural towns for PAI.

(b)   2.0 metres – PAI of other rural areas.

GLOSSARY

A2.65

Accuracy	The relationship of the position of a feature shown on a map to its true position. Accuracy can be absolute or relative and defined mathematically. For a fuller explanation the reader is referred to this Ordnance Survey web page: http://www.ordnancesurvey.co.uk/oswebsite/pai/pdfs/PAI_Companion.pdf.
Air graphic survey (Air ground survey)	A technique of using enlarged vertical aerial photographs to assist the updating of maps by graphic survey methods.
Cartography	The science and art of map making.
Control point	A physically monumented point for which coordinates of a known quality have been defined (for example, triangulation station).
Definitive Map	A map that is a legal record of a public's rights to walk, ride or drive on public rights of way. *NOTE: The duty of the responsible surveying authority is to show on the Definitive Map all footpaths, bridleways, restricted byways, BOATs* and RUPPs** in its area, whether urban or rural. Definitive Maps are prepared everywhere in England and Wales except in the area of the former London County Council (LCC) where their preparation is optional.* BS7666, part 4, 1996. * BOAT = 'Byway Open to All Traffic' ** RUPP = 'Road Used as Public Path', now superseded by 'Restricted Byway'
Definitive Statement	The Definitive Statement is a legal textual record which accompanies the Definitive Map. *NOTE: The Definitive Map and Statement provide conclusive evidence (that is, evidence that can be used in court) of the existence of public rights of way and their extent, legal conditions and limitations.* BS7666, part 4, 1996.
Digital Field Update	A system of updating Digital maps in the surveyor's field office.
Digital map	A map in a form suitable for storage, transmission and manipulation by computers.

Electronic Distance Measurement (EDM)	Distance measurement instruments that transmit narrow beams of light that are reflected back to the receiver. A microprocessor then converts the phase differences of the transmitted and received light waves into a distance measurement. These instruments can measure long distances to within a few millimetres at the press of a button.
Geometric Fidelity	The principle of Geometric Fidelity is that any real-world alignment or shape must be accurately reflected in the data to the required specification. Detail that is square on the ground must be represented as square in the data; shapes must be accurate; alignments that are straight in real life must be represented as straight lines within the data; lines of sight that pass through points on the ground should pass through the map positions of the corresponding points; adjacent features should be in sympathy with each other as regards alignment, distance apart and orientation.
Global Positioning System (GPS)	A radio navigation system that allows land, sea, and airborne users to determine their exact location in all weather conditions, anywhere in the world. GPS is used to support a broad range of military, commercial, and consumer applications. 24 GPS satellites are in orbit. Each satellite contains a computer, an atomic clock, and a radio. With an understanding of its own orbit and the clock, the satellite continually broadcasts its changing position and time. On the ground a GPS receiver contains a computer that fixes its own position by calculating the distance to three or more satellites. Survey quality GPS receivers can fix positions to within a few centimetres.
Graphic survey	A method of survey based upon reproducing the relationship between lines of sight, short measurements and the construction of right angles.
Instrumental survey	Any form of survey using high precision optical or electronic instruments.
Land survey	The science and mathematics of measuring the Earth and features on it, and recording the data in a methodical way.
Large scale survey (map)	A survey (map) at one of the basic scales of 1:1250, 1:2500 or 1:10 000.

OS **MasterMap®**	OS MasterMap® was designed by Ordnance Survey as an intelligent digital map and digital representation of the real world, to be used with geographical information systems (GIS) and database systems. It is a business tool to manage information, aid analysis and speed the decision making process. It provides intelligent data with real-world objects represented as explicit features, each identified by a unique number.
National Grid	A rectangular grid used on most modern Ordnance Survey maps to enable each object on the map to be uniquely referenced in terms of distance east and distance north of a defined origin (see *Ordnance Survey Maps – a descriptive manual* by J B Harley, Ordnance Survey, Southampton 1975).
Optical Tacheometry	A method of measuring distances by use of a theodolite or level.
Ordnance Survey	The National Mapping Agency of Great Britain.
Ordnance Survey Location Map	An updated name for OS Sitemap® (see below).
OS Sitemap®	An Ordnance Survey product which is a printout from the Ordnance Survey digital mapping database of the latest available large scale survey.
Photogrammetry	A high precision technique, used world-wide, for survey applications using photography, (usually vertical, aerial photographs).
Positional Accuracy Improvement (PAI)	The Positional Accuracy Improvement programme dealt with improving the Absolute Accuracy of 1:2500 scale mapping from 1:2500 scale 'Overhaul' accuracies to either 1:1250 scale Resurvey standards (for the built-up areas of defined rural towns) or 1:2500 scale Resurvey standards (the remaining rural areas). However, any surveyed changes also conformed to the Geometric Fidelity and Relative Accuracy of those standards of survey. See this Ordnance Survey web page: http://www.ordnancesurvey.co.uk/oswebsite/pai/pdfs/PAI_Companion.pdf.
Precision	The ability of an instrument or process to repeat measurements to a stated tolerance.
PIES	Portable Interactive Edit System.
PRISM	Portable Revision and Integrated Survey Module. Portable Pen Computers which enable the surveyor to update and edit Digital Maps at the time of survey.

Resurvey	A new survey, not based upon earlier surveys.
Revision	The updating of an earlier survey.
Scale	The relationship between a distance measured on the map and the equivalent distance measured on the ground, for example, a scale of 1:10 000 means that a measurement of one unit on the map represents a measurement on the ground of 10 000 units.
SIM®	Survey Information on Microfilm. A copy of updated Ordnance Survey large scale mapping taken from a microfilm copy of the surveyor's working document for security and archive purposes.
SIP®	Superplan Instant Printout. A copy of updated Ordnance Survey large scale mapping taken from the digital archive for security and archive purposes.
Superplan®	A copy of a large scale Ordnance Survey map printed on demand from the latest Ordnance Survey Landline data.
SUSI®	Supply of Unpublished Survey Information. A copy of the Ordnance Survey surveyor's Master Survey Document produced on demand for a customer.
Theodolite	An instrument used for measuring angles in the horizontal and vertical planes.
Tolerance	The maximum acceptable difference between measurements on a map and the equivalent true measurements on the ground.
Topographic map	A map which depicts physical features on the ground at the time of survey, within the limitations imposed by the particular scale and specification of the map. A topographic map does not show property boundaries.
Validation	The process of quantifying the accuracy and precision of a survey.

USEFUL REFERENCE SOURCES

A2.66 *Ordnance Survey – Map Makers to Britain since 1791*, Tim Owen and Elaine Pilbeam, Ordnance Survey, Southampton, 1992, ISBN 0 31 900249

A History of the Ordnance Survey, WA Seymour, Wm Dawson and Sons Ltd, Kent, 1980, ISBN 0-7129-0979-6

Ordnance Survey maps – a descriptive manual, JB Harley, Ordnance Survey, Southampton, 1975

Map of a Nation – a biography of the Ordnance Survey, Rachel Hewitt, Granta Publications, London; 2010

The early Years of the Ordnance Survey, Col. Sir Charles Close; David & Charles Reprints, Newton Abbot, 1969

The Map of England, Col. Sir Charles Close, Peter Davies, London, 1932

Ordnance Survey Maps – a concise guide for historians, Richard Oliver, The Charles Close Society, London, 1993

Ordnance Survey Maps – a concise guide for historians, second edition, revised and expanded, Richard Oliver, The Charles Close Society, London, 2005

The Historian's Guide to Ordnance Survey Maps, J B Harley & C W Phillips, published for the Standing Conference for Local History by The National Council of Social Service, London, 1964

Ordnance Survey of Great Britain, England & Wales, Indexes to the 1/2500 and 6-inch scale maps, David Archer Maps and Books, Kerry, Wales, 1991

Ordnance Survey of Great Britain, Scotland, Indexes to the 1/2500 and 6-inch scale maps, David Archer Maps and Books, Kerry, Wales, 1993

Elementary Air Survey, W K Kilford, Pitman Publishing Ltd, London, 1977

Maps and Air Photographs, G C Dickinson, Edward Arnold (Publishers) Ltd, London, 1970

The Map Book, edited by Peter Barber, Weidenfield & Nicholson, London

Landmarks of Mapmaking, RV Tooley & Charles Bricker, Wordsworth Editions, Hertfordshire; 1989

Tithe Surveys for Historians, Roger J P Kain & Hugh C Prince; Phillimore & Co Ltd, Chichester, 2000

Road and Way, A W Fry FCA, 2003

Cross Roads; Alec and Margaret Fry, South Pennine Packhorse Trails Trust, 2005

What is a Cross Road?; Susan Taylor, South Pennine Packhorse Trails Trust, 1997

Ordnance Survey website – http://www.ordancesurvey.co.uk

David EM Andrews
Cartographic Survey and Mapping Consultant

Andrews Consulting
Email: andrews.survey@btinternet.com
Website: www.the-expert-witness-surveyor.co.uk

Appendix 3

EXTRACTS FROM LAND REGISTRY PRACTICE GUIDES 40 AND 49

The following extracts set out the land registry requirements for plans in PG 40 and the basis on which an application which includes an inadequate plan will be rejected in PG 49. It is important that a plan comply with registry requirements as if they do not accept the application the applicant may lose rights to or over the land.

The published practice guides are accessible through the land registry webpage and reference should be made to that. They are accompanied by illustrative plans referred to as examples which are not reproduced here.

LAND REGISTRY PRACTICE GUIDE 40 – LAND REGISTRY PLANS – SUPPLEMENT 2 – GUIDANCE FOR PREPARING PLANS FOR LAND REGISTRY APPLICATIONS

A3.1 The following, which covers most eventualities is, however, not an exhaustive list of points that may lead to the application being rejected:

- Where the deed refers to a plan but it is not attached.

- Plans where the scale used makes the extent of the land or easements uncertain.

- Plans that have been reduced from their original scale but that still bear the original scale endorsement (unless a bar scale has been used).

- Plans marked as 'for identification only' or similar wording[2] may be rejected.

- [2] Unless the plan can be accurately related to the OS map and any description in the deed is not at variance with either the OS map or the plan.

- Plans containing a statement of disclaimer under Property Misdescriptions Act 1991.

- Plans where a colouring or marking referred to has been omitted from the plan

- Plans where the extent of any easements is unclear. See *example 7*.

- Plans where we cannot locate the land with any degree of confidence. See *examples 7 and 8*.

- Plans that cannot be orientated to align with the Ordnance Survey Map. See *examples 7 and 9*.

- Plans that have not been drawn to scale. See *examples 7 and 9*.

- Plans with edgings of a thickness that obscures any other detail or that makes the extent any way ambiguous. See *example 8*.

- Plans where the extent is undefined or is unclear. See *example 9*.

- Hand drawn sketches. See *example 9*.

LAND REGISTRY PRACTICE GUIDE 49 – RETURN AND REJECTION OF APPLICATIONS FOR REGISTRATION

6.2 Plans to deeds in dealings of part and leases

A3.2   All these requirements equally apply to plans accompanying searches in form OS2 or OS3.

We reject

Where it is impossible to identify the extent of the land that's the subject of the application. Such as:

- where the deed refers to a plan but it is not attached,

- where the extent on the plan cannot be related to the Ordnance Survey map,

- where the extent on the plan is not clearly defined, e g by edging, colouring or hatching,

- the plan is sufficiently distorted to prevent identification of the extent.

Tips

Transfers, charges and leases of part must be accompanied by a plan unless the part can be clearly identified either:

- beyond doubt on the lessor's or vendor's title plan from the description in the text of the deed, or

- by reference to a precise colouring on the lessor's or vendor's title plan, for example '... shown tinted blue on the title plan of title number ...'. It must not refer to an approved estate plan.

Ensure any edgings are not too thick and do not obscure any other detail on the plan. On a small-scale plan thick lines can be several metres across on the ground. If we cannot determine the precise extent we may reject the application.

We will accept a disclaimer that appears on deed plans created by National Grid Gas plc (Co Regn No 2006000) (formerly Transco plc) where the disclaimer relates to the positioning and/or existence of pipes, equipment and so on.

Please prepare any plan for a new deed or application having regard to the following guidelines. Further information can be found in Practice Guide *40 – Land Registry plans*:

- Draw and show to its actual scale.

- Show its orientation (for example, a north point).

- Use preferred scales of 1/1250–1/500 for urban properties.

- Use preferred scales of 1/2500 for rural properties (fields and farms etc).

- Do not use a scale of imperial measurement (for example, 16 feet to 1 inch).

- Do not reduce in scale (see Practice Guide *40 – Land Registry plans – 6.6 Plans reduced in scale*).

- Do not mark or refer to being for identification only.

- Do not show statements of disclaimer used under the Property Misdescriptions Act 1991.

- Show sufficient detail to be identified on the Ordnance Survey map.

- Show its general location by showing roads, road junctions or other landmarks.

- Show the land of the property, including any garage or garden ground.

- Show buildings in their correct (or intended) position.

- Show access drives or pathways if they form part of the property boundaries.

- Show the land and property clearly (for example, by edging, colouring or hatching).

- Have edgings of a thickness that do not obscure any other detail.

- Show separate parts by suitable plan markings (house, parking space, dustbin space).

- Identify different floor levels (where appropriate).

- Show intricate boundaries with a larger scale or inset plan.

- Show measurements in metric units only, to two decimal places.

- Show undefined boundaries accurately and, where necessary, by reference to measurements.

- Show measurements that correspond, so far as possible, to scaled measurements.

6.3 Plans in deeds in first registrations

A3.3   We reject:

- Where the deed or form FR1 refers to a plan but it is not attached.

- Where there is no plan and the description of the land to be registered is inadequate.

- Where the extent on the plan cannot be related to the Ordnance Survey map.

INDEX

References are to paragraph numbers.